FREE Test Taking Tips DVD Offer

To help us better serve you, we have developed a Test Taking Tips DVD that we would like to give you for FREE. **This DVD covers world-class test taking tips that you can use to be even more successful when you are taking your test.**

All that we ask is that you email us your feedback about your study guide. Please let us know what you thought about it – whether that is good, bad or indifferent.

To get your **FREE Test Taking Tips DVD**, email freedvd@studyguideteam.com with "FREE DVD" in the subject line and the following information in the body of the email:

a. The title of your study guide.

b. Your product rating on a scale of 1-5, with 5 being the highest rating.

c. Your feedback about the study guide. What did you think of it?

d. Your full name and shipping address to send your free DVD.

If you have any questions or concerns, please don't hesitate to contact us at freedvd@studyguideteam.com.

Thanks again!

GED Preparation 2018 All Subjects

GED Book 2018 All Subjects Prep Team

Table of Contents

Quick Overview

As you draw closer to taking your exam, effective preparation becomes more and more important. Thankfully, you have this study guide to help you get ready. Use this guide to help keep your studying on track and refer to it often.

This study guide contains several key sections that will help you be successful on your exam. The guide contains tips for what you should do the night before and the day of the test. Also included are test-taking tips. Knowing the right information is not always enough. Many well-prepared test takers struggle with exams. These tips will help equip you to accurately read, assess, and answer test questions.

A large part of the guide is devoted to showing you what content to expect on the exam and to helping you better understand that content. Near the end of this guide is a practice test so that you can see how well you have grasped the content. Then, answer explanations are provided so that you can understand why you missed certain questions.

Don't try to cram the night before you take your exam. This is not a wise strategy for a few reasons. First, your retention of the information will be low. Your time would be better used by reviewing information you already know rather than trying to learn a lot of new information. Second, you will likely become stressed as you try to gain a large amount of knowledge in a short amount of time. Third, you will be depriving yourself of sleep. So be sure to go to bed at a reasonable time the night before. Being well-rested helps you focus and remain calm.

Be sure to eat a substantial breakfast the morning of the exam. If you are taking the exam in the afternoon, be sure to have a good lunch as well. Being hungry is distracting and can make it difficult to focus. You have hopefully spent lots of time preparing for the exam. Don't let an empty stomach get in the way of success!

When travelling to the testing center, leave earlier than needed. That way, you have a buffer in case you experience any delays. This will help you remain calm and will keep you from missing your appointment time at the testing center.

Be sure to pace yourself during the exam. Don't try to rush through the exam. There is no need to risk performing poorly on the exam just so you can leave the testing center early. Allow yourself to use all of the allotted time if needed.

Remain positive while taking the exam even if you feel like you are performing poorly. Thinking about the content you should have mastered will not help you perform better on the exam.

Once the exam is complete, take some time to relax. Even if you feel that you need to take the exam again, you will be well served by some down time before you begin studying again. It's often easier to convince yourself to study if you know that it will come with a reward!

Test-Taking Strategies

1. Predicting the Answer

When you feel confident in your preparation for a multiple-choice test, try predicting the answer before reading the answer choices. This is especially useful on questions that test objective factual knowledge or that ask you to fill in a blank. By predicting the answer before reading the available choices, you eliminate the possibility that you will be distracted or led astray by an incorrect answer choice. You will feel more confident in your selection if you read the question, predict the answer, and then find your prediction among the answer choices. After using this strategy, be sure to still read all of the answer choices carefully and completely. If you feel unprepared, you should not attempt to predict the answers. This would be a waste of time and an opportunity for your mind to wander in the wrong direction.

2. Reading the Whole Question

Too often, test takers scan a multiple-choice question, recognize a few familiar words, and immediately jump to the answer choices. Test authors are aware of this common impatience, and they will sometimes prey upon it. For instance, a test author might subtly turn the question into a negative, or he or she might redirect the focus of the question right at the end. The only way to avoid falling into these traps is to read the entirety of the question carefully before reading the answer choices.

3. Looking for Wrong Answers

Long and complicated multiple-choice questions can be intimidating. One way to simplify a difficult multiple-choice question is to eliminate all of the answer choices that are clearly wrong. In most sets of answers, there will be at least one selection that can be dismissed right away. If the test is administered on paper, the test taker could draw a line through it to indicate that it may be ignored; otherwise, the test taker will have to perform this operation mentally or on scratch paper. In either case, once the obviously incorrect answers have been eliminated, the remaining choices may be considered. Sometimes identifying the clearly wrong answers will give the test taker some information about the correct answer. For instance, if one of the remaining answer choices is a direct opposite of one of the eliminated answer choices, it may well be the correct answer. The opposite of obviously wrong is obviously right! Of course, this is not always the case. Some answers are obviously incorrect simply because they are irrelevant to the question being asked. Still, identifying and eliminating some incorrect answer choices is a good way to simplify a multiple-choice question.

4. Don't Overanalyze

Anxious test takers often overanalyze questions. When you are nervous, your brain will often run wild, causing you to make associations and discover clues that don't actually exist. If you feel that this may be a problem for you, do whatever you can to slow down during the test. Try taking a deep breath or counting to ten. As you read and consider the question, restrict yourself to the particular words used by the author. Avoid thought tangents about what the author *really* meant, or what he or she was *trying* to say. The only things that matter on a multiple-choice test are the words that are actually in the question. You must avoid reading too much into a multiple-choice question, or supposing that the writer meant something other than what he or she wrote.

5. No Need for Panic

It is wise to learn as many strategies as possible before taking a multiple-choice test, but it is likely that you will come across a few questions for which you simply don't know the answer. In this situation, avoid panicking. Because most multiple-choice tests include dozens of questions, the relative value of a single wrong answer is small. Moreover, your failure on one question has no effect on your success elsewhere on the test. As much as possible, you should compartmentalize each question on a multiple-choice test. In other words, you should not allow your feelings about one question to affect your success on the others. When you find a question that you either don't understand or don't know how to answer, just take a deep breath and do your best. Read the entire question slowly and carefully. Try rephrasing the question a couple of different ways. Then, read all of the answer choices carefully. After eliminating obviously wrong answers, make a selection and move on to the next question.

6. Confusing Answer Choices

When working on a difficult multiple-choice question, there may be a tendency to focus on the answer choices that are the easiest to understand. Many people, whether consciously or not, gravitate to the answer choices that require the least concentration, knowledge, and memory. This is a mistake. When you come across an answer choice that is confusing, you should give it extra attention. A question might be confusing because you do not know the subject matter to which it refers. If this is the case, don't eliminate the answer before you have affirmatively settled on another. When you come across an answer choice of this type, set it aside as you look at the remaining choices. If you can confidently assert that one of the other choices is correct, you can leave the confusing answer aside. Otherwise, you will need to take a moment to try to better understand the confusing answer choice. Rephrasing is one way to tease out the sense of a confusing answer choice.

7. Your First Instinct

Many people struggle with multiple-choice tests because they overthink the questions. If you have studied sufficiently for the test, you should be prepared to trust your first instinct once you have carefully and completely read the question and all of the answer choices. There is a great deal of research suggesting that the mind can come to the correct conclusion very quickly once it has obtained all of the relevant information. At times, it may seem to you as if your intuition is working faster even than your reasoning mind. This may in fact be true. The knowledge you obtain while studying may be retrieved from your subconscious before you have a chance to work out the associations that support it. Verify your instinct by working out the reasons that it should be trusted.

8. Key Words

Many test takers struggle with multiple-choice questions because they have poor reading comprehension skills. Quickly reading and understanding a multiple-choice question requires a mixture of skill and experience. To help with this, try jotting down a few key words and phrases on a piece of scrap paper. Doing this concentrates the process of reading and forces the mind to weigh the relative importance of the question's parts. In selecting words and phrases to write down, the test taker thinks about the question more deeply and carefully. This is especially true for multiple-choice questions that are preceded by a long prompt.

9. Subtle Negatives

One of the oldest tricks in the multiple-choice test writer's book is to subtly reverse the meaning of a question with a word like *not* or *except*. If you are not paying attention to each word in the question, you can easily be led astray by this trick. For instance, a common question format is, "Which of the following is...?" Obviously, if the question instead is, "Which of the following is not...?," then the answer will be quite different. Even worse, the test makers are aware of the potential for this mistake and will include one answer choice that would be correct if the question were not negated or reversed. A test taker who misses the reversal will find what he or she believes to be a correct answer and will be so confident that he or she will fail to reread the question and discover the original error. The only way to avoid this is to practice a wide variety of multiple-choice questions and to pay close attention to each and every word.

10. Reading Every Answer Choice

It may seem obvious, but you should always read every one of the answer choices! Too many test takers fall into the habit of scanning the question and assuming that they understand the question because they recognize a few key words. From there, they pick the first answer choice that answers the question they believe they have read. Test takers who read all of the answer choices might discover that one of the latter answer choices is actually *more* correct. Moreover, reading all of the answer choices can remind you of facts related to the question that can help you arrive at the correct answer. Sometimes, a misstatement or incorrect detail in one of the latter answer choices will trigger your memory of the subject and will enable you to find the right answer. Failing to read all of the answer choices is like not reading all of the items on a restaurant menu: you might miss out on the perfect choice.

11. Spot the Hedges

One of the keys to success on multiple-choice tests is paying close attention to every word. This is never more true than with words like *almost*, *most*, *some*, and *sometimes*. These words are called "hedges" because they indicate that a statement is not totally true or not true in every place and time. An absolute statement will contain no hedges, but in many subjects, like literature and history, the answers are not always straightforward or absolute. There are always exceptions to the rules in these subjects. For this reason, you should favor those multiple-choice questions that contain hedging language. The presence of qualifying words indicates that the author is taking special care with his or her words, which is certainly important when composing the right answer. After all, there are many ways to be wrong, but there is only one way to be right! For this reason, it is wise to avoid answers that are absolute when taking a multiple-choice test. An absolute answer is one that says things are either all one way or all another. They often include words like *every*, *always*, *best*, and *never*. If you are taking a multiple-choice test in a subject that doesn't lend itself to absolute answers, be on your guard if you see any of these words.

12. Long Answers

In many subject areas, the answers are not simple. As already mentioned, the right answer often requires hedges. Another common feature of the answers to a complex or subjective question are qualifying clauses, which are groups of words that subtly modify the meaning of the sentence. If the question or answer choice describes a rule to which there are exceptions or the subject matter is complicated, ambiguous, or confusing, the correct answer will require many words in order to be expressed clearly and accurately. In essence, you should not be deterred by answer choices that seem excessively long. Oftentimes, the author of the text will not be able to write the correct answer without offering some qualifications and modifications. Your job is to read the answer choices thoroughly and completely and to select the one that most accurately and precisely answers the question.

13. Restating to Understand

Sometimes, a question on a multiple-choice test is difficult not because of what it asks but because of how it is written. If this is the case, restate the question or answer choice in different words. This process serves a couple of important purposes. First, it forces you to concentrate on the core of the question. In order to rephrase the question accurately, you have to understand it well. Rephrasing the question will concentrate your mind on the key words and ideas. Second, it will present the information to your mind in a fresh way. This process may trigger your memory and render some useful scrap of information picked up while studying.

14. True Statements

Sometimes an answer choice will be true in itself, but it does not answer the question. This is one of the main reasons why it is essential to read the question carefully and completely before proceeding to the answer choices. Too often, test takers skip ahead to the answer choices and look for true statements. Having found one of these, they are content to select it without reference to the question above. Obviously, this provides an easy way for test makers to play tricks. The savvy test taker will always read the entire question before turning to the answer choices. Then, having settled on a correct answer choice, he or she will refer to the original question and ensure that the selected answer is relevant. The mistake of choosing a correct-but-irrelevant answer choice is especially common on questions related to specific pieces of objective knowledge, like historical or scientific facts. A prepared test taker will have a wealth of factual knowledge at his or her disposal, and should not be careless in its application.

15. No Patterns

One of the more dangerous ideas that circulates about multiple-choice tests is that the correct answers tend to fall into patterns. These erroneous ideas range from a belief that B and C are the most common right answers, to the idea that an unprepared test-taker should answer "A-B-A-C-A-D-A-B-A." It cannot be emphasized enough that pattern-seeking of this type is exactly the WRONG way to approach a multiple-choice test. To begin with, it is highly unlikely that the test maker will plot the correct answers according to some predetermined pattern. The questions are scrambled and delivered in a random order. Furthermore, even if the test maker was following a pattern in the assignation of correct answers, there is no reason why the test taker would know which pattern he or she was using. Any attempt to discern a pattern in the answer choices is a waste of time and a distraction from the real work of taking the test. A test taker would be much better served by extra preparation before the test than by reliance on a pattern in the answers.

FREE DVD OFFER

Don't forget that doing well on your exam includes both understanding the test content and understanding how to use what you know to do well on the test. We offer a completely FREE Test Taking Tips DVD that covers world class test taking tips that you can use to be even more successful when you are taking your test.

All that we ask is that you email us your feedback about your study guide. To get your **FREE Test Taking Tips DVD**, email freedvd@studyguideteam.com with "FREE DVD" in the subject line and the following information in the body of the email:

- The title of your study guide.
- Your product rating on a scale of 1-5, with 5 being the highest rating.
- Your feedback about the study guide. What did you think of it?
- Your full name and shipping address to send your free DVD.

Introduction to the GED

Function of the Test

The General Education Development (GED) test is an exam developed and administered by the GED Testing Service, a joint venture of the American Council on Education and Pearson VUE. The GED offers those without a high school diploma the chance to earn a high school equivalency credential by evaluating their knowledge of core high school subjects. In 2014, the test was updated to become computer-based only and to align with current high school graduation standards.

The GED is the only nationally recognized high school equivalency credential, and GED test takers represent a wide age group with diverse goals. Generally, the GED is appropriate for people who did not graduate from high school but who wish to pursue advancement in their career and/or education. According to MyGED, approximately 98% of U.S. colleges and universities accept a GED as the equivalent of a high school diploma (other schools may require additional preparation courses in addition to a passing GED score in order to be considered for admission). Over 20 million adults have earned GED credentials, and the latest reported pass rates for the 2014 GED are around 60%.

Test Administration

GED tests are widely offered throughout the United States and Canada, although jurisdictions (state, province, etc.) may vary in terms of things like pricing, scheduling, and test rules. For international students and US military, international testing options are also available. Official GED Testing Centers are often operated by community colleges, adult education centers, and local school boards; GED Testing Service offers a comprehensive search of nearby test centers.

Keeping in mind that rules may vary between jurisdictions, all tests are administered in-person and taken on a computer. Tests are scheduled throughout the year; refer to local testing centers for available test times. Generally, test takers are able to take any test module three times without any restrictions on retesting. However, after three failed attempts, testers must wait a minimum of 60 days to retake the test. GED testing centers can also offer accommodations for students with disabilities, such as additional test time or Braille format tests. The GED may also be offered in Spanish or in French (verify availability with local testing centers). (http://www.gedtestingservice.com/testers/mygedfaqs)

Test Format

The GED consists of four sections, or modules: Mathematical Reasoning, Science, Social Studies, and Reasoning Through Language Arts. Although the complete test is offered together, it is not necessary to take all four modules at once. Test subjects vary in length:

Subject	Time	Topics
Math	115 minutes	Quantitative and algebraic problem solving; data analysis of charts, graphs, and tables; geometry
Science	90 minutes	Life science, physical science, earth and space science
Social Studies	70 minutes	Civics and government, U.S. history, economics, world geography
Reasoning Through Language Arts	150 minutes	Ability to closely read, comprehend, and edit written text; ability to write clearly

A ten-minute break is given between each module.

On the testing day, test takers are not permitted to eat, drink, smoke, or use their cell phones during the test. Test takers are permitted to bring a handheld calculator (TI-30XS Multiview Scientific Calculator) to the test; testing centers will not provide handheld calculators, although an on-screen calculator will be available on the computer. Students will also be provided with three erasable note boards to use during the test.

Scoring

Because the GED is now a computer-based test, scores will be available on MyGED within 24 hours of completing the test. The four modules of the GED are scored on a scale of 100–200. In order to earn high school equivalency, it is necessary to achieve a passing score on all of the four modules, and scores cannot be made up between modules—that is, a high score on one subject cannot be used to compensate for a low score on another subject. Scores are divided into four ranges:

1. A score lower than 145 points earns a score of "Not Passing." It is necessary to retake the test to earn high school equivalency.

2. A score at or higher than 145 points earns "GED Passing Score/High School Equivalency."

3. A score of 165-175 is deemed "GED College Ready." This designation advises colleges and universities that the test taker is ready to begin a degree program without further placement testing or preparation courses (policies vary among schools).

4. A score over 175 earns the test taker "GED College Ready + Credit." For some institutions, a score at this level allows the GED graduate to earn college credit for certain courses (policies vary among schools).

Recent/Future Developments

The 2014 GED is the newest version of the test. It was updated to reflect current high school education standards. Initial score results reflected lower pass rates on the 2014 GED compared to earlier versions of the test, so GED Testing Service adjusted score ranges to compensate for the increased difficulty of the exam.

Reasoning through Language Arts

Reading Comprehension

Understanding Literary Interpretation

Literary interpretation is an interpretation and analysis of a literary work, based on the textual evidence in the work. It is often subjective as critical readers may discern different meanings in the details. A test taker needs to be prepared for questions that will test how well he or she can read a passage, make an analysis, and then provide evidence to support that analysis.

Literal and Figurative Meanings

When analyzing and interpreting fiction, readers must be active participants in the experience. Some authors make their messages clearer than others, but the onus is on the reader to add layers to what is read through interpretation. In literary interpretation, the goal is not to offer an opinion as to the inherent value of the work. Rather, the goal is to determine what the text means by analyzing the *literal and figurative meanings* of the text through critical reading.

Critical reading is close reading that elicits questions as the reader progresses. Many authors of fiction use literary elements and devices to further theme and to speak to their audience. These elements often utilize language that has an alternate or figurative meaning in addition to their actual or literal meaning. Readers should be asking questions about these and other important details as a passage is analyzed. What unfamiliar words are there? What is their contextual definition? How do they contribute to the overall feel of the work? How do they contribute to the mood and general message? Literal and figurative meanings are discussed further in the informational texts and rhetoric section.

Drawing Inferences

An *inference* refers to a point that is implied (as opposed to directly-stated) by the evidence presented. It's necessary to use inference in order to draw conclusions about the meaning of a passage. Authors make implications through character dialogue, thoughts, effects on others, actions, and looks.

When making an inference about a passage, it's important to rely only on the information that is provided in the text itself. This helps readers ensure that their conclusions are valid. Drawing inferences is also discussed in the informational texts and rhetoric section.

Textual Evidence

It's helpful to read a passage a few times, noting details that seem important to the piece. Textual evidence within the details helps readers draw a conclusion about a passage. *Textual evidence* refers to information—facts and examples that support the main idea. Textual evidence will likely come from outside sources and can be in the form of quoted or paraphrased material. In order to draw a conclusion from evidence, it's important to examine the credibility and validity of that evidence as well as how (and if) it relates to the main idea. Effective use of textual evidence should connect to the main idea and support a specific point. Textual evidence is examined further in the informational texts and rhetoric section.

Understanding the Development of Themes

Identifying Theme or Central Message

The *theme* is the central message of a fictional work, whether that work is structured as prose, drama, or poetry. It is the heart of what an author is trying to say to readers through the writing, and theme is largely conveyed through literary elements and techniques.

In literature, a theme can often be determined by considering the over-arching narrative conflict within the work. Though there are several types of conflicts and several potential themes within them, the following are the most common:

- *Individual against the self*—relevant to themes of self-awareness, internal struggles, pride, coming of age, facing reality, fate, free will, vanity, loss of innocence, loneliness, isolation, fulfillment, failure, and disillusionment

- *Individual against nature*— relevant to themes of knowledge vs. ignorance, nature as beauty, quest for discovery, self-preservation, chaos and order, circle of life, death, and destruction of beauty

- *Individual against society*— relevant to themes of power, beauty, good, evil, war, class struggle, totalitarianism, role of men/women, wealth, corruption, change vs. tradition, capitalism, destruction, heroism, injustice, and racism

- *Individual against another individual*— relevant to themes of hope, loss of love or hope, sacrifice, power, revenge, betrayal, and honor

For example, in Hawthorne's *The Scarlet Letter*, one possible narrative conflict could be the individual against the self, with a relevant theme of internal struggles. This theme is alluded to through characterization—Dimmesdale's moral struggle with his love for Hester and Hester's internal struggles with the truth and her daughter, Pearl. It's also alluded to through plot—Dimmesdale's suicide and Hester helping the very townspeople who initially condemned her.

Sometimes, a text can convey a *message* or *universal lesson*—a truth or insight that the reader infers from the text, based on analysis of the literary and/or poetic elements. This message is often presented as a statement. For example, a potential message in Shakespeare's *Hamlet* could be "Revenge is what ultimately drives the human soul." This message can be immediately determined through plot and characterization in numerous ways, but it can also be determined through the setting of Norway, which is bordering on war.

How Authors Develop Theme

Authors employ a variety of techniques to present a theme. They may compare or contrast characters, events, places, ideas, or historical or invented settings to speak thematically. They may use analogies, metaphors, similes, allusions, or other literary devices to convey the theme. An author's use of diction, syntax, and tone can also help convey the theme. Authors will often develop themes through the development of characters, use of the setting, repetition of ideas, use of symbols, and through contrasting value systems. Authors of both fiction and nonfiction genres will use a variety of these techniques to develop one or more themes.

Regardless of the literary genre, there are commonalities in how authors, playwrights, and poets develop themes or central ideas.

Authors often do research, the results of which contributes to theme. In prose fiction and drama, this research may include real historical information about the setting the author has chosen or include elements that make fictional characters, settings, and plots seem realistic to the reader. In nonfiction, research is critical since the information contained within this literature must be accurate and, moreover, accurately represented.

In fiction, authors present a narrative conflict that will contribute to the overall theme. In fiction, this conflict may involve the storyline itself and some trouble within characters that needs resolution. In nonfiction, this conflict may be an explanation or commentary on factual people and events.

Authors will sometimes use character motivation to convey theme, such as in the example from *Hamlet* regarding revenge. In fiction, the characters an author creates will think, speak, and act in ways that effectively convey the theme to readers. In nonfiction, the characters are factual, as in a biography, but authors pay particular attention to presenting those motivations to make them clear to readers.

Authors also use literary devices as a means of conveying theme. For example, the use of moon symbolism in Shelley's *Frankenstein* is significant as its phases can be compared to the phases that the Creature undergoes as he struggles with his identity.

The selected point of view can also contribute to a work's theme. The use of first person point of view in a fiction or non-fiction work engages the reader's response differently than third person point of view. The central idea or theme from a first-person narrative may differ from a third-person limited text.

In literary nonfiction, authors usually identify the purpose of their writing, which differs from fiction, where the general purpose is to entertain. The purpose of nonfiction is usually to inform, persuade, or entertain the audience. The stated purpose of a non-fiction text will drive how the central message or theme, if applicable, is presented.

Authors identify an audience for their writing, which is critical in shaping the theme of the work. For example, the audience for J.K. Rowling's *Harry Potter* series would be different than the audience for a biography of George Washington. The audience an author chooses to address is closely tied to the purpose of the work. The choice of an audience also drives the choice of language and level of diction an author uses. Ultimately, the intended audience determines the level to which that subject matter is presented and the complexity of the theme.

Identifying Literary Elements

There is no one, final definition of what literary elements are. They can be considered features or characteristics of fiction, but they are really more of a way that readers can unpack a text for the purpose of analysis and understanding the meaning. The elements contribute to a reader's literary interpretation of a passage as to how they function to convey the central message of a work. The most common literary elements used for analysis are the presented below.

<u>Point of View</u>

The *point of view* is the position the narrator takes when telling the story in prose. If a narrator is incorporated in a drama, the point of view may vary; in poetry, point of view refers to the position the speaker in a poem takes.

First Person
The first person point of view is when the writer uses the word "I" in the text. Poetry often uses first person, e.g., William Wordsworth's "I Wandered Lonely as a Cloud." Two examples of prose written in first person are Suzanne Collins' *The Hunger Games* and Anthony Burgess's *A Clockwork Orange*.

Second Person
The second person point of view is when the writer uses the pronoun "you." It is not widely used in prose fiction, but as a technique, it has been used by writers such as William Faulkner in *Absalom, Absalom!* and Albert Camus in *The Fall*. It is more common in poetry—e.g., Pablo Neruda's "If You Forget Me."

Third Person
Third person point of view is when the writer utilizes pronouns such as him, her, or them. It may be the most utilized point of view in prose as it provides flexibility to an author and is the one with which readers are most familiar. There are two main types of third person used in fiction. *Third person omniscient* uses a narrator that is all-knowing, relating the story by conveying and interpreting thoughts/feelings of all characters. In *third person limited,* the narrator relates the story through the perspective of one character's thoughts/feelings, usually the main character.

Plot
The *plot* is what happens in the story. Plots may be singular, containing one problem, or they may be very complex, with many sub-plots. All plots have exposition, a conflict, a climax, and a resolution. The *conflict* drives the plot and is something that the reader expects to be resolved. The plot carries those events along until there is a resolution to the conflict.

Tone
The *tone* of a story reflects the author's attitude and opinion about the subject matter of the story or text. Tone can be expressed through word choice, imagery, figurative language, syntax, and other details. The emotion or mood the reader experiences relates back to the tone of the story. Some examples of possible tones are humorous, somber, sentimental, and ironic.

Setting
The *setting* is the time, place, or set of surroundings in which the story occurs. It includes time or time span, place(s), climates, geography—man-made or natural—or cultural environments. Emily Dickinson's poem "Because I could not stop for Death" has a simple setting—the narrator's symbolic ride with Death through town towards the local graveyard. Conversely, Leo Tolstoy's *War and Peace* encompasses numerous settings within settings in the areas affected by the Napoleonic Wars, spanning 1805 to 1812.

Characters
Characters are the story's figures that assume primary, secondary, or minor roles. *Central* or *major* characters are those integral to the story—the plot cannot be resolved without them. A central character can be a *protagonist* or hero. There may be more than one protagonist, and he/she doesn't always have to possess good characteristics. A character can also be an *antagonist*—the force against a protagonist.

Dynamic characters change over the course of the plot time. *Static* characters do not change. A *symbolic* character is one that represents an author's idea about society in general—e.g., Napoleon in Orwell's *Animal Farm*. *Stock* characters are those that appear across genres and embrace stereotypes—e.g., the cowboy of the Wild West or the blonde bombshell in a detective novel. A *flat* character is one that does not present a lot of complexity or depth, while a *rounded* character does. Sometimes, the *narrator* of a story or the *speaker* in a poem can be a character—e.g., Nick Carraway in F. Scott Fitzgerald's *The Great Gatsby* or the speaker in Robert Browning's "My Last Duchess." The narrator might also function as a character in prose, though not be part of the story—e.g., Charles Dickens' narrator of *A Christmas Carol*.

Understanding Figurative Language

Whereas literal language is the author's use of precise words, proper meanings, definitions, and phrases that mean exactly what they say, *figurative language* deviates from precise meaning and word definition—often in conjunction with other familiar words and phrases—to paint a picture for the reader. Figurative language is less explicit and more open to reader interpretation.

Some examples of figurative language are included in the following graphic.

	Definition	**Example**
Simile	Compares two things using "like" or "as"	Her hair was like gold.
Metaphor	Compares two things as if they are the same	He was a giant teddy bear.
Idiom	Using words with predictable meanings to create a phrase with a different meaning	The world is your oyster.
Alliteration	Repeating the same beginning sound or letter in a phrase for emphasis	The busy baby babbled.
Personification	Attributing human characteristics to an object or an animal	The house glowered menacingly with a dark smile.
Foreshadowing	Giving an indication that something is going to happen later in the story	I wasn't aware at the time, but I would come to regret those words.
Symbolism	Using symbols to represent ideas and provide a different meaning	The ring represented the bond between us.
Onomatopoeia	Using words that imitate sound	The tire went off with a bang and a crunch.
Imagery	Appealing to the senses by using descriptive language	The sky was painted with red and pink and streaked with orange.
Hyperbole	Using exaggeration not meant to be taken literally	The girl weighed less than a feather.

Figurative language can be used to give additional insight into the theme or message of a text by moving beyond the usual and literal meaning of words and phrases. It can also be used to appeal to the senses of readers and create a more in-depth story.

Understanding Poetic Devices and Structure

<u>Poetic Devices</u>
Rhyme is the poet's use of corresponding word sounds in order to create an effect. Most rhyme occurs at the ends of a poem's lines, which is how readers arrive at the *rhyme scheme*. Each line that has a corresponding rhyming sound is assigned a letter—A, B, C, and so on. When using a rhyme scheme,

poets will often follow lettered patterns. Robert Frost's *"The Road Not Taken"* uses the ABAAB rhyme scheme:

> Two roads diverged in a yellow wood, A
> And sorry I could not travel both B
> And be one traveler, long I stood A
> And looked down one as far as I could A
> To where it bent in the undergrowth; B

Another important poetic device is *rhythm*—metered patterns within poetry verses. When a poet develops rhythm through *meter*, he or she is using a combination of stressed and unstressed syllables to create a sound effect for the reader.

Rhythm is created by the use of *poetic feet*—individual rhythmic units made up of the combination of stressed and unstressed syllables. A line of poetry is made up of one or more poetic feet. There are five standard types in English poetry, as depicted in the chart below.

Foot Type	Rhythm	Pattern
Iamb	buh Buh	Unstressed/stressed
Trochee	Buh buh	Stressed/unstressed
Spondee	Buh Buh	Stressed/stressed
Anapest	buh buh Buh	Unstressed/unstressed/stressed
Dactyl	Buh buh buh	Stressed/unstressed/unstressed

Structure

Poetry is most easily recognized by its structure, which varies greatly. For example, a structure may be strict in the number of lines it uses. It may use rhyming patterns or may not rhyme at all. There are three main types of poetic structures:

- *Verse*—poetry with a consistent meter and rhyme scheme
- *Blank verse*—poetry with consistent meter but an inconsistent rhyme scheme
- *Free verse*—poetry with inconsistent meter or rhyme

Verse poetry is most often developed in the form of *stanzas*—groups of word lines. Stanzas can also be considered *verses*. The structure is usually formulaic and adheres to the protocols for the form. For example, the English *sonnet* form uses a structure of fourteen lines and a variety of different rhyming patterns. The English *ode* typically uses three ten-line stanzas and has a particular rhyming pattern.

Poets choose poetic structure based on the effect they want to create. Some structures—such as the ballad and haiku—developed out of cultural influences and common artistic practice in history, but in more modern poetry, authors choose their structure to best fit their intended effect.

Identifying Reading Strategies

A *reading strategy* is the way a reader interacts with text in order to understand its meaning. It is a skill set that a reader brings to the reading. It employs a reader's ability to use prior knowledge when addressing literature and utilizes a set of methods in order to analyze text. A reading strategy is not simply tackling a text passage as it appears. It involves a more complex system of planning and thought during the reading experience. Current research indicates readers who utilize strategies and a variety of critical reading skills are better thinkers who glean more interpretive information from their reading. Consequently, they are more successful in their overall comprehension.

Pre-reading Strategies

Pre-reading strategies are important, yet often overlooked. Non-critical readers will often begin reading without taking the time to review factors that will help them understand the text. Skipping pre-reading strategies may result in a reader having to re-address a text passage more times than is necessary. Some pre-reading strategies include the following:

- Previewing the text for clues
- Skimming the text for content
- Scanning for unfamiliar words in context
- Formulating questions on sight
- Making predictions
- Recognizing needed prior knowledge

Before reading a text passage, a reader can enhance his or her ability to comprehend material by *previewing the text for clues*. This may mean making careful note of any titles, headings, graphics, notes, introductions, important summaries, and conclusions. It can involve a reader making physical notes regarding these elements or highlighting anything he or she thinks is important before reading. Often, a reader will be able to gain information just from these elements alone. Of course, close reading is required in order to fill in the details. A reader needs to be able to ask what he or she is reading about and what a passage is trying to say. The answers to these general questions can often be answered in previewing the text itself.

It's helpful to use pre-reading clues to determine the main idea and organization. First, any titles, sub-headings, chapter headings should be read, and the test taker should make note of the author's credentials if any are listed. It's important to deduce what these clues may indicate as it pertains to the focus of the text and how it's organized.

During pre-reading, readers should also take special note of how text features contribute to the central idea or thesis of the passage. Is there an index? Is there a glossary? What headings, footnotes, or other visuals are included and how do they relate to the details within the passage? Again, this is where any pre-reading notes come in handy, since a test taker should be able to relate supporting details to these textual features.

Next, a reader should *skim* the text for general ideas and content. This technique does not involve close reading; rather, it involves looking for important words within the passage itself. These words may have something to do with the author's theme. They may have to do with structure—for example, words such as *first, next, therefore*, and *last*. Skimming helps a reader understand the overall structure of a passage and, in turn, this helps him or her understand the author's theme or message.

From there, a reader should quickly *scan* the text for any unfamiliar words. When reading a print text, highlighting these words or making other marginal notation is helpful when going back to read text critically. A reader should look at the words surrounding any unfamiliar ones to see what contextual clues unfamiliar words carry. Being able to define unfamiliar terms through contextual meaning is a critical skill in reading comprehension.

A reader should also *formulate any questions* he or she might have before conducting close reading. Questions such as "What is the author trying to tell me?" or "Is the author trying to persuade my thinking?" are important to a reader's ability to engage critically with the text. Questions will focus a reader's attention on what is important in terms of idea and what is supporting detail.

Along with formulating questions, it is helpful to make predictions of what the answers to these questions and others will be. *Making predictions* involves using information from the text and personal experiences to make a thoughtful guess as to what will happen in the story and what outcomes can be expected.

Last, a reader should recognize that author's assume readers bring a *prior knowledge* set to the reading experience. Not all readers have the same experience, but authors seek to communicate with their readers. In turn, readers should strive to interact with the author of a particular passage by asking themselves what the passage demands they know during reading. This is also known as making a text-to-self connection. If a passage is informational in nature, a reader should ask "What do I know about this topic from other experiences I've had or other works I've read?" If a reader can relate to the content, he or she will better understand it.

All of the above pre-reading strategies will help the reader prepare for a closer reading experience. They will engage a reader in active interaction with the text by helping to focus the reader's full attention on the details that he or she will encounter during the next round or two of critical, closer reading.

<u>Strategies During Reading</u>

After pre-reading, a test taker can employ a variety of other reading strategies while conducting one or more closer readings. These strategies include the following:

- Clarifying during a close read
- Questioning during a close read
- Organizing the main ideas and supporting details
- Summarizing the text effectively

A reader needs to be able to *clarify* what he or she is reading. This strategy demands a reader think about how and what he or she is reading. This thinking should occur during and after the act of reading. For example, a reader may encounter one or more unfamiliar ideas during reading, then be asked to apply thoughts about those unfamiliar concepts after reading when answering test questions.

Questioning during a critical read is closely related to clarifying. A reader must be able to ask questions in general about what he or she is reading and questions regarding the author's supporting ideas. Questioning also involves a reader's ability to self-question. When closely reading a passage, it's not enough to simply try and understand the author. A reader must consider critical thinking questions to ensure he or she is comprehending intent. It's advisable, when conducting a close read, to write out margin notes and questions during the experience. These questions can be addressed later in the thinking process after reading and during the phase where a reader addresses the test questions. A reader who is successful in reading comprehension will iteratively question what he or she reads, search text for clarification, then answer any questions that arise.

A reader should *organize* main ideas and supporting details cognitively as he or she reads, as it will help the reader understand the larger structure at work. The use of quick annotations or marks to indicate what the main idea is and how the details function to support it can be helpful. Understanding the structure of a text passage is sometimes critical to answering questions about an author's approach, theme, messages, and supporting detail. This strategy is most effective when reading informational or nonfiction text. Texts that try to convince readers of a particular idea, that present a theory, or that try to explain difficult concepts are easier to understand when a reader can identify the overarching structure at work.

Post-reading Strategies

After completing a text, a reader should be able to *summarize* the author's theme and supporting details in order to fully understand the passage. Being able to effectively restate the author's message, sub-themes, and pertinent, supporting ideas will help a reader gain an advantage when addressing standardized test questions.

A reader should also evaluate the strength of the predictions that were made in the pre-reading stage. Using textual evidence, predictions should be compared to the actual events in the story to see if the two were similar or not. Employing all of these strategies will lead to fuller, more insightful reading comprehension.

Understanding the Effect of Word Choice

An author's choice of words—also referred to as *diction*—helps to convey his or her meaning in a particular way. Through diction, an author can convey a particular tone—e.g., a humorous tone, a serious tone—in order to support the thesis in a meaningful way to the reader.

Connotation and Denotation

Connotation is when an author chooses words or phrases that invoke ideas or feelings other than their literal meaning. An example of the use of connotation is the word *cheap*, which suggests something is poor in value or negatively describes a person as reluctant to spend money. When something or someone is described this way, the reader is more inclined to have a particular image or feeling about it or him/her. Thus, connotation can be a very effective language tool in creating emotion and swaying opinion. However, connotations are sometimes hard to pin down because varying emotions can be associated with a word. Generally, though, connotative meanings tend to be fairly consistent within a specific cultural group.

Denotation refers to words or phrases that mean exactly what they say. It is helpful when a writer wants to present hard facts or vocabulary terms with which readers may be unfamiliar. Some examples of denotation are the words *inexpensive* and *frugal*. *Inexpensive* refers to the cost of something, not its value, and *frugal* indicates that a person is conscientiously watching his or her spending. These terms do not elicit the same emotions that *cheap* does.

Authors sometimes choose to use both, but what they choose and when they use it is what critical readers need to differentiate. One method isn't inherently better than the other; however, one may create a better effect, depending upon an author's intent. If, for example, an author's purpose is to inform, to instruct, and to familiarize readers with a difficult subject, his or her use of connotation may be helpful. However, it may also undermine credibility and confuse readers. An author who wants to create a credible, scholarly effect in his or her text would most likely use denotation, which emphasizes literal, factual meaning and examples.

Technical Language

Test takers and critical readers alike should be very aware of technical language used within informational text. *Technical language* refers to terminology that is specific to a particular industry and is best understood by those specializing in that industry. This language is fairly easy to differentiate, since it will most likely be unfamiliar to readers. It's critical to be able to define technical language either by the author's written definition, through the use of an included glossary—if offered—or through context clues that help readers clarify word meaning.

Identifying Rhetorical Strategies

Rhetoric refers to an author's use of particular strategies, appeals, and devices to persuade an intended audience. The more effective the use of rhetoric, the more likely the audience will be persuaded.

Determining an Author's Point of View

A *rhetorical strategy*—also referred to as a *rhetorical mode*—is the structural way an author chooses to present his/her argument. Though the terms noted below are similar to the organizational structures noted earlier, these strategies do not imply that the entire text follows the approach. For example, a cause and effect organizational structure is solely that, nothing more. A persuasive text may use cause and effect as a strategy to convey a singular point. Thus, an argument may include several of the strategies as the author strives to convince his or her audience to take action or accept a different point of view. It's important that readers are able to identify an author's thesis and position on the topic in order to be able to identify the careful construction through which the author speaks to the reader. The following are some of the more common rhetorical strategies:

- *Cause and effect*—establishing a logical correlation or causation between two ideas
- *Classification/division*—the grouping of similar items together or division of something into parts
- *Comparison/contrast*—the distinguishing of similarities/differences to expand on an idea
- *Definition*—used to clarify abstract ideas, unfamiliar concepts, or to distinguish one idea from another
- *Description*—use of vivid imagery, active verbs, and clear adjectives to explain ideas
- *Exemplification*—the use of examples to explain an idea
- *Narration*—anecdotes or personal experience to present or expand on a concept
- *Problem/Solution*—presentation of a problem or problems, followed by proposed solution(s)

Rhetorical Strategies and Devices

A *rhetorical device* is the phrasing and presentation of an idea that reinforces and emphasizes a point in an argument. A rhetorical device is often quite memorable. One of the more famous uses of a rhetorical device is in John F. Kennedy's 1961 inaugural address: "Ask not what your country can do for you, ask what you can do for your country." The contrast of ideas presented in the phrasing is an example of the rhetorical device of antimetabole. Some other common examples are provided below, but test takers should be aware that this is not a complete list.

Device	Definition	Example
Allusion	A reference to a famous person, event, or significant literary text as a form of significant comparison	"We are apt to shut our eyes against a painful truth, and listen to the song of that siren till she transforms us into beasts." Patrick Henry
Anaphora	The repetition of the same words at the beginning of successive words, phrases, or clauses, designed to emphasize an idea	"We shall not flag or fail. We shall go on to the end. We shall fight in France, we shall fight on the seas and oceans, we shall fight with growing confidence ... we shall fight in the fields and in the streets, we shall fight in the hills. We shall never surrender." Winston Churchill
Understatement	A statement meant to portray a situation as less important than it actually is to create an ironic effect	"The war in the Pacific has not necessarily developed in Japan's favor." Emperor Hirohito, surrendering Japan in World War II
Parallelism	A syntactical similarity in a structure or series of structures used for impact of an idea, making it memorable	"A penny saved is a penny earned." Ben Franklin
Rhetorical question	A question posed that is not answered by the writer though there is a desired response, most often designed to emphasize a point	"Can anyone look at our reduced standing in the world today and say, 'Let's have four more years of this?'" Ronald Reagan

Literature refers to a collection of written works that are the distinctive voices of peoples, time periods, and cultures. The world has gained great insight into human thought, vices, virtues, and desires through the written word. As the work pertains to the author's approach to these insights, literature can be classified as fiction or non-fiction.

Identifying Major Literary Works and Authors

The GED test assumes test takers will have a familiarity with a wide range of poetic, dramatic, fictional, and nonfiction works. In most cases, the test taker will be presented with a literary passage and be required to answer one or more questions about it. This may involve having to identify the literary work presented from a list of options.

The ability of the test taker to demonstrate familiarity of major literary works is key in success when taking the GED exam. The following chart offers some examples of major works in addition to those listed elsewhere in this guide, but the list not exhaustive.

American

Fictional Prose Before 1920

- Nathaniel Hawthorne | *The Scarlett Letter* (1850)
- Harriet Beecher Stowe | *Uncle Tom's Cabin* (1852)
- Louisa May Alcott | *Little Women* (1868)
- Henry James | *Daisy Miller* (1878)
- Jack London | *The Call of the Wild* (1903)
- William Faulkner | *The Sound and the Fury* (1929)

Fictional Prose After 1920 and Before 1960

- Zora Neale Hurston | *Their Eyes Were Watching God* (1937)
- John Steinbeck | *Grapes of Wrath* (1939)
- Ernest Hemingway | *For Whom the Bell Tolls* (1940)
- J.D. Salinger | *Catcher in the Rye* (1951)
- Herman Melville | *Moby Dick* (1956)

Fictional Prose After 1960

- Harper Lee | *To Kill a Mockingbird* (1960)
- N. Scott Momaday | *The Way to Rainy Mountain* (1969)
- Marilynne Robinson | *Housekeeping* (1980)
- Alice Walker | *The Color Purple* (1982)
- Toni Morrison | *Beloved* (1987)

Drama

- Thornton Wilder I *Our Town* (1938)
- Tennessee Williams | *A Streetcar Named Desire* (1947)
- Eugene O'Neill |*Long Day's Journey into Night* (1956)
- Lorraine Hansberry | *A Raisin in the Sun* (1959)
- Edward Albee | *Who's Afraid of Virginia Woolf?* (1962)
- Amiri Baraka | *Dutchman* (1964)
- Sam Shephard | *Buried Child* (1978)

Poetry

- Anne Bradstreet | "In Reference to her Children, 23 June 1659"
- Phillis Wheatley | "On Being Brought from Africa to America" (1768)
- Edgar Allen Poe | "The Raven" (1845)
- Walt Whitman | "Song of Myself" (1855)

- Emily Dickinson | “Because I could not stop for Death" (1863)
- Robert Frost | “Wild Grapes” (1920)
- Langston Hughes | “Harlem” (1951)
- Richard Wilbur | “Love Calls Us to the Things of This World” (1956)
- Sylvia Plath | “Mirror” (1961)
- Eamon Grennan | “Cat Scat” (1988)
- Sandra Cisneros | “Loose Woman” (1994)
- Anne Carson | “The Glass Essay” (1994)
- Tupac Shakur | “The Rose that Grew from Concrete” (1999)

Literary Non-fiction

- Frederick Douglass | *My Bondage and My Freedom* (1855)
- Anne Frank | *The Diary of Anne Frank* (1947)
- Truman Capote | *In Cold Blood* (1966)
- Maya Angelou | *I Know Why the Caged Bird Sings* (1969)
- Sherman Alexie | *The Absolutely True Diary of a Part-Time Indian* (2007)
- Cynthia Levinson | *We've Got a Job* (2012)
- Malala Yousafzai and Christina Lamb | *I am Malala* (2013)
- Philip Hoose | *The Boys who Challenged Hitler* (2015

Identifying Literary Contexts

Understanding that works of literature emerged either because of a particular context—or perhaps despite a context—is key to analyzing them effectively.

<u>Historical Context</u>

The *historical context* of a piece of literature can refer to the time period, setting, or conditions of living at the time it was written as well as the context of the work. For example, Hawthorne's *The Scarlet Letter* was published in 1850, though the setting of the story is 1642-1649. Historically, then, when Hawthorne wrote his novel, the United States found itself at odds as the beginnings of a potential Civil War were in view. Thus, the historical context is potentially significant as it pertains to the ideas of traditions and values, which Hawthorne addresses in his story of Hester Prynne in the era of Puritanism.

<u>Cultural Context</u>

The *cultural context* of a piece of literature refers to cultural factors, such as the beliefs, religions, and customs that surround and are in a work of literature. The Puritan's beliefs, religion, and customs in Hawthorne's novel would be significant as they are at the core of the plot—the reason Hester wears the A and why Arthur kills himself. The customs of people in the Antebellum Period, though not quite as restrictive, were still somewhat similar. This would impact how the audience of the time received the novel.

<u>Literary Context</u>

Literary context refers to the consideration of the genre, potentially at the time the work was written. In 1850, Realism and Romanticism were the driving forces in literature in the U.S., with depictions of life as it was at the time in which the work was written or the time it was written *about* as well as some works celebrating the beauty of nature. Thus, an audience in Hawthorne's time would have been well satisfied with the elements of both offered in the text. They would have been looking for details about everyday things and people (Realism), but they also would appreciate his approach to description of nature and the focus on the individual (American Romanticism). The contexts would be significant as they would pertain to evaluating the work against those criteria.

Here are some questions to use when considering context:

- When was the text written?
- What was society like at the time the text was written, or what was it like, given the work's identified time period?
- Who or what influenced the writer?
- What political or social influences might there have been?
- What influences may there have been in the genre that may have affected the writer?

Additionally, test takers should familiarize themselves with literary periods such as Old and Middle English, American Colonial, American Renaissance, American Naturalistic, and British and American Modernist and Post-Modernist movements. Most students of literature will have had extensive exposure to these literary periods in history, and while it is not necessary to recognize every major literary work on sight and associate that work to its corresponding movement or cultural context, the test taker should be familiar enough with the historical and cultural significance of each test passage in order to be able to address test questions correctly.

The following brief description of some literary contexts and their associated literary examples follows. It is not an all-inclusive list. The test taker should read each description, then follow up with independent study to clarify each movement, its context, its most familiar authors, and their works.

<u>Metaphysical Poetry</u>

Metaphysical poetry is the descriptor applied to 17th century poets whose poetry emphasized the lyrical quality of their work. These works contain highly creative poetic conceits or metaphoric comparisons between two highly dissimilar things or ideas. Metaphysical poetry is characterized by highly prosaic language and complicated, often layered, metaphor.

Poems such as John Donne's "The Flea," Andrew Marvell's "To His Coy Mistress," George Herbert's "The Collar," Henry Vaughan's "The World," and Richard Crashaw's "A Song" are associated with this type of poetry.

<u>British Romanticism</u>

British Romanticism was a cultural and literary movement within Europe that developed at the end of the 18th century and extended into the 19th century. It occurred partly in response to aristocratic, political, and social norms and partly in response to the Industrial Revolution of the day. Characterized by intense emotion, major literary works of British Romanticism embrace the idea of aestheticism and the beauty of nature. Literary works exalted folk customs and historical art and encouraged spontaneity of artistic endeavor. The movement embraced the heroic ideal and the concept that heroes would raise the quality of society.

Authors who are classified as British Romantics include Samuel Taylor Coleridge, John Keats, George Byron, Mary Shelley, Percy Bysshe Shelley, and William Blake. Well-known works include Samuel Taylor Coleridge's "Kubla Khan," John Keats' "Ode on a Grecian Urn," George Byron's "Childe Harold's Pilgrimage," Mary Shelley's *Frankenstein*, Percy Bysshe Shelley's "Ode to the West Wind," and William Blake's "The Tyger."

American Romanticism

American Romanticism occurred within the American literary scene beginning early in the 19th century. While many aspects were similar to British Romanticism, it is further characterized as having gothic aspects and the idea that individualism was to be encouraged. It also embraced the concept of the *noble savage*—the idea that indigenous culture uncorrupted by civilization is better than advanced society.

Well-known authors and works include Nathanial Hawthorne's *The House of the Seven Gables*, Edgar Allan Poe's "The Raven" and "The Cask of Amontillado," Emily Dickinson's "I Felt a Funeral in My Brain" and James Fenimore Cooper's *The Last of the Mohicans.*

Transcendentalism

Transcendentalism was a movement that applied to a way of thinking that developed within the United States, specifically New England, around 1836. While this way of thinking originally employed philosophical aspects, transcendentalism spread to all forms of art, literature, and even to the ways people chose to live. It was born out of a reaction to traditional rationalism and purported concepts such as a higher divinity, feminism, humanitarianism, and communal living. Transcendentalism valued intuition, self-reliance, and the idea that human nature was inherently good.

Well-known authors include Ralph Waldo Emerson, Henry David Thoreau, Louisa May Alcott, and Ellen Sturgis Hooper. Works include Ralph Waldo Emerson's "Self-Reliance" and "Uriel," Henry David Thoreau's *Walden* and *Civil Disobedience*, Louisa May Alcott's *Little Women*, and Ellen Sturgis Hooper's "I Slept, and Dreamed that Life was Beauty."

The Harlem Renaissance

The Harlem Renaissance is the descriptor given to the cultural, artistic, and social boom that developed in Harlem, New York, at the beginning of the 20th century, spanning the 1920s and 1930s. Originally termed *The New Negro Movement*, it emphasized African-American urban cultural expression and migration across the United States. It had strong roots in African-American Christianity, discourse, and intellectualism. The Harlem Renaissance heavily influenced the development of music and fashion as well. Its singular characteristic was to embrace Pan-American culturalisms; however, strong themes of the slavery experience and African-American folk traditions also emerged. A hallmark of the Harlem Renaissance was that it laid the foundation for the future Civil Rights Movement in the United States.

Well-known authors and works include Zora Neale Hurston's *Their Eyes Were Watching God*, Richard Wright's *Native Son*, Langston Hughes' "I, Too," and James Weldon Johnson's "God's Trombones: Seven Negro Sermons in Verse" and *The Book of American Negro Poetry.*

Understanding the Characteristics of Literary Genres

Classifying literature involves an understanding of the concept of genre. A *genre* is a category of literature that possesses similarities in style and in characteristics. Based on form and structure, there are four basic genres.

Fictional Prose

Fictional prose consists of fictional works written in standard form with a natural flow of speech and without poetic structure. Fictional prose primarily utilizes grammatically complete sentences and a paragraph structure to convey its message.

Drama

Drama is fiction that is written to be performed in a variety of media, intended to be performed for an audience, and structured for that purpose. It might be composed using poetry or prose, often straddling the elements of both in what actors are expected to present. Action and dialogue are the tools used in drama to tell the story.

Poetry

Poetry is fiction in verse that has a unique focus on the rhythm of language and focuses on intensity of feeling. It is not an entire story, though it may tell one; it is compact in form and in function. Poetry can be considered as a poet's brief word picture for a reader. Poetic structure is primarily composed of lines and stanzas. Together, poetic structure and devices are the methods that poets use to lead readers to feeling an effect and, ultimately, to the interpretive message.

Literary Nonfiction

Literary nonfiction is prose writing that is based on current or past real events or real people and includes straightforward accounts as well as those that offer opinions on facts or factual events. The GED exam distinguishes between *literary nonfiction*—a form of writing that incorporates literary styles and techniques to create factually-based narratives—and informational texts, which will be addressed in the next section.

Identifying Characteristics of Major Forms Within Each Genre

Fictional Prose

Fiction written in prose can be further broken down into *fiction genres*—types of fiction. Some of the more common genres of fiction are as follows:

- *Classical Fiction*—a work of fiction considered timeless in its message or theme, remaining noteworthy and meaningful over decades or centuries—e.g., Charlotte *Brontë's Jane Eyre*, Mark Twain's *Adventures of Huckleberry Finn*

- *Fables*— short fiction that generally features animals, fantastic creatures, or other forces within nature that assume human-like characters and has a moral lesson for the reader—e.g., Aesop's Fables

- *Fairy tales*—children's stories with magical characters in imaginary, enchanted lands, usually depicting a struggle between good and evil, a sub-genre of folklore—e.g., Hans Christian Anderson's *The Little Mermaid, Cinderella* by the Brothers Grimm

- *Fantasy*—fiction with magic or supernatural elements that cannot occur in the real world, sometimes involving medieval elements in language, usually includes some form of sorcery or witchcraft and sometimes set on a different world—e.g., J.R.R. Tolkien's *The Hobbit*, J.K. Rowling's *Harry Potter and the Sorcerer's Stone*, George R.R. Martin's *A Game of Thrones*

- *Folklore*—types of fiction passed down from oral tradition, stories indigenous to a particular region or culture, with a local flavor in tone, designed to help humans cope with their condition in life and validate cultural traditions, beliefs, and customs—e.g., William Laughead's *Paul Bunyan and The Blue Ox*, the Buddhist story of "The Banyan Deer"

- *Mythology*—closely related to folklore but more widespread, features mystical, otherworldly characters and addresses the basic question of why and how humans exist, relies heavily on allegory and features gods or heroes captured in some sort of struggle—e.g., Greek myths, Genesis I and II in the *Bible*, Arthurian legends

- *Science fiction*—fiction that uses the principle of *extrapolation*—loosely defined as a form of prediction—to imagine future realities and problems of the human experience—e.g., Robert Heinlein's *Stranger in a Strange Land*, Ayn Rand's *Anthem*, Isaac Asimov's *I, Robot*, Philip K. Dick's *Do Androids Dream of Electric Sheep*?

- *Short stories*—short works of prose fiction with fully-developed themes and characters, focused on mood, generally developed with a single plot, with a short period of time for settings—e.g., Edgar Allan Poe's "Fall of the House of Usher," Shirley Jackson's "The Lottery," Isaac Bashevis Singer's "Gimpel the Fool"

Drama

Drama refers to a form of literature written for the purpose of performance for an audience. Like prose fiction, drama has several genres. The following are the most common ones:

- *Comedy*—a humorous play designed to amuse and entertain, often with an emphasis on the common person's experience, generally resolved in a positive way—e.g., Richard Sheridan's *School for Scandal*, Shakespeare's *Taming of the Shrew*, Neil Simon's *The Odd Couple*

- *History*—a play based on recorded history where the fate of a nation or kingdom is at the core of the conflict—e.g., Christopher Marlowe's *Edward II*, Shakespeare's *King Richard III*, Arthur Miller's *The Crucible*

- *Tragedy*—a serious play that often involves the downfall of the protagonist, in modern tragedies, the protagonist is not necessarily in a position of power or authority—e.g., Jean Racine's *Phèdre*, Arthur Miller's *Death of a Salesman*, John Steinbeck's *Of Mice and Men*

- *Melodrama*—a play that is emphasizes heightened emotion and sensationalism, generally with stereotypical characters in exaggerated or realistic situations and with moral polarization—e.g., Jean-Jacques Rousseau's *Pygmalion*

- *Tragi-comedy*—a play that has elements of both tragedy—a character experiencing a tragic loss—and comedy—the resolution is often positive with no clear distinctive mood for either—e.g., Shakespeare's *The Merchant of Venice*, Anton Chekhov's *The Cherry Orchard*

Poetry

The genre of *poetry* refers to literary works that focus on the expression of feelings and ideas through the use of structure and linguistic rhythm to create a desired effect.

Different poetic structures and devices are used to create the various major forms of poetry. Some of the most common forms are discussed in the following chart.

Type	Poetic Structure	Example
Ballad	A poem or song passed down orally which tells a story and in English tradition usually uses an ABAB or ABCB rhyme scheme	William Butler Yeats' "The Ballad Of Father O'Hart"
Epic	A long poem from ancient oral tradition which narrates the story of a legendary or heroic protagonist	Homer's The Odyssey Virgil's The Aeneid
Haiku	A Japanese poem of three unrhymed lines with five, seven, and five syllables (in English) with nature as a common subject matter	Matsuo Bashō An old silent pond... A frog jumps into the pond, splash! Silence again.
Limerick	A five-line poem written in an AABBA rhyme scheme, with a witty focus	From Edward Lear's Book of Nonsense— "There was a Young Person of Smyrna Whose grandmother threatened to burn her..."
Ode	A formal lyric poem that addresses and praises a person, place, thing, or idea	Edna St. Vincent Millay's "Ode To Silence"
Sonnet	A fourteen-line poem written in iambic pentameter	Shakespeare's Sonnets 18 and 130

Nonfiction works are best characterized by their subject matter, which must be factual and real, describing true life experiences. There are several common types of literary non-fiction.

Biography

A *biography* is a work written about a real person (historical or currently living). It involves factual accounts of the person's life, often in a re-telling of those events based on available, researched factual information. The re-telling and dialogue, especially if related within quotes, must be accurate and reflect reliable sources. A biography reflects the time and place in which the person lived, with the goal of creating an understanding of the person and his/her human experience. Examples of well-known biographies include *The Life of Samuel Johnson* by James Boswell and *Steve Jobs* by Walter Isaacson.

Autobiography

An *autobiography* is a factual account of a person's life written by that person. It may contain some or all of the same elements as a biography, but the author is the subject matter. An autobiography will be told in first person narrative. Examples of well-known autobiographies in literature include *Night* by Elie Wiesel and *Margaret Thatcher: The Autobiography* by Margaret Thatcher.

Memoir

A *memoir* is a historical account of a person's life and experiences written by one who has personal, intimate knowledge of the information. The line between memoir, autobiography, and biography is often muddled, but generally speaking, a memoir covers a specific timeline of events as opposed to the other forms of nonfiction. A memoir is less all-encompassing. It is also less formal in tone and tends to focus on the emotional aspect of the presented timeline of events. Some examples of memoirs in literature include *Angela's Ashes* by Frank McCourt and *All Creatures Great and Small* by James Herriot.

Journalism

Some forms of *journalism* can fall into the category of literary non-fiction—e.g., travel writing, nature writing, sports writing, the interview, and sometimes, the essay. Some examples include Elizabeth Kolbert's "The Lost World, in the Annals of Extinction series for *The New Yorker* and Gary Smith's "Ali and His Entourage" for *Sports Illustrated*.

Informational Texts

Informational texts are a category of texts within the genre of nonfiction. Their intent is to inform, and while they do convey a point of view and may include literary devices, they do not utilize other literary elements, such as characters or plot. An informational text also reflects a *thesis*—an implicit or explicit statement of the text's intent and/or a *main idea*—the overarching focus and/or purpose of the text, generally implied. Some examples of Informational texts are informative articles, instructional/how-to texts, factual reports, reference texts, and self-help texts.

<u>Interpreting Textual Evidence in Informational Text</u>

Literal and Figurative Meanings

It is important when evaluating informational texts to consider the use of both *literal and figurative meanings*. The words and phrases an author chooses to include in a text must be evaluated. How does the word choice affect the meaning and tone? By recognizing the use of literal and figurative language, a reader can more readily ascertain the message or purpose of a text. Literal word choice is the easiest to analyze as it represents the usual and intended way a word or phrase is used. It is also more common in informational texts because it is used to state facts and definitions. While figurative language is typically associated with fiction and poetry, it can be found in informational texts as well. The reader must determine not only what is meant by the figurative language in context, but also how the author intended it to shape the overall text.

Inference in Informational Text

Inference refers to the reader's ability to understand the unwritten text, i.e., "read between the lines" in terms of an author's intent or message. The strategy asks that a reader not take everything he or she reads at face value but instead, add his or her own interpretation of what the author seems to be trying to convey. A reader's ability to make inferences relies on his or her ability to think clearly and logically about the text. It does not ask that the reader make wild speculation or guess about the material but demands that he or she be able to come to a sound conclusion about the material.

An author's use of less literal words and phrases requires readers to make more inference when they read. Since inference involves *deduction*—deriving conclusions from ideas assumed to be true—there's more room for interpretation. Still, critical readers who employ inference, if careful in their thinking, can still arrive at the logical, sound conclusions the author intends.

Textual Evidence in Informational Text

Once a reader has determined an author's thesis or main idea, he or she will need to understand how textual evidence supports interpretation of that thesis or main idea. Test takers will be asked direct questions regarding an author's main idea and may be asked to identify evidence that would support those ideas. This will require test takers to comprehend literal and figurative meanings within the text passage, be able to draw inferences from provided information, and be able to separate important evidence from minor supporting detail. It's often helpful to skim test questions and answer options prior to critically reading informational text; however, test takers should avoid the temptation to solely look for the correct answers. Just trying to find the "right answer" may cause test takers to miss important supporting textual evidence. Making mental note of test questions is only helpful as a guide when reading.

After identifying an author's thesis or main idea, a test taker should look at the supporting details that the author provides to back up his or her assertions, identifying those additional pieces of information that help expand the thesis. From there, test takers should examine that additional information and related details for credibility, the author's use of outside sources, and be able to point to direct evidence that supports the author's claims. It's also imperative that test takers be able to identify what is strong support and what is merely additional information that is nice to know but not necessary. Being able to make this differentiation will help test takers effectively answer questions regarding an author's use of supporting evidence within informational text.

Understanding Organizational Patterns and Structures

Organizational Structure within Informational Text

Informational text is specifically designed to relate factual information, and although it is open to a reader's interpretation and application of the facts, the structure of the presentation is carefully designed to lead the reader to a particular conclusion or central idea. When reading informational text, it is important that readers are able to understand its organizational structure as the structure often directly relates to an author's intent to inform and/or persuade the reader.

The first step in identifying the text's structure is to determine the thesis or main idea. The thesis statement and organization of a work are closely intertwined. *A thesis statement* indicates the writer's purpose and may include the scope and direction of the text. It may be presented at the beginning of a text or at the end, and it may be explicit or implicit.

Once a reader has a grasp of the thesis or main idea of the text, he or she can better determine its organizational structure. Test takers are advised to read informational text passages more than once in order to comprehend the material fully. It is also helpful to examine any text features present in the text including the table of contents, index, glossary, headings, footnotes, and visuals. The analysis of these features and the information presented within them, can offer additional clues about the central idea and structure of a text. The following questions should be asked when considering structure:

- How does the author assemble the parts to make an effective whole argument?
- Is the passage linear in nature and if so, what is the timeline or thread of logic?
- What is the presented order of events, facts, or arguments? Are these effective in contributing to the author's thesis?
- How can the passage be divided into sections? How are they related to each other and to the main idea or thesis?
- What key terms are used to indicate the organization?

Next, test takers should skim the passage, noting the first line or two of each body paragraph—the *topic sentences*—and the conclusion. Key *transitional terms*, such as *on the other hand, also, because, however, therefore, most importantly*, and *first*, within the text can also signal organizational structure. Based on these clues, readers should then be able to identify what type of organizational structure is being used. The following organizational structures are most common:

- *Problem/solution*—organized by an analysis/overview of a problem, followed by potential solution(s)
- *Cause/effect*—organized by the effects resulting from a cause or the cause(s) of a particular effect
- *Spatial order*—organized by points that suggest location or direction—e.g., top to bottom, right to left, outside to inside
- *Chronological/sequence order*—organized by points presented to indicate a passage of time or through purposeful steps/stages
- *Comparison/Contrast*—organized by points that indicate similarities and/or differences between two things or concepts
- *Order of importance*—organized by priority of points, often most significant to least significant or vice versa

Workplace and Community Documents

Workplace and *community* documents help employers to communicate within the business world and foster positive community relations outside of it. Workplace communications typically craft a specific message to a targeted audience while community documents send a broader or more generic message to a wider range of recipients.

<u>Workplace Documents</u>

Even though workplace-related documents are generated in a multitude of paper and electronic formats—memorandums, bulletin boards, presentations, web conferencing, instant messaging, and e-mails—in general all effective business communications share relevant information concisely, accurately, and purposefully. Supervisors rely on workplace documents to communicate expectations to subordinates (downward communication), and subordinates rely on workplace documents to submit progress reports, ask questions, and address concerns with their supervisors (upward communication).

- Memorandums: Designed to communicate information to a wide audience, memorandums inform staff of company-wide policy changes. Similar to an e-mail, a memorandum has a header near the top which identifies the intended audience, the author of the memo, the subject of the memo, and the date it was issued. Unlike an e-mail, though, memorandums are longer, can be submitted in paper or electronic form, and contain an introduction that identifies the topic or problem, a body that expands on the topic, and a conclusion that suggests a course of action or solution.
- Bulletin Boards: Regardless of whether they are in paper or electronic form, bulletin boards provide a less formal setting for supervisors and staff to communicate. Bulletin boards are a perfect medium to post federal and state regulations, employee incentive initiatives, volunteer opportunities, and company news. While paper bulletin boards are limited to a specific office

and personnel, electronic bulletin boards have the capability of broadcasting information nationally and even globally.

- Presentations: Presentations can be created with a variety of software—*PowerPoints*, *Google Slides*, and *Prezi*—and are given extemporaneously. Typically, presentations have an introductory slide, informational slides, and a concluding slide that gives the presenter's audience the opportunity to ask questions or create a dialogue. Presentations relay information in a media-rich format: graphics, tables, and hyperlinked documents and videos are easily imbedded within the slides.

- Web Conferencing: Web conferencing allows for employees to collaborate on projects and tasks. Employees are able to talk or videoconference from different locations, making it possible for remote workers from around the globe to participate simultaneously in one meeting. Web conferencing can be done via telephone with visuals (*PowerPoint* or *Microsoft Word* documents) or via video camera programs like *WebEx®*, *PGI GlobalMeet®*, and *Skype®*.

- Instant Messaging: Many staff outside of centralized locations who cannot communicate verbally with coworkers or supervisors rely, instead, on instant messaging programs. Instant messaging programs can deliver messages one-on-one or in circles and groups, and some software even provides screen-sharing capabilities. Since instant messaging is faster than e-mail, for many employees it has become the preferred method of communicating over long distances.

- E-Mails: In today's fast-paced business world, e-mails are heavily relied upon because they provide a platform that is perfect for quickly communicating brief, concise messages to targeted audiences. E-mails not only detail who the sender and receiver are but also provide a date, time, and subject line. Unlike a memorandum, sender and receiver can communicate back and forth, and, more importantly, they may do so over long distances. Many businesses today rely on *Google*, *Yahoo*, and *Outlook* mail severs.

<u>Community Documents</u>

Where business documents target a specific audience and often contain a higher level of proprietary, confidential, or sensitive information, community documents invite larger groups to discuss business matters in a less restrictive environment. Because community documents often help bridge the gap between businesses and community, an effective newsletter, discussion board, blog, website, and app have the power to influence public perception of private companies.

- Newsletters: Newsletters are used to provide the public information about the business. It can be used to generate excitement, inform or persuade staff or consumers, or give tips on how the public can contact or work with businesses. Newsletters can be mailed or sent electronically. Generally, newsletters are sent weekly, monthly, or quarterly. They can be interactive, providing the community a glance at what is going on with a business that they interact with, and, moreover, newsletters can communicate a company's mission, values, and priorities.

- Discussion Boards: Discussion boards offer a place to go to share information on a specific topic. Discussion boards are organized on menus, submenus, and discussion threads. People visit discussion boards to find out more about a topic. Discussion board members are granted greater access to the site and have greater power to publish and comment, but, still, visitors are welcome, and they often get difficult or obscure questions resolved.

- Blogs: A blog, which is usually centered on a specific topic or theme, is a website where individuals post and update information constantly. Blogs tend to feature the newest posts first while archiving older ones. Articles, editorials, images, videos, surveys, and social media (just to name a few) can all be imbedded within blogs. Menus, sidebars, recent posts, and search boxes help visitors wade through a dizzying array of media formats and topics. Though individuals can hire a web designer to create a blog for them, most people use existing platforms like *WordPress®*, *Blogger®*, and *Tumbler®*.

- Websites: As the world becomes more technologically savvy, a website can be used to house community documents, giving consumers instant access to tools they will need to interact with the business. It can house forms, contact information, discussion boards, surveys, and blogs. It is a one-stop-shop that can assist in the interaction between the business and the consumer. Websites are advantageous because they can be accessed via computer, tablet, or mobile phone.

- Apps: Similar to a website, an application (app) gives businesses yet another method to reach individuals or segments of a community. Apps provide instant access to forms and other documentation. Designed to be downloaded on tablets or mobile phones, apps are streamlined and intuitive, allowing consumers on the go to access information at their convenience. The primary operating systems for apps include *iOS®* and *Android®*.

Practice Questions

Questions 1 – 6 are based on the following passage:

What's About to Happen to Mr. Button?

As long ago as 1860 it was the proper thing to be born at home. At present, so I am told, the high gods of medicine have decreed that the first cries of the young shall be uttered upon the anesthetic air of a hospital, preferably a fashionable one. So young Mr. and Mrs. Roger Button were fifty years ahead of style when they decided, one day in the summer of 1860, that their first baby should be born in a hospital. Whether this anachronism had any bearing upon the astonishing history I am about to set down will never be known.

I shall tell you what occurred, and let you judge for yourself.

The Roger Buttons held an enviable position, both social and financial, in ante-bellum Baltimore. They were related to the This Family and the That Family, which, as every Southerner knew, entitled them to membership in that enormous peerage which largely populated the Confederacy. This was their first experience with the charming old custom of having babies—Mr. Button was naturally nervous. He hoped it would be a boy so that he could be sent to Yale College in Connecticut, at which institution Mr. Button himself had been known for four years by the somewhat obvious nickname of "Cuff."

On the September morning <u>consecrated</u> to the enormous event he arose nervously at six o'clock dressed himself, adjusted an impeccable stock, and hurried forth through the streets of Baltimore to the hospital, to determine whether the darkness of the night had borne in new life upon its bosom.

When he was approximately a hundred yards from the Maryland Private Hospital for Ladies and Gentlemen he saw Doctor Keene, the family physician, descending the front steps, rubbing his hands together with a washing movement—as all doctors are required to do by the unwritten ethics of their profession.

Mr. Roger Button, the president of Roger Button & Co., Wholesale Hardware, began to run toward Doctor Keene with much less dignity than was expected from a Southern gentleman of that picturesque period. "Doctor Keene!" he called. "Oh, Doctor Keene!"

The doctor heard him, faced around, and stood waiting, a curious expression settling on his harsh, medicinal face as Mr. Button drew near.

"What happened?" demanded Mr. Button, as he came up in a gasping rush. "What was it? How is she? A boy? Who is it? What—"

"Talk sense!" said Doctor Keene sharply. He appeared somewhat irritated.

"Is the child born?" begged Mr. Button.

Doctor Keene frowned. "Why, yes, I suppose so—after a fashion." Again he threw a curious glance at Mr. Button.

The Curious Case of Benjamin Button, F.S. Fitzgerald, 1922

1. What major event is about to happen in this story?
   a. Mr. Button is about to go to a funeral.
   b. Mr. Button's wife is about to have a baby.
   c. Mr. Button is getting ready to go to the doctor's office.
   d. Mr. Button is about to go shopping for new clothes.

2. What kind of tone does the above passage have?
   a. Nervous and Excited
   b. Sad and Angry
   c. Shameful and Confused
   d. Grateful and Joyous

3. What is the meaning of the word "consecrated" in paragraph 4?
   a. Numbed
   b. Chained
   c. Dedicated
   d. Moved

4. What does the author mean to do by adding the following statement?

   "rubbing his hands together with a washing movement—as all doctors are required to do by the unwritten ethics of their profession."

   a. Suggesting that Mr. Button is tired of the doctor.
   b. Trying to explain the detail of the doctor's profession.
   c. Hinting to readers that the doctor is an unethical man.
   d. Giving readers a visual picture of what the doctor is doing.

5. Which of the following best describes the development of this passage?
   a. It starts in the middle of a narrative in order to transition smoothly to a conclusion.
   b. It is a chronological narrative from beginning to end.
   c. The sequence of events is backwards—we go from future events to past events.
   d. To introduce the setting of the story and its characters.

6. Which of the following is an example of an imperative sentence?
   a. "Oh, Doctor Keene!"
   b. "Talk sense!"
   c. "Is the child born?"
   d. "Why, yes, I suppose so—"

Questions 7-12 are based on the following passage:

Death or Freedom?

Knowing that Mrs. Mallard was afflicted with heart trouble, great care was taken to break to her as gently as possible the news of her husband's death.

It was her sister Josephine who told her, in broken sentences; veiled hints that revealed in half concealing. Her husband's friend Richards was there, too, near her. It was he who had been in the newspaper office when intelligence of the railroad disaster was received, with Brently Mallard's name leading the list of "killed." He had only taken the time to assure himself of its truth by a second telegram, and had hastened to forestall any less careful, less tender friend in bearing the sad message.

She did not hear the story as many women have heard the same, with a paralyzed inability to accept its significance. She wept at once, with sudden, wild abandonment, in her sister's arms. When the storm of grief had spent itself she went away to her room alone. She would have no one follow her.

There stood, facing the open window, a comfortable, roomy armchair. Into this she sank, pressed down by a physical exhaustion that haunted her body and seemed to reach into her soul.

She could see in the open square before her house the tops of trees that were all aquiver with the new spring life. The delicious breath of rain was in the air. In the street below a peddler was crying his wares. The notes of a distant song which some one was singing reached her faintly, and countless sparrows were twittering in the eaves.

There were patches of blue sky showing here and there through the clouds that had met and piled one above the other in the west facing her window.

She sat with her head thrown back upon the cushion of the chair, quite motionless, except when a sob came up into her throat and shook her, as a child who has cried itself to sleep continues to sob in its dreams.

She was young, with a fair, calm face, whose lines bespoke repression and even a certain strength. But now here was a dull stare in her eyes, whose gaze was fixed away off yonder on one of those patches of blue sky. It was not a glance of reflection, but rather indicated a suspension of intelligent thought.

There was something coming to her and she was waiting for it, fearfully. What was it? She did not know; it was too subtle and elusive to name. But she felt it, creeping out of the sky, reaching toward her through the sounds, the scents, and color that filled the air.

Now her bosom rose and fell tumultuously. She was beginning to recognize this thing that was approaching to possess her, and she was striving to beat it back with her will—as powerless as her two white slender hands would have been. When she abandoned herself a little whispered word escaped her slightly parted lips. She said it over and over under her breath: "free, free, free!" The vacant stare and the look of terror that had followed it went from her eyes. They stayed keen and bright. Her pulses beat fast, and the coursing blood warmed and relaxed every inch of her body.

She did not stop to ask if it were or were not a monstrous joy that held her. A clear and exalted perception enabled her to dismiss the suggestion as trivial. She knew that she would weep again when she saw the kind, tender hands folded in death; the face that had never looked save with love upon her, fixed and gray and dead. But she saw beyond that bitter moment a long procession of years to come that would belong to her absolutely. And she opened and spread her arms out to them in welcome.

Excerpt from "The Story of An Hour," Kate Chopin, 1894

7. What point of view is the above passage told in?
   a. First person
   b. Second person
   c. Third person omniscient
   d. Third person limited

8. What kind of irony are we presented with in this story?
   a. The way Mrs. Mallard reacted to her husband's death.
   b. The way in which Mr. Mallard died.
   c. The way in which the news of her husband's death was presented to Mrs. Mallard.
   d. The way in which nature is compared with death in the story.

9. What is the meaning of the word "elusive" in paragraph 9?
   a. Horrible
   b. Indefinable
   c. Quiet
   d. Joyful

10. What is the best summary of the passage above?
   a. Mr. Mallard, a soldier during World War I, is killed by the enemy and leaves his wife widowed.
   b. Mrs. Mallard understands the value of friendship when her friends show up for her after her husband's death.
   c. Mrs. Mallard combats mental illness daily and will perhaps be sent to a mental institution soon.
   d. Mrs. Mallard, a newly widowed woman, finds unexpected relief in her husband's death.

11. What is the tone of this story?
   a. Confused
   b. Joyful
   c. Depressive
   d. All of the above

12. What is the meaning of the word "tumultuously" in paragraph 10?
   a. Orderly
   b. Unashamedly
   c. Violently
   d. Calmly

Question 13 is based on the following passage:

Which Statement is Correct?

In 2015, 28 countries, including Estonia, Portugal, Slovenia, and Latvia, scored significantly higher than the United States on standardized high school math tests. In the 1960s, the United States consistently ranked first in the world. Today, the United States spends more than $800 billion dollars on education, which exceeds the next highest country by more than $600 billion dollars. The United States also leads the world in spending per school-aged child by an enormous margin.

13. If these statements above are factual, which of the following statements must be correct?
   a. Outspending other countries on education has benefits beyond standardized math tests.
   b. The United States' education system is corrupt and broken.
   c. The standardized math tests are not representative of American academic prowess.
   d. Spending more money does not guarantee success on standardized math tests.

Questions 14 – 17 are based on the following passage:

This article discusses the famous poet and playwright William Shakespeare.

Who Wrote Shakespeare's Plays?

People who argue that William Shakespeare is not responsible for the plays attributed to his name are known as anti-Stratfordians (from the name of Shakespeare's birthplace, Stratford-upon-Avon). The most common anti-Stratfordian claim is that William Shakespeare simply was not educated enough or from a high enough social class to have written plays overflowing with references to such a wide range of subjects like history, the classics, religion, and international culture. William Shakespeare was the son of a glove-maker, he only had a basic grade school education, and he never set foot outside of England—so how could he have produced plays of such sophistication and imagination? How could he have written in such detail about historical figures and events, or about different cultures and locations around Europe? According to anti-Stratfordians, the depth of knowledge contained in Shakespeare's plays suggests a well-traveled writer from a wealthy background with a university education, not a countryside writer like Shakespeare. But in fact, there is not much substance to such speculation, and most anti-Stratfordian arguments can be refuted with a little background about Shakespeare's time and upbringing.

First of all, those who doubt Shakespeare's authorship often point to his common birth and brief education as stumbling blocks to his writerly genius. Although it is true that Shakespeare did not come from a noble class, his father was a very *successful* glove-maker and his mother was from a very wealthy land owning family—so while Shakespeare may have had a country upbringing, he was certainly from a well-off family and would have been educated accordingly. Also, even though he did not attend university, grade school education in Shakespeare's time was actually quite rigorous and exposed students to classic drama through writers like Seneca and Ovid. It is not unreasonable to believe that Shakespeare received a very solid foundation in poetry and literature from his early schooling.

Next, anti-Stratfordians tend to question how Shakespeare could write so extensively about countries and cultures he had never visited before (for instance, several of his most famous works like *Romeo and Juliet* and *The Merchant of Venice* were set in Italy, on the opposite side of Europe!). But again, this criticism does not hold up under scrutiny. For one thing, Shakespeare was living in London, a bustling metropolis of international trade, the most populous city in England, and a political and cultural hub of Europe. In the daily crowds of people, Shakespeare would certainly have been able to meet travelers from other countries and hear firsthand accounts of life in their home country. And, in addition to the influx of information from world travelers, this was also the age of the printing press, a jump in technology that made it possible to print and circulate books much more easily than in the past. This also allowed for a freer flow of information across different countries, allowing people to read about life and ideas from throughout Europe. One needn't travel the continent in order to learn and write about its culture.

14. Which sentence contains the author's thesis?
   a. People who argue that William Shakespeare is not responsible for the plays attributed to his name are known as anti-Stratfordians.
   b. But in fact, there is not much substance to such speculation, and most anti-Stratfordian arguments can be refuted with a little background about Shakespeare's time and upbringing.
   c. It is not unreasonable to believe that Shakespeare received a very solid foundation in poetry and literature from his early schooling.
   d. Next, anti-Stratfordians tend to question how Shakespeare could write so extensively about countries and cultures he had never visited before.

15. In the first paragraph, "How could he have written in such detail about historical figures and events, or about different cultures and locations around Europe?" is an example of which of the following?
   a. Hyperbole
   b. Onomatopoeia
   c. Rhetorical question
   d. Appeal to authority

16. How does the author respond to the claim that Shakespeare was not well-educated because he did not attend university?
   a. By insisting upon Shakespeare's natural genius.
   b. By explaining grade school curriculum in Shakespeare's time.
   c. By comparing Shakespeare with other uneducated writers of his time.
   d. By pointing out that Shakespeare's wealthy parents probably paid for private tutors.

17. The word "bustling" in the third paragraph most nearly means which of the following?
   a. Busy
   b. Foreign
   c. Expensive
   d. Undeveloped

Questions 18 – 23 are based on the following passage:

This article discusses NASA technology.

What is Spinoff Technology?

When researchers and engineers undertake a large-scale scientific project, they may end up making discoveries and developing technologies that have far wider uses than originally intended. This is especially true in NASA, one of the most influential and innovative scientific organizations in America. NASA spinoff technology refers to innovations originally developed for NASA space projects that are now used in a wide range of different commercial fields. Many consumers are unaware that products they are buying are based on NASA research! Spinoff technology proves that it is worthwhile to invest in science research because it could enrich people's lives in unexpected ways.

The first spinoff technology worth mentioning is baby food. In space, where astronauts have limited access to fresh food and fewer options with their daily meals, malnutrition is a serious concern. Consequently, NASA researchers were looking for ways to enhance the nutritional value of astronauts' food. Scientists found that a certain type of algae could be added to food, improving the food's neurological benefits. When experts in the commercial food industry learned of this algae's potential to boost brain health, they were quick to begin their own research. The nutritional substance from algae then developed into a product called life's DHA, which can be found in over 90 percent of infant food sold in America.

Another intriguing example of a spinoff technology can be found in fashion. People who are always dropping their sunglasses may have invested in a pair of sunglasses with scratch resistant lenses—that is, it's impossible to scratch the glass, even if the glasses are dropped on an abrasive surface. This innovation is incredibly advantageous for people who are clumsy, but most shoppers don't know that this technology was originally developed by NASA. Scientists first created scratch resistant glass to help protect costly and crucial equipment from getting scratched in space, especially the helmet visors in space suits. However, sunglass companies later realized that this technology could be profitable for their products, and they licensed the technology from NASA.

18. What is the main purpose of this article?
    a. To advise consumers to do more research before making a purchase
    b. To persuade readers to support NASA research
    c. To tell a narrative about the history of space technology
    d. To define and describe instances of spinoff technology

19. What is the organizational structure of this article?
    a. A general definition followed by more specific examples
    b. A general opinion followed by supporting arguments
    c. An important moment in history followed by chronological details
    d. A popular misconception followed by counterevidence

20. Why did NASA scientists research algae?
    a. They already knew algae was healthy for babies.
    b. They were interested in how to grow food in space.
    c. They were looking for ways to add health benefits to food.
    d. They hoped to use it to protect expensive research equipment.

21. What does the word "neurological" mean in the second paragraph?
    a. Related to the body
    b. Related to the brain
    c. Related to vitamins
    d. Related to technology

22. Why does the author mention space suit helmets?
    a. To give an example of astronaut fashion
    b. To explain where sunglasses got their shape
    c. To explain how astronauts protect their eyes
    d. To give an example of valuable space equipment

23. Which statement would the author probably NOT agree with?
    a. Consumers don't always know the history of the products they are buying.
    b. Sometimes new innovations have unexpected applications.
    c. It is difficult to make money from scientific research.
    d. Space equipment is often very expensive.

Questions 24 – 29 are based upon the following passage:

This excerpt is adaptation from Abraham Lincoln's Address Delivered at the Dedication of the Cemetery at Gettysburg, November 19, 1863.

How Can We Honor Them?

Four score and seven years ago our fathers brought forth on this continent, a new nation, conceived in liberty, and dedicated to the proposition that all men are created equal.

Now we are engaged in a great civil war, testing whether that nation, or any nation so conceived and so dedicated, can long endure. We are met on a great battlefield of that war. We have come to dedicate a portion of that field, as a final resting place for those who here gave their lives that this nation might live. It is altogether fitting and proper that we should do this.

But, in a larger sense, we cannot dedicate—we cannot consecrate that we cannot hallow—this ground. The brave men, living and dead, who struggled here, have consecrated it, far above our poor power to add or detract. The world will little note, nor long remember what we say here, but it can never forget what they did here. It is for us the living, rather, to be dedicated here to the unfinished work which they who fought here have thus far so nobly advanced. It is rather for us to be here and dedicated to the great task remaining before us—that from these honored dead we take increased devotion to that cause for which they gave the last full measure of devotion—that we here highly resolve that these dead shall not have died in vain—that these this nation, under God, shall have a new birth of freedom—and that government of people, by the people, for the people, shall not perish from the earth.

24. The best description for the phrase "Four score and seven years ago" is?
    a. A unit of measurement
    b. A period of time
    c. A literary movement
    d. A statement of political reform

25 What is the setting of this text?
    a. A battleship off of the coast of France
    b. A desert plain on the Sahara Desert
    c. A battlefield in a North American town
    d. The residence of Abraham Lincoln

26. Which war is Abraham Lincoln referring to in the following passage?

> Now we are engaged in a great civil war, testing whether that nation, or any nation so conceived and so dedicated, can long endure.

    a. World War I
    b. The War of Spanish Succession
    c. World War II
    d. The American Civil War

27. What message is the author trying to convey through this address?
    a. The audience should consider the death of the people that fought in the war as an example and perpetuate the ideals of freedom that the soldiers died fighting for.
    b. The audience should honor the dead by establishing an annual memorial service.
    c. The audience should form a militia that would overturn the current political structure.
    d. The audience should forget the lives that were lost and discredit the soldiers.

28. What is the effect of Lincoln's statement in the following passage?

But, in a larger sense, we cannot dedicate—we cannot consecrate that we cannot hallow—this ground. The brave men, living and dead, who struggled here, have consecrated it, far above our poor power to add or detract.

    a. His comparison emphasizes the great sacrifice of the soldiers who fought in the war.
    b. His comparison serves as a remainder of the inadequacies of his audience.
    c. His comparison serves as a catalyst for guilt and shame among audience members.
    d. His comparison attempts to illuminate the great differences between soldiers and civilians.

Read the passage below and answer questions 29 & 30:

To Whom It May Concern:

I'm writing in regards to the Writer/Producer position at Shadow Heat. I graduated with my MA degree in English at the University of Texas in May 2016 where I taught technical writing and writing arguments for my fellowship. My years taking and teaching English courses have enabled me to develop strong writing skills, which I believe will contribute greatly to the position in question.

Although a work in progress, my website, attached below, features technical writing, graphic design, blog writing, and creative writing samples. My passion for writing in order to connect with a specific audience is demonstrated by my various publications as well as my degrees that focus heavily on academic and creative writing. I would love to write for your company and hope you'll consider me for this position.

I'm highly motivated, carrying energy and creativity to my work. My nine years' experience in higher education enables me to adapt to changing ideals and trends while also maintaining personal values. I hope that you'll consider me for this position. I look forward to hearing from you!

Thanks!

29. What type of writing does this passage sound like?
    a. A how-to document on teaching
    b. A consumer email to a corporation
    c. A letter of interest for a resume
    d. A memo concerning employees in the workplace

30. Which of the following is correct information?
    a. The writer of the letter is a writer/producer at Shadow Heat.
    b. The writer of the letter has a Master's degree in English.
    c. The writer of the letter has ten years' experience in higher education.
    d. The writer of the letter is applying to be a website designer.

Questions 31 – 33 are based on the following passage:

Who was George Washington?

George Washington emerged out of the American Revolution as an unlikely champion of liberty. On June 14, 1775, the Second Continental Congress created the Continental Army, and John Adams, serving in the Congress, nominated Washington to be its first commander. Washington fought under the British during the French and Indian War, and his experience and prestige proved instrumental to the American war effort. Washington provided invaluable leadership, training, and strategy during the Revolutionary War. He emerged from the war as the embodiment of liberty and freedom from tyranny.

After vanquishing the heavily favored British forces, Washington could have pronounced himself as the autocratic leader of the former colonies without any opposition, but he famously refused and returned to his Mount Vernon plantation. His restraint proved his commitment to the fledgling state's republicanism. Washington was later unanimously elected as the first American president. But it is Washington's farewell address that cemented his legacy as a visionary worthy of study.

In 1796, President Washington issued his farewell address by public letter. Washington enlisted his good friend, Alexander Hamilton, in drafting his most famous address. The letter expressed Washington's faith in the Constitution and rule of law. He encouraged his fellow Americans to put aside partisan differences and establish a national union. Washington warned Americans against meddling in foreign affairs and entering military alliances. Additionally, he stated his opposition to national political parties, which he considered partisan and counterproductive.

Americans would be wise to remember Washington's farewell, especially during presidential elections when politics hits a fever pitch. They might want to question the political institutions that were not planned by the Founding Fathers, such as the nomination process and political parties themselves.

31. Which of the following statements is logically based on the information contained in the passage above?

a. George Washington's background as a wealthy landholder directly led to his faith in equality, liberty, and democracy.
b. George Washington would have opposed America's involvement in the Second World War.
c. George Washington would not have been able to write as great a farewell address without the assistance of Alexander Hamilton.
d. George Washington would probably not approve of modern political parties.

32. Which of the following statements is the best description of the author's purpose in writing this passage about George Washington?

a. To inform American voters about a Founding Father's sage advice on a contemporary issue and explain its applicability to modern times
b. To introduce George Washington to readers as a historical figure worthy of study
c. To note that George Washington was more than a famous military hero
d. To convince readers that George Washington is a hero of republicanism and liberty

33. In which of the following materials would the author be the most likely to include this passage?
   a. A history textbook
   b. An obituary
   c. A fictional story
   d. A newspaper editorial

Questions 34 – 38 are based on the following passage:

Who First Came to the New World?

Christopher Columbus is often credited for discovering America. This is incorrect. First, it is impossible to "discover" something where people already live; however, Christopher Columbus did explore places in the New World that were previously untouched by Europe, so the term "explorer" would be more accurate. Another correction must be made, as well: Christopher Columbus was not the first European explorer to reach the present day Americas! Rather, it was Leif Erikson who first came to the New World and contacted the natives, nearly five hundred years before Christopher Columbus.

Leif Erikson, the son of Erik the Red (a famous Viking outlaw and explorer in his own right), was born in either 970 or 980, depending on which historian you seek. His own family, though, did not raise Leif, which was a Viking tradition. Instead, one of Erik's prisoners taught Leif reading and writing, languages, sailing, and weaponry. At age 12, Leif was considered a man and returned to his family. He killed a man during a dispute shortly after his return, and the council banished the Erikson clan to Greenland.

In 999, Leif left Greenland and traveled to Norway where he would serve as a guard to King Olaf Tryggvason. It was there that he became a convert to Christianity. Leif later tried to return home with the intention of taking supplies and spreading Christianity to Greenland, however his ship was blown off course and he arrived in a strange new land: present day Newfoundland, Canada.

When he finally returned to his adopted homeland Greenland, Leif consulted with a merchant who had also seen the shores of this previously unknown land we now know as Canada. The son of the legendary Viking explorer then gathered a crew of 35 men and set sail. Leif became the first European to touch foot in the New World as he explored present-day Baffin Island and Labrador, Canada. His crew called the land Vinland since it was plentiful with grapes.

During their time in present-day Newfoundland, Leif's expedition made contact with the natives whom they referred to as Skraelings (which translates to "wretched ones" in Norse). There are several secondhand accounts of their meetings. Some contemporaries described trade between the peoples. Other accounts describe clashes where the Skraelings defeated the Viking explorers with long spears, while still others claim the Vikings dominated the natives. Regardless of the circumstances, it seems that the Vikings made contact of some kind. This happened around 1000, nearly five hundred years before Columbus famously sailed the ocean blue.

Eventually, in 1003, Leif set sail for home and arrived at Greenland with a ship full of timber.

In 1020, seventeen years later, the legendary Viking died. Many believe that Leif Erikson should receive more credit for his contributions in exploring the New World.

34. Which of the following best describes how the author generally presents the information?
    a. Chronological order
    b. Comparison-contrast
    c. Cause-effect
    d. Conclusion-premises

35. Which of the following is an opinion, rather than historical fact, expressed by the author?
    a. Leif Erikson was definitely the son of Erik the Red; however, historians debate the year of his birth.
    b. Leif Erikson's crew called the land Vinland since it was plentiful with grapes.
    c. Leif Erikson deserves more credit for his contributions in exploring the New World.
    d. Leif Erikson explored the Americas nearly five hundred years before Christopher Columbus.

36. Which of the following most accurately describes the author's main conclusion?
    a. Leif Erikson is a legendary Viking explorer.
    b. Leif Erikson deserves more credit for exploring America hundreds of years before Columbus.
    c. Spreading Christianity motivated Leif Erikson's expeditions more than any other factor.
    d. Leif Erikson contacted the natives nearly five hundred years before Columbus.

37. Which of the following best describes the author's intent in the passage?
    a. To entertain
    b. To inform
    c. To alert
    d. To suggest

38. Which of the following can be logically inferred from the passage?
    a. The Vikings disliked exploring the New World.
    b. Leif Erikson's banishment from Iceland led to his exploration of present-day Canada.
    c. Leif Erikson never shared his stories of exploration with the King of Norway.
    d. Historians have difficulty definitively pinpointing events in the Vikings' history.

Questions 39 & 40 are based on the following passage:

Why Should I Stop Smoking?

Smoking tobacco products is terribly destructive. A single cigarette contains over 4,000 chemicals, including 43 known carcinogens and 400 deadly toxins. Some of the most dangerous ingredients include tar, carbon monoxide, formaldehyde, ammonia, arsenic, and DDT. Smoking can cause numerous types of cancer including throat, mouth, nasal cavity, esophagus, stomach, pancreas, kidney, bladder, and cervical.

Cigarettes contain a drug called nicotine, one of the most addictive substances known to man. Addiction is defined as a compulsion to seek the substance despite negative consequences. According to the National Institute of Drug Abuse, nearly 35 million smokers expressed a desire to quit smoking in 2015; however, more than 85 percent of those addicts will not achieve their goal. Almost all smokers regret picking up that first cigarette. You would be wise to learn from their mistake if you have not yet started smoking.

According to the U.S. Department of Health and Human Services, 16 million people in the United States presently suffer from a smoking-related condition and nearly nine million suffer from a serious smoking-related illness. According to the Centers for Disease Control and Prevention (CDC), tobacco products cause nearly six million deaths per year. This number is projected to rise to over eight million deaths by 2030. Smokers, on average, die ten years earlier than their nonsmoking peers.

In the United States, local, state, and federal governments typically tax tobacco products, which leads to high prices. Nicotine addicts sometimes pay more for a pack of cigarettes than for a few gallons of gas. Additionally, smokers tend to stink. The smell of smoke is all-consuming and creates a pervasive nastiness. Smokers also risk staining their teeth and fingers with yellow residue from the tar.

Smoking is deadly, expensive, and socially unappealing. Clearly, smoking is not worth the risks.

39. Which of the following best describes the passage?
    a. Narrative
    b. Persuasive
    c. Expository
    d. Technical

40. Which of the following statements most accurately summarizes the passage?
    a. Tobacco is less healthy than many alternatives.
    b. Tobacco is deadly, expensive, and socially unappealing, and smokers would be much better off kicking the addiction.
    c. In the United States, local, state, and federal governments typically tax tobacco products, which leads to high prices.
    d. Tobacco products shorten smokers' lives by ten years and kill more than six million people per year.

Answer Explanations

1. B: Mr. Button's wife is about to have a baby. The passage begins by giving the reader information about traditional birthing situations. Then, we are told that Mr. and Mrs. Button decide to go against tradition to have their baby in a hospital. The next few passages are dedicated to letting the reader know how Mr. Button dresses and goes to the hospital to welcome his new baby. There is a doctor in this excerpt, as Choice *C* indicates, and Mr. Button does put on clothes, as Choice *D* indicates. However, Mr. Button is not going to the doctor's office nor is he about to go shopping for new clothes.

2. A: The tone of the above passage is nervous and excited. We are told in the fourth paragraph that Mr. Button "arose nervously." We also see him running without caution to the doctor to find out about his wife and baby—this indicates his excitement. We also see him stuttering in a nervous yet excited fashion as he asks the doctor if it's a boy or girl. Though the doctor may seem a bit abrupt at the end, indicating a bit of anger or shame, neither of these choices is the overwhelming tone of the entire passage.

3. C: Dedicated. Mr. Button is dedicated to the task before him. Choice *A*, numbed, Choice *B*, chained, and Choice *D*, moved, all could grammatically fit in the sentence. However, they are not synonyms with *consecrated* like Choice *C* is.

4. D: Giving readers a visual picture of what the doctor is doing. The author describes a visual image—the doctor rubbing his hands together—first and foremost. The author may be trying to make a comment about the profession; however, the author does not "explain the detail of the doctor's profession" as Choice *B* suggests.

5. D: To introduce the setting of the story and its characters. We know we are being introduced to the setting because we are given the year in the very first paragraph along with the season: "one day in the summer of 1860." This is a classic structure of an introduction of the setting. We are also getting a long explanation of Mr. Button, what his work is, who is related to him, and what his life is like in the third paragraph.

6. B: "Talk sense!" is an example of an imperative sentence. An imperative sentence gives a command. The doctor is commanding Mr. Button to talk sense. Choice *A* is an example of an exclamatory sentence, which expresses excitement. Choice *C* is an example of an interrogative sentence—these types of sentences ask questions. Choice *D* is an example of a declarative sentence. This means that the character is simply making a statement.

7. C: The point of view is told in third person omniscient. We know this because the story starts out with us knowing something that the character does not know: that her husband has died. Mrs. Mallard eventually comes to know this, but we as readers know this information before it is broken to her. In third person limited, Choice *D*, we would only see and know what Mrs. Mallard herself knew, and we would find out the news of her husband's death when she found out the news, not before.

8. A: The way Mrs. Mallard reacted to her husband's death. The irony in this story is called situational irony, which means the situation that takes place is different than what the audience anticipated. At the beginning of the story, we see Mrs. Mallard react with a burst of grief to her husband's death. However, once she's alone, she begins to contemplate her future and says the word "free" over and over. This is quite a different reaction from Mrs. Mallard than what readers expected from the first of the story.

9. B: The word "elusive" most closely means "indefinable." Horrible, Choice *A*, doesn't quite fit with the tone of the word "subtle" that comes before it. Choice *C*, "quiet," is more closely related to the word "subtle." Choice *D*, "joyful," also doesn't quite fit the context here. "Indefinable" is the best option.

10. D: Mrs. Mallard, a newly widowed woman, finds unexpected relief in her husband's death. A summary is a brief explanation of the main point of a story. The story mostly focuses on Mrs. Mallard and her reaction to her husband's death, especially in the room when she's alone and contemplating the present and future. All of the other answer choices except Choice *C* are briefly mentioned in the story; however, they are not the main focus of the story.

11. D: The interesting thing about this story is that feelings that are confused, joyful, and depressive all play a unique and almost equal part of this story. There is no one right answer here, because the author seems to display all of these emotions through the character of Mrs. Mallard. She displays feelings of depressiveness by her grief at the beginning; then, when she receives feelings of joy, she feels moments of confusion. We as readers cannot help but go through these feelings with the character. Thus, the author creates a tone of depression, joy, and confusion, all in one story.

12. C: The word "tumultuously" most nearly means "violently." Even if you don't know the word "tumultuously," look at the surrounding context to figure it out. The next few sentences we see Mrs. Mallard striving to "beat back" the "thing that was approaching to possess her." We see a fearful and almost violent reaction to the emotion that she's having. Thus, her chest would rise and fall turbulently, or violently.

13. D: Outspending other countries on education could have other benefits, but there is no reference to this in the passage, so Choice *A* is incorrect. Choice *B* is incorrect because the author does not mention corruption. Choice *C* is incorrect because there is nothing in the passage stating that the tests are not genuinely representative. Choice *D* is accurate because spending more money has not brought success. The United States already spends the most money, and the country is not excelling on these tests. Choice *D* is the correct answer.

14. B: But in fact, there is not much substance to such speculation, and most anti-Stratfordian arguments can be refuted with a little background about Shakespeare's time and upbringing. The thesis is a statement that contains the author's topic and main idea. The main purpose of this article is to use historical evidence to provide counterarguments to anti-Stratfordians. Choice *A* is simply a definition; Choice *C* is a supporting detail, not a main idea; and Choice *D* represents an idea of anti-Stratfordians, not the author's opinion.

15. C: Rhetorical question. This requires readers to be familiar with different types of rhetorical devices. A rhetorical question is a question that is asked not to obtain an answer but to encourage readers to more deeply consider an issue.

16. B: By explaining grade school curriculum in Shakespeare's time. This question asks readers to refer to the organizational structure of the article and demonstrate understanding of how the author provides details to support their argument. This particular detail can be found in the second paragraph: "even though he did not attend university, grade school education in Shakespeare's time was actually quite rigorous."

17. A: Busy. This is a vocabulary question that can be answered using context clues. Other sentences in the paragraph describe London as "the most populous city in England" filled with "crowds of people," giving an image of a busy city full of people. Choice *B* is incorrect because London was in Shakespeare's home country, not a foreign one. Choice *C* is not mentioned in the passage. Choice *D* is not a good answer choice because the passage describes how London was a popular and important city, probably not an underdeveloped one.

18. D: To define and describe instances of spinoff technology. This is an example of a purpose question—*why* did the author write this? The article contains facts, definitions, and other objective information without telling a story or arguing an opinion. In this case, the purpose of the article is to inform the reader. The only answer choice that is related to giving information is Choice *D*: to define and describe.

19. A: A general definition followed by more specific examples. This organization question asks readers to analyze the structure of the essay. The topic of the essay is about spinoff technology; the first paragraph gives a general definition of the concept, while the following two paragraphs offer more detailed examples to help illustrate this idea.

20. C: They were looking for ways to add health benefits to food. This reading comprehension question can be answered based on the second paragraph—scientists were concerned about astronauts' nutrition and began researching useful nutritional supplements. Choice *A* in particular is not true because it reverses the order of discovery (first NASA identified algae for astronaut use, and then it was further developed for use in baby food).

21. B: Related to the brain. This vocabulary question could be answered based on the reader's prior knowledge; but even for readers who have never encountered the word "neurological" before, the passage does provide context clues. The very next sentence talks about "this algae's potential to boost brain health," which is a paraphrase of "neurological benefits." From this context, readers should be able to infer that "neurological" is related to the brain.

22. D: To give an example of valuable space equipment. This purpose question requires readers to understand the relevance of the given detail. In this case, the author mentions "costly and crucial equipment" before mentioning space suit visors, which are given as an example of something that is very valuable. Choice *A* is not correct because fashion is only related to sunglasses, not to NASA equipment. Choice *B* can be eliminated because it is simply not mentioned in the passage. While Choice *C* seems like it could be a true statement, it is also not relevant to what is being explained by the author.

23. C: It is difficult to make money from scientific research. The article gives several examples of how businesses have been able to capitalize on NASA research, so it is unlikely that the author would agree with this statement. Evidence for the other answer choices can be found in the article: for Choice *A*, the author mentions that "many consumers are unaware that products they are buying are based on NASA research"; Choice *B* is a general definition of spinoff technology; and Choice *D* is mentioned in the final paragraph.

24. B: A period of time. "Four score and seven years ago" is the equivalent of eighty-seven years, because the word "score" means "twenty." Choices *A* and *C* are incorrect because the context for describing a unit of measurement or a literary movement is lacking. *D* is incorrect because although Lincoln's speech is a cornerstone in political rhetoric, the phrase "Four score and seven years ago" is better narrowed to a period of time.

25. C: The setting of this text is a battlefield in Gettysburg, PA. Choices *A, B,* and *D* are incorrect because the text specifies that they "met on a great battlefield of that war."

26. D: Abraham Lincoln is the former president of the United States, so the correct answer is *D*, "The American Civil War." Though the U.S. was involved in World War I and II, Choices *A* and *C* are incorrect because a civil war specifically means citizens fighting within the same country. *B* is incorrect, as "The War of Spanish Succession" involved Spain, Italy, Germany, and Holland, and not the United States.

27. A: The speech calls on the audience to consider the soldiers who died on the battlefield as ideas to perpetuate freedom so that their deaths would not be in vain. Choice *B* is incorrect because, although they are there to "dedicate a portion of that field," there is no mention in the text of an annual memorial service. Choice *C* is incorrect because there is no charged language in the text, only reverence for the dead. Choice *D* is incorrect because "forget[ting] the lives that were lost" is the opposite of what Lincoln is suggesting.

28. A: Choice *A* is correct because Lincoln's intention was to memorialize the soldiers who had fallen as a result of war as well as celebrate those who had put their lives in danger for the sake of their country. Choices *B, C,* and *D* are incorrect because Lincoln's speech was supposed to foster a sense of pride among the members of the audience while connecting them to the soldiers' experiences, not to alienate or discourage them.

29. C: A letter of interest for a resume. The passage mentions teaching, Choice *A*, but it does not fit the format of a how-to document. A how-to document is a set of instructions for the reader to follow. Choice *B* is incorrect; the writer of the letter is not a consumer of products, but trying to apply for a certain position within the company. Choice *D* is also incorrect, as the writer of the letter is not yet an employee, and therefore is incapable of writing the company's memo.

30. B: The writer of the letter has a Master's degree in English. Choice *A* is incorrect because the writer of the letter is applying to be a writer/producer at Shad Heat—they aren't currently a writer/producer there. Choice *C* is also incorrect because the passage states that the writer has nine years' experience in higher education, not ten. Choice *D* is incorrect because the position is listed in the very first sentence: writer/producer, not website designer.

31. D: Although Washington is from a wealthy background, the passage does not say that his wealth led to his republican ideals, so Choice *A* is not supported. Choice *B* also does not follow from the passage. Washington's warning against meddling in foreign affairs does not mean that he would oppose wars of every kind, so Choice *B* is wrong. Choice *C* is also unjustified since the author does not indicate that Alexander Hamilton's assistance was absolutely necessary. Choice *D* is correct because the farewell address clearly opposes political parties and partisanship. The author then notes that presidential elections often hit a fever pitch of partisanship. Thus, it is follows that George Washington would not approve of modern political parties and their involvement in presidential elections.

32. A: The author finishes the passage by applying Washington's farewell address to modern politics, so the purpose probably includes this application. Choice *B* is wrong because George Washington is already a well-established historical figure; furthermore, the passage does not seek to introduce him. Choice *C* is wrong because the author is not fighting a common perception that Washington was merely a military hero. Choice *D* is wrong because the author is not convincing readers. Persuasion does not correspond to the passage. Choice *A* states the primary purpose.

33. D: Choice *A* is wrong because the last paragraph is not appropriate for a history textbook. Choice *B* is false because the piece is not a notice or announcement of Washington's death. Choice *C* is clearly false because it is not fiction, but a historical writing. Choice *D* is correct. The passage is most likely to appear in a newspaper editorial because it cites information relevant and applicable to the present day, a popular format in editorials.

34. D: The passage does not proceed in chronological order since it begins by pointing out Leif Erikson's explorations in America so Choice *A* does not work. Although the author compares and contrasts Erikson with Christopher Columbus, this is not the main way the information is presented; therefore, Choice *B* does not work. Neither does Choice *C* because there is no mention of or reference to cause and effect in the passage. However, the passage does offer a conclusion (Leif Erikson deserves more credit) and premises (first European to set foot in the New World and first to contact the natives) to substantiate Erikson's historical importance. Thus, Choice *D* is correct.

35. C: Choice *A* is wrong because it describes facts: Leif Erikson was the son of Erik the Red and historians debate Leif's date of birth. These are not opinions. Choice *B* is wrong; that Erikson called the land Vinland is a verifiable fact as is Choice *D* because he did contact the natives almost 500 years before Columbus. Choice *C* is the correct answer because it is the author's opinion that Erikson deserves more credit. That, in fact, is his conclusion in the piece, but another person could argue that Columbus or another explorer deserves more credit for opening up the New World to exploration. Rather than being an incontrovertible fact, it is a subjective value claim.

36. B: Choice *A* is wrong because the author aims to go beyond describing Erikson as a mere legendary Viking. Choice *C* is wrong because the author does not focus on Erikson's motivations, let alone name the spreading of Christianity as his primary objective. Choice *D* is wrong because it is a premise that Erikson contacted the natives 500 years before Columbus, which is simply a part of supporting the author's conclusion. Choice *B* is correct because, as stated in the previous answer, it accurately identifies the author's statement that Erikson deserves more credit than he has received for being the first European to explore the New World.

37. B: Choice *A* is wrong because the author is not in any way trying to entertain the reader. Choice *D* is wrong because he goes beyond a mere suggestion; "suggest" is too vague. Although the author is certainly trying to alert the readers (make them aware) of Leif Erikson's underappreciated and unheralded accomplishments, the nature of the writing does not indicate the author would be satisfied with the reader merely knowing of Erikson's exploration (Choice *C*). Rather, the author would want the reader to be informed about it, which is more substantial (Choice *B*).

38. D: Choice *A* is wrong because the author never addresses the Vikings' state of mind or emotions. Choice *B* is wrong because the author does not elaborate on Erikson's exile and whether he would have become an explorer if not for his banishment. Choice *C* is wrong because there is not enough information to support this premise. It is unclear whether Erikson informed the King of Norway of his finding. Although it is true that the King did not send a follow-up expedition, he could have simply chosen not to expend the resources after receiving Erikson's news. It is not possible to logically infer whether Erikson told him. Choice *D* is correct because there are two examples—Leif Erikson's date of birth and what happened during the encounter with the natives—of historians having trouble pinning down important dates in Viking history.

39. B: Narrative, Choice *A*, means a written account of connected events. Think of narrative writing as a story. Choice C, expository writing, generally seeks to explain or describe some phenomena, whereas Choice *D*, technical writing, includes directions, instructions, and/or explanations. This passage is definitely persuasive writing, which hopes to change someone's beliefs based on an appeal to reason or emotion. The author is aiming to convince the reader that smoking is terrible. They use health, price, and beauty in their argument against smoking, so Choice *B*, persuasive, is the correct answer.

40. B: The author is clearly opposed to tobacco. He cites disease and deaths associated with smoking. He points to the monetary expense and aesthetic costs. Choice *A* is wrong because alternatives to smoking are not even addressed in the passage. Choice *C* is wrong because it does not summarize the passage but rather is just a premise. Choice *D* is wrong because, while these statistics are a premise in the argument, they do not represent a summary of the piece. Choice *C* is the correct answer because it states the three critiques offered against tobacco and expresses the author's conclusion.

Writing

Extended Response Essay

The Extended Response portion of the test is the second section of the GED. You will be given two short passages with opposing views and asked to choose which argument is better supported. Within the forty-five minute window, you must back up your response with evidence from the passages. At the end of this section is a sample Extended Response question.

Brainstorming

One of the most important steps in writing an essay is prewriting. Before drafting an essay, it's helpful to think about the topic for a moment or two, in order to gain a more solid understanding of what the task is. Then, spending about five minutes jotting down the immediate ideas that could work for the essay is recommended. It is a way to get some words on the page and offer a reference for ideas when drafting. Scratch paper is provided for writers to use any prewriting techniques such as webbing, free writing, or listing. The goal is to get ideas out of the mind and onto the page.

Considering Opposing Viewpoints

In the planning stage, it's important to consider all aspects of the topic, including different viewpoints on the subject. There are more than two ways to look at a topic, and a strong argument considers those opposing viewpoints. Considering opposing viewpoints can help writers present a fair, balanced, and informed essay that shows consideration for all readers. This approach can also strengthen an argument by recognizing and potentially refuting the opposing viewpoint(s).

Drawing from personal experience may help to support ideas. For example, if the goal for writing is a personal narrative, then the story should be from the writer's own life. Many writers find it helpful to draw from personal experience, even in an essay that is not strictly narrative. Personal anecdotes or short stories can help to illustrate a point in other types of essays as well.

Moving from Brainstorming to Planning

Once the ideas are on the page, it's time to turn them into a solid plan for the essay. The best ideas from the brainstorming results can then be developed into a more formal outline. An outline typically has one main point (the thesis) and at least three sub-points that support the main point. Here's an example:

Main Idea

- Point #1
- Point #2
- Point #3

Of course, there will be details under each point, but this approach is the best for dealing with timed writing.

Staying on Track

Basing the essay on the outline aids in both organization and coherence. The goal is to ensure that there is enough time to develop each sub-point in the essay, roughly spending an equal amount of time on each idea. Keeping an eye on the time will help. If there are fifteen minutes left to draft the essay, then it makes sense to spend about 5 minutes on each of the ideas. Staying on task is critical to success, and timing out the parts of the essay can help writers avoid feeling overwhelmed.

Parts of the Essay

The *introduction* has to do a few important things:

- Establish the *topic* of the essay in original wording (i.e., not just repeating the prompt)
- Clarify the significance/importance of the topic or purpose for writing (not too many details, a brief overview)
- Offer a *thesis statement* that identifies the writer's own viewpoint on the topic (typically one-two brief sentences as a clear, concise explanation of the main point on the topic)

Body paragraphs reflect the ideas developed in the outline. Three-four points is probably sufficient for a short essay, and they should include the following:

- A *topic sentence* that identifies the sub-point (e.g., a reason why, a way how, a cause or effect)
- A detailed *explanation* of the point, explaining why the writer thinks this point is valid
- Illustrative *examples*, such as personal examples or real world examples, that support and validate the point (i.e., "prove" the point)
- A *concluding sentence* that connects the examples, reasoning, and analysis to the point being made

The *conclusion*, or final paragraph, should be brief and should reiterate the focus, clarifying why the discussion is significant or important. It is important to avoid adding specific details or new ideas to this paragraph. The purpose of the conclusion is to sum up what has been said to bring the discussion to a close.

Don't Panic!

Writing an essay can be overwhelming, and performance panic is a natural response. The outline serves as a basis for the writing and help writers keep focused. Getting stuck can also happen, and it's helpful to remember that brainstorming can be done at any time during the writing process. Following the steps of the writing process is the best defense against writer's block.

Timed essays can be particularly stressful, but assessors are trained to recognize the necessary planning and thinking for these timed efforts. Using the plan above and sticking to it helps with time management. Timing each part of the process helps writers stay on track. Sometimes writers try to cover too much in their essays. If time seems to be running out, this is an opportunity to determine whether all of the ideas in the outline are necessary. Three body paragraphs is sufficient, and more than that is probably too much to cover in a short essay.

More isn't always *better* in writing. A strong essay will be clear and concise. It will avoid unnecessary or repetitive details. It is better to have a concise, five-paragraph essay that makes a clear point, than a ten-paragraph essay that doesn't. The goal is to write one-two pages of quality writing. Paragraphs should also reflect balance; if the introduction goes to the bottom of the first page, the writing may be going off-track or be repetitive. It's best to fall into the one-two page range, but a complete, well-developed essay is the ultimate goal.

The Final Steps

Leaving a few minutes at the end to revise and proofread offers an opportunity for writers to polish things up. Putting one's self in the reader's shoes and focusing on what the essay actually says helps writers identify problems—it's a movement from the mindset of writer to the mindset of editor. The goal is to have a clean, clear copy of the essay. The following areas should be considered when proofreading:

- Sentence fragments
- Awkward sentence structure
- Run-on sentences
- Incorrect word choice
- Grammatical agreement errors
- Spelling errors
- Punctuation errors
- Capitalization errors

The Short Overview

The essay may seem challenging, but following these steps can help writers focus:

- Take one-two minutes to think about the topic.
- Generate some ideas through brainstorming (three-four minutes).
- Organize ideas into a brief outline, selecting just three-four main points to cover in the essay (eventually the body paragraphs).
- Develop essay in parts:
- Introduction paragraph, with intro to topic and main points
- Viewpoint on the subject at the end of the introduction
- Body paragraphs, based on outline
- Each paragraph: makes a main point, explains the viewpoint, uses examples to support the point
- Brief conclusion highlighting the main points and closing
- Read over the essay (last five minutes).
- Look for any obvious errors, making sure that the writing makes sense.

Authors utilize a wide range of techniques to tell a story or communicate information. Readers should be familiar with the most common of these techniques. Techniques of writing are also commonly known as rhetorical devices.

Types of Appeals

In non-fiction writing, authors employ argumentative techniques to present their opinion to readers in the most convincing way. First of all, persuasive writing usually includes at least one type of appeal: an appeal to logic (logos), emotion (pathos), or credibility and trustworthiness (ethos). When a writer appeals to logic, they are asking readers to agree with them based on research, evidence, and an established line of reasoning. An author's argument might also appeal to readers' emotions, perhaps by including personal stories and anecdotes (a short narrative of a specific event). A final type of appeal, appeal to authority, asks the reader to agree with the author's argument on the basis of their expertise or credentials. Consider three different approaches to arguing the same opinion:

- Logic (Logos)

  Our school should abolish its current ban on cell phone use on campus. This rule was adopted last year as an attempt to reduce class disruptions and help students focus more on their lessons. However, since the rule was enacted, there has been no change in the number of disciplinary problems in class. Therefore, the rule is ineffective and should be done away with.

  The above is an example of an appeal to logic. The author uses evidence to disprove the logic of the school's rule (the rule was supposed to reduce discipline problems; the number of problems has not been reduced; therefore, the rule is not working) and call for its repeal.

- Emotion (Pathos)

  An author's argument might also appeal to readers' emotions, perhaps by including personal stories and anecdotes.

  The next example presents an appeal to emotion. By sharing the personal anecdote of one student and speaking about emotional topics like family relationships, the author invokes the reader's empathy in asking them to reconsider the school rule.

  Our school should abolish its current ban on cell phone use on campus. If they aren't able to use their phones during the school day, many students feel isolated from their loved ones. For example, last semester, one student's grandmother had a heart attack in the morning. However, because he couldn't use his cell phone, the student didn't know about his grandmother's accident until the end of the day—when she had already passed away and it was too late to say goodbye. By preventing students from contacting their friends and family, our school is placing undue stress and anxiety on students.

- Credibility (Ethos)

  Finally, an appeal to authority includes a statement from a relevant expert. In this case, the author uses a doctor in the field of education to support the argument. All three examples begin from the same opinion—the school's phone ban needs to change—but rely on different argumentative styles to persuade the reader.

  Our school should abolish its current ban on cell phone use on campus. According to Dr. Bartholomew Everett, a leading educational expert, "Research studies show that cell phone usage has no real impact on student attentiveness. Rather, phones provide a valuable technological resource for learning. Schools need to learn how to integrate this new technology

> into their curriculum." Rather than banning phones altogether, our school should follow the advice of experts and allow students to use phones as part of their learning.

Rhetorical Questions

Another commonly used argumentative technique is asking rhetorical questions, questions that do not actually require an answer but that push the reader to consider the topic further.

> I wholly disagree with the proposal to ban restaurants from serving foods with high sugar and sodium contents. Do we really want to live in a world where the government can control what we eat? I prefer to make my own food choices.

Here, the author's rhetorical question prompts readers to put themselves in a hypothetical situation and imagine how they would feel about it.

Main Ideas and Supporting Details

When analyzing other writers' arguments, an important thing to look for is the topic of the passage and the main idea of that topic. Topics and main ideas are critical parts of writing. The *topic* is the subject matter of the piece. An example of a topic would be *global warming*.

The main idea is what the writer wants to say about that topic. A writer may make the point that global warming is a growing problem that must be addressed in order to save the planet. Therefore, the topic is global warming, and the main idea is that it's *a serious problem needing to be addressed*. The topic can be expressed in a word or two, but the main idea should be a complete thought.

An author will likely identify the topic immediately within the title or the first sentence of a passage. The main idea is usually presented in the introduction. In a single passage, the main idea may be identified in the first or last sentence, but it will most likely be directly stated and easily recognized by the reader. Because it is not always stated immediately in a passage, it's important to carefully read the entire passage to identify the main idea.

The main idea should not be confused with the thesis statement. A *thesis statement* is a clear statement of the writer's specific stance and can often be found in the introduction of a non-fiction piece. The thesis is a specific sentence (or two) that offers the direction and focus of the discussion.

In order to illustrate the main idea, a writer will use *supporting details*, the details that provide evidence or examples to help make a point. Supporting details often appear in the form of quotations, paraphrasing, or analysis. Authors should connect details and analysis to the main point.

For example, in the example of global warming, where the author's main idea is to show the seriousness of this growing problem and the need for change, the use of supporting details in this piece would be critical in effectively making that point. Supporting details used here might include *statistics* on an increase in global temperatures and *studies* showing the impact of global warming on the planet. The author could also include *projections* for future climate change in order to illustrate potential lasting effects of global warming.

It's important to evaluate the author's supporting details to be sure that they are credible, provide evidence of the author's point, and directly support the main idea. Though shocking statistics grab readers' attention, their use could be ineffective information in the piece. Details like this are crucial to understanding the passage and evaluating how well the author presents his or her argument and evidence.

Also remember that when most authors write, they want to make a point or send a message. This point or message of a text is known as the theme. Authors may state themes explicitly, like in *Aesop's Fables*. More often, especially in modern literature, readers must infer the theme based on text details. Usually after carefully reading and analyzing an entire text, the theme emerges. Typically, the longer the piece, the more themes you will encounter, though often one theme dominates the rest, as evidenced by the author's purposeful revisiting of it throughout the passage.

Evaluating a Passage

Determining conclusions requires being an active reader, as a reader must make a prediction and analyze facts to identify a conclusion. There are a few ways to determine a logical conclusion, but careful reading is the most important. It's helpful to read a passage a few times, noting details that seem important to the piece. A reader should also identify key words in a passage to determine the logical conclusion or determination that flows from the information presented.

Textual evidence within the details helps readers draw a conclusion about a passage. *Textual evidence* refers to information—facts and examples that support the main point. Textual evidence will likely come from outside sources and can be in the form of quoted or paraphrased material. In order to draw a conclusion from evidence, it's important to examine the credibility and validity of that evidence as well as how (and if) it relates to the main idea.

If an author presents a differing opinion or a *counter-argument* in order to refute it, the reader should consider how and why this information is being presented. It is meant to strengthen the original argument and shouldn't be confused with the author's intended conclusion, but it should also be considered in the reader's final evaluation.

Sometimes, authors explicitly state the conclusion they want readers to understand. Alternatively, a conclusion may not be directly stated. In that case, readers must rely on the implications to form a logical conclusion:

> On the way to the bus stop, Michael realized his homework wasn't in his backpack. He ran back to the house to get it and made it back to the bus just in time.

In this example, though it's never explicitly stated, it can be inferred that Michael is a student on his way to school in the morning. When forming a conclusion from implied information, it's important to read the text carefully to find several pieces of evidence in the text to support the conclusion.

Summarizing is an effective way to draw a conclusion from a passage. A summary is a shortened version of the original text, written by the reader in his/her own words. Focusing on the main points of the original text and including only the relevant details can help readers reach a conclusion. It's important to retain the original meaning of the passage.

Like summarizing, *paraphrasing* can also help a reader fully understand different parts of a text. Paraphrasing calls for the reader to take a small part of the passage and list or describe its main points. Paraphrasing is more than rewording the original passage, though. It should be written in the reader's own words, while still retaining the meaning of the original source. This will indicate an understanding of the original source, yet still help the reader expand on his/her interpretation.

Readers should pay attention to the *sequence*, or the order in which details are laid out in the text, as this can be important to understanding its meaning as a whole. Writers will often use transitional words to help the reader understand the order of events and to stay on track. Words like *next, then, after*, and *finally* show that the order of events is important to the author. In some cases, the author omits these transitional words, and the sequence is implied. Authors may even purposely present the information out of order to make an impact or have an effect on the reader. An example might be when a narrative writer uses *flashback* to reveal information.

Responding to a Passage

There are a few ways for readers to engage actively with the text, such as making inferences and predictions. An *inference* refers to a point that is implied (as opposed to directly-stated) by the evidence presented:

> Bradley packed up all of the items from his desk in a box and said goodbye to his coworkers for the last time.

From this sentence, though it is not directly stated, readers can infer that Bradley is leaving his job. It's necessary to use inference in order to draw conclusions about the meaning of a passage. Authors make implications through character dialogue, thoughts, effects on others, actions, and looks. Like in life, readers must assemble all the clues to form a complete picture.

When making an inference about a passage, it's important to rely only on the information that is provided in the text itself. This helps readers ensure that their conclusions are valid.

Readers will also find themselves making predictions when reading a passage or paragraph. *Predictions* are guesses about what's going to happen next. Readers can use prior knowledge to help make accurate predictions. Prior knowledge is best utilized when readers make links between the current text, previously read texts, and life experiences. Some texts use suspense and foreshadowing to captivate readers:

> A cat darted across the street just as the car came careening around the curve.

One unfortunate prediction might be that the car will hit the cat. Of course, predictions aren't always accurate, so it's important to read carefully to the end of the text to determine the accuracy of predictions.

Critical Thinking Skills

It's important to read any piece of writing critically. The goal is to discover the point and purpose of what the author is writing about through analysis. It's also crucial to establish the point or stance the author has taken on the topic of the piece. After determining the author's perspective, readers can then more effectively develop their own viewpoints on the subject of the piece.

It is important to distinguish between *fact and opinion* when reading a piece of writing. A fact is information that can be proven true. If information can be disproved, it is not a fact. For example, water freezes at or below thirty-two degrees Fahrenheit. An argument stating that water freezes at seventy degrees Fahrenheit cannot be supported by data, and is therefore not a fact. Facts tend to be associated with science, mathematics, and statistics. Opinions are information open to debate. Opinions are often tied to subjective concepts like equality, morals, and rights. They can also be controversial. An affirmative argument for a position—such as gun control—can be just as effective as an opposing argument against it.

Authors often use words like *think, feel, believe,* or *in my opinion* when expressing opinion, but these words won't always appear in an opinion piece, especially if it is formally written. An author's opinion may be backed up by facts, which gives it more credibility, but that opinion should not be taken as fact. A critical reader should be suspect of an author's opinion, especially if it is only supported by other opinions.

Fact	**Opinion**
There are 9 innings in a game of baseball.	Baseball games run too long.
James Garfield was assassinated on July 2, 1881.	James Garfield was a good president.
McDonalds has stores in 118 countries.	McDonalds has the best hamburgers.

Critical readers examine the facts used to support an author's argument. They check the facts against other sources to be sure those facts are correct. They also check the validity of the sources used to be sure those sources are credible, academic, and/or peer- reviewed. Consider that when an author uses another person's opinion to support his or her argument, even if it is an expert's opinion, it is still only an opinion and should not be taken as fact. A strong argument uses valid, measurable facts to support ideas. Even then, the reader may disagree with the argument as it may be rooted in his or her personal beliefs.

An authoritative argument may use the facts to sway the reader. In the example of global warming, many experts differ in their opinions of what alternative fuels can be used to aid in offsetting it. Because of this, a writer may choose to only use the information and expert opinion that supports his or her viewpoint.

If the argument is that wind energy is the best solution, the author will use facts that support this idea. That same author may leave out relevant facts on solar energy. The way the author uses facts can influence the reader, so it's important to consider the facts being used, how those facts are being presented, and what information might be left out.

Critical readers should also look for errors in the argument such as logical fallacies and bias. A *logical fallacy* is a flaw in the logic used to make the argument. Logical fallacies include slippery slope, straw man, and begging the question. Authors can also reflect *bias* if they ignore an opposing viewpoint or present their side in an unbalanced way. A strong argument considers the opposition and finds a way to refute it. Critical readers should look for an unfair or one-sided presentation of the argument and be skeptical, as a bias may be present. Even if this bias is unintentional, if it exists in the writing, the reader should be wary of the validity of the argument.

Readers should also look for the use of *stereotypes,* which refer to specific groups. Stereotypes are often negative connotations about a person or place and should always be avoided. When a critical reader finds stereotypes in a piece of writing, they should immediately be critical of the argument and consider the validity of anything the author presents. Stereotypes reveal a flaw in the writer's thinking and may suggest a lack of knowledge or understanding about the subject.

Language Conventions and Usage

Nouns

A noun is a person, place, thing, or idea. All nouns fit into one of two types, common or proper.

A *common noun* is a word that identifies any of a class of people, places, or things. Examples include numbers, objects, animals, feelings, concepts, qualities, and actions. *A, an,* or *the* usually precedes the common noun. These parts of speech are called *articles*. Here are some examples of sentences using nouns preceded by articles.

> *A* building is under construction.
> *The* girl would like to move to *the* city.

A *proper noun* (also called a *proper name*) is used for the specific name of an individual person, place, or organization. The first letter in a proper noun is capitalized. "My name is *Mary*." "I work for *Walmart*."

Nouns sometimes serve as adjectives (which themselves describe nouns), such as "hockey player" and "state government."

Pronouns

A word used in place of a noun is known as a *pronoun*. Pronouns are words like *I, mine, hers,* and *us*.

Pronouns can be split into different classifications (seen below) which make them easier to learn; however, it's not important to memorize the classifications.

- Personal pronouns: refer to people
    - First person: we, I, our, mine
    - Second person: you, yours
    - Third person: he, them
- Possessive pronouns: demonstrate ownership (mine, my, his, yours)
- Interrogative pronouns: ask questions (what, which, who, whom, whose)
- Relative pronouns: include the five interrogative pronouns and others that are relative (whoever, whomever, that, when, where)
- Demonstrative pronouns: replace something specific (this, that, those, these)
- Reciprocal pronouns: indicate something was done or given in return (each other, one another)
- Indefinite pronouns: have a nonspecific status (anybody, whoever, someone, everybody, somebody)

Indefinite pronouns such as *anybody, whoever, someone, everybody,* and *somebody* command a singular verb form, but others such as *all, none,* and *some* could require a singular or plural verb form.

<u>Antecedents</u>
An *antecedent* is the noun to which a pronoun refers; it needs to be written or spoken before the pronoun is used. For many pronouns, antecedents are imperative for clarity. In particular, a lot of the personal, possessive, and demonstrative pronouns need antecedents. Otherwise, it would be unclear who or what someone is referring to when they use a pronoun like *he* or *this*.

Pronoun reference means that the pronoun should refer clearly to one, clear, unmistakable noun (the antecedent).

Pronoun-antecedent agreement refers to the need for the antecedent and the corresponding pronoun to agree in gender, person, and number. Here are some examples:

> The *kidneys* (plural antecedent) are part of the urinary system. *They* (plural pronoun) serve several roles."
>
> The kidneys are part of the *urinary system* (singular antecedent). *It* (singular pronoun) is also known as the renal system.

Pronoun Cases

The subjective pronouns —*I, you, he/she/it, we, they,* and *who*—are the subjects of the sentence.

> Example: *They* have a new house.

The objective pronouns—*me, you (singular), him/her, us, them,* and *whom*—are used when something is being done for or given to someone; they are objects of the action.

> Example: The teacher has an apple for *us*.

The possessive pronouns—*mine, my, your, yours, his, hers, its, their, theirs, our,* and *ours*—are used to denote that something (or someone) belongs to someone (or something).

> Example: It's *their* chocolate cake.
> Even Better Example: It's *my* chocolate cake!

One of the greatest challenges and worst abuses of pronouns concerns *who* and *whom*. Just knowing the following rule can eliminate confusion. *Who* is a subjective-case pronoun used only as a subject or subject complement. *Whom* is only objective-case and, therefore, the object of the verb or preposition.

> *Who* is going to the concert?
>
> You are going to the concert with *whom*?

Hint: When using *who* or *whom*, think of whether someone would say *he* or *him*. If the answer is *he*, use *who*. If the answer is *him*, use *whom*. This trick is easy to remember because *he* and *who* both end in vowels, and *him* and *whom* both end in the letter *M*.

Adjectives

"The *extraordinary* brain is the *main* organ of the central nervous system." The adjective *extraordinary* describes the brain in a way that causes one to realize it is more exceptional than some of other organs while the adjective *main* defines the brain's importance in its system.

An *adjective* is a word or phrase that names an attribute that describes or clarifies a noun or pronoun. This helps the reader visualize and understand the characteristics—size, shape, age, color, origin, etc.—of a person, place, or thing that otherwise might not be known. Adjectives breathe life, color, and depth into the subjects they define. Life would be *drab* and *colorless* without adjectives!

Adjectives often precede the nouns they describe.

She drove her <u>*new*</u> *car.*

However, adjectives can also come later in the sentence.

Her car is <u>*new*</u>*.*

Adjectives using the prefix *a*– can only be used after a verb.

Correct: The dog was alive until the car ran up on the curb and hit him.
Incorrect: The alive dog was hit by a car that ran up on the curb.

Other examples of this rule include *awake, ablaze, ajar, alike,* and *asleep*.

Other adjectives used after verbs concern states of health.

The girl was finally *well* after a long bout of pneumonia.
The boy was *fine* after the accident.

An adjective phrase is not a bunch of adjectives strung together, but a group of words that describes a noun or pronoun and, thus, functions as an adjective. *Very ugly* is an adjective phrase; so are *way too fat* and *faster than a speeding bullet.*

Possessives

In grammar, *possessive nouns* show ownership, which was seen in previous examples like *mine, yours,* and *theirs*.

Singular nouns are generally made possessive with an apostrophe and an *s* (*'s*).

My *uncle's* new car is silver.
The *dog's* bowl is empty.
James's ties are becoming outdated.

Plural nouns ending in *s* are generally made possessive by just adding an apostrophe (*'*):

The pistachio nuts' saltiness is added during roasting. (The saltiness of pistachio nuts is added during roasting.)
The students' achievement tests are difficult. (The achievement tests of the students are difficult.)

If the plural noun does not end in an *s* such as *women,* then it is made possessive by adding an *apostrophe s* (*'s*)—*women's.*

Indefinite possessive pronouns such as *nobody* or *someone* become possessive by adding an *apostrophe s— nobody's* or *someone's.*

Verbs

The *verb* is the part of speech that describes an action, state of being, or occurrence.

A *verb* forms the main part of a predicate of a sentence. This means that the verb explains what the noun (which will be discussed shortly) is doing. A simple example is *time flies*. The verb *flies* explains what the action of the noun, *time*, is doing. This example is a *main* verb.

Helping (*auxiliary*) verbs are words like *have, do, be, can, may, should, must,* and *will.* "I *should* go to the store." Helping verbs assist main verbs in expressing tense, ability, possibility, permission, or obligation.

Particles are minor function words like *not, in, out, up,* or *down* that become part of the verb itself. "I might *not*."

Participles are words formed from verbs that are often used to modify a noun, noun phrase, verb, or verb phrase.

The *running* teenager collided with the cyclist.

Participles can also create compound verb forms.

He is *speaking*.

Verbs have five basic forms: the *base* form, the *-s* form, the *-ing* form, the *past* form, and the *past participle* form.

The *past* forms are either *regular* (*love/loved; hate/hated*) or *irregular* because they don't end by adding the common past tense suffix "-ed" (*go/went; fall/fell; set/set*).

Adverbs

Adverbs have more functions than adjectives because they modify or qualify verbs, adjectives, or other adverbs as well as word groups that express a relation of place, time, circumstance, or cause. Therefore, adverbs answer any of the following questions: *How, when, where, why, in what way, how often, how much, in what condition,* and/or *to what degree. How good looking is he? He is very handsome.*

Here are some examples of adverbs for different situations:

- how: quickly
- when: daily
- where: there
- in what way: easily
- how often: often
- how much: much
- in what condition: badly
- what degree: hardly

As one can see, for some reason, many adverbs end in *-ly*.

Adverbs do things like emphasize (*really, simply,* and *so*), amplify (*heartily, completely,* and *positively*), and tone down (*almost, somewhat,* and *mildly*).

Adverbs also come in phrases.

The dog ran as though his life depended on it.

Prepositions

Prepositions are connecting words and, while there are only about 150 of them, they are used more often than any other individual groups of words. They describe relationships between other words. They are placed before a noun or pronoun, forming a phrase that modifies another word in the sentence. *Prepositional phrases* begin with a preposition and end with a noun or pronoun, the *object of the preposition. A pristine lake is* <u>*near the store*</u> *and* <u>*behind the bank*</u>.

Some commonly used prepositions are *about, after, anti, around, as, at, behind, beside, by, for, from, in, into, of, off, on, to,* and *with.*

Complex prepositions, which also come before a noun or pronoun, consist of two or three words such as *according to, in regards to,* and *because of.*

Interjections

Interjections are words used to express emotion. Examples include *wow*, *ouch*, and *hooray*. Interjections are often separate from sentences; in those cases, the interjection is directly followed by an exclamation point. In other cases the interjection is included in a sentence and followed by a comma. The punctuation plays a big role in the intensity of the emotion that the interjection is expressing. Using a comma or semicolon indicates less excitement than using an exclamation mark

Conjunctions

Conjunctions are vital words that connect words, phrases, thoughts, and ideas. Conjunctions show relationships between components. There are two types:

Coordinating conjunctions are the primary class of conjunctions placed between words, phrases, clauses, and sentences that are of equal grammatical rank; the coordinating conjunctions are for, and, nor, but, or, yes, and so. A useful memorization trick is to remember that the first letter of these conjunctions collectively spell the word *fanboys*.

> I need to go shopping, *but* I must be careful to leave enough money in the bank.
> She wore a black, red, *and* white shirt.

Subordinating conjunctions are the secondary class of conjunctions. They connect two unequal parts, one *main* (or *independent*) and the other *subordinate* (or *dependent*). I must go to the store *even though* I do not have enough money in the bank.

> *Because* I read the review, I do not want to go to the movie.

Notice that the presence of subordinating conjunctions makes clauses dependent. *I read the review* is an independent clause, but *because* makes the clause dependent. Thus, it needs an independent clause to complete the sentence.

Subject-Verb Agreement

The subject of a sentence and its verb must agree. The cornerstone rule of subject-verb agreement is that subject and verb must agree in number. Whether the subject is singular or plural, the verb must follow suit.

Incorrect: The houses is new.
Correct: The houses are new.
Also Correct: The house is new.

In other words, a singular subject requires a singular verb; a plural subject requires a plural verb. The words or phrases that come between the subject and verb do not alter this rule.

Incorrect: The houses built of brick is new.
Correct: The houses built of brick are new.

Incorrect: The houses with the sturdy porches is new.
Correct: The houses with the sturdy porches are new.

The subject will always follow the verb when a sentence begins with *here* or *there*. Identify these with care.

Incorrect: Here *is* the *houses* with sturdy porches.
Correct: Here *are* the *houses* with sturdy porches.

The subject in the sentences above is not *here*, it is *houses*. Remember, *here* and *there* are never subjects. Be careful that contractions such as *here's* or *there're* do not cause confusion!

Two subjects joined by *and* require a plural verb form, except when the two combine to make one thing:

Incorrect: Garrett and Jonathan is over there.
Correct: Garrett and Jonathan are over there.

Incorrect: Spaghetti and meatballs are a delicious meal!
Correct: Spaghetti and meatballs is a delicious meal!

In the example above, *spaghetti and meatballs* is a compound noun. However, *Garrett and Jonathan* is not a compound noun.

Two singular subjects joined by *or, either/or,* or *neither/nor* call for a singular verb form.

Incorrect: Butter or syrup are acceptable.
Correct: Butter or syrup is acceptable.

Plural subjects joined by *or, either/or,* or *neither/nor* are, indeed, plural.

The chairs or the boxes are being moved next.

If one subject is singular and the other is plural, the verb should agree with the closest noun.

Correct: The chair or the boxes are being moved next.
Correct: The chairs or the box is being moved next.

Some plurals of money, distance, and time call for a singular verb.

> Incorrect: Three dollars *are* enough to buy that.
> Correct: Three dollars *is* enough to buy that.

For words declaring degrees of quantity such as *many of, some of,* or *most of,* let the noun that follows *of* be the guide:

> Incorrect: Many of the books is in the shelf.
> Correct: Many of the books are in the shelf.

> Incorrect: Most of the pie *are* on the table.
> Correct: Most of the pie *is* on the table.

For indefinite pronouns like anybody or everybody, use singular verbs.

> Everybody *is* going to the store.

However, the pronouns *few, many, several, all, some,* and *both* have their own rules and use plural forms.

> Some *are* ready.

Some nouns like *crowd* and *congress* are called *collective nouns* and they require a singular verb form.

> Congress *is* in session.
> The news *is* over.

Books and movie titles, though, including plural nouns such as *Great Expectations*, also require a singular verb. Remember that only the subject affects the verb. While writing tricky subject-verb arrangements, say them aloud. Listen to them. Once the rules have been learned, one's ear will become sensitive to them, making it easier to pick out what's right and what's wrong.

Independent and Dependent Clauses

Independent and *dependent* clauses are strings of words that contain both a subject and a verb. An independent clause *can* stand alone as complete thought, but a dependent clause *cannot*. A dependent clause relies on other words to be a complete sentence.

> Independent clause: The keys are on the counter.
> Dependent clause: If the keys are on the counter

Notice that both clauses have a subject (*keys*) and a verb (*are*). The independent clause expresses a complete thought, but the word *if* at the beginning of the dependent clause makes it *dependent* on other words to be a complete thought.

> Independent clause: If the keys are on the counter, please give them to me.

This presents a complete sentence since it includes at least one verb and one subject and is a complete thought. In this case, the independent clause has two subjects (*keys* & an implied *you*) and two verbs (*are* & *give*).

Independent clause: I went to the store.
Dependent clause: Because we are out of milk,

Complete Sentence: Because we are out of milk, I went to the store.
Complete Sentence: I went to the store because we are out of milk.

A *phrase* is a group of words that does not contain both a subject and a verb.

Active and Passive Voice

Active voice is a sentence structure in which the subject performs the action of the sentence. The verbs of these sentences are called *active verbs.*

The deer jumped over the fence.

In the example above, the deer is the one jumping. *Passive voice* is a sentence structure in which the object performs the action of the sentence. The verbs of these sentences are called *passive verbs*.

The fence was jumped by the deer.

In this example, the fence is the subject, but it is not jumping over anything. The deer is still the one performing the action, but it is now the object of the sentence.

Passive voice is helpful when it's unclear who performed an action.

The chair was moved.

While passive voice can add variety to writing, active voice is the generally preferred sentence structure.

Dialogue

Dialogue is a literary device that writers use to show conversations between characters in their stories, books, movies, plays, or other original works.

"Will you go to the store with me?" the young man asked his brother.

Quotation marks written immediately before the beginning and immediately after the end of a statement indicate that these are the exact words spoken or written by someone. They are, thus, a *quote*. Be sure to place the period or comma within the quotations. The comma is used if the author plans to continue writing.

Jackie said, "Get some potatoes at the store."
Jackie said, "Get some potatoes at the store," as she ended the phone call.

Question marks and exclamation points should also go inside quotations if they are part of the quotation.

Jackie asked, "Will you get me some potatoes at the store?" and I responded, "Of course I will."
Was it Jackie that said, "Get some potatoes at the store"?

Quotation marks may also be used to express the unspoken thoughts of a character. An alternative to this is to italicize this type of dialogue.

"I'm so lucky to have such a great sister," thought Sherri.
I'm so lucky to have such a great sister, thought Sherri.

When a quote is used within a quote, just a single quotation mark (looks like the apostrophe ') is used.

"Why did Mrs. Adkins say 'You need be a better team player,' when you were the one that did all of the work on the group project?" Derek asked.

Narrative Voice

An important aspect of writing to keep in mind is perspective. Is it *first* person, *second* person, *third* person, or written from *multiple* points of view?

1st Person
Writing from the *first person* perspective means that the *"I"* or *"me"* of a composition is the main character, narrator, or storyteller. Many challenges are inherent in writing from this perspective, including keeping the audience's attention. How well does that work for someone when he or she is talking? Does it sound like a repetitive "I"? If so, after a while, it's easy for the audience to tune the speaker out. Creativity and knowledge takes a vital role when writing in the first person. Of course, this depends entirely on what genre the writing is and the level of interest in the story.

2nd Person
The *second person* perspective uses the pronoun *"you," "your,"* and *"yours,"* and with it, the author can draw the reader in because he or she is speaking directly to him or her. This perspective is effectively used in advertising, counsel, directions, technical writing, and speeches, provided the author knows his or her audience. Tone also has a pronounced effect in second person. Is the tone accusatory or loving? Is it commanding or counseling?'

3rd Person
Writing in the *third person* calls for the use of pronouns: *he, she, it,* and *they.* Third person is often used for fiction and academics. The third person perspective presents the author with the opportunity to write as one who is omniscient because, writing on behalf of others, he or she can know everything about them and all that's transpiring.

Multiple Points of View
Writing in *multiple points of view* might sound overwhelming. Well, okay, it probably is, but it can be worth it. Many successful novels are written using multiple perspectives. Obviously, great care with structure and continuity is required as one transitions between the points of view.

Context Clues

Context clues help readers understand unfamiliar words, and thankfully, there are many types.

Synonyms are words or phrases that have nearly, if not exactly, the same meaning as other words or phrases

Large boxes are needed to pack *big* items.

Antonyms are words or phrases that have opposite definitions. Antonyms, like synonyms, can serve as context clues, although more cryptically.

Large boxes are not needed to pack *small* items.

Definitions are sometimes included within a sentence to define uncommon words.

They practiced the *rumba, a type of dance,* for hours on end.

Explanations provide context through elaboration.

Large boxes holding items weighing over 60 pounds were stacked in the corner.

Here's an example of *contrast*:

These *minute* creatures were much different than the *huge* mammals that the zoologist was accustomed to dealing with.

Word Usage

Word usage: the way and manner in which writers choose to use words (or phrases). This is a vital consideration in order to create excellence in writing. Context plays a role in the selection of words, as does simple choice.

Correct word usage can be as basic and imperative as making the right grammatical choice.

Incorrect: I never *seen* that play
Correct: I never *saw* that play.

Seen (past participle of see) in place of *saw* (the correct past tense of *see*) is a relatively common and grievous mistake.

Incorrect: *There* going to the store with *there* parents.
Correct: *They're* going to the store with *their* parents.

There (adverb) mistaken for *they're* (contraction for "they are") and *there* (adverb) for *their* (pronoun) are also frequent grammatical errors.

Correct word usage can be as simple as choosing between synonyms. For instance, determining whether to say *for instance* or *for example*! Would it be better to use the word *incongruous* or *inappropriate* for *unsuited,* or when the woman is *uncouth,* would *redneck, uninformed,* or *illiterate* better define her?

Correct word usage can also be as simple as knowing how to access and make good use of dictionaries, thesauruses, grammar correction software, and search engines on computers, tablets, and smartphones.

Word Parts

By analyzing and understanding Latin, Greek, and Anglo-Saxon word roots, prefixes, and suffixes one can better understand word meanings. Of course, people can always look words up if a dictionary or thesaurus if available, but meaning can often be gleaned on the spot if the writer learns to dissect and examine words.

A word can consist of the following:

- root
- root + suffix
- prefix + root
- prefix + root + suffix

For example, if someone was unfamiliar with the word *submarine* they could break the word into its parts.

prefix + root
sub + marine

It can be determined that *sub* means *below* as in *subway* and *subpar*. Additionally, one can determine that *marine* refers to *the sea* as in *marine life*. Thus, it can be figured that *submarine* refers to something below the water.

Roots
Roots are the basic components of words. Many roots can stand alone as individual words, but others must be combined with a prefix or suffix to be a word. For example, *calc* is a root but it needs a suffix to be an actual word (*calcium*).

Prefixes
A *prefix* is a word, letter, or number that is placed before another. It adjusts or qualifies the root word's meaning. When written alone, prefixes are followed by a dash to indicate that the root word follows. Some of the most common prefixes are the following:

Prefix	Meaning	Example
dis-	not or opposite of	disabled
in-, im-, il-, ir-	not	illiterate
re-	again	return
un-	not	unpredictable
anti-	against	antibacterial
fore-	before	forefront
mis-	wrongly	misunderstand
non-	not	nonsense
over-	more than normal	overabundance
pre-	before	preheat
super-	above	superman

Suffixes
A suffix is a letter or group of letters added at the end of a word to form another word. The word created from the root and suffix is either a different tense of the same root (*help + ed = helped*) or a new word (*help + ful = helpful*). When written alone, suffixes are preceded by a dash to indicate that the root word comes before.

Some of the most common suffixes are the following:

Suffix	Meaning	Example
ed	makes a verb past tense	wash*ed*
ing	makes a verb a present participle verb	wash*ing*
ly	to make characteristic of	love*ly*
s/es	to make more than one	chairs, boxes
able	can be done	deplor*able*
al	having characteristics of	comic*al*
est	comparative	great*est*
ful	full of	wonder*ful*
ism	belief in	commun*ism*
less	without	faithless
ment	action or process	accomplish*ment*
ness	state of	happi*ness*
ize, ise	to render, to make	steril*ize*, advert*ise*
cede/ceed/sede	go	concede, proceed, supersede

Here are some helpful tips:

- When adding a suffix that starts with a vowel (for example, *-ed*) to a one-syllable root whose vowel has a short sound and ends in a consonant (for example, *stun*), double the final consonant of the root (*n*).

  stun + ed = stun*n*ed

  Exception: If the past tense verb ends in *x* such as *box*, do not double the *x*.

  box + ed = boxed

- If adding a suffix that starts with a vowel (*-er*) to a multi-syllable word ending in a consonant (*begin*), double the consonant (*n*).

  begin + er = begin*n*er

- If a short vowel is followed by two or more consonants in a word such as *i+t+c+h = itch,* do <u>not</u> double the last consonant.

  itch + ed = itched

- If adding a suffix that starts with a vowel (*-ing*) to a word ending in *e* (for example, *name*), that word's final *e* is generally (but not always) dropped.

  name + ing = naming
  exception: manage + able = manag*e*able

- If adding a suffix that starts with a consonant (*-ness*) to a word ending in *e* (*complete*), the *e* generally (but not always) remains.

  complete + ness = completeness
  exception: judge + ment = judgment

There is great diversity on handling words that end in *y.* For words ending in a vowel + y, nothing changes in the original word.

play + ed = played

For words ending in a consonant + *y*, change the *y* to *i* when adding any suffix except for *–ing*.

marry + ed = married
marry + ing = marrying

Spelling and Punctuation

Spelling might or might not be important to some, or maybe it just doesn't come naturally, but those who are willing to discover some new ideas and consider their benefits can learn to spell better and improve their writing. Misspellings reduce a writer's credibility and can create misunderstandings. Spell checkers built into word processors are not a substitute for accuracy. They are neither foolproof nor without error. In addition, a writer's misspelling of one word may also be a word. For example, a writer intending to spell *herd* might accidentally type *s* instead of *d* and unintentionally spell *hers*. Since *hers* is a word, it would not be marked as a misspelling by a spell checker. In short, use spell check, but don't rely on it.

Guidelines for Spelling

Saying and listening to a word serves as the beginning of knowing how to spell it. Keep these subsequent guidelines in mind, remembering there are often exceptions because the English language is replete with them.

Guideline #1: Syllables must have at least one vowel. In fact, every syllable in every English word has a vowel.

- dog
- h*a*yst*a*ck
- *answering*
- *abstentious*
- s*i*mpl*e*

Guideline #2: The long and short of it. When the vowel has a short vowel sound as in *mad* or *bed,* only the single vowel is needed. If the word has a long vowel sound, add another vowel, either alongside it or separated by a consonant: bed/*bead*; mad/*made.* When the second vowel is separated by two spaces—*madder*—it does not affect the first vowel's sound.

Guideline #3: Suffixes. Refer to the examples listed above.

Guideline #4: Which comes first; the *i* or the *e*? Remember the saying, "*I* before *e* except after *c* or when sounding as *a* as in *neighbor* or *weigh*." Keep in mind that these are only guidelines and that there are always exceptions to every rule.

Guideline #5: Vowels in the right order. Another helpful rhyme is, "When two vowels go walking, the first one does the talking." When two vowels are in a row, the first one often has a long vowel sound and the other is silent. An example is *team*.

If you have difficulty spelling words, determine a strategy to help. Work on spelling by playing word games like Scrabble or Words with Friends. Consider using phonics, which is sounding words out by slowly and surely stating each syllable. Try repeating and memorizing spellings as well as picturing words in your head. Try making up silly memory aids. See what works best.

Homophones

Homophones are two or more words that have no particular relationship to one another except their identical pronunciations. Homophones make spelling English words fun and challenging like these:

Common Homophones		
affect, effect	cell, sell	it's, its
allot, a lot	do, due, dew	knew, new
barbecue, barbeque	dual, duel	libel, liable
bite, byte	eminent, imminent	principal, principle
brake, break	flew, flu, flue	their, there, they're
capital, capitol	gauge, gage	to, too, two
cash, cache	holy, wholly	yoke, yolk

Irregular Plurals

Irregular plurals are words that aren't made plural the usual way.

- Most nouns are made plural by adding *–s* (book*s*, television*s*, skyscraper*s*).
- Most nouns ending in *ch, sh, s, x,* or *z* are made plural by adding *–es* (church*es,* marsh*es*).
- Most nouns ending in a vowel + *y* are made plural by adding *–s* (day*s,* toy*s*).
- Most nouns ending in a consonant + *y,* are made plural by the *-y* becoming *-ies* (baby becomes *babies*).
- Most nouns ending in an *o* are made plural by adding *–s* (piano*s,* photo*s*).
- Some nouns ending in an *o*, though, may be made plural by adding *–es* (example: potato*es,* volcano*es*), and, of note, there is no known rhyme or reason for this!
- Most nouns ending in an *f* or *fe* are made plural by the *-f* or *-fe* becoming *-ves*! (example: wolf becomes *wolves*).

- Some words function as both the singular and plural form of the word (fish, deer).
- Other exceptions include *man* becomes *men, mouse* becomes *mice, goose* becomes *geese,* and *foot* becomes *feet.*

Contractions

The basic rule for making *contractions* is one area of spelling that is pretty straightforward: combine the two words by inserting an apostrophe (') in the space where a letter is omitted. For example, to combine *you* and *are*, drop the *a* and put the apostrophe in its place: *you're*.

> he + is = he's
> you + all = y'all (informal but often misspelled)

Note that *it's*, when spelled with an apostrophe, is always the contraction for *it is*. The possessive form of the word is written without an apostrophe as *its*.

Correcting Misspelled Words

A good place to start looking at commonly misspelled words here is with the word *misspelled*. While it looks peculiar, look at it this way: *mis* (the prefix meaning *wrongly*) + *spelled* = *misspelled.*

Let's look at some commonly misspelled words.

Commonly Misspelled Words					
accept	benign	existence	jewelry	parallel	separate
acceptable	bicycle	experience	judgment	pastime	sergeant
accidentally	brief	extraordinary	library	permissible	similar
accommodate	business	familiar	license	perseverance	supersede
accompany	calendar	February	maintenance	personnel	surprise
acknowledgement	campaign	fiery	maneuver	persuade	symmetry
acquaintance	candidate	finally	mathematics	possess	temperature
acquire	category	forehead	mattress	precede	tragedy
address	cemetery	foreign	millennium	prevalent	transferred
aesthetic	changeable	foremost	miniature	privilege	truly
aisle	committee	forfeit	mischievous	pronunciation	usage
altogether	conceive	glamorous	misspell	protein	valuable
amateur	congratulations	government	mortgage	publicly	vengeance
apparent	courtesy	grateful	necessary	questionnaire	villain
appropriate	deceive	handkerchief	neither	recede	Wednesday
arctic	desperate	harass	nickel	receive	weird
asphalt	discipline	hygiene	niece	recommend	
associate	disappoint	hypocrisy	ninety	referral	
attendance	dissatisfied	ignorance	noticeable	relevant	
auxiliary	eligible	incredible	obedience	restaurant	
available	embarrass	intelligence	occasion	rhetoric	
balloon	especially	intercede	occurrence	rhythm	
believe	exaggerate	interest	omitted	schedule	
beneficial	exceed	irresistible	operate	sentence	

Capitalization

Here's a non-exhaustive list of things that should be capitalized.

- The first word of every sentence
- The first word of every line of poetry
- The first letter of proper nouns (World War II)
- Holidays (Valentine's Day)
- The days of the week and months of the year (Tuesday, March)
- The first word, last word, and all major words in the titles of books, movies, songs, and other creative works (In the novel, *To Kill a Mockingbird*, note that *a* is lowercase since it's not a major word, but *to* is capitalized since it's the first word of the title.)
- Titles when preceding a proper noun (President Roberto Gonzales, Aunt Judy)

When simply using a word such as president or secretary, though, the word is not capitalized.

Officers of the new business must include a *president* and *treasurer*.

Seasons—spring, fall, etc.—are not capitalized.

North, *south*, *east*, and *west* are capitalized when referring to regions but are not when being used for directions. In general, if it's preceded by *the* it should be capitalized.

> I'm from the South.
> I drove south.

Ellipses

An *ellipsis* (...) consists of three handy little dots that can speak volumes on behalf of irrelevant material. Writers use them in place of a word(s), line, phrase, list contents, or paragraph that might just as easily have been omitted from a passage of writing. This can be done to save space or to focus only on the specifically relevant material.

> Exercise is good for some unexpected reasons. Watkins writes, "Exercise has many benefits such as ...reducing cancer risk."

In the example above, the ellipsis takes the place of the other benefits of exercise that are more expected.

The ellipsis may also be used to show a pause in sentence flow.

> "I'm wondering...how this could happen," Dylan said in a soft voice.

Commas

A *comma* (,) is the punctuation mark that signifies a pause—breath—between parts of a sentence. It denotes a break of flow. As with so many aspects of writing structure, authors will benefit by reading their writing aloud or mouthing the words. This can be particularly helpful if one is uncertain about whether the comma is needed.

In a complex sentence—one that contains a subordinate (dependent) clause or clauses—separate the clauses with commas.

> I will not pay for the steak, *because I don't have that much money*.

First, see how the purpose of each comma usage is to designate an interruption in flow. Then, notice how the last clause is dependent because it requires the earlier independent clauses to make sense.

Use a comma on both sides of an interrupting phrase.

> I will pay for the ice cream, chocolate and vanilla, and then will eat it all myself.

The words forming the phrase in italics are nonessential (extra) information. To determine if a phrase is nonessential, try reading the sentence without the phrase and see if it's still coherent.

A comma is not necessary in this next sentence because no interruption—nonessential or extra information—has occurred. Read sentences aloud when uncertain.

I will pay for his chocolate and vanilla ice cream and then will eat it all myself.

If the nonessential phrase comes at the beginning of a sentence, a comma should only go at the end of the phrase. If the phrase comes at the end of a sentence, a comma should only go at the beginning of the phrase.

Other types of interruptions include the following:

- interjections: Oh no, I am not going.
- abbreviations: Barry Potter, M.D., specializes in heart disorders.
- direct addresses: Yes, Claudia, I am tired and going to bed.
- parenthetical phrases: His wife, lovely as she was, was not helpful.
- transitional phrases: Also, it is not possible.

The second comma in the following sentence is called an Oxford comma.

> I will pay for ice cream, syrup, and pop.

It is a comma used after the second-to-last item in a series of three or more items. It comes before the word *or* or *and*. Not everyone uses the Oxford comma; it is optional, but many believe it is needed. The comma functions as a tool to reduce confusion in writing. So, if omitting the Oxford comma would cause confusion, then it's best to include it.

Commas are used in math to mark the place of thousands in numerals, breaking them up so they are easier to read. Other uses for commas are in dates (*March 19, 2016*), letter greetings (*Dear Sally,*), and in between cities and states (*Louisville, KY*).

Semicolons

The *semicolon* (;) might be described as a heavy-handed comma. Take a look at these two examples:

> I will pay for the ice cream, but I will not pay for the steak.
> I will pay for the ice cream; I will not pay for the steak.

What's the difference? The first example has a comma and a conjunction separating the two independent clauses. The second example does not have a conjunction, but there are two independent clauses in the sentence. So something more than a comma is required. In this case, a semicolon is used.

Two independent clauses can only be joined in a sentence by either a comma and conjunction or a semicolon. If one of those tools is not used, the sentence will be a run-on. Remember that while the clauses are independent, they need to be closely related in order to be contained in one sentence.

Another use for the semicolon is to separate items in a list when the items themselves require commas.

> The family lived in Phoenix, Arizona; Oklahoma City, Oklahoma; and Raleigh, North Carolina.

Colons

Colons have many miscellaneous functions. Colons can be used to proceed further information or a list. In these cases, a colon should only follow an independent clause.

> Humans take in sensory information through five basic senses: sight, hearing, smell, touch, and taste.

The meal includes the following components:

- Caesar salad
- spaghetti
- garlic bread
- cake

The family got what they needed: a reliable vehicle.

While a comma is more common, a colon can also proceed a formal quotation.

He said to the crowd: "Let's begin!"

The colon is used after the greeting in a formal letter.

Dear Sir:
To Whom It May Concern:

In the writing of time, the colon separates the minutes from the hour (*4:45 p.m.*). The colon can also be used to indicate a ratio between two numbers (*50:1*).

Hyphens

The *hyphen* (-) is a little hash mark that can be used to join words to show that they are linked.

Hyphenate two words that work together as a single adjective (a compound adjective).

honey-covered biscuits

Some words always require hyphens, even if not serving as an adjective.

merry-go-round

Hyphens always go after certain prefixes like *anti-* & *all-*.

Hyphens should also be used when the absence of the hyphen would cause a strange vowel combination (*semi-engineer*) or confusion. For example, *re-collect* should be used to describe something being gathered twice rather than being written as *recollect*, which means to remember.

Parentheses and Dashes

Parentheses are half-round brackets that look like this: *( )*. They set off a word, phrase, or sentence that is a afterthought, explanation, or side note relevant to the surrounding text but not essential. A pair of commas is often used to set off this sort of information, but parentheses are generally used for information that would not fit well within a sentence or that the writer deems not important enough to be structurally part of the sentence.

The picture of the heart (see above) shows the major parts you should memorize.
Mount Everest is one of three mountains in the world that are over 28,000 feet high (K2 and Kanchenjunga are the other two).

See how the sentences above are complete without the parenthetical statements? In the first example, *see above* would not have fit well within the flow of the sentence. The second parenthetical statement could have been a separate sentence, but the writer deemed the information not pertinent to the topic.

The dash (—) is a mark longer than a hyphen used as a punctuation mark in sentences and to set apart a relevant thought. Even after plucking out the line separated by the dash marks, the sentence will be intact and make sense.

> Looking out the airplane window at the landmarks—Lake Clarke, Thompson Community College, and the bridge—she couldn't help but feel excited to be home.

The dashes use is similar to that of parentheses or a pair of commas. So, what's the difference? Many believe that using dashes makes the clause within them stand out while using parentheses is subtler. It's advised to not use dashes when commas could be used instead.

Quotation Marks

The uses of quotation marks were discussed under the category *Dialogue.* Other uses include:

- around titles of songs, short stories, essays, and chapter in books
- to emphasize a certain word
- to refer to a word as the word itself

> Example: What's the meaning of "indubitably"?

Apostrophes

This punctuation mark, the apostrophe (') is a versatile little mark. It has a few different functions:

- Quotes: Apostrophes are used when a second quote is needed within a quote.

  > In my letter to my friend, I wrote, "The girl had to get a new purse, and guess what Mary did? She said, 'I'd like to go with you to the store.' I knew Mary would buy it for her."

- Contractions: Another use for an apostrophe in the quote above is a contraction. *I'd* is used for *I would.*

- Possession: An apostrophe followed by the letter *s* shows possession (*Mary's* purse). If the possessive word is plural, the apostrophe generally just follows the word.

  > The trees' leaves are all over the ground.

Structure

Sentence Fluency

It's time to take what's been studied and put it all together in order to construct well-written sentences and paragraphs that have correct structure. Learning and utilizing the mechanics of structure will encourage effective, professional results, and adding some creativity will elevate one's writing to a higher level.

First, let's review the basic elements of sentences.

A *sentence* is a set of words that make up a grammatical unit. The words must have certain elements and be spoken or written in a specific order to constitute a complete sentence that makes sense.

1. A sentence must have a *subject* (a noun or noun phrase). The subject tells whom or what the sentence is addressing (i.e. what it is about).

2. A sentence must have an *action* or *state of being* (*a verb*). To reiterate: A verb forms the main part of the predicate of a sentence. This means that it explains what the noun is doing.

3. A sentence must convey a complete thought.

When examining writing, be mindful of grammar, structure, spelling, and patterns. Sentences can come in varying sizes and shapes; so, the point of grammatical correctness is not to stamp out creativity or diversity in writing. Rather, grammatical correctness ensures that writing will be enjoyable and clear. One of the most common methods for catching errors is to mouth the words as you read them. Many typos are fixed automatically by our brain, but mouthing the words often circumvents this instinct and helps one read what's actually on the page. Often, grammar errors are caught not by memorization of grammar rules but by the training of one's mind to know whether something *sounds* right or not.

Types of Sentences

There isn't an overabundance of absolutes in grammar, but here is one: every sentence in the English language falls into one of four categories.

- Declarative: a simple statement that ends with a period

  The price of milk per gallon is the same as the price of gasoline.

- Imperative: a command, instruction, or request that ends with a period

  Buy milk when you stop to fill up your car with gas.

- Interrogative: a question that ends with a question mark

  Will you buy the milk?

- Exclamatory: a statement or command that expresses emotions like anger, urgency, or surprise and ends with an exclamation mark

  Buy the milk now!

Declarative sentences are the most common type, probably because they are comprised of the most general content, without any of the bells and whistles that the other three types contain. They are, simply, declarations or statements of any degree of seriousness, importance, or information.

Imperative sentences often seem to be missing a subject. The subject is there, though; it is just not visible or audible because it is *implied*. Look at the imperative example sentence.

Buy the milk when you fill up your car with gas.

You is the implied subject, the one to whom the command is issued. This is sometimes called *the understood you* because it is understood that *you* is the subject of the sentence.

Interrogative sentences—those that ask questions—are defined as such from the idea of the word *interrogation*, the action of questions being asked of suspects by investigators. Although that is serious business, interrogative sentences apply to all kinds of questions.

To exclaim is at the root of *exclamatory* sentences. These are made with strong emotions behind them. The only technical difference between a declarative or imperative sentence and an exclamatory one is the exclamation mark at the end. The example declarative and imperative sentences can both become an exclamatory one simply by putting an exclamation mark at the end of the sentences.

> The price of milk per gallon is the same as the price of gasoline!
> Buy milk when you stop to fill up your car with gas!

After all, someone might be really excited by the price of gas or milk, or they could be mad at the person that will be buying the milk! However, as stated before, exclamation marks in abundance defeat their own purpose! After a while, they begin to cause fatigue! When used only for their intended purpose, they can have their expected and desired effect.

Lengths

The ideal sentence length—the number of words in a sentence—depends upon the sentence's purpose.

It's okay for a sentence to be brief, and it's fine for a sentence to be lengthy. It's just important to make sure that long sentences do not become run-on sentences or too long to keep up with.

To keep writing interesting, vary sentence lengths, using a mixture of short, medium and long sentences.

Transitions

Transitions are the glue use to make organized thoughts adhere to one another. Transitions are the glue that helps put ideas together seamlessly, within sentences and paragraphs, between them, and (in longer documents) even between sections. Transitions may be single words, sentences, or whole paragraphs (as in the prior example). Transitions help readers to digest and understand what to feel about what has gone on and clue readers in on what is going on, what will be, and how they might react to all these factors. Transitions are like good clues left at a crime scene.

Parallel Structure in a Sentence

Parallel structure, also known as parallelism, refers to using the same grammatical form within a sentence. This is important in lists and for other components of sentences.

> Incorrect: At the recital, the boys and girls were dancing, singing, and played musical instruments.
> Correct: At the recital, the boys and girls were dancing, singing, and playing musical instruments.

Notice that in the second example, *played* is not in the same verb tense as the other verbs nor is it compatible with the helping verb *were*. To test for parallel structure in lists, try reading each item as if it were the only item in the list.

> The boys and girls were dancing.
> The boys and girls were singing.
> The boys and girls were played musical instruments.

Suddenly, the error in the sentence becomes very clear. Here's another example:

> Incorrect: After the accident, I informed the police *that Mrs. Holmes backed* into my car, *that Mrs. Holmes got out* of her car to look at the damage, and *she was driving* off without leaving a note.
>
> Correct: After the accident, I informed the police *that Mrs. Holmes backed* into my car, *that Mrs. Holmes got out* of her car to look at the damage, and *that Mrs. Holmes drove off* without leaving a note.
>
> Correct: After the accident, I informed the police that Mrs. Holmes *backed* into my car, *got out* of her car to look at the damage, and *drove off* without leaving a note.

Note that there are two ways to fix the nonparallel structure of the first sentence. The key to parallelism is consistent structure.

Examples of Transitional Words and Phrases

Transitions have many emphases as can be seen below.

- To show emphasis: truly, in fact
- To show examples: for example, namely, specifically
- To show similarities: also, likewise
- To show dissimilarities: on the other hand, even if, in contrast
- To show progression of time: later, previously, subsequently
- To show sequence or order: next, finally
- To show cause and effect: therefore, so
- To show place or position: above, nearby, there
- To provide evidence: furthermore, then
- To summarize: finally, summarizing

Sentence Structures

- Simple sentence: composed of one independent clause

  Many people watch hummingbirds.

Note that it has one subject and one verb; however, a simple sentence can have a compound subject and/or a compound verb.

  Adults and children often enjoy watching and photographing hummingbirds.

- Compound sentence: composed of two independent clauses

  The wind knocked down lots of trees, but no trees in my yard were affected.

- Complex sentence: composed of one independent clause and one dependent clause

  Although the wind knocked down lots of trees, no trees in my yard were affected.

Forming Paragraphs

A good *paragraph* should have the following characteristics:

- Be logical with organized sentences
- Have a *unified* purpose within itself
- Use sentences as *building blocks*
- Be a *distinct section* of a piece of writing
- Present a *single theme* introduced by a *topic sentence*
- Maintain a *consistent flow* through subsequent, relevant, well-placed sentences
- *Tell a story* of its own or have its own purpose, yet connect with what is written before and after
- *Enlighten, entertain,* and/or *inform*

Though certainly not set in stone, the length should be a consideration for the reader's sake, not merely for the sake of the topic. When paragraphs are especially short, the reader might experience an irregular, uneven effect; when they're much longer than 250 words, the reader's attention span, and probably their retention, is challenged. While a paragraph can technically be a sentence long, a good rule of thumb is for paragraphs to be at least three sentences long and no more than ten sentence long. An optimal word length is 100 to 250 words.

Coherent Paragraphs

Coherence is simply defined as the quality of being logical and consistent. In order to have coherent paragraphs, therefore, authors must be logical and consistent in their writing, whatever the document might be. Two words are helpful to understanding coherence: flow and relationship. Earlier, transitions were referred to as being the "glue" to put organized thoughts together. Now, let's look at the topic sentence from which flow and relationship originate.

The topic sentence, usually the first in a paragraph, holds the essential features that will be brought forth in the paragraph. It is also here that authors either grab or lose readers. It may be the only writing that a reader encounters from that writer, so it is a good idea to summarize and represent ideas accurately.

The coherent paragraph has a logical order. It utilizes transitional words and phrases, parallel sentence structure, clear pronoun references, and reasonable repetition of key words and phrases. Use common sense for repetition. Consider synonyms for variety. Be consistent in verb tense whenever possible.

When writers have accomplished their paragraph's purpose, they prepare it to receive the next paragraph. While writing, read the paragraph over, edit, examine, evaluate, and make changes accordingly. Possibly, a paragraph has gone on too long. If that occurs, it needs to be broken up into other paragraphs, or the length should be reduced. If a paragraph didn't fully accomplish its purpose, consider revising it.

Main Point of a Paragraph

What is the main point of a paragraph? It is *the* point all of the other important and lesser important points should lead up to, and it should be summed up in the topic sentence.

Sometimes there is a fine line between a paragraph's topic sentence and its main point. In fact, they actually might be one and the same. Often, though, they are two separate but closely related aspects of the same paragraph.

Depending upon writer's purpose, they might not fully reveal the topic sentence or the paragraph's main point until the paragraph's conclusion.

Sometimes, while developing paragraphs, authors deviate from the main point, which means they have to delete and rework their materials to stay on point.

Examining Paragraphs

Throughout this text, composing and combining sentences, using basic grammar skills, employing rules and guidelines, identifying differing points of view, using appropriate context, constructing accurate word usage, and discerning correct punctuation have all been discussed. Whew! The types of sentences, patterns, transitions, and overall structure have been covered as well.

While authors write, thoughts coalesce to form words on "paper" (aka a computer screen). Authors strategically place those thoughts in sentences to give them "voice" in an orderly manner, and then they manipulate them into cohesive sentences for cohesion to express ideas. Like a hunk of modeling clay (thanks to computers, people are no longer bound to erasers and whiteout), sentences can be worked and reworked until they cooperate and say what was originally intended.

Before calling a paragraph complete, identify its main point, making sure that related sentences stay on point. Pose questions such as, "Did I sufficiently develop the main point? Did I say it succinctly enough? Did I give it time to develop? *Is* it developed?"

Let's examine the following two paragraphs, each an example of a movie review. Read them and form a critique.

> Example 1: *Eddie the Eagle* is a movie about a struggling athlete. Eddie was crippled at birth. He had a lot of therapy and he had a dream. Eddie trained himself for the Olympics. He went far away to learn how to ski jump. It was hard for him, but he persevered. He got a coach and kept trying. He qualified for the Olympics. He was the only one from Britain who could jump. When he succeeded, they named him, "Eddie the Eagle."

Example 2: The last movie I saw in the theater was *Eddie the Eagle,* a story of extraordinary perseverance inspired by real life events. Eddie was born in England with a birth defect that he slowly but surely overcame, but not without trial and error (not the least of which was his father's perpetual *dis*couragement). In fact, the old man did everything to get him to give up, but Eddie was dogged beyond anyone in the neighborhood; in fact, maybe beyond anyone in the whole town or even the whole world! Eddie, simply, did not know to quit. As he grew up, so did his dream; a strange one, indeed, for someone so unaccomplished: to compete in the Winter Olympics as a ski jumper (which he knew absolutely nothing about). Eddie didn't just keep on dreaming about it. He actually went to Germany and *worked* at it, facing unbelievable odds, defeats, and put-downs by Dad and the other Men in Charge, aka the Olympic decision-makers. Did that stop him? No way! Eddie got a coach and persevered. Then, when he failed, he persevered some more, again and again. You should be able to open up a dictionary, look at the word "persevere," and see a picture of Eddie the Eagle because, when everybody told him he couldn't, he did. The result? He is forever dubbed, "Eddie the Eagle."

Both reviews tell something about the movie *Eddie the Eagle*. Does one motivate the reader to want to see the movie more than the other? Does one just provide a few facts while the other paints a virtual picture of the movie? Does one give a carrot and the other a rib eye steak, mashed potatoes, and chocolate silk pie?

Paragraphs sometimes only give facts. Sometimes that's appropriate and all that is needed. Sometimes, though, writers want to use the blank documents on their computer screens to paint a picture. Writers must "see" the painting come to life. To do so, pick a familiar topic, write a simple sentence, and add to it. Pretend, for instance, there's a lovely view. What does one see? Is it a lake? Try again – picture it as though it were the sea! Visualize a big ship sailing out there. Is it sailing away or approaching ? Who is on it? Is it dangerous? Is it night and are there crazy pirates on board? Uh-oh! Did one just jump ship and start swimming toward shore?

Simple Sentences

A *simple sentence* has one independent clause.

I am going to win.

A *compound sentence* has two independent clauses. A conjunction—*for, and, nor, but, or, yet, so*—links them together. Note that each of the independent clauses has a subject and a verb.

I am going to win, but the odds are against me.

A *complex sentence* has one independent clause and one or more dependent clauses.

I am going to win, even though I don't deserve it.

Even though I don't deserve it is a dependent clause. It does not stand on its own. Some conjunctions that link an independent and a dependent clause are *although, because, before, after, that, when, which*, and *while*.

A *compound-complex sentence* has at least three clauses, two of which are independent and at least one that is a dependent clause.

While trying to dance, I tripped over my partner's feet, but I regained my balance quickly.

The dependent clause is *While trying to dance*.

Writing Sample

There are two passages below. Read both of the passages carefully all the way through. Then, choose which passage you think is better supported by evidence. In your response, be sure to use your own evidence from the passages. You will have forty-five minutes to plan, write, and edit your response. Your essay should be around 500 words.

Passage #1:

People who share their lives on social media sites are edging into dangerous territory. Social media sites such as Facebook, Instagram, and Snapchat are black holes for those easily addicted to validation and acceptance. Society should be wary of allowing their kids to have open access to social media sites.

So many people feel a sense of joy at being "liked" or having a certain amount of friends or comments on their pages. This feeling may lead to a false sense of acceptance by peers, and the feeling that one has accomplished something. Friends post vacations, what they ate for lunch, who they are dating, and pictures of themselves and their families. They say that if it's not on social media, it didn't happen. Sharing so much personal information is an invasion of privacy and could prove dangerous. They think sharing personal pictures and details invites predators, cyberbullying, and identity theft.

People should take care to stay away from social media and get their validation and acceptance from entities that truly matter, like from themselves or a higher being. Being outside and getting exercise is a good alternative to staring at a screen all day. Those who get out and expand their worlds will definitely experience happier lives.

Passage #2:

Although there are many negative side effects to social media, such as predatory accounts, cyberbullying, and identity theft, there are many positive sides to social media as well. Carrying around information 24/7 has its perks and can't be all bad—in fact, we are a society thriving on technology and connection. Social media can be seen as a good thing due to its connecting us with family and peers, its possibilities for political support, and its support for at-home businesses and marketers.

Social media is great for staying in touch with family and peers. Last year, when I moved to California, I had bouts of loneliness trying to cope without my family and friends. This is where Skype and Facebook came in handy—I could reach out to family and friends anytime I wanted, with just a click of a button!

Social media is also beneficial for giving and receiving political support. In 2011, young persons in the Egyptian Revolution used social media to form protests and request outside help. They used Twitter and YouTube to reach out to the world and let everyone what was going on with their events and the requests they made to their government. Social media was used as a platform for regular citizens to be heard by their government.

Another reasons social media is beneficial is because many men and women use it to start and maintain at-home businesses. The platforms of Facebook and YouTube are easy ways to set up shop, to create and events, and to create videos to reach out to a particular audience. People can Google certain terms, and those terms will bring them straight to the social media site they are looking for. According to

SocialMediaStatsForAtHomeBusiness.org, 75 percent of businesses use social media to supplement their consumer market.

All in all, people should not be afraid of social media when it's able to bring so much opportunity to society. Staying in touch with family and friends, supporting political cries, and creating business opportunities are just some of the ways social media is beneficial to the community.

Mathematical Reasoning

Number Operations/Number Sense

Numbers and Their Classifications

Rational numbers are any number that can be written as a fraction or ratio. Within the set of rational numbers, several subsets exist that are referenced throughout the mathematics topics. Counting numbers are the first numbers learned as a child. Counting numbers consist of 1,2,3,4, and so on. Whole numbers include all counting numbers and zero (0,1,2,3,4,...). Integers include counting numbers, their opposites, and zero (...,-3,-2,-1,0,1,2,3,...). Rational numbers are inclusive of integers, fractions, and decimals that terminate, or end (1.7, 0.04213) or repeat ($0.136\overline{5}$).

A number line typically consists of integers (...3,2,1,0,-1,-2,-3...), and is used to visually represent the value of a rational number. Each rational number has a distinct position on the line determined by comparing its value with the displayed values on the line. For example, if plotting -1.5 on the number line below, it is necessary to recognize that the value of -1.5 is .5 less than -1 and .5 greater than -2. Therefore, -1.5 is plotted halfway between -1 and -2.

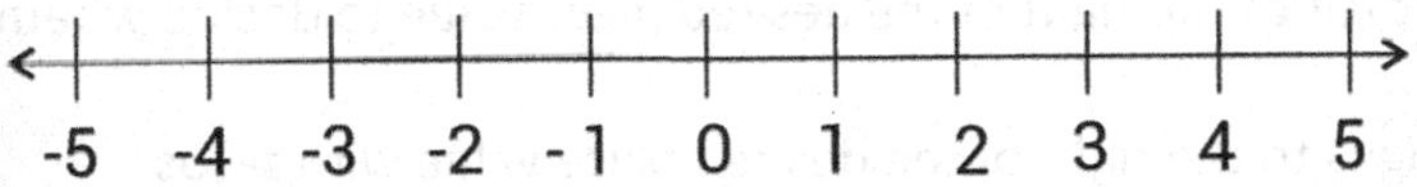

The number system that is used consists of only ten different digits or characters. However, this system is used to represent an infinite number of values. The place value system makes this infinite number of values possible. The position in which a digit is written corresponds to a given value. Starting from the decimal point (which is implied, if not physically present), each subsequent place value to the left represents a value greater than the one before it. Conversely, starting from the decimal point, each subsequent place value to the right represents a value less than the one before it.

The names for the place values to the left of the decimal point are as follows:

...	Billions	Hundred-Millions	Ten-Millions	Millions	Hundred-Thousands	Ten-Thousands	Thousands	Hundreds	Tens	Ones

*Note that this table can be extended infinitely further to the left.

The names for the place values to the right of the decimal point are as follows:

Decimal Point (.)	Tenths	Hundredths	Thousandths	Ten-Thousandths	...

*Note that this table can be extended infinitely further to the right.

When given a multi-digit number, the value of each digit depends on its place value. Consider the number 682,174.953. Referring to the chart above, it can be determined that the digit 8 is in the ten-thousands place. It is in the fifth place to the left of the decimal point. Its value is 8 ten-thousands or 80,000. The digit 5 is two places to the right of the decimal point. Therefore, the digit 5 is in the hundredths place. Its value is 5 hundredths or $\frac{5}{100}$ (equivalent to .05).

In accordance with the base-10 system, the value of a digit increases by a factor of ten each place it moves to the left. For example, consider the number 7. Moving the digit one place to the left (70), increases its value by a factor of 10 ($7 \times 10 = 70$). Moving the digit two places to the left (700) increases its value by a factor of 10 twice ($7 \times 10 \times 10 = 700$). Moving the digit three places to the left (7,000) increases its value by a factor of 10 three times ($7 \times 10 \times 10 \times 10 = 7{,}000$), and so on.

Conversely, the value of a digit decreases by a factor of ten each place it moves to the right. (Note that multiplying by $\frac{1}{10}$ is equivalent to dividing by 10). For example, consider the number 40. Moving the digit one place to the right (4) decreases its value by a factor of 10 ($40 \div 10 = 4$). Moving the digit two places to the right (0.4), decreases its value by a factor of 10 twice ($40 \div 10 \div 10 = 0.4$) or ($40 \times \frac{1}{10} \times \frac{1}{10} = 0.4$). Moving the digit three places to the right (0.04) decreases its value by a factor of 10 three times ($40 \div 10 \div 10 \div 10 = 0.04$) or ($40 \times \frac{1}{10} \times \frac{1}{10} \times \frac{1}{10} = 0.04$), and so on.

<u>Rounding</u>

Rounding numbers changes the given number to a simpler and less accurate number than the exact given number. Rounding allows for easier calculations which estimate the results of using the exact given number. The accuracy of the estimate and ease of use depends on the place value to which the number is rounded. Rounding numbers consists of:

- Determining what place value the number is being rounded to
- Examining the digit to the right of the desired place value to decide whether to round up or keep the digit
- Replacing all digits to the right of the desired place value with zeros

To round 746,311 to the nearest ten thousands, the digit in the ten thousands place should be located first. In this case, this digit is 4 (7<u>4</u>6,311). Then, the digit to its right is examined. If this digit is 5 or greater, the number will be rounded up by increasing the digit in the desired place by one. If the digit to the right of the place value being rounded is 4 or less, the number will be kept the same. For the given example, the digit being examined is a 6, which means that the number will be rounded up by increasing the digit to the left by one. Therefore, the digit 4 is changed to a 5. Finally, to write the rounded number, any digits to the left of the place value being rounded remain the same and any to its right are replaced with zeros. For the given example, rounding 746,311 to the nearest ten thousand will produce 750,000. To round 746,311 to the nearest hundred, the digit to the right of the three in the hundreds place is examined to determine whether to round up or keep the same number. In this case, that digit is a one, so the number will be kept the same and any digits to its right will be replaced with zeros. The resulting rounded number is 746,300.

Rounding place values to the right of the decimal follows the same procedure, but digits being replaced by zeros can simply be dropped. To round 3.752891 to the nearest thousandth, the desired place value is located (3.75<u>2</u>891) and the digit to the right is examined. In this case, the digit 8 indicates that the number will be rounded up, and the 2 in the thousandths place will increase to a 3. Rounding up and replacing the digits to the right of the thousandths place produces 3.753000 which is equivalent to 3.753. Therefore, the zeros are not necessary and the rounded number should be written as 3.753.

When rounding up, if the digit to be increased is a 9, the digit to its left is increased by 1 and the digit in the desired place value is changed to a zero. For example, the number 1,598 rounded to the nearest ten is 1,600. Another example shows the number 43.72961 rounded to the nearest thousandth is 43.730 or 43.73.

Operations

Addition combines two quantities together. With whole numbers, this is taking two sets of things and merging them into one, then counting the result. For example, 4 + 3 = 7. When adding numbers, the order does not matter: 3 + 4 = 7, also. Longer lists of whole numbers can also be added together. The result of adding numbers is called the *sum*.

With fractions, the number on top is the *numerator*, and the number on the bottom is the *denominator*. To add fractions, the denominator must be the same—a *common denominator*. To find a common denominator, the existing numbers on the bottom must be considered, and the lowest number they will both multiply into must be determined. Consider the following equation:

$$\frac{1}{3} + \frac{5}{6} = ?$$

The numbers 3 and 6 both multiply into 6. Three can be multiplied by 2, and 6 can be multiplied by 1. The top and bottom of each fraction must be multiplied by the same number. Then, the numerators are added together to get a new numerator. The following equation is the result:

$$\frac{1}{3} + \frac{5}{6} = \frac{2}{6} + \frac{5}{6} = \frac{7}{6}$$

Subtraction is taking one quantity away from another, so it is the opposite of addition. The expression 4 – 3 means taking 3 away from 4. So, 4 – 3 = 1. In this case, the order matters, since it entails taking one quantity away from the other, rather than just putting two quantities together. The result of subtraction is also called the *difference*.

To subtract fractions, the denominator must be the same. Then, subtract the numerators together to get a new numerator. Here is an example:

$$\frac{1}{3} - \frac{5}{6} = \frac{2}{6} - \frac{5}{6} = \frac{-3}{6} = -\frac{1}{2}$$

Multiplication is a kind of repeated addition. The expression 4×5 is taking four sets, each of them having five things in them, and putting them all together. That means $4 \times 5 = 5 + 5 + 5 + 5 = 20$. As with addition, the order of the numbers does not matter. The result of a multiplication problem is called the *product*.

To multiply fractions, the numerators are multiplied to get the new numerator, and the denominators are multiplied to get the new denominator:

$$\frac{1}{3} \times \frac{5}{6} = \frac{1 \times 5}{3 \times 6} = \frac{5}{18}$$

When multiplying fractions, common factors can *cancel* or *divide into one another*, when factors that appear in the numerator of one fraction and the denominator of the other fraction. Here is an example:

$$\frac{1}{3} \times \frac{9}{8} = \frac{1}{1} \times \frac{3}{8} = 1 \times \frac{3}{8} = \frac{3}{8}$$

The numbers 3 and 9 have a common factor of 3, so that factor can be divided out.

Division is the opposite of multiplication. With whole numbers, it means splitting up one number into sets of equal size. For example, $16 \div 8$ is the number of sets of eight things that can be made out of sixteen things. Thus, $16 \div 8 = 2$. As with subtraction, the order of the numbers will make a difference, here. The answer to a division problem is called the *quotient*, while the number in front of the division sign is called the *dividend* and the number behind the division sign is called the *divisor*.

To divide fractions, the first fraction must be multiplied with the reciprocal of the second fraction. The *reciprocal* of the fraction $\frac{x}{y}$ is the fraction $\frac{y}{x}$. Here is an example:

$$\frac{1}{3} \div \frac{5}{6} = \frac{1}{3} \times \frac{6}{5} = \frac{6}{15} = \frac{2}{5}$$

The value of a fraction does not change if multiplying or dividing both the numerator and the denominator by the same number (other than 0). In other words, $\frac{x}{y} = \frac{a \times x}{a \times y} = \frac{x \div a}{y \div a}$, as long as *a* is not 0. This means that $\frac{2}{5} = \frac{4}{10}$, for example. If *x* and *y* are integers that have no common factors, then the fraction is said to be *simplified*. This means $\frac{2}{5}$ is simplified, but $\frac{4}{10}$ is not.

Often when working with fractions, the fractions need to be rewritten so that they all share a single denominator—this is called finding a *common denominator* for the fractions. Using two fractions, $\frac{a}{b}$ and $\frac{c}{d}$, the numerator and denominator of the left fraction can be multiplied by *d*, while the numerator and denominator of the right fraction can be multiplied by *b*. This provides the fractions $\frac{a \times d}{b \times d}$ and $\frac{c \times b}{d \times b}$ with the common denominator $b \times d$.

A fraction whose numerator is smaller than its denominator is called a *proper fraction*. A fraction whose numerator is bigger than its denominator is called an *improper fraction*. These numbers can be rewritten as a combination of integers and fractions, called a *mixed number*. For example, $\frac{6}{5} = \frac{5}{5} + \frac{1}{5} = 1 + \frac{1}{5}$, and can be written as $1\frac{1}{5}$.

Estimation is finding a value that is close to a solution but is not the exact answer. For example, if there are values in the thousands to be multiplied, then each value can be estimated to the nearest thousand and the calculation performed. This value provides an approximate solution that can be determined very quickly.

Sometimes when multiplying numbers, the result can be estimated by *rounding*. For example, to estimate the value of 11.2×2.01, each number can be rounded to the nearest integer. This will yield a result of 22.

The *decimal system* is a way of writing out numbers that uses ten different numerals: 0, 1, 2, 3, 4, 5, 6, 7, 8, and 9. This is also called a "base ten" or "base 10" system. Other bases are also used. For example, computers work with a base of 2. This means they only use the numerals 0 and 1.

The *decimal place* denotes how far to the right of the decimal point a numeral is. The first digit to the right of the decimal point is in the *tenths* place. The next is the *hundredths*. The third is the *thousandths*.

So, 3.142 has a 1 in the tenths place, a 4 in the hundredths place, and a 2 in the thousandths place.

The *decimal point* is a period used to separate the *ones* place from the *tenths* place when writing out a number as a decimal.

A *decimal number* is a number written out with a decimal point instead of as a fraction, for example, 1.25 instead of $\frac{5}{4}$. Depending on the situation, it can sometimes be easier to work with fractions and sometimes easier to work with decimal numbers.

A decimal number is *terminating* if it stops at some point. It is called *repeating* if it never stops, but repeats a pattern over and over. It is important to note that every rational number can be written as a terminating decimal or as a repeating decimal.

To add decimal numbers, each number in columns needs to be lined up by the decimal point. For each number being added, the zeros to the right of the last number need to be filled in so that each of the numbers has the same number of places to the right of the decimal. Then, the columns can be added together. Here is an example of 2.45 + 1.3 + 8.891 written in column form:

$$\begin{array}{r} 2.450 \\ 1.300 \\ \underline{+\ 8.891} \end{array}$$

Zeros have been added in the columns so that each number has the same number of places to the right of the decimal.

Added together, the correct answer is 12.641:

$$\begin{array}{r} 2.450 \\ 1.300 \\ \underline{+\ 8.891} \\ 12.641 \end{array}$$

Subtracting decimal numbers is the same process as adding decimals. Here is 7.89 – 4.235 written in column form:

$$\begin{array}{r} 7.890 \\ -\ \underline{4.235} \\ 3.655 \end{array}$$

A zero has been added in the column so that each number has the same number of places to the right of the decimal.

Decimals can be multiplied as if there were no decimals points in the problem. For example, 0.5 x 1.25 can be rewritten and multiplied as 5 x 125, which equals 625.

The final answer will have the same number of decimal *points* as the total number of decimal *places* in the problem. The first number has one decimal place, and the second number has two decimal places. Therefore, the final answer will contain three decimal places:

$0.5 \times 1.25 = 0.625$

Dividing a decimal by a whole number entails using long division first by ignoring the decimal point. Then, the decimal point is moved the number of places given in the problem.

For example, $6.8 \div 4$ can be rewritten as $68 \div 4$, which is 17. There is one non-zero integer to the right of the decimal point, so the final solution would have one decimal place to the right of the solution. In this case, the solution is 1.7.

Dividing a decimal by another decimal requires changing the divisor to a whole number by moving its decimal point. The decimal place of the dividend should be moved by the same number of places as the divisor. Then, the problem is the same as dividing a decimal by a whole number.

For example, $5.72 \div 1.1$ has a divisor with one decimal point in the denominator. The expression can be rewritten as $57.2 \div 11$ by moving each number one decimal place to the right to eliminate the decimal. The long division can be completed as $572 \div 11$ with a result of 52. Since there is one non-zero integer to the right of the decimal point in the problem, the final solution is 5.2.

In another example, $8 \div 0.16$ has a divisor with two decimal points in the denominator. The expression can be rewritten as $800 \div 16$ by moving each number two decimal places to the right to eliminate the decimal in the divisor. The long division can be completed with a result of 50.

Algebra, Functions, and Patterns

Working With Positive and Negative Numbers

When adding integers and negative rational numbers, there are some basic rules to determine if the solution is negative or positive:

Adding two positive numbers results in a positive number: $3.3 + 4.8 = 8.1$.

Adding two negative numbers results in a negative number: $(-8) + (-6) = -14$.

Adding one positive and one negative number requires taking the absolute values and finding the difference between them. Then, the sign of the number that has the higher absolute value for the final solution is used.

For example, $(-9) + 11$, has a difference of absolute values of 2. The final solution is 2 because 11 has the higher absolute value. Another example is $9 + (-11)$, which has a difference of absolute values of 2. The final solution is -2 because 11 has the higher absolute value.

When subtracting integers and negative rational numbers, one has to change the problem to adding the opposite and then apply the rules of addition.

Subtracting two positive numbers is the same as adding one positive and one negative number.

For example, $4.9 - 7.1$ is the same as $4.9 + (-7.1)$. The solution is -2.2 since the absolute value of -7.1 is greater. Another example is $8.5 - 6.4$ which is the same as $8.5 + (-6.4)$. The solution is 2.1 since the absolute value of 8.5 is greater.

Subtracting a positive number from a negative number results in negative value.

For example, (-12) – 7 is the same as (-12) + (-7) with a solution of -19.

Subtracting a negative number from a positive number results in a positive value.

For example, 12 – (-7) is the same as 12 + 7 with a solution of 19.

For multiplication and division of integers and rational numbers, if both numbers are positive or both numbers are negative, the result is a positive value.

For example, (-1.7)(-4) has a solution of 6.8 since both numbers are negative values.

If one number is positive and another number is negative, the result is a negative value.

For example, (-15)/5 has a solution of -3 since there is one negative number.

Order of Operations

Exponents are shorthand for longer multiplications or divisions. The exponent is written to the upper right of a number. In the expression 2^3, the exponent is 3. The number with the exponent is called the *base*.

When the exponent is a whole number, it means to multiply the base by itself as many times as the number in the exponent. So, $2^3 = 2 \times 2 \times 2 = 8$.

If the exponent is a negative number, it means to take the reciprocal of the positive exponent:

$$2^{-3} = \frac{1}{2^3} = \frac{1}{8}$$

When the exponent is 0, the result is always 1: $2^0 = 1, 5^0 = 1$, and so on.

When the exponent is 2, the number is *squared*, and when the exponent is 3, it is *cubed*.

When working with longer expressions, parentheses are used to show the order in which the operations should be performed. Operations inside the parentheses should be completed first. Thus, $(3 - 1) \div 2$ means one should first subtract 1 from 3, and then divide that result by 2.

The *order of operations* gives an order for how a mathematical expression is to be simplified:

- Parentheses
- Exponents
- Multiplication
- Division
- Addition
- Subtraction

To help remember this, many students like to use the mnemonic PEMDAS. Some students associate this word with a phrase to help them, such as "Pirates Eat Many Donuts at Sea." Here is a quick example:

$$\text{Evaluate } 2^2 \times (3-1) \div 2 + 3.$$

$$\text{Parenthesis: } 2^2 \times 2 \div 2 + 3.$$

$$\text{Exponents: } 4 \times 2 \div 2 + 3$$

$$\text{Multiply: } 8 \div 2 + 3.$$

$$\text{Divide: } 4 + 3.$$

$$\text{Addition: } 7$$

Percentages, Ratios, and Proportions

The word *percent* comes from the Latin phrase for "per one hundred." A *percent* is a way of writing out a fraction. It is a fraction with a denominator of 100. Thus, $65\% = \frac{65}{100}$.

To convert a fraction to a percent, the denominator is written as 100. For example, $\frac{3}{5} = \frac{60}{100} = 60\%$.

In converting a percent to a fraction, the percent is written with a denominator of 100, and the result is simplified. For example, $30\% = \frac{30}{100} = \frac{3}{10}$.

The basic percent equation is the following:

$$\frac{is}{of} = \frac{\%}{100}$$

The placement of numbers in the equation depends on what the question asks.

Example 1

Find 40% of 80.

Basically, the problem is asking, "What is 40% of 80?" The 40% is the percent, and 80 is the number to find the percent "of." The equation is:

$$\frac{x}{80} = \frac{40}{100}$$

Solving the equation by cross-multiplication, the problem becomes 100x = 80(40). Solving for x gives the answer: x = 32.

Example 2

What percent of 100 is 20?

The 20 fills in the "is" portion, while 100 fills in the "of." The question asks for the percent, so that will be x, the unknown. The following equation is set up:

$$\frac{20}{100} = \frac{x}{100}$$

Cross-multiplying yields the equation 100x = 20(100). Solving for x gives the answer of 20%.

Example 3
30% of what number is 30?

The following equation uses the clues and numbers in the problem:

$$\frac{30}{x} = \frac{30}{100}$$

Cross-multiplying results in the equation 30(100) = 30x. Solving for x gives the answer x = 100.

A *ratio* compares the size of one group to the size of another. For example, there may be a room with 4 tables and 24 chairs. The ratio of tables to chairs is 4: 24. Such ratios behave like fractions in that both sides of the ratio by the same number can be multiplied or divided. Thus, the ratio 4:24 is the same as the ratio 2:12 and 1:6.

One quantity is *proportional* to another quantity if the first quantity is always some multiple of the second. For instance, the distance travelled in five hours is always five times to the speed as travelled. The distance is proportional to speed in this case.

One quantity is *inversely proportional* to another quantity if the first quantity is equal to some number divided by the second quantity. The time it takes to travel one hundred miles will be given by 100 divided by the speed travelled. The time is inversely proportional to the speed.

When dealing with word problems, there is no fixed series of steps to follow, but there are some general guidelines to use. It is important that the quantity that to be found is identified. Then, it can be determined how the given values can be used and manipulated to find the final answer.

Example 1
Jana wants to travel to visit Alice, who lives one hundred and fifty miles away. If she can drive at fifty miles per hour, how long will her trip take?

The quantity to find is the *time* of the trip. The time of a trip is given by the distance to travel divided by the speed to be traveled. The problem determines that the distance is one hundred and fifty miles, while the speed is fifty miles per hour. Thus, 150 divided by 50 is $150 \div 50 = 3$. Because *miles* and *miles per hour* are the units being divided, the miles cancel out. The result is 3 hours.

Example 2
Bernard wishes to paint a wall that measures twenty feet wide by eight feet high. It costs ten cents to paint one square foot. How much money will Bernard need for paint?

The final quantity to compute is the *cost* to paint the wall. This will be ten cents ($0.10) for each square foot of area needed to paint. The area to be painted is unknown, but the dimensions of the wall are given; thus, it can be calculated.

The dimensions of the wall are 20 feet wide and 8 feet high. Since the area of a rectangle is length multiplied by width, the area of the wall is 8 x 20 = 160 square feet. Multiplying 0.1 x 160 yields $16 as the cost of the paint.

To convert a fraction to a decimal, the numerator is divided by the denominator. For example, $\frac{3}{8}$ can be converted to a decimal by dividing 3 by 8 ($\frac{3}{8} = 0.375$). To convert a decimal to a fraction, the decimal point is dropped and the value is written as the numerator. The denominator is the place value farthest to the right with a digit other than zero. For example, to convert .48 to a fraction, the numerator is 48 and the denominator is 100 (the digit 8 is in the hundredths place). Therefore, .48 = $\frac{48}{100}$. Fractions should be written in the simplest form, or reduced. To reduce a fraction, the numerator and denominator are divided by the largest common factor. In the previous example, 48 and 100 are both divisible by 4. Dividing the numerator and denominator by 4 results in a reduced fraction of $\frac{12}{25}$.

To convert a decimal to a percent, the number is multiplied by 100. To convert .13 to a percent, .13 is multiplied by 100 to get 13 percent. To convert a fraction to a percent, the fraction is converted to a decimal and then multiplied by 100. For example, $\frac{1}{5}$ = .20 and .20 multiplied by 100 produces 20 percent.

To convert a percent to a decimal, the value is divided by 100. For example, 125 percent is equal to 1.25 ($\frac{125}{100}$). To convert a percent to a fraction, the percent sign is dropped and the value is written as the numerator with a denominator of 100. For example, 80% = $\frac{80}{100}$. This fraction can be reduced ($\frac{80}{100} = \frac{4}{5}$).

Scientific Notation

Scientific Notation is used to represent numbers that are either very small or very large. For example, the distance to the sun is approximately 150,000,000,000 meters. Instead of writing this number with so many zeros, it can be written in scientific notation as $1.5 * 10^{11}$meters. The same is true for very small numbers, but the exponent becomes negative. If the mass of a human cell is 0.000000000001 kilograms, that measurement can be easily represented by $1.0 * 10^{-12}$ kilograms. In both situations, scientific notation makes the measurement easier to read and understand. Each number is translated to an expression with one digit in the tens place times an expression corresponding to the zeros.

When two measurements are given and both involve scientific notation, it is important to know how these interact with each other:

- In addition and subtraction, the exponent on the ten must be the same before any operations are performed on the numbers. For example, $(1.3 * 10^4) + (3.0 * 10^3)$ cannot be added until one of the exponents on the ten is changed. The $3.0 * 10^3$ can be changed to $0.3 * 10^4$, then the 1.3 and 0.3 can be added. The answer comes out to be $1.6 * 10^4$.

- For multiplication, the first numbers can be multiplied and then the exponents on the tens can be added. Once an answer is formed, it may have to be converted into scientific notation again depending on the change that occurred.

- The following is an example of multiplication with scientific notation:

$$(4.5 * 10^3) * (3.0 * 10^{-5}) = 13.5 * 10^{-2}$$

- Since this answer is not in scientific notation, the decimal is moved over to the left one unit, and 1 is added to the ten's exponent. This results in the final answer: $1.35 * 10^{-1}$.

- For division, the first numbers are divided, and the exponents on the tens are subtracted. Again, the answer may need to be converted into scientific notation form, depending on the type of changes that occurred during the problem.

- *Order of magnitude* relates to scientific notation and is the total count of powers of 10 in a number. For example, there are 6 orders of magnitude in 1,000,000. If a number is raised by an order of magnitude, it is multiplied times 10. Order of magnitude can be helpful in estimating results using very large or small numbers. An answer should make sense in terms of its order of magnitude.

- For example, if area is calculated using two dimensions with 6 orders of magnitude, because area involves multiplication, the answer should have around 12 orders of magnitude. Also, answers can be estimated by rounding to the largest place value in each number. For example, 5,493,302 * 2,523,100 can be estimated by 5 * 3 = 15 with 6 orders of magnitude.

Properties of Operations

Properties of operations exist that make calculations easier and solve problems for missing values. The following table summarizes commonly used properties of real numbers.

Property	Addition	Multiplication
Commutative	$a+b = b+a$	$a\times b = b\times a$
Associative	$(a+b)+c = a+(b+c)$	$(a\times b)\times c = a\times (bc)$
Identity	$a+0 = a;\ 0+a=a$	$a\times 1 = a;\ 1\times a = a$
Inverse	$a+(-a) = 0$	$a\times\frac{1}{a} = 1;\ a \neq 0$
Distributive	$a(b+c) = ab+ac$	

The commutative property of addition states that the order in which numbers are added does not change the sum. Similarly, the commutative property of multiplication states that the order in which numbers are multiplied does not change the product. The associative property of addition and multiplication state that the grouping of numbers being added or multiplied does not change the sum or product, respectively. The commutative and associative properties are useful for performing calculations. For example, $(47+25)+3$ is equivalent to $(47+3)+25$, which is easier to calculate.

The identity property of addition states that adding zero to any number does not change its value. The identity property of multiplication states that multiplying a number by one does not change its value. The inverse property of addition states that the sum of a number and its opposite equals zero. Opposites are numbers that are the same with different signs (ex. 5 and -5; $-\frac{1}{2}$ and $\frac{1}{2}$). The inverse property of multiplication states that the product of a number (other than zero) and its reciprocal equals one. Reciprocal numbers have numerators and denominators that are inverted (ex. $\frac{2}{5}$ and $\frac{5}{2}$). Inverse properties are useful for canceling quantities to find missing values (see algebra content). For example, $a+7=12$ is solved by adding the inverse of 7(-7) to both sides in order to isolate a.

The distributive property states that multiplying a sum (or difference) by a number produces the same result as multiplying each value in the sum (or difference) by the number and adding (or subtracting) the products. Consider the following scenario: You are buying three tickets for a baseball game. Each ticket costs \$18. You are also charged a fee of \$2 per ticket for purchasing the tickets online. The cost is calculated: $3 \times 18 + 3 \times 2$. Using the distributive property, the cost can also be calculated $3(18 + 2)$.

Factors and Multiples

The factors of a number are all integers that can be multiplied by another integer to produce the given number. For example, 2 is multiplied by 3 to produce 6. Therefore, 2 and 3 are both factors of 6. Similarly, $1 \times 6 = 6$ and $2 \times 3 = 6$, so one, 2, 3, and 6 are all factors of 6. Another way to explain a factor is to say that a given number divides evenly by each of its factors to produce an integer. For example, 6 does not divide evenly by 5. Therefore, 5 is not a factor of 6.

Multiples of a given number are found by taking that number and multiplying it by any other whole number. For example, 3 is a factor of 6, 9, and 12. Therefore, 6, 9, and 12 are multiples of 3. The multiples of any number are an infinite list. For example, the multiples of 5 are 5, 10, 15, 20, and so on. This list continues without end. A list of multiples is used in finding the least common multiple, or LCM, for fractions when a common denominator is needed. The denominators are written down and their multiples listed until a common number is found in both lists. This common number is the LCM.

Prime factorization breaks down each factor of a whole number until only prime numbers remain. All composite numbers can be factored into prime numbers. For example, the prime factors of 12 are 2, 2, and 3 ($2 \times 2 \times 3 = 12$). To produce the prime factors of a number, the number is factored and any composite numbers are continuously factored until the result is the product of prime factors only. A factor tree, such as the one below, is helpful when exploring this concept.

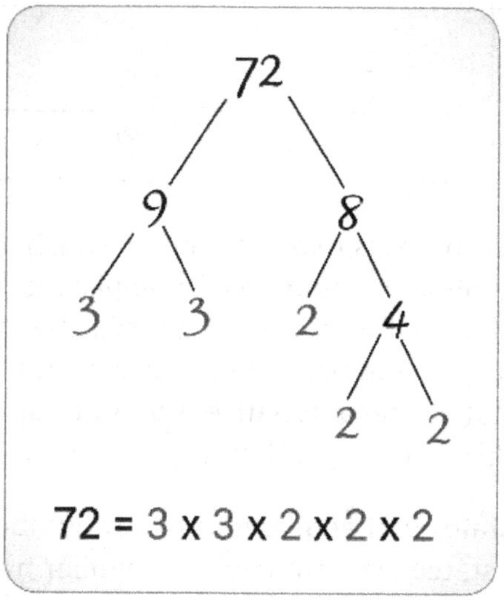

Roots and Square Roots

An *exponent* is written as a^b. In this expression, *a* is called the *base* and *b* is called the *exponent*. It is properly stated that *a* is raised to the *n*-th power. Therefore, in the expression 2^3, the exponent is 3, while the base is 2. Such an expression is called an *exponential expression*. Note that when the exponent is 2, it is called *squaring* the base, and when it is 3, it is called *cubing* the base.

When the exponent is a positive integer, this indicates the base is multiplied by itself the number of times written in the exponent. So, in the expression 2^3, multiply 2 by itself with 3 copies of 2: $2^3 = 2 \cdot 2 \cdot 2 = 8$. One thing to notice is that, for positive integers *n* and *m*, $a^n a^m = a^{n+m}$ is a rule. In order to make this rule be true for an integer of 0, $a^0 = 1$, so that $a^n a^0 = a^{n+0} = a^n$. And, in order to make this rule be true for negative exponents, $a^{-n} = \frac{1}{a^n}$.

Another rule for simplifying expressions with exponents is shown by the following equation: $(a^m)^n = a^{mn}$. This is true for fractional exponents as well. So, for a positive integer, define $a^{\frac{1}{n}}$ to be the number that, when raised to the *n*-th power, provides *a*. In other words, $(a^{\frac{1}{n}})^n = a$ is the desired equation. It should be noted that $a^{\frac{1}{n}}$ is the *n*-th root of *a*. This also can be written as $a^{\frac{1}{n}} = \sqrt[n]{a}$. The symbol on the right-hand side of this equation is called a *radical*. If the root is left out, assume that the 2nd root should be taken, also called the *square* root: $a^{\frac{1}{2}} = \sqrt[2]{a} = \sqrt{a}$. Additionally, $\sqrt[3]{a}$ is also called the *cube* root.

Note that when multiple roots exist, $a^{\frac{1}{n}}$ is defined to be the *positive* root. So, $4^{\frac{1}{2}} = 2$. Also note that negative numbers do not have even roots in the real numbers.

This also enables finding exponents for any rational number: $a^{\frac{m}{n}} = (a^{\frac{1}{n}})^m = (a^m)^{\frac{1}{n}}$. In fact, the exponent can be any real number. In general, the following rules for exponents should be used for any numbers a, b, m, and n.

- $a^1 = a$.
- $1^a = 1$.
- $a^0 = 1$.
- $a^m a^n = a^{m+n}$.
- $\frac{a^m}{a^n} = a^{m-n}$
- $(a^m)^n = a^{m \times n}$.
- $(ab)^m = a^m b^m$.
- $(\frac{a}{b})^m = \frac{a^m}{b^m}$.

As an example of applying these rules, consider the problem of simplifying the expression $(3x^2y)^3(2xy^4)$. Start by simplifying the left term using the sixth rule listed. Applying this rule yields the following expression: $27x^6y^3(2xy^4)$. The exponents can now be combined with base *x* and the exponents with base *y*. Multiply the coefficients to yield $54x^7y^7$.

Polynomial Algebra

An expression of the form ax^n, where *n* is a non-negative integer, is called a *monomial* because it contains one term. A sum of monomials is called a *polynomial*. For example, $-4x^3 + x$ is a polynomial, while $5x^7$ is a monomial. A function equal to a polynomial is called a *polynomial function*.

The monomials in a polynomial are also called the *terms* of the polynomial.

The constants that precede the variables are called *coefficients*.

The highest value of the exponent of *x* in a polynomial is called the *degree* of the polynomial. So, $-4x^3 + x$ has a degree of 3, while $-2x^5 + x^3 + 4x + 1$ has a degree of 5. When multiplying polynomials, the degree of the result will be the sum of the degrees of the two polynomials being multiplied.

To add polynomials, add the coefficients of like powers of *x*. For example:

$$(-2x^5 + x^3 + 4x + 1) + (-4x^3 + x) = -2x^5 + (1 - 4)x^3 + (4 + 1)x + 1 = -2x^5 - 3x^3 + 5x + 1$$

Likewise, subtraction of polynomials is performed by subtracting coefficients of like powers of *x*. So, $(-2x^5 + x^3 + 4x + 1) - (-4x^3 + x) = -2x^5 + (1 + 4)x^3 + (4 - 1)x + 1 = -2x^5 + 5x^3 + 3x + 1$.

To multiply two polynomials, multiply each term of the first polynomial by each term of the second polynomial and add the results. For example:

$$(4x^2 + x)(-x^3 + x) = 4x^2(-x^3) + 4x^2(x) + x(-x^3) + x(x) = -4x^5 + 4x^3 - x^4 + x^2$$

In the case where each polynomial has two terms, like in this example, some students find it helpful to remember this as multiplying the First terms, then the Outer terms, then the Inner terms, and finally the Last terms, with the mnemonic FOIL. For longer polynomials, the multiplication process is the same, but there will be, of course, more terms, and there is no common mnemonic to remember each combination.

The process of *factoring* a polynomial means to write the polynomial as a product of other (generally simpler) polynomials. Here is an example: $x^2 - 4x + 3 = (x - 1)(x - 3)$. If a certain monomial divides every term of the polynomial, factor it out of each term, for example:

$$4x^3 + 16x^2 = 4x^2(x + 4).$$

$$x^2 + 2xy + y^2 = (x + y)^2 \text{ or } x^2 - 2xy + y^2 = (x - y)^2$$

$$x^2 - y^2 = (x + y)(x - y)$$

$$x^3 + y^3 = (x + y)(x^2 - xy + y^2)$$

$$x^3 - y^3 = (x - y)(x^2 + xy + y^2)$$

$$x^3 + 3x^2y + 3xy^2 + y^3 = (x + y)^3 \text{ and } x^3 - 3x^2y + 3xy^2 - y^3 = (x - y)^3$$

It sometimes can be necessary to rewrite the polynomial in some clever way before applying the above rules. Consider the problem of factoring $x^4 - 1$. This does not immediately look like any of the cases for which there are rules. However, it's possible to think of this polynomial as $x^4 - 1 = (x^2)^2 - (1^2)^2$, and now apply the third rule in the above list to simplify this:

$$(x^2)^2 - (1^2)^2 = (x^2 + 1^2)(x^2 - 1^2) = (x^2 + 1)(x^2 - 1)$$

<u>Rational Expressions</u>

A fraction, or ratio, wherein each part is a polynomial, defines *rational expressions*. Some examples include $\frac{2x+6}{x}$, $\frac{1}{x^2-4x+8}$, and $\frac{z^2}{x+5}$. Exponents on the variables are restricted to whole numbers, which means roots and negative exponents are not included in rational expressions.

Rational expressions can be transformed by factoring. For example, the expression $\frac{x^2-5x+6}{(x-3)}$ can be rewritten by factoring the numerator to obtain $\frac{(x-3)(x-2)}{(x-3)}$. Therefore, the common binomial $(x - 3)$ can cancel so that the simplified expression is $\frac{(x-2)}{1} = (x - 2)$.

Additionally, other rational expressions can be rewritten to take on different forms. Some may be factorable in themselves, while others can be transformed through arithmetic operations. Rational expressions are closed under addition, subtraction, multiplication, and division by a nonzero expression. *Closed* means that if any one of these operations is performed on a rational expression, the result will still be a rational expression. The set of all real numbers is another example of a set closed under all four operations.

Adding and subtracting rational expressions is based on the same concepts as adding and subtracting simple fractions. For both concepts, the denominators must be the same for the operation to take place. For example, here are two rational expressions:

$$\frac{x^3 - 4}{(x-3)} + \frac{x+8}{(x-3)}$$

Since the denominators are both $(x - 3)$, the numerators can be combined by collecting like terms to form:

$$\frac{x^3 + x + 4}{(x-3)}$$

If the denominators are different, they need to be made common (the same) by using the Least Common Denominator (LCD). Each denominator needs to be factored, and the LCD contains each factor that appears in any one denominator the greatest number of times it appears in any denominator. The original expressions need to be multiplied times a form of 1, which will turn each denominator into the LCD. This process is like adding fractions with unlike denominators. It is also important when working with rational expressions to define what value of the variable makes the denominator zero. For this particular value, the expression is undefined.

Multiplication of rational expressions is performed like multiplication of fractions. The numerators are multiplied; then, the denominators are multiplied. The final fraction is then simplified. The expressions are simplified by factoring and cancelling out common terms. In the following example, the numerator of the second expression can be factored first to simplify the expression before multiplying:

$$\frac{x^2}{(x-4)} * \frac{x^2 - x - 12}{2}$$

$$\frac{x^2}{(x-4)} * \frac{(x-4)(x+3)}{2}$$

The $(x - 4)$ on the top and bottom cancel out:

$$\frac{x^2}{1} * \frac{(x+3)}{2}$$

Then multiplication is performed, resulting in:

$$\frac{x^3 + 3x^2}{2}$$

Dividing rational expressions is similar to the division of fractions, where division turns into multiplying by a reciprocal. So the following expression can be rewritten as a multiplication problem:

$$\frac{x^2 - 3x + 7}{x - 4} \div \frac{x^2 - 5x + 3}{x - 4}$$

$$\frac{x^2 - 3x + 7}{x - 4} * \frac{x - 4}{x^2 - 5x + 3}$$

The $x - 4$ cancels out, leaving:

$$\frac{x^2 - 3x + 7}{x^2 - 5x + 3}$$

The final answers should always be completely simplified. If a function is composed of a rational expression, the zeros of the graph can be found from setting the polynomial in the numerator as equal to zero and solving. The values that make the denominator equal to zero will either exist on the graph as a hole or a vertical asymptote.

Equations and Inequalities

An equation contains two sides separated by an equal sign. Equations can be solved to determine the value(s) of the variable for which the statement is true.

Assume the sum of a number and 5 is equal to 10 times the number. To find this unknown number, a simple equation can be written to represent the problem. Key words such as *sum*, *equal*, and *times* are used to form the following equation with one variable: $n + 5 = 10n$. When solving for n, opposite operations are used. First, n is subtracted from $10n$ across the equals sign, resulting in $5 = 9n$. Then, 9 is divided on both sides, leaving $n = \frac{5}{9}$. This solution can be graphed on the number line with a dot as shown below:

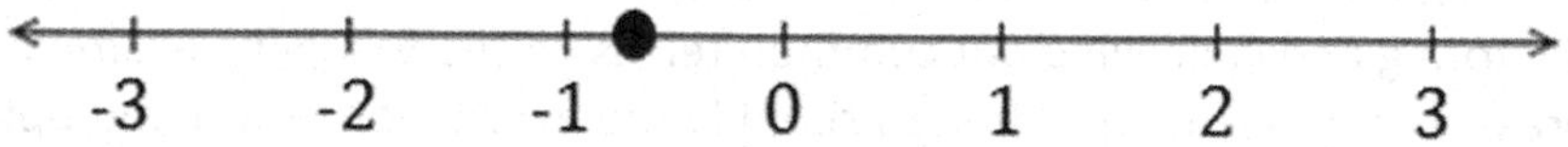

If the problem were changed to say, "The sum of a number and 5 is greater than 10 times the number," then an inequality would be used instead of an equation. Using key words again, *greater than* is represented by the symbol >. The inequality $n + 5 > 10n$ can be solved using the same techniques, resulting in $n < \frac{5}{9}$. The only time solving an inequality differs from solving an equation is when a negative number is either multiplied times or divided by each side of the inequality. The sign must be switched in this case. For this example, the graph of the solution changes to the following graph because the solution represents all real numbers less than $\frac{5}{9}$. Not included in this solution is $\frac{5}{9}$ because it is a *less than* symbol, not *equal to*.

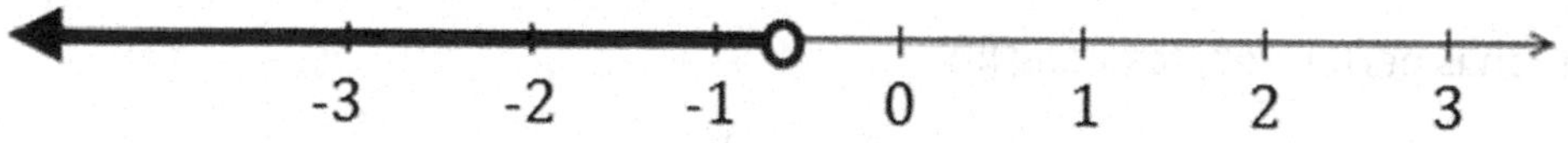

Equations and inequalities in two variables represent a relationship. Jim owns a car wash and charges $40 per car. The rent for the facility is $350 per month. An equation can be written to relate the number of cars Jim cleans to the money he makes per month. Let x represent the number of cars and y represent the profit Jim makes each month from the car wash. The equation $y = 40x - 350$ can be used to show Jim's profit or loss. Since this equation has two variables, the coordinate plane can be used to show the relationship and predict profit or loss for Jim. The following graph shows that Jim must wash at least nine cars to pay the rent, where $x = 9$.

Anything nine cars and above will yield a profit as shown by the value on the y-axis.

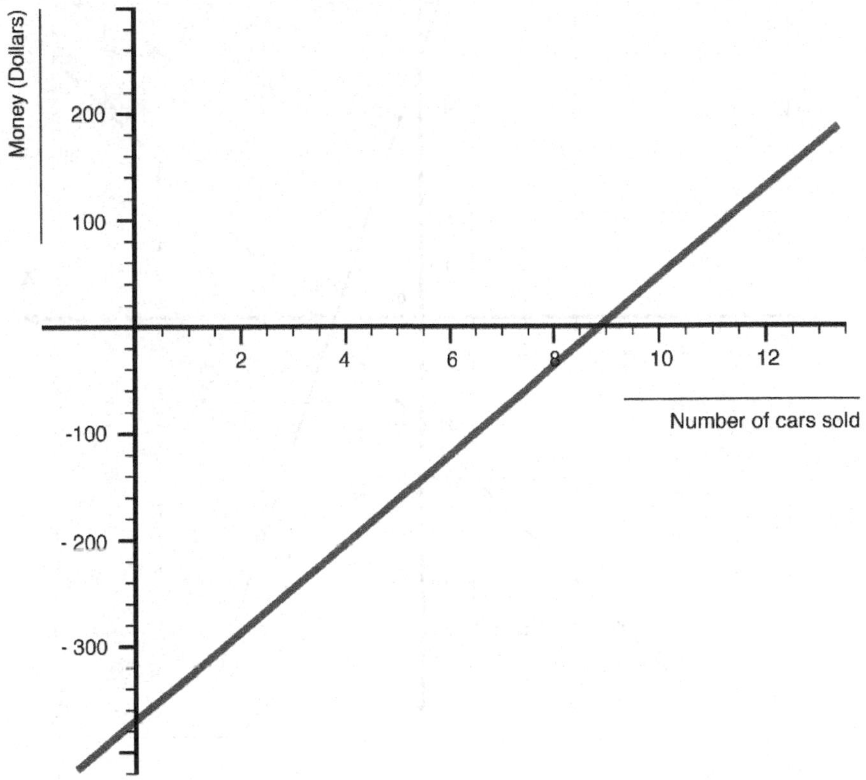

With a single equation in two variables, the solutions are limited only by the situation the equation represents. When two equations or inequalities are used, more constraints are added. For example, in a system of linear equations, there is often—although not always—only one answer. The point of intersection of two lines is the solution. For a system of inequalities, there are infinitely many answers.

The intersection of two solution sets gives the solution set of the system of inequalities. In the following graph, the darker shaded region is where two inequalities overlap. Any set of x and y found in that region satisfies both inequalities. The line with the positive slope is solid, meaning the values on that line are included in the solution.

The line with the negative slope is dotted, so the coordinates on that line are not included.

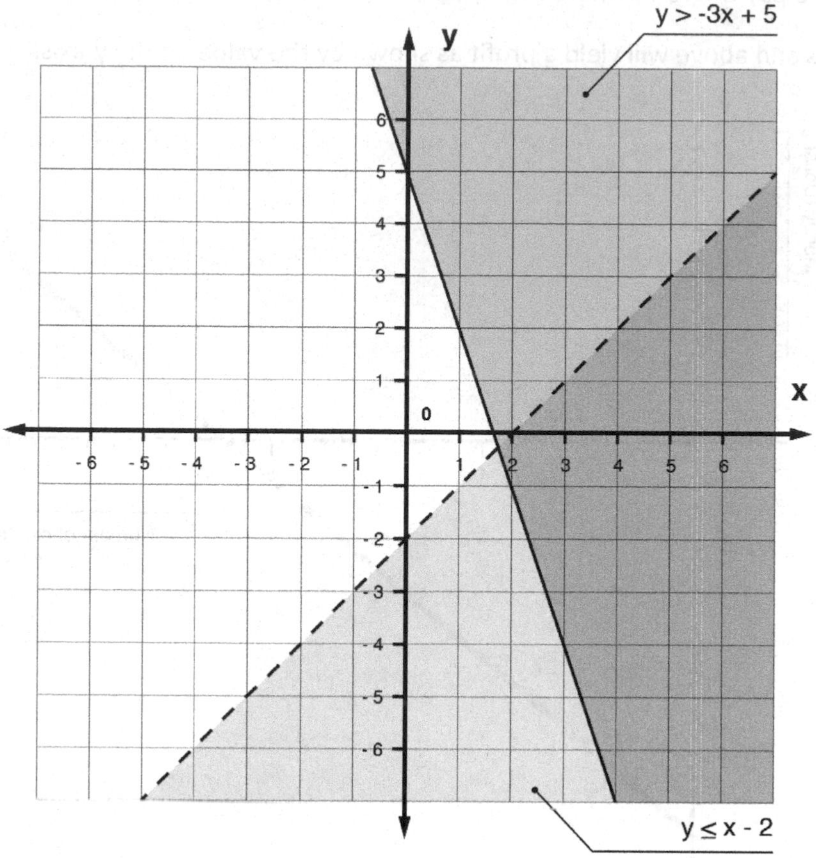

Formulas with two variables are equations used to represent a specific relationship. For example, the formula $d = rt$ represents the relationship between distance, rate, and time. If Bob travels at a rate of 35 miles per hour on his road trip from Westminster to Seneca, the formula $d = 35t$ can be used to represent his distance traveled in a specific length of time. Formulas can also be used to show different roles of the variables, transformed without any given numbers. Solving for r, the formula becomes $\frac{d}{t} = r$. The t is moved over by division so that *rate* is a function of distance and time.

<u>Solving Equations</u>

Solving equations in one variable is the process of For example, in $3x - 7 = 20$, the variable x needs to be isolated. Using opposite operations, the -7 is moved to the right side of the equation by adding seven to both sides:

$$3x - 7 + 7 = 20 + 7$$

$$3x = 27$$

Dividing by three on each side, $\frac{3x}{3} = \frac{27}{3}$, results in isolation of the variable. It is important to note that if an operation is performed on one side of the equals sign, it has to be performed on the other side to maintain equality. The solution is found to be $x = 9$. This solution can be checked for accuracy by plugging x=7 in the original equation. After simplifying the equation, $20 = 20$ is found, which is a true statement.

When solving radical and rational equations, extraneous solutions must be accounted for when finding the answers. For example, the equation $\frac{x}{x-5} = \frac{3x}{x+3}$ has two values that create a 0 denominator: $x \neq 5, -3$. When solving for x, these values must be considered because they cannot be solutions. In the given equation, solving for x can be done using cross-multiplication, yielding the equation:

$$x(x+3) = 3x(x-5)$$

Distributing results in the quadratic equation yields $x^2 + 3x = 3x^2 - 15x$; therefore, all terms must be moved to one side of the equals sign. This results in $2x^2 - 18x = 0$, which in factored form is $2x(x-9) = 0$. Setting each factor equal to zero, the apparent solutions are $x = 0$ and $x = 9$. These two solutions are neither 5 nor -3, so they are viable solutions. Neither 0 nor 9 create a 0 denominator in the original equation.

A similar process exists when solving radical equations. One must check to make sure the solutions are defined in the original equations. Solving an equation containing a square root involves isolating the root and then squaring both sides of the equals sign. Solving a cube root equation involves isolating the radical and then cubing both sides. In either case, the variable can then be solved for because there are no longer radicals in the equation.

Equations with one variable can be solved using the addition principle and multiplication principle. If $a = b$, then $a + c = b + c$, and $ac = bc$. Given the equation $2x - 3 = 5x + 7$, the first step is to combine the variable terms and the constant terms. Using the principles, expressions can be added and subtracted onto and off both sides of the equals sign, so the equation turns into $-10 = 3x$. Dividing by 3 on both sides through the multiplication principle with $c = \frac{1}{3}$ results in the final answer of $x = \frac{-10}{3}$.

Some equations have a higher degree and are not solved by simply using opposite operations. When an equation has a degree of 2, completing the square is an option. For example, the quadratic equation $x^2 - 6x + 2 = 0$ can be rewritten by completing the square. A *quadratic equation* is an equation in the form $ax^2 + bx + c = 0$. The goal of completing the square is to get the equation into the form $(x-p)^2 = q$. Using the example, the constant term 2 first needs to be moved over to the opposite side by subtracting. Then, the square can be completed by adding 9 to both sides, which is the square of half of the coefficient of the middle term $-6x$. The current equation is $x^2 - 6x + 9 = 7$. The left side can be factored into a square of a binomial, resulting in $(x-3)^2 = 7$. To solve for x, the square root of both sides should be taken, resulting in:

$$(x-3) = \pm\sqrt{7}$$

$$x = 3 \pm \sqrt{7}$$

Other ways of solving quadratic equations include graphing, factoring, and using the quadratic formula. The equation $y = x^2 - 4x + 3$ can be graphed on the coordinate plane, and the solutions can be observed where it crosses the x-axis. The graph will be a parabola that opens up with two solutions at 1 and 3.

The equation can also be factored to find the solutions. The original equation, $y = x^2 - 4x + 3$ can be factored into $y = (x-1)(x-3)$. Setting this equal to zero, the x-values are found to be 1 and 3, just as on the graph. Solving by factoring and graphing are not always possible. The quadratic formula is a method of solving quadratic equations that always results in exact solutions.

The formula is:

$$x = \frac{-b \pm \sqrt{b^2 - 4ac}}{2a}$$

where $a, b,$ and c are the coefficients in the original equation in standard form $y = ax^2 + bx + c$. For this example,

$$x = \frac{4 \pm \sqrt{(-4)^2 - 4(1)(3)}}{2(1)} = \frac{4 \pm \sqrt{16 - 12}}{2} = \frac{4 \pm 2}{2} = 1, 3$$

The expression underneath the radical is called the *discriminant*. Without working out the entire formula, the value of the discriminant can reveal the nature of the solutions. If the value of the discriminant $b^2 - 4ac$ is positive, then there will be two real solutions. If the value is zero, there will be one real solution. If the value is negative, the two solutions will be imaginary or complex. If the solutions are complex, it means that the parabola never touches the x-axis. An example of a complex solution can be found by solving the following quadratic: $y = x^2 - 4x + 8$. By using the quadratic formula, the solutions are found to be:

$$x = \frac{4 \pm \sqrt{(-4)^2 - 4(1)(8)}}{2(1)} = \frac{4 \pm \sqrt{16 - 32}}{2} = \frac{4 \pm \sqrt{-16}}{2} = 2 \pm 2i$$

The solutions both have a real part, 2, and an imaginary part, $2i$.

Systems of Equations

A *system of equations* is a group of equations that have the same variables or unknowns. These equations can be linear, but they are not always so. Finding a solution to a system of equations means finding the values of the variables that satisfy each equation. For a linear system of two equations and two variables, there could be a single solution, no solution, or infinitely many solutions.

A single solution occurs when there is one value for x and y that satisfies the system. This would be shown on the graph where the lines cross at exactly one point. When there is no solution, the lines are parallel and do not ever cross. With infinitely many solutions, the equations may look different, but they are the same line. One equation will be a multiple of the other, and on the graph, they lie on top of each other.

The process of elimination can be used to solve a system of equations. For example, the following equations make up a system:

$$x + 3y = 10 \text{ and } 2x - 5y = 9$$

Immediately adding these equations does not eliminate a variable, but it is possible to change the first equation by multiplying the whole equation by -2. This changes the first equation to

$$-2x - 6y = -20$$

The equations can be then added to obtain $-11y = -11$. Solving for y yields $y = 1$. To find the rest of the solution, 1 can be substituted in for y in either original equation to find the value of $x = 7$. The solution to the system is (7, 1) because it makes both equations true, and it is the point in which the lines intersect. If the system is *dependent*—having infinitely many solutions—then both variables will cancel out when the elimination method is used, resulting in an equation that is true for many values of x and y. Since the system is dependent, both equations can be simplified to the same equation or line.

A system can also be solved using *substitution*. This involves solving one equation for a variable and then plugging that solved equation into the other equation in the system. This equation can be solved for one variable, which can then be plugged in to either original equation and solved for the other variable. For example, $x - y = -2$ and $3x + 2y = 9$ can be solved using substitution. The first equation can be solved for x, where $x = -2 + y$. Then it can be plugged into the other equation:

$$3(-2 + y) + 2y = 9$$

Solving for y yields:

$$-6 + 3y + 2y = 9$$

That shows that $y = 3$. If $y = 3$, then $x = 1$.

This solution can be checked by plugging in these values for the variables in each equation to see if it makes a true statement.

Finally, a solution to a system of equations can be found graphically. The solution to a linear system is the point or points where the lines cross. The values of x and y represent the coordinates (x, y) where the lines intersect. Using the same system of equation as above, they can be solved for y to put them in slope-intercept form, $y = mx + b$. These equations become $y = x + 4$ and $y = -\frac{3}{2}x + 4.5$. The slope is the coefficient of x, and the y-intercept is the constant value. This system with the solution is shown below:

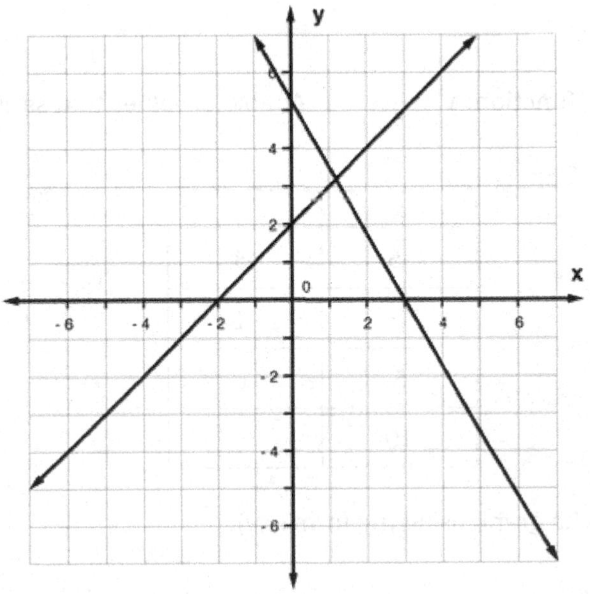

A system of equations may also be made up of a linear and a quadratic equation. These systems may have one solution, two solutions, or no solutions. The graph of these systems involves one straight line and one parabola. Algebraically, these systems can be solved by solving the linear equation for one variable and plugging that answer in to the quadratic equation. If possible, the equation can then be solved to find part of the answer. The graphing method is commonly used for these types of systems. On a graph, these two lines can be found to intersect at one point, at two points across the parabola, or at no points.

<u>Equations and Graphing</u>
A function is called *linear* if it can take the form of the equation $f(x) = ax + b$, or $y = ax + b$, for any two numbers a and b. A linear equation forms a straight line when graphed on the coordinate plane. An example of a linear function is shown below on the graph.

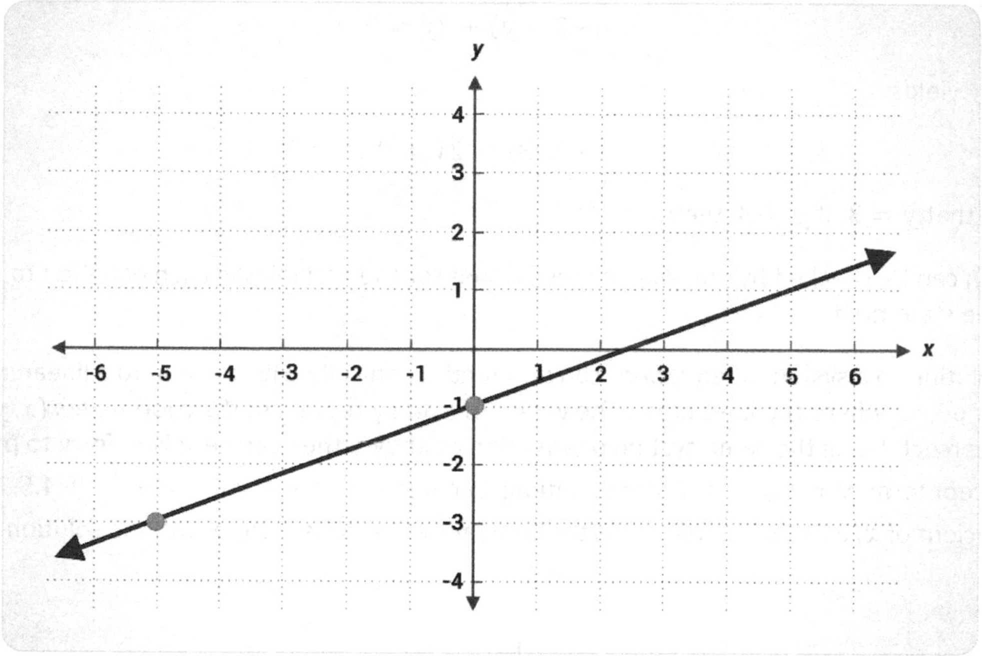

This is a graph of the following function: $y = \frac{2}{5}x - 1$. A table of values that satisfies this function is shown below.

x	y
-5	-3
0	-1
5	1
10	3

These points can be found on the graph using the form (x,y).

To graph relations and functions, the Cartesian plane is used. This means to think of the plane as being given a grid of squares, with one direction being the *x*-axis and the other direction the *y*-axis. Generally, the independent variable is placed along the horizontal axis, and the dependent variable is placed along the vertical axis. Any point on the plane can be specified by saying how far to go along the *x*-axis and how far along the *y*-axis with a pair of numbers (x, y). Specific values for these pairs can be given names such as $C = (-1, 3)$. Negative values mean to move left or down; positive values mean to move right or up. The point where the axes cross one another is called the *origin*. The origin has coordinates $(0, 0)$ and is usually called *O* when given a specific label. An illustration of the Cartesian plane, along with graphs of $(2, 1)$ and $(-1, -1)$, are below.

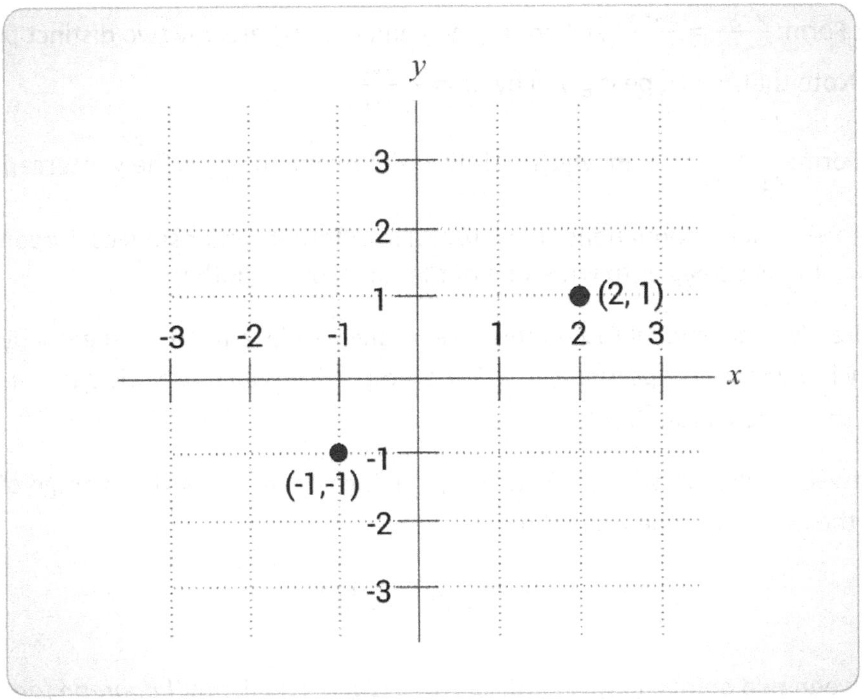

Relations also can be graphed by marking each point whose coordinates satisfy the relation. If the relation is a function, then there is only one value of *y* for any given value of *x*. This leads to the *vertical line test*: if a relation is graphed, then the relation is a function if every vertical line touches the graph at either zero or one point. Conversely, when graphing a function, then every vertical line will touch the graph at no points or just one point.

When graphing a linear function, note that the ratio of the change of the *y* coordinate to the change in the *x* coordinate is constant between any two points on the resulting line, no matter which two points are chosen. In other words, in a pair of points on a line, (x_1, y_1) and (x_2, y_2), with $x_1 \neq x_2$ so that the two points are distinct, then the ratio $\frac{y_2 - y_1}{x_2 - x_1}$ will be the same, regardless of which particular pair of points are chosen. This ratio, $\frac{y_2 - y_1}{x_2 - x_1}$, is called the *slope* of the line and is frequently denoted with the letter m. If slope *m* is positive, then the line goes upward when moving to the right, while if slope *m* is negative, then the line goes downward when moving to the right. If the slope is 0, then the line is called *horizontal*, and the *y* coordinate is constant along the entire line. In lines where the *x* coordinate is constant along the entire line, *y* is not actually a function of *x*. For such lines, the slope is not defined. These lines are called *vertical* lines.

Linear functions may take forms other than $y = ax + b$. The most common forms of linear equations are explained below:

1. Standard Form: $Ax + By = C$, in which the slope is given by $m = \frac{-A}{B}$, and the y-intercept is given by $\frac{C}{B}$.

2. Slope-Intercept Form: $y = mx + b$, where the slope is m and the y intercept is b.

3. Point-Slope Form: $y - y_1 = m(x - x_1)$, where the slope is m and (x_1, y_1) is any point on the chosen line.

4. Two-Point Form: $\frac{y-y_1}{x-x_1} = \frac{y_2-y_1}{x_2-x_1}$, where (x_1, y_1) and (x_2, y_2) are any two distinct points on the chosen line. Note that the slope is given by $m = \frac{y_2-y_1}{x_2-x_1}$.

5. Intercept Form: $\frac{x}{x_1} + \frac{y}{y_1} = 1$, in which x_1 is the x-intercept and y_1 is the y-intercept.

These five ways to write linear equations are all useful in different circumstances. Depending on the given information, it may be easier to write one of the forms over another.

If $y = mx$, y is directly proportional to x. In this case, changing x by a factor changes y by that same factor. If $y = \frac{m}{x}$, y is inversely proportional to x. For example, if x is increased by a factor of 3, then y will be decreased by the same factor, 3.

The *midpoint* between two points, (x_1, y_1) and (x_2, y_2), is given by taking the average of the x coordinates and the average of the y coordinates:

$$\left(\frac{x_1 + x_2}{2}, \frac{y_1 + y_2}{2}\right)$$

The *distance* between two points, (x_1, y_1) and (x_2, y_2), is given by the *Pythagorean formula*, $\sqrt{(x_2 - x_1)^2 + (y_2 - y_1)^2}$.

To find the perpendicular distance between a line $Ax + By = C$ and a point (x_1, y_1) not on the line, we need to use the formula

$$\frac{|Ax_1 + By_1 + C|}{\sqrt{A^2 + B^2}}$$

Functions

A *function* is defined as a relationship between inputs and outputs where there is only one output value for a given input. The input is called the *independent variable*. If the variable is set equal to the output, as in $y = f(x)$, then this is called the *dependent variable*. To indicate the dependent value a function, y, gives for a specific independent variable, x, the notation y = $f(x)$ is used.

As an example, the following function is in function notation: $f(x) = 3x - 4$. The $f(x)$ represents the output value for an input of x. If $x = 2$, the equation becomes:

$$f(2) = 3(2) - 4 = 6 - 4 = 2$$

The input of 2 yields an output of 2, forming the ordered pair $(2, 2)$. The following set of ordered pairs corresponds to the given function: $(2, 2), (0, -4), (-2, -10)$. The set of all possible inputs of a function is its *domain*, and all possible outputs is called the *range*. By definition, each member of the domain is paired with only one member of the range.

Functions can also be defined recursively. In this form, they are not defined explicitly in terms of variables. Instead, they are defined using previously-evaluated function outputs, starting with either $f(0)$ or $f(1)$. An example of a recursively-defined function is:

$$f(1) = 2, f(n) = 2f(n-1) + 2n, n > 1$$

The domain of this function is the set of all integers.

The domain and range of a function can be found visually by its plot on the coordinate plane. In the function $f(x) = x^2 - 3$, for example, the domain is all real numbers because the parabola stretches as far left and as far right as it can go, with no restrictions. This means that any input value from the real number system will yield an answer in the real number system. For the range, the inequality $y \geq -3$ would be used to describe the possible output values because the parabola has a minimum at $y = -3$. This means there will not be any real output values less than -3 because -3 is the lowest value it reaches on the y-axis.

These same answers for domain and range can be found by observing a table. The table below shows that from input values $x = -1$ to $x = 1$, the output results in a minimum of -3. On each side of $x = 0$, the numbers increase, showing that the range is all real numbers greater than or equal to -3.

x (domain/input)	**y (range/output)**
-2	1
-1	-2
0	-3
-1	-2
2	1

Different types of functions behave in different ways. The quadratic function described above can be described as decreasing from left to right until the input value of zero, then increasing after that. A function is defined to be increasing over a subset of its domain if for all $x_1 \geq x_2$ in that interval, $f(x_1) \geq f(x_2)$. Also, a function is decreasing over an interval if for all $x_1 \geq x_2$ in that interval, $f(x_1) \leq f(x_2)$. A point in which a function changes from increasing to decreasing can also be labeled as the *maximum value* of a function if it is the largest point the graph reaches on the y-axis. A point in which a function changes from decreasing to increasing can be labeled as the minimum value of a function if it is the smallest point the graph reaches on the y-axis. Maximum values are also known as *extreme values*. The graph of a continuous function does not have any breaks or jumps in the graph. This description is not true of all functions. A radical function, for example, $f(x) = \sqrt{x}$, has a restriction for the domain and range because there are no real negative inputs or outputs for this function. The domain can be stated as $x \geq 0$, and the range is $y \geq 0$.

A piecewise-defined function also has a different appearance on the graph. In the following function, there are three equations defined over different intervals. It is a function because there is only one y-value for each x-value, passing the Vertical Line Test. The domain is all real numbers less than or equal

to 6. The range is all real numbers greater than zero. From left to right, the graph decreases to zero, then increases to almost 4, and then jumps to 6.
From input values greater than 2, the input decreases just below 8 to 4, and then stops.

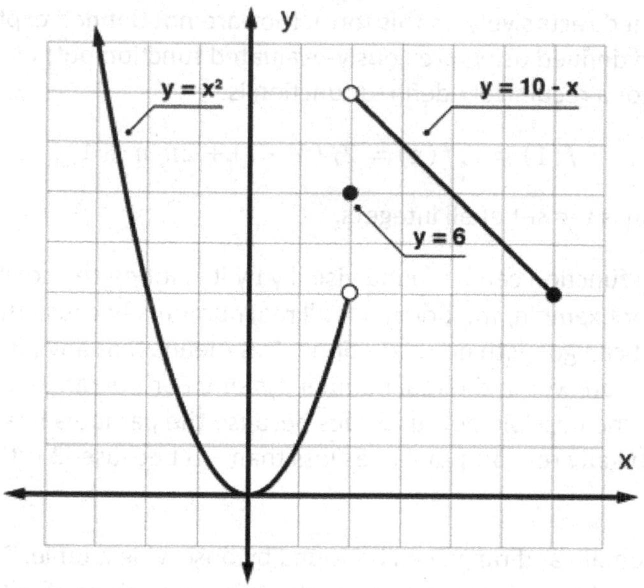

Logarithmic and exponential functions also have different behavior than other functions. These two types of functions are inverses of each other. The *inverse* of a function can be found by switching the place of x and y, and solving for y. When this is done for the exponential equation, $y = 2^x$, the function $y = \log_2 x$ is found. The general form of a *logarithmic function* is $y = log_b x$, which says b raised to the y power equals x.

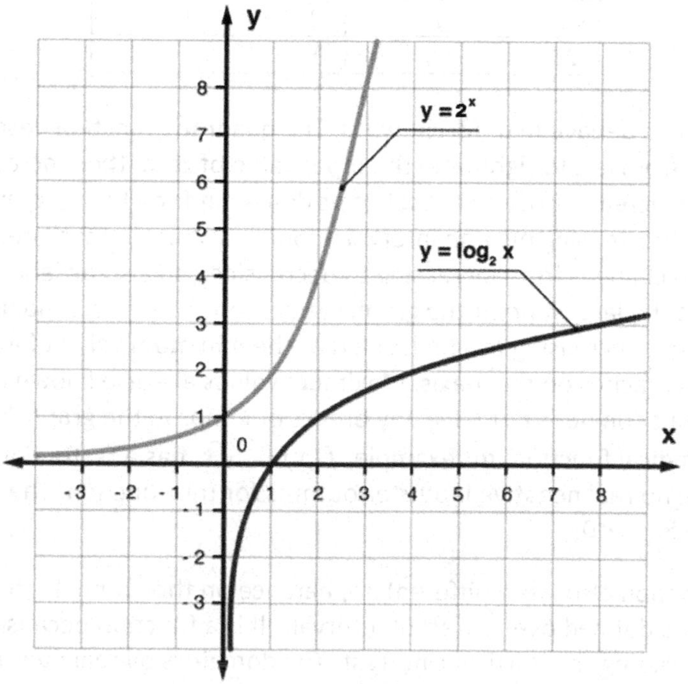

The thick black line on the graph above represents the logarithmic function $y = \log_2 x$. This curve passes through the point $(1, 0)$, just as all log functions do, because any value $b^0 = 1$. The graph of this logarithmic function starts very close to zero, but does not touch the y-axis. The output value will never be zero by the definition of logarithms. The thinner gray line seen above represents the exponential function $y = 2^x$. The behavior of this function is opposite the logarithmic function because the graph of an inverse function is the graph of the original function flipped over the line $y = x$. The curve passes through the point $(0, 1)$ because any number raised to the zero power is one. This curve also gets very close to the x-axis but never touches it because an exponential expression never has an output of zero. The x-axis on this graph is called a horizontal asymptote. An *asymptote* is a line that represents a boundary for a function. It shows a value that the function will get close to, but never reach.

Functions can also be described as being even, odd, or neither. If $f(-x) = f(x)$, the function is even. For example, the function $f(x) = x^2 - 2$ is even. Plugging in $x = 2$ yields an output of $y = 2$. After changing the input to $x = -2$, the output is still $y = 2$. The output is the same for opposite inputs. Another way to observe an even function is by the symmetry of the graph. If the graph is symmetrical about the axis, then the function is even. If the graph is symmetric about the origin, then the function is odd. Algebraically, if $f(-x) = -f(x)$, the function is odd.

Finally, a function can be described as *periodic* if it repeats itself in regular intervals. Common periodic functions are trigonometric functions. For example, $y = \sin x$ is a periodic function with period 2π because it repeats itself every 2π units along the x-axis.

<u>Building Functions</u>

Functions can be built out of the context of a situation. For example, the relationship between the money paid for a gym membership and the months that someone has been a member can be described through a function. If the one-time membership fee is \$40 and the monthly fee is \$30, then the function can be written $f(x) = 30x + 40$. The x-value represents the number of months the person has been part of the gym, while the output is the total money paid for the membership. The table below shows this relationship. It is a representation of the function because the initial cost is \$40 and the cost increases each month by \$30.

x (months)	y (money paid to gym)
0	40
1	70
2	100
3	130

Functions can also be built from existing functions. For example, a given function $f(x)$ can be transformed by adding a constant, multiplying by a constant, or changing the input value by a constant. The new function $g(x) = f(x) + k$ represents a vertical shift of the original function. In $f(x) = 3x - 2$, a vertical shift 4 units up would be:

$$g(x) = 3x - 2 + 4 = 3x + 2$$

Multiplying the function times a constant k represents a vertical stretch, based on whether the constant is greater than or less than 1. The following function represents a stretch:

$$g(x) = kf(x) = 4(3x - 2) = 12x - 8$$

Changing the input x by a constant forms the function:

$$g(x) = f(x + k) = 3(x + 4) - 2 = 3x + 12 - 2 = 3x + 10$$

and this represents a horizontal shift to the left 4 units. If $(x - 4)$ was plugged into the function, it would represent a vertical shift.

A composition function can also be formed by plugging one function into another. In function notation, this is written:

$$(f \circ g)(x) = f(g(x))$$

For two functions $f(x) = x^2$ and $g(x) = x - 3$, the composition function becomes:

$$f(g(x)) = (x - 3)^2 = x^2 - 6x + 9$$

The composition of functions can also be used to verify if two functions are inverses of each other. Given the two functions $f(x) = 2x + 5$ and $g(x) = \frac{x-5}{2}$, the composition function can be found $(f \circ g)(x)$. Solving this equation yields:

$$f(g(x)) = 2\left(\frac{x - 5}{2}\right) + 5 = x - 5 + 5 = x$$

It also is true that $g(f(x)) = x$. Since the composition of these two functions gives a simplified answer of x, this verifies that $f(x)$ and $g(x)$ are inverse functions. The domain of $f(g(x))$ is the set of all x-values in the domain of $g(x)$ such that $g(x)$ is in the domain of $f(x)$. Basically, both $f(g(x))$ and $g(x)$ have to be defined.

To build an inverse of a function, $f(x)$ needs to be replaced with y, and the x and y values need to be switched. Then, the equation can be solved for y. For example, given the equation $y = e^{2x}$, the inverse can be found by rewriting the equation $x = e^{2y}$. The natural logarithm of both sides is taken down, and the exponent is brought down to form the equation:

$$\ln(x) = \ln(e)\, 2y$$

$\ln(e)$=1, which yields the equation $\ln(x) = 2y$. Dividing both sides by 2 yields the inverse equation

$$\frac{\ln(x)}{2} = y = f^{-1}(x)$$

The domain of an inverse function is the range of the original function, and the range of an inverse function is the domain of the original function. Therefore, an ordered pair (x, y) on either a graph or a table corresponding to $f(x)$ means that the ordered pair (y, x) exists on the graph of $f^{-1}(x)$. Basically, if $f(x) = y$, then $f^{-1}(y) = x$. For a function have an inverse, it must be one-to-one. That means it must pass the *Horizontal Line Test*, and if any horizontal line passes through the graph of the function twice, a function is not one-to-one. The domain of a function that is not one-to-one can be restricted to an interval in which the function is one-to-one, to be able to define an inverse function.

Functions can also be formed from combinations of existing functions.

Given $f(x)$ and $g(x)$, the following can be built:

$$f + g$$

$$f - g$$

$$fg$$

$$\frac{f}{g}$$

The domains of $f + g, f - g,$ and fg are the intersection of the domains of f and g. The domain of $\frac{f}{g}$ is the same set, excluding those values that make $g(x) = 0$.

For example, if:

$$f(x) = 2x + 3$$

$$g(x) = x + 1$$

then

$$\frac{f}{g} = \frac{2x + 3}{x + 1}$$

Its domain is all real numbers except -1.

Common Functions

Three common functions used to model different relationships between quantities are linear, quadratic, and exponential functions. Linear functions are the simplest of the three, and the independent variable x has an exponent of 1. Written in the most common form, $y = mx + b$, the coefficient of x tells how fast the function grows at a constant rate, and the b-value tells the starting point. A quadratic function has an exponent of 2 on the independent variable x. Standard form for this type of function is $y = ax^2 + bx + c$, and the graph is a parabola. These type functions grow at a changing rate. An exponential function has an independent variable in the exponent $y = ab^x$. The graph of these types of functions is described as *growth* or *decay*, based on whether the base, b, is greater than or less than 1. These functions are different from quadratic functions because the base stays constant. A common base is base *e*.

The following three functions model a linear, quadratic, and exponential function respectively: $y = 2x$, $y = x^2$, and $y = 2^x$. Their graphs are shown below. The first graph, modeling the linear function, shows that the growth is constant over each interval. With a horizontal change of 1, the vertical change is 2. It models a constant positive growth. The second graph shows the quadratic function, which is a curve that is symmetric across the y-axis. The growth is not constant, but the change is mirrored over the axis. The last graph models the exponential function, where the horizontal change of 1 yields a vertical change that increases more and more. The exponential graph gets very close to the x-axis, but never touches it, meaning there is an asymptote there. The y-value can never be zero because the base of 2 can never be raised to an input value that yields an output of zero.

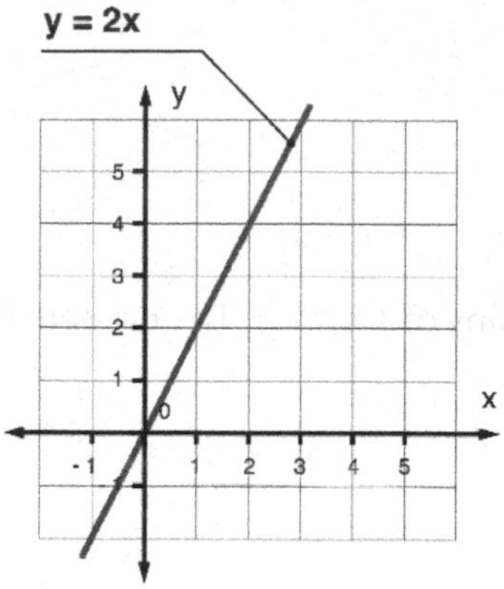

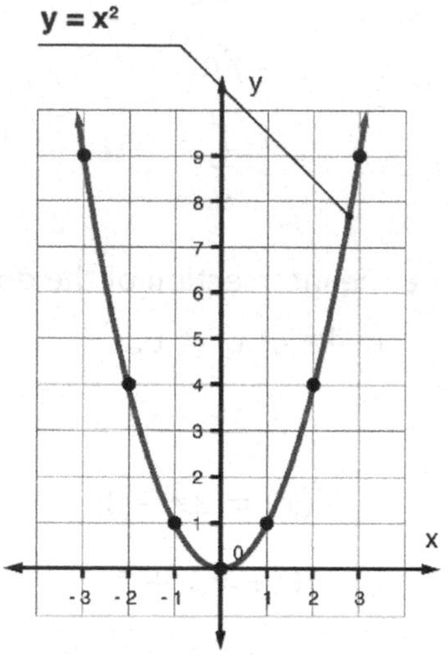

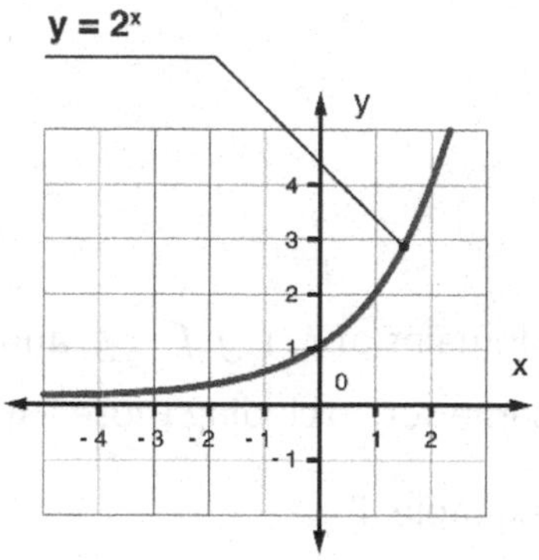

The three tables below show specific values for three types of functions. The third column in each table shows the change in the y-values for each interval. The first table shows a constant change of 2 for each equal interval, which matches the slope in the equation $y = 2x$. The second table shows an increasing change, but it also has a pattern. The increase is changing by 2 more each time, so the change is quadratic. The third table shows the change as factors of the base, 2. It shows a continuing pattern of factors of the base.

y = 2x		
x	y	Δy
1	2	
2	4	2
3	6	2
4	8	2
5	10	2

$y = x^2$		
x	y	Δy
1	1	
2	4	3
3	9	5
4	16	7
5	25	9

$y = 2^x$		
x	y	Δy
1	2	
2	4	2
3	8	4
4	16	8
5	32	16

Given a table of values, the type of function can be determined by observing the change in y over equal intervals. For example, the tables below model two functions. The changes in interval for the x-values is 1 for both tables. For the first table, the y-values increase by 5 for each interval. Since the change is constant, the situation can be described as a linear function. The equation would be $y = 5x + 3$. For the second table, the change for y is 5, 20, 100, and 500, respectively. The increases are multiples of 5, meaning the situation can be modeled by an exponential function. The equation $y = 5^x + 3$ models this situation.

x	y
0	3
1	8
2	13
3	18
4	23

x	y
0	3
1	8
2	28
3	128
4	628

Quadratic equations can be used to model real-world area problems. For example, a farmer may have a rectangular field that he needs to sow with seed. The field has length $x + 8$ and width $2x$. The formula for area should be used: $A = lw$. Therefore:

$$A = (x + 8) * 2x = 2x^2 + 16x$$

The possible values for the length and width can be shown in a table, with input x and output A. If the equation was graphed, the possible area values can be seen on the y-axis for given x-values.

Exponential growth and decay can be found in real-world situations. For example, if a piece of notebook paper is folded 25 times, the thickness of the paper can be found. To model this situation, a table can be used. The initial point is one-fold, which yields a thickness of 2 papers. For the second fold, the thickness is 4. Since the thickness doubles each time, the table below shows the thickness for the next few folds. Notice the thickness changes by the same factor each time. Since this change for a constant interval of folds is a factor of 2, the function is exponential. The equation for this is $y = 2^x$. For twenty-five folds, the thickness would be 33,554,432 papers.

x (folds)	**y (paper thickness)**
0	1
1	2
2	4
3	8
4	16
5	32

One exponential formula that is commonly used is the *interest formula*: $A = Pe^{rt}$. In this formula, interest is compounded continuously. A is the value of the investment after the time, t, in years. P is the initial amount of the investment, r is the interest rate, and e is the constant equal to approximately 2.718. Given an initial amount of $200 and a time of 3 years, if interest is compounded continuously at a rate of 6%, the total investment value can be found by plugging each value into the formula. The invested value at the end is $239.44. In more complex problems, the final investment may be given, and the rate may be the unknown. In this case, the formula becomes $239.44 = 200e^{r3}$. Solving for r requires isolating the exponential expression on one side by dividing by 200, yielding the equation

$1.20 = e^{r3}$. Taking the natural log of both sides results in $\ln(1.2) = r3$. Using a calculator to evaluate the logarithmic expression, $r = 0.06 = 6\%$.

When working with logarithms and exponential expressions, it is important to remember the relationship between the two. In general, the logarithmic form is $y = log_b x$ for an exponential form $b^y = x$. Logarithms and exponential functions are inverses of each other.

Patterns

Patterns within a sequence can come in 2 distinct forms: the items (shapes, numbers, etc.) either repeat in a constant order, or the items change from one step to another in some consistent way. The core is the smallest unit, or number of items, that repeats in a repeating pattern. For example, the pattern ○○▲○○▲○... has a core that is ○○▲. Knowing only the core, the pattern can be extended. Knowing the number of steps in the core allows the identification of an item in each step without drawing/writing the entire pattern out. For example, suppose the tenth item in the previous pattern must be determined. Because the core consists of three items (○○▲), the core repeats in multiples of 3. In other words, steps 3, 6, 9, 12, etc. will be ▲ completing the core with the core starting over on the next step. For the above example, the 9th step will be ▲ and the 10th will be ○.

The most common patterns in which each item changes from one step to the next are arithmetic and geometric sequences. An arithmetic sequence is one in which the items increase or decrease by a constant difference. In other words, the same thing is added or subtracted to each item or step to produce the next. To determine if a sequence is arithmetic, determine what must be added or subtracted to step one to produce step two. Then, check if the same thing is added/subtracted to step two to produce step three. The same thing must be added/subtracted to step three to produce step four, and so on. Consider the pattern 13, 10, 7, 4 . . . To get from step one (13) to step two (10) by adding or subtracting requires subtracting by 3. The next step is checking if subtracting 3 from step two (10) will produce step three (7), and subtracting 3 from step three (7) will produce step four (4). In this case, the pattern holds true. Therefore, this is an arithmetic sequence in which each step is produced by subtracting 3 from the previous step. To extend the sequence, 3 is subtracted from the last step to produce the next. The next three numbers in the sequence are 1, -2, -5.

A geometric sequence is one in which each step is produced by multiplying or dividing the previous step by the same number. To determine if a sequence is geometric, decide what step one must be multiplied or divided by to produce step two. Then check if multiplying or dividing step two by the same number produces step three, and so on. Consider the pattern 2, 8, 32, 128 . . . To get from step one (2) to step two (8) requires multiplication by 4. The next step determines if multiplying step two (8) by 4 produces step three (32), and multiplying step three (32) by 4 produces step four (128). In this case, the pattern holds true. Therefore, this is a geometric sequence in which each step is produced by multiplying the previous step by 4. To extend the sequence, the last step is multiplied by 4 and repeated. The next three numbers in the sequence are 512; 2,048; 8,192.

Although arithmetic and geometric sequences typically use numbers, these sequences can also be represented by shapes. For example, an arithmetic sequence could consist of shapes with three sides, four sides, and five sides (add one side to the previous step to produce the next). A geometric sequence could consist of eight blocks, four blocks, and two blocks (each step is produced by dividing the number of blocks in the previous step by 2).

An arithmetic or geometric sequence can be written as a formula and used to determine unknown steps without writing out the entire sequence. An arithmetic sequence progresses by a *common difference*. To determine the common difference, any step is subtracted by the step that precedes it. In the sequence 4, 9, 14, 19 . . . the common difference, or *d*, is 5. By expressing each step as a_1, a_2, a_3, etc., a formula can be written to represent the sequence. a_1 is the first step. To produce step two, step 1 (a_1) is added to the common difference (*d*): $a_2 = a_1 + d$. To produce step three, the common difference (*d*) is added twice to a_1: $a_3 = a_1 + 2d$. To produce step four, the common difference (*d*) is added three times to a_1: $a_4 = a_1 + 3d$. Following this pattern allows a general rule for arithmetic sequences to be written. For any term of the sequence (a_n), the first step (a_1) is added to the product of the common difference (*d*) and one less than the step of the term ($n - 1$): $a_n = a_1 + (n - 1)d$. Suppose the 8th term (a_8) is to be found in the previous sequence. By knowing the first step (a_1) is 4 and the common difference (*d*) is 5, the formula can be used: $a_n = a_1 + (n - 1)d \rightarrow a_8 = 4 + (7)5 \rightarrow a_8 = 39$.

In a geometric sequence, each step is produced by multiplying or dividing the previous step by the same number. The *common ratio*, or (*r*), can be determined by dividing any step by the previous step. In the sequence 1, 3, 9, 27 . . . the common ratio (*r*) is $3(\frac{3}{1} = 3$ or $\frac{9}{3} = 3$ or $\frac{27}{9} = 3)$. Each successive step can be expressed as a product of the first step (a_1) and the common ratio (*r*) to some power. For example, $a_2 = a_1 \times r; a_3 = a_1 \times r \times r$ or $a_3 = a_1 \times r^2; a_4 = a_1 \times r \times r \times r$ or $a_4 = a\_1 \times r^3$. Following this pattern, a general rule for geometric sequences can be written. For any term of the sequence (a_n), the first step (a_1) is multiplied by the common ratio (*r*) raised to the power one less than the step of the term ($n - 1$): $a_n = a_1 \times r^{(n-1)}$. Suppose for the previous sequence, the 7th term (a_7) is to be found. Knowing the first step (a_1) is one, and the common ratio (*r*) is 3, the formula can be used: $a_n = a_1 \times r^{(n-1)} \rightarrow a_7 = (1) \times 3^6 \rightarrow a_7 = 729$.

Data Analysis, Probability, and Statistics

<u>Statistics</u>

The field of statistics describes relationships between quantities that are related, but not necessarily in a deterministic manner. For example, a graduating student's salary will often be higher when the student graduates with a higher GPA, but this is not always the case. Likewise, people who smoke tobacco are more likely to develop lung cancer, but, in fact, it is possible for non-smokers to develop the disease as well. *Statistics* describes these kinds of situations, where the likelihood of some outcome depends on the starting data.

Descriptive statistics involves analyzing a collection of data to describe its broad properties such average (or mean), what percent of the data falls within a given range, and other such properties. An example of this would be taking all of the test scores from a given class and calculating the average test score. *Inferential statistics* attempts to use data about a subset of some population to make inferences about the rest of the population. An example of this would be taking a collection of students who received tutoring and comparing their results to a collection of students who did not receive tutoring, then using that comparison to try to predict whether the tutoring program in question is beneficial.

To be sure that inferences have a high probability of being true for the whole population, the subset that is analyzed needs to resemble a miniature version of the population as closely as possible. For this reason, statisticians like to choose random samples from the population to study, rather than picking a specific group of people based on some similarity. For example, studying the incomes of people who live in Portland does not tell anything useful about the incomes of people who live in Tallahassee.

<u>Measures of Central Tendency</u>

Suppose that *X* is a set of data points $(x_1, x_2, x_3, ... x_n)$ and some description of the general properties of this data need to be found.

The first property that can be defined for this set of data is the *mean*. To find the mean, add up all the data points, then divide by the total number of data points. This can be expressed using *summation notation* as:

$$\bar{X} = \frac{x_1 + x_2 + x_3 + \cdots + x_n}{n} = \frac{1}{n}\sum_{i=1}^{n} x_i$$

For example, suppose that in a class of 10 students, the scores on a test were 50, 60, 65, 65, 75, 80, 85, 85, 90, 100. Therefore, the average test score will be $\frac{1}{10}(50 + 60 + 65 + 65 + 75 + 80 + 85 + 85 + 90 + 100) = 75.5$.

The mean is a useful number if the distribution of data is normal (more on this later), which roughly means that the frequency of different outcomes has a single peak and is roughly equally distributed on both sides of that peak. However, it is less useful in some cases where the data might be split or where there are some *outliers*. Outliers are data points that are far from the rest of the data. For example, suppose there are 90 employees and 10 executives at a company. The executives make \$1000 per hour, and the employees make \$10 per hour. Therefore, the average pay rate will be $\frac{1000 \cdot 10 + 10 \cdot 90}{100} = 109$, or \$109 per hour. In this case, this average is not very descriptive.

Another useful measurement is the *median*. In a data set *X* consisting of data points $x_1, x_2, x_3, \dots x_n$, the median is the point in the middle. The middle refers to the point where half the data comes before it and half comes after, when the data is recorded in numerical order. If *n* is odd, then the median is $x_{\frac{n+1}{2}}$. If *n* is even, it is defined as $\frac{1}{2}\left(x_{\frac{n}{2}} + x_{\frac{n}{2}+1}\right)$, the mean of the two data points closest to the middle of the data points. In the previous example of test scores, the two middle points are 75 and 80. Since there is no single point, the average of these two scores needs to be found. The average is $\frac{75+80}{2} = 77.5$. The median is generally a good value to use if there are a few outliers in the data. It prevents those outliers from affecting the "middle" value as much as when using the mean.

Since an outlier is a data point that is far from most of the other data points in a data set, this means an outlier also is any point that is far from the median of the data set. The outliers can have a substantial effect on the mean of a data set, but usually do not change the median or mode, or do not change them by a large quantity. For example, consider the data set (3, 5, 6, 6, 6, 8). This has a median of 6 and a mode of 6, with a mean of $\frac{34}{6} \approx 5.67$. Now, suppose a new data point of 1000 is added so that the data set is now (3, 5, 6, 6, 6, 8, 1000). This does not change the median or mode, which are both still 6. However, the average is now $\frac{1034}{7}$, which is approximately 147.7. In this case, the median and mode will be better descriptions for most of the data points.

The reason for outliers in a given data set is a complicated problem. It is sometimes the result of an error by the experimenter, but often they are perfectly valid data points that must be taken into consideration.

One additional measure to define for *X* is the *mode*. This is the data point that appears more frequently. If two or more data points all tie for the most frequent appearance, then each of them is considered a mode. In the case of the test scores, where the numbers were 50, 60, 65, 65, 75, 80, 85, 85, 90, 100, there are two modes: 65 and 85.

The *first quartile* of a set of data *X* refers to the largest value from the first ¼ of the data points. In practice, there are sometimes slightly different definitions that can be used, such as the median of the first half of the data points (excluding the median itself if there are an odd number of data points). The term also has a slightly different use: when it is said that a data point lies *in the first quartile*, it means it is less than or equal to the median of the first half of the data points. Conversely, if it lies *at* the first quartile, then it is equal to the first quartile.

When it is said that a data point lies in the *second quartile*, it means it is between the first quartile and the median.

The *third quartile* refers to data that lies between ½ and ¾ of the way through the data set. Again, there are various methods for defining this precisely, but the simplest way is to include all of the data that lie between the median and the median of the top half of the data.

Data that lies in the *fourth quartile* refers to all of the data above the third quartile.

Percentiles may be defined in a similar manner to quartiles. Generally, this is defined in the following manner:

If a data point lies *in the n-th percentile*, this means it lies in the range of the first *n*% of the data.

If a data point lies *at* the *n*-th percentile, then it means that *n*% of the data lies below this data point.

Given a data set *X* consisting of data points $(x_1, x_2, x_3, \dots x_n)$, the *variance* of *X* is defined to be:

$$\frac{\sum_{i=1}^{n}(x_i - \bar{X})^2}{n}$$

This means that the variance of *X* is the average of the squares of the differences between each data point and the mean of *X*. In the formula, $\bar{X}$ is the mean of the values in the data set, and x_i represents each individual value in the data set. The sigma notation indicates that the sum should be found with n being the number of values to add together. $i = 1$ means that the values should begin with the first value.

Given a data set *X* consisting of data points $(x_1, x_2, x_3, \dots x_n)$, the *standard deviation* of *X* is defined to be

$$s_x = \sqrt{\frac{\sum_{i=1}^{n}(x_i - \bar{X})^2}{n}}$$

In other words, the standard deviation is the square root of the variance.

Both the variance and the standard deviation are measures of how much the data tend to be spread out. When the standard deviation is low, the data points are mostly clustered around the mean. When the standard deviation is high, this generally indicates that the data are quite spread out, or else that there are a few substantial outliers.

As a simple example, compute the standard deviation for the data set (1, 3, 3, 5). First, compute the mean, which will be $\frac{1+3+3+5}{4} = \frac{12}{4} = 3$.

Now, find the variance of X with the formula:

$\sum_{i=1}^{4}(x_i - \bar{X})^2 = (1-3)^2 + (3-3)^2 + (5-3)^2 = -2^2 + 0^2 + 0^2 + 2^2 = 8$. Therefore, the variance is $\frac{8}{4} = 2$. Taking the square root, the standard deviation will be $\sqrt{2}$.

Note that the standard deviation only depends upon the mean, not upon the median or mode(s). Generally, if there are multiple modes that are far apart from one another, the standard deviation will be high. A high standard deviation does not always mean there are multiple modes, however.

Describing a Set of Data

A set of data can be described in terms of its center, spread, shape and any unusual features. The center of a data set can be measured by its mean, median, or mode. The spread of a data set refers to how far the data points are from the center (mean or median). The spread can be measured by the range or the quartiles and interquartile range. A data set with data points clustered around the center will have a small spread. A data set covering a wide range will have a large spread.

When a data set is displayed as a histogram or frequency distribution plot, the shape indicates if a sample is normally distributed, symmetrical, or has measures of skewness or kurtosis. When graphed, a data set with a normal distribution will resemble a bell curve.

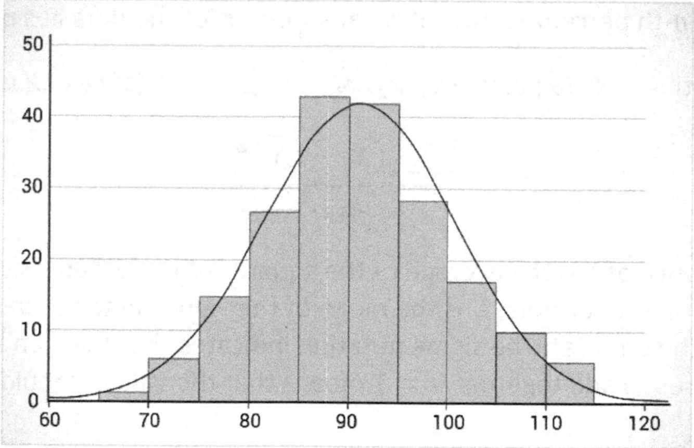

If the data set is symmetrical, each half of the graph when divided at the center is a mirror image of the other. If the graph has fewer data points to the right, the data is skewed right. If it has fewer data points to the left, the data is skewed left.

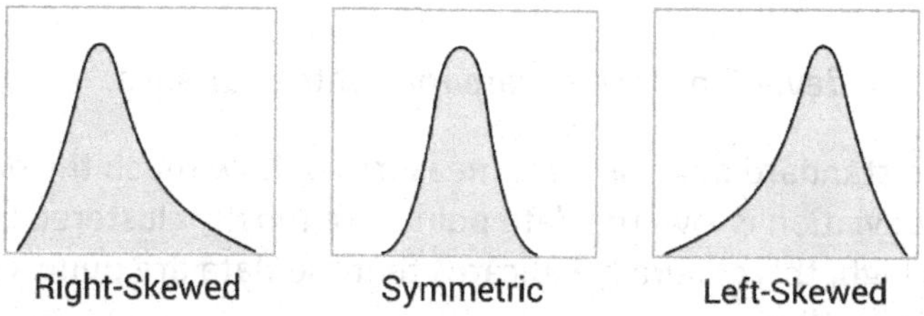

Kurtosis is a measure of whether the data is heavy-tailed with a high number of outliers, or light-tailed with a low number of outliers.

A description of a data set should include any unusual features such as gaps or outliers. A gap is a span within the range of the data set containing no data points. An outlier is a data point with a value either extremely large or extremely small when compared to the other values in the set.

Common Charts and Graphs

A set of data can be visually displayed in various forms allowing for quick identification of characteristics of the set. Histograms, such as the one shown below, display the number of data points (vertical axis) that fall into given intervals (horizontal axis) across the range of the set. The histogram below displays the heights of black cherry trees in a certain city park. Each rectangle represents the number of trees with heights between a given five-point span. For example, the furthest bar to the right indicates that two trees are between 85 and 90 feet. Histograms can describe the center, spread, shape, and any unusual characteristics of a data set.

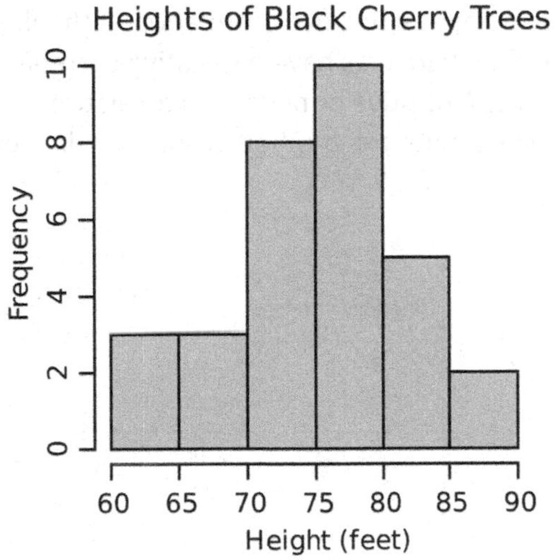

A box plot, also called a box-and-whisker plot, divides the data points into four groups and displays the five number summary for the set, as well as any outliers. The five number summary consists of:

- The lower extreme: the lowest value that is not an outlier
- The higher extreme: the highest value that is not an outlier
- The median of the set: also referred to as the second quartile or Q_2
- The first quartile or Q_1: the median of values below Q_2
- The third quartile or Q_3: the median of values above Q_2

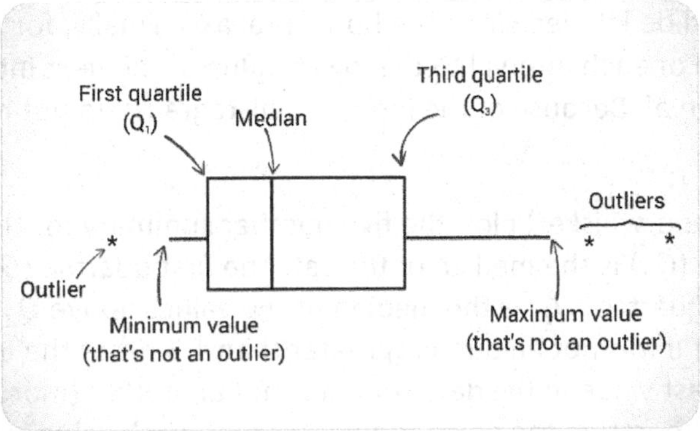

Suppose the box plot displays IQ scores for 12th grade students at a given school. The five number summary of the data consists of: lower extreme (67); upper extreme (127); Q_2or median (100); Q_1 (91); Q_3 (108); and outliers (135 and 140). Although all data points are not known from the plot, the points are divided into four quartiles each, including 25% of the data points. Therefore, 25% of students scored between 67 and 91, 25% scored between 91 and 100, 25% scored between 100 and 108, and 25% scored between 108 and 127. These percentages include the normal values for the set and exclude the outliers. This information is useful when comparing a given score with the rest of the scores in the set.

A scatter plot is a mathematical diagram that visually displays the relationship or connection between two variables. The independent variable is placed on the *x*-axis, or horizontal axis, and the dependent variable is placed on the *y*-axis, or vertical axis. When visually examining the points on the graph, if the points model a linear relationship, or a line of best-fit can be drawn through the points with the points relatively close on either side, then a correlation exists. If the line of best-fit has a positive slope (rises from left to right), then the variables have a positive correlation. If the line of best-fit has a negative slope (falls from left to right), then the variables have a negative correlation. If a line of best-fit cannot be drawn, then no correlation exists. A positive or negative correlation can be categorized as strong or weak, depending on how closely the points are graphed around the line of best-fit.

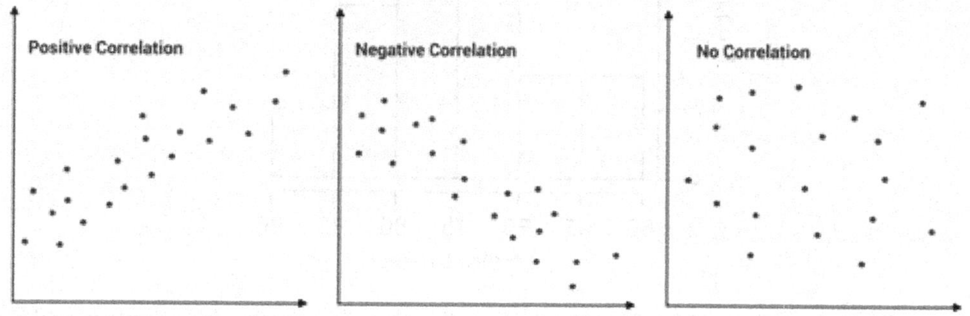

Graphical Representation of Data

Various graphs can be used to visually represent a given set of data. Each type of graph requires a different method of arranging data points and different calculations of the data. To construct a histogram, the range of the data points is divided into equal intervals. The frequency for each interval is then determined, which reveals how many points fall into each interval. A graph is constructed with the vertical axis representing the frequency and the horizontal axis representing the intervals. The lower value of each interval should be labeled along the horizontal axis. Finally, for each interval, a bar is drawn from the lower value of each interval to the lower value of the next interval with a height equal to the frequency of the interval. Because of the intervals, histograms do not have any gaps between bars along the horizontal axis.

To construct a box (or box-and-whisker) plot, the five number summary for the data set is calculated as follows: the second quartile (Q_2) is the median of the set. The first quartile (Q_1) is the median of the values below Q_2. The third quartile (Q_3) is the median of the values above Q_2. The upper extreme is the highest value in the data set if it is not an outlier (greater than 1.5 times the interquartile range Q_3 - Q_1). The lower extreme is the least value in the data set if it is not an outlier (more than 1.5 times lower than the interquartile range). To construct the box-and-whisker plot, each value is plotted on a number line, along with any outliers. The *box* consists of Q_1 and Q_3 as its *top* and *bottom* and Q_2 as the dividing line inside the box. The *whiskers* extend from the lower extreme to Q_1 and from Q_3 to the upper extreme.

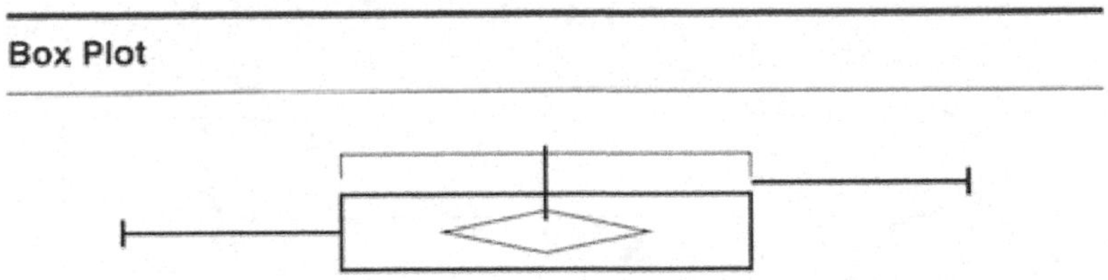

A scatter plot displays the relationship between two variables. Values for the independent variable, typically denoted by *x*, are paired with values for the dependent variable, typically denoted by *y*. Each set of corresponding values are written as an ordered pair (*x*, *y*). To construct the graph, a coordinate grid is labeled with the *x*-axis representing the independent variable and the *y*-axis representing the dependent variable. Each ordered pair is graphed.

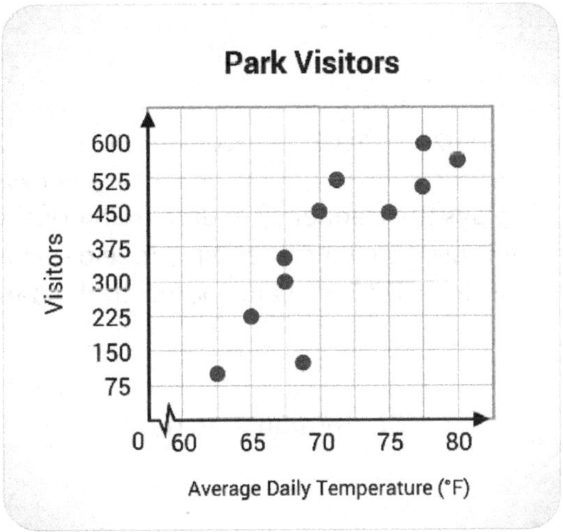

Like a scatter plot, a line graph compares variables that change continuously, typically over time. Paired data values (ordered pair) are plotted on a coordinate grid with the *x*- and *y*-axis representing the variables. A line is drawn from each point to the next, going from left to right. The line graph below displays cell phone use for given years (two variables) for men, women, and both sexes (three data sets).

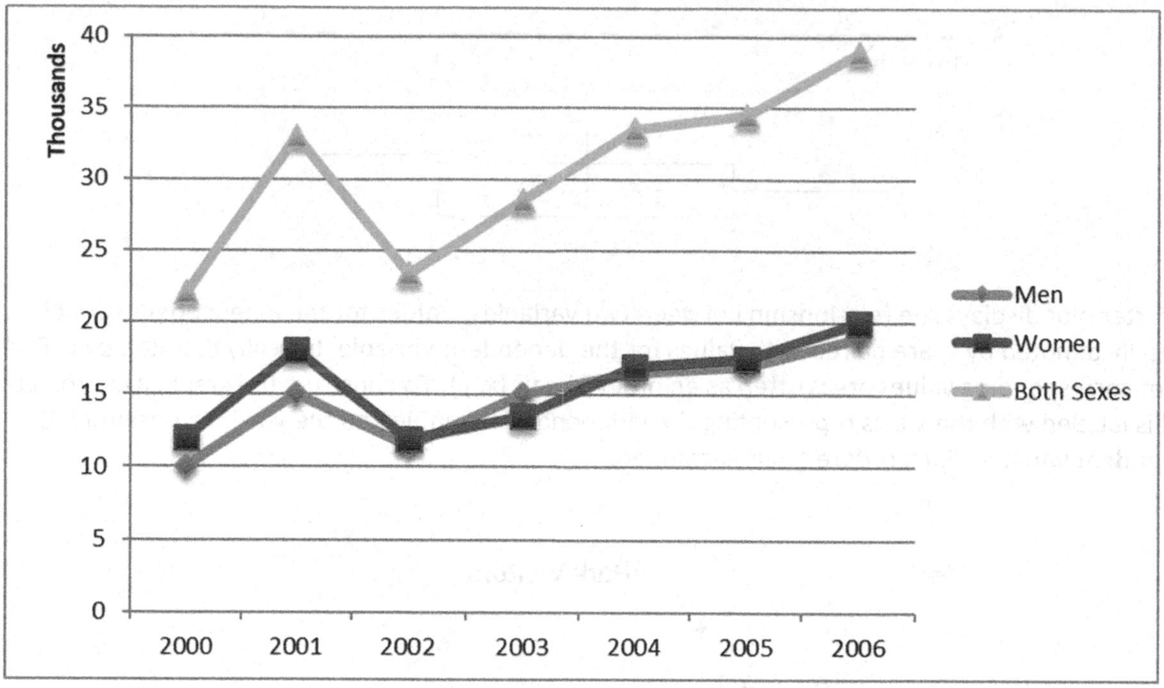

A line plot, also called dot plot, displays the frequency of data (numerical values) on a number line. To construct a line plot, a number line is used that includes all unique data values. It is marked with x's or dots above the value the number of times that the value occurs in the data set.

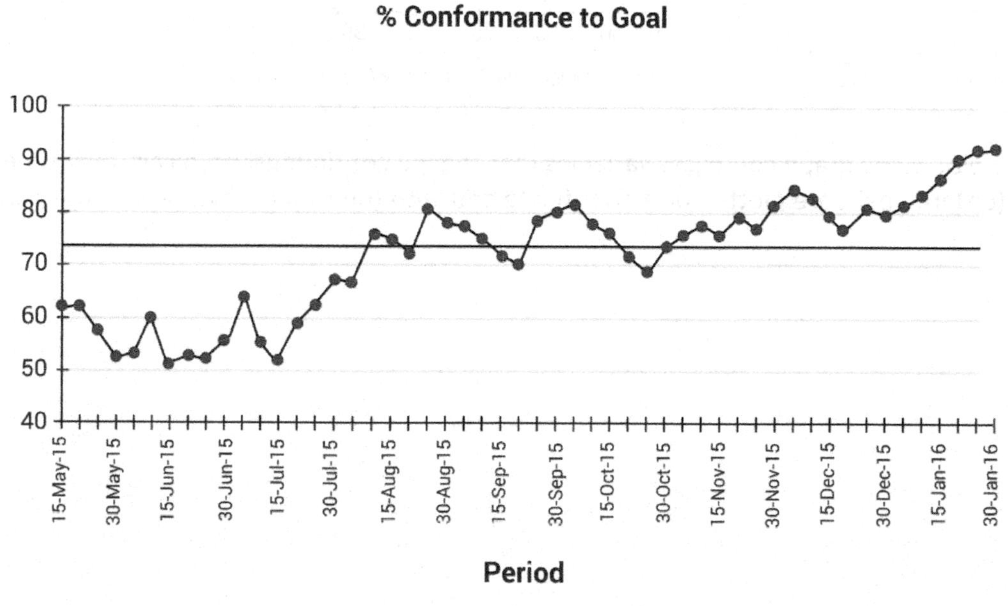

A *bar graph* is a diagram in which the quantity of items within a specific classification is represented by the height of a rectangle. Each type of classification is represented by a rectangle of equal width. Here is an example of a bar graph:

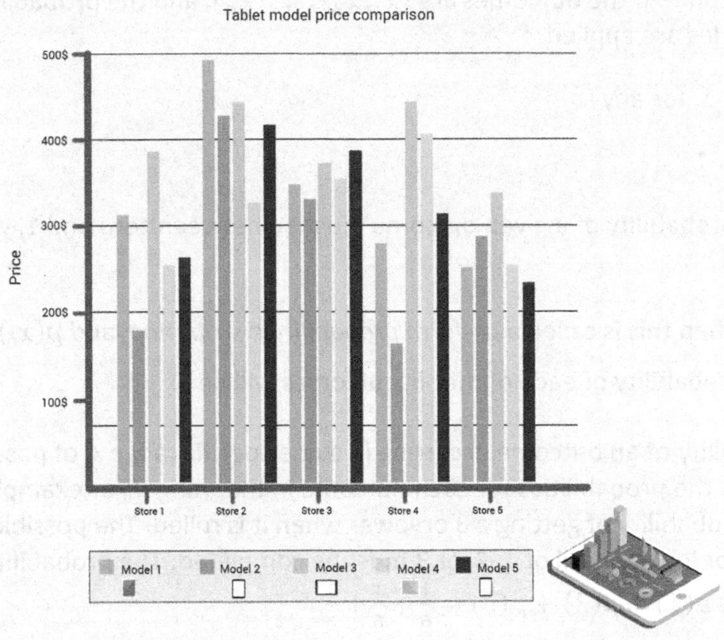

A circle graph, also called a pie chart, shows categorical data with each category representing a percentage of the whole data set. To make a circle graph, the percent of the data set for each category must be determined. To do so, the frequency of the category is divided by the total number of data points and converted to a percent. For example, if 80 people were asked what their favorite sport is and 20 responded basketball, basketball makes up 25% of the data ($\frac{20}{80}$ =.25=25%). Each category in a data set is represented by a *slice* of the circle proportionate to its percentage of the whole.

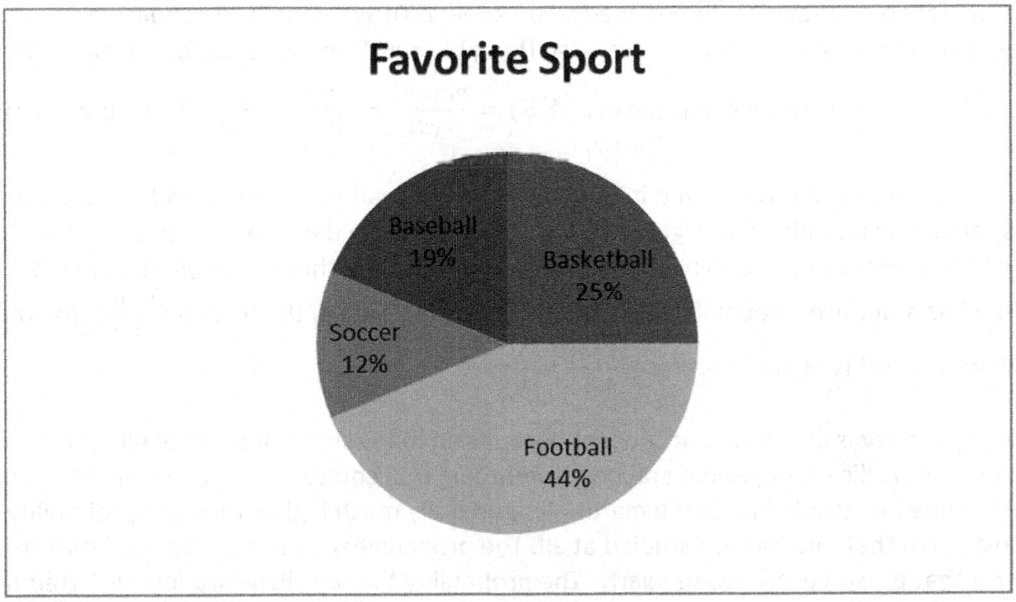

Probability

Given a set of possible outcomes *X*, a *probability distribution* on *X* is a function that assigns a probability to each possible outcome. If the outcomes are $(x_1, x_2, x_3, \dots x_n)$, and the probability distribution is *p*, then the following rules are applied.

- $0 \leq p(x_i) \leq 1$, for any i.
- $\sum_{i=1}^{n} p(x_i) = 1$.

In other words, the probability of a given outcome must be between zero and 1, while the total probability must be 1.

If $p(x_i)$ is constant, then this is called a *uniform probability distribution*, and $p(x_i) = \frac{1}{n}$. For example, on a six-sided die, the probability of each of the six outcomes will be $\frac{1}{6}$.

If seeking the probability of an outcome occurring in some specific range *A* of possible outcomes, written $P(A)$, add up the probabilities for each outcome in that range. For example, consider a six-sided die, and figure the probability of getting a 3 or lower when it is rolled. The possible rolls are 1, 2, 3, 4, 5, and 6. So, to get a 3 or lower, a roll of 1, 2, or 3 must be completed. The probabilities of each of these is $\frac{1}{6}$, so add these to get $p(1) + p(2) + p(3) = \frac{1}{6} + \frac{1}{6} + \frac{1}{6} = \frac{1}{2}$.

An outcome occasionally lies within some range of possibilities *B*, and the probability that the outcomes also lie within some set of possibilities *A* needs to be figured. This is called a *conditional probability*. It is written as $P(A|B)$, which is read "the probability of *A* given *B*." The general formula for computing conditional probabilities is $P(A|B) = \frac{P(A \cap B)}{P(B)}$.

However, when dealing with uniform probability distributions, simplify this a bit. Write $|A|$ to indicate the number of outcomes in *A*. Then, for uniform probability distributions, write $P(A|B) = \frac{|A \cap B|}{|B|}$ (recall that $A \cap B$ means "*A* intersect *B*," and consists of all of the outcomes that lie in both *A* and *B*). This means that all possible outcomes do not need to be known. To see why this formula works, suppose that the set of outcomes *X* is $(x_1, x_2, x_3, \dots x_n)$, so that $|X| = n$. Then, for a uniform probability distribution, $P(A) = \frac{|A|}{n}$. However, this means $(A|B) = \frac{P(A \cap B)}{P(B)} = \frac{\frac{|A \cap B|}{n}}{\frac{|B|}{n}} = \frac{|A \cap B|}{|B|}$, since the *n*'s cancel out.

For example, suppose a die is rolled and it is known that it will land between 1 and 4. However, how many sides the die has is unknown. Figure the probability that the die is rolled higher than 2. To figure this, $P(3)$ or $P(4)$ does not need to be determined, or any of the other probabilities, since it is known that a fair die has a uniform probability distribution. Therefore, apply the formula $\frac{|A \cap B|}{|B|}$. So, in this case *B* is (1, 2, 3, 4) and $A \cap B$ is (3, 4). Therefore $\frac{|A \cap B|}{|B|} = \frac{2}{4} = \frac{1}{2}$.

Conditional probability is an important concept because, in many situations, the likelihood of one outcome can differ radically depending on how something else comes out. The probability of passing a test given that one has studied all of the material is generally much higher than the probability of passing a test given that one has not studied at all. The probability of a person having heart trouble is much lower if that person exercises regularly. The probability that a college student will graduate is higher when his or her SAT scores are higher, and so on. For this reason, there are many people who are interested in conditional probabilities.

Note that in some practical situations, changing the order of the conditional probabilities can make the outcome very different. For example, the probability that a person with heart trouble has exercised regularly is quite different than the probability that a person who exercises regularly will have heart trouble. The probability of a person receiving a military-only award, given that he or she is or was a soldier, is generally not very high, but the probability that a person being or having been a soldier, given that he or she received a military-only award, is 1.

However, in some cases, the outcomes do not influence one another this way. If the probability of *A* is the same regardless of whether *B* is given; that is, if $P(A|B) = P(A)$, then *A* and *B* are considered *independent*. In this case, $P(A|B) = \frac{P(A \cap B)}{P(B)} = P(A)$, so $P(A \cap B) = P(A)P(B)$. In fact, if $P(A \cap B) = P(A)P(B)$, it can be determined that $P(A|B) = P(A)$ and $P(A|B) = P(B)$ by working backward. Therefore, *B* is also independent of *A*.

An example of something being independent can be seen in rolling dice. In this case, consider a red die and a green die. It is expected that when the dice are rolled, the outcome of the green die should not depend in any way on the outcome of the red die. Or, to take another example, if the same die is rolled repeatedly, then the next number rolled should not depend on which numbers have been rolled previously. Similarly, if a coin is flipped, then the next flip's outcome does not depend on the outcomes of previous flips.

This can sometimes be counter-intuitive, since when rolling a die or flipping a coin, there can be a streak of surprising results. If, however, it is known that the die or coin is fair, then these results are just the result of the fact that over long periods of time, it is very likely that some unlikely streaks of outcomes will occur. Therefore, avoid making the mistake of thinking that when considering a series of independent outcomes, a particular outcome is "due to happen" simply because a surprising series of outcomes has already been seen.

There is a second type of common mistake that people tend to make when reasoning about statistical outcomes: the idea that when something of low probability happens, this is surprising. It would be surprising that something with low probability happened after just one attempt. However, with so much happening all at once, it is easy to see at least something happen in a way that seems to have a very low probability. In fact, a lottery is a good example. The odds of winning a lottery are very small, but the odds that somebody wins the lottery each week are actually fairly high. Therefore, no one should be surprised when some low probability things happen.

The *addition rule* for probabilities states that the probability of *A* or *B* happening is $P(A \cup B) = P(A) + P(B) - P(A \cap B)$. Note that the subtraction of $P(A \cap B)$ must be performed, or else it would result in double counting any outcomes that lie in both *A* and in *B*. For example, suppose that a 20-sided die is being rolled. Fred bets that the outcome will be greater than 10, while Helen bets that it will be greater than 4 but less than 15. What is the probability that at least one of them is correct?

We apply the rule $P(A \cup B) = P(A) + P(B) - P(A \cap B)$, where *A* is that outcome *x* is in the range $x > 10$, and *B* is that outcome *x* is in the range $4 < x < 15$. $P(A) = 10 \cdot \frac{1}{20} = \frac{1}{2}$. $P(B) = 10 \cdot \frac{1}{20} = \frac{1}{2}$. $P(A \cap B)$ can be computed by noting that $A \cap B$ means the outcome *x* is in the range $10 < x < 15$, so $P(A \cap B) = 4 \cdot \frac{1}{20} = \frac{1}{5}$. Therefore, $P(A \cup B) = P(A) + P(B) - P(A \cap B) = \frac{1}{2} + \frac{1}{2} - \frac{1}{5} = \frac{4}{5}$.

Note that in this particular example, we could also have directly reasoned about the set of possible outcomes $A \cup B$, by noting that this would mean that x must be in the range $5 \leq x$. However, this is not always the case, depending on the given information.

The *multiplication rule* for probabilities states the probability of A and B both happening is $P(A \cap B) = P(A)P(B|A)$. As an example, suppose that when Jamie wears black pants, there is a ½ probability that she wears a black shirt as well, and that she wears black pants ¾ of the time. What is the probability that she is wearing both a black shirt and black pants?

To figure this, use the above formula, where A will be "Jamie is wearing black pants," while B will be "Jamie is wearing a black shirt." It is known that $P(A)$ is ¾. It is also known that $P(B|A) = \frac{1}{2}$. Multiplying the two, the probability that she is wearing both black pants and a black shirt is $P(A)P(B|A) = \frac{3}{4} \cdot \frac{1}{2} = \frac{3}{8}$.

Measurement and Geometry

Measurement

The United States customary system and the metric system each consist of distinct units to measure lengths and volume of liquids. The U.S. customary units for length, from smallest to largest, are: inch (in), foot (ft), yard (yd), and mile (mi). The metric units for length, from smallest to largest, are: millimeter (mm), centimeter (cm), decimeter (dm), meter (m), and kilometer (km). The relative size of each unit of length is shown below.

U.S. Customary	Metric	Conversion
12in = 1ft	10mm = 1cm	1in = 254cm
36in = 3ft = 1yd	10cm = 1dm(decimeter)	1m ≈ 3.28ft ≈ 1.09yd
5,280ft = 1,760yd = 1mi	100cm = 10dm = 1m	1mi ≈ 1.6km
	1000m = 1km	

The U.S. customary units for volume of liquids, from smallest to largest, are: fluid ounces (fl oz), cup (c), pint (pt), quart (qt), and gallon (gal). The metric units for volume of liquids, from smallest to largest, are: milliliter (mL), centiliter (cL), deciliter (dL), liter (L), and kiloliter (kL). The relative size of each unit of liquid volume is shown below.

U.S. Customary	Metric	Conversion
8fl oz = 1c	10mL = 1cL	1pt ≈ 0.473L
2c = 1pt	10cL = 1dL	1L ≈ 1.057qt
4c = 2pt = 1qt	1,000mL = 100cL = 10dL = 1L	1gal ≈ 3,785L
4qt = 1gal	1,000L = 1kL	

The U.S. customary system measures weight (how strongly Earth is pulling on an object) in the following units, from least to greatest: ounce (oz), pound (lb), and ton. The metric system measures mass (the quantity of matter within an object) in the following units, from least to greatest: milligram (mg), centigram (cg), gram (g), kilogram (kg), and metric ton (MT). The relative sizes of each unit of weight and mass are shown below.

U.S. Measures of Weight	Metric Measures of Mass
16oz = 1lb	10mg = 1cg
2,000lb = 1 ton	100cg = 1g
	1,000g = 1kg
	1,000kg = 1MT

Note that weight and mass DO NOT measure the same thing.

Time is measured in the following units, from shortest to longest: second (sec), minute (min), hour (h), day (d), week (wk), month (mo), year (yr), decade, century, millennium. The relative sizes of each unit of time is shown below.

- 60sec = 1min
- 60min = 1h
- 24hr = 1d
- 7d = 1wk
- 52wk = 1yr
- 12mo = 1yr
- 10yr = 1 decade
- 100yrs = 1 century
- 1,000yrs = 1 millennium

- When working with different systems of measurement, conversion from one unit to another may be necessary. The conversion rate must be known to convert units. One method for converting units is to write and solve a proportion. The arrangement of values in a proportion is extremely important. Suppose that a problem requires converting 20 fluid ounces to cups. To do so, a proportion can be written using the conversion rate of 8fl oz = 1c with *x* representing the missing value. The proportion can be written in any of the following ways:

- $\frac{1}{8} = \frac{x}{20}\left(\frac{c\ for\ conversion}{fl\ oz\ for\ conversion} = \frac{unknown\ c}{fl\ oz\ given}\right); \frac{8}{1} = \frac{20}{x}\left(\frac{fl\ oz\ for\ conversion}{c\ for\ conversion} = \frac{fl\ oz\ given}{unknown\ c}\right);$

- $\frac{1}{x} = \frac{8}{20}\left(\frac{c\ for\ conversion}{unknown\ c} = \frac{fl\ oz\ for\ conversion}{fl\ oz\ given}\right); \frac{x}{1} = \frac{20}{8}\left(\frac{unknown\ c}{c\ for\ conversion} = \frac{fl\ oz\ given}{fl\ oz\ for\ conversion}\right)$

- To solve a proportion, the ratios are cross-multiplied and the resulting equation is solved. When cross-multiplying, all four proportions above will produce the same equation: $(8)(x) = (20)(1) \rightarrow 8x = 20$. Dividing by 8 to isolate the variable *x*, the result is *x* = 2.5. The variable *x* represented the unknown number of cups. Therefore, the conclusion is that 20 fluid ounces converts (is equal) to 2.5 cups.

- Sometimes converting units requires writing and solving more than one proportion. Suppose an exam question asks to determine how many hours are in 2 weeks. Without knowing the conversion rate between hours and weeks, this can be determined knowing the conversion rates between weeks and days, and between days and hours. First, weeks are converted to days, then days are converted to hours. To convert from weeks to days, the following proportion can be written $\frac{7}{1}=\frac{x}{2}\left(\frac{days\ conversion}{weeks\ conversion}=\frac{days\ unknown}{weeks\ given}\right)$.

- Cross-multiplying produces: $(7)(2)=(x)(1)\rightarrow 14=x$. Therefore, 2 weeks is equal to 14 days. Next, a proportion is written to convert 14 days to hours: $\frac{24}{1}=\frac{x}{14}\left(\frac{conversion\ hours}{conversion\ days}=\frac{unknown\ hours}{given\ days}\right)$. Cross-multiplying produces: $(24)(14)=(x)(1)\rightarrow 336=x$. Therefore, the answer is that there are 336 hours in 2 weeks.

Lines and Planes

The basic unit of geometry is a point. These are locations on the plane that have no width or breadth. The position of a point is indicated with a dot and usually named with a single uppercase letter, such as point *A* or point *T*. A point is a place, not a thing, and therefore has no dimensions or size. A set of points that lies on the same line is called collinear. A set of points that lies on the same plane is called coplanar.

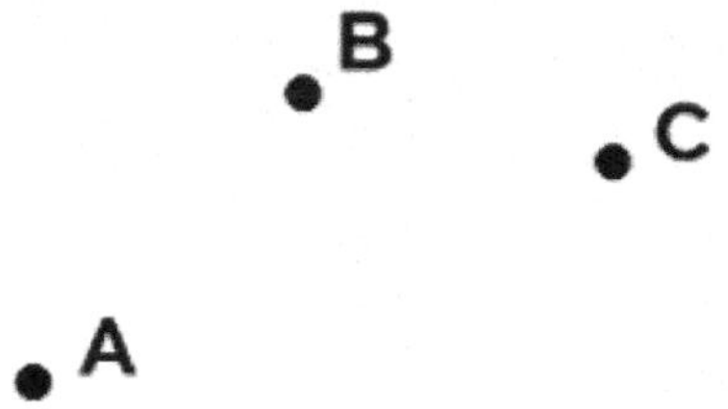

The image above displays point *A*, point *B*, and point *C*.

Any pair of points *A*, *B* on the plane will determine a unique straight line between them. This line is denoted *AB*. Sometimes to emphasize a line is being considered, this will be written as $\overleftrightarrow{AB}$.

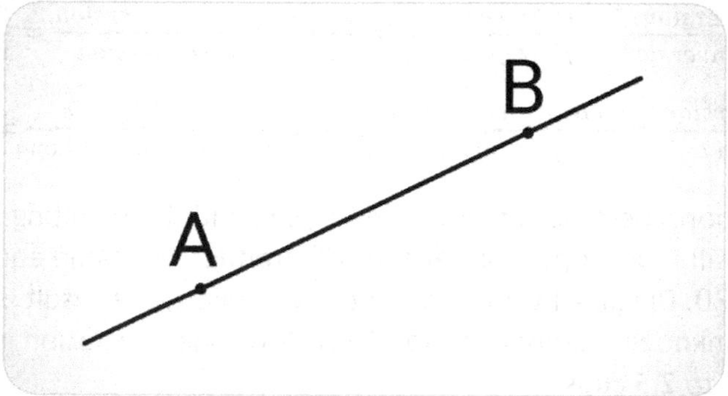

If the Cartesian coordinates for *A* and *B* are known, then the distance $d(A,B)$ along the line between them can be measured using the *Pythagorean formula*, which states that if $A=(x_1,y_1)$ and $B=(x_2,y_2)$, then the distance between them is $d(A,B)=\sqrt{(x_2-x_1)^2+(y_2-y_1)^2}$.

The part of a line that lies between *A* and *B* is called a *line segment*. It has two endpoints, one at *A* and one at *B*. *Rays* also can be formed. Given points *A* and *B*, a *ray* is the portion of a line that starts at one of these points, passes through the other, and keeps on going. Therefore, a ray has a single endpoint, but the other end goes off to infinity.

Two lines are considered parallel to each other if, while extending infinitely, they will never intersect (or meet). Parallel lines point in the same direction and are always the same distance apart. Two lines are considered perpendicular if they intersect to form right angles. Right angles are 90°. Typically, a small box is drawn at the intersection point to indicate the right angle.

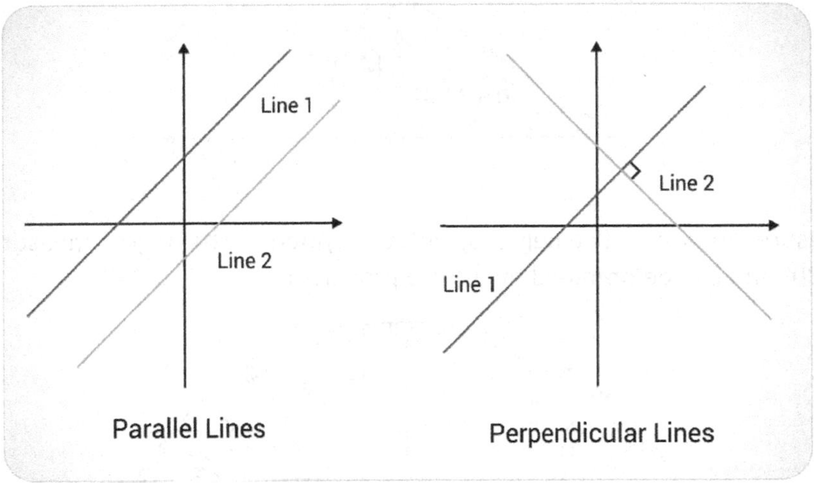

Line 1 is parallel to line 2 in the left image and is written as line 1 || line 2. Line 1 is perpendicular to line 2 in the right image and is written as line 1 ⊥ line 2.

Angles

An angle consists of two rays that have a common endpoint. This common endpoint is called the vertex of the angle. The two rays can be called sides of the angle. The angle below has a vertex at point *B* and the sides consist of ray *BA* and ray *BC*. An angle can be named in three ways:

1. Using the vertex and a point from each side, with the vertex letter in the middle.
2. Using only the vertex. This can only be used if it is the only angle with that vertex.
3. Using a number that is written inside the angle.

The angle below can be written $\angle ABC$ (read angle *ABC*), $\angle CBA$, $\angle B$, or $\angle 1$.

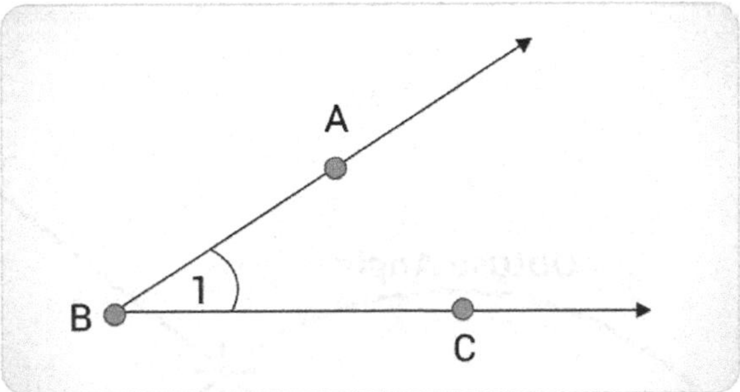

An angle divides a plane, or flat surface, into three parts: the angle itself, the interior (inside) of the angle, and the exterior (outside) of the angle. The figure below shows point *M* on the interior of the angle and point *N* on the exterior of the angle.

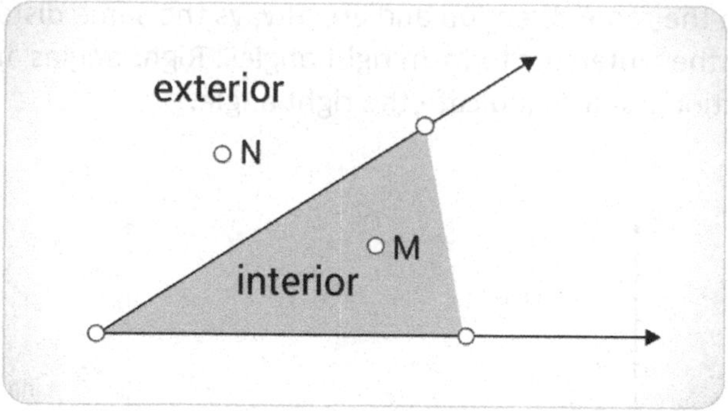

Angles can be measured in units called degrees, with the symbol °. The degree measure of an angle is between 0° and 180° and can be obtained by using a protractor.

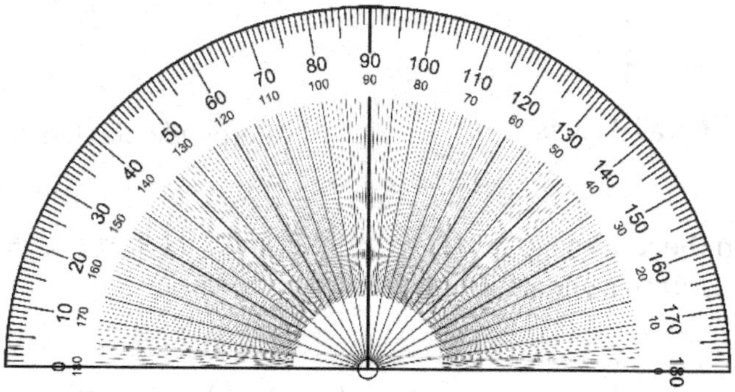

A straight angle (or simply a line) measures exactly 180°. A right angle's sides meet at the vertex to create a square corner. A right angle measures exactly 90° and is typically indicated by a box drawn in the interior of the angle. An acute angle has an interior that is narrower than a right angle. The measure of an acute angle is any value less than 90° and greater than 0°. For example, 89.9°, 47°, 12°, and 1°. An obtuse angle has an interior that is wider than a right angle. The measure of an obtuse angle is any value greater than 90° but less than 180°. For example, 90.1°, 110°, 150°, and 179.9°.

- Acute angles: Less than 90°
- Obtuse angles: Greater than 90°
- Right angles: 90°
- Straight angles: 180°

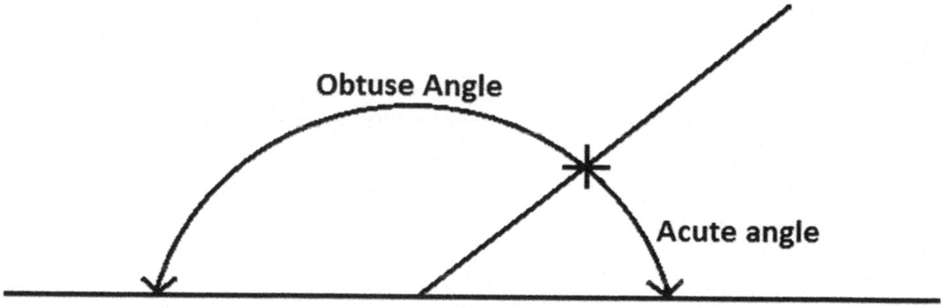

Adjacent angles are two side-by-side angles formed from the same ray that have the same endpoint.

Polygons

A *polygon* is a closed figure (meaning it divides the plane into an inside and an outside) consisting of a collection of line segments between points. These points are called the *vertices* of the polygon. These line segments must not overlap one another. Note that the number of sides is equal to the number of angles, or vertices of the polygon. The angles between line segments meeting one another in the polygon are called *interior angles*.

A *regular polygon* is a polygon whose edges are all the same length and whose interior angles are all of equal measure.

Polygons can be classified by the number of sides (also equal to the number of angles) they have. The following are the names of polygons with a given number of sides or angles:

# of sides	**3**	**4**	**5**	**6**	**7**	**8**	**9**	**10**
Name of polygon	Triangle	Quadrilateral	Pentagon	Hexagon	Septagon (or heptagon)	Octagon	Nonagon	Decagon

A *triangle* is a polygon with three sides. A *quadrilateral* is a polygon with four sides.

Quadrilaterals can be further classified according to their sides and angles. A quadrilateral with exactly one pair of parallel sides is called a trapezoid. A quadrilateral that shows both pairs of opposite sides parallel is a parallelogram. Parallelograms include rhombuses, rectangles, and squares. A rhombus has four equal sides. A rectangle has four equal angles (90° each). A square has four 90° angles and four equal sides. Therefore, a square is both a rhombus and a rectangle.

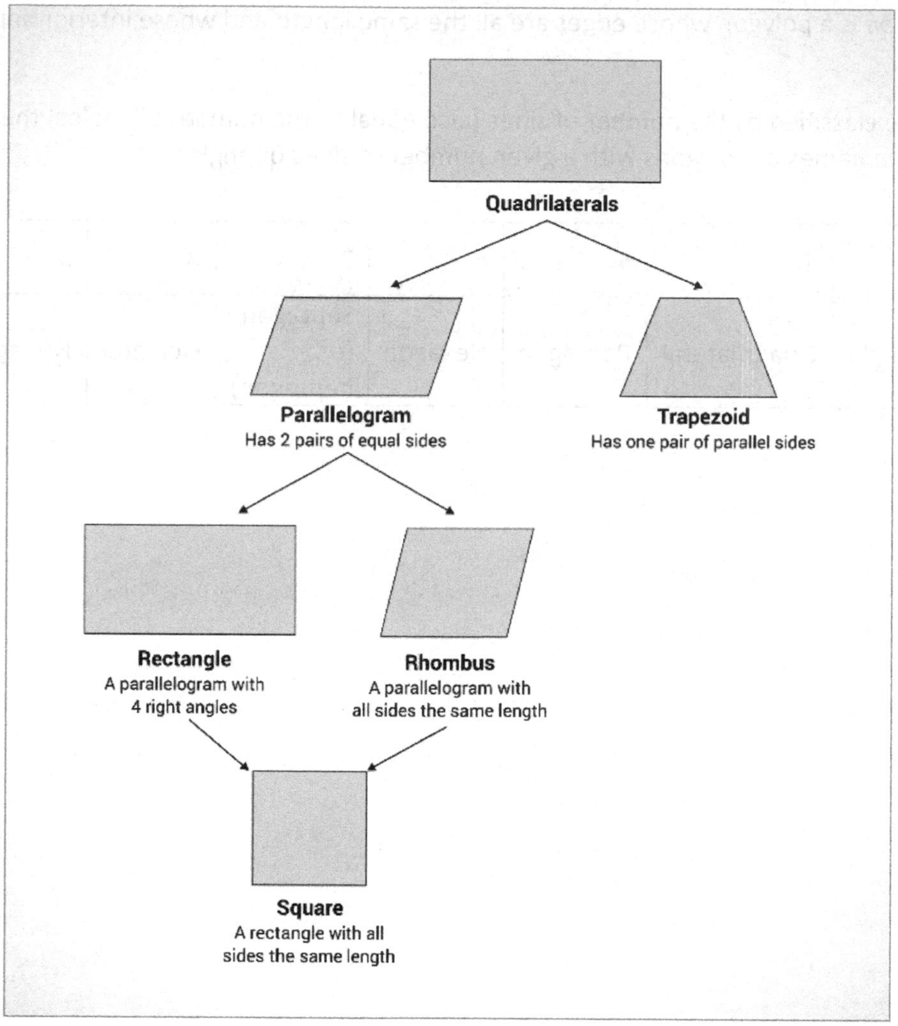

Triangles

A *right triangle* is a triangle that has one 90° angle.

The sum of the interior angles of any triangle must add up to 180°.

An *isosceles triangle* is a triangle in which two of the sides are the same length. In this case, it will always have two congruent interior angles. If a triangle has two congruent interior angles, it will always be isosceles.

An *equilateral triangle* is a triangle whose sides are all the same length and whose angles are all equivalent to one another, equal to 60°. Equilateral triangles are examples of regular polygons. Note that equilateral triangles are also isosceles. A triangle with no equal sides or angles is a scalene triangle.

Angles that add up to 90 degrees are *complementary*. Within a right triangle, two complementary angles exist because the third angle is always 90 degrees.

Pythagorean Theorem

The Pythagorean theorem is an important result in geometry. It states that for right triangles, the sum of the squares of the two shorter sides will be equal to the square of the longest side (also called the *hypotenuse*). The longest side will always be the side opposite to the 90° angle. If this side is called *c*, and the other two sides are *a* and *b*, then the Pythagorean theorem states that $c^2 = a^2 + b^2$. Since lengths are always positive, this also can be written as $c = \sqrt{a^2 + b^2}$.

A diagram to show the parts of a triangle using the Pythagorean theorem is below.

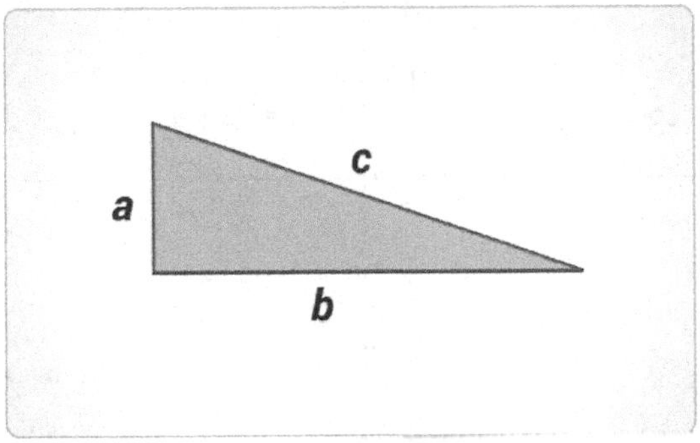

As an example of the theorem, suppose that Shirley has a rectangular field that is 5 feet wide and 12 feet long, and she wants to split it in half using a fence that goes from one corner to the opposite corner. How long will this fence need to be? To figure this out, note that this makes the field into two right triangles, whose hypotenuse will be the fence dividing it in half. Therefore, the fence length will be given by $\sqrt{5^2 + 12^2} = \sqrt{169} = 13$ feet long.

Transformations of a Plane

Given a figure drawn on a plane, many changes can be made to that figure, including *rotation*, *translation*, and *reflection*. Rotations turn the figure about a point, translations slide the figure, and reflections flip the figure over a specified line. When performing these transformations, the original figure is called the *pre-image*, and the figure after transformation is called the *image*.

More specifically, *translation* means that all points in the figure are moved in the same direction by the same distance. In other words, the figure is slid in some fixed direction. Of course, while the entire figure is slid by the same distance, this does not change any of the measurements of the figures involved. The result will have the same distances and angles as the original figure.

In terms of Cartesian coordinates, a translation means a shift of each of the original points (x, y) by a fixed amount in the *x* and *y* directions, to become $(x + a, y + b)$.

Another procedure that can be performed is called *reflection*. To do this, a line in the plane is specified, called the *line of reflection*. Then, take each point and flip it over the line so that it is the same distance from the line but on the opposite side of it. This does not change any of the distances or angles involved, but it does reverse the order in which everything appears.

To reflect something over the *x*-axis, the points (x, y) are sent to $(x, -y)$. To reflect something over the *y*-axis, the points (x, y) are sent to the points $(-x, y)$. Flipping over other lines is not something easy to express in Cartesian coordinates. However, by drawing the figure and the line of reflection, the distance to the line and the original points can be used to find the reflected figure.

Example: Reflect this triangle with vertices (-1, 0), (2, 1), and (2, 0) over the *y*-axis. The pre-image is shown below.

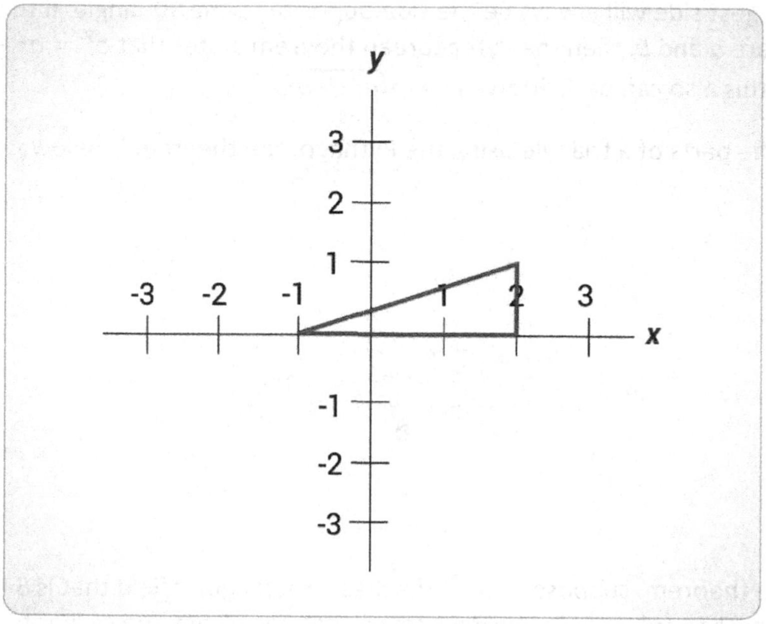

To do this, flip the *x* values of the points involved to the negatives of themselves, while keeping the *y* values the same. The image is shown here.

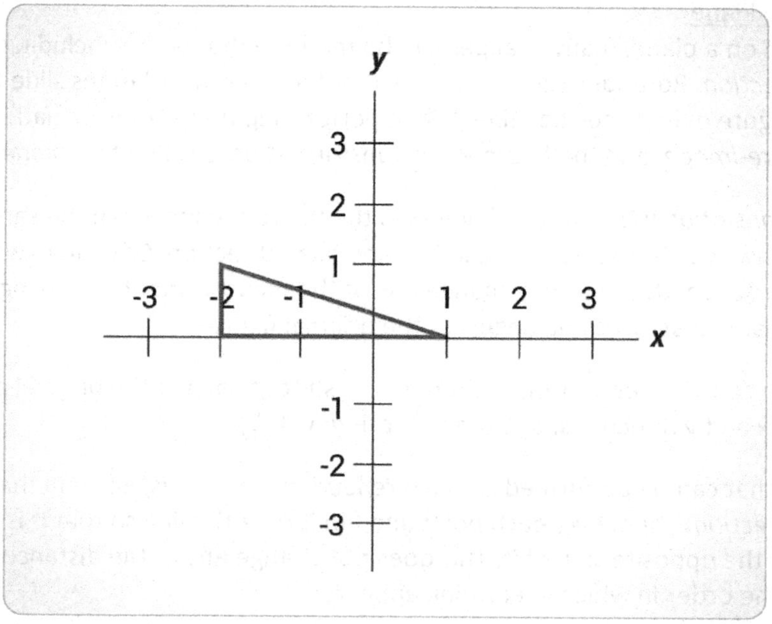

The new vertices will be (1, 0), (-2, 1), and (-2, 0).

Another procedure that does not change the distances and angles in a figure is *rotation*. In this procedure, pick a center point, then rotate every vertex along a circle around that point by the same angle. This procedure is also not easy to express in Cartesian coordinates, and this is not a requirement on this test. However, as with reflections, it's helpful to draw the figures and see what the result of the rotation would look like. This transformation can be performed using a compass and protractor.

Each one of these transformations can be performed on the coordinate plane without changes to the original dimensions or angles.

If two figures in the plane involve the same distances and angles, they are called *congruent figures*. In other words, two figures are congruent when they go from one form to another through reflection, rotation, and translation, or a combination of these.

Remember that rotation and translation will give back a new figure that is identical to the original figure, but reflection will give back a mirror image of it.

To recognize that a figure has undergone a rotation, check to see that the figure has not been changed into a mirror image, but that its orientation has changed (that is, whether the parts of the figure now form different angles with the *x* and *y* axes).

To recognize that a figure has undergone a translation, check to see that the figure has not been changed into a mirror image, and that the orientation remains the same.

To recognize that a figure has undergone a reflection, check to see that the new figure is a mirror image of the old figure.

Keep in mind that sometimes a combination of translations, reflections, and rotations may be performed on a figure.

A *dilation* is a transformation that preserves angles, but not distances. This can be thought of as stretching or shrinking a figure. If a dilation makes figures larger, it is called an *enlargement*. If a dilation makes figures smaller, it is called a *reduction*. The easiest example is to dilate around the origin. In this case, multiply the *x* and *y* coordinates by a *scale factor*, k, sending points (x, y) to (kx, ky).

Note that after a dilation, the distances between the vertices of the figure will have changed, but the angles remain the same. The two figures that are obtained by dilation, along with possibly translation, rotation, and reflection, are all *similar* to one another. Another way to think of this is that similar figures have the same number of vertices and edges, and their angles are all the same. Similar figures have the same basic shape, but are different in size.

Using the types of transformations above, if an object can undergo these changes and not appear to have changed, then the figure is symmetrical. If an object can be split in half by a line and flipped over that line to lie directly on top of itself, it is said to have *line symmetry*. An example of both types of figures is seen below.

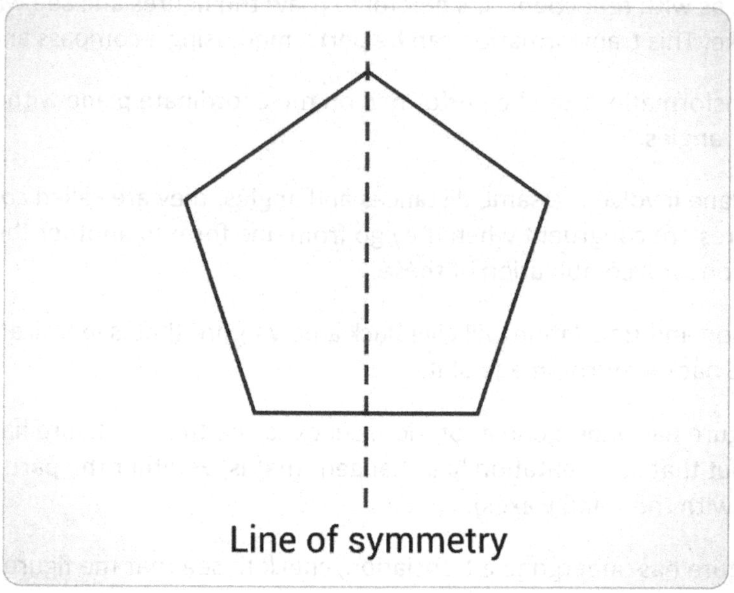

Similar Figures

Sometimes, two figures are similar, meaning they have the same basic shape and the same interior angles, but they have different dimensions. If the ratio of two corresponding sides is known, then that ratio, or scale factor, holds true for all of the dimensions of the new figure.

Here is an example of applying this principle. Suppose that Lara is 5 feet tall and is standing 30 feet from the base of a light pole, and her shadow is 6 feet long. How high is the light on the pole? To figure this, it helps to make a sketch of the situation:

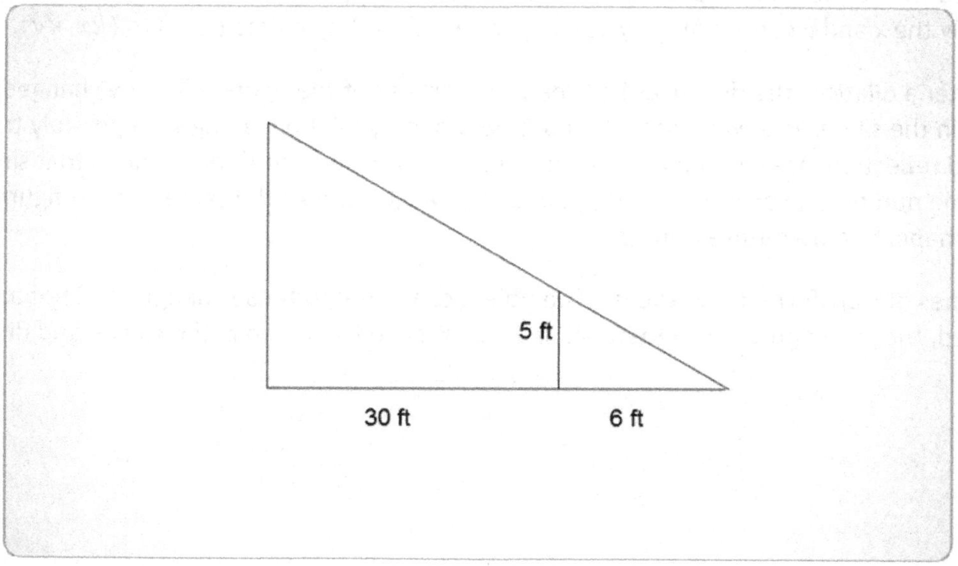

The light pole is the left side of the triangle. Lara is the 5-foot vertical line. Notice that there are two right triangles here, and that they have all the same angles as one another. Therefore, they form similar triangles. So, figure the ratio of proportionality between them.

The bases of these triangles are known. The small triangle, formed by Lara and her shadow, has a base of 6 feet. The large triangle, formed by the light pole along with the line from the base of the pole out to the end of Lara's shadow is $30 + 6 = 36$ feet long. So, the ratio of the big triangle to the little triangle will be $\frac{36}{6} = 6$. The height of the little triangle is 5 feet. Therefore, the height of the big triangle will be $6 \cdot 5 = 30$ feet, meaning that the light is 30 feet up the pole.

Notice that the perimeter of a figure changes by the ratio of proportionality between two similar figures, but the area changes by the *square* of the ratio. This is because if the length of one side is doubled, the area is quadrupled.

As an example, suppose two rectangles are similar, but the edges of the second rectangle are three times longer than the edges of the first rectangle. The area of the first rectangle is 10 square inches. How much more area does the second rectangle have than the first?

To answer this, note that the area of the second rectangle is $3^2 = 9$ times the area of the first rectangle, which is 10 square inches. Therefore, the area of the second rectangle is going to be $9 \cdot 10 = 90$ square inches. This means it has $90 - 10 = 80$ square inches more area than the first rectangle.

As a second example, suppose *X* and *Y* are similar right triangles. The hypotenuse of *X* is 4 inches. The area of *Y* is $\frac{1}{4}$ the area of *X*. What is the hypotenuse of *Y*?

First, realize the area has changed by a factor of $\frac{1}{4}$. The area changes by a factor that is the *square* of the ratio of changes in lengths, so the ratio of the lengths is the square root of the ratio of areas. That means that the ratio of lengths must be is $\sqrt{\frac{1}{4}} = \frac{1}{2}$, and the hypotenuse of *Y* must be $\frac{1}{2} \cdot 4 = 2$ inches.

Volumes between similar solids change like the cube of the change in the lengths of their edges. Likewise, if the ratio of the volumes between similar solids is known, the ratio between their lengths is known by finding the cube root of the ratio of their volumes.

For example, suppose there are two similar rectangular pyramids *X* and *Y*. The base of *X* is 1 inch by 2 inches, and the volume of *X* is 8 inches. The volume of *Y* is 64 inches. What are the dimensions of the base of *Y*?

To answer this, first find the ratio of the volume of *Y* to the volume of *X*. This will be given by $\frac{64}{8} = 8$. Now the ratio of lengths is the cube root of the ratio of volumes, or $\sqrt[3]{8} = 2$. So, the dimensions of the base of *Y* must be 2 inches by 4 inches.

<u>Circles</u>
A *circle* can be defined as the set of all points that are the same distance (known as the radius, *r*) from a single point (known as the center of the circle). The center has coordinates (h, k), and any point on the circle can be labelled with coordinates (x, y).

The *circumference* of a circle is the distance traveled by following the edge of the circle for one complete revolution, and the length of the circumference is given by $2\pi r$, where *r* is the radius of the circle. The formula for circumference is $C = 2\pi r$.

Given two points on the circumference of a circle, the path along the circle between those points is called an *arc* of the circle. For example, the arc between *B* and *C* is denoted by a thinner line:

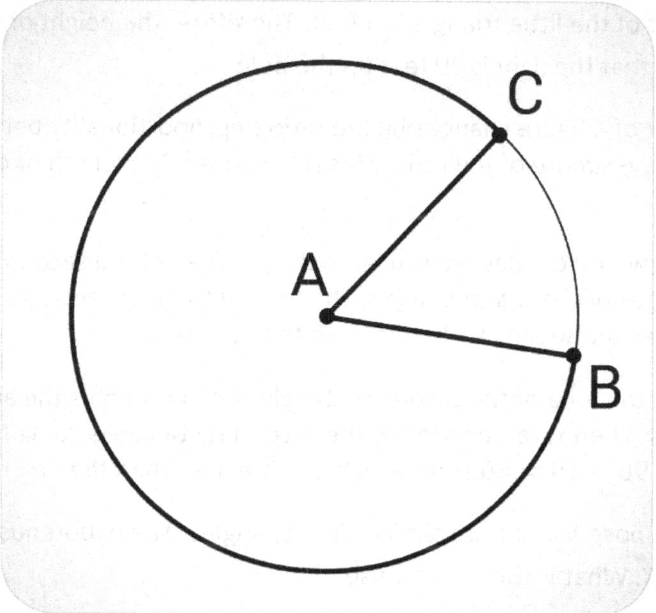

The length of the path along an arc is called the *arc length*. If the circle has radius *r*, then the arc length is given by multiplying the measure of the angle in radians by the radius of the circle.

The area of a circle can be calculated using the formula $A = \pi r^2$, where *r* is the radius of the circle.

Area and Perimeter

The perimeter of a polygon is the distance around the outside of the two-dimensional figure. Perimeter is a one-dimensional measurement and is therefore expressed in linear units such as centimeters (*cm*), feet (*ft*), and miles (*mi*). The perimeter (*P*) of a figure can be calculated by adding together each of the sides.

Properties of certain polygons allow that the perimeter may be obtained by using formulas. A rectangle consists of two sides called the length (*l*), which have equal measures, and two sides called the width (*w*), which have equal measures. Therefore, the perimeter (*P*) of a rectangle can be expressed as $P = l + l + w + w$. This can be simplified to produce the following formula to find the perimeter of a rectangle: $P = 2l + 2w$ or $P = 2(l + w)$.

A regular polygon is one in which all sides have equal length and all interior angles have equal measures, such as a square and an equilateral triangle. To find the perimeter of a regular polygon, the length of one side is multiplied by the number of sides. For example, to find the perimeter of an equilateral triangle with a side of length of 4 feet, 4 feet is multiplied by 3 (number of sides of a triangle). The perimeter of a regular octagon (8 sides) with a side of length of $\frac{1}{2}$cm is $\frac{1}{2} cm \times 8 = 4cm$.

The area of a polygon is the number of square units needed to cover the interior region of the figure. Area is a two-dimensional measurement. Therefore, area is expressed in square units, such as square centimeters (cm^2), square feet (ft^2), or square miles (mi^2). Regarding the area of a rectangle with sides of length *x* and *y*, the area is given by xy. For a triangle with a base of length *b* and a height of length *h*, the area is $\frac{1}{2}bh$. To find the area (*A*) of a parallelogram, the length of the base (*b*) is multiplied by the length of the height (*h*) $\rightarrow A = b \times h$. Similar to triangles, the height of the parallelogram is measured from one base to the other at a 90° angle (or perpendicular).

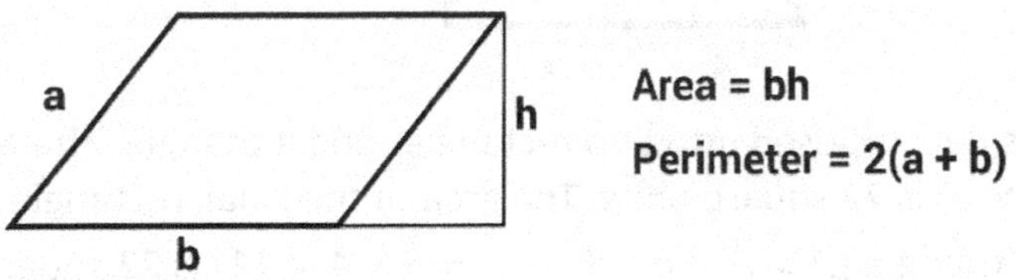

The area of a trapezoid can be calculated using the formula: $A = \frac{1}{2} \times h(b_1 + b_2)$, where *h* is the height and b_1 and b_2 are the parallel bases of the trapezoid.

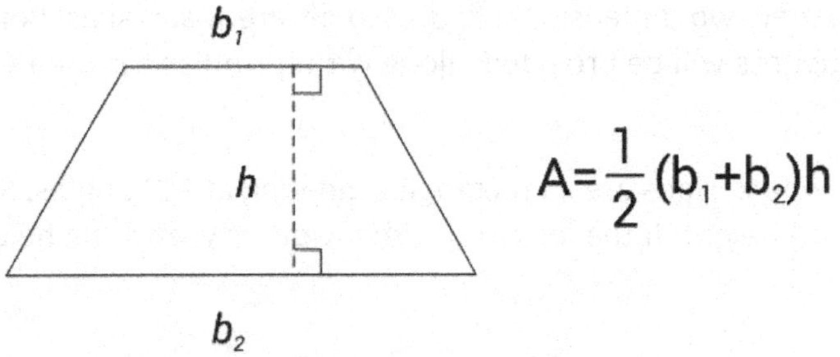

The area of a regular polygon can be determined by using its perimeter and the length of the apothem. The apothem is a line from the center of the regular polygon to any of its sides at a right angle. (Note that the perimeter of a regular polygon can be determined given the length of only one side.) The formula for the area (*A*) of a regular polygon is $A = \frac{1}{2} \times a \times P$, where *a* is the length of the apothem and *P* is the perimeter of the figure. Consider the following regular pentagon:

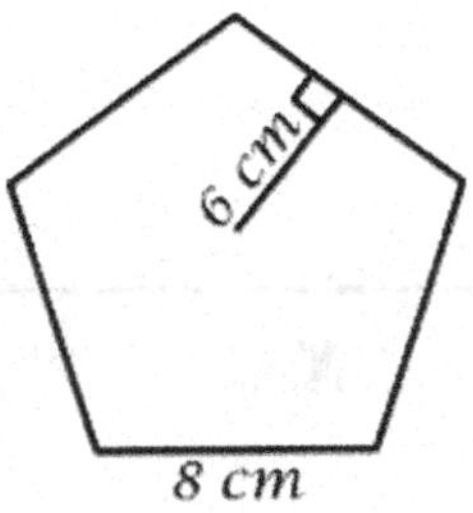

To find the area, the perimeter (*P*) is calculated first: $8cm \times 5 \rightarrow P = 40cm$. Then the perimeter and the apothem are used to find the area (*A*): $A = \frac{1}{2} \times a \times P \rightarrow A = \frac{1}{2} \times (6cm) \times (40cm) \rightarrow A = 120cm^2$. Note that the unit is $cm^2 \rightarrow cm \times cm = cm^2$.

The area of irregular polygons is found by decomposing, or breaking apart, the figure into smaller shapes. When the area of the smaller shapes is determined, the area of the smaller shapes will produce the area of the original figure when added together. Consider the example below:

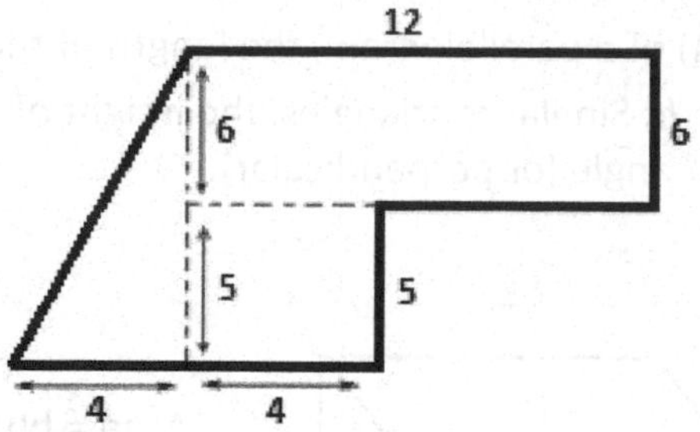

The irregular polygon is decomposed into two rectangles and a triangle. The area of the large rectangles ($A = l \times w \rightarrow A = 12 \times 6$) is 72 square units. The area of the small rectangle is 20 square units ($A = 4 \times 5$). The area of the triangle ($A = \frac{1}{2} \times b \times h \rightarrow A = \frac{1}{2} \times 4 \times 11$) is 22 square units. The sum of the areas of these figures produces the total area of the original polygon: $A = 72 + 20 + 22 \rightarrow A = 114$ square units.

Surface Area and Volume

Geometry in three dimensions is similar to geometry in two dimensions. The main new feature is that three points now define a unique *plane* that passes through each of them. Three dimensional objects can be made by putting together two dimensional figures in different surfaces. Below, some of the possible three dimensional figures will be provided, along with formulas for their volumes and surface areas.

A rectangular prism is a box whose sides are all rectangles meeting at 90° angles. Such a box has three dimensions: length, width, and height. If the length is *x*, the width is *y*, and the height is *z*, then the volume is given by $V = xyz$.

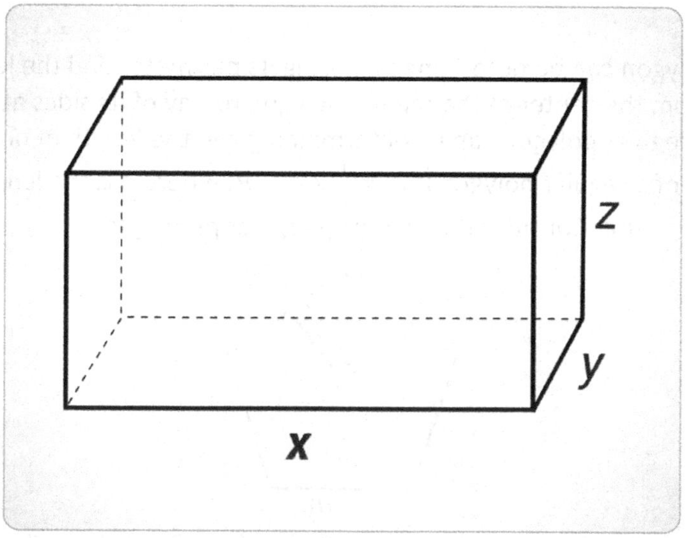

The surface area will be given by computing the surface area of each rectangle and adding them together. There are a total of six rectangles. Two of them have sides of length *x* and *y*, two have sides of length y and z, and two have sides of length x and z. Therefore, the total surface area will be given by $SA = 2xy + 2yz + 2xz$.

A *cube* is a special type of rectangular solid in which its length, width, and height are the same. If this length is s, then the formula for the volume of a cube is $V = s \times s \times s$. The surface area of a cube is $SA = 6s^2$.

A *rectangular pyramid* is a figure with a rectangular base and four triangular sides that meet at a single vertex. If the rectangle has sides of length x and y, then the volume will be given by $V = \frac{1}{3}xyh$.

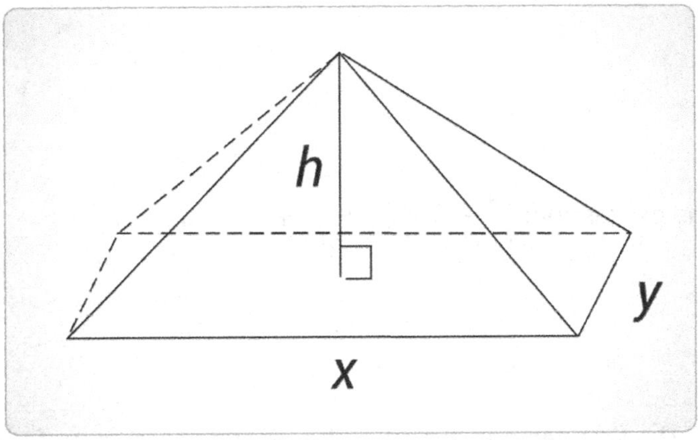

To find the surface area, the dimensions of each triangle need to be known. However, these dimensions can differ depending on the problem in question. Therefore, there is no general formula for calculating total surface area.

A *sphere* is a set of points all of which are equidistant from some central point. It is like a circle, but in three dimensions. The volume of a sphere of radius r is given by $V = \frac{4}{3}\pi r^3$. The surface area is given by $A = 4\pi r^2$.

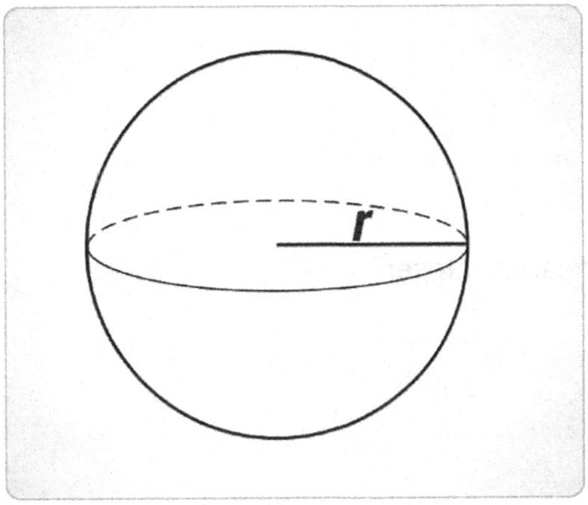

Practice Questions

1. $5.88 \times 3.2 =$
   a. 18.816
   b. 16.44
   c. 20.352
   d. 17

2. How will the following number be written in standard form: $(1 \times 10^4) + (3 \times 10^3) + (7 \times 10^1) + (8 \times 10^0)$
   a. 137
   b. 13,078
   c. 1,378
   d. 8,731

3. What is the value of the expression: $7^2 - 3 \times (4 + 2) + 15 \div 5$?
   a. 12.2
   b. 40.2
   c. 34
   d. 58.2

4. Four people split a bill. The first person pays for $\frac{1}{5}$, the second person pays for $\frac{1}{4}$, and the third person pays for $\frac{1}{3}$. What fraction of the bill does the fourth person pay?
   a. $\frac{13}{60}$
   b. $\frac{47}{60}$
   c. $\frac{1}{4}$
   d. $\frac{4}{15}$

5. A student gets an 85% on a test with 20 questions. How many answers did the student solve correctly?
   a. 15
   b. 16
   c. 17
   d. 18

6. What is $\frac{420}{98}$ rounded to the nearest integer?
   a. 4
   b. 3
   c. 5
   d. 6

7. If Danny takes 48 minutes to walk 3 miles, how long should it take him to walk 5 miles maintaining the same speed?

a. 32 min
b. 64 min
c. 80 min
d. 96 min

8. If $\sqrt{1+x}=4$, what is x?

a. 10
b. 15
c. 20
d. 25

9. What is the simplified quotient of the following equation?

$$\frac{5x^3}{3x^2y} \div \frac{25}{3y^9}$$

a. $\frac{125x}{9y^{10}}$
b. $\frac{x}{5y^8}$
c. $\frac{5}{xy^8}$
d. $\frac{xy^8}{5}$

10. Which of the following is a factor of both x^2+4x+4 and x^2-x-6?

a. $x-3$
b. $x+2$
c. $x-2$
d. $x+3$

11. Which of the following shows the correct result of simplifying the following expression:

$$(7n+3n^3+3)+(8n+5n^3+2n^4)$$

a. $9n^4+15n-2$
b. $2n^4+5n^3+15n-2$
c. $9n^4+8n^3+15n$
d. $2n^4+8n^3+15n+3$

12. Which of the following inequalities is equivalent to $3-\frac{1}{2}x \geq 2$?

a. $x \geq 2$
b. $x \leq 2$
c. $x \geq 1$
d. $x \leq 1$

13. If $4x - 3 = 5$, then $x =$

a. 1
b. 2
c. 3
d. 4

14. What is the solution to the following system of equations?

$$x^2 - 2x + y = 8$$
$$x - y = -2$$

a. $(-2, 3)$
b. There is no solution.
c. $(-2, 0)$ $(1, 3)$
d. $(-2, 0)$ $(3, 5)$

15. A line passes through the point (1, 2) and crosses the *y*-axis at *y* = 1. Which of the following is an equation for this line?

a. $y = 2x$
b. $y = x + 1$
c. $x + y = 1$
d. $y = \frac{x}{2} - 2$

16. A company invests $50,000 in a building where they can produce saws. If the cost of producing one saw is $40, then which function expresses the amount of money the company pays? The variable *y* is the money paid and *x* is the number of saws produced.

a. $y = 50{,}000x + 40$
b. $y + 40 = x - 50{,}000$
c. $y = 40x - 50{,}000$
d. $y = 40x + 50{,}000$

17. If $g(x) = x^3 - 3x^2 - 2x + 6$ and $f(x) = 2$, then what is $g(f(x))$?

a. -26
b. 6
c. $2x^3 - 6x^2 - 4x + 12$
d. -2

18. Is the following function even, odd, neither, or both?

$$y = \frac{1}{2}x^4 + 2x^2 - 6$$

a. Even
b. Odd
c. Neither
d. Both

19. An investment of $2,000 is made into an account with an annual interest rate of 5%, compounded continuously. What is the total value for the investment after eight years?

a. $4,707
b. $3,000
c. $2,983.65
d. $10, 919.63

20. What is the 42nd item in the pattern: ▲oo□▲oo□▲...?

a. o

b. ▲

c. □

d. None of the above

21. For a group of 20 men, the median weight is 180 pounds and the range is 30 pounds. If each man gains 10 pounds, which of the following would be true?

a. The median weight will increase, and the range will remain the same.

b. The median weight and range will both remain the same.

c. The median weight will stay the same, and the range will increase.

d. The median weight and range will both increase.

22. Five students take a test. The scores of the first four students are 80, 85, 75, and 60. If the median score is 80, which of the following could NOT be the score of the fifth student?

a. 60

b. 80

c. 85

d. 100

23. Ten students take a test. Five students get a 50. Four students get a 70. If the average score is 55, what was the last student's score?

a. 20

b. 40

c. 50

d. 60

24. Given the value of a given stock at monthly intervals, which graph should be used to best represent the trend of the stock?

a. Box plot

b. Line plot

c. Line graph

d. Circle graph

25. A six-sided die is rolled. What is the probability that the roll is 1 or 2?

a. $\frac{1}{6}$

b. $\frac{1}{4}$

c. $\frac{1}{3}$

d. $\frac{1}{2}$

26. What is the probability of randomly picking the winner and runner-up from a race of 4 horses and distinguishing which is the winner?

a. $\frac{1}{4}$

b. $\frac{1}{2}$

c. $\frac{1}{16}$

d. $\frac{1}{12}$

27. A grocery store is selling individual bottles of water, and each bottle contains 750 milliliters of water. If 12 bottles are purchased, what conversion will correctly determine how many liters that customer will take home?

a. 100 milliliters equals 1 liter
b. 1,000 milliliters equals 1 liter
c. 1,000 liters equals 1 milliliter
d. 10 liters equals 1 milliliter

28. Which of the following statements is true about the two lines below?

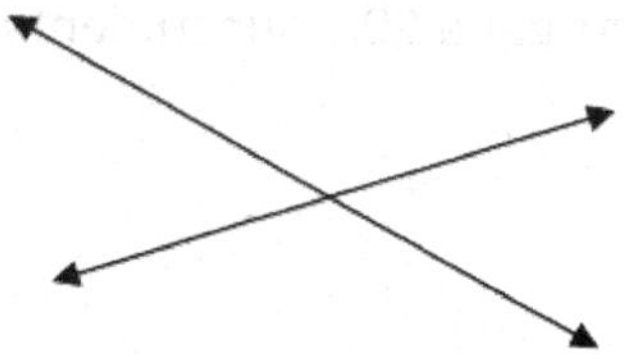

a. The two lines are parallel but not perpendicular.
b. The two lines are perpendicular but not parallel.
c. The two lines are both parallel and perpendicular.
d. The two lines are neither parallel nor perpendicular.

29. The perimeter of a 6-sided polygon is 56 cm. The length of three sides is 9 cm each. The length of two other sides is 8 cm each. What is the length of the missing side?

a. 11 cm
b. 12 cm
c. 13 cm
d. 10 cm

30. An equilateral triangle has a perimeter of 18 feet. If a square whose sides have the same length as one side of the triangle is built, what will be the area of the square?

a. 6 square feet
b. 36 square feet
c. 256 square feet
d. 1000 square feet

31. The area of a given rectangle is 24 centimeters. If the measure of each side is multiplied by 3, what is the area of the new figure?

a. 48cm
b. 72cm
c. 216cm
d. 13,824cm

32. Apples cost $2 each, while oranges cost $3 each. Maria purchased 10 fruits in total and spent $22. How many apples did she buy?

a. 5
b. 6
c. 7
d. 8

33. $(4x^2y^4)^{\frac{3}{2}}$ can be simplified to which of the following?

a. $8x^3y^6$
b. $4x^{\frac{5}{2}}y$
c. $4xy$
d. $32x^{\frac{7}{2}}y^{\frac{11}{2}}$

34. A line passes through the origin and through the point (-3, 4). What is the slope of the line?

a. $-\frac{4}{3}$
b. $-\frac{3}{4}$
c. $\frac{4}{3}$
d. $\frac{3}{4}$

35. $3\frac{2}{3} - 1\frac{4}{5} =$

a. $1\frac{13}{15}$
b. $\frac{14}{15}$
c. $2\frac{2}{3}$
d. $\frac{4}{5}$

36. What is the value of $x^2 - 2xy + 2y^2$ when $x = 2, y = 3$?

a. 8
b. 10
c. 12
d. 14

37. The square and circle have the same center. The circle has a radius of r. What is the area of the shaded region?

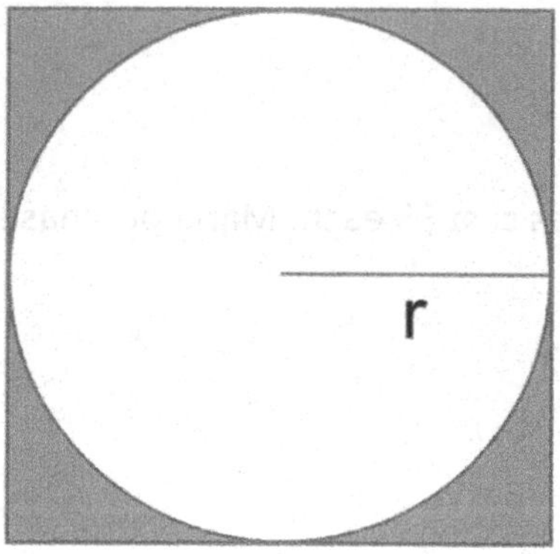

a. $r^2 - \pi r^2$
b. $4r^2 - 2\pi r$
c. $(4 - \pi)r^2$
d. $(\pi - 1)r^2$

38. What is the expression that represents three times the sum of twice a number and one minus 6?
a. $2x + 1 - 6$
b. $3x + 1 - 6$
c. $3(x + 1) - 6$
d. $3(2x + 1) - 6$

39. What are the coordinates of the two points marked with green dots on this coordinate plane?

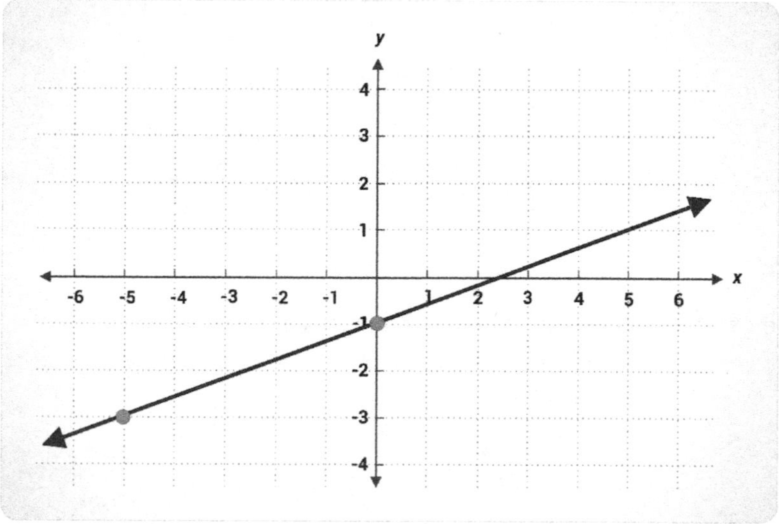

a. (-3, -5) and (-1, 0)
b. (5, 3) and (0, 1)
c. (-5, -3) and (0, -1)
d. (-3, -5) and (0, -1)

40. What is the value of x for the right triangle shown below?

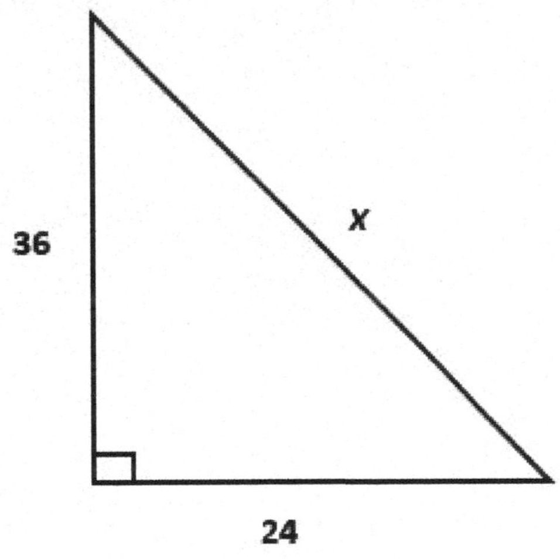

a. 43.3
b. 26.8
c. 42.7
d. 44.1

41. A cube has sides that are 7 inches long. What is the cube's volume?
a. $49in^3$
b. $343in^3$
c. $294in^3$
d. $28in^3$

No Calculator Questions

1. 3.4+2.35+4=
a. 5.35
b. 9.2
c. 9.75
d. 10.25

2. $\frac{3}{25} =$
a. 0.15
b. 0.1
c. 0.9
d. 0.12

3. 6 is 30% of what number?
a. 18
b. 20
c. 24
d. 26

4. What is the value of the following expression?

$$\sqrt{8^2 + 6^2}$$

a. 14
b. 10
c. 9
d. 100

5. $864 \div 36 =$

a. 24
b. 25
c. 34
d. 18

Answer Explanations

1. A: This problem can be multiplied as 588×32, except at the end, the decimal point needs to be moved three places to the left. Performing the multiplication will give 18,816, and moving the decimal place over three places results in 18.816.

2. B: 13,078. The power of 10 by which a digit is multiplied corresponds with the number of zeros following the digit when expressing its value in standard form. Therefore, $(1 \times 10^4) + (3 \times 10^3) + (7 \times 10^1) + (8 \times 10^0) = 10{,}000 + 3{,}000 + 70 + 8 = 13{,}078$.

3. C: 34. When performing calculations consisting of more than one operation, the order of operations should be followed: *P*arenthesis, *E*xponents, *M*ultiplication/*D*ivision, *A*ddition/*S*ubtraction. Parenthesis: $7^2 - 3 \times (4 + 2) + 15 \div 5 = 7^2 - 3 \times (6) + 15 \div 5$. Exponents: $7^2 - 3 \times 6 + 15 \div 5 = 49 - 3 \times 6 + 15 \div 5$. Multiplication/Division (from left to right): $49 - 3 \times 6 + 15 \div 5 = 49 - 18 + 3$. Addition/Subtraction (from left to right): $49 - 18 + 3 = 34$.

4. A: To find the fraction of the bill that the first three people pay, the fractions need to be added, which means finding common denominator. The common denominator will be 60. $\frac{1}{5} + \frac{1}{4} + \frac{1}{3} = \frac{12}{60} + \frac{15}{60} + \frac{20}{60} = \frac{47}{60}$. The remainder of the bill is $1 - \frac{47}{60} = \frac{60}{60} - \frac{47}{60} = \frac{13}{60}$.

5. C: 85% of a number means multiplying that number by 0.85. So, $0.85 \times 20 = \frac{85}{100} \times \frac{20}{1}$, which can be simplified to $\frac{17}{20} \times \frac{20}{1} = 17$.

6. A: Dividing by 98 can be approximated by dividing by 100, which would mean shifting the decimal point of the numerator to the left by 2. The result is 4.2 and rounds to 4.

7. C: 80 min. To solve the problem, a proportion is written consisting of ratios comparing distance and time. One way to set up the proportion is: $\frac{3}{48} = \frac{5}{x} \left(\frac{distance}{time} = \frac{distance}{time}\right)$ where x represents the unknown value of time. To solve a proportion, the ratios are cross-multiplied: $(3)(x) = (5)(48) \rightarrow 3x = 240$. The equation is solved by isolating the variable, or dividing by 3 on both sides, to produce $x = 80$.

8. B: Start by squaring both sides to get $1 + x = 16$. Then subtract 1 from both sides to get $x = 15$.

9. D: Dividing rational expressions follows the same rule as dividing fractions. The division is changed to multiplication, and the reciprocal is found in the second fraction. This turns the expression into $\frac{5x^3}{3x^2} * \frac{3y^9}{25}$. Multiplying across and simplifying, the final expression is $\frac{xy^8}{5}$.

10. B: To factor $x^2 + 4x + 4$, the numbers needed are those that add to 4 and multiply to 4. Therefore, both numbers must be 2, and the expression factors to $x^2 + 4x + 4 = (x + 2)^2$. Similarly, the expression factors to $x^2 - x - 6 = (x - 3)(x + 2)$, so that they have $x + 2$ in common.

11. D: The expression is simplified by collecting like terms. Terms with the same variable and exponent are like terms, and their coefficients can be added.

12. B: To simplify this inequality, subtract 3 from both sides to get $-\frac{1}{2}x \geq -1$. Then, multiply both sides by -2 (remembering this flips the direction of the inequality) to get $x \leq 2$.

13. B: Add 3 to both sides to get $4x = 8$. Then divide both sides by 4 to get $x = 2$.

14. D: This system of equations involves one quadratic function and one linear function, as seen from the degree of each equation. One way to solve this is through substitution. Solving for y in the second equation yields $y = x + 2$. Plugging this equation in for the y of the quadratic equation yields $x^2 - 2x + x + 2 = 8$. Simplifying the equation, it becomes $x^2 - x + 2 = 8$. Setting this equal to zero and factoring, it becomes $x^2 - x - 6 = 0 = (x - 3)(x + 2)$. Solving these two factors for x gives the zeros $x = 3, -2$. To find the y-value for the point, each number can be plugged in to either original equation. Solving each one for y yields the points $(3, 5)$ and $(-2, 0)$.

15. B: From the slope-intercept form, $y = mx + b$, it is known that b is the y-intercept, which is 1. Compute the slope as $\frac{2-1}{1-0} = 1$, so the equation should be $y = x + 1$.

16. D: For manufacturing costs, there is a linear relationship between the cost to the company and the number produced, with a y-intercept given by the base cost of acquiring the means of production, and a slope given by the cost to produce one unit. In this case, that base cost is \$50,000, while the cost per unit is \$40. So, $y = 40x + 50{,}000$.

17. D: This problem involves a composition function, where one function is plugged into the other function. In this case, the $f(x)$ function is plugged into the $g(x)$ function for each x-value. The composition equation becomes $g\big(f(x)\big) = 2^3 - 3(2^2) - 2(2) + 6$. Simplifying the equation gives the answer $g\big(f(x)\big) = 8 - 3(4) - 2(2) + 6 = 8 - 12 - 4 + 6 = -2$.

18. A: The equation is *even* because $f(-x) = f(x)$. Plugging in a negative value will result in the same answer as when plugging in the positive of that same value. The function:

$$f(-2) = \frac{1}{2}(-2)^4 + 2(-2)^2 - 6 = 8 + 8 - 6 = 10$$

yields the same value as:

$$f(2) = \frac{1}{2}(2)^4 + 2(2)^2 - 6 = 8 + 8 - 6 = 10$$

19. C: The formula for continually compounded interest is $A = Pe^{rt}$. Plugging in the given values to find the total amount in the account yields the equation $A = 2000e^{0.05*8}$ = 2983.65.

20. A: ○. The core of the pattern consists of 4 items: ▲○○□. Therefore, the core repeats in multiples of 4, with the pattern starting over on the next step. The closest multiple of 4 to 42 is 40. Step 40 is the end of the core (□), so step 41 will start the core over (▲) and step 42 is ○.

21. A: If each man gains 10 pounds, every original data point will increase by 10 pounds. Therefore, the man with the original median will still have the median value, but that value will increase by 10. The smallest value and largest value will also increase by 10 and, therefore, the difference between the two won't change. The range does not change in value and, thus, remains the same.

22. A: Lining up the given scores provides the following list: 60, 75, 80, 85, and one unknown. Because the median needs to be 80, it means 80 must be the middle data point out of these five. Therefore, the unknown data point must be the fourth or fifth data point, meaning it must be greater than or equal to 80. The only answer that fails to meet this condition is 60.

23. A: Let the unknown score be x. The average will be $\frac{5 \cdot 50 + 4 \cdot 70 + x}{10} = \frac{530 + x}{10} = 55$. Multiply both sides by 10 to get $530 + x = 550$, or $x = 20$.

24. C: Line graph. The scenario involves data consisting of two variables, month, and stock value. Box plots display data consisting of values for one variable. Therefore, a box plot is not an appropriate choice. Both line plots and circle graphs are used to display frequencies within categorical data. Neither can be used for the given scenario. Line graphs display two numerical variables on a coordinate grid and show trends among the variables.

25. C: A die has an equal chance for each outcome. Since it has six sides, each outcome has a probability of $\frac{1}{6}$. The chance of a 1 or a 2 is therefore $\frac{1}{6} + \frac{1}{6} = \frac{1}{3}$.

26. D: $\frac{1}{12}$. The probability of picking the winner of the race is $\frac{1}{4}\left(\frac{\textit{number of favorable outcomes}}{\textit{number of total outcomes}}\right)$. Assuming the winner was picked on the first selection, three horses remain from which to choose the runner-up (these are dependent events). Therefore, the probability of picking the runner-up is $\frac{1}{3}$. To determine the probability of multiple events, the probability of each event is multiplied: $\frac{1}{4} \times \frac{1}{3} = \frac{1}{12}$.

27. B: $12 \times 750 = 9{,}000$. Therefore, there are 9,000 milliliters of water, which must be converted to liters. 1,000 milliliters equals 1 liter; therefore, 9 liters of water are purchased.

28. D: The two lines are neither parallel nor perpendicular. Parallel lines will never intersect or meet. Therefore, the lines are not parallel. Perpendicular lines intersect to form a right angle (90°). Although the lines intersect, they do not form a right angle, which is usually indicated with a box at the intersection point. Therefore, the lines are not perpendicular.

29. C: Perimeter is found by calculating the sum of all sides of the polygon. $9 + 9 + 9 + 8 + 8 + s = 56$, where s is the missing side length. Therefore, 43 plus the missing side length is equal to 56. The missing side length is 13 cm.

30. B: An equilateral triangle has three sides of equal length, so if the total perimeter is 18 feet, each side must be 6 feet long. A square with sides of 6 feet will have an area of $6^2 = 36$ square feet.

31. C: 216cm. Because area is a two-dimensional measurement, the dimensions are multiplied by a scale that is squared to determine the scale of the corresponding areas. The dimensions of the rectangle are multiplied by a scale of 3. Therefore, the area is multiplied by a scale of 3^2 (which is equal to 9): $24cm \times 9 = 216cm$.

32. D: Let a be the number of apples and o the number of oranges. Then, the total cost is $2a + 3o = 22$, while it also known that $a + o = 10$. Using the knowledge of systems of equations, cancel the o variables by multiplying the second equation by -3. This makes the equation $-3a - 3o = -30$. Adding this to the first equation, the o values cancel to get $-a = -8$, which simplifies to $a = 8$.

33. A: Simplify this to $(4x^2y^4)^{\frac{3}{2}} = 4^{\frac{3}{2}}(x^2)^{\frac{3}{2}}(y^4)^{\frac{3}{2}}$. Now, $4^{\frac{3}{2}} = (\sqrt{4})^3 = 2^3 = 8$. For the other, recall that the exponents must be multiplied, so this yields $8x^{2 \cdot \frac{3}{2}}y^{4 \cdot \frac{3}{2}} = 8x^3y^6$.

34. A: The slope is given by $m = \frac{y_2 - y_1}{x_2 - x_1} = \frac{0-4}{0-(-3)} = -\frac{4}{3}$.

35. A: These numbers to improper fractions: $\frac{11}{3} - \frac{9}{5}$. Take 15 as a common denominator: $\frac{11}{3} - \frac{9}{5} =: \frac{55}{15} - \frac{27}{15} = \frac{28}{15} = 1\frac{13}{15}$ (when rewritten to get rid of the partial fraction).

36. B: Each instance of *x* is replaced with a 2, and each instance of *y* is replaced with a 3 to get $2^2 - 2 \cdot 2 \cdot 3 + 2 \cdot 3^2 = 4 - 12 + 18 = 10$.

37. C: The area of the shaded region is the area of the square, minus the area of the circle. The area of the circle will be πr^2. The side of the square will be $2r$, so the area of the square will be $4r^2$. Therefore, the difference is $4r^2 - \pi r^2 = (4 - \pi)r^2$.

38. D: The expression is three times the sum of twice a number and 1, which is $3(2x + 1)$. Then, 6 is subtracted from this expression.

39: C. The two points are at -5 and 0 for the x-axis and at -3 and at -1 for y-axis respectively. Therefore, the two points have the coordinates of (-5, -3) and (0, -1).

40. A: The Pythagorean theorem states that for right triangles $c^2 = a^2 + b^2$, with *c* being the side opposite the 90° angle. Substituting 24 as *a* and 36 as *b,* the equation becomes $c^2 = 24^2 + 36^2 = 576 + 1296 = 1872$. The last step is to square both sides to remove the exponent, $c = \sqrt{1872} = 43.3$.

41. B: The formula for the volume of a cube is $V = s^3$. Substitute the side length of $7in$ to get $V = 7^3 = 343in^3$.

No Calculator Questions

1. C: The decimal points are lined up, with zeroes put in as needed. Then, the numbers are added just like integers:

$$\begin{array}{r} 3.40 \\ 2.35 \\ +4.00 \\ \hline 9.75 \end{array}$$

2. D: The fraction is converted so that the denominator is 100 by multiplying the numerator and denominator by 4, to get $\frac{3}{25} = \frac{12}{100}$. Dividing a number by 100 just moves the decimal point two places to the left, with a result of 0.12.

3. B: 30% is 3/10. The number itself must be 10/3 of 6, or $\frac{10}{3} \times 6 = 10 \times 2 = 20$.

4. B: 8 squared is 64, and 6 squared is 36. These should be added together to get $64 + 36 = 100$. Then, the last step is to find the square root of 100 which is 10.

5. A: The long division would be completed as follows:

$$\begin{array}{r} 24 \\ 36\overline{)864} \\ -\underline{72\downarrow} \\ 144 \end{array}$$

Science

Life Science

Biology Basics

Biology is the study of living organisms and the processes that are vital for life. Scientists who study biology are interested in the origin, evolution, structure, function, growth, and distribution of these living organisms. They study these organisms on a cellular level, individually or as populations, and look at the effects they have on their surrounding environment.

There are five foundations of modern biology: cell theory, evolution, genetics, homeostasis, and energy.

Cell theory is the idea that the cell is the fundamental unit of life. Living organisms are made up of one or more cells, and the products that are generated by those cells. Cells have processes that both produce and use energy, known as metabolism. They also contain deoxyribonucleic acid (DNA), which is hereditary information that gets passed on to subsequent generations.

Evolution is the theory that all living organisms descended from one common ancestor. Charles Darwin generated a viable scientific model of evolution based on the concept of natural selection. Natural selection is the idea that certain species with more advantageous phenotypes are more likely to survive than those species with less advantageous phenotypes. Over long periods of time, populations of species can develop phenotypes specialized for their environment.

Genetics is the study of genes. Genes are the primary unit of inheritance between generations or organisms. They are regions of DNA that encode ribonucleic acid (RNA) and proteins, all of which have specific forms and functions. DNA is present in all living cells and is important for the cell's own functions, as well as for its ability to divide and pass on information to subsequent daughter cells.

Homeostasis is the ability of a system, such as a cell or organism, to regulate itself so that its internal conditions remain stable even when its external environment may be changing. By maintaining homeostasis, systems are able to function normally even in adverse conditions.

The constant flow of energy is important for the survival of living organisms. All organisms have vital functions that require the input of energy and other functions that release energy. These processes work together to drive all chemical reactions required for life.

Water

Most cells are primarily composed of water and live in water-rich environments. Since water is such a familiar substance, it is easy to overlook its unique properties. Chemically, water is made up of two hydrogen atoms bonded to one oxygen atom by covalent bonds. The three atoms join to make a V-shaped molecule. Water is a polar molecule, meaning it has an unevenly distributed overall charge due to an unequal sharing of electrons. Due to oxygen's electronegativity and its more substantial positively charged nucleus, hydrogen's electrons are pulled closer to the oxygen. This causes the hydrogen atoms to have a slight positive charge and the oxygen atom to have a slight negative charge. In a glass of water, the molecules constantly interact and link for a fraction of a second due to intermolecular bonding between the slightly positive hydrogen atoms of one molecule and the slightly negative oxygen of a different molecule. These weak intermolecular bonds are called hydrogen bonds.

Water has several important qualities, including: cohesive and adhesive behaviors, temperature moderation ability, expansion upon freezing, and diverse use as a solvent.

Cohesion is the interaction of many of the same molecules. In water, cohesion occurs when there is hydrogen bonding between water molecules. Water molecules use this bonding ability to attach to each other and can work against gravity to transport dissolved nutrients to the top of a plant. A network of water-conducting cells can push water from the roots of a plant up to the leaves. Adhesion is the linking of two different substances. Water molecules can form a weak hydrogen bond with, or adhere to, plant cell walls to help fight gravity. The cohesive behavior of water also causes surface tension. If a glass of water is slightly overfull, water can still stand above the rim. This is because of the unique bonding of water molecules at the surface — they bond to each other and to the molecules below them, making it seem like it is covered with an impenetrable film. A raft spider could actually walk across a small body of water due to this surface tension.

Another important property of water is its ability to moderate temperature. Water can moderate the temperature of air by absorbing or releasing stored heat into the air. Water has the distinctive capability of being able to absorb or release large quantities of stored heat while undergoing only a small change in temperature. This is because of the relatively high specific heat of water, where specific heat is the amount of heat it takes for one gram of a material to change its temperature by 1 degree Celsius. The specific heat of water is one calorie per gram per degree Celsius, meaning that for each gram of water, it takes one calorie of heat to raise or lower the temperature of water by 1 degree Celsius.

When the temperature of water is reduced to freezing levels, water displays another interesting property: It expands instead of contracts. Most liquids become denser as they freeze because the molecules move around slower and stay closer together. Water molecules, however, form hydrogen bonds with each other as they move together. As the temperature lowers and they begin to move slower, these bonds become harder to break apart. When water freezes into ice, molecules are frozen with hydrogen bonds between them and they take up about 10 percent more volume than in their liquid state. The fact that ice is less dense than water is what makes ice float to the top of a glass of water.

Lastly, the polarity of water molecules makes it a versatile solvent. Ionic compounds, such as salt, are made up of positively and negatively charged atoms, called cations and anions, respectively. Cations and anions are easily dissolved in water because of their individual attractions to the slight positive charge of the hydrogen atoms or the slight negative charge of the oxygen atoms in water molecules. Water molecules separate the individually charged atoms and shield them from each other so they don't bond to each other again, creating a homogenous solution of the cations and anions. Nonionic compounds, such as sugar, have polar regions, so are easily dissolved in water. For these compounds, the water molecules form hydrogen bonds with the polar regions (hydroxyl groups) to create a homogenous solution. Any substance that is attracted to water is termed hydrophilic. Substances that repel water are termed hydrophobic.

Structure and Function of Cell Membranes

All cells are surrounded by a cell membrane that is formed from two layers of phospholipids. *Phospholipids* are two fatty acid chains connected to a glycerol molecule with a phosphate group. The membrane is amphiphilic because the fatty acid chains are hydrophobic and the phosphate group is hydrophilic. This creates a unique environment that protects the cell's inner contents while still allowing material to pass through the membrane. Because the outside of a cell, known as the *extracellular space*, and the inside of a cell, the *intercellular space*, are aqueous, the lipid bilayer forms with the two phospholipid heads facing the outside and the inside of the cell. This allows the phospholipids to interact with water; the fatty acid tails face the middle, so they can interact with each other and avoid water.

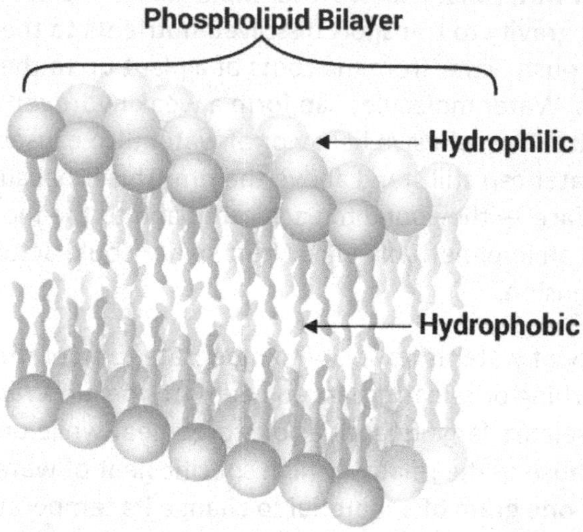

Molecules can pass through the cell membrane by either active or passive transport. *Active transport* requires chemical energy to move molecules in or out of the cell from areas of low concentration to areas of high concentration, or in instances where the molecules would not be able to pass through by themselves, such as with large non-lipid soluble molecules. Ions, amino acids, and complex sugars use active transport mechanisms. Molecules that are soluble in lipids, water, and oxygen use *passive transport* to move in and out of the cell, which means that cellular energy is not required for their movement. Examples of passive transport include diffusion, facilitated diffusion, and osmosis. *Diffusion* is the net movement of particles from an area of high concentration to lower concentration. *Facilitated diffusion* is the movement of molecules through cell membranes with the use of special transport proteins. Finally, *osmosis* is the movement of water molecules across partially permeable membranes.

Structure and Function of Animal and Plant Cell Organelles

Animal and plant cells contain many of the same or similar *organelles*, which are membrane enclosed structures that each have a specific function; however, there are a few organelles that are unique to either one or the other general cell type. The following cell organelles are found in both animal and plant cells, unless otherwise noted in their description:

- *Nucleus*: The nucleus consists of three parts: the nuclear envelope, the nucleolus, and chromatin. The *nuclear envelope* is the double membrane that surrounds the nucleus and separates its contents from the rest of the cell. The *nucleolus* produces ribosomes. *Chromatin* consists of DNA and protein, which form chromosomes that contain genetic information. Most cells have only one nucleus; however, some cells, such as skeletal muscle cells, have multiple nuclei.

- *Endoplasmic reticulum (ER)*: The ER is a network of membranous sacs and tubes that is responsible for membrane synthesis. It is also responsible for packaging and transporting proteins into vesicles that can move out of the cell. It folds and transports other proteins to the

Golgi apparatus. It contains both smooth and rough regions; the rough regions have ribosomes attached, which are the sites of protein synthesis.

- *Flagellum*: Flagellum are found only in animal cells. They are made up of a cluster of microtubules projected out of the plasma membrane, and they aid in cell mobility.
- *Centrosome*: The centrosome is the area of the cell where *microtubules*, which are filaments that are responsible for movement in the cell, begin to be formed. Each centrosome contains two centrioles. Each cell contains one centrosome.
- *Cytoskeleton*: The cytoskeleton in animal cells is made up of microfilaments, intermediate filaments, and microtubules. In plant cells, the cytoskeleton is made up of only microfilaments and microtubules. These structures reinforce the cell's shape and aid in cell movement.
- *Microvilli*: Microvilli are found only in animal cells. They are protrusions in the cell membrane that increase the cell's surface area. They have a variety of functions, including absorption, secretion, and cellular adhesion. They are found on the apical surface of epithelial cells, such as in the small intestine. They are also located on the plasma surface of a female's eggs to help anchor sperm that are attempting fertilization.
- *Peroxisome*: A peroxisome contains enzymes that are involved in many of the cell's metabolic functions, one of the most important being the breakdown of very long chain fatty acids. Peroxisomes produces hydrogen peroxide as a byproduct of these processes and then converts the hydrogen peroxide to water. There are many peroxisomes in each cell.
- *Mitochondrion*: The mitochondrion is often called the powerhouse of the cell and is one of the most important structures for maintaining regular cell function. It is where aerobic cellular respiration occurs and where most of the cell's adenosine triphosphate (ATP) is generated. The number of mitochondria in a cell varies greatly from organism to organism, and from cell to cell. In human cells, the number of mitochondria can vary from zero in a red blood cell, to 2000 in a liver cell.
- *Lysosome*: Lysosomes are exclusively found in animal cells. They are responsible for digestion and can hydrolyze macromolecules. There are many lysosomes in each cell.
- *Golgi apparatus*: The Golgi apparatus is responsible for the composition, modification, organization, and secretion of cell products. Because of its large size, it was actually one of the first organelles to be studied in detail. There are many Golgi apparati in each cell.
- *Ribosomes*: Ribosomes are found either free in the cytosol, bound to the rough ER, or bound to the nuclear envelope. They manufacture proteins within the cell.
- *Plasmodesmata*: The plasmodesmata are found only in plant cells. They are cytoplasmic channels, or tunnels, that go through the cell wall and connect the cytoplasm of adjacent cells.
- *Chloroplast*: Chloroplasts are found only in plant cells. They are responsible for *photosynthesis*, which is the process of converting sunlight to chemical energy that can be stored and used later to drive cellular activities.

- *Central vacuole*: A central vacuole is found only in plant cells. It is responsible for storing material and waste. This is the only vacuole found in a plant cell.
- *Plasma membrane*: The plasma membrane is a phospholipid bilayer that encloses the cell.
- *Cell wall*: Cell walls are only present in plant cells. The cell wall is made up of strong fibrous substances including cellulose and other polysaccharides, and protein. It is a layer outside of the plasma membrane, which protects the cell from mechanical damage and helps maintain the cell's shape.

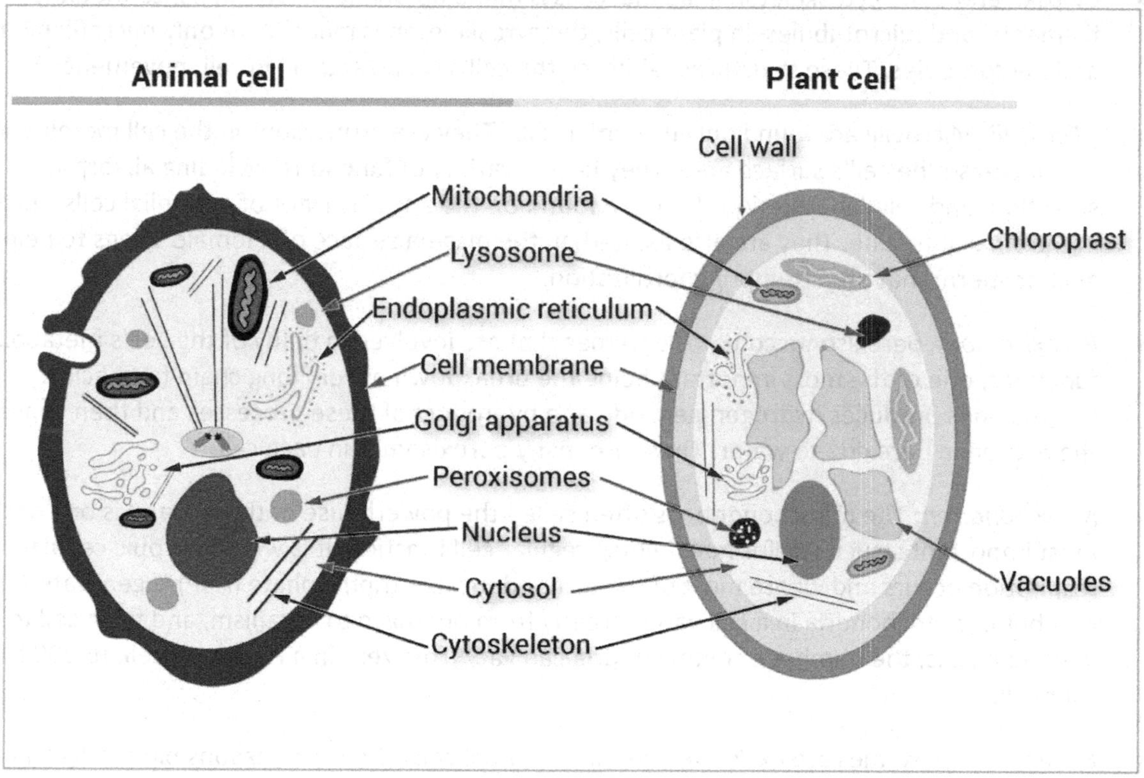

Levels of Organization

There are about two hundred different types of cells in the human body. Cells group together to form *biological tissues*, and tissues combine to form *organs*, such as the heart and kidneys. Organs that work together to perform vital functions of the human body form *organ systems*. There are eleven organ systems in the human body: skeletal, muscular, urinary, nervous, digestive, endocrine, reproductive, respiratory, cardiovascular, integumentary, and lymphatic. Although each system has its own unique function, they all rely on each other, either directly or indirectly, to operate properly.

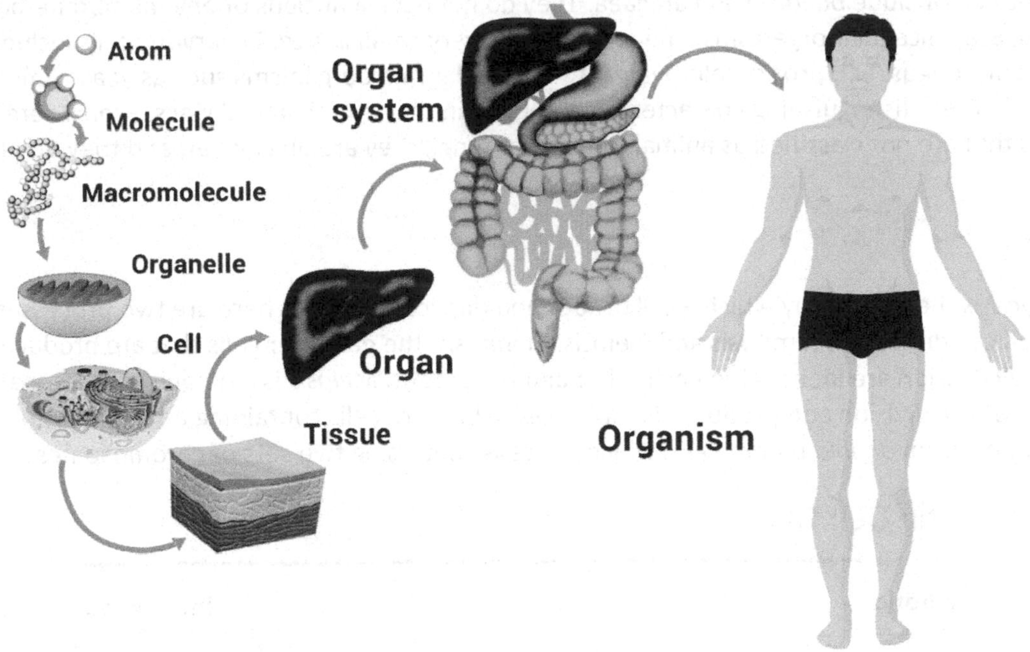

Major Features of Common Animal Cell Types

The most common animal cell types are blood, muscle, nerve, epithelial, and gamete cells. The three main blood cells are *red blood cells (RBCs), white blood cells (WBCs),* and *platelets*. RBCs transport oxygen and carbon dioxide through the body. They do not have a nucleus and they live for about 120 days in the blood. WBCs defend the body against diseases. They do have a nucleus and live for only three to four days in the human body. Platelets help with the formation of blood clots following an injury. They do not have a nucleus and live for about eight days after formation. *Muscle cells* are long, tubular cells that form muscles, which are responsible for movement in the body. On average, they live for about fifteen years, but this number is highly dependent on the individual body. There are three main types of muscle tissue: skeletal, cardiac, and smooth. *Skeletal muscle cells* have multiple nuclei and are the only voluntary muscle cell, which means that the brain consciously controls the movement of skeletal muscle. *Cardiac muscle cells* are only found in the heart; they have a single nucleus and are involuntary. *Smooth muscle cells* make up the walls of the blood vessels and organs. They have a single nucleus and are involuntary. *Nerve cells* conduct electrical impulses that help send information and instructions from the brain to the rest of the body. They contain a single nucleus and have a specialized membrane that allows for this electrical signaling between cells. *Epithelial* cells cover exposed surfaces, and line internal cavities and passageways. *Gametes* are specialized cells that are responsible for reproduction. In the human body, the gametes are the egg and the sperm.

Prokaryotes and Eukaryotes

There are two distinct types of cells that make up most living organisms: *prokaryotic* and *eukaryotic*. Both types of cells are enclosed by plasma membranes with cytosol on the inside. They both contain *ribosomes* and DNA. One major difference between these types of cells is that in eukaryotic cells, the cell's DNA is enclosed in a membrane-bound nucleus, whereas in prokaryotic cells, the cell's DNA is in a region—called the *nucleoid*—that is not enclosed by a membrane. Another major difference is that eukaryotic cells contain organelles, while prokaryotic cells do not have organelles.

Prokaryotic cells include *bacteria* and archaea. They do not have a nucleus or any membrane-bound organelles, are unicellular organisms, and are generally very small in size. Eukaryotic cells include animal, plant, fungus, and protist cells. *Fungi* are unicellular microorganisms such as yeasts, molds, and mushrooms. Their distinguishing characteristic is the chitin that is in their cell walls. *Protists* are organisms that are not classified as animals, plants, or fungi; they are unicellular; and they do not form tissues.

Cell Cycle

The *cell cycle* is the process by which a cell divides and duplicates itself. There are two processes by which a cell can divide itself: mitosis and meiosis. In *mitosis*, the daughter cells that are produced from parental cell division are identical to each other and the parent. *Meiosis* is a unique process that involves two stages of cell division and produces *haploid cells*, which are cells containing only one set of chromosomes, from *diploid parent cells*, which are cells containing two sets of chromosomes.

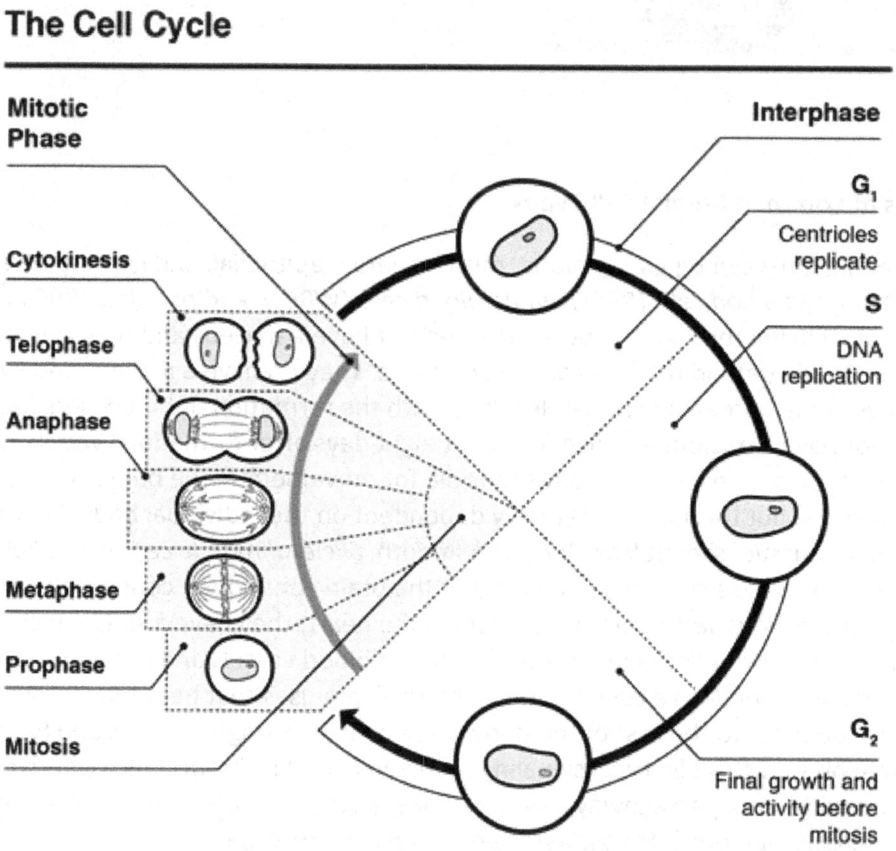

Mitosis

Mitosis can be broken down into five stages: prophase, prometaphase, metaphase, anaphase, and telophase.

- *Prophase*: During this phase, the mitotic spindles begin to form from centrosomes and microtubules. As the microtubules lengthen, the centrosomes move farther away from each other. The nucleolus disappears and the chromatin fibers begin to coil up and form chromosomes. Two sister chromatids, which are two copies of one chromosome, are joined together.

- *Prometaphase*: The nuclear envelope begins to break down and the microtubules enter the nuclear area. Each pair of chromatin fibers develops a *kinetochore*, which is a specialized protein structure in the middle of the adjoined fibers. The chromosomes are further condensed.
- *Metaphase*: In this stage, the microtubules are stretched across the cell and the centrosomes are at opposite ends of the cell. The chromosomes align at the *metaphase plate*, which is a plane that is exactly between the two centrosomes. The kinetochore of each chromosome is attached to the kinetochore of the microtubules that are stretching from each centrosome to the metaphase plate.
- *Anaphase*: The sister chromatids break apart, forming full-fledged chromosomes. The two daughter chromosomes move to opposite ends of the cell. The microtubules shorten toward opposite ends of the cell as well, and the cell elongates.
- *Telophase*: Two nuclei form at each end of the cell and nuclear envelopes begin to form around each nucleus. The nucleoli reappear and the chromosomes become less condensed. The microtubules are broken down by the cell and mitosis is complete.

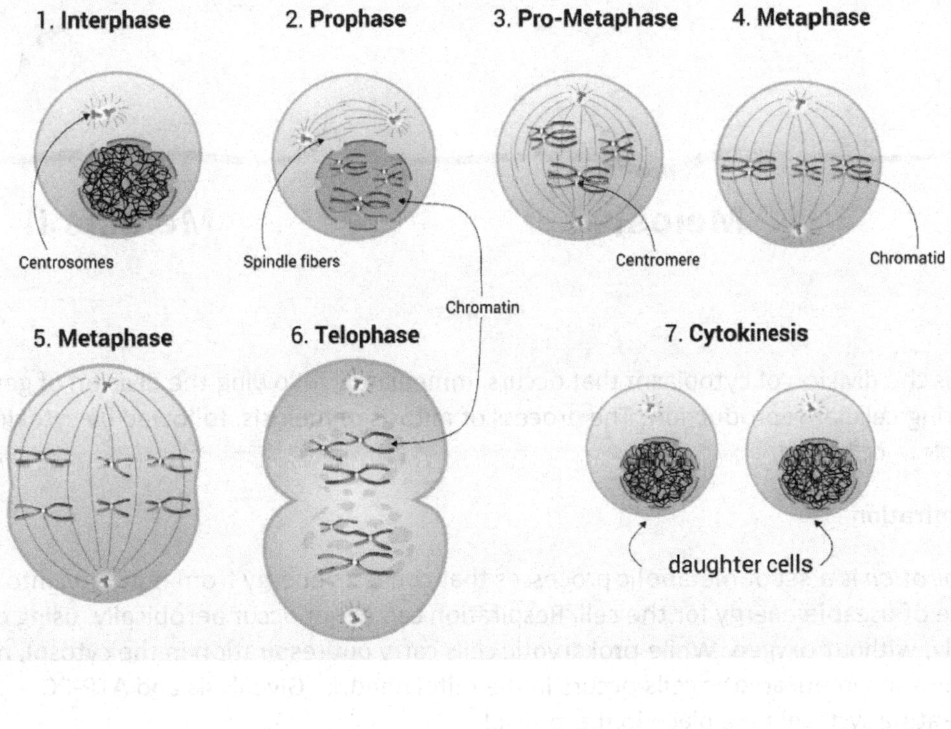

Meiosis

Meiosis is a type of cell division in which the daughter cells have half as many sets of chromosomes as the parent cell. In addition, one parent cell produces four daughter cells. Meiosis has the same phases as mitosis, except that they occur twice—once in meiosis I and once in meiosis II. The diploid parent has two sets of chromosomes, set A and set B. During meiosis I, each chromosome set duplicates, producing a second set of A chromosomes and a second set of B chromosomes, and the cell splits into two. Each cell contains two sets of chromosomes. Next, during meiosis II, the two intermediate daughter cells divide again, producing four total haploid cells that each contain one set of chromosomes. Two of the haploid cells each contain one chromosome of set A and the other two cells each contain one chromosome of set B.

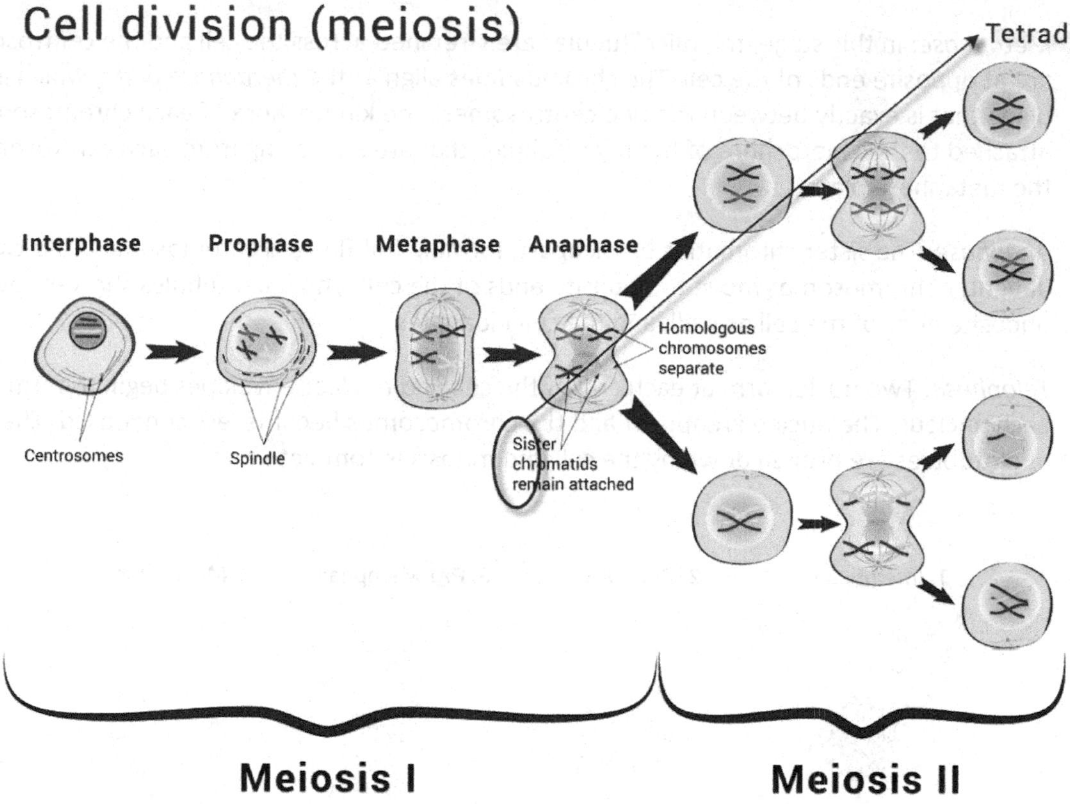

Cytokinesis

Cytokinesis is the division of cytoplasm that occurs immediately following the division of genetic material during cellular reproduction. The process of mitosis or meiosis, followed by cytokinesis, makes up the complete cell cycle.

Cellular Respiration

Cellular respiration is a set of metabolic processes that converts energy from nutrients into ATP, which is the molecule of useable energy for the cell. Respiration can either occur aerobically, using oxygen, or anaerobically, without oxygen. While prokaryotic cells carry out respiration in the cytosol, most of the aerobic respiration in eukaryotic cells occurs in the mitochondria. Glycolysis and ATP-PC (phosphocreatine system) take place in the cytosol.

<u>Anaerobic Respiration</u>
Some organisms do not live in oxygen-rich environments and must find alternate methods of respiration. *Anaerobic respiration* occurs in certain prokaryotic organisms, and while it does occur in eukaryotic organisms, it happens in them much less frequently. The organisms utilize an electron

transport chain similar to that of the aerobic respiration pathway; the terminal acceptor molecule, however, is an electronegative substance that is not an oxygen molecule. Some bacteria, for example, use the sulfate ion (SO_4^{2-}) as the final electron accepting molecule and the resulting byproduct is hydrogen sulfide (H_2S), instead of water.

Aerobic Respiration

There are two main steps in *aerobic cellular respiration*: the *citric acid cycle*, also known as the *Krebs cycle*, and *oxidative phosphorylation*. A process called *glycolysis* converts glucose molecules into pyruvate molecules and those pyruvate molecules then enter the citric acid cycle. The pyruvate molecules are broken down to produce ATP, as well as NADH and $FADH_2$—molecules that are used energetically to drive the next step of oxidative phosphorylation. During this phase of aerobic respiration, an electron transport chain pumps electrons and protons across the inner mitochondrial matrix. The electrons are accepted by an oxygen molecule, and water is produced. This process then fuels *chemiosmosis*, which helps convert ADP molecules to ATP. The total number of ATP molecules generated through aerobic respiration can be as many as thirty-eight, if none are lost during the process. Aerobic respiration is up to fifteen times more efficient than anaerobic respiration.

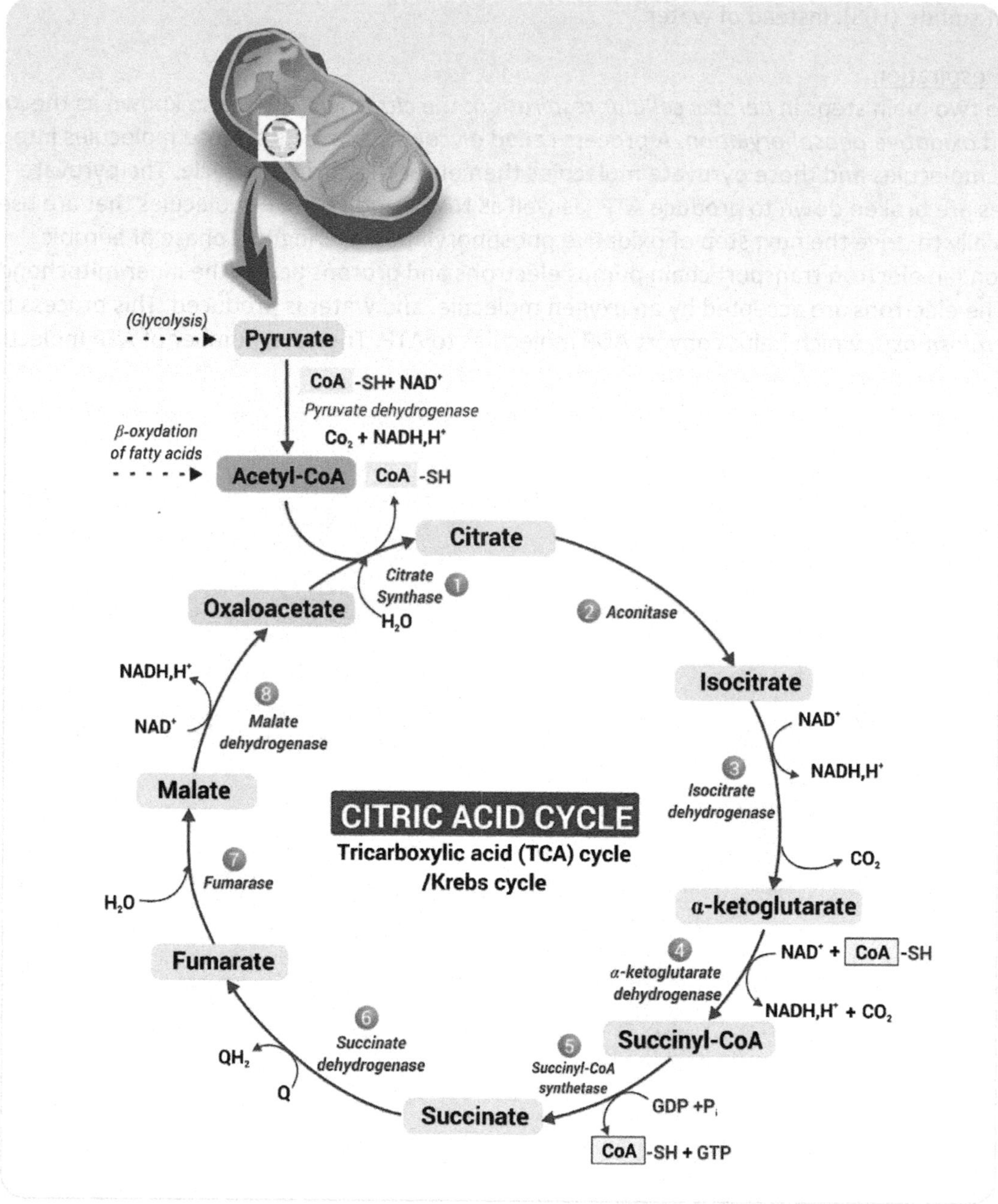

Photosynthesis

Photosynthesis is the process of converting light energy into chemical energy, which is then stored in sugar and other organic molecules. It can be divided into two stages called the *light reactions* and the *Calvin cycle*. The photosynthetic process takes place in the chloroplast in plants. Inside the chloroplast, there are membranous sacs called *thylakoids*. *Chlorophyll* is a green pigment that lives in the thylakoid membranes, absorbs photons from light, and starts an electron transport chain in order to produce energy in the form of ATP and NADPH. The ATP and NADPH produced from the light reactions are used as energy to form organic molecules in the Calvin cycle.

The Calvin cycle takes place in the *stroma*, or inner space, of the chloroplasts. The process consumes nine ATP molecules and six NADPH molecules for every one molecule of glyceraldehyde 3-phosphate (G3P) that it produces. The G3P that is produced can be used as the starting material to build larger organic compounds, such as glucose. The complex series of reactions that takes place in photosynthesis can be simplified into the following equation: $6CO_2 + 12\ H_2O + \text{Light Energy} \rightarrow C_6H_{12}O_6 + 6O_2 + 6H_2O$.

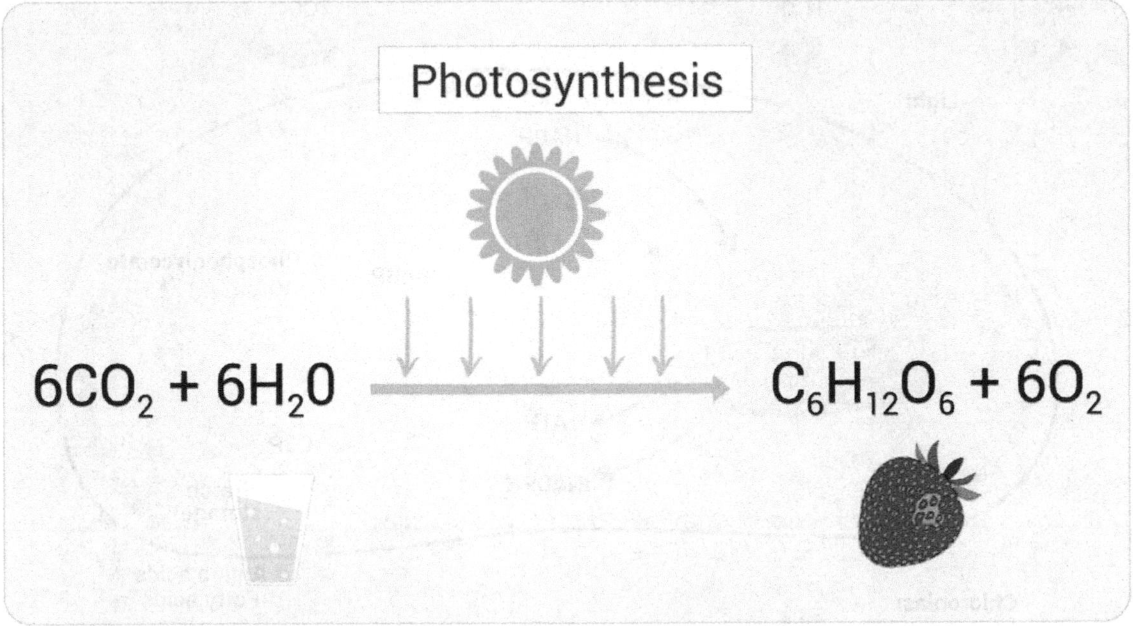

Basically, carbon dioxide and water mix with light energy inside the chloroplast to produce organic molecules, oxygen, and water. It is interesting to note that water is on both sides of the equation. Twelve water molecules are consumed during this process and six water molecules are newly formed as byproducts. Although the Calvin cycle itself is not dependent on light energy, both steps of photosynthesis usually occur during daylight because the Calvin cycle is dependent upon the ATP and NADPH that is produced by the light reactions.

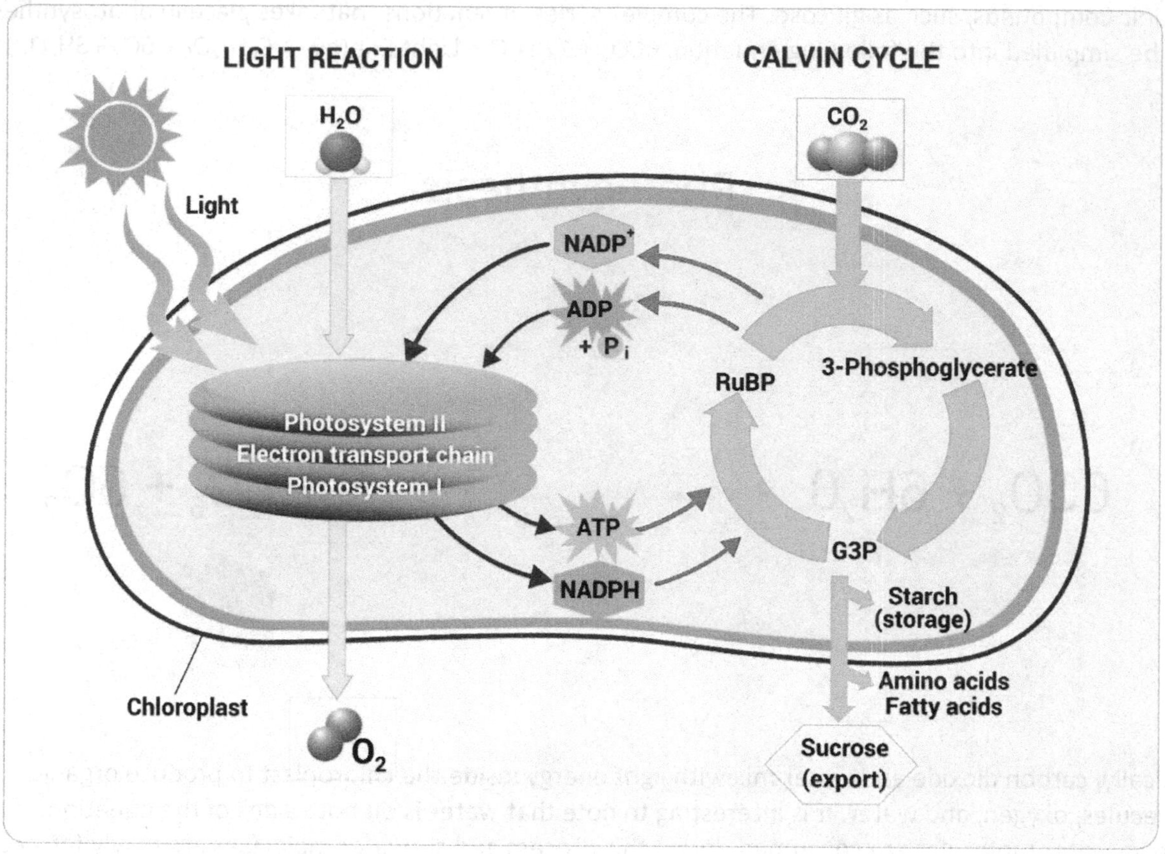

Biological Molecules

Repeating units of monomers (small molecules that bond with identical small molecules) that are linked together are called *polymers*. The most important polymers found in all living things can be divided into five categories: nucleic acids (such as DNA), carbohydrates, proteins, lipids, and enzymes. Carbon (C), hydrogen (H), oxygen (O), nitrogen (N), sulfur (S), and phosphorus (P) are the major elements of most biological molecules. Carbon is a common backbone of large molecules because of its ability to bond to four different atoms.

<u>DNA and RNA</u>

Nucleotides consist of a five-carbon sugar, a nitrogen-containing base, and one or more phosphate groups. *Deoxyribonucleic acid (DNA)* is made up of two strands of nucleotides coiled together in a double-helix structure. It plays a major role in enabling living organisms to pass their genetic information and complex components on to subsequent generations. There are four nitrogenous bases that make up DNA: adenine, thymine, guanine, and cytosine. Adenine always pairs with thymine, and guanine always pairs with cytosine. *Ribonucleic acid (RNA)* is often made up of only one strand of nucleotides folded in on itself. Like DNA, RNA has four nitrogenous bases; however, in RNA, thymine is replaced by uracil.

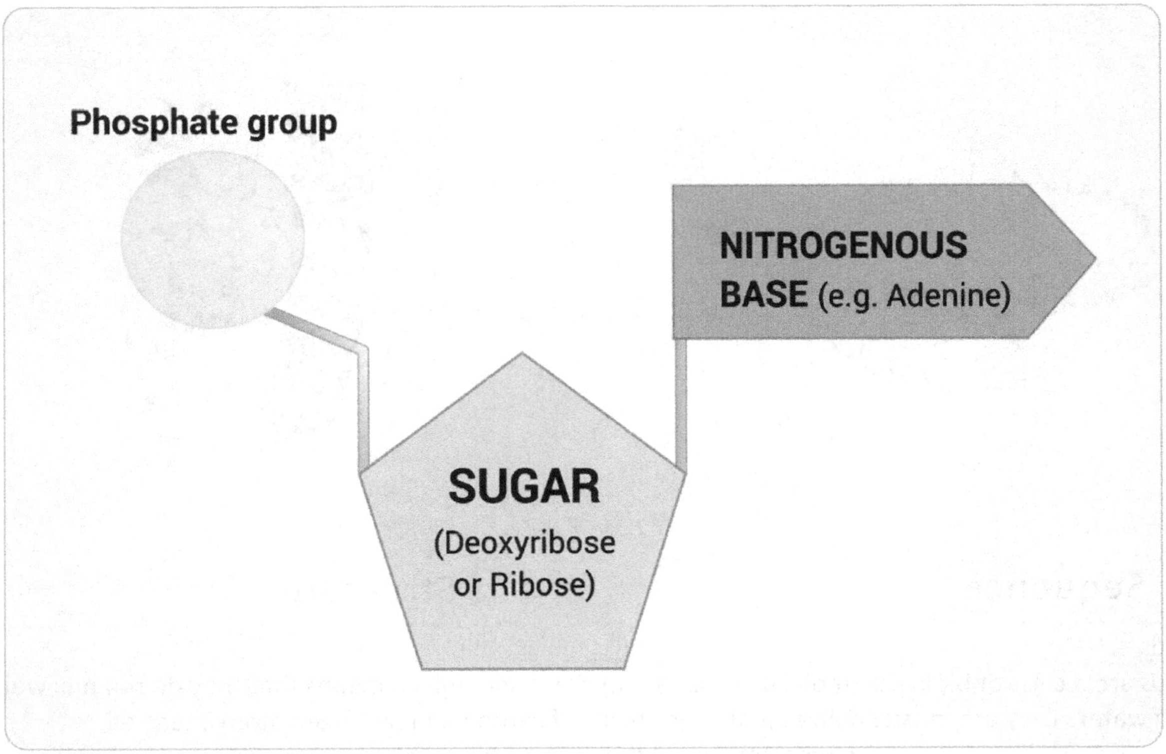

<u>Carbohydrates</u>
Carbohydrates consist of sugars and polymers of sugars, such as starches, which make up the cell walls of plants. The simplest sugar is called a *monosaccharide* and has the molecular formula of CH_2O, or a multiple of that formula. Monosaccharides are important molecules for cellular respiration. Their carbon skeleton can also be used to rebuild new small molecules. *Polysaccharides* are made up of a few hundred to a few thousand monosaccharides linked together.

<u>Proteins</u>
Proteins are essential for almost all functions in living beings. All proteins are made from a set of twenty *amino acids* that are linked in *unbranched polymers*. The amino acids are linked by *peptide bonds*, and polymers of amino acids are called *polypeptides*. These polypeptides, either individually or in linked combination with each other, fold up and form coils of biologically functional molecules.

There are four levels of protein structure: primary, secondary, tertiary, and quaternary. The *primary structure* is the sequence of amino acids, similar to the letters in a long word. The *secondary structure* comprises the folds and coils that are formed by hydrogen bonding between the slightly charged atoms of the polypeptide backbone. *Tertiary structure* is the overall shape of the molecule that results from the interactions between the side chains that are linked to the polypeptide backbone. *Quaternary structure* is the overall protein structure that occurs when a protein is made up of two or more polypeptide chains.

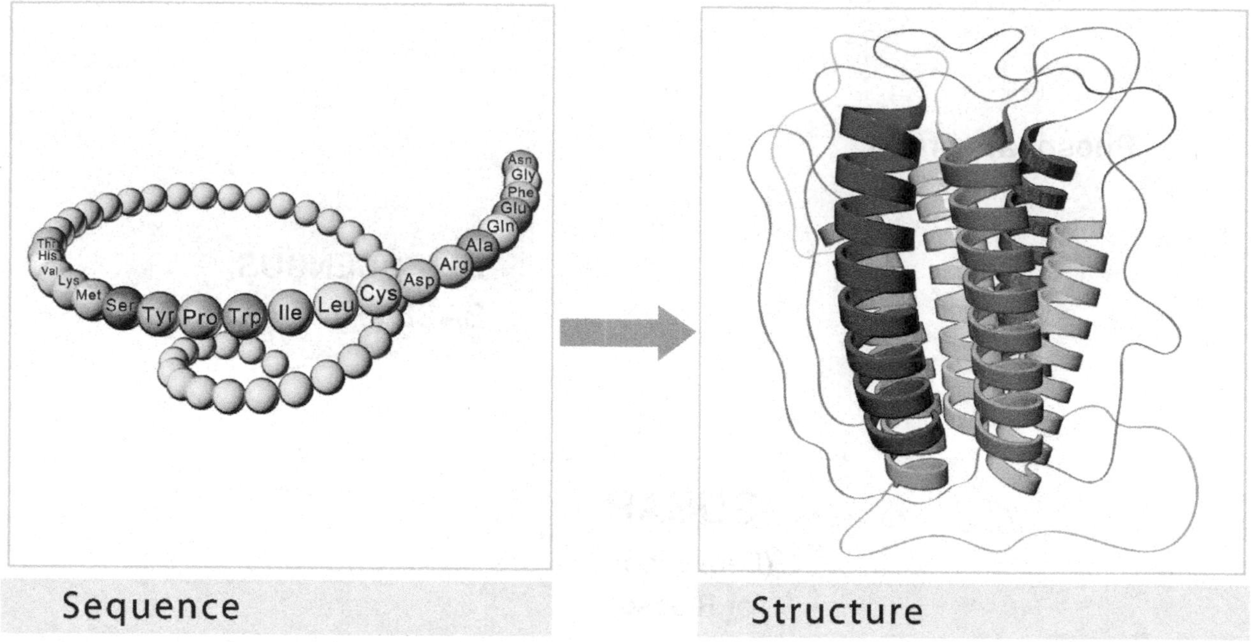

Lipids

Lipids are a class of biological molecules that are *hydrophobic*, which means that they do not mix well with water. They are mostly made up of large chains of carbon and hydrogen atoms, termed *hydrocarbon chains*. The three most important types of lipids are fats, phospholipids, and steroids.

Fats are made up of two types of smaller molecules: three fatty acids and one glycerol molecule. Saturated fats do not have double bonds between the carbons in the fatty acid chain, such as glycerol, pictured below. They are fairly straight molecules and can pack together closely, so they form solids at room temperature. Unsaturated fats have one or more double bonds between carbons in the fatty acid chain. Since they cannot pack together as tightly as saturated fats, they take up more space and are called oils. They remain liquid at room temperature.

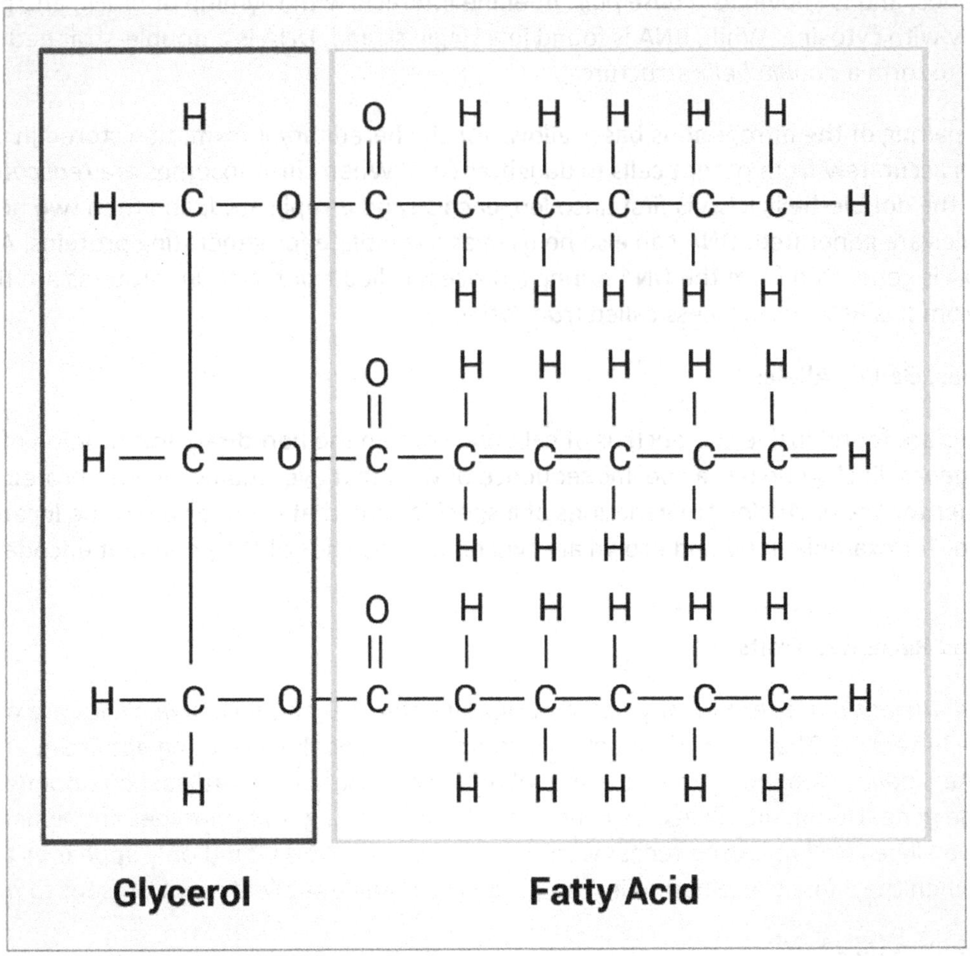

Phospholipids are made up of two fatty acid molecules linked to one glycerol molecule. When phospholipids are mixed with water, they inherently create double-layered structures, called *bilayers*, which shield their hydrophobic regions from the water molecules.

Steroids are lipids that consist of four fused carbon rings. They can mix in between the phospholipid bilayer cell membrane and help maintain its structure, as well as aid in cell signaling.

<u>Enzymes</u>

Enzymes are biological molecules that accelerate the rate of chemical reactions by lowering the activation energy needed to make the reaction proceed. Although most enzymes can be classified as proteins, some are ribonucleic acid (RNA) molecules. Enzymes function by interacting with a specific substrate in order to create a different molecule, or product. Most reactions in cells need enzymes to make them occur at rates fast enough to sustain life.

Structure and Function of DNA and RNA

DNA and RNA are made up of *nucleotides*, which are formed from a five-carbon sugar, a nitrogenous base, and one or more phosphate group. While DNA is made up of the sugar deoxyribose, RNA is made up of the sugar ribose. Deoxyribose has one fewer oxygen atom than ribose. DNA and RNA each comprise four nitrogenous bases, three of which they have in common: adenine, guanine, and cytosine. Thymine is found only in DNA and uracil is found only in RNA. Each base has a specific pairing formed by hydrogen bonds, and is known as a *base pair*. Adenine interacts with thymine or uracil, and guanine interacts only with cytosine. While RNA is found in a single strand, DNA is a double-stranded molecule that coils up to form a *double helix* structure.

The specific pairing of the nitrogenous bases allows for the hereditary information stored in DNA to be passed down accurately from parent cells to daughter cells. When chromosomes are *replicated* during cell division, the double-helix DNA is first uncoiled, each strand is replicated, and then two new identical DNA molecules are generated. DNA can also be used as a template for generating proteins. A *single-stranded* RNA is generated from the DNA during a process called *transcription*; proteins are then generated from this RNA in a process called *translation*.

Chromosomes, Genes, Alleles

Chromosomes are found inside the nucleus of cells and contain the hereditary information of the cell in the form of *genes*. Each gene has a specific sequence of DNA that eventually encodes proteins and results in inherited traits. *Alleles* are variations of a specific gene that occur at the same location on the chromosome. For example, blue and brown are two different alleles of the gene that encodes for eye color.

Dominant and Recessive Traits

In genetics, *dominant alleles* are mostly noted in capital letters (A) and *recessive alleles* are mostly noted in lower case letters (a). There are three possible combinations of alleles among dominant and recessive alleles: AA, Aa, and aa. Dominant traits are phenotypes that appear when at least one dominant allele is present in the gene. Dominant alleles are considered to have stronger phenotypes and, when mixed with recessive alleles, will mask the recessive trait. The recessive trait would only appear as the phenotype when the allele combination is "aa" because a dominant allele is not present to mask it.

Mendelian Inheritance

A monk named Gregor Mendel is referred to as the father of genetics. He was responsible for coming up with one of the first models of inheritance in the 1860s. His model included two laws to determine which traits are inherited. These laws still apply today, even after genetics has been studied much more in depth.

- *The Law of Segregation*: Each characteristic has two versions that can be inherited. When two parent cells form daughter cells, the two alleles of the gene segregate and each daughter cell can inherit only one of the alleles from each parent.

- *The Law of Independent Assortment*: The alleles for different traits are inherited independent of one another. In other words, the biological selection of one allele by a daughter cell is not linked to the biological selection of an allele for a different trait by the same daughter cell. The genotype that is inherited is the alleles that are encoded on the gene, and the phenotype is the outward appearance of the physical trait for that gene. For example, "A" is the dominant allele for brown eyes and "a" is the recessive allele for blue eyes; the phenotype of brown eyes would occur for two different genotypes: both "AA" and "Aa."

Punnett Squares

For simple genetic combinations, a *Punnett square* can be used to assess the phenotypic ratios of subsequent generations. In a 2 x 2 cell square, one parent's alleles are set up in columns and the other parent's alleles are set up in rows. The resulting allele combinations are shown in the four internal cells.

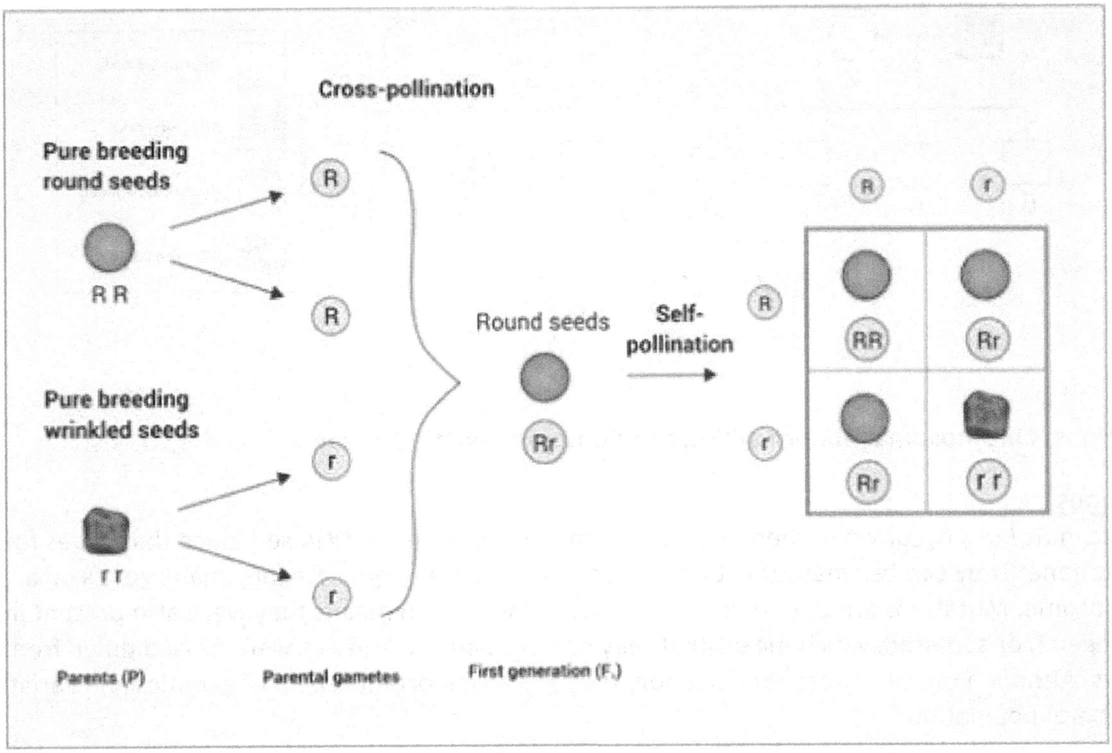

Pedigree

For existing populations where genetic crosses cannot be controlled, phenotype information can be collected over several generations and a *pedigree analysis* can be done to investigate the dominant and recessive characteristics of specific traits. There are several rules to follow when determining the pedigree of a trait. For dominant alleles:

- Affected individuals have at least one affected parent;
- The phenotype appears in every generation; and
- If both parents are unaffected, their offspring will always be unaffected.

For recessive alleles:

- Unaffected parents can have affected offspring; and
- Affected offspring are male and female.

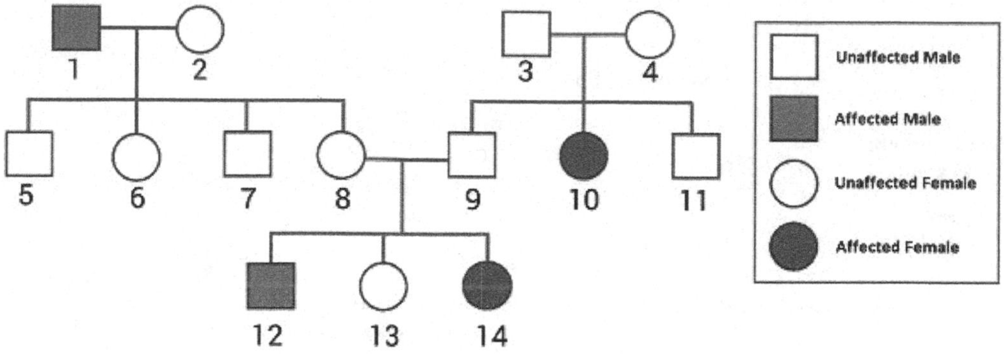

Mutations, Chromosomal Abnormalities, and Common Genetic Disorders

Mutations

Genetic *mutations* occur when there is a permanent alteration in the DNA sequence that codes for a specific gene. They can be small, affecting only one base pair, or large, affecting many genes on a chromosome. Mutations are classified as either hereditary, which means they were also present in the parent gene, or acquired, which means that they occurred after the genes were passed down from the parents. Although mutations are not common, they are an important aspect of genetics and variation in the general population.

Chromosomal Abnormalities and Common Genetic Disorders

Structural chromosomal abnormalities are mutations that affect a large chromosomal segment of more than one gene. This often occurs due to an error in cell division. Acute myelogenous leukemia is caused by a *translocation error*, which is when a segment of one chromosome is moved to another chromosome.

There can also be an abnormal number of chromosomes, which is referred to as *aneuploidy*. Down syndrome is an example of an aneuploidy in which there are three copies of chromosome 21 instead of two copies. Turner syndrome is another example of aneuploidy, in which a female is completely or partially missing an X chromosome. Without the second X chromosome, these females do not develop all of the typical female physical characteristics and are unable to bear children.

Mechanisms of Evolution

Evolution is the concept that there is one common ancestor for all living organisms, and, over time, genetic variation and mutations cause the development of different species. Charles Darwin came up with a scientific model of evolution based on the idea that individuals within a population can have longer lives (better survival) and higher reproduction rates based on certain specific traits that they have inherited, called *natural selection*. The variation of a trait that enhances survival and reproduction in the environment is the one that gets passed on. The survival and inheritance of these traits through many subsequent generations causes a change in the overall population. The traits that are more advantageous for survival and reproduction become more common in subsequent generations and increase the diversity of the population. For example, when there was a drought in the Galapagos

Islands, the finches with large beaks became more populous because they were able to survive on the larger, rougher seeds that were remaining.

Speciation and Isolation Methods

Speciation is the method by which one species splits into two or more species due to either geographic separation, called allopatric speciation, or a reduction in gene flow between varying members of the population, called sympatric speciation. In *allopatric speciation*, one population is divided into two subpopulations. For example, if a drought occurs and a large lake becomes divided into two smaller lakes, each lake is left with its own population that cannot intermingle with the population of the other lake. When the genes of these two subpopulations are no longer mixing with each other, new mutations can arise and natural selection can take place.

In *sympatric speciation*, gene flow in the population is reduced by polyploidy, sexual selection, and habitat differentiation. *Polyploidy* is more common in plants than animals and results when cell division during reproduction creates an extra set of chromosomes. In *sexual selection*, organisms of one sex choose their mate of the opposite sex based on certain traits. If there is high selection for two extreme variations of a trait, sympatric speciation may occur. *Habitat differentiation* occurs when a subpopulation exploits a resource that is not used by the parent population. Both allopatric and sympatric speciation can occur quickly or slowly, and may involve just a few gene changes or many gene changes between the new species.

One important distinguishing factor in the formation of two species is their *reproductive isolation*. Species are characterized by their members' ability to breed and produce viable offspring. When speciation occurs and new species are formed, there must have been a biological barrier that prevented the two species from producing viable offspring.

Following speciation, there are two types of *reproductive barriers* that keep the two populations from mating with each other. These are classified as either prezygotic barriers or postzygotic barriers. *Prezygotic barriers* prevent fertilization via habitat isolation, temporal isolation, and behavioral isolation. Through habitat isolation, two species may inhabit the same area but don't often encounter each other. *Temporal isolation* is when species breed at different times of the day, during different seasons, or during different years, so their mating patterns never coincide. *Behavioral isolation* refers to mating rituals that prevent an organism from recognizing a different species as potential mate.

Other prezygotic barriers block fertilization after a mating attempt. *Mechanical isolation* occurs when anatomical differences prevent fertilization. *Gametic isolation* occurs when the gametes of two species are incompatible.

Supporting Evidence

<u>The Fossil Record</u>
Fossils are the preserved remains of animals and organisms from the distant past. They provide evidence of evolution and can elucidate the homology of both living and extinct species. Looking at the *fossil record* over time can help identify how quickly or slowly evolutionary changes occurred, and can also help match those changes to environmental changes that were occurring concurrently.

<u>Comparative Genetics</u>
In *comparative genetics*, different organisms are compared at a genetic level to look for similarities and differences. DNA sequence, genes, gene order, and other structural features are among the features

that may be analyzed in order to look for evolutionary relationships and common ancestors between the organisms. Comparative genetics was useful in elucidating the similarities between humans and chimpanzees and linking their evolutionary history.

Homology

Organisms that developed from a common ancestor often have similar characteristics that function differently. This similarity is known as *homology*. For example, humans, cats, whales, and bats all have bones arranged in the same manner from their shoulders to their digits. However, the bones form arms in humans, forelegs in cats, flippers in whales, and wings in bats, and these forelimbs are used for lifting, walking, swimming, and flying, respectively. The similarity of the bone structure shows a common ancestry, but the functional differences are the product of evolution.

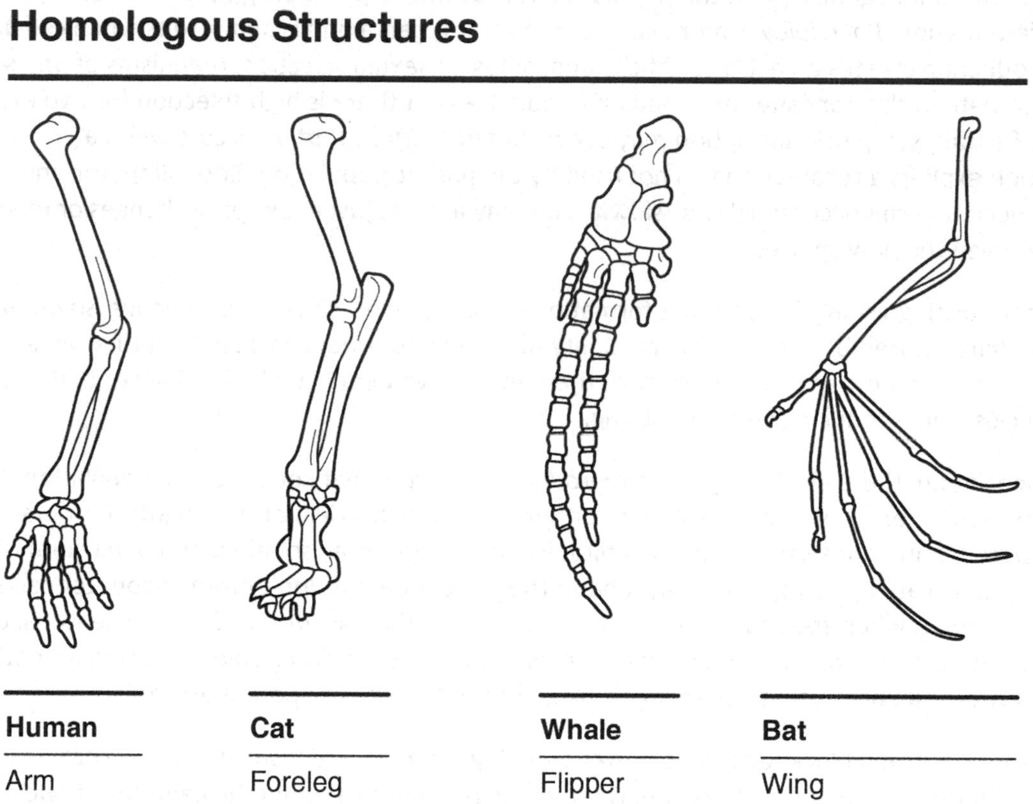

Classification Schemes

Taxonomy is the science behind the biological names of organisms. Biologists often refer to organisms by their Latin scientific names to avoid confusion with common names, such as with fish. Jellyfish, crayfish, and silverfish all have the word “fish” in their name, but belong to three different species. In the eighteenth century, Carl Linnaeus invented a naming system for species that included using the Latin scientific name of a species, called the *binomial*, which has two parts: the *genus*, which comes first, and the *specific epithet*, which comes second. Similar species are grouped into the same genus. The Linnean system is the commonly used taxonomic system today and, moving from comprehensive similarities to more general similarities, classifies organisms into their species, genus, family, order, class, phylum, kingdom, and domain. *Homo sapiens* is the Latin scientific name for humans.

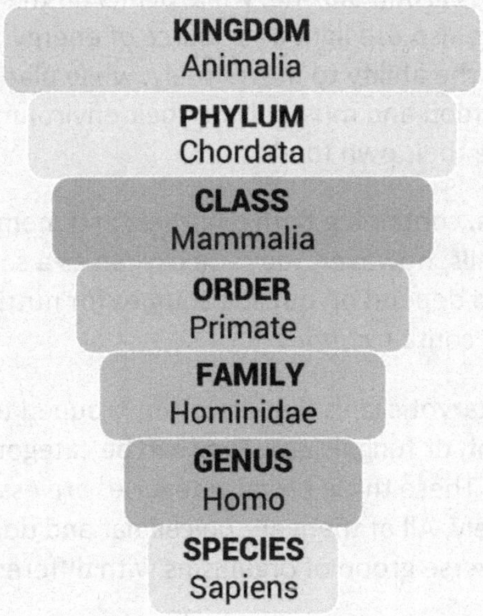

Phylogenetic trees are branching diagrams that represent the evolutionary history of a species. The branch points most often match the classification groups set forth by the Linnean system. Using this system helps elucidate the relationship between different groups of organisms. The diagram below is that of an empty phylogenetic tree:

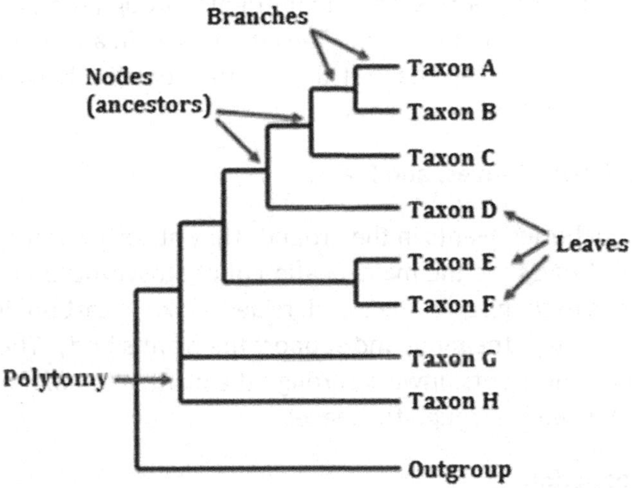

Each branch of the tree represents the divergence of two species from a common ancestor. For example, the coyote is known as Canis latrans and the gray wolf is known as Canis lupus. Their common ancestor, the Canis lepophagus, which is now extinct, is where their shared genus derived.

Characteristics of Bacteria, Animals, Plants, Fungi, and Protists

As discussed earlier, there are two distinct types of cells that make up most living organisms: prokaryotic and eukaryotic. Bacteria (and archaea) are classified as prokaryotic cells, whereas animal, plant, fungi, and protist cells are classified as eukaryotic cells.

Although animal cells and plant cells are both eukaryotic, they each have several distinguishing characteristics. *Animal cells* are surrounded by a plasma membrane, while *plant cells* have a cell wall made up of cellulose that provides more structure and an extra layer of protection for the cell. Animals use oxygen to breathe and give off carbon dioxide, while plants do the opposite—they take in carbon dioxide and give off oxygen. Plants also use light as a source of energy. Animals have highly developed sensory and nervous systems and the ability to move freely, while plants lack both abilities. Animals, however, cannot make their own food and must rely on their environment to provide sufficient nutrition, whereas plants do make their own food.

Fungal cells are typical eukaryotes, containing both a nucleus and membrane-bound organelles. They have a cell wall, similar to plant cells; however, they use oxygen as a source of energy and cannot perform photosynthesis. They also depend on outside sources for nutrition and cannot produce their own food. Of note, their cell walls contain *chitin.*

Protists are a group of diverse eukaryotic cells that are often grouped together because they do not fit into the categories of animal, plant, or fungal cells. They can be categorized into three broad categories: protozoa, protophyta, and molds. These three broad categories are essentially "animal -like," "plant-like," and "fungus-like," respectively. All of them are unicellular and do not form tissues. Besides this simple similarity, protists are a diverse group of organisms with different characteristics, life cycles, and cellular structures.

Characteristics of Vascular and Nonvascular Plants

Plants that have an extensive vascular transport system are called *vascular plants*. Those plants without a transport system are called *nonvascular plants*. Approximately ninety-three percent of plants that are currently living and reproducing are vascular plants. The cells that comprise the vascular tissue in vascular plants form tubes that transport water and nutrients through the entire plant. Nonvascular plants include mosses, liverworts, and hornworts. They do not retain any water; instead, they transport water using other specialized tissue. They have structures that look like leaves, but are actually just single sheets of cells without a cuticle or stomata.

Structure and Function of Roots, Leaves, and Stems

Roots are responsible for anchoring plants in the ground. They absorb water and nutrients and transport them up through the plant. *Leaves* are the main location of photosynthesis. They contain *stomata*, which are pores used for gas exchange, on their underside to take in carbon dioxide and release oxygen. *Stems* transport materials through the plant and support the plant's body. They contain *xylem*, which conducts water and dissolved nutrients upward through the plant, and *phloem*, which conducts sugars and metabolic products downward through the leaves.

Asexual and Sexual Reproduction

Plants can generate future generations through both asexual and sexual reproduction. Asexually, plants can go through an artificial reproductive technique called *budding*, in which parts from two or more plants of the same species are joined together with the hope that they will begin to grow as a single plant.

Sexual reproduction of flowers can happen in a couple of ways. *Angiosperms* are flowering plants that have seeds. The flowers have male parts that make pollen and female parts that contain ovules. Wind, insects, and other animals carry the pollen from the male part to the female part in a process called *pollination*. Once the ovules are pollinated, or fertilized, they develop into seeds that then develop into new plants. In many angiosperms, the flowers develop into fruit, such as oranges, or even hard nuts, which protect the seeds inside of them.

Nonvascular plants reproduce by sexual reproduction involving *spores*. Parent plants send out spores that contain a set of chromosomes. The spores develop into sperm or eggs, and fertilization is similar to that in humans. Sperm travel to the egg through water in the environment. An embryo forms and then a new plant grows from the embryo. Generally, this happens in damp places.

Growth

Germination is the process of a plant growing from a seed or spore, such as when a seedling sprouts from a seed or a sporeling grows from a spore. Plants then grow by *elongation*. Plant cell walls are modified by the hormone auxin, which allows for cell elongation. This process is regulated by light and phytohormones, which are plant hormones that regulate growth, so plants are often seen growing toward the sun.

Uptake and Transport of Nutrients and Water

Plant roots are responsible for bringing nutrients and water into the plant from the ground. The nutrients are not used as food for the plant, but rather to maintain the plant's health so that the plant can make its own food during photosynthesis. The xylem and phloem in the stem help with transport of water and other substances throughout the plant.

Responses to Stimuli

Because plants have limited mobility, they often respond to stimuli through changes in their growth behavior. *Tropism* is a response to stimuli that causes the plant to grow toward or away from the stimuli:

- *Phototropism*: A reaction to light that causes plants to grow toward the source of the light
- *Thermotropism*: A response to changes in temperature
- *Hydrotropism*: A response to a change in water concentration
- *Gravitropism*: A response to gravity that causes roots to follow the pull of gravity and grow downward, but also causes plant shoots to act against gravity and grow upward

General Terminology

Anatomy is the study of external and internal body parts and structures, and their physical relationships to each other. Physiology is the study of the function of living organisms and their body parts. Understanding these areas of study is easier after learning the specific terms relating to the field.

Types of Anatomy and Physiology

Gross Anatomy: The study of large structures and features visible to the naked eye. It is also known as macroscopic anatomy.

Microscopic: The study of structures and their functions that can only be seen with magnification, such as through a magnifying glass or microscope.

Systemic: The study of a major organ system.

Developmental: The study of the physical changes that occur between conception and physical maturity. It includes gross anatomy, microscopic anatomy and physiology, because of the broad range of anatomical structures that undergo changes during this time.

Comparative: The study of structural organization and their functions among different types of animals. Animals that look different now but have the same internal structures with similar functions may have an evolutionary relationship.

Pathophysiology: The study of the effects of diseases on how an organ or organ system functions.

Body Positions

Anatomical Position: The person stands with legs together, feet flat on the floor, and hands at the sides with palms facing forward.

Supine: The person is lying down, face up, in the anatomical position.

Prone: The person is lying face down in the anatomical position.

Regional and Directional Terms

Anterior: The front; can also mean before.

Ventral: The belly side.

Posterior: The back; can also mean behind.

Dorsal: The back side.

Cranial or Cephalic: Toward the head.

Superior: Above; can also mean at a higher level.

Caudal: The tail.

Inferior: Below; can also mean at a lower level; can also mean toward the feet.

Medial: Toward the midline.

Lateral: Away from the midline.

Proximal: Toward an attached base.

Distal: Away from an attached base.

Sections of the Body

Transverse or horizontal: A horizontal section in the anatomical position that separates superior and inferior portions of the body.

Sagittal: A vertical section in the anatomical position that separates right and left portions of the body. A midsagittal section separates the body into equal parts, while a parasagittal section separates it into unequal parts.

Frontal or coronal: A vertical section in the anatomical position that separates the anterior and posterior portions of the body.

Histology

Histology is the examination of specialized cells and cell groups that perform a specific function by working together. Although there are trillions of cells in the human body, there are only 200 different types of cells. Groups of cells form biological tissues, and tissues combine to form organs, such as the heart and kidney. Organs are structures that have many different functions that are vital to living creatures. There are four primary types of tissue: epithelial, connective, muscle, and neural. Each tissue type has specific characteristics that enable organs and organ systems to function properly.

Epithelial Tissue

Epithelial tissue includes epithelia and glands. Epithelia are the layers of cells that cover exposed surfaces and line internal cavities and passageways. Glands are structures that are involved in secretion of fluids. Epithelia do not contain blood vessels and can often regenerate quickly to replace dead and damaged cells.

Connective Tissue

Connective tissue fills internal spaces and is not exposed to the outside of the body. It provides structural support for the body and stores energy. Fluid can be transported by connective tissue between different regions of the body. This type of tissue is also a protective barrier for delicate organs and for the body against microorganisms.

Muscle Tissue

Muscle tissue has characteristics that allow motion. Skeletal muscles are long fibers of actin and myosin that slide past each other to cause a contraction, which shortens the muscle. They are filled with mitochondria, because they expend a lot of energy. Smooth muscle tissue is structured differently, because its movement is in the form of peristalsis. For example, the esophagus moves food in a wave-like contraction, as opposed to a shortening of muscle to bring structures together. Smooth muscle tissues make up internal organs, with the exception of the heart, which is composed of thick, contracting muscle tissue.

Neural Tissue

Neural tissue conducts electrical impulses which help send information and instructions throughout the body. Most of it is concentrated in the brain and spinal cord. The changes in frequency and patterns of the impulse are important distinctions in the messages being sent. Its structure is composed of message-receiving projections called dendrites and a long, myelinated axon. The myelin sheath surrounds the axon to conduct the action potential, ultimately causing neurotransmitter release at the synapse, or the boundary between the axon of one cell and the dendrite of another.

Mitosis and Meiosis

The human body is made of trillions of cells. Cell division and replication are responsible for growth of the body. There are many different types of cells in the body, and most undergo mitosis to divide and replicate. Mitosis also occurs to replenish damaged and dying cells. In mitosis, one cell replicates its own genetic material and splits into two identical daughter cells. It is an important part of both growth and the maintenance of homeostasis within the body.

Although the majority of cells undergo mitosis when replicating, gamete cells (reproductive cells) undergo a more complicated process, called meiosis. In the human body, the gametes are the egg and the sperm. Human reproduction happens by sexual reproduction, which means one gamete fertilizes another gamete. The resulting cell is not identical to either of its parent cells, which is in contrast to daughter cells produced by mitosis. Eggs and sperm cells contain twenty-three chromosomes each. They combine to form a diploid cell that contains all forty-six chromosomes. The diploid cell replicates its chromosomes and splits into two cells, each containing forty-six chromosomes. Those two cells split again to create four cells, each containing twenty-three chromosomes. None of the daughter gamete cells are identical to either of the parent gamete cells. During the process of meiosis, the chromosomes from each parent get mixed together, then split into the daughter gamete cells randomly. This process explains why children are not exactly identical to their parents, but instead have characteristics from each of them.

Membranes

Membranes are formed by the combination of epithelia and connective tissues. They consist of an underlying connective tissue layer covered by an epithelial sheet, and together they cover and protect structures and tissues in the body. There are four types of membranes: mucous, serous, cutaneous, and synovial. Mucous membranes line cavities that connect with the exterior part of the body and form a barrier against pathogens. The epithelial layer is always moist with mucus or glandular secretions. The loose connective tissue layer is called the lamina propria and connects the epithelium to the underlying structures. Serous membranes consist of a mesothelium connected to loose connective tissue. These membranes line the subdivisions of the ventral body cavity. They are very thin and are firmly attached to both the body wall and the organs they are covering. Serous membranes are covered in fluid, called transudate, which helps minimize friction between the organs and the body wall and is the main function of the membrane. The cutaneous membrane is also known as skin. It consists of epithelium and an underlying layer of loose connective tissue that is reinforced by a layer of dense connective tissue and covers the entire surface of the body. It is a thick membrane and is usually dry. Synovial membranes consist of large areas of loose connective tissue bound by an incomplete layer of squamous or cuboidal cells. It is found between the joint capsule and joint cavity of synovial joints. Synovial fluid lubricates this area and distributes oxygen and nutrients, as well as cushions shocks at the joints.

Glands

Glands are organs that synthesize and secrete chemical substances, such as hormones, for use inside the body or discharge outside the body. There are two types of glands: endocrine and exocrine. Endocrine glands secrete hormones into the bloodstream and are important in maintaining homeostasis within the body. They do not have a duct system. Examples of endocrine glands are the pancreas, the pineal gland, the thymus gland, the pituitary gland, the thyroid gland, and the adrenal gland. Exocrine glands have ducts that are used to secrete substances to the surface of the body and can be classified into three types: apocrine, holocrine, and merocrine. In apocrine glands, part of the cell's body is lost during secretion; in holocrine glands, the whole cell body disintegrates during secretion; and in merocrine glands, cells use exocytosis to secrete fluids. Exocytosis occurs when the chemical substance is carried in a vacuole across the cell membrane for release outside of the cell. The cells remain intact in merocrine glands.

Cartilage

Cartilage is a firm gel substance that contains complex polysaccharides, called chondroitin sulfates. It contains collagen fibers, which provide tensile strength, and chondrocytes, which are cartilage cells. It is an avascular material, because the chondrocytes do not allow blood vessels to form within the fibrous network. There are three types of cartilage: hyaline cartilage, elastic cartilage, and fibrocartilage. Hyaline cartilage is the body's most common cartilage, and is made of tightly packed collagen fibers. It is tough and flexible, but is also the weakest type of cartilage. Elastic cartilage contains elastic fibers that make is very resilient and flexible. Fibrocartilage has densely woven collagen fibers that make it very durable and tough.

Integumentary System (Skin)

Skin consists of three layers: epidermis, dermis, and the hypodermis. There are four types of cells that make up the keratinized stratified squamous epithelium in the epidermis. They are keratinocytes, melanocytes, Merkel cells, and Langerhans cells. Skin is composed of many layers, starting with a basement membrane. On top of that sits the stratum germinativum, the stratum spinosum, the stratum granulosum, the stratum lucidum, and then the stratum corneum at the outer surface. Skin can be classified as thick or thin. These descriptions refer to the epidermis layer. Most of the body is covered with thin skin, but areas such as the palm of the hands are covered with thick skin. The dermis consists of a superficial papillary layer and a deeper reticular layer. The papillary layer is made of loose connective tissue, containing capillaries and the axons of sensory neurons. The reticular layer is a meshwork of tightly packed irregular connective tissue, containing blood vessels, hair follicles, nerves, sweat glands, and sebaceous glands. The hypodermis is a loose layer of fat and connective tissue. Since it is the third layer, if a burn reaches this third degree, it has caused serious damage.

Sweat glands and sebaceous glands are important exocrine glands found in the skin. Sweat glands regulate temperature, and remove bodily waste by secreting water, nitrogenous waste, and sodium salts to the surface of the body. Some sweat glands are classified as apocrine glands. Sebaceous glands are holocrine glands that secrete sebum, which is an oily mixture of lipids and proteins. Sebum protects the skin from water loss, as well as bacterial and fungal infections.

The three major functions of skin are protection, regulation, and sensation. Skin acts as a barrier and protects the body from mechanical impacts, variations in temperature, microorganisms, and chemicals. It regulates body temperature, peripheral circulation, and fluid balance by secreting sweat. It also contains a large network of nerve cells that relay changes in the external environment to the body.

Skeletal System

The skeletal system consists of the 206 bones that make up the skeleton, as well as the cartilage, ligaments, and other connective tissues that stabilize them. Bone is made of collagen fibers and calcium salts. The calcium salts are strong but brittle, and the collagen fibers are weak but flexible, so the combination makes bone resistant to shattering. There are two types of bone: compact and spongy. Compact bone has a basic functional unit, called the Haversian system. Osteocytes, or bone cells, are arranged in concentric circles around a central canal, called the Haversian canal, which contains blood vessels. While Haversian canals run parallel to the surface of the bone, perforating canals, also known as the canals of Volkmann, run perpendicularly between the central canal and the surface of the bone. The concentric circles of bone tissue that surround the central canal within the Haversian system are called lamellae. The spaces that are found between the lamellae are called lacunae. The Haversian system is a reservoir for calcium and phosphorus for blood. Spongy bone, in contrast to compact bone, is lightweight and porous. It covers the outside of the bone and it gives it a shiny, white appearance. It has a branching network of parallel lamellae, called trabeculae.

Although spongy bone forms an open framework around the compact bone, it is still quite strong. Different bones have different ratios of compact-to-spongy bone, depending on their functions. The outside of the bone is covered by a periosteum, which has four major functions. It isolates and protects bones from the surrounding tissue; provides a place for attachment of the circulatory and nervous system structures; participates in growth and repair of the bone; and attaches the bone to the deep fascia. An endosteum is found inside the bone, covers the trabeculae of the spongy bone and lines the inner surfaces of the central canals.

One major function of the skeletal system is to provide structural support for the entire body. It provides a framework for the soft tissues and organs to attach to. The skeletal system also provides a reserve of important nutrients, such as calcium and lipids. Normal concentrations of calcium and phosphate in body fluids are partly maintained by the calcium salts stored in bone. Lipids that are stored in yellow bone marrow can be used as a source of energy. Red bone marrow produces red blood cells, white blood cells, and platelets that circulate in the blood. Certain groups of bones form protective barriers around delicate organs. The ribs, for example, protect the heart and lungs, the skull encloses the brain, and the vertebrae cover the spinal cord.

Muscular System

The muscular system of the human body is responsible for all movement that occurs. There are approximately 700 muscles in the body that are attached to the bones of the skeletal system and that make up half of the body's weight. Muscles are attached to the bones through tendons. Tendons are made up of dense bands of connective tissue and have collagen fibers that firmly attach to the bone on one side and the muscle on the other. Their fibers are actually woven into the coverings of the bone and muscle so they can withstand the large forces that are put on them when muscles are moving. There are three types of muscle tissue in the body: Skeletal muscle tissue pulls on the bones of the skeleton and causes body movement; cardiac muscle tissue helps pump blood through veins and arteries; and smooth muscle tissue helps move fluids and solids along the digestive tract and contributes to movement in other body systems. All of these muscle tissues have four important properties in common: They are excitable, meaning they respond to stimuli; contractile, meaning they can shorten and pull on connective tissue; extensible, meaning they can be stretched repeatedly, but maintain the ability to contract; and elastic, meaning they rebound to their original length after a contraction.

Muscles begin at an origin and end at an insertion. Generally, the origin is proximal to the insertion and the origin remains stationary while the insertion moves. For example, when bending the elbow and moving the hand up toward the head, the part of the forearm that is closest to the wrist moves and the part closer to the elbow is stationary. Therefore, the muscle in the forearm has an origin at the elbow and an insertion at the wrist.

Body movements occur by muscle contraction. Each contraction causes a specific action. Muscles can be classified into one of three muscle groups based on the action they perform. Primary movers, or agonists, produce a specific movement, such as flexion of the elbow. Synergists are in charge of helping the primary movers complete their specific movements. They can help stabilize the point of origin or provide extra pull near the insertion. Some synergists can aid an agonist in preventing movement at a joint. Antagonists are muscles whose actions are the opposite of that of the agonist. If an agonist is contracting during a specific movement, the antagonist is stretched. During flexion of the elbow, the biceps' brachii muscle contracts and acts as an agonist, while the triceps' brachii muscle on the opposite side of the upper arm acts as an antagonist and stretches.

Skeletal muscle tissue has several important functions. It causes movement of the skeleton by pulling on tendons and moving the bones. It maintains body posture through the contraction of specific muscles responsible for the stability of the skeleton. Skeletal muscles help support the weight of internal organs and protect these organs from external injury. They also help to regulate body temperature within a normal range. Muscle contractions require energy and produce heat, which heats the body when cold.

Nervous System

Although the nervous system is one of the smallest organ systems in the human body, it is the most complex. It consists of all of the neural tissue, and is in charge of controlling and adjusting the activities of all of the other systems of the body. Neural responses to stimuli are often fast, but disappear quickly once the neural activity stops. Neural tissue contains two types of cells: neurons and neuroglia. Neurons, or nerve cells, are the main cells responsible for transferring and processing information in the nervous system. Neuroglia support the neurons by providing a framework around them and isolating them from the surrounding environment. They also act as phagocytes and protect neurons from harmful substances.

The nervous system is made of the central nervous system (CNS) and the peripheral nervous system (PNS). The CNS includes the brain and the spinal cord, while the PNS includes the rest of the neural tissue not included in the CNS. The CNS is where intelligence, memory, learning, and emotions are processed. It is responsible for processing and coordinating sensory data and motor commands. The PNS is responsible for relaying sensory information and motor commands between the CNS and peripheral tissues and systems. The PNS has two subdivisions, known as the afferent and efferent divisions. While the afferent division relays sensory information to the CNS, the efferent division transmits motor commands to muscles and glands. The efferent division consists of the somatic nervous system (SNS), which controls skeletal muscle contractions, and the autonomic nervous system (ANS), which regulates activity of smooth muscle, cardiac muscle, and glands.

Two types of pathways are used to communicate information between the brain and the peripheral tissues. Sensory pathways start in a peripheral system and end in the brain. Motor pathways carry information from the brain to peripheral systems. Motor commands often occur in response to the information transmitted through a sensory pathway. Processing in both pathways happens at several points along the way, where neurons pass the information to each other.

The nervous system is responsible for processing both general senses and specialized senses. General senses include temperature, pain, touch, pressure, vibration and proprioception. Specialized senses include olfaction (smell), gustation (taste), equilibrium, hearing, and vision. The information from each sense is processed through a specific receptor for that sense. A receptor that is sensitive to touch may not be responsive to chemical stimuli, for example. The specificity of the receptor is developed either from its individual structure or from accessory cells or structures creating a shield against other senses.

Endocrine System

The endocrine system is made of the ductless tissues and glands that secrete hormones into the interstitial fluids of the body. Interstitial fluid is the solution that surrounds tissue cells within the body. This system works closely with the nervous system to regulate the physiological activities of the other systems of the body to maintain homeostasis. While the nervous system provides quick, short-term responses to stimuli, the endocrine system acts by releasing hormones into the bloodstream that get distributed to the whole body. The response is slow but long-lasting, ranging from a few hours to a few weeks.

Hormones are chemical substances that change the metabolic activity of tissues and organs. While regular metabolic reactions are controlled by enzymes, hormones can change the type, activity, or quantity of the enzymes involved in the reaction. They bind to specific cells and start a biochemical chain of events that changes the enzymatic activity. Hormones can regulate development and growth, digestive metabolism, mood, and body temperature, among other things. Often small amounts of hormone will lead to large changes in the body.

Major Endocrine Glands

Hypothalamus: A part of the brain, the hypothalamus connects the nervous system to the endocrine system via the pituitary gland. Although it is considered part of the nervous system, it plays a dual role in regulating endocrine organs.

Pituitary Gland: A pea-sized gland found at the bottom of the hypothalamus. It has two lobes, called the anterior and posterior lobes. It plays an important role in regulating the function of other endocrine glands. The hormones released control growth, blood pressure, certain functions of the sex organs, salt concentration of the kidneys, internal temperature regulation, and pain relief.

Thyroid Gland: This gland releases hormones, such as thyroxine, that are important for metabolism, growth and development, temperature regulation, and brain development during infancy and childhood. Thyroid hormones also monitor the amount of circulating calcium in the body.

Parathyroid Glands: These are four pea-sized glands located on the posterior surface of the thyroid. The main hormone secreted is called parathyroid hormone (PTH) and helps with the thyroid's regulation of calcium in the body.

Thymus Gland: The thymus is located in the chest cavity, embedded in connective tissue. It produces several hormones important for development and maintenance of normal immunological defenses. One hormone promotes the development and maturation of lymphocytes, which strengthens the immune system.

Adrenal Gland: One adrenal gland is attached to the top of each kidney. It produces adrenaline and is responsible for the "fight or flight" reactions in the face of danger or stress. The hormones epinephrine and norepinephrine cooperate to regulate states of arousal.

Pancreas: The pancreas is an organ that has both endocrine and exocrine functions. The endocrine functions are controlled by the pancreatic islets of Langerhans, which are groups of beta cells scattered throughout the gland that secrete insulin to lower blood sugar levels in the body. Neighboring alpha cells secrete glucagon to raise blood sugar.

Pineal Gland: The pineal gland secretes melatonin, a hormone derived from the neurotransmitter serotonin. Melatonin can slow the maturation of sperm, oocytes, and reproductive organs. It also regulates the body's circadian rhythm, which is the natural awake/asleep cycle. It also serves an important role in protecting the CNS tissues from neural toxins.

Testes and Ovaries: These glands secrete testosterone and estrogen, respectively, and are responsible for secondary sex characteristics, as well as reproduction.

Circulatory System

The circulatory system is composed of the heart and blood vessels of the body. The heart is the main organ of the circulatory system. It acts as a pump and works to circulate blood throughout the body. Gases, nutrients, and waste are constantly exchanged between the circulating blood and interstitial fluid, keeping tissues and organs alive and healthy. The circulatory system is divided into the pulmonary and systemic circuits. The pulmonary circuit is responsible for carrying carbon dioxide-rich blood to the lungs and returning oxygen-rich blood to the heart. The systemic circuit transports the oxygen-rich blood to the rest of the body and returns carbon dioxide-rich blood to the heart.

Heart

The heart is located posterior to the sternum, on the left side, in the front of the chest. The heart wall is made of three distinct layers. The outer layer, the epicardium, is a *serous* membrane that is also known as the visceral pericardium. The middle layer is called the myocardium, and contains connective tissue, blood vessels, and nerves within its layers of cardiac muscle tissue. The inner layer is the endocardium, and is made of a simple squamous epithelium. This layer includes the heart valves, and is continuous with the endothelium of the attached blood vessels.

The heart has four chambers: the right atrium, the right ventricle, the left atrium, and the left ventricle. An interatrial septum, or wall, separates the right and left atria, and the right and left ventricles are separated by an interventricular septum. The atrium and ventricle on the same side of the heart have an opening between them that is regulated by a valve. The valve maintains blood flow in only one direction, moving from the atrium to the ventricle, and prevents backflow. The systemic circuit pumps oxygen-poor blood into the right atrium, then pumps it into the right ventricle. From there, the blood enters the pulmonary trunk and then flows into the pulmonary arteries, where it can become re-oxygenated. Oxygen-rich blood from the lungs flows into the left atrium and then passes into the left ventricle. From there, blood enters the aorta and is pumped to the entire systemic circuit.

Blood

Blood circulates throughout the body in a system of vessels that includes arteries, veins, and capillaries. It distributes oxygen, nutrients, and hormones to all the cells in the body. The vessels are muscular tubes that allow gas exchange to occur. Arteries carry oxygen-rich blood from the heart to the other tissues of the body. The largest artery is the aorta. Veins collect oxygen-depleted blood from tissues and organs, and return it to the heart. The walls of veins are thinner and less elastic than arteries, because the blood pressure in veins is lower than in arteries. Capillaries are the smallest of the blood vessels and do not function individually; instead, they work together in a unit, called a capillary bed. This network of capillaries provides oxygen-rich blood from arterioles to tissues and feeds oxygen-poor blood from tissues back to venules.

Blood comprises plasma and formed elements, which include red blood cells (RBCs), white blood cells (WBCs), and platelets. Plasma is the liquid matrix of the blood and contains dissolved proteins. RBCs transport oxygen and carbon dioxide. WBCs are part of the immune system and help fight diseases. Platelets contain enzymes and other factors that help with blood clotting.

Respiratory System

The respiratory system mediates the exchange of gas between the air and the blood, mainly by the act of breathing. This system is divided into the upper respiratory system and the lower respiratory system. The upper system comprises the nose, the nasal cavity and sinuses, and the pharynx. The lower respiratory system comprises the larynx (voice box), the trachea (windpipe), the small passageways leading to the lungs, and the lungs. The upper respiratory system is responsible for filtering, warming, and humidifying the air that gets passed to the lower respiratory system, protecting the lower respiratory system's more delicate tissue surfaces.

The Lungs

The right lung is divided into three lobes: superior, middle, and inferior. The left lung is divided into two lobes: superior and inferior. The left lung is smaller than the right, likely because it shares its space in the chest cavity with the heart. Together, the lungs contain approximately 1500 miles of airway passages. The bronchi, which carry air into the lungs, branch into bronchioles and continue to divide into smaller and smaller passageways, until they become alveoli, which are the smallest passages. Most of the gas exchange in the lungs occurs between the blood-filled pulmonary capillaries and the air-filled alveoli.

Functions of the Respiratory System

The respiratory system has many functions. Most importantly, it provides a large area for gas exchange between the air and the circulating blood. It protects the delicate respiratory surfaces from environmental variations and defends them against pathogens. It is responsible for producing the sounds that the body makes for speaking and singing, as well as for non-verbal communication. It also helps regulate blood volume, blood pressure, and body fluid pH.

Breathing

When a breath of air is inhaled, oxygen enters the nose or mouth, and passes into the sinuses, where the temperature and humidity of the air get regulated. The air then passes into the trachea and is filtered. From there, the air travels into the bronchi and reaches the lungs. Bronchi are tubes that lead from the trachea to each lung, and are lined with cilia and mucus that collect dust and germs along the way. Within the lungs, oxygen and carbon dioxide are exchanged between the air in the alveoli and the blood in the pulmonary capillaries. Oxygen-rich blood returns to the heart and is pumped through the systemic circuit. Carbon dioxide-rich air is exhaled from the body.

Breathing is possible due to the muscular diaphragm pulling on the lungs, increasing their volume and decreasing their pressure. Air flows from the external high-pressure system to the low-pressure system inside the lungs. When breathing out, the diaphragm releases its pressure difference, decreases the lung volume, and forces the stale air back out.

Digestive System

The digestive system is a group of organs that work together to transform food and liquids into energy, which can then be used by the body as fuel. Food is ingested and then passes through the alimentary canal, or GI tract, which comprises the mouth, pharynx, esophagus, stomach, small intestine, and large intestine. The digestive system has accessory organs, including the liver, gallbladder, and pancreas, that help with the processing of food and liquids, but do not have food pass directly through them. These accessory organs and the digestive system organs work together in the following functions:

Ingestion: Food and liquids enter the alimentary canal through the mouth.

Introductory Mechanical and Chemical Processing: Teeth grind the food and the tongue swirls it to facilitate swallowing. Enzymes in saliva begin chemical digestion.

Advanced Mechanical and Chemical Digestion: The muscular stomach uses physical force and enzymes, which function at low pH levels, to break down the food and liquid's complex molecules, such as sugars, lipids, and proteins, into smaller molecules that can be absorbed by the small intestine.

Secretion: Most of the acids, buffers, and enzymes that aid in digestion are secreted by the accessory organs, but some are provided by the digestive tract. Bile from the liver facilitates fat digestion.

Absorption: Vitamins, electrolytes, organic molecules, and water are absorbed by the villi and microvilli lining in the small intestine and are moved to the interstitial fluid of the digestive tract.

Compaction: Indigestible materials and organic wastes are dehydrated in the large intestine and compacted before elimination from the body.

Excretion: Waste products are excreted from the digestive tract.

Major Organs of the Alimentary Canal

Stomach: This organ stores food so the body has time to digest large meals. Its highly acidic environment and enzyme secretions, such as pepsin and trypsin, aid in digestion. It also aids in mechanical processing through muscular contractions.

Small Intestine: This organ is a thin tube that is approximately ten feet long. It secretes enzymes to aid in digestion and has many folds that increase its surface area and allows for maximum absorption of nutrients from the digested food.

Large Intestine: This organ is a long thick tube that is about five feet long. It absorbs water from the digested food and transports waste to be excreted from the body. It also contains symbiotic bacteria that further breaks down the waste products, allowing for any extra nutrients to be absorbed.

Major Accessory Organs

Liver: The liver produces and secretes bile, which is important for the digestion of lipids. It also plays a large role in the regulation of circulating levels of carbohydrates, amino acids, and lipids in the body. Excess nutrients are removed by the liver and deficiencies are corrected with its stored nutrients.

Gallbladder: This organ is responsible for storing and concentrating bile before it gets secreted into the small intestine. While the gallbladder is storing bile, it can regulate the bile's composition by absorbing water, thereby increasing the concentration of bile salts and other components.

Pancreas: The Pancreas has exocrine cells that secrete buffers and digestive enzymes. It contains specific enzymes for each type of food molecule, such as carbohydrases for carbohydrates, lipases for lipids, and proteinases for proteins.

Urinary System

The urinary system is made up of the kidneys, ureters, urinary bladder, and the urethra. It is the main system responsible for getting rid of the organic waste products, excess water and electrolytes are generated by the body's other systems. The kidneys are responsible for producing urine, which is a fluid waste product containing water, ions, and small soluble compounds. The urinary system has many important functions related to waste excretion. It regulates the concentrations of sodium, potassium, chloride, calcium, and other ions in the plasma by controlling the amount of each that is excreted in urine. This also contributes to the maintenance of blood pH. It regulates blood volume and pressure by controlling the amount of water lost in the urine, and releasing erythropoietin and renin. It eliminates toxic substances, drugs, and organic waste products, such as urea and uric acid. It also synthesizes calcitriol, which is a hormone derivative of vitamin D3 that aids in calcium ion absorption by the intestinal epithelium.

The Kidneys

Under normal circumstances, humans have two functioning kidneys. They are the main organs are responsible for filtering waste products out of the blood and transferring them to urine. Every day, the kidneys filter approximately 120 to 150 quarts of blood and produce one to two quarts of urine. Kidneys are made of millions of tiny filtering units, called nephrons. Nephrons have two parts: a glomerulus, which is the filter, and a tubule. As blood enters the kidneys, the glomerulus allows fluid and waste products to pass through it and enter the tubule. Blood cells and large molecules, such as proteins, do not pass through and remain in the blood. The filtered fluid and waste then pass through the tubule, where any final essential minerals are sent back to the bloodstream. The final product at the end of the tubule is called urine.

Waste Excretion

Once urine accumulates, it leaves the kidneys. The urine travels through the ureters into the urinary bladder, a muscular organ that is hollow and elastic. As more urine enters the urinary bladder, its walls stretch and become thinner so there is no significant difference in internal pressure. The urinary bladder stores the urine until the body is ready for urination, at which time the muscles contract and force the urine through the urethra and out of the body.

Reproductive System

The reproductive system is responsible for producing, storing, nourishing, and transporting functional reproductive cells, or gametes, in the human body. It includes the reproductive organs, also known as gonads, the reproductive tract, the accessory glands and organs that secrete fluids into the reproductive tract, and the perineal structures, which are the external genitalia. The human male and female reproductive systems are very different from each other.

The Male System

The male gonads are called testes. The testes secrete androgens, mainly testosterone, and produce and store 500 million sperms cells, which are the male gametes, each day. An androgen is a steroid hormone that controls the development and maintenance of male characteristics. Once the sperm are mature, they move through a duct system, where they mix with additional fluids secreted by accessory glands, forming a mixture called semen. The sperm cells in semen are responsible for fertilization of the female gametes to produce offspring.

The Female System

The female gonads are the ovaries. Ovaries generally produce one immature gamete, or oocyte, per month. They are also responsible for secreting the hormones estrogen and progesterone. When the oocyte is released from the ovary, it travels along the uterine tubes, or Fallopian tubes, and then into the uterus. The uterus opens into the vagina. When sperm cells enter the vagina, they swim through the uterus and may fertilize the oocyte in the Fallopian tubes. The resulting zygote travels down the tube and implants into the uterine wall. The uterus protects and nourishes the developing embryo for nine months until it is ready for the outside environment. If the oocyte is not fertilized, it is released in the uterine, or menstrual, cycle. The menstrual cycle occurs monthly and involves the shedding of the functional part of the uterine lining.

Mammary glands are a specialized accessory organ of the female reproductive system. The mammary glands are located in the breast tissue, and during pregnancy begin to grow, and the cells proliferate in preparation for lactation. After pregnancy, the cells begin to secrete nutrient-filled milk, which is transferred into a duct system and out through the nipple for nourishment of the baby.

Population Dynamics

Population dynamics is the study of the composition of populations, including size, age, and the biological and environmental processes that cause changes. These can include immigration, emigration, births, and deaths.

Growth Curves and Carrying Capacity

Population dynamics can be characterized by *growth curves*. Growth can either be *unrestricted*, which is modeled by an exponential curve, or *restricted*, which is modeled by a logistic curve. Population growth can be restricted by environmental factors such as the availability of food and water sources, habitat, and other necessities. The *carrying capacity* of a population is the maximum population size that an environment can sustain indefinitely, given all of the above factors.

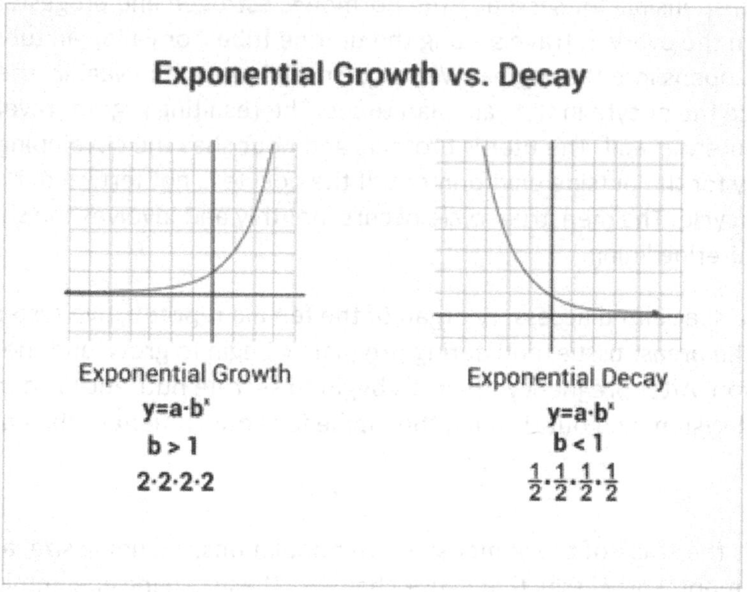

Behavior

Different species within a population can act differently regarding their environment. Some species display *territoriality*, which is a specific type of competition that excludes other species from a given area. It can be shown through specific animal calls, intimidating behavior, or marking an area with scents, and is often a display of defense.

Intraspecific Relationships

Intraspecific relationships is a term that describes the competition and cooperation between organisms that belong to the same species. They may compete for the same food sources, or for mates that are necessary for their personal survival and reproduction. Stronger organisms may display dominance that allows them to reside at the top of a social hierarchy and obtain better food and higher quality mates. However, organisms may also cooperate with each other in order to benefit the larger group; for instance, they may divide laborious activities among themselves.

Community Ecology

An *ecological community* is a group of species that interact and live in the same location. Because of their shared environment, they tend to have a large influence on each other.

Niche

An *ecological niche* is the role that a species plays in its environment, including how it finds its food and shelter. It could be a predator of a different species, or prey for a larger species.

Species Diversity

Species diversity is the number of different species that cohabitate in an ecological community. It has two different facets: *species richness*, which is the general number of species, and *species evenness*, which accounts for the population size of each species.

Interspecific Relationships

Interspecific relationships include the interactions between organisms of different species. The following list defines the common relationships that can occur:

- *Commensalism*: One organism benefits while the other is neither benefited nor harmed
- *Mutualism*: Both organisms benefit
- *Parasitism*: One organism benefits and the other is harmed
- *Competition*: Two or more species compete for limited resources that are necessary for their survival
- *Predation (Predator-Prey)*: One species is a food source for another species

Ecosystems

An *ecosystem* includes all of the living organisms and nonliving components of an environment (each community) and their interactions with each other.

Biomes

A *biome* is a group of plants and animals that are found in many different continents and have the same characteristics because of the similar climates in which they live. Each biome is composed of all of the ecosystems in that area. Five primary types of biomes are aquatic, deserts, forests, grasslands, and tundra. The sum total of all biomes comprises the Earth's biosphere.

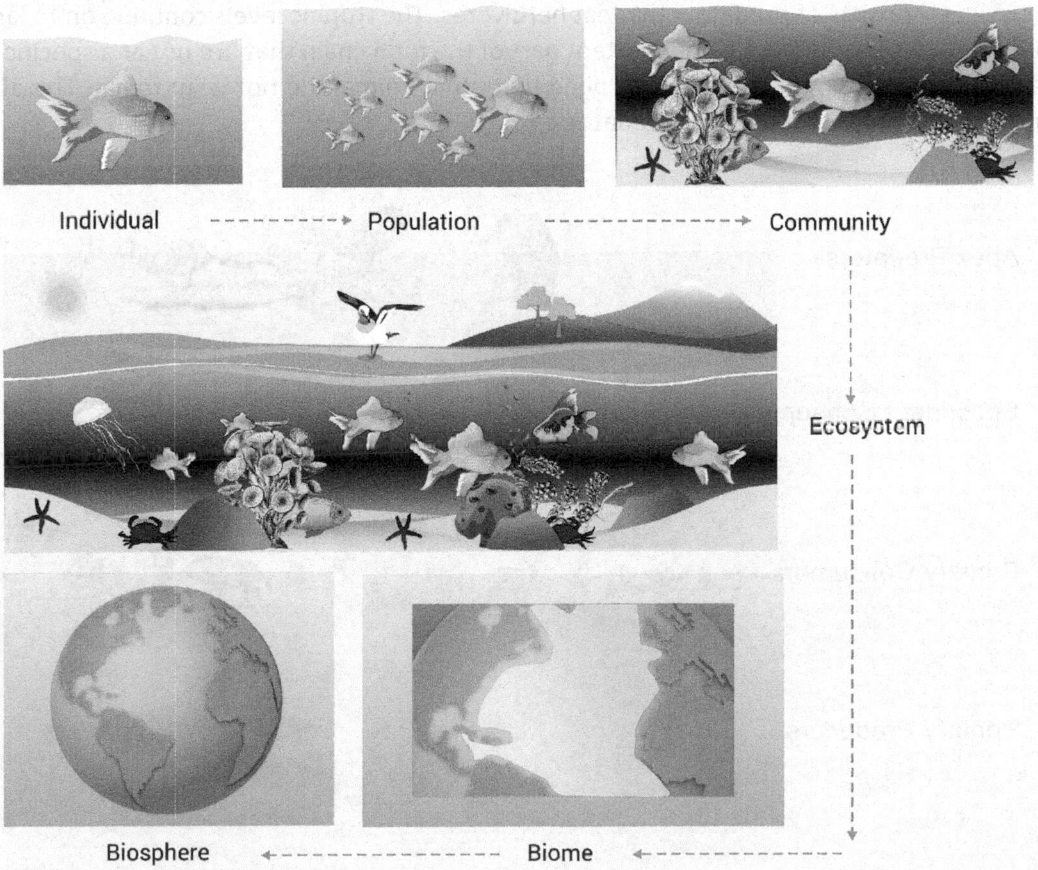

Stability and Disturbances

Ecological stability is the ability of an ecosystem to withstand changes that are occurring within it. With *regenerative stability*, an ecosystem may change, but then quickly return to its previous state. *Constant stability* occurs in ecosystems that remain unchanged despite the changes going on around them.

An *ecological disturbance* is a change in the environment that causes a larger change in the ecosystem. Smaller disturbances include fires and floods. Larger disturbances include the *climate change* that is currently occurring. Gas emissions from human activity are causing the atmosphere to warm up, which is changing the Earth's water systems and making weather more extreme. The increase in temperature is causing greater evaporation of the water sources on Earth, creating droughts and depleting natural water sources. This has also caused many of the Earth's glaciers to begin melting, which can change the salinity of the oceans.

Changes in the environment can cause an *ecological succession* to occur, which is the change in structure of the species that coexist in an ecological community. When the environment changes, resources available to the different species also change. For example, the formation of sand dunes or a forest fire would change the environment enough to allow a change in the social hierarchy of the coexisting species.

Energy Flow

Ecosystems are maintained by cycling the energy and nutrients that they obtain from external sources. The process can be diagramed in a *food web*, which represents the feeding relationship between species in a community. The different levels of the food web are called *trophic levels*. The first trophic level generally consists of plants, algae, and bacteria. The second trophic level consists of herbivores. The third trophic level consists of predators that eat herbivores. The trophic levels continue on to larger and larger predators. *Decomposers* are an important part of the food chain that are not at a specific trophic level. They eat decomposing things on the ground that other animals do not want to eat. This allows them to provide nutrients to their own predators.

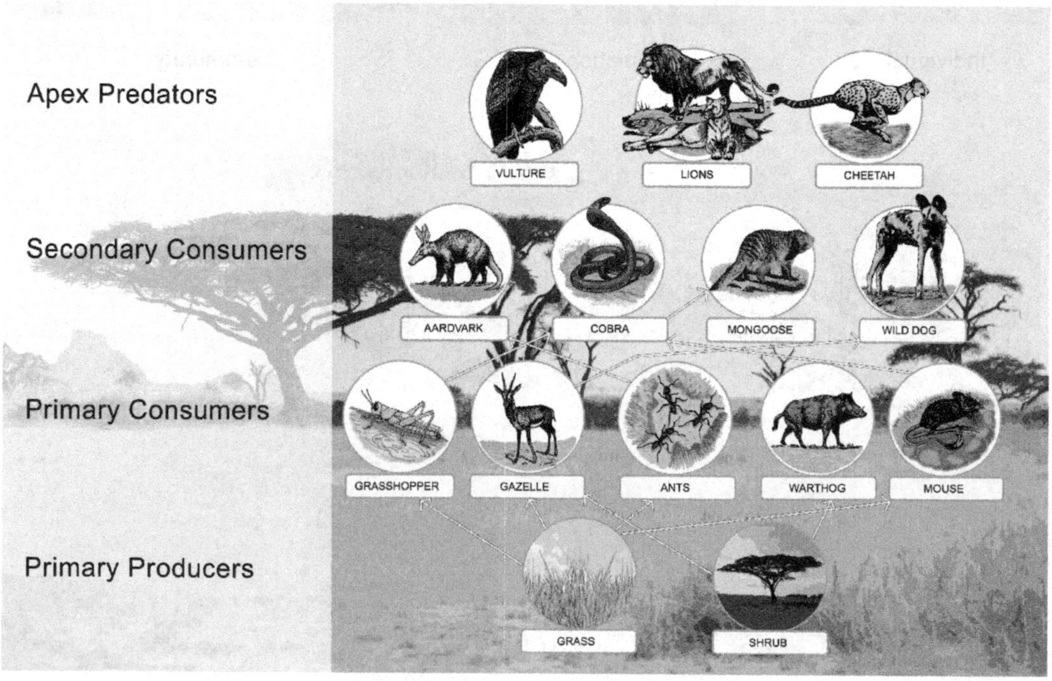

Biogeochemical Cycles

Biogeochemical cycles are the pathways by which chemicals move through the *biotic*, or biospheric, and *abiotic*, or atmospheric, parts of the Earth. The most important biogeochemical cycles include the water, carbon, and nitrogen cycles. *Water* goes through an evaporation, condensation, and precipitation cycle. *Nitrogen* makes up seventy-eight percent of the Earth's atmosphere and can affect the rate of many ecosystem processes, such as production of the primary producers at the first trophic level of the food web. The *carbon cycle* has many steps that are vitally important for sustaining life on Earth.

The water cycle:

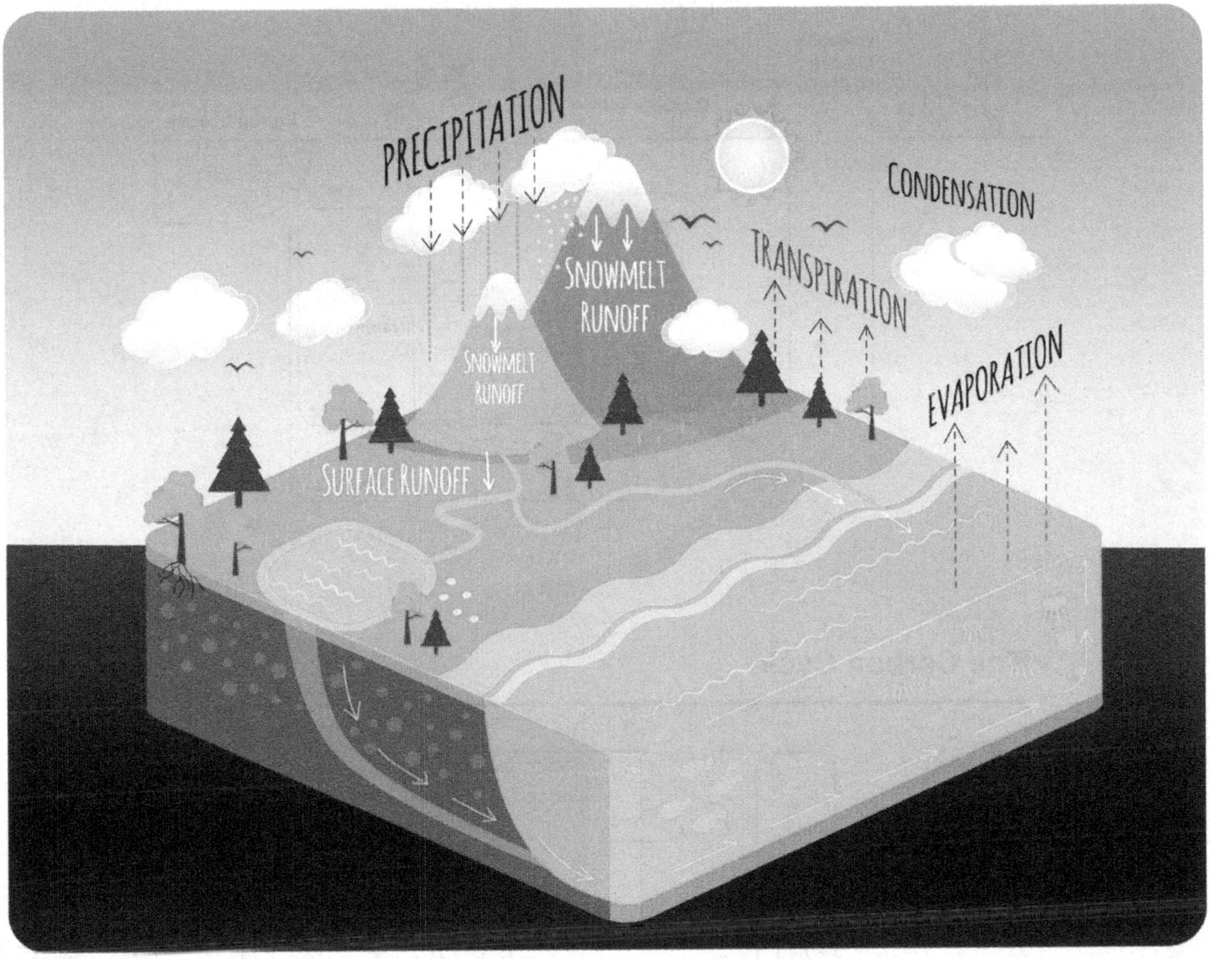

The nitrogen cycle:

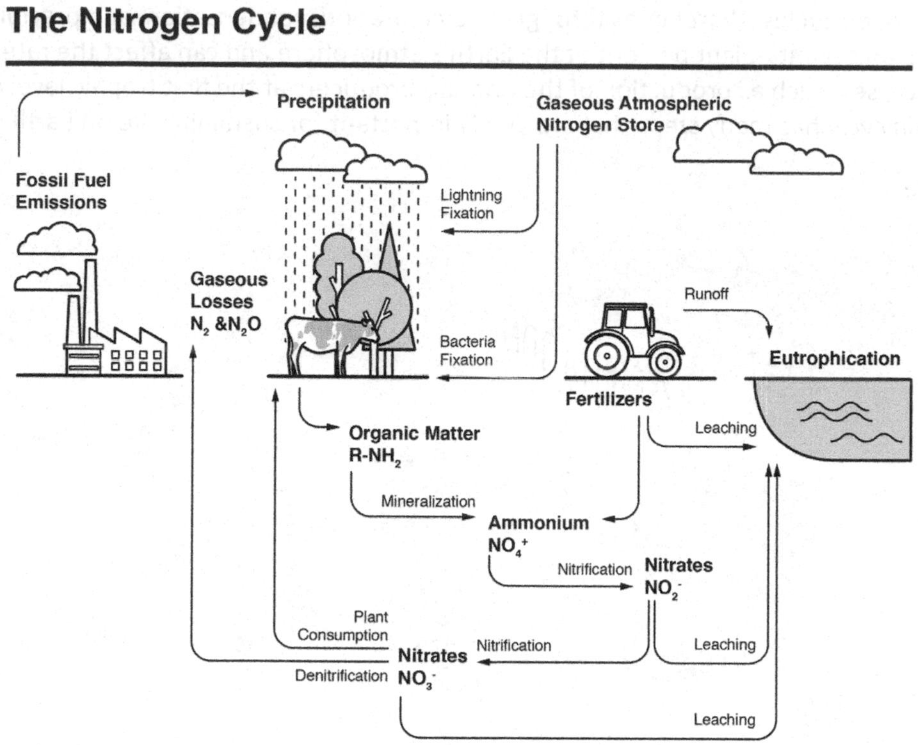

The carbon cycle:

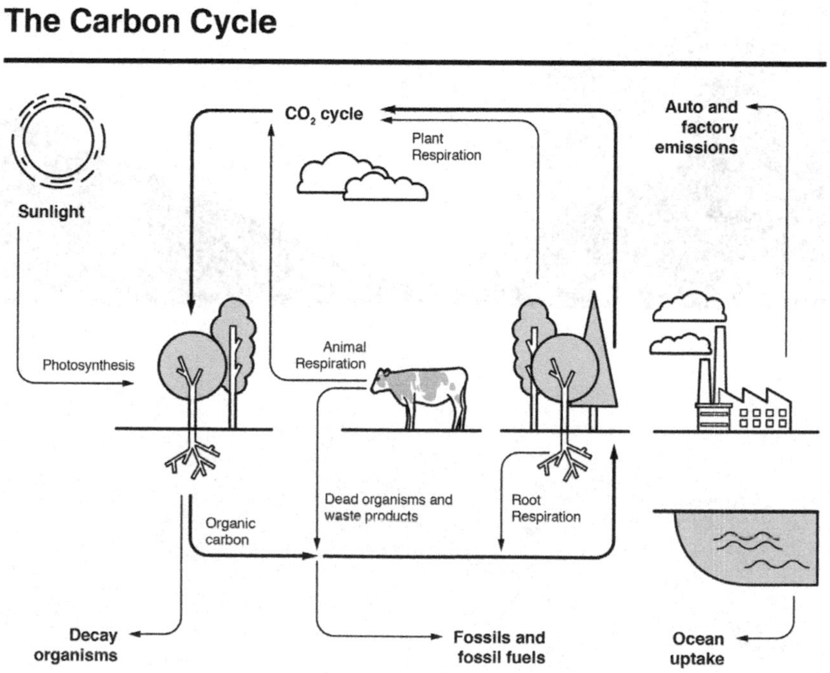

Physical Science

Structure of Matter

Elements, Compounds, and Mixtures

Everything that takes up space and has mass is composed of *matter*. Understanding the basic characteristics and properties of matter helps with classification and identification.

An *element* is a substance that cannot be chemically decomposed to a simpler substance, while still retaining the properties of the element.

Compounds are composed of two or more elements that are chemically combined. The constituent elements in the compound are in constant proportions by mass.

When a material can be separated by physicals means (such as sifting it through a colander), it is called a *mixture*. Mixtures are categorized into two types: *heterogeneous* and *homogeneous*. Heterogeneous mixtures have physically distinct parts, which retain their different properties. A mix of salt and sugar is an example of a heterogeneous mixture. With heterogenous mixtures, it is possible that different samples from the same parent mixture may have different proportions of each component in the mixture. For example, in the sugar and salt mixture, there may be uneven mixing of the two, causing one random tablespoon sample to be mostly salt, while a different tablespoon sample may be mostly sugar.

A homogeneous mixture, also called a *solution*, has uniform properties throughout a given sample. An example of a homogeneous solution is salt fully dissolved in warm water. In this case, any number of samples taken from the parent solution would be identical.

Atoms, Molecules, and Ions

The basic building blocks of matter are *atoms*, which are extremely small particles that retain their identity during chemical reactions. Atoms can be singular or grouped to form elements. Elements are composed of one type of atom with the same properties.

Molecules are a group of atoms—either the same or different types—that are chemically bonded together by attractive forces. For example, hydrogen and oxygen are both atoms but, when bonded together, form water.

Ions are electrically-charged particles that are formed from an atom or a group of atoms via the loss or gain of electrons.

Basic Properties of Solids, Liquids, and Gases

Matter exists in certain *states*, or physical forms, under different conditions. These states are called *solid*, *liquid*, or *gas*.

A solid has a rigid, or set, form and occupies a fixed shape and volume. Solids generally maintain their shape when exposed to outside forces.

Liquids and gases are considered fluids, which have no set shape. Liquids are fluid, yet are distinguished from gases by their incompressibility (incapable of being compressed) and set volume. Liquids can be transferred from one container to another, but cannot be forced to fill containers of different volumes via compression without causing damage to the container. For example, if one attempts to force a given volume or number of particles of a liquid, such as water, into a fixed container, such as a small water bottle, the container would likely explode from the extra water.

A gas can easily be compressed into a confined space, such as a tire or an air mattress. Gases have no fixed shape or volume. They can also be subjected to outside forces, and the number of gas molecules that can fill a certain volume vary with changes in temperature and pressure.

Basic Structure of an Atom

Atomic Models

Theories of the atomic model have developed over the centuries. The most commonly referenced model of an atom was proposed by Niels Bohr. Bohr studied the models of J.J. Thomson and Ernest Rutherford and adapted his own theories from these existing models. Bohr compared the structure of the atom to that of the Solar System, where there is a center, or nucleus, with various sized orbitals circulating around this nucleus. This is a simplified version of what scientists have discovered about atoms, including the structures and placements of any orbitals. Modern science has made further adaptations to the model, including the fact that orbitals are actually made of electron "clouds."

Atomic Structure: Nucleus, Electrons, Protons, and Neutrons

Following the Bohr model of the atom, the nucleus, or core, is made up of positively charged *protons* and neutrally charged *neutrons*. The neutrons are theorized to be in the nucleus with the protons to provide greater "balance" at the center of the atom. The nucleus of the atom makes up the majority (more than 99%) of the mass of an atom, while the orbitals surrounding the nucleus contain negatively charged *electrons*. The entire structure of an atom is incredibly small.

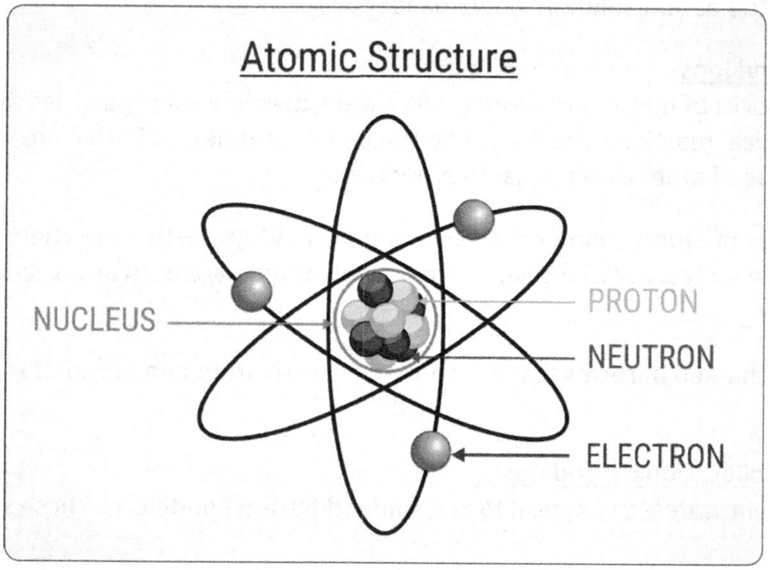

Atomic Number, Atomic Mass, and Isotopes

The *atomic number* of an atom is determined by the number of protons within the nucleus. When a substance is composed of atoms that all have the same atomic number, it is called an *element*. Elements are arranged by atomic number and grouped by properties in the *periodic table*.

An atom's *mass number* is determined by the sum of the total number of protons and neutrons in the atom. Most nuclei have a net neutral charge, and all atoms of one type have the same atomic number. However, there are some atoms of the same type that have a different mass number, due to an imbalance of neutrons. These are called *isotopes*. In isotopes, the atomic number, which is determined by the number of protons, is the same, but the mass number, which is determined by adding the protons and neutrons, is different due to the irregular number of neutrons.

Electron Arrangements

Electrons are most easily organized into distributions of subshells called *electron configurations*. Subshells fill from the inside (closest to the nucleus) to the outside. Therefore, once a subshell is filled, the next shell farther from the nucleus begins to fill, and so on. Atoms with electrons on the outside of a noble gas core (an atom with an electron inner shell that corresponds to the configuration of one of the noble gases, such as Neon) and pseudo-noble gas core (an atom with an electron inner shell that is similar to that of a noble gas core along with (n -1) d^{10} electrons), are called *valence* electrons. Valence electrons are primarily the electrons involved in chemical reactions. The similarities in their configurations account for similarities in properties of groups of elements. Essentially, the groups (vertical columns) on the periodic table all have similar characteristics, such as solubility and reactivity, due to their similar electron configurations.

Basic Characteristics of Radioactive Materials

Radioisotopes

As mentioned, an isotope is a variation of an element with a different number of neutrons in the nucleus, causing the nucleus to be unstable. When an element is unstable, it will go through decay or disintegration. All manmade elements are unstable and will break down. The length of time for an unstable element to break down is called the *half-life*. As an element breaks down, it forms other elements, known as daughters. Once a stable daughter is formed, the radioactive decay stops.

Characteristics of Alpha Particles, Beta Particles, and Gamma Radiation

As radioactive decay is occurring, the unstable element emits *alpha*, *beta*, and *gamma* radiation. Alpha and beta radiation are not as far-reaching or as powerful as gamma radiation. Alpha radiation is caused by the emission of two protons and two neutrons, while beta radiation is caused by the emission of either an electron or a positron. In contrast, gamma radiation is the release of photons of energy, not particles. This makes it the farthest-reaching and the most dangerous of these emissions.

Fission and Fusion

The splitting of an atom is referred to as fission, whereas the combination of two atoms into one is called fusion. To achieve fission and break apart an isotope, the unstable isotope is bombarded with high-speed particles. This process releases a large amount of energy and is what provides the energy in a nuclear power plant. Fusion occurs when two nuclei are merged to form a larger nucleus. The action of fusion also creates a tremendous amount of energy. To put the difference in the levels of energy between fission and fusion into perspective, the level of energy from fusion is what provides energy to the Earth's sun.

Basic Concepts and Relationships Involving Energy and Matter

The study of energy and matter, including heat and temperature, is called *thermodynamics*. There are four fundamental laws of thermodynamics, but the first two are the most commonly discussed.

First Law of Thermodynamics

The first law of thermodynamics is also known as the *conservation of energy*. This law states that energy cannot be created or destroyed, but is just transferred or converted into another form through a thermodynamic process. For example, if a liquid is boiled and then removed from the heat source, the liquid will eventually cool. This change in temperature is not because of a loss of energy or heat, but from a transfer of energy or heat to the surroundings. This can include the heating of nearby air molecules, or the transfer of heat from the liquid to the container or to the surface where the container is resting.

This law also applies to the idea of perpetual motion. A self-powered perpetual motion machine cannot exist. This is because the motion of the machine would inevitably lose some heat or energy to friction, whether from materials or from the air.

Second Law of Thermodynamics

The second law of thermodynamics is also known as the *law of entropy*. Entropy means chaos or disorder. In simple terms, this law means that all systems tend toward chaos. When one or more systems interacts with another, the total entropy is the sum of the interacting systems, and this overall sum also tends toward entropy.

Conservation of Matter in Chemical Systems

The conservation of energy is seen in the conservation of matter in chemical systems. This is helpful when attempting to understand chemical processes, since these processes must balance out. This means that extra matter cannot be created or destroyed, it must all be accounted for through a chemical process.

Kinetic and Potential Energy

The conservation of energy also applies to the study of energy in physics. This is clearly demonstrated through the kinetic and potential energy involved in a system.

The energy of motion is called *kinetic energy*. If an object has height, or is raised above the ground, it has *potential energy*. The total energy of any given system is the sum of the potential energy and the kinetic energy of the subject (object) in the system.

Potential energy is expressed by the equation:

$$PE = mgh$$

Where m equals the object's mass, g equals acceleration caused by the gravitational force acting on the object, and h equals the height of the object above the ground.

Kinetic energy is expressed by the following equation:

$$KE = \frac{1}{2} mv^2$$

Where m is the mass of the object and v is the velocity of the object.

Conservation of energy allows the total energy for any situation to be calculated by the following equation:

$$KE + PE$$

For example, a roller coaster poised at the top of a hill has all potential energy, and when it reaches the bottom of that hill, as it is speeding through its lowest point, it has all kinetic energy. Halfway down the hill, the total energy of the roller coaster is about half potential energy and half kinetic energy.

Therefore, the total energy is found by calculating both the potential energy and the kinetic energy and then adding them together.

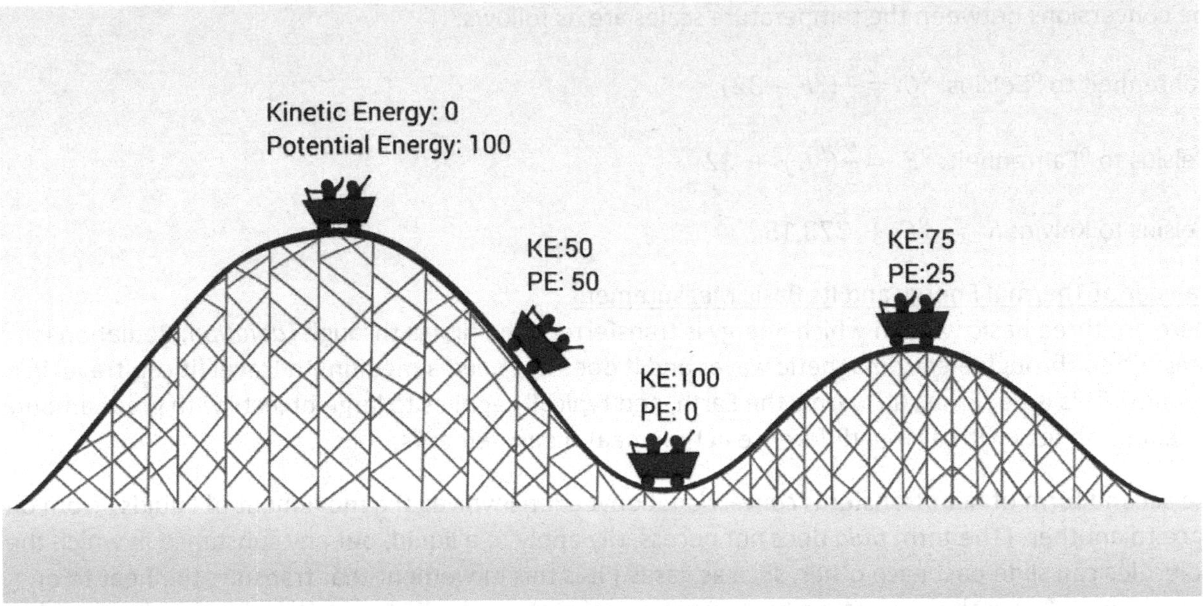

<u>Transformations Between Different Forms of Energy</u>
As stated by the conservation of energy, energy cannot be created or destroyed. If a system gains or loses energy, it is transformed within a single system from one type of energy to another or transferred from one system to another. For example, if the roller coaster system has potential energy that transfers to kinetic energy, the kinetic energy can then be transferred into thermal energy or heat released through braking as the coaster descends the hill. Energy can also transform from the chemical energy inside of a battery into the electrical energy that lights a train set. The energy released through nuclear fusion (when atoms are joined together, they release heat) is what supplies power plants with the energy for electricity. All energy is transferred from one form to another through different reactions. It can also be transferred through the simple action of atoms bumping into each other, causing a transfer of heat.

<u>Differences Between Chemical and Physical Properties/Changes</u>
A change in the physical form of matter, but not in its chemical identity, is known as a *physical change*. An example of a physical change is tearing a piece of paper in half. This changes the shape of the matter, but it is still paper.

Conversely, a *chemical change* alters the chemical composition or identity of matter. An example of a chemical change is burning a piece of paper. The heat necessary to burn the paper alters the chemical composition of the paper. This chemical change cannot be easily undone, since it has created at least one form of matter different than the original matter.

<u>Temperature Scales</u>
There are three main temperature scales used in science. The scale most often used in the United States is the *Fahrenheit* scale. This scale is based on the measurement of water freezing at 32^{0} F and water boiling at 212^{0} F. The Celsius scale uses 0^{0} C as the temperature for water freezing and 100^{0} C for water boiling. The accepted measurement by the International System of Units (from the French *Système international d'unités*), or SI, for temperature is the Kelvin scale. This is the scale employed in

thermodynamics, since its zero is the basis for *absolute zero*, or the unattainable temperature, when matter no longer exhibits degradation.

The conversions between the temperature scales are as follows:

^{o}Fahrenheit to ^{o}Celsius: $^{0}C = \frac{5}{9}(^{0}F - 32)$

^{o}Celsius to ^{o}Fahrenheit: $^{0}F = \frac{9}{5}(^{0}C) + 32$

^{o}Celsius to Kelvin: $K = {}^{0}C + 273.15$

<u>Transfer of Thermal Energy and Its Basic Measurement</u>

There are three basic ways in which energy is transferred. The first is through *radiation*. Radiation is transmitted through electromagnetic waves and it does not need a medium to travel (it can travel in a vacuum). This is how the sun warms the Earth, and typically applies to large objects with great amounts of heat or objects with a large difference in their heat measurements.

The second form of heat transfer is *convection*. Convection involves the movement of "fluids" from one place to another. (The term *fluid* does not necessarily apply to a liquid, but any substance in which the molecules can slide past each other, such as gases.) It is this movement that transfers the heat to or from an area. Generally, convective heat transfer occurs through diffusion, which is when heat moves from areas of higher concentrations of particles to those of lower concentrations of particles and less heat. This process of flowing heat can be assisted or amplified through the use of fans and other methods of forcing the molecules to move.

The final process is called *conduction*. Conduction involves transferring heat through the touching of molecules. Molecules can either bump into each other to transfer heat, or they may already be touching each other and transfer the heat through this connection. For example, imagine a circular burner on an electric stove top. The coil begins to glow orange near the base of the burner that is connected to the stove because it heats up first. Since the burner is one continuous piece of metal, the molecules are touching each other. As they pass heat along the coil, it begins to glow all the way to the end.

To determine the amount of heat required to warm the coil in the above example, the type of material from which the coil is made must be known. The quantity of heat required to raise one gram of a substance one degree Celsius (or Kelvin) at a constant pressure is called *specific heat*. This measurement can be calculated for masses of varying substances by using the following equation:

$$q = s \times m \times \Delta t$$

Where q is the specific heat, s is the specific heat of the material being used, m is the mass of the substance being used, and Δt is the change in temperature.

A calorimeter is used to measure the heat of a reaction (either expelled or absorbed) and the temperature changes in a controlled system. A simple calorimeter can be made by using an insulated coffee cup with a thermometer inside. For this example, a lid of some sort would be preferred to prevent any escaping heat that could be lost by evaporation or convection.

Applications of Energy and Matter Relationships

When considering the cycling of matter in ecosystems, the flow of energy and atoms is from one organism to another. The *trophic level* of an organism refers to its position in a food chain. The level shows the relationship between it and other organisms on the same level and how they use and transfer energy to other levels in the food chain. This includes consumption and decomposition for the transfer of energy among organisms and matter. The sun provides energy through radiation to the Earth, and plants convert this light energy into chemical energy, which is then released to fuel the organism's activities.

Naturally occurring elements deep within the Earth's mantle release heat during their radioactive decay. This release of heat drives convection currents in the Earth's magma, which then drives plate tectonics. The transfer of heat from these actions causes the plates to move and create convection currents in the oceans. This type of cycling can also be seen in transformations of rocks. Sedimentary rocks can undergo significant amounts of heat and pressure to become metamorphic rocks. These rocks can melt back into magma, which then becomes igneous rock or, with extensive weathering and erosion, can revert to sediment and form sedimentary rocks over time. Under the right conditions (weathering and erosion), igneous rocks can also become sediment, which eventually compresses into sedimentary rock. Erosion helps the process by redepositing rocks into sediment on the sea floor.

All of these cycles are examples of the transfer of energy from one type into another, along with the conservation of mass from one level to the next.

Describing Matter

Chemistry is the study of matter, including its properties and behavior. As mentioned, matter is the material that the universe is made of; it is any object that occupies space and has mass. Despite the diversity of items found in the universe, matter is comprised of only about 100 substances, known as elements. Elements cannot be broken down into simpler substances. Hydrogen and oxygen are two examples of elements. When different elements join together, they form compounds. Water is a compound made from hydrogen and oxygen. Atoms and molecules are among the smallest forms of matter.

Matter can be found in three different states: gas, liquid, or solid. Gas is a state that does not have a fixed volume or shape. It can expand to fill large containers or compress to fill smaller ones. Gas molecules are far apart from each other and float around at high speeds. They collide with each other and the container they are in, filling the container uniformly. When the gas is compressed, the space between the molecules decreases and the frequency of collisions between them increases. A liquid has an exact volume. It molds to the shape of the container that holds it. Liquid molecules are close together but still move rapidly. They cannot be compressed and slide over each other easily when liquids are poured. Solids have a definitive shape and volume. Similar to liquids, solids cannot be compressed. The molecules are packed together tightly in a specific arrangement that does not allow for much movement. When environmental changes occur, such as temperature or pressure changes, one state of matter can convert to another. For example, when water, a liquid, freezes, it becomes a solid, ice. When water is heated up to a certain temperature, it becomes water vapor, a gas.

The physical and chemical properties of matter can help distinguish different substances. Physical properties include color, odor, density, and hardness. These are properties that can be observed without changing the substance's identity or composition. When a substance undergoes a physical change, its physical appearance changes but its composition remains the same. Chemical properties are those that describe the way a substance might change to form another substance. Examples of chemical properties are flammability, toxicity, and ability to oxidize. These properties are observed by changing the environment of the substance and seeing how the substance reacts. A substance's composition is changed when it undergoes a chemical change.

Many properties of matter can be measured quantitatively, meaning the measurement is associated with a number. When a property of matter is represented by a number, it is important to include the unit of measure, otherwise the number is meaningless. For example, saying a pencil measures 10 is meaningless. It could be referring to 10 of something very short or 10 of something very long. The correct measurement notation would be 10 centimeters, because a centimeter has a designated length. Other examples of properties of matter that can be measured quantitatively are mass, time, and temperature, among others.

Chemical Equations and Reactions

Chemical reactions are represented by chemical equations. The equations help to explain how the molecules change during the reaction. For example, when hydrogen gas (H_2) combines with oxygen gas (O_2), two molecules of water are formed. The equation is written as follows, where the "+" sign means *reacts with* and the "→" means *produces*:

$$2\ H_2 + O_2 \rightarrow 2\ H_2O$$

Two hydrogen molecules react with an oxygen molecule to produce two water molecules. In all chemical equations, the quantity of each element on the reactant side of the equation should equal the quantity of the same element on the product side of the equation due to the law of conservation of matter. If this is true, the equation is described as balanced. To figure out how many of each element there is on each side of the equation, the coefficient of the element should be multiplied by the subscript next to the element. Coefficients and subscripts are noted for quantities larger than one. The coefficient is the number located directly to the left of the element. The subscript is the small-sized number directly to the right of the element. In the equation above, on the left side, the coefficient of the hydrogen is two and the subscript is also two, which makes a total of four hydrogen atoms. Using the same method, there are two oxygen atoms. On the right side, the coefficient two is multiplied by the subscript in each element of the water molecule, making four hydrogen atoms and two oxygen atoms. This equation is balanced because there are four hydrogen atoms and two oxygen atoms on each side. The states of the reactants and products can also be written in the equation: gas (g), liquid (l), solid (s), and dissolved in water (aq). If they are included, they are noted in parentheses on the right side of each molecule in the equation.

There are several types of chemical reactions: combination, decomposition, combustion single replacement, double replacement, and oxidation-reduction reactions. Reactions where two or more reactants combine to form one product, $A + B \rightarrow C$, are called combination reactions. When one substance is broken down into two or more substances, $C \rightarrow B + A$, it is known as a decomposition reaction. Combustion reactions involve oxygen gas as a reactant and generally involve the burning of a substance. One example is the combustion of propane: $C_3H_8(g) + 5O_2 \rightarrow 3CO_2(g) + 4H_2O$. Oxygen is combined with propane gas to from carbon dioxide and water. Double and single replacement reactions involve ionic compounds and metals and the rearranging of cations and anions, and oxidation-reduction reactions involve the passing of electrons.

Periodic Table

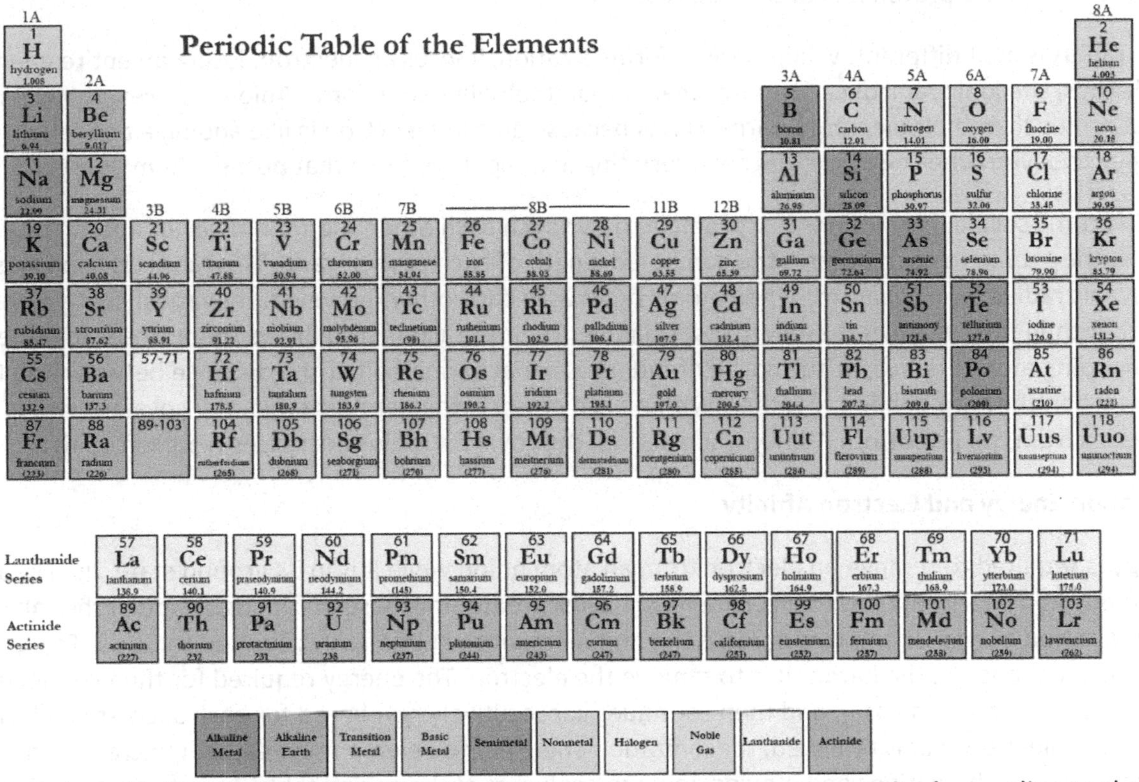

The periodic table is a chart of all 118 known elements. The elements are organized according to their quantity of protons, also known as their atomic number, their electron configurations, and their chemical properties. The rows are called periods and the columns are called groups. Groups have similar chemical behavior. For example, Group 8 is the noble gases, and because their outer electron shell is full, they are non-reactive. The closer the element is to having a full set of valence electrons it is, the more reactive it is. Group 1, the alkali metals, and Group 7, the halogens, are both highly reactive for that reason. The alkali metals form cations and lose their lone electron while halogens pick up an electron.

In each box in the period table, an element's symbol is the abbreviation in the center and its full name is located directly below that. The number in the top left corner is the atomic number and the atomic mass of the element is the number underneath. The atomic mass of the element is noted in atomic mass units, or amu, which represents the number of protons and neutrons combined. The number of protons defines the element, but the mass number can be different due to the existence of elements with a different number of neutrons, also called isotopes. The amu shown on the periodic table is a weighted mass (based on abundance) of all known isotopes of a particular element.

Atomic Radii

Atomic radius refers to the size of an atom. Going down a group, because each level represents an energy level, atomic radii increase. For example, when comparing lithium and potassium, potassium will have a greater atomic radius because it has two more energy levels.

Contrary to what might be predicted, going from left to right on the periodic table across a period, atomic radius actually decreases. This is due to proton pull. As each element gains a proton in its nucleus, it is like gaining a positive magnet in the middle. The more magnets in the middle, the stronger they will suck in any outer electrons. Comparing carbon and fluorine, fluorine has a smaller atomic radius due to more proton pull of the nucleus.

Ionic radius is a bit different. When sodium forms a cation, it loses an electron, losing an entire energy level. Thus, the ionic radii of cations are smaller than their elemental form. Anions, however, have a larger radius than their elemental form. This is because an extra electron is like adding a negative magnet to seven other negative magnets, resulting in a repulsive force that pushes them apart.

When atoms collide, in solutions, for example, they touch each other and then ricochet apart. The closest they come to each other is the combined length of each of their radii. This radius is known as van der Waals radius for each atom. When atoms bond with each other, however, they must come closer together than they would if they were just colliding. Their attraction also draws them closer together. The bonding atomic radius, or the covalent radius, is equal to one-half of the distance between the two atoms when they are bonded together. Within each group in the periodic table, the covalent radius increases from top to bottom. Within each period, the covalent radius decreases from left to right.

Ionization Energy and Electron Affinity

Energy is required to remove an electron from an atom or ion while it is in its ground state, usually as a gas. Ionization energy applies to all elements; it is just greater for those on the right side of the table. The ionization energy of an atom or ion is the minimum amount of energy required to do so. The greater the ionization energy, the harder it is to remove the electron. The energy required for the first electron is noted as I_1, the second as I_2, and then continues consecutively numbered for each successive electron. With each electron that is removed, the ionization energy of the element increases. I_1 increases in elements across the periods and moving down the columns of the period table. In contrast to ionization energy, energy is released from an atom when an electron is added. This negative change in energy is known as electron affinity. Ionization energies are always positive, because atoms require more energy to let go of an electron than to add one.

Looking at the periodic table, elements on the left, the alkali metals and alkali earth metals, have a low ionization energy. It takes little energy to peel off of their electron, because they have the least proton pull in their period. Elements on the right, like halogens (gases), have an extremely high ionization energy, because they have a very strong proton pull pulling electrons in, so it would require even more energy to peel off an electron. Noble gases have an extremely high ionization energy.

Going down a group, as energy levels increase, proton pull becomes less affected, so ionization energy decreases.

Molecular Weight

Elements can exist alone or combine to form compounds and molecules. Using the atomic mass, or atomic weights, that are noted on the periodic table, the molecular weight of a substance can be found by multiplying the subscript of each element by the atomic mass of that element and then adding together the weights of all of the elements in the molecule together. For example, to find the molecular weight of one glucose molecule, $C_6H_{12}O_6$, the atomic mass of carbon is multiplied by six, the atomic mass of hydrogen is multiplied by twelve, the atomic mass of oxygen is multiplied by six and then the three resulting numbers are added together. The answer is one glucose molecule has a molecular weight of 180 amu.

Atomic Structure

Atoms are made up of three subatomic particles: protons, neutrons, and electrons. The protons have a positive charge and are located in the nucleus of the atom. Neutrons have a neutral charge and are also located in the nucleus. Electrons have a negative charge, are the smallest of the three parts, and are located in orbitals that surround the nucleus. An atom is neutral if it has an equal number of electrons and protons. If an atom does not have an equal number of electrons and protons, it is an ion. When there are fewer electrons than protons, leaving it with a positive charge, it is termed a cation. When there are more electrons than protons, leaving a negative charge, it is an anion.

There are many levels of orbitals that surround the nucleus and house electrons. Each orbital has a distinct shape and three quantum numbers that characterize it: n, l, and m_l. The n is the principal quantum number and is always a positive integer, or whole number. As n increases, the size of the orbital increases and the electrons are less tightly bound to the nucleus. The angular momentum quantum number is represented by l and defines the shape of the orbital. There are four numerical values of l that correspond to four letter representations of the orbital: 0 or s, 1 or p, 2 or d, and 3 or f. Lastly, m_l represents the magnetic quantum number and describes the orientation of the orbital in space. It has a value in between $-l$ and l, including zero.

Electrons exist outside the nucleus in energy levels, and with each increasing period, there is additional energy level. Hydrogen and helium are the only elements that have only one energy level, which is an s orbital that can only hold two electrons. Their relative electron configurations are $1s^1$ and $1s^2$. Each orbital holds two electrons with opposite spins.

Energy level two can hold a total of eight electrons: two in the s orbital, and six in the p orbital, of which there are three, since electrons pair up: $p_xp_yp_z$. All alkali metals and alkali Earth metals have an electron configuration that ends in either s^1 or s^2. For example, magnesium ends in $3s^s$ and cesium ends in $6s^1$. Groups 3A to 8A all end in the Xp^y configuration, with X representing the energy level and y representing how for inland it is. For example, oxygen is $2p^4$. The third energy level has s, p, and d orbitals, and together can hold 18 electrons, since d can hold 10. D orbitals start with the transition metals, and even though it appears that they are in the fourth energy level, they actually are on the third. The energy level for the whole d block is actually the period number minus one.

<u>Example</u>
Mn: $1s^2 2s^2 2p^6 3s^2 3p^6 4s^2 3d^5$

The f block, which can hold 14 electrons, has a similar pattern for its preceding number, except two are subtracted from the period number.

Nuclear Chemistry

Nuclear chemistry is the study of reactions in which the nuclei of atoms are transformed and their identities are changed. These reactions can involve large changes in energy — much larger than the energy changes that occur when chemical bonds between atoms are made or broken. Nuclear chemistry is also used to create electricity.

Nuclear reactions are described by nuclear equations, which have different notations than regular chemical equations. Nuclear equations are written as follows, with the superscript being the mass number and the subscript being the atomic number for each element:

$$^{238}_{92}U \longrightarrow {}^{234}_{90}Th + {}^{4}_{2}He$$

The equation describes the spontaneous decomposition of uranium into thorium and helium via alpha decay. When this happens, the process is referred to as nuclear decay. Similar to chemical equations, nuclear equations must be balanced on each side; the sum of the mass numbers and the sum of the atomic numbers should be equal on both sides of the equation.

In some cases, the nucleus of an atom is unstable and constantly emits particles due to this instability. These atoms are described as radioactive and the isotopes are referred to as radioisotopes. There are three types of radioactive decay that occur most frequently: alpha (α), beta (β), and gamma (γ). Alpha radiation is emitted when a nucleus releases a stream of alpha particles, which are helium-4 nuclei. Beta radiation occurs when a stream of high-speed electrons is emitted by an unstable nucleus. The beta particles are often noted as β^-. Gamma radiation occurs when the nucleus emits high-energy photons. In gamma radiation, the atomic number and the mass remain the same for the unstable nucleus. This type of radiation represents a rearrangement of an unstable nucleus into a more stable one and often accompanies other types of radioactive emission. Radioactive decay is often described in terms of its half-life, which is the time that it takes for half of the radioactive substance to react. For example, the radioisotope strontium-90 has a half-life of 28.8 years. If there are 10 grams of strontium-90 to start with, after 28.8 years, there would be 5 grams left.

There are two distinct types of nuclear reactions: fission and fusion reactions. Both involve a large energy release. In fission reactions, a large atom is split into two or more smaller atoms. The nucleus absorbs slow-moving neutrons, resulting in a larger nucleus that is unstable. The unstable nucleus then undergoes fission. Nuclear power plants depend on nuclear fission reactions for energy. Fusion reactions involve the combination of two or more lighter atoms into a larger atom. Fusion reactions do not occur in Earth's nature due to the extreme temperature and pressure conditions required to make them happen. Fusion products are generally not radioactive. Fusion reactions are responsible for the energy that is created by the Sun.

Chemical Bonding

Chemical bonding occurs between two or more atoms that are joined together. There are three types of chemical bonds: ionic, covalent, and metallic. The characteristics of the different bonds are determined by how electrons behave in a compound. Lewis structures were developed to help visualize the electrons in molecules; they are a method of writing a compound structure formula and including its electron composition. A Lewis symbol for an element consists of the element symbol and a dot for each valence electron. The dots are located on all four sides of the symbol, with a maximum of two dots per side, and eight dots, or electrons, total. The octet rule states that atoms tend to gain, lose, or share electrons until they have a total of eight valence electrons.

Ionic Bonds

Ionic bonds are formed from the electrostatic attractions between oppositely charged atoms. They result from the transfer of electrons from a metal on the left side of the periodic table to a nonmetal on the right side. The metallic substance often has low ionization energy and will transfer an electron easily to the nonmetal, which has a high electron affinity. An example of this is the compound NaCl, which is sodium chloride or table salt, where the Na atom transfers an electron to the Cl atom. Due to strong bonding, ionic compounds have several distinct characteristics. They have high melting and boiling points, and are brittle and crystalline. They are arranged in rigid, well-defined structures, which allow them to break apart along smooth, flat surfaces. The formation of ionic bonds is a reaction that is exothermic. In the opposite scenario, the energy it takes to break up a one mole quantity of an ionic compound is referred to as lattice energy, which is generally endothermic. The Lewis structure for NaCl is written as follows:

Covalent Bonds

Covalent bonds are formed when two atoms share electrons, instead of transferring them as in ionic compounds. The atoms in covalent compounds have a balance of attraction and repulsion between their protons and electrons, which keeps them bonded together. Two atoms can be joined by single, double, or even triple covalent bonds. As the number of electrons that are shared increases, the length of the bond decreases. Covalent substances have low melting and boiling points, and are poor conductors of heat and electricity.

The Lewis structure for Cl_2 is written as follows:

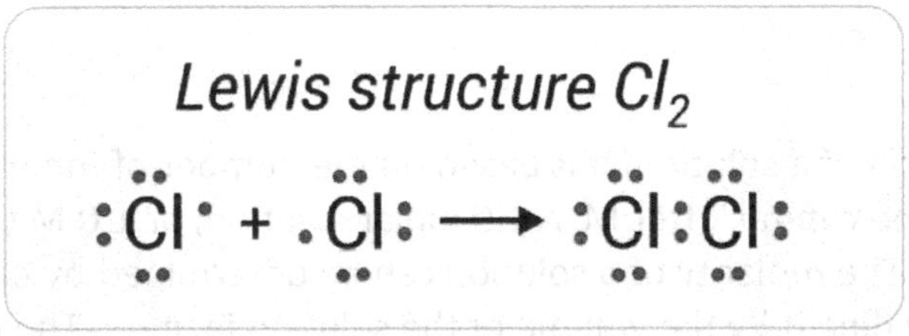

Metallic Bonds

Metallic bonds are formed by electrons that move freely through metal. They are the product of the force of attraction between electrons and metal ions. The electrons are shared by many metal cations and act like glue that holds the metallic substance together, similar to the attraction between oppositely charged atoms in ionic substances, except the electrons are more fluid and float around the bonded metals and form a sea of electrons. Metallic compounds have characteristic properties that include strength, conduction of heat and electricity, and malleability. They can conduct electricity by passing energy through the freely moving electrons, creating a current. These compounds also have high melting and boiling points. Lewis structures are not common for metallic structures because of the free-roaming ability of the electrons.

Molar Relationships

One mole is the amount of matter contained in 6.02×10^{23} of any object, such as atoms, ions, or molecules. It is a useful unit of measure for items in large quantities. This number is also known as Avogadro's number. One mole of ^{12}C atoms is equivalent to 6.02×10^{23} ^{12}C atoms. Avogadro's number is often written as an inverse mole, or as $6.02 \times 10^{23}/mol$.

Molar Mass

A mole is always the same number, equivalent to Avogadro's number. The molar mass of a substance is the mass in grams of one mole of molecules of that substance. It is numerically equivalent to the molecular weight of the substance. The molecular weight of glucose ($C_6H_{12}O_6$) is 180 amu. Therefore, the molar mass of glucose is 180 grams per mole, written as 180 g/mol. In other words, one mole of glucose, or 6.02×10^{23} molecules of glucose, has a mass of 180 grams. Two substances with different molecular weights will have two different molar masses. Compared to glucose, O_2 has a molecular weight of 32 amu, which is less than that of glucose. So, the molar mass of O_2 is 32 g/mol. One mole of O_2 has an equivalent number of molecules as one mole of glucose, but it weighs less.

A simple calculation can determine how many moles are in a certain number of grams of a substance. The amount of substance in grams is divided by the molar mass of that substance and the result is the number of moles of the substance. Similarly, to convert the number of moles of a substance to the amount of grams, multiply the number of moles by the molar mass of the substance. The result is the amount of grams of the substance.

It is also possible to calculate the number of molecules in a certain number of grams of substance using Avogadro's number and the molar mass. The number of known grams is divided by the molar mass and then multiplied by Avogadro's number. The result is the number of molecules in the starting amount of grams.

Molarity

Molarity is the concentration of a solution. It is based on the number of moles of solute in one liter of solution and is written as the capital letter M. A 1.0 molar solution, or 1.0 M solution, has one mole of solute per liter of solution. The molarity of a solution can be determined by calculating the number of moles of the solute and dividing it by the volume of the solution in liters. The resulting number is the mol/L or M for molarity of the solution.

Ionic solutions can also be described by molarity values. Since ionic compounds dissolve in solution, the chemical formula of the compound can be used to determine the relative concentrations of the ions in the solution. For example, in a 1.0 M solution of NaCl, there is 1.0 M Na^+ ions and 1.0 M Cl^- ions. In a 1.0 M solution of Na_2SO_4, there are two Na^+ ions (2.0 M) for every one SO_4^{2-} ion (1.0 M).

Stoichiometry

Stoichiometry investigates the quantities of chemicals that are consumed and produced in chemical reactions. Chemical equations are made up of reactants and products; stoichiometry helps elucidate how the changes from reactants to products occur, as well as how to ensure the equation is balanced.

Limiting Reactants

Chemical reactions are limited by the amount of starting material, or reactants, available to drive the process forward. The reactant that has the smallest amount of substance is called the limiting reactant. The limiting reactant is completely consumed by the end of the reaction. The other reactants are called excess reactants. For example, gasoline is used in a combustion reaction to make a car move and is the limiting reactant of the reaction. If the gasoline runs out, the combustion reaction can no longer take place, and the car stops.

Reaction Yield

The quantity of product that should be produced after using up all of the limiting reactant can be calculated, and is called the theoretical yield of the reaction. Since the reactants do not always act as they should, the actual amount of resulting product is called the actual yield. The actual yield is divided by the theoretical yield and then multiplied by 100 to find the percent yield for the reaction.

Solution Stoichiometry

Solution stoichiometry deals with quantities of solutes in chemical reactions that occur in solutions. The quantity of a solute in a solution can be calculated by multiplying the molarity of the solution by the volume. Similar to chemical equations involving simple elements, the number of moles of the elements that make up the solute should be equivalent on both sides of the equation.

When the concentration of a particular solute in a solution is unknown, a titration is used to determine that concentration. In a titration, the solution with the unknown solute is combined with a standard solution, which is a solution with a known solute concentration. The point at which the unknown solute has completely reacted with the known solute is called the equivalence point. Using the known information about the standard solution, including the concentration and volume, and the volume of the unknown solution, the concentration of the unknown solute is determined in a balanced equation. For example, in the case of combining acids and bases, the equivalence point is reached when the resulting solution is neutral. HCl, an acid, combines with NaOH, a base, to form water, which is neutral, and a solution of Cl^- ions and Na^+ ions. Before the equivalence point, there are an unequal number of cations and anions and the solution is not neutral.

Reaction Rates

The rate of a reaction is the measure of the change in concentration of the reactants or products over a certain period of time. Many factors affect how fast or slow a reaction occurs, such as concentration, pressure, or temperature. As the concentration of a reactant increases, the rate of the reaction also increases, because the frequency of collisions between elements increases. High-pressure situations for reactants that are gases cause the gas to compress and increase the frequency of gas molecule collisions, similar to solutions with higher concentrations. Reactions rates are then increased with the higher frequency of gas molecule collisions. Higher temperatures usually increase the rate of the reaction, adding more energy to the system with heat and increasing the frequency of molecular collisions.

Equilibrium

Equilibrium is described as the state of a system when no net changes occur. Chemical equilibrium occurs when opposing reactions occur at equal rates. In other words, the rate of reactants forming products is equal to the rate of the products breaking down into the reactants — the concentration of reactants and products in the system doesn't change. Although the concentrations are not changing, the forward and reverse reactions are likely still occurring. This type of equilibrium is called a dynamic equilibrium. In situations where all reactions have ceased, a static equilibrium is reached. Chemical equilibriums are also described as homogeneous or heterogeneous. Homogeneous equilibrium involves substances that are all in the same phase, while heterogeneous equilibrium means the substances are in different phases when equilibrium is reached.

When a reaction reaches equilibrium, the conditions of the equilibrium are described by the following equation, based on the chemical equation $aA + bB \leftrightarrow cC + dD$:

$$K_c = \frac{[C]^c[D]^d}{[A]^a[B]^b}$$

This equation describes the law of mass action. It explains how the reactants and products react during dynamic equilibrium. K_c is the equilibrium constant and is obtained when molarity values are put into the equation for the reactants and products. It is important to note that K_c is only dependent on the stoichiometry of the equation. If K_c is greater than 1, the equilibrium occurs when there are more products generated; the equilibrium lies to the right. If K_c is less than 1, the equilibrium occurs when there are more reactants generated and the equilibrium is to the left.

Similar to finding K_c, the quantity of reactants and products, as well as the direction of the reaction can be determined at any point of time by finding Q, the reaction quotient. Q_c is substituted for the K_c in the equation above. If Q is less than K, the concentration of the reactants is too large and the concentration of the products is too small, so the reaction must move from left to right to achieve equilibrium. If Q is equal to K, the system is at equilibrium. If Q is greater than K, the concentration of the products is too large and the concentration of the reactants is too small; the reaction must move from right to left to reach equilibrium.

Oxidation and Reduction

Oxidation and reduction reactions, also known as redox reactions, are those in which electrons are transferred from one element to another. Batteries and fuel cells are two energy-related technologies that utilize these reactions. When an atom, ion, or molecule loses its electrons and becomes more positively charged, it is described as being oxidized. When a substance gains electrons and becomes more negatively charged, it is reduced. In chemical reactions, if one element or molecule is oxidized, another must be reduced for the equation to be balanced. Although the transfer of electrons is obvious in some reactions where ions are formed, redox reactions also include those in which electrons are transferred but the products remain neutral.

Oxidation Numbers

Keep track of oxidation states or oxidation numbers to ensure the chemical equation is balanced. Oxidation numbers are assigned to each atom in a neutral substance or ion. For ions made up of a single atom, the oxidation number is equal to the charge of the ion. For atoms in their original elemental form, the oxidation number is always zero. Each hydrogen atom in an H_2 molecule, for example, has an oxidation number of zero. The sum of the oxidation numbers in a molecule should be equal to the overall charge of the molecule. If the molecule is a positively charged ion, the sum of the oxidation number should be equal to overall positive charge of the molecule. In ionic compounds that have a cation and anion joined, the sum of the oxidation numbers should equal zero.

Balancing Redox Reactions

All chemical equations must have the same number of elements on each side of the equation to be balanced. Redox reactions have an extra step of counting the electrons on both sides of the equation to be balanced. Separating redox reactions into oxidation reactions and reduction reactions is a simple way to account for all of the electrons involved. The individual equations are known as half-reactions. The number of electrons lost in the oxidation reaction must be equal to the number of electrons gained in the reduction reaction for the redox reaction to be balanced. The oxidation of tin (Sn) by iron (Fe) can be balanced by the following half-reactions:

Oxidation: $Sn^{2+} \longrightarrow Sn^{4+} + 2e^-$

Reduction: $2Fe^{3+} + 2e^- \longrightarrow 2Fe^{2+}$

Complete redox reaction: $Sn^{2+} + 2Fe^{3+} \longrightarrow Sn^{4+} + 2Fe^{2+}$

Acids and Bases

Acids and bases are defined in many different ways. An acid can be described as a substance that increases the concentration of H^+ ions when it is dissolved in water, as a proton donor in a chemical equation, or as an electron-pair acceptor. A base can be a substance that increases the concentration of OH^- ions when it is dissolved in water, accepts a proton in a chemical reaction, or is an electron-pair donor.

Autoionization of Water

Water can act as either an acid or a base. When mixed with an acid, water can accept a proton and become an H_3O^+ ion. When mixed with a base, water can donate a proton and become an OH^- ion. Sometimes water molecules donate and accept protons from each other; this process is called autoionization. The chemical equation is written as follows: $H_2O + H_2O \longrightarrow OH^- + H_3O^+$.

PH Scale

The pH scale is a numeric scale that determines whether a solution is acidic, basic, or neutral. The pH of a solution is equal to the inverse base 10 logarithm of its activity of H^+ ions ($pH = \log_{10}(1/(H^+ \text{ activity}))$). Solutions with a pH value greater than seven are considered basic and those with a pH value less than seven are considered acidic. Water is neutral and has a pH of 7.0.

Strength of Acids and Bases

Acids and bases are characterized as strong, weak, or somewhere in between. Strong acids and bases completely or almost completely ionize in aqueous solution. The chemical reaction is driven completely forward, to the right side of the equation, where the acidic or basic ions are formed. Weak acids and bases do not completely disassociate in aqueous solution. They only partially ionize and the solution becomes a mixture of the acid or base, water, and the acidic or basic ions. Strong acids are complemented by weak bases, and vice versa. A conjugate acid is an ion that forms when its base pair gains a proton. For example, the conjugate acid NH_4^+ is formed from the base NH_3. The conjugate base that pairs with an acid is the ion that is formed when an acid loses a proton. NO_2^- is the conjugate base of the acid HNO_2.

Mechanics

Description of Motion in One and Two Dimensions

The description of motion is known as *kinetics*, and the causes of motion are known as *dynamics*. Motion in one dimension is known as a *scalar* quantity. It consists of one measurement such as length (length or distance is also known as displacement), speed, or time. Motion in two dimensions is known as a *vector* quantity. This would be a speed with a direction, or velocity.

Velocity is the measure of the change in distance over the change in time. All vector quantities have a direction that can be relayed through the sign of an answer, such as -5.0 m/s or +5.0 m/s. The objects registering these velocities would be in opposite directions, where the change in distance is denoted by Δx and the change in time is denoted by Δt:

$$v = \frac{\Delta x}{\Delta t}$$

Acceleration is the measure of the change in an object's velocity over a change in time, where the change in velocity, $v_2 - v_1$, is denoted by Δv and the change in time, $t_1 - t_2$, is denoted by Δt:

$$a = \frac{\Delta v}{\Delta t}$$

The linear momentum, *p*, of an object is the result of the objects mass, *m*, multiplied by its velocity, *v*, and is described by the equation:

$$p = mv$$

This aspect becomes important when one object hits another object. For example, the linear momentum of a small sports car will be much smaller than the linear momentum of a large semi-truck. Thus, the semi-truck will cause more damage to the car than the car to the truck.

Newton's Three Laws of Motion

Sir Isaac Newton summarized his observations and calculations relating to motion into three concise laws.

First Law of Motion: Inertia

This law states that an object in motion tends to stay in motion or an object at rest tends to stay at rest, unless the object is acted upon by an outside force.

For example, a rock sitting on the ground will remain in the same place, unless it is pushed or lifted from its place.

The First Law also includes the relation of weight to gravity and force between objects relative to the distance separating them.

$$Weight = G\frac{Mm}{r^2}$$

In this equation, *G* is the gravitational constant, *M* and *m* are the masses of the two objects, and *r* is the distance separating the two objects.

Second Law of Motion: F = ma

This law states that the force on a given body is the result of the object's mass multiplied by any acceleration acting upon the object. For objects falling on Earth, an acceleration is caused by gravitational force (9.8 m/s^2).

Third Law of Motion: Action-Reaction

This law states that for every action there is an equal and opposite reaction. For example, if a person punches a wall, the wall exerts a force back on the person's hand equal and opposite to his or her punching force. Since the wall has more mass, it absorbs the impact of the punch better than the person's hand.

Mass, Weight, and Gravity

Mass is a measure of how much of a substance exists, or how much inertia an object has. The mass of an object does not change based on the object's location, but the weight of an object does vary with its location.

For example, a 15-kg mass has a weight that is determined by acceleration from the force of gravity here on Earth. However, if that same 15-kg mass were to be weighed on the moon, it would weigh much less, since the acceleration force from the moon's gravity is approximately one-sixth of that on Earth.

Weight = mass × acceleration

$$W_{Earth} = 15\text{ kg} \times 9.8\text{ m/s}^2 \quad > \quad W_{Moon} = 15\text{ kg} \times 1.62\text{ m/s}^2$$

$$W_{Earth} = 147\text{N} \quad > \quad 24.3\text{N}$$

Analysis of Motion and Forces

Projectile Motion describes the path of an object in the air. Generally, it is described by two-dimensional movement, such as a stone thrown through the air. This activity maps to a parabolic curve. However, the definition of projectile motion also applies to free fall, or the non-arced motion of an object in a path straight up and/or straight down. When an object is thrown horizontally, it is subject to the same influence of gravity as an object that is dropped straight down. The farther the projectile motion, the farther the distance of the object's flight.

Friction is a force that opposes motion. It can be caused by a number of materials; there is even friction caused by air. Whenever two differing materials touch, rub, or pass by each other, it will create friction, or an oppositional force, unless the interaction occurs in a true vacuum. To move an object across a floor, the force exerted on the object must overcome the frictional force keeping the object in place. Friction is also why people can walk on surfaces. Without the oppositional force of friction to a shoe pressing on the floor, a person would not be able to grip the floor to walk—similar to the challenge of walking on ice. Without friction, shoes slip and are unable to help people propel forward and walk.

When calculating the effects of objects hitting (or colliding with) each other, several things are important to remember. One of these is the definition of momentum: the mass of an object multiplied by the object's velocity. As mentioned, it is expressed by the following equation:

$$p = mv$$

Here, *p* is equal to an object's momentum, *m* is equal to the object's mass, and *v* is equal to the object's velocity.

Another important thing to remember is the principle of the conservation of linear momentum. The total momentum for objects in a situation will be the same before and after a collision. There are two primary types of collisions: elastic and inelastic. In an elastic collision, the objects collide and then travel in different directions. During an inelastic collision, the objects collide and then stick together in their final direction of travel. The total momentum in an elastic collision is calculated by using the following formula:

$$m_1v_1 + m_2v_2 = m_1v_1 + m_2v_2$$

Here, m_1 and m_2 are the masses of two separate objects, and v_1 and v_2 are the velocities, respectively, of the two separate objects.

The total momentum in an inelastic collision is calculated by using the following formula:

$$m_1v_1 + m_2v_2 = (m_1 + m_2)v_f$$

Here, v_f is the final velocity of the two masses after they stick together post-collision.

Example:

If two bumper cars are speeding toward each other, head-on, and collide, they are designed to bounce off of each other and head in different directions. This would be an elastic collision.

If real cars are speeding toward each other, head-on, and collide, there is a good chance their bumpers might get caught together and their direction of travel would be together in the same direction.

An *axis* is an invisible line on which an object can rotate. This is most easily observed with a toy top. There is actually a point (or rod) through the center of the top on which the top can be observed to be spinning. This is called the axis.

When objects move in a circle by spinning on their own axis, or because they are tethered around a central point (also an axis), they exhibit circular motion. Circular motion is similar in many ways to linear (straight line) motion; however, there are a few additional points to note. A spinning object is always accelerating because it is always changing direction. The force causing this constant acceleration on or around an axis is called *centripetal force* and is often associated with centripetal acceleration. Centripetal force always pulls toward the axis of rotation. An imaginary reactionary force, called *centrifugal force*, is the outward force felt when an object is undergoing circular motion. This reactionary force is not the real force; it just feels like it is there. For this reason, it has also been referred to as a "fictional force." The true force is the one pulling inward, or the centripetal force.

The terms *centripetal* and *centrifugal* are often mistakenly interchanged. If the centripetal force acting on an object moving with circular motion is removed, the object will continue moving in a straight line tangent to the point on the circle where the object last experienced the centripetal force. For example, when a traditional style washing machine spins a load of clothes to expunge the water from the load, it rapidly spins the machine barrel. A force is pulling in toward the center of the circle (centripetal force). At the same time, the wet clothes, which are attempting to move in a straight line, are colliding with the outer wall of the barrel that is moving in a circle. The interaction between the wet clothes and barrel wall cause a reactionary force to the centripetal force and this expels the water out of the small holes that line the outer wall of the barrel.

Conservation of Angular Momentum

An object moving in a circular motion also has momentum; for circular motion, it is called *angular momentum*. This is determined by rotational inertia, rotational velocity, and the distance of the mass from the axis or center of rotation. When objects exhibit circular motion, they also demonstrate the *conservation of angular momentum*, meaning that the angular momentum of a system is always constant, regardless of the placement of the mass. Rotational inertia can be affected by how far the mass of the object is placed with respect to the axis of rotation. The greater the distance between the mass and the axis of rotation, the slower the rotational velocity. Conversely, if the mass is closer to the axis of rotation, the rotational velocity is faster. A change in one affects the other, thus conserving the angular momentum. This holds true as long as no external forces act upon the system.

For example, ice skaters spinning in on one ice skate extends their arms out for a slower rotational velocity. When skaters bring their arms in close to their bodies (which lessens the distance between the mass and the axis of rotation), their rotational velocity increases and they spin much faster. Some skaters extend their arms straight up above their head, which causes an extension of the axis of rotation, thus removing any distance between the mass and the center of rotation, which maximizes their rotational velocity.

Another example is when a person selects a horse on a merry-go-round: the placement of their horse can affect their ride experience. All of the horses are traveling with the same rotational speed, but in order to travel along the same plane as the merry-go-round turns, a horse on the outside will have a greater linear speed because it is further away from the axis of rotation. Essentially, an outer horse has to cover a lot more ground than a horse on the inside in order to keep up with the rotational speed of the merry-go-round platform. Thrill seekers should always select an outer horse.

The center of mass is the point that provides the average location for the total mass of a system. The word "system" can apply to just one object/particle or to many. The center of mass for a system can be calculated by finding the average of the mass of each object and multiplying by its distance from an origin point using the following formula:

$$x_{centerofmass} = \frac{m_1 x_1 + m_2 x_2}{m_1 + m_2}$$

In this case, *x* is the distance from the point of origin for the center of mass and each respective object, and *m* is the mass of each object.

To calculate for more than one object, the pattern can be continued by adding additional masses and their respective distances from the origin point.

Simple Machines

A simple machine is a mechanical device that changes the direction or magnitude of a force. There are six basic types of simple machines: lever, wedge, screw, inclined plane, wheel and axle, and pulley.

Here is how each type works and an example:

- A lever helps lift heavy items higher with less force, such as a crowbar lifting a large cast iron lid.
- A wedge helps apply force to a specific area by focusing the pressure, such as an axe splitting a tree.
- An inclined plane, such as a loading dock ramp, helps move heavy items up vertical distances with less force.
- A screw is an inclined plane wrapped around an axis and allows more force to be applied by extending the distance of the plane. For example, a screw being turned into a piece of wood provides greater securing strength than hitting a nail into the wood.
- A wheel and axle allows the use of rotational force around an axis to assist with applying force. For example, a wheelbarrow makes it easier to haul large loads by employing a wheel and axle at the front.
- A pulley is an application of a wheel and axle with the addition of cords or ropes and it helps move objects vertically. For example, pulling a bucket out of a well is easier with a pulley and ropes.

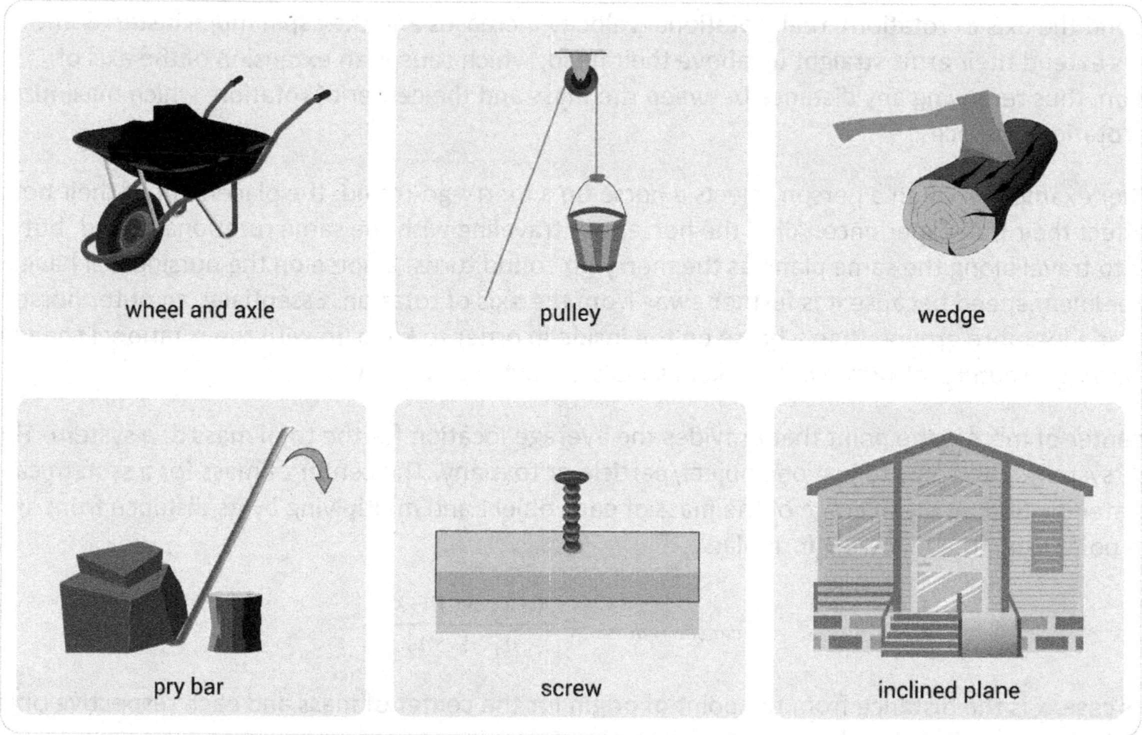

Using a simple machine employs an advantage to the user. This is referred to as the mechanical advantage. It can be calculated by comparing the force input by the user to the simple machine with the force output from the use of the machine (also displayed as a ratio).

$$Mechanical\ Advantage = \frac{output\ force}{input\ force}$$

$$MA = \frac{F_{out}}{F_{in}}$$

In the following instance of using a lever, it can be helpful to calculate the torque, or circular force, necessary to move something. This is also employed when using a wrench to loosen a bolt.

$$Torque = F \times distance\ of\ lever\ arm\ from\ the\ axis\ of\ rotation\ (called\ the\ moment\ arm)$$

$$T = F \times d$$

Electricity and Magnetism

Electrical Nature of Common Materials

Generally, an atom carries no net charge because the positive charges of the protons in the nucleus balance the negative charges of the electrons in the outer shells of the atom. This is considered to be electrically neutral. However, since electrons are the only portion of the atom known to have the freedom to "move," this can cause an object to become electrically charged. This happens either through a gain or a loss of electrons. Electrons have a negative charge, so a gain creates a net negative charge for the object. On the contrary, a loss of electrons creates a positive charge for the object. This charge can also be focused on specific areas of an object, causing a notable interaction between charged objects. For example, if a person rubs a balloon on a carpet, the balloon transfers some of is electrons to the carpet. So, if that person were to hold a balloon near his or her hair, the electrons in the "neutral" hair would make the hair stand on end. This is due to the electrons wanting to fill the deficit of electrons on the balloon. Unless electrically forced into a charged state, most natural objects in nature tend toward reestablishing and maintaining a neutral charge.

When dealing with charges, it is easiest to remember that *like charges repel* each other and *opposite charges attract* each other. Therefore, negatives and positives attract, while two positives or two negatives will repel each other. Similarly, when two charges come near each other, they exert a force on one another. This is described through *Coulomb's Law*:

$$F = k\frac{q_1 q_2}{r^2}$$

In this equation, F is equal to the force exerted by the interaction, k is a constant ($k = 8.99 \times 10^9$ N m^2/C^2), q_1 and q_2 are the measure of the two charges, and r is the distance between the two charges.

When materials readily transfer electricity or electrons, or can easily accept or lose electrons, they are considered to be good conductors. The transferring of electricity is called *conductivity*. If a material does not readily accept the transfer of electrons or readily loses electrons, it is considered to be an *insulator*. For example, copper wire easily transfers electricity because copper is a good conductor. However, plastic does not transfer electricity because it is not a good conductor. In fact, plastic is an insulator.

Basic Electrical Concepts

In an electrical circuit, the flow from a power source, or the voltage, is "drawn" across the components in the circuit from the positive end to the negative end. This flow of charge creates an electric current (*I*), which is the time (*t*) rate of flow of net charge (*q*). It is measured with the formula:

$$I = \frac{q}{t}$$

Current is measured in amperes (amps). There are two main types of currents:

1. *Direct current* (DC): a unidirectional flow of charges through a circuit

2. *Alternating current* (AC): a circuit with a changing directional flow of charges or magnitude

Every circuit will show a loss in voltage across its conducting material. This loss of voltage is from resistance within the circuit and can be caused by multiple factors, including resistance from wiring and components such as light bulbs and switches. To measure the resistance in a given circuit, Ohm's law is used:

$$Resistance = \frac{Voltage}{current} = R = \frac{V}{I}$$

Resistance (*R*) is measured in Ohms (Ω).

Components in a circuit can be wired *in series* or *in parallel*. If the components are wired in series, a single wire connects each component to the next in line. If the components are wired in parallel, two wires connect each component to the next. The main difference is that the voltage across those in series is directly related from one component to the next. Therefore, if the first component in the series becomes inoperable, no voltage can get to the other components. Conversely, the components in parallel share the voltage across each other and are not dependent on the prior component wired to allow the voltage across the wire.

To calculate the resistance of circuit components wired in series or parallel, the following equations are used:

Resistance in series:

$$R_{total} = R_1 + R_2 + R_3 + \cdots$$

Resistance in parallel:

$$R_{total} = \frac{1}{R_1} + \frac{1}{R_2} + \frac{1}{R_3} + \cdots$$

To make electrons move so that they can carry their charge, a change in voltage must be present. On a small scale, this is demonstrated through the electrons traveling from the light switch to a person's finger. This might happen in a situation where a person runs his or her socks on a carpet, touches a light switch, and receives a small jolt from the electrons that run from the switch to the finger. This minor jolt is due to the deficit of electrons created by rubbing the socks on the carpet, and then the electrons going into the ground. The difference in charge between the switch and the finger caused the electrons to move.

If this situation were to be created on a larger and more sustained scale, the factors would need to be more systematic, predictable, and harnessed. This could be achieved through batteries/cells and generators. Batteries or cells have a chemical reaction that occurs inside, causing energy to be released and charges to be able to move freely. Batteries generally have nodes (one positive and one negative), where items can be hooked up to complete a circuit and allow the charge to travel freely through the item. Generators convert mechanical energy into electric energy using power and movement.

<u>Basic Properties of Magnetic Fields and Forces</u>

Magnetic forces can occur naturally in certain types of materials. If two straight rods are made from iron, they will naturally have a negative end (pole) and a positive end (pole). These charged poles react just like any charged item: opposite charges attract and like charges repel. They will attract each other when arranged positive pole to negative pole. However, if one rod is turned around, the two rods will now repel each other due to the alignment of negative to negative and positive to positive. These types of forces can also be created and amplified by using an electric current. For example, sending an electric current through a stretch of wire creates an electromagnetic force around the wire from the charge of the current. This force exists as long as the flow of electricity is sustained. This magnetic force can also attract and repel other items with magnetic properties. Depending on the strength of the current in the wire, a greater or smaller magnetic force can be generated around the wire. As soon as the current is stopped, the magnetic force also stops.

Optics and Waves

<u>Electromagnetic Spectrum</u>

The movement of light is described like the movement of waves. Light travels with a wave front, has an amplitude (height from the neutral), a cycle or wavelength, a period, and energy. Light travels at approximately 3.00×10^8 m/s and is faster than anything created by humans thus far.

Light is commonly referred to by its measured wavelengths, or the distance between two successive crests or troughs in a wave. Types of light with the longest wavelengths include radio, TV, and micro, and infrared waves. The next set of wavelengths are detectable by the human eye and create the *visible spectrum*. The visible spectrum has wavelengths of 10^{-7} m, and the colors seen are red, orange, yellow, green, blue, indigo, and violet. Beyond the visible spectrum are shorter wavelengths (also called the *electromagnetic spectrum*) containing ultraviolet light, X-rays, and gamma rays. The wavelengths outside of the visible light range can be harmful to humans if they are directly exposed or are exposed for long periods of time. For example, the light from the Sun has a small percentage of ultraviolet (UV) light, which is mostly absorbed by the UV layer of the Earth's atmosphere. When this layer does not filter out the UV rays, the exposure to the wavelengths can be harmful to humans' skin. When there is an extra layer of pollutants, and the light from the sun is trapped by repeated reflection to the Earth (so that it is unable to bounce back into space), it creates another harmful condition for the Earth called the *greenhouse effect*. This is an overexposure to the Sun's light and contributes to *global warming* by increasing the temperature on Earth.

<u>Basic Characteristics and Types of Waves</u>

A *mechanical wave* is a type of wave that passes through a medium (solid, liquid, or gas). There are two basic types of mechanical waves: longitudinal and transverse.

A *longitudinal wave* has motion that is parallel to the direction of the wave's travel. This can best be visualized by compressing one side of a tethered spring and then releasing that end. The movement travels in a bunching/un-bunching motion across the length of the spring and back.

A *transverse wave* has motion that is perpendicular to the direction of the wave's travel. The particles on a transverse wave do not move across the length of the wave; instead, they oscillate up and down, creating peaks and troughs.

A wave with a combination of both longitudinal and transverse motion can be seen through the motion of a wave on the ocean—with peaks and troughs, and particles oscillating up and down.

Mechanical waves can carry energy, sound, and light, but they need a medium through which transport can occur. An electromagnetic wave can transmit energy without a medium, or in a vacuum.

A more recent addition in the study of waves is the *gravitational wave*. Its existence has been proven and verified, yet the details surrounding its capabilities are still somewhat under inquiry. Gravitational waves are purported to be ripples that propagate as waves outward from their source and travel in the curvature of space/time. They are thought to carry energy in a form of radiant energy called *gravitational radiation*.

Basic Wave Phenomena

When a wave crosses a boundary or travels from one medium to another, certain things occur. If the wave can travel through one medium into another medium, it experiences *refraction*. This is the bending of the wave from one medium to another due to a change in density of the mediums, and thus, the speed of the wave changes. For example, when a pencil is sitting in half of a glass of water, a side view of the glass makes the pencil appear to be bent at the water level. What the viewer is seeing is the refraction of light waves traveling from the air into the water. Since the wave speed is slowed in water, the change makes the pencil appear bent.

When a wave hits a medium that it cannot penetrate, it is bounced back in an action called *reflection*. For example, when light waves hit a mirror, they are reflected, or bounced, off the mirror. This can cause it to seem like there is more light in the room, since there is a "doubling back" of the initial wave. This same phenomenon also causes people to be able to see their reflection in a mirror.

When a wave travels through a slit or around an obstacle, it is known as *diffraction*. A light wave will bend around an obstacle or through a slit and cause what is called a *diffraction pattern*. When the waves bend around an obstacle, it causes the addition of waves and the spreading of light on the other side of the opening.

Dispersion is used to describe the splitting of a single wave by refracting its components into separate parts. For example, if a wave of white light is sent through a dispersion prism, the light appears as its separate rainbow-colored components, due to each colored wavelength being refracted in the prism.

When wavelengths hit boundaries, different things occur. Objects will absorb certain wavelengths of light and reflect others, depending on the boundaries. This becomes important when an object appears to be a certain color. The color of an object is not actually within that object, but rather, in the wavelengths being transmitted by that object. For example, if a table appears to be red, that means the table is absorbing all other wavelengths of visible light except those of the red wavelength. The table is reflecting, or transmitting, the wavelengths associated with red back to the human eye, and so it appears red.

Interference describes when an object affects the path of a wave, or another wave interacts with a wave. Waves interacting with each other can result in either *constructive interference* or *destructive interference*, based on their positions. With constructive interference, the waves are in sync with each other and combine to reinforce each other. In the case of deconstructive interference, the waves are out of sync and reduce the effect of each other to some degree. In *scattering*, the boundary can change the direction or energy of a wave, thus altering the entire wave. *Polarization* changes the oscillations of a wave and can alter its appearance in light waves. For example, polarized sunglasses remove the "glare" from sunlight by altering the oscillation pattern observed by the wearer.

When a wave hits a boundary and is completely reflected, or if it cannot escape from one medium to another, it is called *total internal reflection*. This effect can be seen in the diamonds with a brilliant cut. The angle cut on the sides of the diamond causes the light hitting the diamond to be completely reflected back inside the gem, making it appear brighter and more colorful than a diamond with different angles cut into its surface.

The *Doppler effect* applies to situations with both light and sound waves. The premise of the Doppler effect is that, based upon the relative position or movement of a source and an observer, waves can seem shorter or longer than they actually are. When the Doppler effect is noted with sound, it warps the noise being heard by the observer. This makes the pitch or frequency seem shorter or higher as the source is approaching, and then longer or lower as the source is getting farther away. The frequency/pitch of the source never actually changes, but the sound in respect to the observer makes it seem like the sound has changed. This can be observed when a siren passes by an observer on the road. The siren sounds much higher in pitch as it approaches the observer and then lower after it passes and is getting farther away.

The Doppler effect also applies to situations involving light waves. An observer in space would see light approaching as being shorter wavelengths than the light actually is, causing it to look blue. When the light wave gets farther away, the light would appear red because of the apparent elongation of the wavelength. This is called the *red-blue shift*.

Basic Optics

When reflecting light, a mirror can be used to observe a virtual (not real) image. A *plane mirror* is a piece of glass with a coating in the background to create a reflective surface. An image is what the human eye sees when light is reflected off the mirror in an unmagnified manner. If a *curved mirror* is used for reflection, the image seen will not be a true reflection. Instead, the image will either be enlarged or miniaturized compared to its actual size. Curved mirrors can also make the object appear closer or farther away than the actual distance the object is from the mirror.

Lenses can be used to refract or bend light to form images. Examples of lenses are the human eye, microscopes, and telescopes. The human eye interprets the refraction of light into images that humans understand to be actual size. *Microscopes* allow objects that are too small for the unaided human eye to be enlarged enough to be seen. *Telescopes* allow objects to be viewed that are too far away to be seen with the unaided eye. *Prisms* are pieces of glass that can have a wavelength of light enter one side and appear to be divided into its component wavelengths on the other side. This is due to the ability of the prism to slow certain wavelengths more than others.

Sound

Sound travels in waves and is the movement of vibrations through a medium. It can travel through air (gas), land, water, etc. For example, the noise a human hears in the air is the vibration of the waves as they reach the ear. The human brain translates the different frequencies (pitches) and intensities of the vibrations to determine what created the noise.

A tuning fork has a predetermined frequency because of the length and thickness of its tines. When struck, it allows vibrations between the two tines to move the air at a specific rate. This creates a specific tone, or note, for that size of tuning fork. The number of vibrations over time is also steady for that tuning fork and can be matched with a frequency. All pitches heard by the human ear are categorized by using frequency and are measured in Hertz (cycles per second).

The level of sound in the air is measured with sound level meters on a decibel (dB) scale. These meters respond to changes in air pressure caused by sound waves and measure sound intensity. One decibel is 1/10th of a *bel*, named after Alexander Graham Bell, the inventor of the telephone. The decibel scale is logarithmic, so it is measured in factors of 10. This means, for example, that a 10 dB increase on a sound meter equates to a 10-fold increase in sound intensity.

Earth and Space Science

Types and Basic Characteristics of Rocks and Minerals and Their Formation Processes

The Rock Cycle

Although it may not always be apparent, rocks are constantly being destroyed while new ones are created in a process called the *rock cycle*. This cycle is driven by plate tectonics and the water cycle, which are discussed in detail later. The rock cycle starts with *magma*, the molten rock found deep within the Earth. As magma moves toward the Earth's surface, it hardens and transforms into igneous rock. Then, over time, igneous rock is broken down into tiny pieces called *sediment* that are eventually deposited all over the surface. As more and more sediment accumulates, the weight of the newer sediment compresses the older sediment underneath and creates sedimentary rock. As sedimentary rock is pushed deeper below the surface, the high pressure and temperature transform it into metamorphic rock. This metamorphic rock can either rise to the surface again or sink even deeper and melt back into magma, thus starting the cycle again.

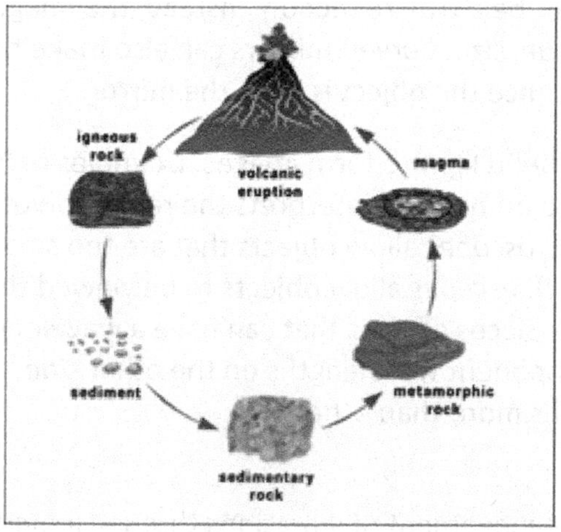

Characteristics of Rocks and Their Formation Processes

There are three main types of rocks: sedimentary, igneous, and metamorphic. Aside from physical characteristics, one of their main differences is how they are created. *Sedimentary rocks* are formed at the surface, on land and in bodies of water, through processes called deposition and cementation. They can be classified as clastic, biochemical, and chemical. *Clastic rocks*, such as sandstone, are composed of other pieces of inorganic rocks and sediment. *Biochemical rocks* are created from an organic material, such as coal, forming from dead plant life. *Chemical rocks* are created from the deposition of dissolved minerals, such as calcium salts that form stalagmites and stalactites in caves.

Igneous rocks are created when magma solidifies at or near the Earth's surface. When they're formed at the surface, (i.e. from volcanic eruption), they are *extrusive*. When they form below the surface, they're called *intrusive*. Examples of extrusive rocks are obsidian and tuff, while rocks like granite are intrusive.

Metamorphic rocks are the result of a transformation from other rocks. Based on appearance, these rocks are classified as foliated or non-foliated. *Foliated rocks* are created from compression in one direction, making them appear layered or folded like slate. *Non-foliated rocks* are compressed from all directions, giving them a more homogenous appearance, such as marble.

<u>Characteristics of Minerals and Their Formation Processes</u>
A *mineral*, such as gold, is a naturally occurring inorganic solid composed of one type of molecule or element that's organized into a crystalline structure. Rocks are aggregates of different types of minerals. Depending on their composition, minerals can be mainly classified into one of the following eight groups:

- *Carbonates*: formed from molecules that have either a carbon, nitrogen, or boron atom at the center.
- *Elements*: formed from single elements that occur naturally; includes metals such as gold and nickel, as well as metallic alloys like brass.
- *Halides:* formed from molecules that have halogens; halite, which is table salt, is a classic example.
- *Oxides*: formed from molecules that contain oxygen or hydroxide and are held together with ionic bonds; encompasses the phosphates, silicates, and sulfates.
- *Phosphates*: formed from molecules that contain phosphates; the apatite group minerals are in this class.
- *Silicates*: formed from molecules that contain silicon, silicates are the largest class and usually the most complex minerals; topaz is an example of a silicate.
- *Sulfates*: formed from molecules that contain either sulfur, chromium, tungsten, selenium, tellurium, and/or molybdenum.
- *Sulfides*: formed from molecules that contain sulfide (S^{2-}); includes many of the important metal ores, such as lead and silver.

One important physical characteristic of a mineral is its *hardness*, which is defined as its resistance to scratching. When two crystals are struck together, the harder crystal will scratch the softer crystal. The most common measure of hardness is the Mohs Hardness Scale, which ranges from 1 to 10, with 10 being the hardest. Diamonds are rated 10 on the Mohs Hardness Scale, and talc, which was once used to make baby powder, is rated 1. Other important characteristics of minerals include *luster* or shine, *color,* and *cleavage*, which is the natural plane of weakness at which a specific crystal breaks.

Erosion, Weathering, and Deposition of Earth's Surface Materials and Soil Formation

Erosion and Deposition

Erosion is the process of moving rock and occurs when rock and sediment are picked up and transported. Wind, water, and ice are the primary factors for erosion. *Deposition* occurs when the particles stop moving and settle onto a surface, which can happen through gravity or involve processes such as precipitation or flocculation. *Precipitation* is the solidification or crystallization of dissolved ions that occurs when a solution is oversaturated. *Flocculation* is similar to coagulation and occurs when colloid materials (materials that aren't dissolved but are suspended in the medium) aggregate or clump until they are too heavy to remain suspended.

Chemical and Physical (Mechanical) Weathering

Weathering is the process of breaking down rocks through mechanical or chemical changes. Mechanical forces include animal contact, wind, extreme weather, and the water cycle. These physical forces don't alter the composition of rocks. In contrast, chemical weathering transforms rock composition. When water and minerals interact, they can start chemical reactions and form new or secondary minerals from the original rock. In chemical weathering, the processes of oxidation and hydrolysis are important. When rain falls, it dissolves atmospheric carbon dioxide and becomes acidic. With sulfur dioxide and nitrogen oxide in the atmosphere from volcanic eruptions or burning fossil fuels, the rainfall becomes even more acidic and creates acid rain. Acidic rain can dissolve the rock that it falls upon.

Characteristics of Soil

Soil is a combination of minerals, organic materials, liquids, and gases. There are three main types of soil, as defined by their compositions, going from coarse to fine: sand, silt, and clay. Large particles, such as those found in sand, affect how water moves through the soil, while tiny clay particles can be chemically active and bind with water and nutrients. An important characteristic of soil is its ability to form a crust when dehydrated. In general, the finer the soil, the harder the crust, which is why clay (and not sand) is used to make pottery.

There are many different classes of soil, but the components are always sand, silt, or clay. Below is a chart used by the United States Department of Agriculture (USDA) to define soil types:

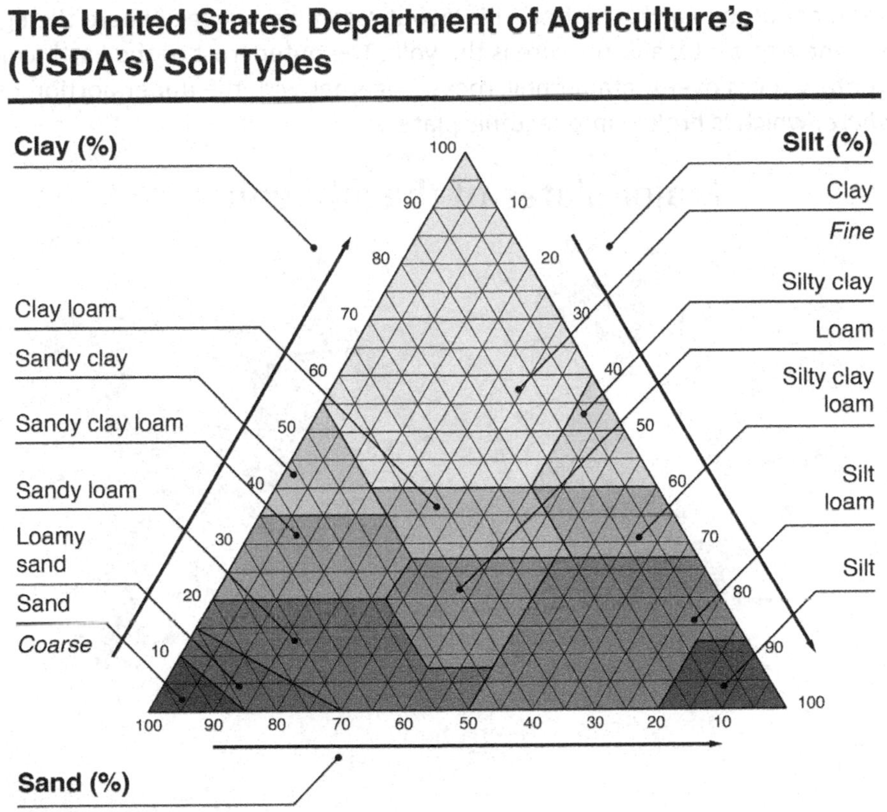

Loam is a term for soil that is a mixture of sand, silt, and clay. It's also the soil most commonly used for agriculture and gardening.

Porosity and Permeability

Porosity and permeability refer to how water moves through rock and soil underground. *Porosity* is a measure of the open space in a rock. This space can be between grains or within cracks and cavities in the rock. *Permeability* is a measure of the ease with which water can move through a porous rock. Therefore, rock that's more porous is also more permeable. When a rock is more permeable, it's less effective as a water purifier because dirty particles in the water can pass through porous rock.

Runoff and Infiltration

An important function of soil is to absorb water to be used by plants or released into groundwater. *Infiltration capacity* is the maximum amount of water that can enter soil at any given time and is regulated by the soil's porosity and composition. For example, sandy soils have larger pores than clays, allowing water to infiltrate them easier and faster. *Runoff* is water that moves across land's surface and may end up in a stream or a rut in the soil. Runoff generally occurs after the soil's infiltration capacity is reached. However, during heavy rainfalls, water may reach the soil's surface at a faster rate than infiltration can occur, causing runoff without soil saturation. In addition, if the ground is frozen and the soil's pores are blocked by ice, runoff may occur without water infiltrating the soil.

Earth's Basic Structure and Internal Processes

Earth's Layers

Earth has three major layers: a thin solid outer surface or *crust*, a dense *core,* and a *mantle* between them that contains most of the Earth's matter. This layout resembles an egg, where the eggshell is the crust, the mantle is the egg white, and the core is the yolk. The outer crust of the Earth consists of igneous or sedimentary rocks over metamorphic rocks. Together with the upper portion of the mantle, it forms the *lithosphere*, which is broken into tectonic plates.

Major plates of the lithosphere

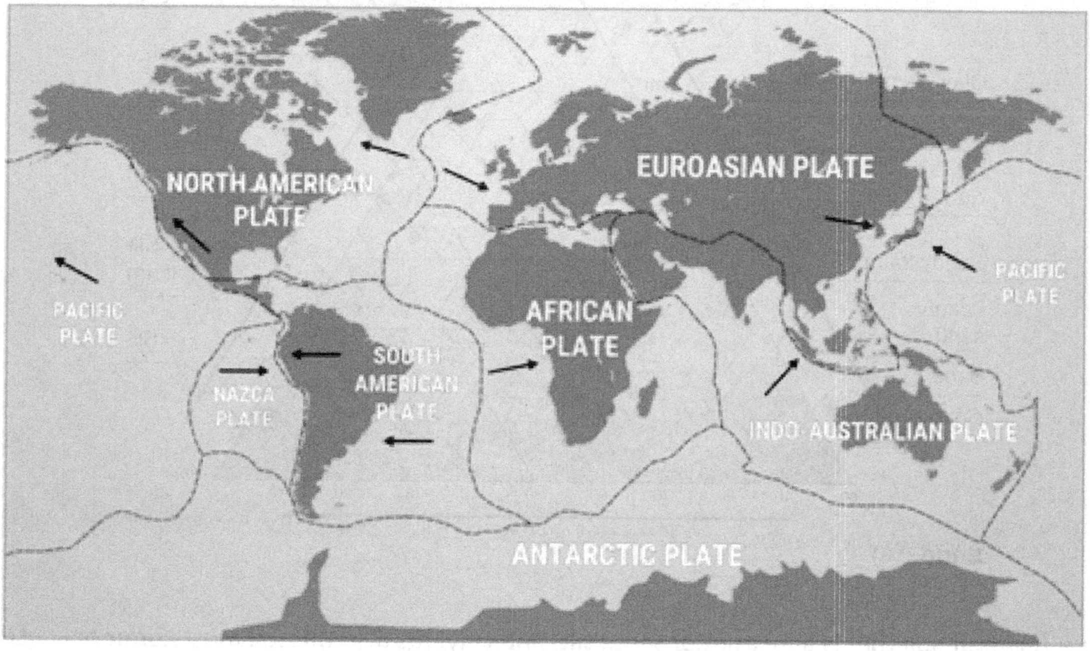

The mantle can be divided into three zones. The *upper mantle* is adjacent to the crust and composed of solid rock. Below the upper mantle is the *transition zone*. The *lower mantle* below the transition zone is a layer of completely solid rock. Underneath the mantle is the molten *outer core* followed by the compact, solid *inner core*. The inner and outer cores contain the densest elements, consisting of mostly iron and nickel.

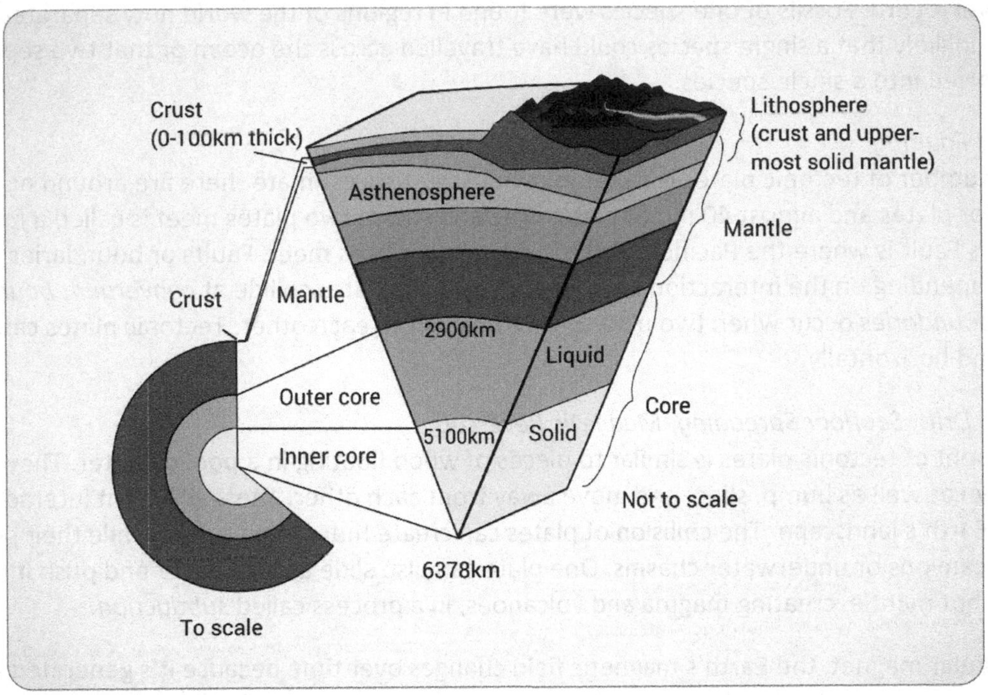

<u>Shape and Size of the Earth</u>
The Earth isn't a perfect sphere; it's slightly elliptical. From center to surface, its radius is almost 4,000 miles, and its circumference around the equator is about 24,902 miles. In comparison, the Sun's radius is 432,288 miles—over 1,000 times larger than the Earth's—and the Moon's radius is about 1,000 miles.

<u>Geographical Features</u>
The Earth's surface is dynamic and consists of various landforms. As tectonic plates are pushed together, *mountains* are formed. *Canyons* are deep trenches that are usually created by plates moving apart, but can also be created by constant weathering and erosion from rivers and runoff. *Deltas* are flat, triangular stretches of land formed by rivers that deposit sediment and water into the ocean. *Sand dunes* are mountains of sand located in desert areas or the bottom of the ocean. They are formed by wind and water movement when there's an absence of plants or other features that would otherwise hold the sand in place.

<u>The Earth's Magnetic Field</u>
The Earth's magnetic field is created by the magnetic forces that extend from the Earth's interior to outer space. It can be modeled as a magnetic dipole tilted about 10 degrees from the Earth's rotational axis, as if a bar magnet was placed at an angle inside the Earth's core. The geomagnetic pole located near Greenland in the northern hemisphere is actually the south pole of the Earth's magnetic field, and vice versa for the southern geomagnetic pole. The *magnetosphere* is the Earth's magnetic field, which extends tens of thousands of kilometers into space and protects the Earth and the atmosphere from damaging solar wind and cosmic rays.

Plate Tectonics Theory and Evidence

The theory of *plate tectonics* hypothesizes that the continents weren't always separated like they are today, but were once joined and slowly drifted apart. Evidence for this theory is based upon evolution and the fossil record. Fossils of one species were found in regions of the world now separated by an ocean. It's unlikely that a single species could have travelled across the ocean or that two separate species evolved into a single species.

Folding and Faulting

The exact number of tectonic plates is debatable, but scientists estimate there are around nine to fifteen major plates and almost 40 minor plates. The line where two plates meet is called a *fault*. The San Andreas Fault is where the Pacific and North American plates meet. Faults or boundaries are classified depending on the interaction between plates. Two plates collide at *convergent boundaries. Divergent boundaries* occur when two plates move away from each other. Tectonic plates can move vertically and horizontally.

Continental Drift, Seafloor Spreading, Magnetic Reversals

The movement of tectonic plates is similar to pieces of wood floating in a pool of water. They can bob up and down as well as bump, slide, and move away from each other. These different interactions create the Earth's landscape. The collision of plates can create mountain ranges, while their separation can create canyons or underwater chasms. One plate can also slide atop another and push it down into the Earth's hot mantle, creating magma and volcanoes, in a process called *subduction*.

Unlike a regular magnet, the Earth's magnetic field changes over time because it's generated by the motion of molten iron alloys in the outer core. Although the magnetic poles can wander geographically, they do so at such a slow rate that they don't affect the use of compasses in navigation. However, at irregular intervals that are several hundred thousand years long, the fields can reverse, with the north and south magnetic poles switching places.

Characteristics of Volcanoes

Volcanoes are mountainous structures that act as vents to release pressure and magma from the Earth's crust. During an *eruption*, the pressure and magma are released, and volcanoes smoke, rumble, and throw ash and *lava*, or molten rock, into the air. *Hot spots* are volcanic regions of the mantle that are hotter than surrounding regions.

Characteristics of Earthquakes

Earthquakes occur when tectonic plates slide or collide as a result of the crust suddenly releasing energy. Stress in the Earth's outer layer pushes together two faults. The motion of the planes of the fault continues until something makes them stop. The *epicenter* of an earthquake is the point on the surface directly above where the fault is slipping. If the epicenter is located under a body of water, the earthquake may cause a *tsunami*, a series of large, forceful waves.

Seismic waves and Triangulation

Earthquakes cause *seismic waves*, which travel through the Earth's layers and give out low-frequency acoustic energy. Triangulation of seismic waves helps scientists determine the origin of an earthquake.

The Water Cycle

Evaporation and Condensation

The *water cycle* is the cycling of water between its three physical states: solid, liquid, and gas. The Sun's thermal energy heats surface water so it evaporates. As water vapor collects in the atmosphere from evaporation, it eventually reaches a saturation level where it condenses and forms clouds heavy with water droplets.

<u>Precipitation</u>

When the droplets condense as clouds get heavy, they fall as different forms of precipitation, such as rain, snow, hail, fog, and sleet. *Advection* is the process of evaporated water moving from the ocean and falling over land as precipitation.

<u>Runoff and Infiltration</u>

Runoff and *infiltration* are important parts of the water cycle because they provide water on the surface available for evaporation. Runoff can add water to oceans and aid in the advection process. Infiltration provides water to plants and aids in the transpiration process.

<u>Transpiration</u>

Transpiration is an evaporation-like process that occurs in plants and soil. Water from the stomata of plants and from pores in soil evaporates into water vapor and enters the atmosphere.

Historical Geology

<u>Principle of Uniformitarianism</u>

Uniformitarianism is the assumption that natural laws and processes haven't changed and apply everywhere in the universe. In geology, uniformitarianism includes the *gradualist model*, which states that "the present is the key to the past" and claims that natural laws functioned at the same rates as observed today.

<u>Basic Principles of Relative Age Dating</u>

Relative age dating is the determination of the relative order of past events without determining absolute age. The Law of Superposition states that older geological layers are deeper than more recent layers. Rocks and fossils can be used to compare one stratigraphic column with another. A *stratigraphic column* is a drawing that describes the vertical location of rocks in a cliff wall or underground. Correlating these columns from different geographic areas allows scientists to understand the relationships between different areas and strata. Before the discovery of radiometric dating, geologists used this technique to determine the ages of different materials. Relative dating can only determine the sequential order of events, not the exact time they occurred. The Law of Fossil Succession states that when the same kinds of fossils are found in rocks from different locations, the rocks are likely the same age.

<u>Absolute (Radiometric) Dating</u>

Absolute or *radiometric dating* is the process of determining age on a specified chronology in archaeology and geology. It provides a numerical age by measuring the radioactive decay of elements (such as carbon-14) trapped in rocks or minerals and using the known rate of decay to determine how much time has passed. *Uranium-lead dating* can be used to date some of the oldest rocks on Earth, from 1 million to over 4.5 billion years old.

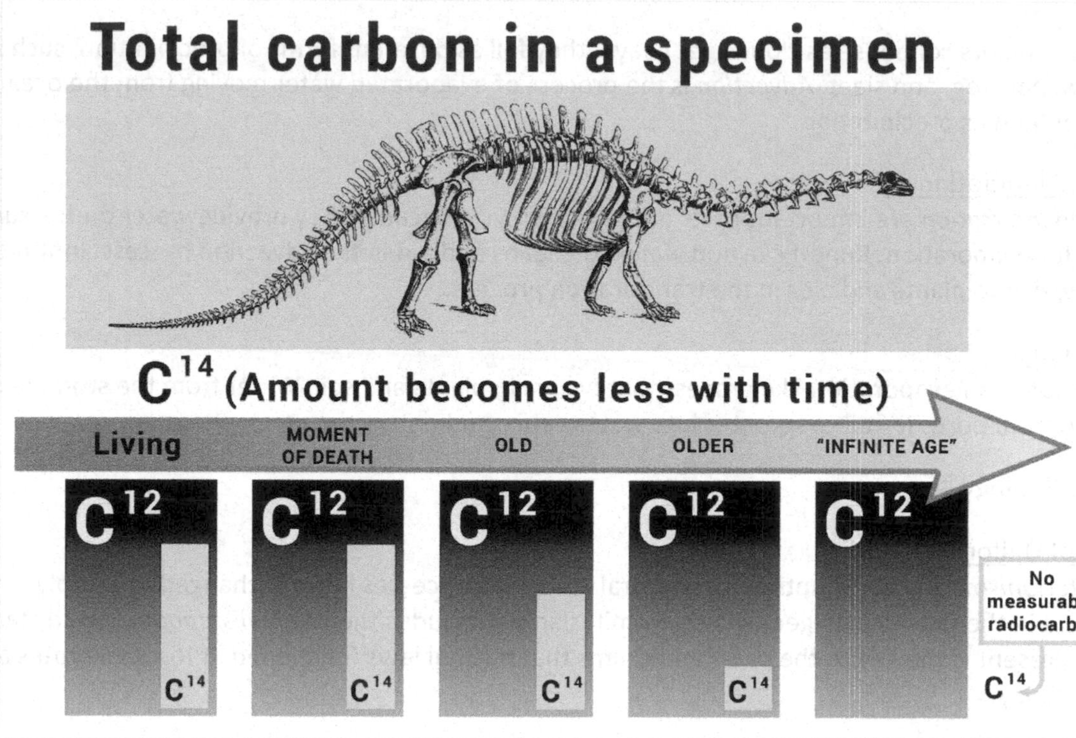

Geologic Time Scale

The *geological time scale* is a system that correlates geological strata to time. It's used by scientists to describe the timing and relationships of past natural events. Radiometric dating calculates that the Earth is around 4.55 billion years old. The geology of the Earth's past is organized into units following events that occurred in each period. The diagram below is geologic time scale represented in a clock-face format. The 12 o'clock position represents the formation of the Earth as well as present time. It shows important events in the Earth's history in relation to each other. In the picture, Ma represents millions of years and Ga represents billions of years.

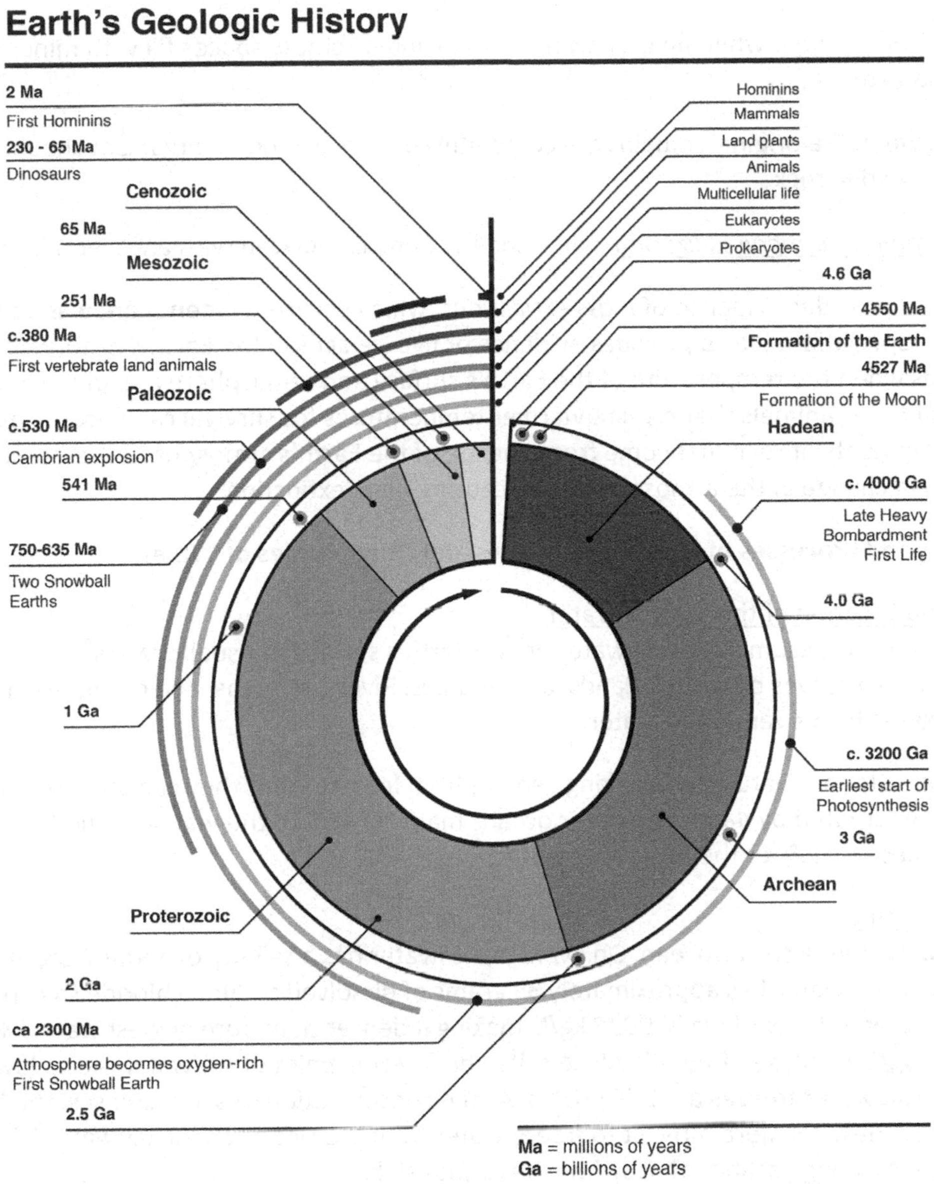

Fossil Record as Evidence of the Origin and Development of Life
The *fossil record* is the location of fossils throughout the Earth's surface layers. Deeper fossils are older than the fossils above. Scientists use the fossil record to determine when certain organisms existed and how they evolved. There are several ways a fossil can form:

- *Perimineralization:* when an organism is buried and its empty spaces fill with mineral-rich groundwater
- *Casts:* when the original remains are completely destroyed and an organism-shaped hole is left in the existing rock
- *Replacement or recrystallization:* when shell or bone is replaced with another mineral

The fossil record provides evidence of *mass extinctions*, which occurred when there was a faster rate of extinction than speciation. It also provides evidence of five ice ages in the Earth's history. *Ice ages* are lengthy periods when the temperature of the Earth's surface and atmosphere are greatly reduced. During these periods, animals that require warmer temperatures for survival can become extinct. *Meteors* are fragments of rock that come from outside of the Earth's atmosphere. A meteor impact can induce a massive change in the atmosphere, also causing mass extinction.

Characteristics and Processes of the Earth's Oceans and Other Bodies of Water

Distribution and Location of the Earth's Water
A *body of water* is any accumulation of water on the Earth's surface. It usually refers to oceans, seas, and lakes, but also includes ponds, wetlands, and puddles. Rivers, streams, and canals are bodies of water that involve the movement of water.

Most bodies of water are naturally occurring geographical features, but they can also be artificially created like lakes created by dams. Saltwater oceans make up 96% of the water on the Earth's surface. Freshwater makes up 2.5% of the remaining water.

Seawater Composition
Seawater is water from a sea or ocean. On average, seawater has a salinity of about 3.5%, meaning every kilogram of seawater has approximately 35 grams of dissolved sodium chloride salt. The average density of saltwater at the surface is 1.025 kg/L, making it denser than pure or freshwater, which has a density of 1.00 kg/L. Because of the dissolved salts, the freezing point of saltwater is also lower than that of pure water; salt water freezes at −2 °C (28 °F). As the concentration of salt increases, the freezing point decreases. Thus, it's more difficult to freeze water from the Dead Sea—a saltwater lake known to have water with such high salinity that swimmers cannot sink.

Coastline Topography and the Topography of Ocean Floor
Topography is the study of natural and artificial features comprising the surface of an area. *Coastlines* are an intermediate area between dry land and the ocean floor. The ground progressively slopes from the dry coastal area to the deepest depth of the ocean floor. At the continental shelf, there's a steep descent of the ocean floor. Although it's often believed that the ocean floor is flat and sandy like a beach, its topography includes mountains, plateaus, and valleys.

Tides, Waves, and Currents
Tides are caused by the pull of the Moon and the Sun. When the Moon is closer in its orbit to the Earth, its gravity pulls the oceans away from the shore. When the distance between the Moon and the Earth is

greater, the pull is weaker, and the water on Earth can spread across more land. This relationship creates low and high tides. Waves are influenced by changes in tides as well as the wind. The energy transferred from wind to the top of large bodies of water creates *crests* on the water's surface and *waves* below. Circular movements in the ocean are called *currents*. They result from the Coriolis Effect, which is caused by the Earth's rotation. Currents spin in a clockwise direction above the equator and counterclockwise below the equator.

Estuaries and Barrier Islands

An *estuary* is an area of water located on a coast where a river or stream meets the sea. It's a transitional area that's partially enclosed, has a mix of salty and fresh water, and has calmer water than the open sea. *Barrier islands* are coastal landforms created by waves and tidal action parallel to the mainland coast. They usually occur in chains, and they protect the coastlines and create areas of protected waters where wetlands may flourish.

Islands, Reefs, and Atolls

Islands are land that is completely surrounded by water. *Reefs* are bars of rocky, sandy, or coral material that sit below the surface of water. They may form from sand deposits or erosion of underwater rocks. An *atoll* is a coral reef in the shape of a ring (but not necessarily circular) that encircles a lagoon. In order for an atoll to exist, the rate of its erosion must be slower than the regrowth of the coral that composes the atoll.

Polar Ice, Icebergs, Glaciers

Polar ice is the term for the sheets of ice that cover the poles of a planet. *Icebergs* are large pieces of freshwater ice that break off from glaciers and float in the water. A *glacier* is a persistent body of dense ice that constantly moves because of its own weight. Glaciers form when snow accumulates at a faster rate than it melts over centuries. They form only on land, in contrast to *ice caps*, which can form from sheets of ice in the ocean. When glaciers deform and move due to stresses created by their own weight, they can create crevasses and other large distinguishing land features.

Lakes, Ponds, and Wetlands

Lakes and *ponds* are bodies of water that are surrounded by land. They aren't part of the ocean and don't contain flowing water. Lakes are larger than ponds, but otherwise the two bodies don't have a scientific distinction. *Wetlands* are areas of land saturated by water. They have a unique soil composition and provide a nutrient-dense area for vegetation and aquatic plant growth. They also play a role in water purification and flood control.

Streams, Rivers, and River Deltas

A *river* is a natural flowing waterway usually consisting of freshwater that flows toward an ocean, sea, lake, or another river. Some rivers flow into the ground and become dry instead of reaching another body of water. Small rivers are usually called *streams* or *creeks*. River *deltas* are areas of land formed from the sediment carried by a river and deposited before it enters another body of water. As the river reaches its end, the flow of water slows, and the river loses the power to transport the sediment so it falls out of suspension.

Geysers and Springs

A *spring* is a natural occurrence where water flows from an aquifer to the Earth's surface. A *geyser* is a spring that intermittently and turbulently discharges water. Geysers form only in certain hydrogeological conditions. They require proximity to a volcanic area or magma to provide enough heat to boil or vaporize the water. As hot water and steam accumulate, pressure grows and creates the spraying geyser effect.

Properties of Water that Affect Earth Systems

Water is a chemical compound composed of two hydrogen atoms and one oxygen atom (H_2O) and has many unique properties. In its solid state, water is less dense than its liquid form; therefore, ice floats in water. Water also has a very high heat capacity, allowing it to absorb a high amount of the Sun's energy without getting too hot or evaporating. Its chemical structure makes it a polar compound, meaning one side has a negative charge while the other is positive. This characteristic—along with its ability to form strong intermolecular hydrogen bonds with itself and other molecules—make water an effective solvent for other chemicals.

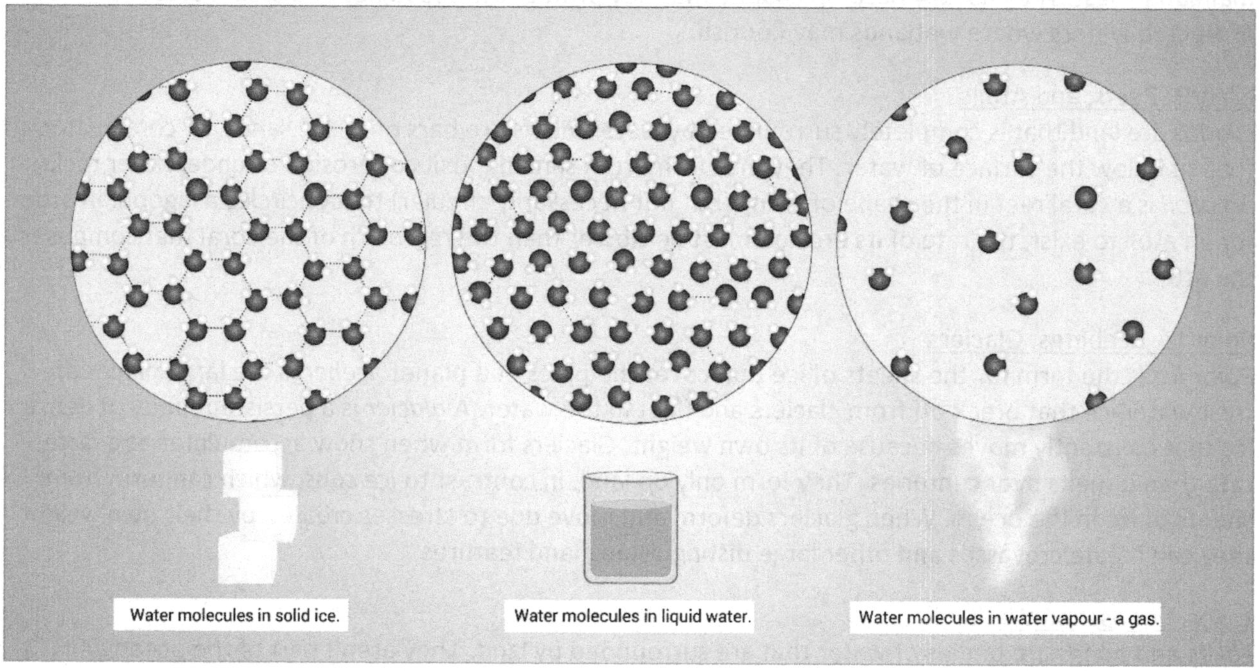

Basic Structure and Composition of the Earth's Atmosphere

Layers

The Earth's atmospheric layers are determined by their temperatures but are reported by their distance above sea level. Listed from closest to sea level on upward, the levels are:

- Troposphere: sea level to 11 miles above sea level
- Stratosphere: 11 miles to 31 miles above sea level
- Mesosphere: 31 miles to 50 miles above sea level
- Ionosphere: 50 miles to 400 miles above sea level
- Exosphere: 400 miles to 800 miles above sea level

The ionosphere and exosphere are together considered the thermosphere. The ozone layer is in the stratosphere and weather experienced on Earth's surface is a product of factors in the troposphere.

Composition of the Atmosphere

The Earth's atmosphere is composed of gas particles: 78% nitrogen, 21% oxygen, 1% other gases such as argon, and 0.039% carbon dioxide. The atmospheric layers are created by the number of particles in the air and gravity's pull upon them.

Atmospheric Pressure and Temperature

The lower atmospheric levels have higher atmospheric pressures due to the mass of the gas particles located above. The air is less dense (it contains fewer particles per given volume) at higher altitudes. The temperature changes from the bottom to top of each atmospheric layer. The tops of the troposphere and mesosphere are colder than their bottoms, but the reverse is true for the stratosphere and thermosphere. Some of the warmest temperatures are actually found in the thermosphere because of a type of radiation that enters that layer.

Basic Concepts of Meteorology

Relative Humidity

Relative humidity is the ratio of the partial pressure of water vapor to water's equilibrium vapor pressure at a given temperature. At low temperatures, less water vapor is required to reach a high relative humidity. More water vapor is needed to reach a high relative humidity in warm air, which has a greater capacity for water vapor. At ground level or other areas of higher pressure, relative humidity increases as temperatures decrease because water vapor condenses as the temperature falls below the dew point. As relative humidity cannot be greater than 100%, the dew point temperature cannot be greater than the air temperature.

Dew Point

The *dew point* is the temperature at which the water vapor in air at constant barometric pressure condenses into liquid water due to saturation. At temperatures below the dew point, the rate of condensation will be greater than the rate of evaporation, forming more liquid water. When condensed water forms on a surface, it's called *dew*; when it forms in the air, it's called *fog* or *clouds*, depending on the altitude.

Wind

Wind is the movement of gas particles across the Earth's surface. Winds are generated by differences in atmospheric pressure. Air inherently moves from areas of higher pressure to lower pressure, which is what causes wind to occur. Surface friction from geological features, such as mountains or man-made features can decrease wind speed. In meteorology, winds are classified based on their strength, duration, and direction. *Gusts* are short bursts of high-speed wind, *squalls* are strong winds of intermediate duration (around one minute), and winds with a long duration are given names based on their average strength. *Breezes* are the weakest, followed by *gales*, *storms*, and *hurricanes*.

Cloud Types and Formation

Water in the atmosphere can exist as visible masses called *clouds* composed of water droplets, tiny crystals of ice, and various chemicals. Clouds exist primarily in the troposphere. They can be classified based on the altitude at which they occur:

- *High clouds*—between 5,000 and 13,000 meters above sea level
    - Cirrus: thin and wispy "mare's tail" appearance
    - Cirrocumulus: rows of small puffy pillows
    - Cirrostratus: thin sheets that cover the sky

- *Middle clouds*—between 2,000 and 7,000 meters above sea level
    - Altocumulus: gray and white and made up of water droplets
    - Altostratus: grayish or bluish gray clouds
- *Low clouds*—below 2,000 meters above sea level
    - Stratus: gray clouds made of water droplets that can cover the sky
    - Stratocumulus: gray and lumpy low-lying clouds
    - Nimbostratus: dark gray with uneven bases; typical of rain or snow clouds

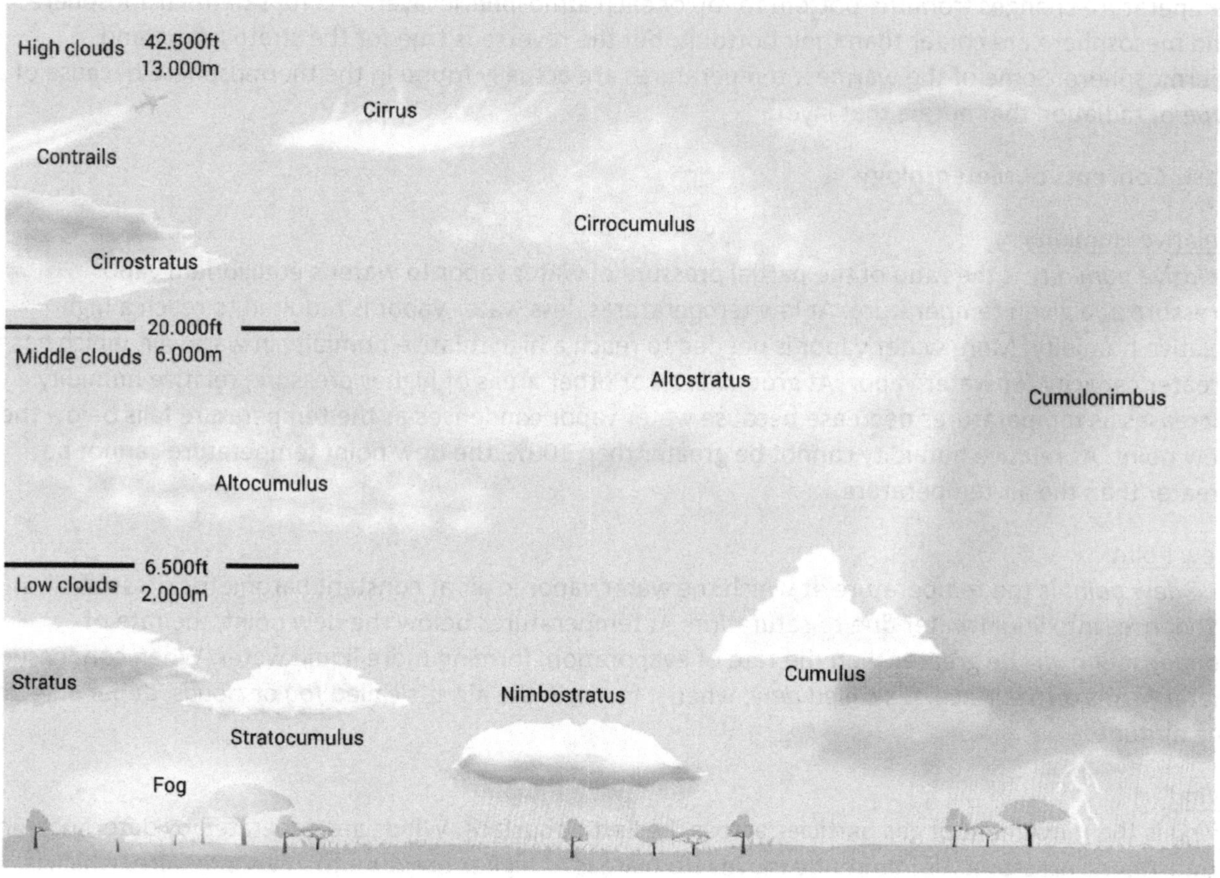

Types of Precipitation

There are three distinct processes by which precipitation occurs. *Convection precipitation* occurs when air rises vertically in a forceful manner, quickly overturning the atmosphere and resulting in heavy precipitation. It's generally more intense and shorter in duration than *stratiform precipitation*, which occurs when large masses of air move over each other. *Orographic precipitation* occurs when moist air is forced upwards over rising terrain, such as a mountain. Most storms are a result of convection precipitation.

Precipitation can fall in liquid or solid phases, as well as any form in between. Liquid precipitation includes rain and drizzle. Frozen precipitation includes snow, sleet, and hail. Intensity is classified by rate of fall or visibility restriction. The forms of precipitation are:

- *Rain*: water vapor that condenses on dust particles in the troposphere until it becomes heavy enough to fall to Earth
- *Sleet*: rain that freezes on its way down; it starts as ice that melts and then freezes again before hitting the ground
- *Hail*: balls of ice thrown up and down several times by turbulent winds, so that more and more water vapor can condense and freeze on the original ice; hail can be as large as golf balls or even baseballs
- *Snow*: loosely packed ice crystals that fall to Earth

Air Masses, Fronts, Storms, and Severe Weather

Air masses are volumes of air defined by their temperature and the amount of water vapor they contain. A *front* is where two air masses of different temperatures and water vapor content meet. Fronts can be the site of extreme weather, such as thunderstorms, which are caused by water particles rubbing against each other. When they do so, electrons are transferred and energy and electrical currents accumulate. When enough energy accumulates, thunder and lightning occur. *Lightning* is a massive electric spark created by a cloud, and *thunder* is the sound created by an expansion of air caused by the sudden increase in pressure and temperature around lightning.

Extreme weather includes tornadoes and hurricanes. *Tornadoes* are created by changing air pressure and winds that can exceed 300 miles per hour. *Hurricanes* occur when warm ocean water quickly evaporates and rises to a colder, low-pressure portion of the atmosphere. Hurricanes, typhoons, and tropical cyclones are all created by the same phenomena but they occur in different regions. *Blizzards* are similar to hurricanes in that they're created by the clash of warm and cold air, but they only occur when cold Arctic air moves toward warmer air. They usually involve large amounts of snow.

Development and Movement of Weather Patterns

A *weather pattern* is weather that's consistent for a period of time. Weather patterns are created by fronts. A *cold front* is created when two air masses collide in a high-pressure system. A *warm front* is created when a low-pressure system results from the collision of two air masses; they are usually warmer and less dense than high-pressure systems. When a cold front enters an area, the air from the warm front is forced upwards. The temperature of the warm front's air decreases, condenses, and often creates clouds and precipitation. When a warm front moves into an area, the warm air moves slowly upwards at an angle. Clouds and precipitation form, but the precipitation generally lasts longer because of how slowly the air moves.

Major Factors that Affect Climate and Seasons

Effects of Latitude, Geographical Location, and Elevation

The climate and seasons of different geographical areas are primarily dictated by their sunlight exposure. Because the Earth rotates on a tilted axis while travelling around the Sun, different latitudes get different amounts of direct sunlight throughout the year, creating different climates. Polar regions experience the greatest variation, with long periods of limited or no sunlight in the winter and up to 24 hours of daylight in the summer. Equatorial regions experience the least variance in direct sunlight exposure. Coastal areas experience breezes in the summer as cooler ocean air moves ashore, while areas southeast of the Great Lakes can get "lake effect" snow in the winter, as cold air travels over the warmer water and creates snow on land. Mountains are often seen with snow in the spring and fall. Their high elevation causes mountaintops to stay cold. The air around the mountaintop is also cold and holds less water vapor than air at sea level. As the water vapor condenses, it creates snow.

Effects of Atmospheric Circulation

Global winds are patterns of wind circulation and they have a major influence on global weather and climate. They help influence temperature and precipitation by carrying heat and water vapor around the Earth. These winds are driven by the uneven heating between the polar and equatorial regions created by the Sun. Cold air from the polar regions sinks and moves toward the equator, while the warm air from the equator rises and moves toward the poles. The other factor driving global winds is the *Coriolis Effect*. As air moves from the North Pole to the equator, the Earth's rotation makes it seem as if the wind is also moving to the right, or westbound, and eastbound from South Pole to equator.

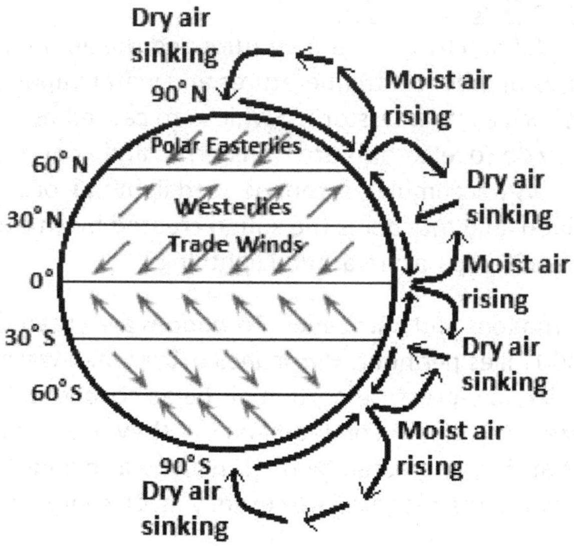

Global wind patterns are given names based on which direction they blow. There are three major wind patterns in each hemisphere. Notice the image above diagraming the movement of warm (dry) air and moist (cold) air.

Trade winds—easterly surface winds found in the troposphere near the equator—blow predominantly from the northeast in the Northern Hemisphere and from the southeast in the Southern Hemisphere. These winds direct the tropical storms that develop over the Atlantic, Pacific, and Indian Oceans and land in North America, Southeast Asia, and eastern Africa, respectively. *Jet streams* are westerly winds that follow a narrow, meandering path. The two strongest jet streams are the polar jets and the subtropical jets. In the Northern Hemisphere, the polar jet flows over the middle of North America, Europe, and Asia, while in the Southern Hemisphere, it circles Antarctica.

Effects of Ocean Circulation

Ocean currents are similar to global winds because winds influence how the oceans move. Ocean currents are created by warm water moving from the equator towards the poles while cold water travels from the poles to the equator. The warm water can increase precipitation in an area because it evaporates faster than the colder water.

Characteristics and Locations of Climate Zones

Climate zones are created by the Earth's tilt as it travels around the Sun. These zones are delineated by the equator and four other special latitudinal lines: the Tropic of Cancer or Northern Tropic at 23.5° North; the Tropic of Capricorn or Southern Tropic at 23.5° South; the Arctic Circle at 66.5° North; and the Antarctic Circle at 66.5° South. The areas between these lines of latitude represent different climate zones. Tropical climates are hot and wet, like rainforests, and tend to have abundant plant and animal life, while polar climates are cold and usually have little plant and animal life. Temperate zones can vary and experience the four seasons.

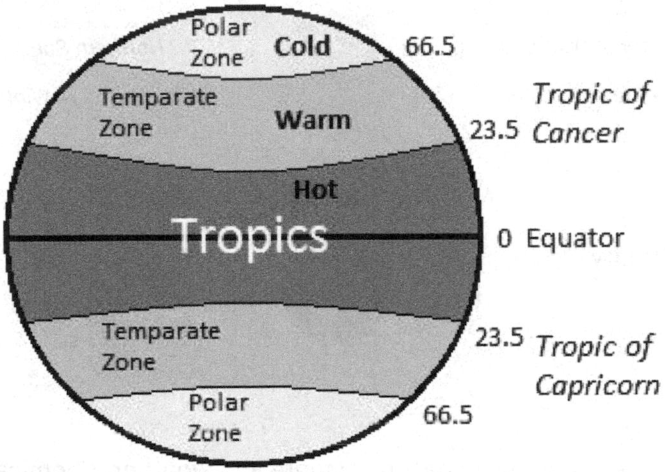

Effect of the Tilt of the Earth's Axis on Seasons

In addition to the equator and the prime meridian, other major lines of latitude and longitude divide the world into regions relative to the direct rays of the Sun. These lines correspond with the Earth's 23.5-degree tilt, and are responsible—along with the Earth's revolution around the Sun—for the seasons. For example, the Northern Hemisphere is tilted directly toward the Sun from June 22 to September 23, which creates the summer. Conversely, the Southern Hemisphere is tilted away from the Sun and experiences winter during those months. The area between the Tropic of Cancer and the Tropic of Capricorn tends to be warmer and experiences fewer variations in seasonal temperatures because it's constantly subject to the direct rays of the Sun, no matter which direction the Earth is tilted.

The area between the Tropic of Cancer and the Arctic Circle, which is at 66.5° North, and the Antarctic Circle, which is at 66.5° South, is where most of Earth's population resides and is called the *middle latitudes*. Here, the seasons are more pronounced, and milder temperatures generally prevail. When the Sun's direct rays are over the equator, it's known as an *equinox*, and day and night are almost equal throughout the world. Equinoxes occur twice a year: the fall, or autumnal equinox, occurs on September 22, while the spring equinox occurs on March 20.

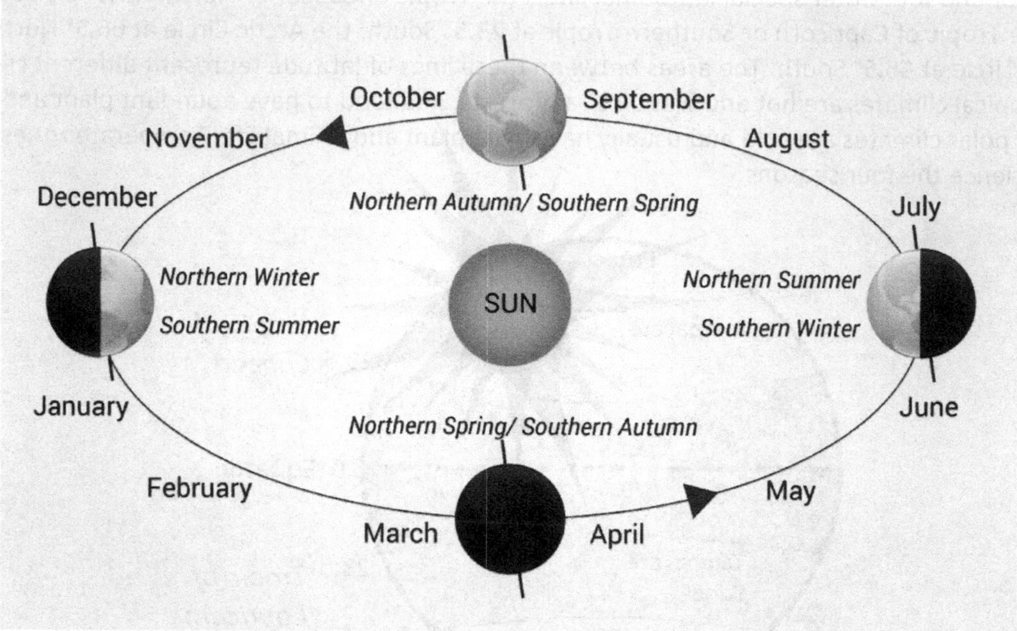

Effects of Natural Phenomena

Natural phenomena can have a sizeable impact on climate and weather. Chemicals released from volcanic eruptions can fall back to Earth in acid rain. In addition, large amounts of carbon dioxide released into the atmosphere can warm the climate. Carbon dioxide creates the *greenhouse effect* by trapping solar energy from sunlight reflected off the Earth's surface within the atmosphere. The amount of solar radiation emitted from the Sun varies and has recently been discovered to be cyclical.

El Niño and La Niña

El Niño and *La Niña* are terms for severe weather anomalies associated with torrential rainfall in the Pacific coastal regions, mainly in North and South America. These events occur irregularly every few years, usually around December, and are caused by a band of warm ocean water that accumulates in the central Pacific Ocean around the equator. The warm water changes the wind patterns over the Pacific and stops cold water from rising toward the American coastlines. The rise in ocean temperature also leads to increased evaporation and rain. These events are split into two phases—a warm, beginning phase called El Niño and a cool end phase called La Niña.

Major Features of the Solar System

Structure of the Solar System

The *solar system* is an elliptical planetary system with a large sun in the center that provides gravitational pull on the planets. It was formed 4.568 billion years ago from the gravitational collapse of a region within a giant molecular cloud that likely birthed other suns. This region of collapse is called a *pre-solar nebula*. As it started to collapse in the center, the nebula accumulated more energy and became hotter and heavier, providing more gravitational energy to the rest of the cloud, eventually becoming the Sun. The planets likely formed in a similar fashion, starting as small clumps called *protoplanets* that revolved around the Sun and then smashed together to form larger planets and, eventually, the Solar System seen today.

Laws of Motion

Planetary motion is governed by three scientific laws called Kepler's laws:

1. The orbit of a planet is elliptical in shape, with the Sun as one focus.

2. An imaginary line joining the center of a planet and the center of the Sun sweeps out equal areas during equal intervals of time.

3. For all planets, the ratio of the square of the orbital period is the same as the cube of the average distance from the Sun.

The most relevant of these laws is the first. Planets move in elliptical paths because of gravity; when a planet is closer to the Sun, it moves faster because it has built up gravitational speed. As illustrated in the diagram below, the second law states that it takes planet 1 the same time to travel along the A1 segment as the A2 segment, even though the A2 segment is shorter.

Kepler's Laws of Planetary Motion

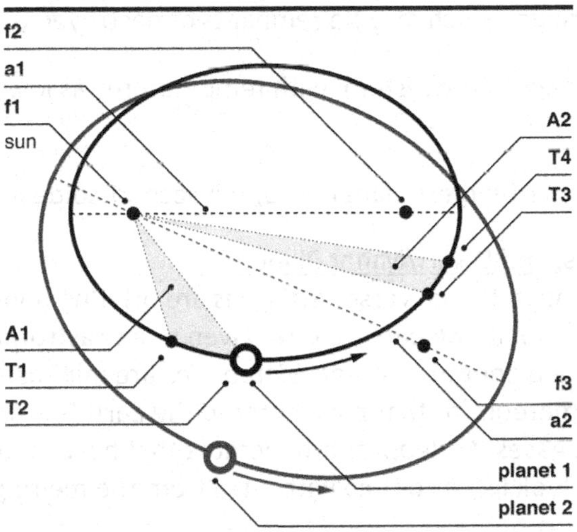

(T2 - T1) = (T4 - T3)

Δ TA1 = Δ TA2

Characteristics of the Sun, Moon, and Planets

The Sun is comprised mainly of hydrogen and helium. Metals make up only about 2% of its total mass. The Sun is 1.3 million kilometers wide, weighs 1.989 x 10^{30} kilograms, and has temperatures of 5,800 Kelvin (9980 °F) on the surface and 15,600,000 Kelvin (28 million °F) at the core. The Sun's enormous size and gravity give it the ability to provide sunlight. The gravity of the Sun compresses hydrogen and helium atoms together through nuclear fusion and releases energy and light.

The Moon has a distinct core, mantle, and crust. It has elevations and craters created by impacts with large objects in the solar system. The Moon makes a complete orbit around the Earth every 27.3 days. It's relatively large compared to other moons in the Solar System, with a diameter one-quarter of the Earth and a mass 1/81 of the Earth.

The eight planets of the Solar System are divided into four inner (or terrestrial) planets and four outer (or Jovian) planets. In general, terrestrial planets are small, and Jovian planets are large and gaseous. The planets in the Solar System are listed below from nearest to farthest from the Sun:

- Mercury: the smallest planet in the Solar System; it only takes about 88 days to completely orbit the Sun.
- Venus: around the same size, composition, and gravity as Earth and orbits the Sun every 225 days.
- Earth: the only known planet with life
- Mars: called the Red Planet due to iron oxide on the surface; takes around 365 days to complete its orbit
- Jupiter: the largest planet in the system; made up of mainly hydrogen and helium
- Saturn: mainly composed of hydrogen and helium along with other trace elements; has 61 moons; has beautiful rings, which may be remnants of destroyed moons
- Uranus: the coldest planet in the system, with temperatures as low as -224.2 °Celsius (-371.56 °F)
- Neptune: the last and third-largest planet; also, the second-coldest planet

Asteroids, Meteoroids, Comets, and Dwarf/Minor Planets

Several other bodies travel through the universe. *Asteroids* are orbiting bodies composed of minerals and rock. They're also known as *minor planets*—a term given to any astronomical object in orbit around the Sun that doesn't resemble a planet or a comet. *Meteoroids* are mini-asteroids with no specific orbiting pattern. *Meteors* are meteoroids that have entered the Earth's atmosphere and started melting from contact with greenhouse gases. *Meteorites* are meteors that have landed on Earth. *Comets* are composed of dust and ice and look like a comma with a tail from the melting ice as they streak across the sky.

Theories of Origin of the Solar System

One theory of the origins of the Solar System is the *nebular hypothesis*, which posits that the Solar System was formed by clouds of extremely hot gas called a *nebula*. As the nebula gases cooled, they became smaller and started rotating. Rings of the nebula left behind during rotation eventually condensed into planets and their satellites. The remaining nebula formed the Sun.

Another theory of the Solar System's development is the *planetesimal hypothesis*. This theory proposes that planets formed from cosmic dust grains that collided and stuck together to form larger and larger bodies. The larger bodies attracted each other, growing into moon-sized protoplanets and eventually planets.

Interactions of the Earth-Moon-Sun System

The Earth's Rotation and Orbital Revolution Around the Sun

Besides revolving around the Sun, the Earth also spins like a top. It takes one day for the Earth to complete a full spin, or rotation. The same is true for other planets, except that their "days" may be shorter or longer. One Earth day is about 24 hours, while one Jupiter day is only about nine Earth hours, and a Venus day is about 241 Earth days. Night occurs in areas that face away from the Sun, so one side of the planet experiences daylight and the other experiences night. This phenomenon is the reason that the Earth is divided into time zones. The concept of time zones was created to provide people around the world with a uniform standard time, so the Sun would rise around 7:00 AM, regardless of location.

<u>Effect on Seasons</u>

The Earth's tilted axis creates the seasons. When Earth is tilted toward the Sun, the Northern Hemisphere experiences summer while the Southern Hemisphere has winter—and vice versa. As the Earth rotates, the distribution of direct sunlight slowly changes, explaining how the seasons gradually change.

<u>Phases of the Moon</u>

The Moon goes through two phases as it revolves around Earth: waxing and waning. Each phase lasts about two weeks:

- Waxing—the right side of the Moon is illuminated
    - New moon (dark): the Moon rises and sets with the Sun
    - Crescent: a tiny sliver of illumination on the right
    - First quarter: the right half the Moon is illuminated
    - Gibbous: more than half of the Moon is illuminated
    - Full moon: the Moon rises at sunset and sets at sunrise
- Waning—the left side of the Moon is illuminated
    - Gibbous: more than half is illuminated, only here it is the left side that is illuminated
    - Last quarter: the left half of the Moon is illuminated
    - Crescent: a tiny sliver of illumination on the left
- New moon (dark)—the Moon rises and sets with the Sun

<u>Effect on Tides</u>

Although the Earth is much larger, the Moon still has a significant gravitational force that pulls on Earth's oceans. At its closest to Earth, the Moon's gravitation pull is greatest and creates high tide. The opposite is true when the Moon is farthest from the Earth: less pull creates low tide.

<u>Solar and Lunar Eclipses</u>

Eclipses occur when the Earth, the Sun, and the Moon are all in line. If the three bodies are perfectly aligned, a total eclipse occurs; otherwise, it's only a partial eclipse. A *solar eclipse* occurs when the Moon is between the Earth and the Sun, blocking sunlight from reaching the Earth. A *lunar eclipse* occurs when the Earth interferes with the Sun's light reflecting off the full moon. The Earth casts a shadow on the

Moon, but the particles of the Earth's atmosphere refract the light, so some light reaches the Moon, causing it to look yellow, brown, or red.

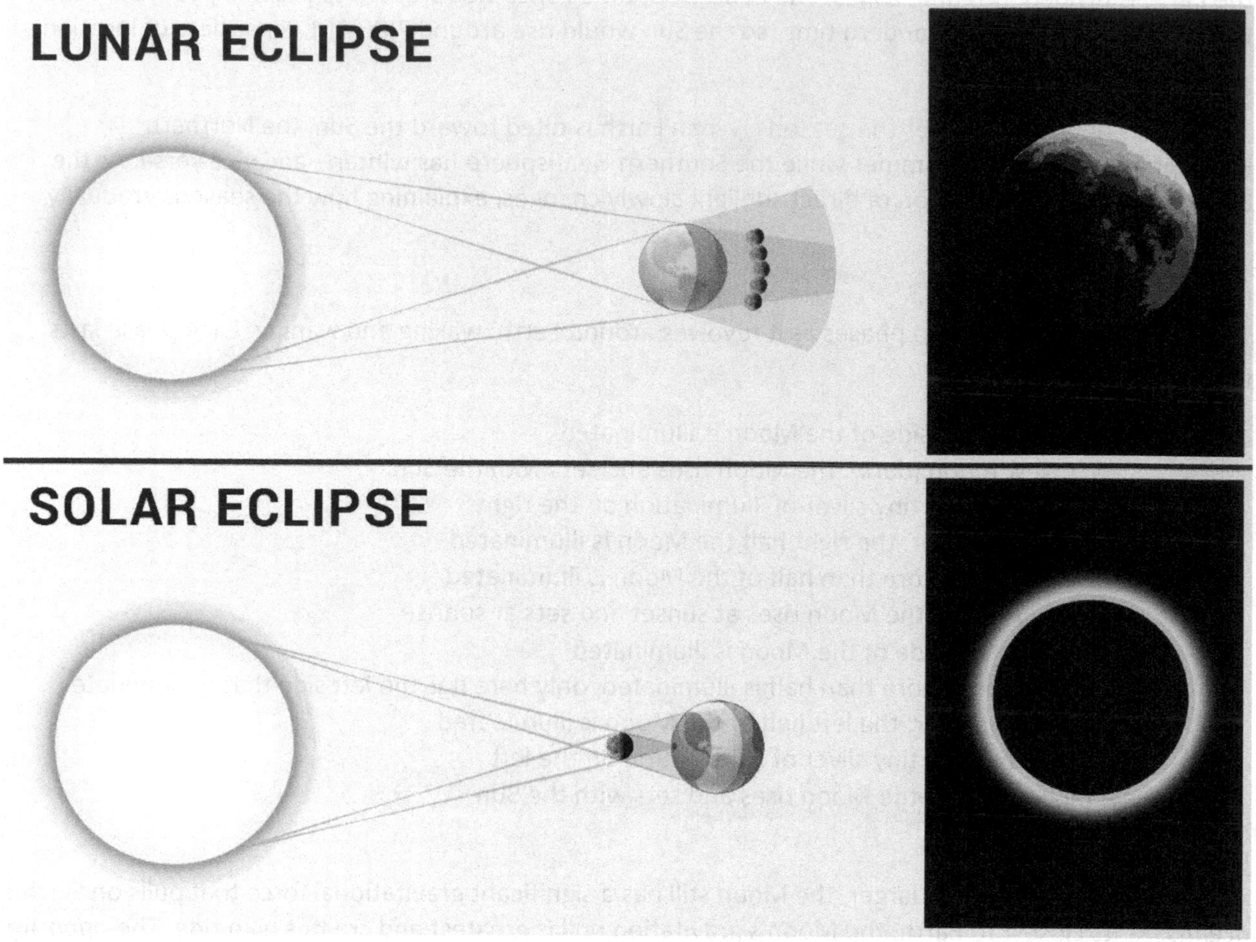

<u>Time Zones</u>

Longitudinal, or vertical, lines determine how far east or west different regions are from each other. These lines, also known as *meridians,* are the basis for time zones, which allocate different times to regions depending on their position eastward and westward of the prime meridian.

<u>Effect of Solar Wind on the Earth</u>

Solar winds are streams of charged particles emitted by the Sun, consisting of mostly electrons, protons, and alpha particles. The Earth is largely protected from solar winds by its magnetic field. However, the winds can still be observed, as they create phenomena like the beautiful Northern Lights (or Aurora Borealis).

Major Features of the Universe

<u>Galaxies</u>

Galaxies are clusters of stars, rocks, ice, and space dust. Like everything else in space, the exact number of galaxies is unknown, but there could be as many as a hundred billion. There are three types of galaxies: spiral, elliptical, and irregular. Most galaxies are *spiral galaxies*; they have a large, central galactic bulge made up of a cluster of older stars. They look like a disk with spinning arms. *Elliptical galaxies* are groups of stars with no pattern of rotation. They can be spherical or extremely elongated, and they don't have arms. *Irregular galaxies* vary significantly in size and shape.

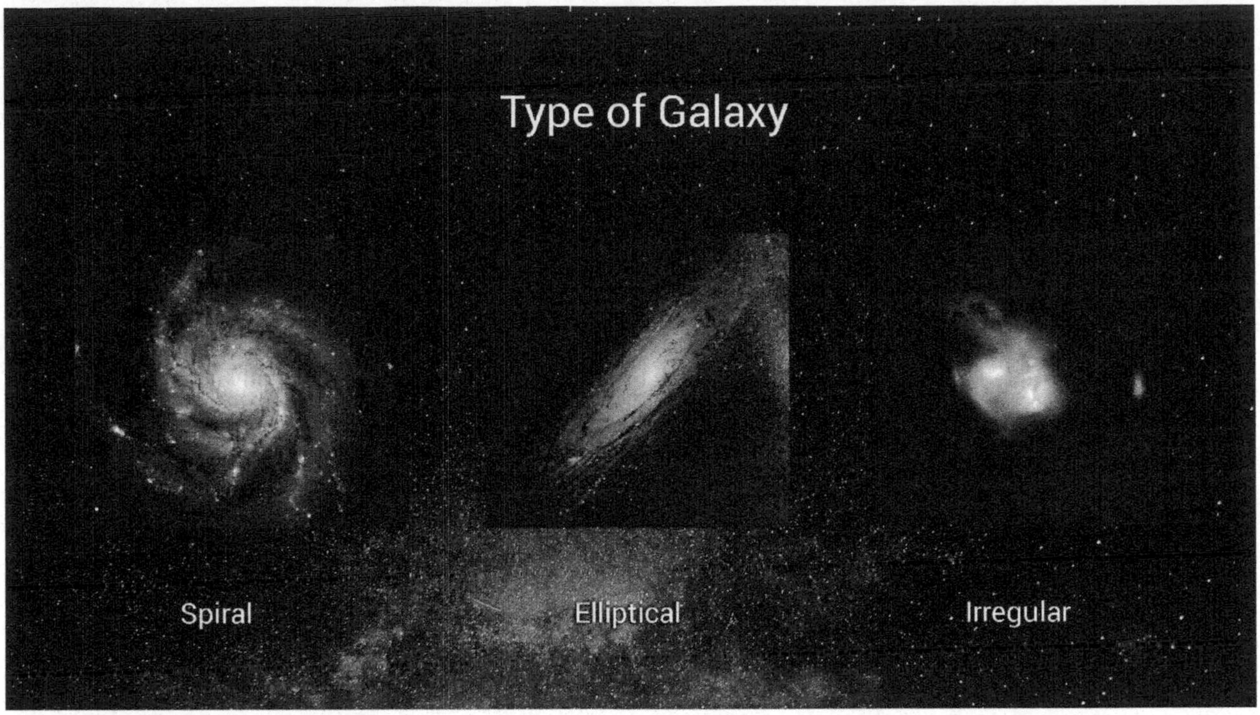

To say that galaxies are large is an understatement. Most galaxies are 1,000 to 100,000 parsecs in diameter, with one *parsec* equal to about 19 trillion miles. The Milky Way is the galaxy that contains Earth's Solar System. It's one of the smaller galaxies that has been studied. The diameter of the Milky Way is estimated to be between 31,000 to 55,000 parsecs.

<u>Characteristics of Stars and Their Life Cycles</u>

Life Cycle of Stars

All stars are formed from nebulae. Depending on their mass, stars take different pathways during their evolution. Low- and medium-mass stars start as nebulae and then become red giants and white dwarfs. High-mass stars become red supergiants, supernovas, and then either neutron stars or black holes. Official stars are born as red dwarves because they have plentiful amounts of gas—mainly hydrogen—to undergo nuclear fusion. Red dwarves mature into white dwarves before expending their hydrogen fuel source. When the fuel is spent, it creates a burst of energy that expands the star into a red giant. Red giants eventually condense to form white dwarves, which is the final stage of a star's life.

Stars that undergo nuclear fusion and energy expenditure extremely quickly can burst in violent explosions called *supernovas*. These bursts can release as much energy in a few seconds as the Sun can release in its entire lifetime. The particles from the explosion then condense into the smallest type of star—a neutron star—and eventually form a *black hole*, which has such a high amount of gravity that not even light energy can escape. The Sun is currently a red dwarf, early in its life cycle.

Color, Temperature, Apparent Brightness, Absolute Brightness, and Luminosity

The color of a star depends on its surface temperature. Stars with cooler surfaces emit red light, while the hottest stars give off blue light. Stars with temperatures between these extremes, such as the Sun, emit white light. The *apparent brightness* of a star is a measure of how bright a star appears to an observer on the Earth. The *absolute brightness* is a measure of the intrinsic brightness of a star and is measured at a distance of exactly 10 parsecs away. The *luminosity* of a star is the amount of light emitted from its surface.

Hertzsprung-Russell Diagrams

Hertzsprung-Russell diagrams are scatterplots that show the relationship of a star's brightness and temperature, or color. The general layout shows stars of greater luminosity toward the top of the diagram. Stars with higher surface temperatures appear toward the left side of the diagram. The diagonal area from the top-left of the diagram to the bottom-right is called the *main sequence*. Stars may or may not follow the main sequence during their evolutionary period.

Dark Matter

Dark matter is an unidentified type of matter that comprises approximately 27% of the mass and energy in the observable universe. As the name suggests, dark matter is so dense and small that it doesn't emit or interact with electromagnetic radiation, such as light, making it electromagnetically invisible. Although dark matter has never been directly observed, its existence and properties can be inferred from its gravitational effects on visible objects as well as the cosmic microwave background. Patterns of movement have been observed in visible objects that would only be possible if dark matter exerted a gravitational pull.

Theories About the Origin of the Universe

The *Big Bang theory* is the most plausible cosmological model for the origin of the universe. It theorizes that the universe expanded from a high-density and high-temperature state. The theory offers comprehensive explanations for a wide range of astronomical phenomena, such as the cosmic microwave background and Hubble's Law. From detailed measurements of the expansion rate of the universe, it's estimated that the Big Bang occurred approximately 13.8 billion years ago, which is considered the age of the universe. The theory states that after the initial expansion, the universe cooled enough for subatomic particles and atoms to form and aggregate into giant clouds. These clouds coalesced through gravity and formed the stars and galaxies. If this theory holds true, it's predicted that the universe will reach a point where it will stop expanding and start to pull back toward the center due to gravity.

Contributions of Space Exploration and Technology to our Understanding of the Universe

Remote Sensing Devices

Scientists and astronomers use satellites and other technology to explore the universe because humans cannot yet safely travel far into space. The *telescope* allows observation beyond what the naked eye can see. With information from the Planck satellite, astronomers were able to determine that the observable universe is actually smaller than earlier believed; they estimated that the universe is smaller by 320 million light years, giving it a total radius of 45.34 billion light years. *Astronomical spectroscopy* uses spectroscopy techniques to measure visible light and radiation from stars and other hot celestial objects. This information allows scientists to determine the physical properties of stars that would otherwise be impossible to measure, including chemical composition, temperature, density, and mass.

Search for Water and Life on Other Planets

Even the smallest microorganisms on Earth cannot live without liquid water. Water is essential to life, which is why scientists believe the search for water is the best way to find life on other planets. Water can be found throughout the universe in the form of ice. For example, some of Saturn's rings are composed of ice, and comets streaking through the sky release ice particles through their tails. Until recently, it was believed that the Earth was the only place with liquid water. Through the use of satellites and telescopes, astronomers have discovered that two of Jupiter's moons—Europa and Callisto—may contain liquid water below their surfaces.

Practice Questions

1. What types of molecules can move through a cell membrane by passive transport?
    a. Complex sugars
    b. Non-lipid soluble molecules
    c. Oxygen
    d. Molecules moving from areas of low concentration to areas of high concentration

2. What is ONE feature that both prokaryotes and eukaryotes have in common?
    a. A plasma membrane
    b. A nucleus enclosed by a membrane
    c. Organelles
    d. A nucleoid

3. What is the LAST phase of mitosis?
    a. Prophase
    b. Telophase
    c. Anaphase
    d. Metaphase

4. How many daughter cells are formed from one parent cell during meiosis?
    a. One
    b. Two
    c. Three
    d. Four

5. In which organelle do eukaryotes carry out aerobic respiration?
    a. Golgi apparatus
    b. Nucleus
    c. Mitochondrion
    d. Cytosol

6. What kind of energy do plants use in photosynthesis to create chemical energy?
    a. Light
    b. Electric
    c. Nuclear
    d. Cellular

7. What type of biological molecule is a monosaccharide?
    a. Protein
    b. Carbohydrate
    c. Nucleic acid
    d. Lipid

8. Which level of protein structure is defined by the folds and coils of the protein's polypeptide backbone?
   a. Primary
   b. Secondary
   c. Tertiary
   d. Quaternary

9. Which base pairs with adenine in RNA?
   a. Thymine
   b. Guanine
   c. Cytosine
   d. Uracil

10. With which genotype would the recessive phenotype appear, if the dominant allele is marked with "A" and the recessive allele is marked with "a"?
   a. AA
   b. aa
   c. Aa
   d. aA

11. What is ONE reason why speciation can occur?
   a. Geographic separation
   b. Seasons
   c. Daylight
   d. A virus

12. What is the broadest, or LEAST specialized, classification of the Linnean taxonomic system?
   a. Species
   b. Family
   c. Domain
   d. Phylum

13. How are fungi similar to plants?
   a. They have a cell wall
   b. They contain chloroplasts
   c. They perform photosynthesis
   d. They use carbon dioxide as a source of energy

14. What important function are the roots of plants responsible for?
   a. Absorbing water from the surrounding environment
   b. Performing photosynthesis
   c. Conducting sugars downward through the leaves
   d. Supporting the plant body

15. Which of the following would occur in response to a change in water concentration?
   a. Phototropism
   b. Thermotropism
   c. Gravitropism
   d. Hydrotropism

16. What is the MAIN function of the respiratory system?
    a. To eliminate waste through the kidneys and bladder
    b. To exchange gas between the air and circulating blood
    c. To transform food and liquids into energy
    d. To excrete waste from the body

17. What type of vessel carries oxygen-rich blood from the heart to other tissues of the body?
    a. Veins
    b. Intestines
    c. Bronchioles
    d. Arteries

18. Which system comprises the 206 bones of the body?
    a. Skeletal
    b. Muscular
    c. Endocrine
    d. Reproductive

19. Which factor is NOT a consideration in population dynamics?
    a. Size and age of population
    b. Immigration
    c. Hair color
    d. Number of births

20. Which type of diagram describes the cycling of energy and nutrients of an ecosystem?
    a. Food web
    b. Phylogenetic tree
    c. Fossil record
    d. Pedigree chart

21. Which blood component is chiefly responsible for clotting?
    a. Platelets
    b. Red blood cells
    c. Antigens
    d. Plasma cells

22. Which is the first event to happen in a primary immune response?
    a. Macrophages phagocytose pathogens and present their antigens.
    b. Neutrophils aggregate and act as cytotoxic, nonspecific killers of pathogens.
    c. B lymphocytes make pathogen-specific antibodies.
    d. Helper T cells secrete interleukins to activate pathogen-fighting cells.

23. Where does sperm maturation take place in the male reproductive system?
    a. Seminal vesicles
    b. Prostate gland
    c. Epididymis
    d. Vas Deferens

24. What is the total mechanical energy of a system?
   a. The total potential energy
   b. The total kinetic energy
   c. Kinetic energy plus potential energy
   d. Kinetic energy minus potential energy

25. What does the Lewis Dot structure of an element represent?
   a. The outer electron valence shell population
   b. The inner electron valence shell population
   c. The positioning of the element's protons
   d. The positioning of the element's neutrons

26. What is the name of the scale used in sound level meters to measure the intensity of sound waves?
   a. Doppler
   b. Electron
   c. Watt
   d. Decibel

27. Which statement is true regarding electrostatic charges?
   a. Like charges attract.
   b. Like charges repel.
   c. Like charges are neutral.
   d. Like charges neither attract nor repel.

28. What is the name of this compound: CO?
   a. Carbonite oxide
   b. Carbonic dioxide
   c. Carbonic oxide
   d. Carbon monoxide

29. What is the molarity of a solution made by dissolving 4.0 grams of NaCl into enough water to make 120 mL of solution? The atomic mass of Na is 23.0 g/mol and Cl is 35.5 g/mol.
   a. 0.34 M
   b. 0.57 M
   c. 0.034 M
   d. 0.057 M

30. Considering a gas in a closed system, at a constant volume, what will happen to the temperature if the pressure is increased?
   a. The temperature will stay the same
   b. The temperature will decrease
   c. The temperature will increase
   d. It cannot be determined with the information given

31. What is the current when a 3.0 V battery is wired across a lightbulb that has a resistance of 6.0 ohms?
   a. 0.5 A
   b. 18.0 A
   c. 0.5 J
   d. 18.0 J

32. What is the chemical reaction when a compound is broken down into its elemental components called?

a. A synthesis reaction
b. A decomposition reaction
c. An organic reaction
d. An oxidation reaction

33. Which of the following is a balanced chemical equation?

a. $Na + Cl_2 \rightarrow NaCl$
b. $2Na + Cl_2 \rightarrow NaCl$
c. $2Na + Cl_2 \rightarrow 2NaCl$
d. $2Na + 2Cl_2 \rightarrow 2NaCl$

34. What effect changes the oscillations of a wave and can alter the appearance of light waves?

a. Reflection
b. Refraction
c. Dispersion
d. Polarization

35. The Sun transferring heat to the Earth through space is an example of which of the following?

a. Convection
b. Conduction
c. Induction
d. Radiation

36. What is the acceleration of a vehicle starting from rest and reaching a velocity of 15 m/s in 5.0 s?

a. 3.0 m/s
b. 75 m/s
c. 3.0 m/s^2
d. 75 m/s^2

37. What is the force that opposes motion?

a. Reactive force
b. Responsive force
c. Friction
d. Momentum

38. What type of chemical reaction produces a salt?

a. An oxidation reaction
b. A neutralization reaction
c. A synthesis reaction
d. A decomposition reaction

39. Car A (mass 100 kg) traveling at 5 m/s hits Car B (mass 110 kg) traveling at 8 m/s in a head-on collision. The bumpers hook together during the collision so that Car A and Car B travel together after the impact. What is their combined velocity after impact?

a. 13.0 m/s
b. 3.0 m/s
c. 6.6 m/s
d. 16.6 m/s

40. How is mechanical advantage calculated?
   a. The force input divided by the force output
   b. The force input multiplied by the force output
   c. The force output divided by 100
   d. The force output divided by the force input

41. Which rock is formed from cooling magma underneath the Earth's surface?
   a. Extrusive sedimentary rocks
   b. Sedimentary rocks
   c. Igneous rocks
   d. Metamorphic rocks

42. Pure gold is an example of which class of mineral?
   a. Carbonate
   b. Silicates
   c. Elements
   d. Oxides

43. Water that has seeped into rock cracks and freezes will most likely result in what process?
   a. Chemical weathering
   b. Mechanical weathering
   c. Erosion
   d. Deposition

44. Which soil is the least permeable to water?
   a. Pure sand
   b. Pure silt
   c. Pure clay
   d. Loam

45. Which of the Earth's layers is thickest?
   a. The crust
   b. The shell
   c. The mantle
   d. The inner core

46. Dew point is a measure of which of the following?
      I. Pressure
      II. Temperature at which water vapor condenses
      III. Temperature at which water evaporates
   a. I and III
   b. I and II
   c. II and III
   d. All the above

47. Dark storm clouds are usually located where?
   a. Between 5,000 and 13,000 meters above sea level
   b. Between 2,000 and 7,000 meters above sea level
   c. Below 2,000 meters above sea level
   d. Outer space

48. What is transpiration?
   a. Evaporation from moving water
   b. Evaporation from plant life
   c. Movement of water through the ground
   d. Precipitation that falls on trees

49. Absolute dating involves which of the following?
   a. Measuring radioactive decay
   b. Comparing rock stratification
   c. Fossil location
   d. Fossil record

50. Which of the following will freeze last?
   a. Freshwater from a pond
   b. Pure water
   c. Seawater from the Pacific Ocean
   d. Seawater from the Dead Sea

Answers and Explanations

1. C: Molecules that are soluble in lipids, like fats, sterols, and vitamins (A, D, E and K), for example, are able to move in and out of a cell using passive transport. Water and oxygen are also able to move in and out of the cell without the use of cellular energy. Complex sugars and non-lipid soluble molecules are too large to move through the cell membrane without relying on active transport mechanisms. Molecules naturally move from areas of high concentration to those of lower concentration. It requires active transport to move molecules in the opposite direction, as suggested by Choice *D*.

2. A: Both types of cells are enclosed by plasma membranes with cytosol on the inside. Prokaryotes contain a nucleoid and do not have organelles; eukaryotes contain a nucleus enclosed by a membrane, as well as organelles.

3. B: During telophase, two nuclei form at each end of the cell and nuclear envelopes begin to form around each nucleus. The nucleoli reappear, and the chromosomes become less compact. The microtubules are broken down by the cell, and mitosis is complete. The process begins with prophase as the mitotic spindles begin to form from centrosomes. Prometaphase follows, with the breakdown of the nuclear envelope and the further condensing of the chromosomes. Next, metaphase occurs when the microtubules are stretched across the cell and the chromosomes align at the metaphase plate. Finally, in the last step before telophase, anaphase occurs as the sister chromatids break apart and form chromosomes.

4. D: Meiosis has the same phases as mitosis, except that they occur twice—once in meiosis I and once in meiosis II. During meiosis I, the cell splits into two. Each cell contains two sets of chromosomes. Next, during meiosis II, the two intermediate daughter cells divide again, producing four total haploid cells that each contain one set of chromosomes.

5. C: The mitochondrion is often called the powerhouse of the cell and is one of the most important structures for maintaining regular cell function. It is where aerobic cellular respiration occurs and where most of the cell's ATP is generated. The number of mitochondria in a cell varies greatly from organism to organism and from cell to cell. Cells that require more energy, like muscle cells, have more mitochondria.

6. A: Photosynthesis is the process of converting light energy into chemical energy, which is then stored in sugar and other organic molecules. The photosynthetic process takes place in the thylakoids inside chloroplast in plants. Chlorophyll is a green pigment that lives in the thylakoid membranes and absorbs photons from light.

7. B: Carbohydrates consist of sugars. The simplest sugar molecule is called a monosaccharide and has the molecular formula of CH_2O, or a multiple of that formula. Monosaccharides are important molecules for cellular respiration. Their carbon skeleton can also be used to rebuild new small molecules. Lipids are fats, proteins are formed via amino acids, and nucleic acid is found in DNA and RNA.

8. B: The secondary structure of a protein refers to the folds and coils that are formed by hydrogen bonding between the slightly charged atoms of the polypeptide backbone. The primary structure is the sequence of amino acids, similar to the letters in a long word. The tertiary structure is the overall shape of the molecule that results from the interactions between the side chains that are linked to the polypeptide backbone. The quaternary structure is the complete protein structure that occurs when a protein is made up of two or more polypeptide chains.

9. D: DNA and RNA each contain four nitrogenous bases, three of which they have in common: adenine, guanine, and cytosine. Thymine is only found in DNA, and uracil is only found in RNA. Adenine interacts with uracil in RNA, and with thymine in DNA. Guanine always pairs with cytosine in both DNA and RNA.

10. B: Dominant alleles are considered to have stronger phenotypes and, when mixed with recessive alleles, will mask the recessive trait. The recessive trait would only appear as the phenotype when the allele combination is "aa" because a dominant allele is not present to mask it.

11. A: Speciation is the method by which one species splits into two or more species. In allopatric speciation, one population is divided into two subpopulations. If a drought occurs and a large lake becomes divided into two smaller lakes, each lake is left with its own population that cannot intermingle with the population of the other lake. When the genes of these two subpopulations are no longer mixing with each other, new mutations can arise and natural selection can take place.

12. C: In the Linnean system, organisms are classified as follows, moving from comprehensive and specific similarities to fewer and more general similarities: species, genus, family, order, class, phylum, kingdom, and domain. A popular mnemonic device to remember the Linnean system is "Dear King Philip came over for good soup."

13. A: Fungal cells have a cell wall, similar to plant cells; however, they use oxygen as a source of energy and cannot perform photosynthesis. Because they do not perform photosynthesis, fungal cells do not contain chloroplasts.

14. A: Roots are responsible for absorbing water and nutrients that will get transported up through the plant. They also anchor the plant to the ground. Photosynthesis occurs in leaves, stems transport materials through the plant and support the plant body, and phloem moves sugars downward to the leaves.

15. D: Tropism is a response to stimuli that causes the plant to grow toward or away from the stimuli. Hydrotropism is a response to a change in water concentration. Phototropism is a reaction to light that causes plants to grow toward the source of the light. Thermotropism is a response to changes in temperature. Gravitropism is a response to gravity that causes roots to follow the pull of gravity and grow downward, but also causes plant shoots to act against gravity and grow upward.

16. B: The respiratory system mediates the exchange of gas between the air and the circulating blood, mainly by the act of breathing. It filters, warms, and humidifies the air that gets breathed in and then passes it into the blood stream. The digestive system transforms food and liquids into energy and helps excrete waste from the body. Eliminating waste via the kidneys and bladder is a function of the urinary system.

17. D: Arteries carry oxygen-rich blood from the heart to the other tissues of the body. Veins carry oxygen-poor blood back to the heart. Intestines carry digested food through the body. Bronchioles are passageways that carry air from the nose and mouth to the lungs.

18. A: The skeletal system consists of the 206 bones that make up the skeleton, as well as the cartilage, ligaments, and other connective tissues that stabilize the bones. The skeletal system provides structural support for the entire body, a framework for the soft tissues and organs to attach to, and acts as a protective barrier for some organs, such as the ribs protecting the heart and lungs, and the vertebrae protecting the spinal cord. The muscular system includes skeletal muscles, cardiac muscle, and the smooth muscles found on the inside of blood vessels. The endocrine system uses ductless glands to produce hormones that help maintain hemostasis, and the reproductive system is responsible for the productions of egg and sperm cells.

19. C: Population dynamics looks at the composition of populations, including size and age, and the biological and environmental processes that cause changes. These can include immigration, emigration, births, and deaths.

20. A: Ecosystems are maintained by cycling the energy and nutrients that they obtain from external sources. The process can be diagramed in a food web, which represents the feeding relationship between the species in a community. A phylogenetic tree shows inferred evolutionary relationships among species and is similar to the fossil record. A pedigree chart shows occurrences of phenotypes of a particular gene through the generations of an organism.

21. A: Platelets are the blood components responsible for clotting. There are between 150,000 and 450,000 platelets in healthy blood. When a clot forms, platelets adhere to the injured area of the vessel and promote a molecular cascade that results in adherence of more platelets. Ultimately, the platelet aggregation results in recruitment of a protein called fibrin, which adds structure to the clot. Too many platelets can cause clotting disorders. Not enough leads to bleeding disorders.

22. A: Choice B might be an attractive answer choice, but neutrophils are part of the innate immune system and are not considered part of the primary immune response. The first event that happens in a primary immune response is that macrophages ingest pathogens and display their antigens. Then, they secrete interleukin 1 to recruit helper T cells. Once helper T cells are activated, they secrete interleukin 2 to simulate plasma B and killer T cell production. Only then can plasma B make the pathogen specific antibodies.

23. C: The epididymis stores sperm and is a coiled tube located near the testes. The immature sperm that enters the epididymis from the testes migrates through the 20-foot long epididymis tube in about two weeks, where viable sperm are concentrated at the end. The vas deferens is a tube that transports mature sperm from the epididymis to the urethra. Seminal vesicles are pouches attached that add fructose to the ejaculate to provide energy for sperm. The prostate gland excretes fluid that makes up about a third of semen released during ejaculation. The fluid reduces semen viscosity and contains enzymes that aid in sperm functioning; both effects increase sperm motility and ultimate success.

24. C: In any system, the total mechanical energy is the sum of the potential energy and the kinetic energy. Either value could be zero but it still must be included in the total. Choices *A* and *B* only give the total potential or kinetic energy, respectively. Choice *D* gives the difference in the kinetic and potential energy.

25. A: A Lewis Dot diagram shows the alignment of the valence (outer) shell electrons and how readily they can pair or bond with the valence shell electrons of other atoms to form a compound. Choice *B* is incorrect because the Lewis Dot structure aids in understanding how likely an atom is to bond or not bond with another atom, so the inner shell would add no relevance to understanding this likelihood. The positioning of protons and neutrons concerns the nucleus of the atom, which again would not lend information to the likelihood of bonding.

26. D: The decibel scale is used to measure the intensity of sound waves. The decibel scale is a ratio of a particular sound's intensity to a standard value. Since it is a logarithmic scale, it is measured by a factor of 10. Choice *A* is the name of the effect experienced by an observer of a moving wave; Choice *B* is a particle in an atom; and Choice *C* is a unit for measuring power.

27. B: For charges, *like charges repel* each other and *opposite charges attract* each other. Negatives and positives will attract, while two positive charges or two negative charges will repel each other. Charges have an effect on each other, so Choices *C* and *D* are incorrect.

28. D: The naming of compounds focuses on the second element in a chemical compound. Elements from the non-metal category are written with an "ide" at the end. The compound CO has one carbon and one oxygen, so it is called carbon monoxide. Choice *B* represents that there are two oxygen atoms, and Choices *A* and *B* incorrectly alter the name of the first element, which should remain as carbon.

29. B: To solve this, the number of moles of NaCl needs to be calculated:

First, to find the mass of NaCl, the mass of each of the molecule's atoms is added together as follows:

$$23.0\text{g (Na)} + 35.5\text{g (Cl)} = 58.8\text{g NaCl}$$

Next, the given mass of the substance is multiplied by one mole per total mass of the substance:

$$4.0\text{g NaCl} \times (1\text{ mol NaCl}/58.5\text{g NaCl}) = 0.068\text{ mol NaCl}$$

Finally, the moles are divided by the number of liters of the solution to find the molarity:

$$(0.068\text{ mol NaCl})/(0.120\text{L}) = 0.57\text{ M NaCl}$$

Choice *A* incorporates a miscalculation for the molar mass of NaCl, and Choices *C* and *D* both incorporate a miscalculation by not converting mL into liters (L), so they are incorrect by a factor of 10.

30. C: According to the *ideal gas law* ($PV = nRT$), if volume is constant, the temperature is directly related to the pressure in a system. Therefore, if the pressure increases, the temperature will increase in direct proportion. Choice *A* would not be possible, since the system is closed and a change is occurring, so the temperature will change. Choice *B* incorrectly exhibits an inverse relationship between pressure and temperature, or $P = 1/T$. Choice *D* is incorrect because even without actual values for the variables, the relationship and proportions can be determined.

31. A: According to Ohm's Law: $V = IR$, so using the given variables: $3.0\text{ V} = \text{I} \times 6.0\ \Omega$

Solving for I: $\text{I} = 3.0\text{ V}/6.0\ \Omega = 0.5\text{ A}$

Choice *B* incorporates a miscalculation in the equation by multiplying 3.0 V by 6.0 Ω, rather than dividing these values. Choices *C* and *D* are labeled with the wrong units; Joules measure energy, not current.

32. B: A decomposition reaction breaks down a compound into its constituent elemental components. Choice *A* is incorrect because a synthesis reaction joins two or more elements into a single compound. Choice *C*, an organic reaction, is not possible, since it needs carbon and hydrogen for a reaction. Choice *D*, oxidation/reduction (redox or half) reaction, is incorrect because it involves the loss of electrons from one species (oxidation) and the gain of electrons to the other species (reduction). There is no notation of this occurring within the given reaction, so it is not correct.

33. C:

$$2Na + Cl_2 \longrightarrow 2NaCl$$

The number of each element must be equal on both sides of the equation:

Choice *C* is the only correct option: $2Na + Cl_2 \rightarrow 2NaCl$

2 Na + 2 Cl does equal 2 Na + 2 Cl (the number of sodium atoms and chlorine atoms match)

Choice *A*: $Na + Cl_2 \rightarrow NaCl$

1 Na + 2 Cl does not equal 1 Na + 1 Cl (the number of chlorine atoms do not match)

Choice *B*: $2Na + Cl_2 \rightarrow NaCl$

2 Na + 2 Cl does not equal 1 Na + 1 Cl (neither the number of sodium atoms nor chlorine atoms match)

Choice *D*: $2Na + 2Cl_2 \rightarrow 2NaCl$

2 Na + 4 Cl does not equal 2 Na + 2 Cl (the number of chlorine atoms do not match)

34. D: Polarization changes the oscillations of a wave and can alter the appearance in light waves. For example, polarized sunglasses remove the "glare" from sunlight by altering the oscillation pattern observed by the wearer. Choice *A*, reflection, is the bouncing back of a wave, such as in a mirror; Choice *B* is the bending of a wave as it travels from one medium to another, such as going from air to water; and Choice *C*, dispersion, is the spreading of a wave through a barrier or a prism.

35. D: Radiation can be transmitted through electromagnetic waves and needs no medium to travel; it can travel in a vacuum. This is how the Sun warms the Earth and it typically applies to large objects with great amounts of heat, or objects that have a large difference in their heat measurements. Choice *A*, convection, involves atoms or molecules traveling from areas of high concentration to those of low concentration and transferring energy or heat with them. Choice *B*, conduction, involves the touching or bumping of atoms or molecules to transfer energy or heat. Choice *C*, induction, deals with charges and does not apply to the transfer of energy or heat. Choices *A*, *B*, and *C* need a medium in which to travel, while radiation requires no medium.

36. C: Review the following:

$$a = \frac{\Delta v}{\Delta t}$$

$$a = \frac{15 - 0}{5 - 0}$$

$$a = \frac{15}{5}$$

$$= 3.0\ m/s^2$$

Choices *A* and *B* have the wrong units for acceleration; they are labeled with the units for velocity. Choices *B* and *D* integrate a miscalculation with the formula—multiplying, rather than dividing, 15 and 5.

37. C: The force that opposes motion is called *friction*. It also provides the resistance necessary for walking, running, braking, etc. In order for something to slide down a ramp, it must be acted upon by a force stronger than that of friction. Choices *A* and *B* are not actual terms, and Choice *C* is the measure of mass multiplied by velocity ($p = mv$).

38. B: A solid produced during a reaction is called a precipitate. In a neutralization reaction, the products (an acid and a base) react to form a salt and water. Choice A, an oxidation reaction, involves the transfer of an electron. Choice C, a synthesis reaction, involves the joining of two molecules to form a single molecule. Choice D, a decomposition reaction, involves the separation of a molecule into two other molecules.

39. A: Using the equation for the conservation of momentum for an inelastic collision:

$$m_1v_1 + m_2v_2 = (m_1 + m_2)v_f$$

$m_1 = 100$ kg

$m_2 = 110$ kg

$v_1 = 5$ m/s

$v_2 = 8$ m/s

$(100 \times 5) + (110 \times 8) = (100 + 110) \times v_f$

$(500) + (880) = (210) \times v_f$

$1380 = 210 \times v_f$

$1380/210 = v_f$

$v_f = 6.6$ m/s

Choices *A*, *B*, and *D* are answers created from possible mathematical errors when calculating the results.

40. D: The *mechanical advantage* is calculated by comparing the force input by the user to the simple machine with the force output from the use of the machine. This calculation is performed through a ratio:

$$Mechanical\ Advantage = \frac{output\ force}{input\ force}$$

$$MA = \frac{F_{out}}{F_{in}}$$

Choice *A*, the force input divided by the force output, is the reciprocal of the mechanical advantage. Choice *B* is an incorrect equation and would result in a force, not a ratio. Choice *C* is not used for any calculation.

41. C: Igneous rocks are formed from the cooling of magma, both on and below the Earth's surface, which are classified as extrusive and intrusive, respectively. Sedimentary rocks are formed from deposition and cementation on the surface, and metamorphic rocks are formed from the transformation of sedimentary or igneous rocks through heat and pressure.

42. C: Elements are minerals formed by elements that occur naturally and aren't combined with other elements or substances. This group contains metals such as gold and nickel.

43. B: Freezing water expands because ice is less dense than liquid water. This expansion can break up solid rocks, which describes a form of mechanical weathering. Chemical weathering occurs when water dissolves rocks. Erosion is the movement of broken rock, and deposition is the process of laying down rocks from erosion.

44. C: Pure clay has small particles that pack together tightly and are impermeable to water. Sand is the least permeable type of soil because it has the largest grains. Loam is a combination of all three types of soil in relatively equal proportions.

45. C: The mantle is the Earth's thickest layer; it holds most of the Earth's material. The crust is thin, and the inner core is also small compared to the mantle. There is no such thing as Earth's shell.

46. C: The dew point is the temperature at which the water vapor in a sample of air at constant barometric pressure condenses into water at the same rate at which it evaporates. It isn't a measure of pressure.

47. C: Dark storm clouds are considered nimbostratus clouds, which are located below 2,000 meters above sea level. There are no atmospheric clouds in outer space.

48. B: Transpiration is water that evaporates from pores in plants called stomata. Evaporation of moving water is still called evaporation. Infiltration is the process of water moving into the ground, and precipitation that falls on trees is called canopy interception.

49. A: Absolute dating involves measuring radioactive decay of elements such as carbon-14 trapped in rocks or minerals and using the known rate of decay to determine how much time has passed. Another element used is uranium-lead, which allows dating for some of the oldest rocks on the Earth.

50. D: Water with a higher salinity has more dissolved salt and a lower freezing point. Water from the Dead Sea has the highest salinity of the answer choices.

Civics and Government

Political Theory

Major Political Concepts

Politics is the process of governance, typically exercised through the enactment and enforcement of laws, over a community, most commonly a state. Political theory involves the study of politics, especially concerning the efficacy and legitimacy of those responsible for governance. The major concepts in political theory include *power* and *authority*. The concepts of power and authority are closely related but possess certain significant distinctions.

Power is the ability of a ruling body or political entity to influence the actions, behavior, and attitude of a person or group of people; in short, power implies a degree of control over a human community. In order to possess *authority*, the ruling body or political entity must be recognized as having the right and justification to exercise power. This is commonly referred to as *legitimacy*. In representative governments, authority is garnered from the citizens through democratic processes, but in more autocratic regimes, influential elites grant that authority. In some cases, a ruling body or political entity may possess authority recognized by its citizens or influential elites but lack the power to influence those citizens and political entities or effect change within the system of governance. When power and authority are not properly aligned, governments are extremely weak, often deadlocked, and at risk of collapse or revolution.

Government is the result of the decisions made by a society during the political process and is a physical manifestation of the political entity or ruling body. The government determines and enforces the power of the state. A government includes the formal institutions of a society with the power and authority to enact, enforce, and interpret laws. The many different forms of government are determined based on this delegation of power between those institutions. Government encompasses the functions of *law*, *order*, and *justice* and is responsible for maintaining the society.

Sovereignty refers to a political entity's right and power to self-govern, including enacting and enforcing its own taxes and laws without interference from external forces. A political entity may possess varying degrees of sovereignty, as some sovereign states may still be subject to influence by outside political entities. For example, the members of the European Union cede some sovereignty in order to enjoy membership. A state's sovereignty is legitimate when outside political entities recognize the right of the state to self-govern. Both sovereignty and legitimacy are requirements to form a state.

The terms *nation* and *state* are often used interchangeably, but in political theory, they are two very distinct concepts. *Nation* refers to a people's cultural identity, while *state* refers to a territory's political organization and government.

Unlike states, there are no definitive requirements to be a nation; the nation just needs to include a group that is bound together by some shared defining characteristics such as the following:

- Language
- Culture and traditions
- Beliefs and religion
- Homeland
- Ethnicity
- History
- Mythology

The term *state* is commonly used to reference a nation-state, especially in regard to their government. There are four requirements for a political entity to be recognized as a state:

- Territory: a clearly defined geographic area with distinct borders

- Population: citizens and noncitizens living within the borders of the territory with some degree of permanence

- Legitimacy: legal authority to rule that is recognized by the citizens of the state and by other states

- Sovereignty: a political entity's right and power to self-govern without interference from external forces

Nation-state is the term used to describe a political entity with both a clearly defined nation and state. In a nation-state, the majority population of the state is a nation that identifies the territory as their homeland and shares a common history and culture. It is also possible to have several nations in the same nation-state. For example, there are Canadians in Canada and nations of Aboriginal peoples. The presence of multiple nations raises issues related to sovereignty.

Example of a nation: Sikhs in India

Example of a state: Vatican City

Example of a nation-state: Germany

Liberty and Freedom

Governments provide different *liberty* and *freedom*, depending on the form of government that, in turn, is influenced by the states' shared history and culture. Philosophers started articulating defined rights and liberties and arguing for their adoption and protection by the government during the Enlightenment. Liberalism advocates for increasing liberty and freedom in society and economics, while authoritarian regimes offer considerably less protection. The terms liberty and freedom both reference the same thing in society. Examples of liberty and freedom relate to speech, religion, press, economic pursuits, etc. The degrees and breadth of protections are context dependent, and they might be fluid and influenced by the political process. Many states delineate liberty and freedoms in their constitution. Rights and privileges are different because they involve something that is legal to do or possible according to the government sanctioning the action; thus, rights and privileges are typically more easily revoked from both specific individuals and larger communities.

Rights and Privileges
A *right* is a freedom, protection, or entitlement afforded to a person. In political theory, a right or *privilege* specifically refers to that which is granted to the citizens of a political territory according to the legal system or the social conventions of the society. Rights and privileges typically cannot be removed without due process under the law, although this depends on the form of government. Like the distinction between liberty and freedom, the difference between rights and privileges is indistinguishable. They are often the concrete representations of liberty and freedom in a society; as rights and privileges grow in number and strength, the society enjoys more liberty and freedom. Rights are the privileges provided by the government; however, the term right is commonly used to refer to a privilege of higher status that receives more scrutiny and protection from the state, usually requiring more due process to revoke or alter.

Example of a right: the right to vote

Example of a privilege: the privilege to receive a driver's license

Law, Order, and Justice
Governments must establish *law*, *order*, and *justice* through the government's political institutions. Protecting citizens' rights under the systems of laws, as well as effectively punishing the violators, is one of government's foundational responsibilities. Establishing law, order, and justice is an exercise in sovereignty—states that do not impose law and order under a reasonable standard of justice risk public unrest and challenges to the regime's legitimacy.

Law is the system of rules, policies, and regulations that govern behavior that is enacted by a political entity and enforced by the formal institutions created by the political entity. *Order* refers to each citizen, institution, and political entity acting as the law. Political entities secure order through the execution of laws through its enforcing institutions, like the police and justice system.

The term *justice* often refers to the fairness in the political entity's treatment of its citizens. When discussing its relation to law and order, justice refers to the necessary, agreed-upon consequences for failure to act according to the law. In political theory, justice is the social contract between the political entity and its citizens in which all parties involved have agreed upon what is considered "fair" in a society and what the consequences of acting contrary to the law should be.

Citizenship and Nationality
Citizenship is the political term referring to the legal status of an individual recognized by the state or government as a protected member. *Citizens* are subject to the laws of their state and granted the rights and liberties afforded by that state, including the right to vote and be elected to office.

Citizenship does not necessarily denote *nationality*, which refers to the relationship between an individual and a nation, rather than a legal status. Nationality is a component of citizenship, but nationality does not afford an individual any of the rights associated with citizenship of a state without official sanction from the state.

<u>Major Political Theorists</u>
Aristotle, 384 BC to 322 BC
A student of Plato, Aristotle was a Greek philosopher best known for his theories of rationality and ethics. In *Politics*, Aristotle asserted that "man is a political animal" and that man must actively participate in politics to further the political well-being of the city-state. He believed that man could only attain the happy life that nature intended through noble acts that bettered the community in which

they lived. To this end, he envisioned an ideal society in which the most virtuous and knowledgeable men ruled and the citizens lived virtuous lives in the service of their city-state. Aristotle is one of the leading contributors to Western philosophy and, later, Liberalism. The Roman Republic applied much of his theories on ethics and civics to their government.

Niccolo Machiavelli, 1469-1527
Machiavelli was an Italian diplomat, politician, and historian during the Italian Renaissance. He is most known for his infamous political treatise, *The Prince,* which inspired the political philosophy known as Machiavellianism. In *The Prince,* Machiavelli instructed rulers that it is "better to be feared than to be loved" and asserted that a ruler must be willing to commit any acts necessary to maintain power and establish the stability of their society. He advocated violence, deceit, and immoral acts and advised rulers to seek out and eliminate any potential political rivals within the community. Machiavellianism prioritizes maintaining and consolidating power over all else.

Thomas Hobbes, 1588-1679
Thomas Hobbes was an English philosopher most notable as being the founder of social contract theory. In his 1651 book, *Leviathan,* Hobbes stated that without a strong central authority, the people would live in constant fear; they would go without industry, knowledge, or commodities if there was no system for enforcing good behavior As such, he asserted that the people enacted social contracts with ruling bodies, in which the people agreed to submit to the laws and limitations imposed by the ruling body in exchange for the protection and quality of life afforded to them. Hobbes was responsible for founding many of the fundamentals of liberal thought, stating that all men are naturally equal and that a ruling body may only gain legitimacy through the consent of the people.

John Locke, 1632-1704
John Locke was an English philosopher influenced by Thomas Hobbes' social contract theory. Though he agreed with the theory on some points, he argued against Hobbes' assertion that man requires protection from a ruling body in order to maintain a civilized society, Instead, Locke believed that men are rational and tolerant beings by nature. Locke is considered the "Father of Liberalism." His works on political theory include the famous *Two Treatises on Government*, which contributed significantly to modern ideals of liberal theory, including espousing the need to protect the right to life, liberty, health, and possessions. Locke's philosophy on rights and self-government influenced the writers of the Declaration of Independence.

Jean-Jacques Rousseau, 1712-1778
Jean-Jacques Rousseau was a philosopher, writer, and composer during the Enlightenment in France whose political writings, *Discourse on Equality* and *The Social Contract,* influenced aspects of the French Revolutionary War and many modern political theories. Rousseau thought man was free in the more primitive stage, and this freedom could only be maintained in a state if the people remained sovereign through representative government. He advocated for religious equality and argued that the people are sovereign, rather than a divinely empowered monarch, and that the people should have the right to rule themselves. His work was banned in France, but his ideals influenced the people and inspired many of the political reforms that led to the Revolutionary War.

Immanuel Kant, 1724-1804
A German philosopher, Kant is best known for the set of ideas known as Kantianism, which states that individuals possess dignity and deserve respect. Although more famous for his philosophy, Kant discussed political theory in his essay, *Perpetual Peace: A Philosophical Sketch,* where he argued that world peace may be achieved through universal democracy and international cooperation. In this work,

he explained that, in order to end all wars and create lasting peace, all states must form constitutional republics in which elected officials adhere to the rule of the constitutional law to govern the state.

John Stuart Mills, 1806-1873

John Stuart Mills, an English philosopher and political economist, was considered the "most influential English-speaking philosopher of the nineteenth century" and was best known for being the first member of Parliament to advocate women's suffrage. His book *On Liberty* promoted utilitarianism, which advocates that people should always make decisions based on what would be the most net positive. In his work, Mills sought to limit the power exercised upon the individual by any ruling body and stated that moral actions are those that promote utility and increase individuals' and society's well-being. He called for limited constraints upon individual behavior that only restrict those actions that cause harm to others.

Karl Marx, 1818-1883

Karl Marx, a philosopher, social scientist, historian, and revolutionary, is considered one of the most influential Socialist thinkers of the nineteenth century. His ideas became known as Marxism, and Marx heavily influenced powerful Socialist and Communist leaders, such as Vladimir Lenin, with his 1848 pamphlet *The Communist Manifesto.* In this pamphlet, he explained that, in a capitalist society, perpetual "class struggle" exists in which a ruling class (bourgeois) controls the means of production and exploits the working class (proletariat), who are forced to sell labor for wages. He advocated for the working class to rebel against the ruling class and establish a classless society with collective ownership of the means of production. He envisioned world history as a series of stages in which capitalism eventually collapses into Communism.

Vladimir Lenin, 1870-1924

As a leading figure in the Russian Revolution and eventual founding of the Soviet Union, Lenin was one of the most controversial and influential political figures in the international Communist movement. Strongly influenced by Karl Marx, Lenin established the one-party system of government, which advocates pure Communism: a classless, egalitarian society in which the people abide by one rule—from "each according to his ability, to each according to his needs," a slogan coined by Marx. Lenin led the Bolsheviks into power after the Russian Revolution, and his Communist Party dominated the centralized one-party system. Lenin redistributed land among the peasants and nationalized most private industries, and he suppressed all political opposition with aggression, most notably during the Red Terror. Lenin advocated for Communist revolution across the world. Joseph Stalin, who further consolidated power of the increasingly authoritarian centralized government, succeeded Lenin as head of the Soviet Union.

<u>Political Orientations</u>

A *political orientation* is a set of ideals, principles, and doctrines that inform how government should be organized, specifically the balance between individual rights, government power, and economic policy. Thus, the country's dominant orientation will largely shape the state form of government. Orientations are also known as political ideologies and are commonly plotted on a political system to provide a visual representation for comparative purposes. The simplest political spectrum orders political orientations on a left-to-right axis. The far left and far right represent the most extreme political orientations, while the center is more moderate.

Left Axis

In general, the orientations on the left emphasize social and economic equality and advocate for government intervention to achieve it. Examples of "leftist" ideologies include Communism, Socialism, Progressivism, and Liberalism.

Communism

Communism is a radical political ideology that seeks to establish common ownership over production and abolish social status and money. Communists believe that the world is split between two social classes—capitalists and the working class (often referred to as the proletariat). Communist politics assert that conflict arises from the inequality between the ruling class and the working class; thus, Communism favors a classless society. Political philosophers Karl Marx and Friedrich Engels argued that Communism is society's destiny since capitalism would ultimately collapse. The collapse of the Soviet Union weakened Communism across the world.

Socialism

Socialists prioritize the health of the community over the rights of individuals, seeking collective and equitable ownership over the means of production. Consequently, Socialism is closely tied to an economic system. Under the political philosopher Karl Marx, Socialism is the transitional stage between capitalism and Communism. In general, Socialism is less extreme than Communism. Socialists are more willing to work within the framework of democracy to elect Socialist policies, like social security, universal health care, unemployment benefits, and other programs related to building a societal safety net. Most modern countries include some degree of Socialism, such as progressive taxation and welfare systems. The Scandinavian countries of Denmark, Finland, Sweden, and Norway are examples of countries with a socialized welfare system.

Progressivism

Progressive ideals maintain that progress in the form of scientific and technological advancement, social change, and economic development improve the quality of human life. Progressive ideals include the view that the political and economic interests of the ruling class suppress progress, which results in perpetual social and economic inequality.

Liberalism

Liberalism developed during the Age of Enlightenment in opposition to absolute monarchy, royal privilege, and state religion. In general, Liberalism emphasizes liberty and equality, and liberals support freedom of speech, freedom of religion, free markets, civil rights, gender equality, and secular governance. Liberals support government intervention into private matters to further social justice and fight inequality; thus, liberals often favor social welfare organizations and economic safety nets to combat income inequality. A popular form of Liberalism is Populism, which advocates for incorporating advances in technology, social organization, science, and economics into the government to benefit society.

Right Axis

Orientations on the right of the spectrum generally value the existing and historical political institutions and oppose government intervention, especially in regard to the economy. Examples include Conservatism, Libertarianism, and Fascism.

Conservatism

Conservatism is a political ideology that prioritizes traditional institutions within a culture and civilization. In general, Conservatives oppose modern developments and value stability. Since

Conservatism depends on the traditional institution, this ideology differs greatly from country to country. Conservatives often emphasize the traditional family structure and the importance of individual self-reliance. Fiscal Conservatism is one of the most common variants, and in general, the proponents of fiscal Conservatism oppose government spending and public debt.

Libertarianism
Libertarianism opposes state intervention on society and the economy. Libertarians advocate for a weak central government, favoring more local rule, and seek to maximize personal autonomy and protect personal freedom. Libertarians often follow a conservative approach to government, especially in the context of power and intervention, but favor a progressive approach to rights and freedom, especially those tied to personal liberty, like freedom of speech.

Fascism
Fascism is a form of totalitarianism that became popular in Europe after World War I. Fascists advocate for a centralized government led by an all-powerful dictator, tasked with preparing for total war and mobilizing all resources to benefit the state. This orientation's distinguishing features include a consolidated and centralized government. In addition, Fascists show more willingness to use violence as a means to accomplish state goals. Popular support for Fascism fell drastically after World War II. There is widespread disagreement among historians, political theorists, and other commentators as to whether governments or political movements qualify as Fascist regimes. Kim Jong-un's status as the supreme leader of North Korea is often cited as a Fascist regime due to the extreme consolidation of totalitarian power. Similarly, Vladimir Putin's Russia is often characterized as Fascist. There are also many European political parties—typically, nationalist parties that oppose immigration and international governance—that advocate for policies widely considered to be Fascist, like the Golden Dawn in Greece. However, few modern movements and regimes would describe themselves as Fascist. Fascism implies some comfort with totalitarian government, and it is most closely associated with the Fascist regimes during World War II, especially Adolf Hitler's Nazi Party.

Off the Spectrum
Some political orientations do not fit within the political spectrum because they can fit alongside other orientations and ideologies. For example, Nazism is both a Fascist and nationalist ideology. Examples include nationalism, internationalism, and anarchism.

Nationalism
Nationalism is an ideology that prioritizes a loyalty and devotion to the home country. Typically, nationalists exalt their country over all others; thus, nationalism prioritizes promoting its own culture over all other cultures and foreign interests. Nationalism developed alongside the growth of the European nation-state during the nineteenth century. Nationalists can be on the far right or far left. Nationalism is a powerful unifying force within a country or region. In modern times, nationalist groups oppose globalism, such as free trade agreements and supranational political entities, viewing global cooperation as a threat to their national culture.

Internationalism
Internationalist ideals support strong social, political, and economic unity among the states, nations, and people of the world. Internationalists value political institutions on an international level, commonly referred to as supranational political entities. Member states cede some degree of sovereignty to the international entity and receive the associated benefits. Internationalism advocates for free trade and globalism. Nongovernmental organizations play an important role in internationalism's approach to

global problems. Examples of supranational organizations include the United Nations, European Union, North Atlantic Treaty Organization (NATO), and World Trade Organization (WTO).

Anarchism
Anarchism is a radical political orientation that advocates for self-government and abolishment of existing political institutions; instead, society would be based on voluntary institutions. Anarchists oppose the state, arguing that political institutions organize society hierarchically, which creates the conflict. Thus, law and order is then accomplished by freeing the people from the state's corruption.

United States Government and Politics

Constitutional Underpinnings
The role of government is to maintain a society and provide public services through its formal institutions, protect the citizens of the state, and regulate the economic system. To determine how a government should perform these functions and to protect the rights and liberties of the citizens, states enact a *constitution*, a written document that typically establishes the form of government and delegation of powers within the government, delineates limits on government, and defines protected rights, liberties, and privileges.

The many underpinnings, or foundations, upon which the *Constitution* of the United States was founded include:

Articles of Confederation (1781-1789)
The Articles of Confederation established a formal agreement or confederation between the original thirteen states. The Articles of Confederation established a central government composed of a unicameral legislative assembly in which each state was granted a single representative. Passing a bill required votes from nine of the thirteen representatives. Under the Articles of Confederation, the centralized government, the Continental Congress, was granted very limited powers, rendering it largely ineffective. Those powers included:

- Borrowing money from states or foreign government
- Creating post offices
- Appointing military offices
- Declaring war
- Signing treaties with foreign states

The weak central government established under the Articles of Confederation lacked the power to impose taxes, enforce a draft to staff the new army and navy, regulate trade, or enforce the laws enacted in Congress. As such, the sovereignty remained primarily with the states. Under the Articles, the states reserved the powers to impose taxes upon each other and the citizens of their states, regulate trade within their states, coin and print money, and sign treaties with foreign states. The states also often ignored the laws enacted by the Congress because there was no executive branch to enforce the law.

This imbalance of power between the central government and the states led to crisis within the states, resulting in economic difficulties and violence. The lack of common currency and investment in interstate infrastructure greatly hindered economic growth. In the years 1786 and 1787, farmers in several states staged a series of protests over local tax and debt collection imposed on struggling farms, commonly known as Shay's Rebellion.

Constitutional Convention, 1787

The failures of the Articles of Confederation to effectively govern on a national level directly led to the Constitutional Convention, and those experiences influenced the founders' decision to include a more robust federal government in the United States Constitution. The Constitutional Convention faced several challenges, including disputes over representation between large and small states, tension between the southern and northern states over slavery, differing visions of how power would be delegated within the government, and opposition to ceding states' sovereignty to a national federal government.

New Jersey Plan

Led by William Patterson, the New Jersey Plan called for a unicameral legislature that would grant each state a single vote. It proposed a plural executive power selected by the legislature, which would possess no veto power over the legislature, as well as judges appointed by the executive power for the duration of their lives.

The Virginia Plan

Drafted by James Madison, the Virginia Plan featured a bicameral legislature with two houses. The representatives of the lower house were to be selected by the people, and then the lower house would elect the upper house. The number of representatives of each house would be based upon population or the amount of money contributed to the federal government by each state; thus, large states supported the Virginia Plan. In this plan, the legislature could appoint judges and select a single executive with veto power.

<u>Compromises</u>

Connecticut Compromise

This compromise included aspects of both the New Jersey Plan and Virginia Plan in a bicameral legislature. Representation in the House of Representatives was proportional to a state's population, and in the Senate, states enjoyed equal representation with two senators per state.

Slavery Compromises

Several other compromises were made during the Convention, including the *Three-Fifths Compromise,* which, in an effort to appease both the South states who wanted slaves to be counted as part of the population for the purpose of representation but not counted for the purpose of taxes, and the North, who demanded slaves be counted for taxes but not representation, the framers of the Constitution determined that three-fifths of the slave population of each state would be counted for the purpose of both taxes and representation. In an additional compromise called the *Commerce and Slave Trade Compromise*, Congress agreed not to tax exports from states or ban the trading of slaves for twenty years. This eased Southerners' fears that if the Northern states controlled the federal government, then they could enforce antislavery policies.

Constitution vs. Articles of Confederation

The Constitution addressed the weaknesses of the Articles of Confederation in the following ways:

- Unlike the sovereign states under the Articles of Confederation, the people are now the sovereign, and they bestow sovereignty to both the states and federal government, according to principles of Federalism.
- The Constitution creates a robust central government with many specific and implied powers.
- The Constitution empowers the federal government to levy taxes against the states.

- The Constitution establishes an executive branch of the federal government to enforce the laws; it is led by a president who serves as the commander-in-chief.

- The Constitution establishes a federal judiciary branch with a Supreme Court and lower courts to interpret the laws enacted by the legislative branch.

- The Constitution removes the states' power to coin and print money and establishes a national currency; Congress may regulate interstate and international commerce.

- The Constitution specifies representation in Congress based on population and equal representation for each state in the Senate.

- The Constitution requires a simple majority in both houses to enact laws rather than a vote of at least nine out of thirteen, as specified in the Articles of Confederation. In addition, senators vote separately under the Constitution, while states vote as a single bloc in the Constitution.

- The Constitution requires a two-thirds majority vote in Congress and a three-fourths majority in the Senate to amend the Constitution, while the Articles of Confederation required a unanimous vote.

<u>Federalism</u>
To strengthen the central government, while still appeasing the individual states who preferred to remain sovereign over their territories, the framers of the Constitution based the new government upon the principles of *Federalism*—a compound government system that divides powers between a central government and various regional governments. The Constitution clearly defined the roles of both the state governments and the new federal government, specifying the limited power of the federal government and reserving all other powers not restricted by the Constitution to the states in the Tenth Amendment to the Constitution, commonly referred to as the Reservation Clause.

The Constitution establishes the specific powers granted to the federal and state governments.

- Delegated powers: the specific powers granted to the federal government by the Constitution
- Implied powers: the unstated powers that can be reasonably inferred from the Constitution
- Inherent powers: the reasonable powers required by the government to manage the nation's affairs and maintain sovereignty
- Reserved powers: the unspecified powers belonging to the state that are not expressly granted to the federal government or denied to the state by the Constitution
- Concurrent powers: the powers shared between the federal and state governments

The Constitution would delegate the following expanded powers to the federal government:

- Coin money
- Declare war
- Establish lower federal courts
- Sign foreign treaties
- Expand the territories of the United States, and admit new states into the union
- Regulate immigration
- Regulate interstate commerce

The following powers were reserved for the states:

- Establish local governments
- Hold elections
- Implement welfare and benefit programs
- Create public school systems
- Establish licensing standards and requirements
- Regulate state corporations
- Regulate commerce within the state

The *concurrent* powers granted to both the federal and state governments in the Constitution include:

- The power to levy taxes
- The power to borrow money
- The power to charter incorporations

Ratifying the Constitution
The framers of the Constitution signed the Constitution on September 17, 1787, but the Articles of Confederation required nine of the thirteen states to ratify the document. Conventions were held in all thirteen states and sparked heated debates between those who supported and those who opposed the new system of government. The Federalists supported the expansion of the federal government, and the anti-Federalists feared that a stronger central government would weaken the states. The anti-Federalists also sought additional protection for civil liberties. The debates between these two parties continued for two years and inspired a series of essays known as the *Federalist Papers* and *Anti-Federalist Papers* authored anonymously by leaders of their respective party.

Notable Federalists and authors of the *Federalist Papers* include:

- Alexander Hamilton: founder of the Federalist Party and advocate for a centralized financial system

- George Washington: commander-in-chief of the Continental Army and future first president of the United States

- James Madison: one of the primary drafters of the Constitution and the future fourth president of the United States

- John Jay: president of the Continental Congress and future first chief justice of the United States

- John Adams: future second president of the United States

Notable anti-Federalists and authors of the *Anti-Federalist Papers* include:

- Thomas Jefferson: primary author of the Declaration of Independence and future third president of the United States

- Patrick Henry: governor of Virginia (1776-1779, 1784-1786)

- Samuel Adams: governor of Massachusetts (1794-1797), lieutenant governor of Massachusetts (1789-1794), and president of the Massachusetts Senate (1782-1785, 1787-1788)
- George Mason: one of only three delegates who did not sign the Constitution at the Constitutional Convention and author of Objections to This Constitution of Government (1787) and the Virginia Declaration of Rights of 1776, which served as the basis for the Bill of Rights

The first state to ratify the Constitution was Delaware in a unanimous vote on December 7, 1787. Several other states followed, and eventually, after ten months, New Hampshire became the ninth state to ratify the Constitution in June 1788. However, some states still remained divided between Federalist and anti-Federalist sentiments and had yet to approve the document, including the two most populous states, Virginia and New York. To reconcile their differing views, the Federalists agreed to include a bill of rights if anti-Federalists supported the new Constitution. Federalist sentiment prevailed, and the remaining states approved the document. On May 29, 1790, the last holdout, Rhode Island, ratified the Constitution by two votes. As promised, the Bill of Rights—the first 10 amendments to the Constitution—was added in 1791, providing expanded civil liberty protection and due process of law.

Powers, Structure, and Processes of National Political Institutions

A *political institution* is an organization created by the government to enact and enforce laws, act as a mediator during conflict, create economic policy, establish social systems, and carry out some power. These institutions maintain a rigid structure of internal rules and oversight, especially if the power is delegated, like agencies under the executive branch.

The Constitution established a federal government divided into three branches: legislative, executive, and judicial.

The Three Branches of the U.S. Government

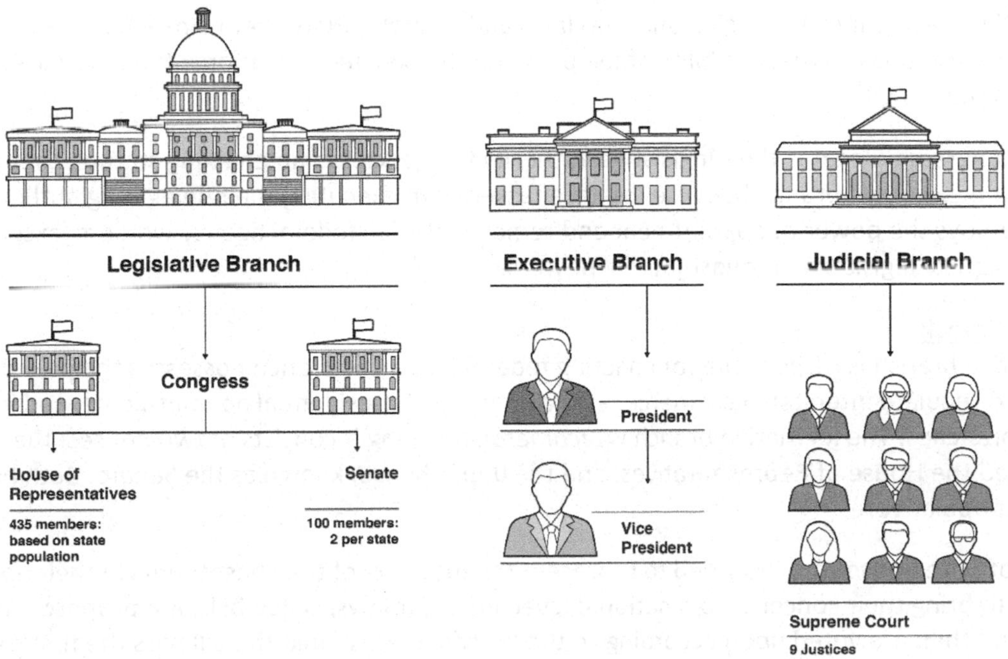

Executive Branch

The executive branch is responsible for enforcing the laws. The executive branch consists of the president, the vice president, the president's cabinet, and federal agencies created by Congress to execute some delegated.

The president of the United States:

- Serves a four-year term and is limited to two terms in office
- Is the chief executive officer of the United States and commander-in-chief of the armed forces
- Is elected by the Electoral College
- Appoints cabinet members, federal judges, and the heads of federal agencies
- Vetoes or signs bills into law
- Handles foreign affairs, including appointing diplomats and negotiating treaties
- Must be thirty-five years old, a natural-born U.S. citizen, and have lived in the United States for at least fourteen years

The vice president:

- Serves four-year terms alongside and at the will of the president
- Acts as president of the Senate
- Assumes the presidency if the president is incapacitated
- Assumes any additional duties assigned by the president

The cabinet members:

- Are appointed by the president
- Act as heads for the fifteen executive departments
- Advise the president in matters relating to their departments and carry out delegated power

Note that the president can only sign and veto laws and cannot initiate them himself. As head of the executive branch, it is the responsibility of the president to execute and enforce the laws passed by the legislative branch.

Although Congress delegates their legislative authority to agencies in an enabling statute, they are located in the executive branch because they are tasked with executing their delegating authority. The president enjoys the power of appointment and removal over all federal agency workers, except those tasked with quasi-legislative or quasi-judicial powers.

Legislative Branch

The legislative branch is responsible for enacting federal laws. This branch possesses the power to declare war, regulate interstate commerce, approve or reject presidential appointments, and investigate the other branches. The legislative branch is *bicameral*, meaning it consists of two houses: the lower house, called the House of Representatives, and the upper house, known as the Senate. Both houses are elected by popular vote.

Members of both houses are intended to represent the interests of the constituents in their home states and to bring their concerns to a national level. Ideas for laws, called bills, are proposed in one chamber and then are voted upon according to the body's rules; should the bill pass the first round of voting, the other legislative chamber must approve it before it can be sent to the president.

The two houses (or chambers) are similar though they differ on some procedures such as how debates on bills take place.

House of Representatives

The House of Representatives is responsible for enacting bills relating to revenue, impeaching federal officers including the president and Supreme Court justices, and electing the president in the case of no candidate reaching a majority in the Electoral College.

In the House of Representatives:

- Each state's representation in the House of Representatives is determined proportionally by population, with the total number of voting seats limited to 435.
- There are six nonvoting members from Washington, D.C., Puerto Rico, American Samoa, Guam, Northern Mariana Islands, and the U.S. Virgin Islands.
- The Speaker of the House is elected by the other representatives and is responsible for presiding over the House. In the event that the president and vice president are unable to fulfill their duties, the Speaker of the House will succeed to the presidency.
- The representatives of the House serve two-year terms.
- The requirements for eligibility in the House include:
    - Must be twenty-five years of age
    - Must have been a U.S. citizen for at least seven years
    - Must be a resident of the state they are representing by the time of the election

Senate

The Senate has the exclusive powers to confirm or reject all presidential appointments, ratify treaties, and try impeachment cases initiated by the House of Representatives.

In the Senate:

- The number of representatives is one hundred, with two representatives from each state.
- The vice president presides over the Senate and breaks the tie, if necessary.
- The representatives serve six-year terms.
- The requirements for eligibility in the Senate include:
    - Must be thirty years of age
    - Must have been a U.S. citizen for the past nine years
    - Must be a resident of the state they are representing at the time of their election

Legislative Process

Although all members of the houses make the final voting, the senators and representatives serve on committees and subcommittees dedicated to specific areas of policy. These committees are responsible for debating the merit of bills, revising bills, and passing or killing bills that are assigned to their committee. If it passes, they then present the bill to the entire Senate or House of Representatives (depending on which they are a part of). In most cases, a bill can be introduced in either the Senate or the House, but a majority vote of both houses is required to approve a new bill before the president may sign the bill into law.

Judicial Branch

The *judicial branch*, though it cannot pass laws itself, is tasked with interpreting the law and ensuring citizens receive due process under the law. The judicial branch consists of the Supreme Court, the highest court in the country, overseeing all federal and state courts. Lower federal courts are the district courts and court of appeals.

The Supreme Court:

- Judges are appointed by the president and confirmed by the Senate.
- Judges serve until retirement, death, or impeachment.
- Judges possess sole power to judge the constitutionality of a law.
- Judges set precedents for lower courts based on their decisions.
- Judges try appeals that have proceeded from the lower district courts.

Checks and Balances

Notice that a system of checks and balances between the branches exists. This is to ensure that no branch oversteps its authority. They include:

- Checks on the Legislative Branch:
  - The president can veto bills passed by Congress.
  - The president can call special sessions of Congress.
  - The judicial branch can rule legislation unconstitutional.
- Checks on the Executive Branch:
  - Congress has the power to override presidential vetoes by a two-thirds majority vote.
  - Congress can impeach or remove a president, and the chief justice of the Supreme Court presides over impeachment proceedings.
  - Congress can refuse to approve presidential appointments or ratify treaties.
- Checks on the Judicial Branch:
  - The president appoints justices to the Supreme Court, as well as district court and court of appeals judges.
  - The president can pardon federal prisoners.
  - The executive branch can refuse to enforce court decisions.
  - Congress can create federal courts below the Supreme Court.
  - Congress can determine the number of Supreme Court justices.
  - Congress can set the salaries of federal judges.
  - Congress can refuse to approve presidential appointments of judges.
  - Congress can impeach and convict federal judges.

The three branches of government operate separately, but they must rely on each other to create, enforce, and interpret the laws of the United States.

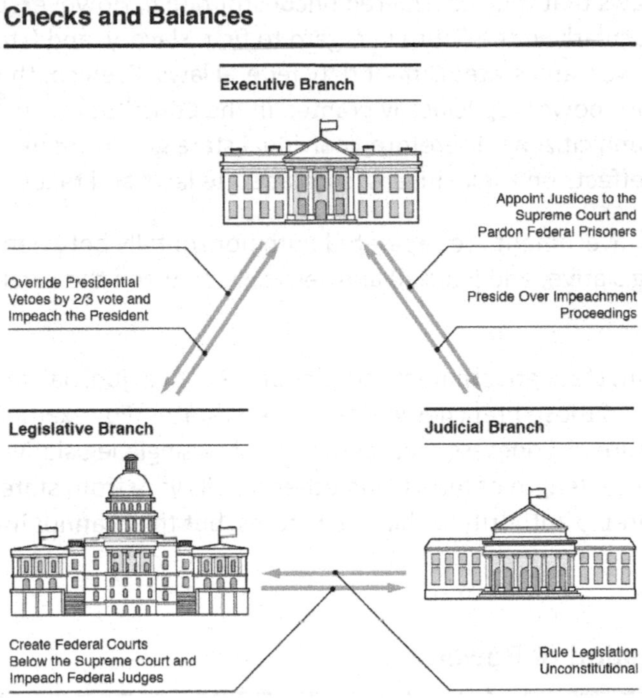

<u>How Laws are Enacted and Enforced</u>

To enact a new law:

- The bill is introduced to Congress.
- The bill is sent to the appropriate committee for review and revision.
- The approved bill is sent to the Speaker of the House and the majority party leader of the Senate, who places the bill on the calendar for review.
- The houses debate the merits of the bill and recommend amendments.
    - In the House of Representatives, those who wish to debate about a bill are allowed only a few minutes to speak, and amendments to the bill are limited.
    - In the Senate, debates and amendments are unlimited, and those who wish to postpone a vote may do so by filibuster, refusing to stop speaking.
- The approved bill is revised in both houses to ensure identical wording in both bills.
- The revised bill is returned to both houses for final approval.
- The bill is sent to the president, who may
    - Sign the bill into law
    - Veto the bill
    - Take no action, resulting in the bill becoming law if Congress remains in session for ten days or dying if Congress adjourns before ten days have passed

The Role of State Government

While the federal government manages the nation as a whole, state governments address issues pertaining to their specific territory. In the past, states claimed the right, known as nullification, to refuse to enforce federal laws that they considered unconstitutional. However, conflicts between state and federal authority, particularly in the South in regard to first, slavery, and later, discrimination, have led to increased federal power, and states cannot defy federal laws. Even so, the Tenth Amendment limits federal power to those powers specifically granted in the Constitution, and the rest of the powers are retained by the states and citizens. Therefore, individual state governments are left in charge of decisions with immediate effects on their citizens, such as state laws and taxes.

In this way, the powers of government are separated both horizontally between the three branches of government (executive, legislative, and judicial) and vertically between the levels of government (federal, state, and local).

Like the federal government, state governments consist of executive, judicial, and legislative branches, but the exact configuration of those branches varies between states. For example, while most states follow the bicameral structure of Congress, Nebraska has only a single legislative chamber. Additionally, requirements to run for office, length of terms, and other details vary from state to state. State governments have considerable authority within their states, but they cannot impose their power on other states.

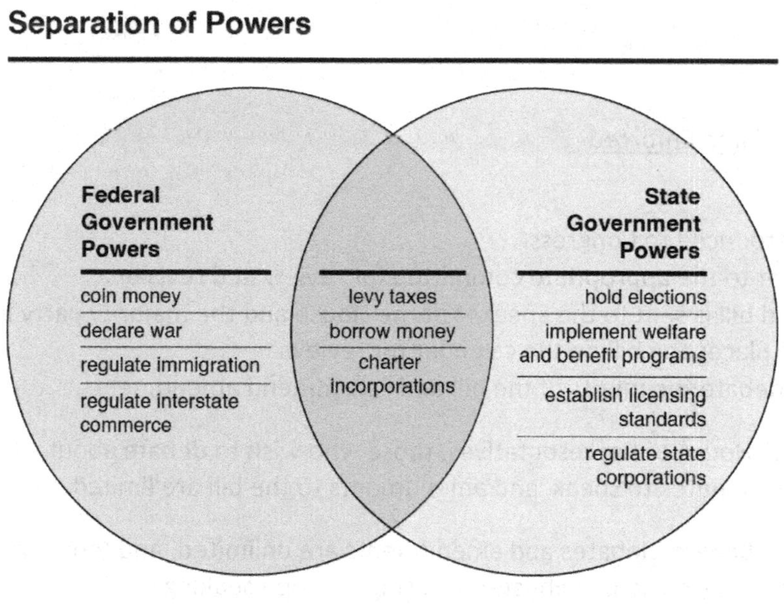

Civil Liberties and Civil Rights

The protection of *civil liberties* is one of the most important political values upon which American society is based. Though the terms *civil liberties* and *civil rights* are commonly used interchangeably, they describe two very distinct types of protections. Civil liberties refer to the legal protections afforded to U.S. citizens against government action, while civil rights refer to equal treatment under the law, especially in relation to minority groups, like women, African Americans, and Hispanics.

Civil Liberties

A civil liberty is a protection from legal action by the government. Civil liberties are granted by the Constitution in the first ten amendments, collectively known as the Bill of Rights, which were added to the Constitution in 1791. Civil liberties are conditional and do not afford protection from government action in every scenario. They can be restricted when they infringe on the rights of others; for example, with defamation, child pornography, or "fighting words." They also may be suspended with just cause, such as in the case of limiting the freedom of press to protect national security.

The Bill of Rights

The first ten amendments of the Constitution are called the Bill of Rights. They were passed to win over anti-Federalists during the ratification of the Constitution. Anti-Federalists wanted assurances that the federal government would protect certain fundamental civil liberties. The Bill of Rights includes:

- Amendment I: Establishes freedom of religion, speech, and press; the right to assemble in peaceful protest; and the right to petition the government without fear of reprisal
- Amendment II: Establishes the right to bear arms
- Amendment III: Establishes the right to refuse to quarter, or house, soldiers in time of war
- Amendment IV: Establishes protection against unreasonable search and seizure and requires a warrant based on probable cause supported by specific information
- Amendment V: Protects against self-incrimination in criminal trials, except in cases of military court martial; protects against being tried more than once for the same crime, known as double jeopardy; and protects against seizure of private property for public use without compensation
- Amendment VI: Establishes extensive set of rights to protect defendants in a criminal trial—the right to a speedy and timely trial before a judge and impartial jury of peers, the right to be informed of criminal accusations, the right to present and compel witnesses in defense of the accused, the right to confront witnesses against the accused, and the right to assistance of counsel
- Amendment VII: Protects the right to a trial by jury in civil cases exceeding a dollar amount of $20
- Amendment VIII: Protects against cruel and unusual punishment and excessive fines
- Amendment IX: Establishes the existence of additional fundamental rights unnamed in the Constitution; protects those rights that are not enumerated
- Amendment X: Reserves all powers that are not specified to the federal government or prohibited to the states or the people, establishing the principles of separation of powers and Federalism

Civil Rights

Civil rights concern who is protected, while *civil liberties* concern what is protected. Civil rights refer to protection against unfair treatment based on characteristics such as gender, race, ethnicity, religion, sexual orientation, and disability. The struggle for civil rights has a long history in the United States. Following the Civil War, the ratification of three amendments—Thirteenth, Fourteenth, and Fifteenth, collectively known as the Reconstruction Amendments—expanded the constitutional protection of equal civil rights.

The Thirteenth Amendment abolished slavery and involuntary servitude, except as punishment for a crime. The issue of slavery was no longer in the states' hands. Although the Emancipation Proclamation freed slaves in the Confederacy, the status of former slaves remained uncertain as the war neared its conclusion. Many Northerners did not hold strong views on slavery, but most wanted to punish the South and resolve the primary cause of the bloody Civil War. The Northern states all immediately ratified the amendment, and in December 1865, enough reconstructed Southern states ratified the amendment for it to be adopted into law.

The Fourteenth Amendment prohibited states from depriving life, liberty, or property without due process and from violating equal protection based on race, color, or previous condition of servitude. Now, all persons born or naturalized in the United States were considered legal citizens. Although revolutionary for the theoretical rights of all American citizens, newly freed or otherwise, the Fourteenth Amendment did not provide actual federally enforced equal protection until the Civil Rights Act of 1964.

The Fifteenth Amendment prohibits the government from denying a citizen the right to vote for reasons of race, color, or previous condition of servitude. Adopted in 1870, the last of the Reconstruction Amendments, the Fifteenth Amendment sought to protect newly freed slaves' right to vote. As discussed below, most states interpreted the amendment to only apply to male suffrage. In addition, Southern states passed a series of laws to systematically disenfranchise African Americans, like poll taxes, literacy tests, and residency rules. The use of violence and intimidation for political purpose was also common. Meaningful change did not occur until the Civil Rights Movement, nearly one hundred years later. In 1964, the Twenty-Fourth Amendment prohibited the states and federal government from charging a poll tax or fee to vote. Later, the Voting Rights Act of 1965 empowered the federal government to enforce the Fifteenth Amendment on the states for the first time.

Women's Suffrage

The Fourteenth Amendment specified equal treatment for all citizens; however, it did not establish women's right to vote in elections, known as women's suffrage. Although landowning women were allowed to vote in New Jersey in the late eighteenth century, the right was removed in 1807. The fight for women's suffrage continued in the middle of the nineteenth century. Famous women's rights activists include Susan B. Anthony, Lucy Stone, and Elizabeth Cady Stanton, who authored the *Declaration of Rights and Sentiments*, which demanded access to the civil liberties granted to all men. Women gained the right to vote in 1869 in Wyoming and 1870 in Utah.

The women's suffrage movement gained momentum in the early twentieth century after their increased participation in the economy during World War I when much of the workforce went overseas to fight. The National Women's Party picketed outside the White House and led a series of protests in Washington, resulting in the imprisonment of the party's leader, Alice Paul. In 1918, Woodrow Wilson declared his support for women's suffrage despite earlier opposition, and in 1920, Congress passed the Nineteenth Amendment, which made it illegal for states to withhold voting rights based on gender.

Jim Crow Laws

Southern states circumvented the Fourteenth Amendment and imposed what were referred to as Jim Crow laws, which established racial segregation of public facilities. These "separate but equal" facilities included the military, workplaces, public schools, restaurants, restrooms, transportation, and recreational facilities. Despite the label of "separate but equal," most facilities reserved for African Americans were considerably inferior.

In 1896, the Supreme Court handed down a decision in the case of *Plessy vs. Ferguson*, in which Homer Plessy, a Louisiana man of mixed race, attempted to board a railway car reserved for "whites only" and was charged for violating the separate car law. Plessy subsequently filed suit against the state, claiming they violated his Fourteenth Amendment rights. The Supreme Court decided in favor of the state, ruling that the law was not unconstitutional. The Supreme Court upheld separate but equal laws until the 1954 case of *Brown vs. the Board of Education of Topeka* where the Supreme Court ruled that racial segregation of public schools violated the Fourteenth Amendment.

Civil Rights Movement
Brown vs. the Board of Education prohibited segregation in 1954, but the Civil Rights Movement, led by the National Association for the Advancement of Colored People (NAACP) and such famous activists as Martin Luther King Jr. and Malcolm X, did not secure the enforcement of the Fourteenth Amendment until the passage of the Civil Rights Act of 1964, which outlawed discrimination based on gender, race, ethnicity, and religion. African American and Native American women, however, did not gain the right to vote until the Voting Rights Act of 1965, which enforced the voting rights articulated in the Fourteenth Amendment and Fifteenth Amendment. Section 5 of the Voting Rights Act prevented states with a history of discrimination from altering their voting laws without getting approval from the attorney general or a federal district court.

<u>Political Beliefs and Behaviors</u>
Political beliefs are the beliefs held by the citizens of a nation about the government, leaders, policies, and the related political issues of their state. Political beliefs differ among individual citizens, but in America, a strong basis of democracy shapes the political beliefs, behaviors, and attitudes.

Democratic Values
The foundation of democratic values upon which the United States is based include:

- The people are sovereign, and they elect a representative government to exercise that sovereignty.
- The citizens of the nation are equal under the law.
- The peaceful transition of power is valued regardless of election results.
- The private property of individuals cannot be taken by force by the government without due process or fair compensation.
- The civil liberties of the citizens of the state cannot be abridged or violated by the government without due process.
- The government should be accountable to the citizenry.

Political Socialization
American citizens undergo a process of *political socialization* from early childhood to adulthood during which they develop their individual sense of political identity and civic pride. Children learn about politics in the home from an early age, whether from the views, opinions, and facts of family and friends, or through the media to which they are exposed.

In school, they learn about the nation's political history, basic politics, and democratic values, as well as the ideals of patriotism and the processes of government. As they grow older, they join interest groups, labor unions, religious groups, and political organizations that further influence their political beliefs.

This socialization shapes not only the political beliefs and values of individual citizens and groups but the political ideals of the nation and public opinion.

Public Opinion

Public opinion is the shared political ideals, opinions, and attitudes of the people of a state regarding the politics, current events, and social issues that influence policy and shape the political atmosphere of a state. Public opinion is the result of political beliefs, socialization, and current events. Political scientists measure public opinion through:

- Distribution of opinion across demographics such as age, race, gender, and religion
- Strength of the opinion
- Stability of the opinion over time

Public opinion refers to the majority opinion in a democratic state. Citizens express public opinion through the interest groups they join, the media they consume and interact with, and the leaders they elect. To measure public opinion, scientists use polls to gather data. Accurate polling requires:

- Random sampling of representative populations
- Unbiased questions
- Clear instructions for how to answer questions
- Controlled procedures such as the use of telephone, mail, Internet, or in-person interviews with an unbiased pollster
- Accurate reporting of the results, including information about methods, inconsistencies, respondents, and possible sources and degree of error

Political Participation

Citizens express their political beliefs and public opinion through participation in politics. The conventional ways citizens can participate in politics in a democratic state include:

- Obeying laws
- Voting in elections
- Running for public office
- Staying interested and informed of current events
- Learning U.S. history
- Attending public hearings to be informed and to express their opinions on issues, especially on the local level
- Forming interest groups to promote their common goals
- Forming political action committees (PACs) that raise money to influence policy decisions
- Petitioning government to create awareness of issues
- Campaigning for a candidate
- Contributing to campaigns
- Using mass media to express political ideas, opinions, and grievances

Voting

In a democratic state, the most common way to participate in politics is by voting for candidates in an election. Voting allows the citizens of a state to influence policy by selecting the candidates who share their views and make policy decisions that best suit their interests, or candidates who they believe are most capable of leading the country. In the United States, all citizens—regardless of gender, race, or religion—are allowed to vote unless they have lost their right to vote through due process, such as felons.

Since the Progressive movement and the increased social activism of the 1890s to the 1920s that sought to eliminate corruption in government, direct participation in politics through voting has increased. Citizens can participate by voting in the following types of elections:

- Direct primaries: Citizens can nominate candidates for public office.
- National, state, and municipal elections: Citizens elect their representatives in government.
- Recall elections: Citizens can petition the government to vote an official out of office before their term ends.
- Referendums: Citizens can vote directly on proposed laws or amendments to the state constitution.
- Voter initiatives: Citizens can petition their local or state government to propose laws that will be approved or rejected by voters.

<u>Electoral Process, Political Parties, Interest Groups, and Mass Media</u>

Electoral Process

During the *electoral process*, the citizens of a state decide who will represent them at the local, state, and federal level. Different political officials that citizens elect through popular vote include but are not limited to:

- City mayor
- City council members
- State representative
- State governor
- State senator
- House member
- U.S. Senator
- President

The Constitution grants the states the power to hold their own elections, and the voting process often varies from city to city and state to state.

While a popular vote decides nearly all local and state elections, the president of the United States is elected by the *Electoral College*, rather than by popular vote. Presidential elections occur every four years on the first Tuesday after the first Monday in November.

The electoral process for the president of the United States includes:

Primary Elections and Caucuses

In a presidential election, *nominees* from the two major parties, as well as some third parties, run against each other. To determine who will win the nomination from each party, the states hold *primary elections* or *caucuses*.

During the primary elections, the states vote for who they want to win their party's nomination. In some states, primary elections are closed, meaning voters may only vote for candidates from their registered party, but other states hold *open primaries* in which voters may vote in either party's primary.

Some states hold *caucuses* in which the members of a political party meet in small groups, and the decisions of those groups determine the party's candidate.

Each state holds a number of delegates proportional to its population, and the candidate with the most delegate votes receives the domination. Some states give all of their delegates (*winner-take-all*) to the primary or caucus winner, while some others split the votes more proportionally.

Conventions

The two major parties hold national conventions to determine who will be the nominee to run for president from each party. The *delegates* each candidate won in the primary elections or caucuses are the voters who represent their states at the national conventions. The candidate who wins the most delegate votes is given the nomination. Political parties establish their own internal requirements and procedures for how a nominee is nominated.

Conventions are typically spread across several days, and leaders of the party give speeches, culminating with the candidate accepting the nomination at the end.

Campaigning

Once the nominees are selected from each party, they continue campaigning into the national election. Prior to the mid-1800s, candidates did not actively campaign for themselves, considering it dishonorable to the office, but campaigning is now rampant. Modern campaigning includes, but is not limited to:

- Raising money
- Meeting with citizens and public officials around the country
- Giving speeches
- Issuing policy proposals
- Running internal polls to determine strategy
- Organizing strategic voter outreach in important districts
- Participating in debates organized by a third-party private debate commission
- Advertising on television, through mail, or on the Internet

General Election

On the first Tuesday after the first Monday in November of an election year, every four years, the people cast their votes by secret ballot for president in a *general election*. Voters may vote for any candidate, regardless of their party affiliation. The outcome of the popular vote does not decide the election; instead, the winner is determined by the Electoral College.

Electoral College

When the people cast their votes for president in the general election, they are casting their votes for the *electors* from the *Electoral College* who will elect the president. In order to win the presidential election, a nominee must win 270 of the 538 electoral votes. The number of electors is equal to the total number of senators and representatives from each state plus three electoral votes for Washington D.C. which does not have any voting members in the legislative branch.

The electors typically vote based on the popular vote from their states. Although the Constitution does not require electors to vote for the popular vote winner, no elector voting against the popular vote has ever changed the outcome of an election. Due to the Electoral College, a nominee may win the popular vote and still lose the election.

For example, let's imagine that there only two states, Wyoming and Nebraska, in a presidential election. Wyoming has three electoral votes and awards them all to the winner of the election by majority vote. Nebraska has five electoral votes and also awards them all to the winner of the election by majority vote. If 500,000 people in Wyoming vote and the Republican candidate wins by a vote of 300,000 to 200,000, the Republican candidate will win the three electoral votes for the state. If the same number of people vote in Nebraska, but the Republican candidate loses the state by a vote of 249,000 to 251,000, the Democratic candidate wins the five electoral votes from that state. This means the Republican candidate will have received 549,000 popular votes but only three electoral votes, while the Democratic candidate will have received 451,000 popular votes but will have won five electoral votes. Thus, the Republican won the popular vote by a considerable margin, but the Democratic candidate will have been awarded more electoral votes, which are the only ones that matter.

	Wyoming	**Nebraska**	**Total # of Votes**
Republican Votes	300,000	249,000	**549,000**
Democratic Votes	200,000	251,000	**451,000**
Republican Electoral Votes	3	0	**3**
Democratic Electoral Votes	0	5	**5**

If no one wins the majority of electoral votes in the presidential election, the House of Representatives decides the presidency, as required by the Twelfth Amendment. They may only vote for the top three candidates, and each state delegation votes as a single bloc. Twenty-six votes, a simple majority, are required to elect the president. The House has only elected the president twice, in 1801 and 1825.

Here how many electoral votes each state and the District of Columbia have:

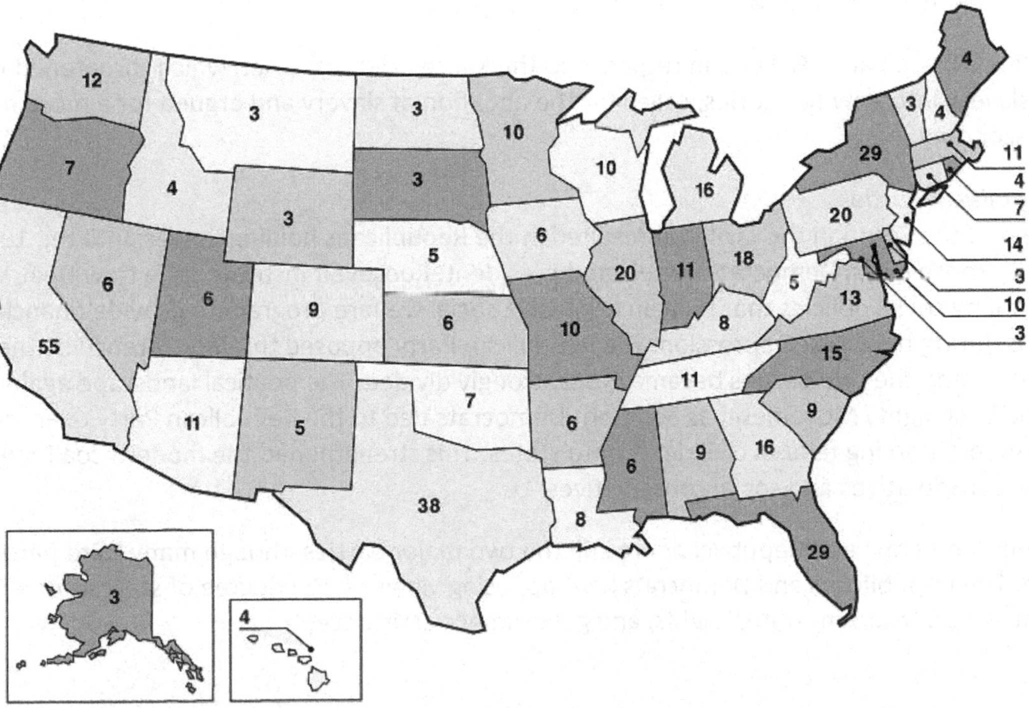

Political Parties

A *political party* is an organized group of voters who share the same political values and support or oppose the same policies. Members of a political party vote for the candidates from their party who they believe share their values and will approve or reject the policies they support or oppose. Political parties often determine the positions party members take on issues of policy, such as the economy, taxation, and social services.

The Founding Fathers of the United States opposed the divisiveness they associated with political parties, and President George Washington railed against the evil of political parties in his Farewell Address. However, the ratification of the Constitution led to the creation of the first two American political parties, the Federalists and the anti-Federalist Democratic-Republican Party. When Andrew Jackson became the fourth president of the United States as a Democrat, his opposition organized under the Whig Party. The Whigs asserted Congress' supremacy over the president and primarily focused on economic concerns, like banking and violations.

Slavery divided the nation and created unrest among the political parties, as members took opposing views and splintered into separate sects of the party or started new parties with members who shared their views. The Whig Party, so divided by the differing views of the members, collapsed. Former Whigs joined or formed the following parties:

- Constitutional Union Party: Devoted itself to a single-issue platform of preserving the Union and recognizing the Constitution as the supreme rule of law. The party did not take a firm issue on slavery, but vigorously opposed secession.

- Democratic Party: Divided into northern and southern factions over slavery, but the Democrats sought to compromise and remain unified.

- Know-Nothing Party: Advocated for an anti-immigration single-party platform, especially immigrants from Catholic countries.

- Republican Party: Formed in response to the Kansas-Nebraska Act, which threatened to extend slavery into new territories, called for the abolition of slavery and argued for a more modernized economy.

Modern Political Parties

The defeat of the South in the Civil War resulted in the Republicans holding power until the 1930s, when Franklin D. Roosevelt, a Democrat, was elected president. Roosevelt instituted the New Deal, which included many social policies that built an expansive social welfare program to provide financial support to citizens during the Great Depression. The Republican Party opposed this interference by the government, and the two parties became more strongly divided. The political landscape again shifted during the Civil Rights Movement, as Southern Democrats fled to the Republican Party over their opposition to enforcing federal civil rights onto states. This strengthened the modern coalition between economic conservatives and social conservatives.

Today, the Democrats and Republicans are still the two major parties, though many third parties have emerged. The Republicans and Democrats hold opposing views on the degree of state intervention into private business, taxation, states' rights, and government assistance.

The ideals of these parties include:

Republican (or the Grand Old Party [GOP])

- Founded by abolitionists
- Support capitalism, free enterprise, and a policy of noninterference by the government
- Support strong national defense
- Support deregulation and restrictions of labor unions
- Advocate for states' rights
- Oppose abortion
- Support traditional values, often based on Judeo-Christian foundations, including considerable opposition to same-sex marriage

Democrat

- Founded by anti-Federalists and rooted in classical Liberalism
- Promote civil rights, equal opportunity and protection under the law, and social justice
- Support government-instituted social programs and safety nets
- Support environmental issues
- Support government intervention and regulation, and advocate for labor unions
- Support universal health care

Some prominent third parties include:

- Reform Party: support political reform of the two-party system
- Green Party: support environmental causes
- Libertarian Party: support a radical policy of nonintervention and small, localized government

Interest Groups

An *interest group* is an organization with members who share similar social concerns or political interests. Members of political interest groups work together to influence policy decisions that benefit a particular segment of society or cause. Interest groups might include:

- Activist groups, like the NAACP, American Civil Liberties Union (ACLU), or People for the Ethical Treatment of Animals (PETA)
- Corporations, like pharmaceutical companies or banks
- Small-business advocates
- Religious groups, like the Concerned Women PAC and the Muslim Public Affairs Council
- Unions, such as the Association of Teacher Educators and International Brotherhood of Electrical Workers

Lobbyists

To promote their causes and influence policy in their favor, many interest groups employ *lobbyists*, paid advocates who work to influence lawmakers. Lobbying is a controversial practice, but it is sanctioned and protected as free speech. Lobbying from interest groups has a powerful impact on many policy decisions made in the United States. Examples of lobbyist groups include American Israel Public Affairs Committee (AIPAC) and Pharmaceutical Research and Manufacturers of America.

Mass Media

Mass media refers to the various methods by which the majority of the general public receives news and information. Mass media includes television, newspapers, radio, magazines, online news outlets, and social media networks. The general public relies on mass media for political knowledge and cultural socialization, as well as the majority of their knowledge of current events, social issues, and political news.

Evolution of Mass Media

- Until the end of the nineteenth century, print media such as newspapers and magazines was the only form of mass communication.
- In the 1890s, after the invention of the radio, broadcast media become a popular form of communication, particularly among illiterate people.
- In the 1940s, television superseded both print and broadcast media as the most popular form of mass media.
- In 1947, President Harry Truman gave the first political speech on television.
- In 1952, Dwight Eisenhower was the first political candidate to air campaign ads on television.
- Today, the Internet is the most widespread mass media technology, and citizens have instant access to news and information, as well as interactive platforms on which they can communicate directly with political leaders or share their views through social media, blogs, and independent news sites.

Influence of Mass Media on Politics

Mass media has a powerful effect on public opinion and politics. Mass media:

- Shapes public interests
- Enables candidates to reach voters wherever they are
- Determines what is and is not considered important in society based on how it prioritizes events and issues
- Provides the context in which to report events
- Is paid for by advertisers who may pressure news outlets to suppress or report information in their own interests

Comparative Politics and International Relations

Forms of Government and Types of Regimes

Government is the physical manifestation of the political entity or ruling body of a state. It includes the formal institutions that operate to manage and maintain a society. The form of government does not determine the state's *economic system*, though these concepts are often closely tied. Many forms of government are based on a society's economic system. However, while the form of government refers to the methods by which a society is managed, the term *economy* refers to the management of resources in a society. Many forms of government exist, often as hybrids of two or more forms of government or economic systems. Forms of government can be distinguished based on protection of civil liberties, protection of rights, distribution of power, power of government, and principles of Federalism.

Regime is the term used to describe the political conditions under which the citizens live under the ruling body. A regime is defined by the amount of power the government exerts over the people and the number of people who comprise the ruling body. It is closely related to the form of government because the form of government largely creates the political conditions. Regimes are governmental bodies that control both the form and the limit of term of their office. For example, authoritarianism is an example of a form of government and type of regime. A regime is considered to be ongoing until the culture, priorities, and values of the government are altered, ranging from the peaceful transitions of power between democratic political parties to the violent overthrow of the current regime.

The forms of government operated by regimes of government include:

Aristocracy

An *aristocracy* is a form of government composed of a small group of wealthy rulers, either holding hereditary titles of nobility or membership in a higher class. Variations of aristocratic governments include:

- Oligarchy: form of government where political power is consolidated in the hands of a small group of people
- Plutocracy: type of oligarchy where a wealthy elite class dominates the state and society

Though no aristocratic governments exist today, it was the dominant form of government during ancient times, including the:

- Vassals and lords during the Middle Ages, especially in relation to feudalism
- City-state of Sparta in ancient Greece

Authoritarian

An authoritarian state is one in which a single party rules indefinitely. The ruling body operates with unrivaled control and complete power to make policy decisions, including the restriction of denying civil liberties such as freedom of speech, press, religion, and protest. Forms of authoritarian governments include *autocracy*, *dictatorship*, and *totalitarian*—states or societies ruled by a single person with complete power over society.

Examples of states with authoritarian governments:

- Soviet Union
- Nazi Germany
- Modern-day North Korea

Democracy

Democracy is a form of government in which the people act as the ruling body by electing representatives to voice their views. Forms of democratic governments include:

- Direct democracy: democratic government in which the people make direct decisions on specific policies by majority vote of all eligible voters, like in ancient Athens
- Representative democracy: democratic government in which the people elect representatives to vote in a legislative body. This form of soft government providing for the election of representatives is also known as representative republic or indirect democracy. Representative democracy is currently the most popular form of government in the world.

The presidential and parliamentary systems are the most common forms of representative democracy. In the presidential system, the executive operates in its own distinct branch. Although the executive and legislative branches might enjoy powers checking each other, as in the American presidential system, the two functions are clearly separated. In addition, the president is typically both the head of state and head of government. Examples of presidential systems include Brazil, Nigeria, and the United States.

In the parliamentary system, the prime minister serves as the head of the government. The legislative branch, typically a parliament, elects the prime minister; thus, unlike in the presidential system, the parliament can replace the prime minister with a vote of no confidence. This practically means that the parliament has considerable influence over the office of prime minister. Parliamentary systems often include a president as the head of state, but the office is mostly ceremonial, functioning like a figurehead. Examples of parliamentary systems include Germany, Australia, and Pakistan.

The presidential system is a form of government better designed to distribute power between separate branches of government. This theoretically provides more stability. The president serves for a limited term of years, while prime ministers serve until replaced after receiving a vote of no confidence.

In the parliamentary system, the interdependence and interconnectedness between the parliament and prime minister facilitates efficient and timely governance, capable of adjusting to developing and fluid situations. In contrast, the presidential system is more prone to political gridlock because there is no direct connection between the legislative and executive branches. The legislature in a presidential system cannot replace the executive, like in the parliamentary system. The separation of powers in a presidential system can lead to disagreement between the executive and legislature, causing gridlock and other delays in governance.

Federalism is a set of principles that divides power between a central government and regional governments. Sovereign states often combine into a federation, and to do so, they cede some degree of sovereignty to establish a functional central government to handle broad national policies. The United States Constitution structures the central government according to principles of Federalism. Canada is another example of a form of government with a Federalist structure.

<u>Monarchy</u>

Monarchy is a form of government in which the state is ruled by a *monarch*, typically a hereditary ruler. Monarchs have often justified their power due to some divine right to rule. Types of monarchies include:

- Absolute monarchy: a monarchy in which the monarch has complete power over the people and the state

- Constitutional monarchy: a type of monarchy in which the citizens of the state are protected by a constitution, and a separate branch, typically a parliament, makes legislative decisions. The monarch and legislature share power.

- Crowned republic: a type of monarchy in which the monarch holds only a ceremonial position and the people hold sovereignty over the state. It is defined by the monarch's lack of executive power.

Examples of monarchies:

- Kingdom of Saudi Arabia is an absolute monarchy.
- Australia is a crowned republic.

Major Types of Electoral Systems

An *electoral system* defines the procedures by which voters make decisions regarding who will rule a state and how those elected officials will make policy decisions for the state. Electoral systems dictate how the members of the ruling body are selected, how votes translate into positions, and how seats are filled in the political offices at each level of government. States use three types of electoral systems to determine the outcomes of elections: plurality, majority, and proportional representation.

Plurality

In a *plurality* electoral system, a candidate must receive a plurality, or highest percent, of votes in order to win a political seat. For example, if three candidates are running for election to a single-seat political office and Candidate A receives 37 percent, Candidate B receives 39 percent, and Candidate C receives 24 percent, Candidate B will win the seat, even though the majority of the electorate actually voted *against* them.

One benefit of a plurality electoral system is that additional rounds of voting are not required if none of the candidates receive a majority vote. However, a plurality does not reflect the majority opinion, as in the example above, where most voters voted against the winner. Plurality electoral systems often lead to a wide variety of political parties because it is possible to win without a majority.

Majority

In a majority electoral system, a candidate must receive a majority of votes in order to be awarded a seat. If none of the candidates hit the mark, another round of voting is called, also referred to as a runoff. Some states only include the two candidates with the most votes to participate in the second round, while other states only require a candidate to reach a certain threshold of votes (for example, 15 percent) in order to be included as a candidate in the second round of voting.

A benefit of majority electoral systems is that they are more representative of public opinion than a plurality, as no candidate may win if the majority has voted against them. However, until a candidate receives a vote of 50 percent plus 1, additional rounds of voting must occur, which can lead to confusion. In addition, the second round of voting can lead to the less popular candidate winning. The Twelfth Amendment of the United States mandates that if no presidential candidate wins a majority of electoral delegates, then the House determines the winner by majority vote. The House could then elect a candidate that received considerably less support in the first round, such as a third-party candidate.

Proportional Representation

A proportional representation electoral system is often used for elections in which more than one seat in a legislative body is open. Proportional representation awards seats in proportion to the percent of votes each party receives. It is most common in parliamentary systems. For example, if there are ten seats and Party A receives 40 percent, Party B receives 20 percent, Party C receives 30 percent, and Party D receives 10 percent, Party A is awarded four seats, Party B is awarded two, Party C is awarded three, and Party D is awarded one.

A benefit of proportional representation is that it is the most representative of the people. However, it requires complex procedures and formulas to allocate votes and award seats, causing some confusion in the process. There are two types of proportional representation electoral systems—party list systems and single transferable systems.

Party List Systems: This method employs the *highest average method,* in which the votes received by each party are divided based on a formula (for example, the number of seats), and the highest quotient values are used to determine which parties receive a seat. In some party list systems, the voters directly select a political party, while others pool the total vote of the candidates from the party. The political parties typically issue lists of candidates that would serve in the government if their political party wins the seats.

Single Transferable Systems: In this method, voters rank the candidates in order of preference. To determine the number of votes to qualify, a candidate must receive a number of votes equal to $[v/(s + 1)] + 1$ in which v represents the number of votes and s represents the number of seats.

The number 1 rankings are counted first, and the first candidate to receive the required votes is awarded a seat. Any further votes that ranked that candidate number 1 will instead be awarded to the candidate ranked number 2. When a second candidate receives the required votes, any votes for them will be transferred to the next candidate on the list, and so on, until all the seats are filled. In this system, if no one receives the required number of votes, the candidate with the lowest number of #1 ranking votes is dropped, and the process begins again.

Countries that use proportional representation electoral systems:

- Ireland
- Belgium

Foreign Policy

Foreign policy refers to a state's international policy governing and informing their interactions with other states. A state's foreign policy typically defines the methods they employ to safeguard the state against foreign states, the social and economic goals of the state, and how the state will achieve these goals in the global arena through their relations with foreign states. Foreign policy is typically an executive function, either through the head of state or delegated to the foreign minister.

A state's foreign policy is influenced by several factors, including:

- Public opinion
- Economic and domestic stability
- Current events
- Social and humanitarian interests

The foreign policy of the United States has changed dramatically since the Founding Fathers established a policy of isolationism, which persisted well into the nineteenth century. After World War II, the United States emerged alongside the Soviet Union as the lone remaining global support powers. The United States led Europe and her allies during the Cold War's fight against the spread of Communism. When the Cold War ended after the collapse of the Soviet Union, the United States was left as the only true superpower, enjoying an unrivaled military and one of the world's most productive economies. American foreign policy shifted toward funding sustainable development economic projects in struggling countries and supporting democracy across the globe. The United States remains the leader of the NATO and has entered into several free trade agreements, most notably the North American Free Trade Association between Mexico, America, and Canada.

The president and secretary of state of the United States determine and enforce the U.S. foreign policy. The goals of U.S. foreign policy include:

- Maintain national security
- Promote world peace

- Promote civil rights and democracy
- Ally with other states to solve international problems
- Promote global cooperation and trade

To accomplish these goals, the State Department:

- Employs foreign diplomats to meet and talk with officials from foreign countries
- Maintains U.S. embassies in foreign nations from which to practice diplomacy
- Joins and supports international organizations such as:
    - NATO
    - WTO
    - United Nations

<u>Theories of International Relations</u>
The study of international relations involves analyzing the methods and effectiveness of different countries' approaches to international relations. Those approaches are informed by theories of international relations. The foundational theories of international relations are Realism and Liberalism.

Realism
Realism believes that states' foreign policy is guided by principles of "realpolitik"—the idea that states' politics and foreign relations are based primarily on the specific circumstances and factors. Realism advocates for studying international relations through the inevitable conflict between states pursuing power.

There are four basic tenets common to all schools of Realism.

1. States are the central actors, not individuals or international institutions.
2. There is no supreme authority guiding international relations, so the system is anarchic.
3. States act rationally to advance their self-interest.
4. All states are interested in maintaining or expanding their power as a means to self-preservation.

Liberalism
Liberalism has roots dating back to the Enlightenment, advocating for equality between states of the world. Liberals assert that global cooperation and interdependence is a force of world peace. Liberals seek to form international organizations to respond to international issues. There are three foundational principles common to all schools of Liberalism.

- Rejects "realpolitik" and the assumption that conflict is the inevitable outcome for international relations

- Supports international cooperation for the states' mutual benefit

- Seeks to establish international organizations and nongovernmental organizations to influence states' policy decisions and respond to international issues

<u>International Relations in Practice</u>
Examples of practices related to the execution of states' foreign policy, and the subject of the study of international relations, include diplomacy, conflict, treaties, and cooperation.

Diplomacy is the act of meeting with officials from foreign states to:

- Discuss matters of international interest
- Foster harmonious relationships
- Organize international partnerships
- Broker agreements
- Resolve disputes

States conduct diplomacy to negotiate compromises between states; accomplish militaristic, economic, environmental, and humanitarian goals; and garner allies in case of future crisis or conflict.

Conflict

International *conflict* refers to disputes between states. If not defused with international intervention and diplomacy, conflicts often lead to violence and armed conflict. The causes of international conflict might include:

- Territorial disputes
- Economic interests
- Religious or cultural tensions
- Social or humanitarian interests
- Political differences
- Civil rights and liberties
- Struggle for power

Treaties

To promote harmonious international relations, solve disputes, or protect against foreign invasions, states enter into *treaties* with other states. Treaties resolve armed conflict, establish trade agreements, or form defense alliances by:

- Creating compromises between the states for mutual benefit because treaties are invalid when signed under coercion
- Outlining the responsibilities and benefits of membership
- Limiting the actions of the states
- Describing the consequences of breaking the treaty agreement

Cooperation

To achieve common goals, states *cooperate*, or work together. When states cooperate, they form military alliances to protect each other against other states and make trade agreements that outline how trade is conducted fairly between the states to benefit both states' economies. States form international organizations that regulate military action and trade between states. Some of the most powerful of these include:

- United Nations: a global organization created after World War II in an effort to prevent another world war, foster cooperation among the nations of the world, and protect human rights across the world
- WTO: a global organization created to encourage, regulate, and promote fair trade among the nations of the world
- NATO: an organization of states from North America and Europe, led by the United States, formed after the end of World War II to counter the Soviet Union and Warsaw Pact's efforts to spread Communism across the world

Power and Problems of International Organizations and International Law

States form *international organizations* to foster cooperation among the nations of the world. These include organizations that are dedicated to regulating trade, outlining rules for dealing with conflict among states, settling territory disputes, solving global problems, and promoting social or humanitarian efforts around the world. International organizations also develop the body of *international laws*—the rules and regulations for interactions between the states. International organizations are important for the enforcement of international agreements and treaties. Without these organizations, there would be no way to enforce obligations and rights, effectively rendering those agreements useless.

Benefits of international organizations:

- States gain a forum to discuss matters of international politics and peacefully settle disputes.
- States increase their political power and wealth by combining their power with other powerful nations.
- States collaborate to solve global issues.
- States protect each other against more powerful foreign enemies; conflict is less likely due to the threat of stronger collective action.

Problems of International Law Enforcement

International laws enacted by international organizations are difficult to enforce, as no international enforcement agency exists to ensure states abide by the rules and regulations agreed upon by the organization. As such, states are bound only by the understanding that it is in their best interest to comply with the rules of the organization, rather than out of fear of retaliation from other states, except in the most extreme cases. There are also issues related to the balance of sovereignty between international organizations and states.

The methods by which organizations can punish state members who fail to follow the rules of the organization include:

- Reciprocal action: If a state acts against another state, the offended state may reciprocate the act.
- Economic boycott: If a state fails to comply with the organization's rules, the other states may refuse to trade with the offending state.

- Damaged reputation: If a state fails to follow the rules, the organization speaks out publicly to shame the offending state; thus, other states are less likely to do future business with the violating state.
- Collective military action: If a state violates the rules of the organization to an extreme extent, such as by committing government-sanctioned genocide or interfering with the territorial integrity of another state, states and international organizations may use military force to punish the offending state.

United States History

North American Geography, Peoples, and Cultures Prior to European Colonization

During the last Ice Age, large glaciers covered much of North America, trapping seawater and lowering the sea level. This exposed a land bridge between northwest Asia and North America that has been named Beringia. Nomadic peoples from Siberia used the Beringia land bridge to cross into North America. When the Ice Age ended a few thousand years later, the glaciers melted, the sea level rose, and Beringia disappeared beneath the ocean. The nomads who had crossed into North America before the Ice Age ended were searching for prey such as mastodons and wooly mammoths. These nomadic peoples lived in small groups and slowly spread out across North and South America during the next several millennia.

Several thousand years ago, the Neolithic Revolution occurred. This event occurred at different times in different places around the world, but it marked an important turning point in human history. The Neolithic Revolution included the development of agriculture and the domestication of animals. In North America, the primary crops were maize (corn), tomatoes, pumpkins, chilies, potatoes, and beans. There were only a few animals for Native Americans to domesticate, including the dog (in North America) and the llama (in Central America). Dogs were used to guard and hunt, and llamas produced wool and also transported goods.

The development of agriculture and domesticated animals led to a major change in North American societies: instead of small nomadic bands of hunter-gatherers, many native peoples became semi-sedentary. They began to form settlements, create social hierarchies, and develop new religious beliefs. However, many Native Americans remained semi-nomadic and lived in villages for only part of the year. Most Native American villages engaged in long distance trade with other groups. In general, most Native American peoples practiced animist beliefs—in other words, they thought that everything in the natural world had some spiritual power, including plants, animals, and rocks. In most Native American societies, women were responsible for farming while men hunted and fished.

Although most Native Americans continued to live in small villages, some larger settlements eventually developed. In Central America in 1325 A.D., the Aztec built the city of Tenochtitlan, located on the site of present day Mexico City, which was thought to contain more than 200,000 inhabitants. This meant it could have been one of the largest cities in the world before Spanish conquistadors destroyed it in 1521. In North America, Native Americans built the city of Cahokia (near the modern city of St. Louis), which may have had up to 40,000 residents before it was abandoned sometime around 1300. Cahokia also included a large circle of timber posts that may have had been used for astronomical predictions, similar to Stonehenge in Britain.

North and South America were rich in natural resources and also featured a variety of climates and geographies. This led to the development of various Native American societies before European colonists arrived.

The Iroquois and Algonquians were the major tribes in the eastern part of North America. They spoke different languages and frequently fought each other. The vast forests, especially in the Northeast, Midwest, and Southeast, provided wood for building wigwams and longhouses, as well as tools and weapons. Native Americans also used major waterways such as the Ohio and Mississippi Rivers to engage in trade, participate in small- and large-scale fishing activities, and launch raids against each other.

Several different tribes also lived between the Mississippi River and the Rocky Mountains—an area later known as the Great Plains. The Sioux, Comanche, Blackfoot, and Cheyenne were among these more nomadic peoples who hunted buffalo. They lived in teepees that were easy to take apart and rebuild in a new location as the tribe moved across the vast prairies. Native Americans sometimes set fire to the grasslands in order to control vegetation and improve grazing conditions.

The Pueblo people—including the Zuni, Hope, and Acoma tribes—lived in the deserts of the southwest. They used clay bricks to build large apartment complexes called pueblos, digging into the side of cliffs to create shelter. Since the environment was so dry, they had to build complex irrigation systems in order to grow crops.

The Tlingit, Chinook, and Salish people lived on the Pacific coast where they survived by hunting and fishing. Salmon were a staple of their diet and culture, playing an important part in their eating habits as well as their religious beliefs. The tribes developed techniques to create waterproof baskets and woven raincoats due to the wet climate of the Pacific Northwest.

The Aleuts and Inuit lived in the arctic and subarctic regions of North America where they hunted seals and whales. Because of the harsh conditions, they built semi-subterranean shelters that were insulated against the cold.

Founding and Development of European Colonies in North America

European monarchs began dispatching naval expeditions in the 15th century in an effort to bypass Muslim powers in the Middle East, such as the Ottoman Empire, which controlled the overland trade routes that led to Asia. European nation-states were competing against each other for wealth and power and wanted to have direct contact with Asia. The spice trade was especially lucrative, but Europeans also sought to spread Christianity and earn a reputation for making exciting discoveries. Several technological improvements helped European explorers establish trading outposts in Africa, Asia, and the Americas. Tools such as the astrolabe and quadrant allowed sailors to navigate more accurately, and the Portuguese built a new ship called a caravel that was faster and more maneuverable.

Europeans had discovered a route around the southern tip of Africa that led to Asia. However, the journey was long and dangerous. Christopher Columbus, a Genoese sailor, lobbied several European monarchs and sought financial support for an expedition across the Atlantic Ocean. He mistakenly believed he could reach Asia much more quickly via a western route across the Atlantic and was unaware that his path was blocked. Eventually, King Ferdinand and Queen Isabella of Castile accepted his proposal and provided funding for three ships as well as sailors and provisions. They agreed to appoint Columbus governor of any territory he discovered and granted him ten percent of the revenue from the new lands. After five weeks at sea, Columbus landed on San Salvador and explored the Caribbean islands for about three months before returning home.

Interaction of European, Native American, and African Peoples During the Colonial Period

News of his success sparked a number of other expeditions and the British, French, Dutch, Spanish, and Portuguese all eventually laid claim to lands in the New World. Columbus himself made three more voyages to the Americas. The French and Dutch focused mostly on the lucrative fur trade in North America. The Spanish and Portuguese sought gold in Central and South America but also tried to convert Native Americans to Christianity. British settlers also sought economic opportunity and created the first British colony at Jamestown, Virginia, in 1607. However, the Puritans who landed at Plymouth Rock in 1620 left for the New World in order to establish their ideal religious community.

Connecticut, New Hampshire, Massachusetts, and Rhode Island were considered the "New England colonies." The settlements in New England were based around an economy focused on fishing and lumber. These colonies maintained puritanical and Congregationalist religious beliefs. While English Puritans mostly settled in New England, a wide variety of colonists settled in the mid-Atlantic region. English, Scottish, Dutch, and Swedish settlers came to Delaware, New York, New Jersey, and Pennsylvania. As a result, the mid-Atlantic colonies were more religiously diverse and tolerant than the settlements in New England. Agriculture was the foundation of the economy in mid-Atlantic colonies. This meant that settlements were more dispersed. Government and administration were based on counties instead of towns.

The southern colonies, including Virginia, Maryland, the Carolinas, and Georgia, were also organized by county. The southern economy focused on labor-intensive crops such as tobacco and rice, and as a result, landowners relied on indentured servants and African slaves. Slaves were present in most colonies, but were more common in the south.

Political power was also distributed differently among the colonies. Some colonies, such as New York and Virginia, were royal colonies ruled directly by the king. Pennsylvania was a proprietary colony—the king allowed William Penn to appoint officials and govern the colony as he saw fit. Corporate colonies, such as Rhode Island and Connecticut, were administered by a group of investors. But, by the early 1700s, the king had revoked the charters of most proprietary and corporate colonies and assumed direct control himself.

Native Americans continued to play an important role in the early history of Britain's North American colonies. Squanto was an Algonquian Indian who helped English settlers in Massachusetts survive by teaching them how to plant native crops. Some Native American tribes were friendly towards the colonists and traded with them.

However, Native Americans and Europeans often came into conflict, frequently over land disputes. The Native Americans and Europeans had very different concepts of land use and ownership. Native Americans did not understand the concept of landownership or sale. When they entered into agreements with the colonists, Native Americans thought they were allowing the settlers to farm the land temporarily, rather than retain it in perpetuity. On the other hand, colonists were frustrated when Native Americans continued to hunt and fish on lands they had "sold." These, and other disagreements, eventually led to bloody conflicts that gradually weakened Native American tribes.

Native Americans were also vulnerable to diseases to which the Europeans had developed immunity. These diseases included bubonic plague, cholera, chicken pox, pneumonic plague, influenza, measles, scarlet fever, typhus, smallpox, and tuberculosis. These diseases killed millions of Native Americans and were sometimes used as a biological weapon. Historians estimate that as much as 80 percent of the Native American population died through disease and warfare.

Origins of the American Revolution and Founding of the United States

The French colonies in Canada also threatened the British settlements. France and Britain had been enemies for centuries. Religious differences reinforced their hostility; the British were Protestant and the French were mostly Catholic. Far fewer colonists settled in "New France," but they often clashed with the British, especially over the lucrative fur trade. Both the British and French sought to dominate the trade in beaver pelts, which were used to make hats in Europe. The British and French fought a series of colonial wars between 1689 and 1748 that failed to resolve the struggle for dominance in North America.

Eventually, the contest culminated in the French and Indian War (also known as the Seven Years' War), which ended in 1763. The French initially enjoyed the upper hand because they were able to persuade more Native American tribes to support them. The Native Americans felt the French were less likely to encroach on their territory than the land-hungry British. The Native Americans launched devastating raids along the British colonial frontier. However, the British eventually emerged victorious after they blockaded the French colonies in Canada. This prevented the French from bringing in reinforcements or from resupplying their Native American allies with gunpowder and ammunition. Native American raids subsided and eventually the French surrendered almost all of their colonial possessions in North America. Some historians consider this war the first global conflict because battles were also fought in Europe, Asia, and Africa.

The French defeat radically altered the balance of power in North America. Previously, Native Americans had been able to play the French and British against each other, but now they were without many of their French allies. In addition, the French and Indian War also set the stage for the American Revolution. Although victorious, the British monarchy spent an enormous amount of money and the war doubled the national debt. In order to pay off the debts, King George III began imposing taxes upon the North American colonies, which eventually led to revolution.

Since 1651, the British crown had tried to control trade within its empire, which eventually led to tension and discontent in the North American colonies. That year, the monarchy introduced the Navigation Acts, which prevented the North American colonies from trading directly with other European powers—all goods had to be shipped to Britain first. This was an attempt to keep wealth within the British Empire and to prevent other empires from profiting from their colonies. This was an example of mercantilism—an economic policy that formed the foundation of Britain's empire. Mercantilism called for government regulation in the form of tariffs, a tax on imports from other countries. This raised prices on foreign goods and encouraged British imperial subjects to purchase goods made in Britain or the colonies. This reduced imports and maximized exports, thus enriching the British Empire.

The Molasses Act in 1731 was another outgrowth of mercantilism. This law imposed a higher tax on the molasses that colonists purchased from the Dutch, French, or Spanish colonies. The tax was unpopular with the colonists and British imperial officials eventually decided not to enforce the tax. The Molasses Act had threatened to disrupt the pattern of triangular trade that had emerged in the Atlantic world. First, ships from Britain's North American colonies carried rum to Africa where it was traded for slaves and gold. Then, the ships took the slaves to French and Spanish colonies in the Caribbean and exchanged them for sugar or molasses. In the last part of the triangular trade system, merchants sailed back to North America where the sugar and molasses was used to make rum, and the cycle could start over again.

In addition to economic connections, many other bonds also bridged the Atlantic Ocean. Most colonists shared a common language, common religion, and common culture. However, as the colonies grew in population, they began to develop local institutions and a separate sense of identity. For example, it became common for ministers to receive their education at seminaries in North America rather than Britain. Newspapers also began to focus on printing more local news as well. Perhaps most importantly, the colonies began to exercise more control over their own political affairs. The British government retained control over international issues, such as war and trade, but the colonists controlled their own domestic affairs. Colonies began to form their own political assemblies and elect landowners who represented local districts. In addition, communications between the colonies and Britain were very slow because it took months for a ship to cross the Atlantic and return with a response.

A number of political acts by the British monarchy also led to more discontent among the colonies. After the French and Indian War ended in 1763, the king declared that the colonists could not settle west of the Appalachian Mountains. This was known as the Proclamation of 1763. Many colonists were frustrated because they had expected this territory would be open for expansion after the French had been defeated.

Additionally, taxes were imposed in an effort to help reduce the debt Britain amassed during the French and Indian War. In 1764, Parliament passed the Sugar Act, which reduced the tax on molasses but also provided for greater enforcement powers. Some colonists protested by organizing boycotts on British goods. One year later, in 1765, Parliament passed the Quartering Act, which required colonists to provide housing and food to British troops. This law was also very unpopular and led to protests in the North American colonies.

The Stamp Act of 1765 required the colonists to pay a tax on legal documents, newspapers, magazines and other printed materials. Colonial assemblies protested the tax and petitioned the British government in order to have it repealed. Merchants also organized boycotts and established correspondence committees in order to share information. Eventually, Parliament repealed the Stamp Act but simultaneously reaffirmed the Crown's right to tax the colonies.

In 1767, Parliament introduced the Townshend Acts, which imposed a tax on goods the colonies imported from Britain, such as tea, lead, paint, glass, and paper. The colonies protested again and British imperial officials were assaulted in some cases. The British government sent additional troops to North America to restore order. The arrival of troops in Boston only led to more tension that eventually culminated in the Boston Massacre in 1770, where five colonists were killed and eight were wounded. Except for the duty on tea, most of Townshend Act taxes were repealed after the Boston Massacre.

Parliament passed the Tea Act in 1773 and, although it actually reduced the tax on tea, it was another unpopular piece of legislation. The Tea Act allowed the British East India Company to sell its products directly, effectively cutting out colonial merchants and stirring more Anglo-American anger and resentment. This resulted in the Boston Tea Party in 1773, an incident in which colonial tea merchants disguised themselves as Indians before storming several British ships that were anchored in Boston harbor. Once aboard, the disguised colonists dumped more than 300 chests of tea into the water.

Because the British government was unable to identify the perpetrators, Parliament passed a series of laws that punished the entire colony of Massachusetts. These acts were known as the Coercive or

Intolerable Acts. The first law closed the port of Boston until the tea had been paid for (an estimated $1.7 million in today's currency). The second act curtailed the authority of Massachusetts' colonial government. Instead of being elected by colonists, most government officials were now appointed by the king. In addition, the act restricted town meetings, the basic form of government in Massachusetts, and limited most villages to one meeting per year. This act angered colonists throughout the thirteen colonies because they feared their rights could be stripped away as well. A third act allowed for British soldiers to be tried in Britain if they were accused of a crime. The fourth act once again required colonists to provide food and shelter to British soldiers.

Colonists responded by forming the First Continental Congress in 1774, and all the colonies except for Georgia sent delegates. The delegates sought a compromise with the British government instead of launching an armed revolt. The First Continental Congress sent a petition to King George III affirming their loyalty but demanding the repeal of the Intolerable Acts. The delegates organized a boycott of imports from and exports to Britain until their demands were met.

The colonists began to form militias and gather weapons and ammunition. The first battle of the revolution began at Lexington and Concord in April 1775 when British troops tried to seize a supply of gunpowder and were confronted by about eighty Minutemen. A brief skirmish left eight colonists dead and ten wounded. Colonial reinforcements poured in and harassed the British force as they retreated to Boston. Although the battle did not result in many casualties, it marked the beginning of war.

A month later, the Second Continental Congress convened in Philadelphia. The delegates formed an army and appointed George Washington as commander in chief. Delegates were still reluctant to repudiate their allegiance to King George III and did not do so until they issued the Declaration of Independence on July 4, 1776. The Declaration drew on the ideas of the Enlightenment and declared that the colonists had the right to life, liberty, and the pursuit of happiness. The Declaration stated that the colonists had to break away from Britain because King George III had violated their rights.

After the Battle of Lexington and Concord, British troops retreated to Boston and the colonial militias laid siege to the city. Colonists built fortifications on Bunker Hill outside the city and British troops attacked the position in June 1775. The colonists inflicted heavy casualties on the British and killed a number of officers. However, the defenders ran out of ammunition and British troops captured Bunker Hill on the third assault. Although it was a defeat for the colonists, the Battle of Bunker Hill demonstrated that they could stand and fight against the disciplined and professional British army.

The British army initially had the upper hand and defeated colonial forces in a number of engagements. The Americans did not achieve a victory until the Battle of Trenton in December 1776. Washington famously crossed the Delaware River on Christmas Day and launched a surprise attack against Hessian mercenaries. They captured more than 1,000 soldiers and suffered very minimal casualties. The victory at Trenton bolstered American morale and showed that they could defeat professional European soldiers.

The Battle of Saratoga in New York in the fall of 1777 was an important turning point in the American War for Independence. American troops surrounded and captured more than 6,000 British soldiers. This victory convinced the French king to support the revolutionaries by sending troops, money, weapons, and ships to the American continent. French officers who fought alongside the Patriots brought back many ideas with them that eventually sparked a revolution in France in 1789.

French support was very important in the last major battle of the revolution at Yorktown, Virginia, in 1781. American troops laid siege to General Cornwallis's British forces at Yorktown. The French fleet defeated a British naval squadron sent to relieve Cornwallis. French and American troops began attacking the British fortifications in Yorktown; a sustained artillery bombardment by American guns eventually forced Cornwallis to surrender. This ended the Revolutionary War, and in 1783 the British signed the Treaty of Paris. Britain recognized the United States as an independent country and set the Mississippi River as the nation's western border. However, British troops continued to occupy several forts in the Great Lakes region.

In addition, tens of thousands of colonists who remained loyal to the British Empire fled the United States after the war. They were known as loyalists and many thousands had joined militias and fought against the patriots. Some loyalists fled to Canada or Britain but many remained in the United States. Many Native American tribes had sided with the British as well in an attempt to curb western expansion. No Native American leaders signed the Treaty of Paris and they refused to give up their territories, which led to further conflict as the new American nation began to expand westward.

Adoption of the Constitution and Bill of Rights

America's first system of government was actually laid out in the Articles of Confederation, and not the Constitution. The Articles of Confederation were ratified during the Revolutionary War and went into effect in 1781. The Articles of Confederation created a relatively weak central government and allowed individual states to retain most of the power. Under this system, the national government did not have a president or judiciary. Each state had only one vote in the Confederation Congress and most major decisions required unanimous approval by all thirteen states. Despite this requirement, the Confederation Congress did pass some important legislation, including the Northwest Ordinance, which organized the land west of Appalachian Mountains. The territories eventually became the states of Ohio, Indiana, Michigan, Illinois, Wisconsin, and Minnesota. However, Congress did not have the power to tax and could only request money from the states without any way to enforce its demands. A Revolutionary War veteran named Daniel Shays led an armed insurrection in western Massachusetts in 1787. Although Shay's Rebellion was defeated, it drew attention to the weaknesses of the Articles of Confederation.

The Constitutional Convention met in Philadelphia a few months after the rebellion in order to create a stronger federal government. However, delegates disagreed over how to structure the new system. The Virginia Plan was one proposal that included a bicameral legislature where states were awarded representation based on their population size. This would benefit more populous states at the expense of smaller states. The other main proposal was the New Jersey Plan, which retained many elements of the Articles of Confederation, including a unicameral legislature with one vote per state. This plan would put states on an equal footing regardless of population.

Eventually, delegates agreed to support the Connecticut Compromise (also known as the Great Compromise), which incorporated elements from both the Virginia and New Jersey Plans. Under the new Constitution, Congress would be a bicameral body. In the House of Representatives, states would be allocated seats based on population, but in the Senate each state would have two votes. The Constitution also included a president and judiciary that would each serve to check the power of other branches of government. In addition, Congress had the power to tax and had more enforcement powers.

Slavery was another contentious issue during the Constitutional Convention. Slavery was more common in the Southern states and less common in the North. The Southern states wanted slaves to be counted when calculating representation in Congress but not when it came to assessing taxes. Northern states wanted the opposite and eventually the two sides agreed to the Three-Fifths Compromise where slaves were counted as three-fifths of a person for the purposes of both taxation and representation. The Constitution also included a provision that allowed slave owners to recover slaves who had escaped and permitted the international slave trade to continue until 1808.

Once the Constitution had been drafted, nine of the thirteen states had to ratify it. Vigorous debate erupted over whether or not the Constitution should be approved. Two different political factions emerged. The Federalists supported the Constitution because they felt a stronger central government was necessary in order to promote economic growth and improve national security. Several leading federalists, including Alexander Hamilton, John Jay, and James Madison, published a series of articles urging voters to support the Constitution. However, the Anti-Federalists, including Thomas Jefferson and Patrick Henry, felt that the Constitution took too much power away from the states and gave it to the national government. They also thought there weren't enough protections for individual rights and lobbied for the addition of a Bill of Rights that guaranteed basic liberties. Ultimately, the Constitution was ratified in 1788 and the Bill of Rights was approved a year later.

The Electoral College unanimously elected George Washington as the nation's first president in 1789. Despite this appearance of unity, deep political divisions led to the formation of the nation's first party system. Washington supported the Federalist ideology and appointed several Federalists to his cabinet, including Alexander Hamilton as secretary of the treasury. The Anti-Federalist faction evolved into the Democratic-Republican Party and favored stronger state governments instead of a powerful federal government. As settlers moved into the new Northwest Territories, Washington helped pacify Indians who opposed further expansion. He also successfully put down a rebellion in western Pennsylvania by farmers opposed to a federal tax on whiskey.

A number of different issues divided the Federalists and the Democratic-Republicans, including the French Revolution, which began in 1789. Initially, many Americans supported the French effort to replace their monarchy and create a republican government. However, the French Revolution quickly became more violent, as thousands of suspected opponents of the revolution were executed during the Reign of Terror. The Federalists, including Washington, were horrified by the violence, while Jefferson and the Democratic-Republicans thought the United States should help its former ally. Washington ensured that the country remain officially neutral.

Washington declined to seek a third term and another Federalist, John Adams, became our second president. Adams signed the Alien and Sedition Acts, which made it a criminal offense to criticize the government, and allowed the president to deport aliens suspected of treason. Adams and the Federalists argued that the laws were necessary in order to improve security as Europe became embroiled in a war against the new French republic. Jefferson and the Democratic-Republicans said the laws restricted free speech. Jefferson made the acts an important topic in 1800 when he successfully ran for president.

Jefferson's victory marked a turning point in the political system because the Democratic-Republicans gained more power while the Federalists went into decline. He repealed the Alien and Sedition Acts when he was elected. The Federalists were further weakened when Hamilton was killed in a duel in 1804.

Jefferson accomplished several significant achievements during his presidency, and one of the most important was the Louisiana Purchase in 1803. For $15 million, Jefferson bought French territory west of the Mississippi River that doubled the size of the United States. He then appointed Meriwether Lewis and William Clark to lead an expedition to explore the vast new territory and study its geography, vegetation, and plant life. Clark also brought his African-American slave, York, on the journey. York helped hunt and even saved Clark's life during a flood. The expedition was also aided by Sacagawea, a Shoshone woman, who acted as a guide and interpreter. The explorers also established relations with Native American tribes and set the stage for further western expansion in the 1800s.

Several key Supreme Court decisions were also issued during this time. The case of *Marbury vs. Madison* established the policy of judicial review, which declared that the Supreme Court could rule whether or not an act of Congress was constitutional. The case of *McCullough vs. Maryland* affirmed that Congress had the power to pass laws that were "necessary and proper" in order to carry out its other duties. The case also upheld the supremacy of federal laws over state laws when they came into conflict.

War between the United States and Britain broke out in 1812 because the United States was drawn into a conflict between Britain and France. Britain refused to stop interfering with American ships bound for France and had begun forcibly recruiting American citizens into the British navy. Furthermore, the British still occupied several forts near the Great Lakes and continued to encourage Indians to attack American settlements in the Northwest Territories.

This led to war in 1812, and many Native American leaders allied themselves with the British, including the Shawnee warrior Tecumseh. Tecumseh temporarily united several tribes but his confederacy fell apart when he was killed in battle. This further weakened Native American resistance and facilitated American settlement in the Northwest Territory after the war.

The United States also achieved a victory at the Battle of Lake Erie where several American ships routed a British squadron. However, an American attempt to invade Canada failed, and the British humiliated the nation by invading Washington D.C. and burning down several public buildings, including the White House. The United States did achieve another victory after hostilities had ceased when future president Andrew Jackson repulsed a British attack at New Orleans. The war did not result in any major territorial gains or losses, but it did reaffirm American independence and gave America its national anthem, the "Star Spangled Banner." It also led to the collapse of the Federalist Party, which had opposed the war. The Democratic-Republicans dominated politics for the next decade, which was known as the "Era of Good Feelings," thus marking the end of the first party system.

Causes and Consequences of Territorial Expansion

Constant immigration meant that land prices in the eastern United States rose, and people sought new economic opportunities on the frontier where land was cheaper. The United States government tried purchasing land from Native Americans, but most refused to relinquish their territories. Native Americans continued to defend their land until Tecumseh was defeated in the War of 1812. This defeat helped secure the Northwest Territory, and more settlers began pouring in. After the Louisiana Purchase, Lewis and Clark paved the way for expansion into the Great Plains and further west.

The Cherokee, Chickasaw, Choctaw, Creek, and Seminole tribes of the Southeastern United States were known as the "Five Civilized Tribes" because they had developed a written language and many members had become Christians. Nevertheless, Andrew Jackson signed the Indian Removal Act of 1830, which gave him the power to continue buying land from various tribes. The Cherokee filed a lawsuit to protect their territory and won their arguments before the Supreme Court. However, President Andrew Jackson ignored the ruling and eventually used troops to force many tribes off their land and sent them west to Oklahoma during the 1830s. This was known as the "Trail of Tears" because thousands of Native Americans died from starvation, exposure, and disease along the way.

Furthermore, the concept of Manifest Density emerged during the 1800s and introduced the idea that God wanted Americans to civilize and control the entire continent. This led to conflict when the province of Texas declared its independence from Mexico and asked to be annexed by the United States. President James K. Polk tried to buy Texas, but when Mexico refused, he sent troops into the disputed territory. Mexican troops responding by attacking an American unit, which led to war in 1846.

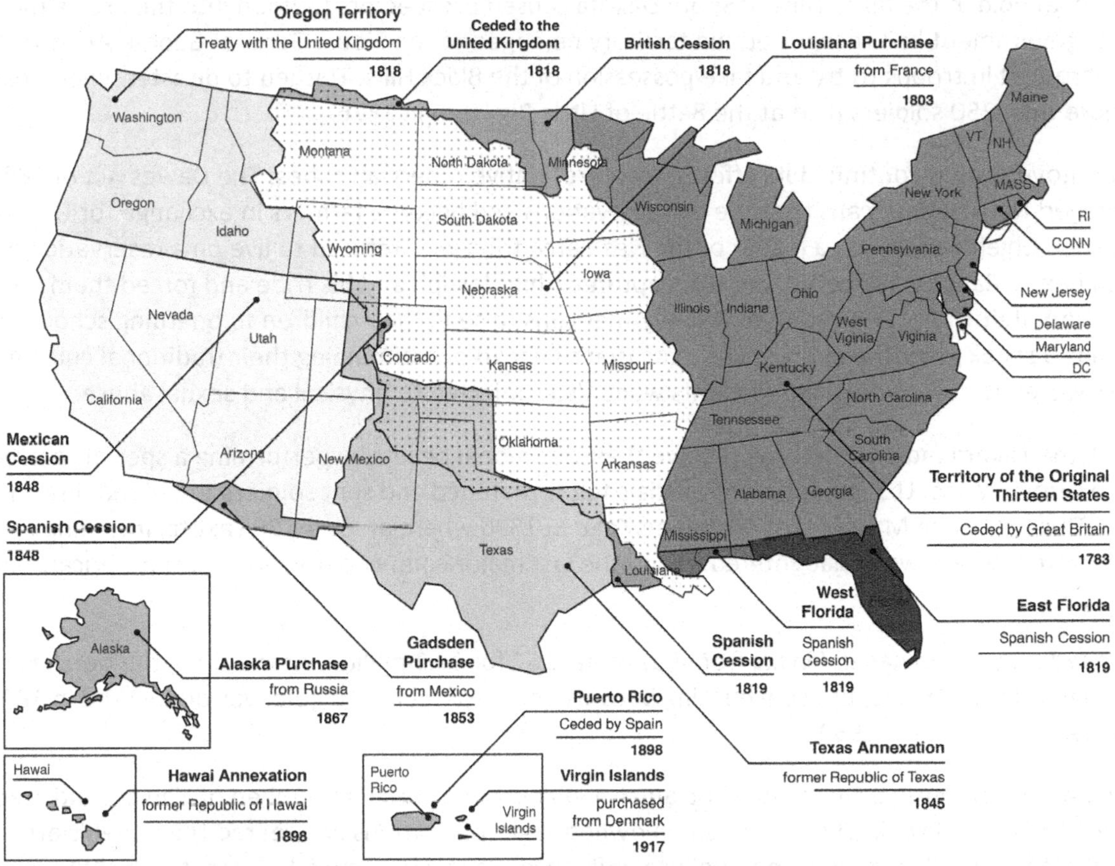

In the Mexican-American War, American troops won several battles although the Mexican army usually outnumbered them. The Mexican troops were poorly armed and trained, but, on the other hand, the Americans made use of their highly skilled artillery force. They eventually captured Mexico City and forced the Mexican government to sign the Treaty of Guadalupe-Hidalgo in 1848. The treaty recognized American control over Texas and also ceded California, Utah, Colorado, Arizona, New Mexico, and Nevada in exchange for $15 million. Tens of thousands of prospectors flooded into California when gold was discovered there in 1849. The prospectors often encroached on Native American lands, which led to further conflict. In 1854, the United States also acquired additional territories as part of the Gadsden Purchase. The acquisition of so much new territory sparked a debate over whether the land would be open or closed to slavery.

Manifest Destiny also sparked a desire to expand American influence into Central and South America. Adventurers launched several unsuccessful attempts to invade Nicaragua and Cuba.

Several important laws also stimulated western expansion during the second half of the 19th century. Congress passed the Homestead Act in 1862, which allowed citizens to claim 160 acres for only $1.25 per acre. The settler also had to live on the land for five years and make improvements. That same year,

Congress also passed the Pacific Railroad Act, which supported the construction of a transcontinental railroad. The United States government provided land and financial support to railroad companies and the first transcontinental link was established in 1869. This facilitated trade and communication between the eastern and western United States.

As Americans poured westward, conflict again broke out between settlers and Native Americans. The discovery of gold in the Black Hills of South Dakota caused prospectors to flood into the area although the U.S. government had recognized the territory belonged to the Sioux. General George Armstrong Custer brought in troops to try and take possession of the Black Hills. This led to disaster when Custer and more than 250 soldiers died at the Battle of Little Big Horn in 1876.

The U.S. government continued its efforts to control Native American tribes. The Dawes Act of 1887 encouraged Native Americans to settle on reservations and become farmers in exchange for U.S. citizenship. Chief Joseph was a leader of the Nez Perce tribe who refused to live on a reservation and tried to flee to Canada. However, the U.S. captured Chief Joseph and his tribe and forced them onto a reservation. Reformers also required Native Americans to send their children to boarding schools where they had to speak English and dress like Caucasians instead of maintaining their traditional culture. The schools were often crowded, and students were also subjected to physical and sexual abuse.

In 1890, the Lakota Indians tried to preserve their traditional beliefs by performing a special ceremony called a Ghost Dance. U.S. government officials felt threatened and sent soldiers to try and disarm the Lakota. This led to the Massacre at Wounded Knee in 1890 where at least 150 Lakota, including many women and children, were slaughtered. It was the last major conflict between Native Americans and U.S. forces.

The United States purchased Alaska from Russia in 1867 for $7.2 million. At the time, the purchase was unpopular with the public, but seal hunting became very profitable and gold was discovered in 1896. Alaska became a state in 1959.

In 1893, American businessmen launched an armed coup, overthrew the queen of Hawaii, and asked Congress to annex Hawaii. The businessmen owned sugar plantations and feared the queen's attempts to enact reform would threaten their political influence. Hawaii became a U.S. territory in 1898 and a state in 1959.

The last phase of American territorial expansion occurred as a result of the Spanish-American War in 1898. New ideas arose in the late 19th century that helped justify further expansion. Some intellectuals applied Charles Darwin's ideas of "survival of the fittest" to the human race and called this new concept Social Darwinism. They used this idea to justify why stronger groups of people colonized and exploited weaker groups. In addition, imperialists also used the idea of the White Man's Burden to justify further expansion. They claimed that Caucasians were obligated to civilize and govern groups thought to be less advanced.

These ideas were used to justify America's new status as a colonial power as a result of the Spanish-American War. Although Spain had once been a powerful empire, it had been in decline. The United States went to war against Spain in 1898 when the American battleship USS Maine exploded in Havana Harbor and killed more than 250 sailors. The U.S. Navy defeated the Spanish fleet in several engagements and then the Army followed up with a victory at San Juan Hill, which included the famous charge by Teddy Roosevelt and the Rough Riders.

The war lasted less than four months and made the United States a world power. The U.S. also acquired several Spanish colonies, including Puerto Rico, Guam, and the Philippines. Guam became an important refueling station for American naval forces in the Pacific and remains a U.S. territory today, along with Puerto Rico. When the United States occupied the Philippines, the Filipino people launched a rebellion in order to obtain their independence. The U.S. Army put down the insurrection, but in doing so, they committed many atrocities against the Filipino people. The Philippines would remain an American territory until 1946.

Causes and Consequences of 19th-Century Sectionalism, the Civil War, and Reconstruction

In the early 1800s, political and economic differences between the North and South became more apparent. Politically, a small but vocal group of abolitionists emerged in the North who demanded a complete end to slavery throughout the United States. William Lloyd Garrison edited the abolitionist newspaper *The Liberator* and vehemently denounced the brutality of slavery. His criticism was so vicious that the legislature of Georgia offered a $5,000 bounty to anyone who could capture Garrison and deliver him to state authorities. Other activists participated in the Underground Railroad—a network that helped fugitive slaves escape to the Northern United States or Canada.

Economic differences emerged as the North began to industrialize, especially in the textile industry where factories increased productivity. However, the Southern economy remained largely agricultural and focused on labor-intensive crops such as tobacco and cotton. This meant that slavery remained an essential part of the Southern economy. In addition, the North built more roads, railroads, and canals, while the Southern transportation system lagged behind. The Northern economy was also based on cash, while many Southerners still bartered for goods and services. This led to growing sectional tension between the North and South as their economies began to diverge further apart.

These economic differences led to political tension as well, especially over the debate about the expansion of slavery. This debate became more important as the United States expanded westward into the Louisiana Purchase and acquired more land after the Mexican-American War. Most Northerners were not abolitionists. However, many opposed the expansion of slavery into the western territories because it would limit their economic opportunities. If a territory was open to slavery, it would be more attractive to wealthy slave owners who could afford to buy up the best land. In addition, the presence of slave labor would make it hard for independent farmers, artisans, and craftsman to make a living, because they would have to compete against slaves who did not earn any wages. For their part, Southerners felt it was essential to continue expanding in order to strengthen the southern economy and ensure that the Southern way of life survived. As intensive farming depleted the soil of nutrients, Southern slave owners sought more fertile land in the west.

Both the North and South also feared losing political power as more states were admitted to the nation. For example, neither side wanted to lose influence in the United States senate if the careful balance of free and slave state representation was disrupted. Several compromises were negotiated in Congress, but they only temporarily quieted debate. The first such effort, called the Missouri Compromise, was passed in 1820, and it maintained political parity in the U.S. Senate by admitting Missouri as a slave state and Maine as a free state. The Missouri Compromise banned slavery in the portion of the Louisiana Purchase that was north of the 36°30′ parallel and permitted slavery in the portion south of that line as well as Missouri.

However, the slavery debate erupted again after the acquisition of new territory during the Mexican-American War. The Compromise of 1850 admitted California as a free state and ended the slave trade, but not slavery itself, in Washington D.C., in order to please Northern politicians. In return, Southern politicians were able to pass a stronger fugitive slave law and demanded that New Mexico and Utah be allowed to vote on whether or not slavery would be permitted in their state constitutions. This introduced the idea of popular sovereignty where the residents of each new territory, and not the federal government, could decide whether or not they would become a slave state or a free state. This essentially negated the Missouri Compromise of 1820. The enhanced fugitive slave law also angered many Northerners, because it empowered federal marshals to deputize anyone, even residents of a free state, and force them to help recapture escaped slaves. Anyone who refused would be subject to a $1,000 fine (equivalent to more than $28,000 in 2015).

The debate over slavery erupted again only a few years later when the territories of Kansas and Nebraska were created in 1854. The application of popular sovereignty meant that pro- and anti-slavery settlers flooded into these two territories to ensure that their faction would have a majority when it came time to vote on the state constitution. Tension between pro- and anti-slavery forces in Kansas led to an armed conflict known as "Bleeding Kansas."

John Brown was a militant abolitionist who fought in "Bleeding Kansas" and murdered five pro-slavery settlers there in 1856. He returned to the eastern United States and attacked the federal arsenal at Harper's Ferry, Virginia, in 1859. He hoped to seize the weapons there and launch a slave rebellion, but federal troops killed or captured most of Brown's accomplices and Brown was executed. The attack terrified Southerners and reflected the increasing hostility between North and South.

The sectional differences that emerged in the last several decades culminated in the presidential election of 1860. Abraham Lincoln led the new Republican Party, which opposed slavery on moral and economic grounds. The question of how best to expand slavery into new territories split the Democratic Party into two different factions that each nominated a presidential candidate. A fourth candidate also ran on a platform of preserving the union by trying to ignore the slavery controversy.

Lincoln found little support outside of the North but managed to win the White House since the Democratic Party was divided. Southern states felt threatened by Lincoln's anti-slavery stance and feared he would abolish slavery throughout the country. South Carolina was the first Southern state to secede from the Union and ten more eventually followed. Lincoln declared that the Union could not be dissolved and swore to defend federal installations. The Civil War began when Confederate troops fired on Fort Sumter in Charleston in 1861.

The Civil War

The First Battle of Bull Run (also known as the First Battle of Manassas) in 1861 was the first major infantry engagement of the Civil War. Both the Northern and Southern troops were inexperienced and although they had equal numbers, the Confederates emerged victorious. Many had thought the war would be short, but it continued for another four years.

The Union navy imposed a blockade on the Confederacy and captured the port of New Orleans in 1862. The Union navy was much stronger than the Confederate fleet and prevented the Southern states from selling cotton to foreign countries or buying weapons.

In 1862, Union forces thwarted a Confederate invasion of Maryland at the Battle of Antietam. This engagement was the single bloodiest day of the war and more than 23,000 men on both sides were killed or wounded. Union troops forced the Confederates to retreat, and that gave Lincoln the political capital he needed to issue the Emancipation Proclamation in 1863. This declaration did not abolish slavery, but it did free slaves in Southern territory. It also allowed African Americans to join the Union navy and about 200,000 did so. The 54th Massachusetts Infantry was a famous unit of African American soldiers who led an assault on Fort Wagner in South Carolina in 1863. Although the attack failed, the 54th Massachusetts witnessed African American troops fighting bravely under fire.

The Siege of Vicksburg in 1863 was a major Union victory because they gained control of the Mississippi River and cut the Confederacy in half. This made it difficult the Confederacy to move troops around and communicate with their forces. Grant commanded the Northern forces in the siege and eventually became the Union army's top general.

The Battle of Gettysburg in 1863 marked the turning point of the Civil War. Robert E. Lee led Confederate troops into Pennsylvania, but in three days of heavy fighting, the Union army forced them to retreat. The victory bolstered Northern morale and weakened Southern resolve. Never again would Confederate forces threaten Northern territory.

In 1864, Union general William T. Sherman captured Atlanta and then marched more than 200 miles to Savannah. Along the way, he destroyed anything that could support the Southern war effort, such as railroads and cotton mills. At this point, the Southern economy was beginning to collapse. The North had more manpower than the South and could afford to sustain more casualties. The North also had more industrial capacity to produce weapons and supplies and more railroads to transport men and equipment.

Eventually, Robert E. Lee surrendered to Ulysses S. Grant at Appomattox, Virginia, on April 9, 1865. Five days later, John Wilkes Booth assassinated Lincoln in Washington D.C. Vice President Andrew Johnson, a Democrat, succeeded him and soon came into conflict with Republicans in Congress about how to reintegrate Southern states into the nation. This process was known as Reconstruction and lasted from 1865 to 1877.

Reconstruction

Johnson opposed equal rights for African Americans and pardoned many Confederate leaders. However, many Congressional Republicans wanted to harshly punish Southerners for their attempts to secede from the Union. They were known as Radical Republicans because they also wanted to give former slaves equal rights.

Johnson vetoed bills that were designed to protect the rights of freed slaves, but Congress overrode his vetoes. This led to increasing conflict between Johnson and Congress, which eventually caused Radical Republicans to impeach him. Although Johnson was acquitted in 1868, he had very little power, and Radical Republicans took control of the Reconstruction process.

Republicans passed three important constitutional amendments as part of the Reconstruction process. The 13th amendment was ratified in 1865, and it abolished slavery throughout the country. The 14th Amendment was ratified in 1868 and gave equal rights to all citizens. The 15th Amendment was ratified in 1870 and specifically granted all men the right to vote regardless of race.

Southerners resisted these demands and passed laws that prohibited freed slaves from owning weapons or testifying against whites. They also formed militias and vigilante groups, such as the Ku Klux Klan, in order to intimidate African Americans who tried to vote. Congress sent federal troops into Southern states in order to enforce the law and prevent vigilante violence.

After the much-disputed election of 1876, the Democrats offered to let the Republicans have the White House if they agreed to end Reconstruction. After the Republicans agreed, federal troops were withdrawn and African Americans in the South were subjected to discrimination until the Civil Rights movement of the 1960s. Scholars often consider the Reconstruction era the beginning of Jim Crow and a transition into a new form of "institutionalized racism" that still pervades much of modern U.S. society.

Relationships among Industrialization, Urbanization, and Immigration in the Late 19th and Early 20th Centuries

After the end of the Civil War, America experienced a period of intense industrialization, immigration, and urbanization, and all three trends were interrelated. The process of industrialization had begun before the Civil War but expanded into more sectors of the economy in the later part of the century. This era is often called the Second Industrial Revolution and included growth in the chemical, petroleum, iron, steel, and telecommunications industries. For example, the Bessemer process made it much easier to produce high quality steel by removing impurities during the smelting process.

The writer Mark Twain called the late 19th century the Gilded Age because the era was also one of extreme social inequality. Some corporations expanded and began to control entire industries. For example, by 1890, the Standard Oil Company produced 88 percent of all the refined oil in the nation. This made a few individuals, such as John D. Rockefeller who owned Standard Oil, extremely wealthy. On the other hand, many workers earned low wages and began to form labor unions, such as the American Federation of Labor in 1886, in order to demand better working conditions and higher pay. Strikes were one of the most common ways workers could express their dissatisfaction, and the Pullman Strike of 1894 was one of the largest such incidents in the 19th century. Workers went on strike after the Pullman Company, which manufactured railroad cars, cut wages by about 25 percent. More than 125,000 workers around the country walked off the job and attacked workers hired to replace them. Federal troops were sent in to end the strike, and more than eighty workers were killed or wounded during confrontations. The strike was unsuccessful, but Congress passed a law making Labor Day a federal holiday in order to placate union members.

Immigration also played an important part in the economic and social changes that occurred during the late 19th century. Immigration patterns changed during this time and immigrants from Southern and Eastern Europe, such as Italy and Poland, began to surpass the number of arrivals from Northern and Western Europe. The immigrants sought economic opportunity in the United States because wages for unskilled workers were higher than in their home countries. Some Americans resented the influx of immigrants because they spoke different languages and practiced Catholicism. In 1924, Congress passed a law that restricted immigration from Southern and Eastern Europe.

Increased urbanization was the last factor that contributed to the rapid changes of the Gilded Age. Factories were located near cities in order to draw upon a large pool of potential employees. Immigrants flooded into cities in search of work, and new arrivals often settled in the same neighborhoods where their compatriots lived. Between 1860 and 1890, the urbanization rate increased from about 20 percent to 35 percent. Cities struggled to keep up with growing populations, and services such as sanitation and water often lagged behind demand. Immigrants often lived in crowded living conditions that facilitated the spread of diseases.

Political, Economic, Social, and Cultural Developments from the Progressive Era Through the New Deal

The social inequalities and economic abuses of the Gilded Age did not go unnoticed, and in the 1890s many reformers began to demand change. This period was called the Progressive Era and included activists in both the Democratic and Republican parties. The Progressives wanted to use scientific methods and government regulation to improve society. For example, they advocated the use of initiative, referendum, and recall to make government more responsive to its citizens. Progressives also argued that it was necessary to breakup large monopolies (known as trust busting) in order to promote equal economic competition. In 1911, Rockefeller's Standard Oil was split up into thirty-four different companies in order to promote competition, and the Federal Trade Commission was established in 1914 in order to prevent other monopolies from forming. Many Progressives also supported several constitutional amendments that were ratified in early 20th century, including the 17th amendment, which established the direct election of U.S. Senators in 1913 (previously state legislatures had elected senators). They also favored the Prohibition of alcohol that went into effect with the 18th Amendment in 1919. Progressives also advocated for women's rights and backed the 19th Amendment, which gave women the right to vote in 1920.

Many journalists who supported the reform movement of the Progressives were known as Muckrackers because they helped expose political corruption and social inequality. Upton Sinclair wrote a novel in 1906 called "The Jungle," which exposed poor working conditions and health violations in the Chicago meatpacking industry. His exposé led to the passages of the Pure Food and Drug Act in 1906, which authorized the federal government to inspect the purity of foodstuffs and medicines. Jacob Riis was a photographer who documented the crowded and unhealthy living conditions that many immigrants and poor workers endured.

World War I, from 1914 to 1918, led to a communist revolution in Russia in 1917. Many Americans wanted to prevent political radicals from gaining influence in the United States. A number of strikes and bombings around the country led the federal government to crack down on anarchists, socialists, and communists in an event known as the First Red Scare. In 1919, U.S. Attorney General A. Mitchell Palmer launched a series of raids and arrested resident aliens suspected of belonging to radical groups. About 500 resident aliens were eventually deported.

In 1933, President Franklin D. Roosevelt introduced the New Deal, which was a series of executive orders and laws passed by Congress in response to the Great Depression. The programs focused on relief, recovery, and reform, and were enacted until 1938. The second New Deal from 1935-1938 promoted the Social Security Act, labor unions, and aided tenant farmers and migrant workers who were struggling from the economic devastation of the Great Depression.

<u>Social Developments</u>

With the ratification of the 19th Amendment in 1920, women obtained the right to vote. This achievement was partly due to women's contributions on the home front during World War I. Women served as Army nurses and worked in factories to help produce weapons, ammunition, and equipment. As more women entered the workforce, they became more financially independent and began to socialize without being supervised by a chaperone, as was the norm during the 19th century. Overall, women during this period, known as "New Women," took on a more active role in public life, pursued higher education in greater numbers, and sought more sexual freedom. During the 1920s, women, known as "flappers," began to flaunt social conventions by wearing short skirts, bobbing hair, smoking cigarettes, and driving automobiles. Nevertheless, a "glass ceiling" still remains in place decades after women's suffrage in regards to a gender wage gap.

Millions of African Americans also moved north during and after World War I in search of work in a phenomenon known as the Great Migration. This led to increased racial tension as whites and blacks competed for jobs and housing. This culminated in a wave of race riots that swept across the country in the summer of 1919. In Chicago, conflict broke out between whites and blacks at a segregated beach, which led to five days of violence during which thirty-eight people were killed and more than 500 injured. The impact of the Great Migration can still be seen in contemporary, heavily segregated Rust Belt cities such as Gary, IN and Milwaukee, WI.

The invention of the automobile also contributed to social change. Henry Ford applied the method of assembly line construction and scientific management to the automobile manufacturing industry. This made it much cheaper to manufacture cars and allowed more people to purchase them. Automobiles allowed young men and women to socialize and date without adult supervision. Automobiles also improved transportation, increased mobility, and spawned the first suburbs.

Cultural Developments

Motion picture cameras were invented in the late 19th century, and the film industry experienced significant growth in the early 20th century. Because the first movies were silent, dialogue was displayed on intertitles and a live orchestra usually performed during a screening. "Birth of a Nation," by D.W. Griffith, was one of the first major cinema blockbusters, and it portrayed the Ku Klux Klan in a heroic light. Millions of Americans saw the film, which helped the Klan spread throughout the Northern and Western United States.

The Great Migration also led to cultural changes during the 1920s known as the Harlem Renaissance. The movement was based in the neighborhood of Harlem and led to a rebirth of black literature, art, music, and fashion. Jazz was an important feature of the Harlem Renaissance and challenged musical conventions by emphasizing improvisation and spontaneity. Jazz became very popular with both whites and blacks during the 1920s. Langston Hughes was a poet of the Harlem Renaissance who encouraged his readers to take pride in their black identity.

Economic Developments

The Panic of 1893 was a worldwide economic depression that devastated the American economy. Businesses went bankrupt, banks collapsed, and unemployment rose to approximately 17 percent. The economy began to recover by 1897, and the beginning of World War I boosted the U.S. economy as European nations bought American goods.

In 1918, the United States emerged from World War I as a major economic power because it had helped finance the Allied war effort and produced large amounts of weapons and equipment. The American agricultural sector also prospered because European farms had been devastated by the war. This sent crop prices up, and farmers used the money to buy more land and equipment. Although the 1920s is usually depicted as an era of economic prosperity, agricultural prices fell after World War I, and farmers were unable to pay back their debts.

Stock market speculation increased during the 1920s, and investors borrowed money in order to purchase shares. This did not cause any concern as long as the stock market went up, but it led to disaster when stock prices fell sharply in October 1929 and investors were unable to repay their loans. The stock market crash may have triggered the Great Depression, but it did not cause it. The Great Depression spread around the globe as nations stopped trading with each other. In the United States, families lost their savings when banks failed because there was no federal insurance. The economy went into a downward spiral because as more people lost their jobs, they had little money to spend, which led to further layoffs and more economic contraction. Unemployment peaked at 25 percent between 1932 and 1933.

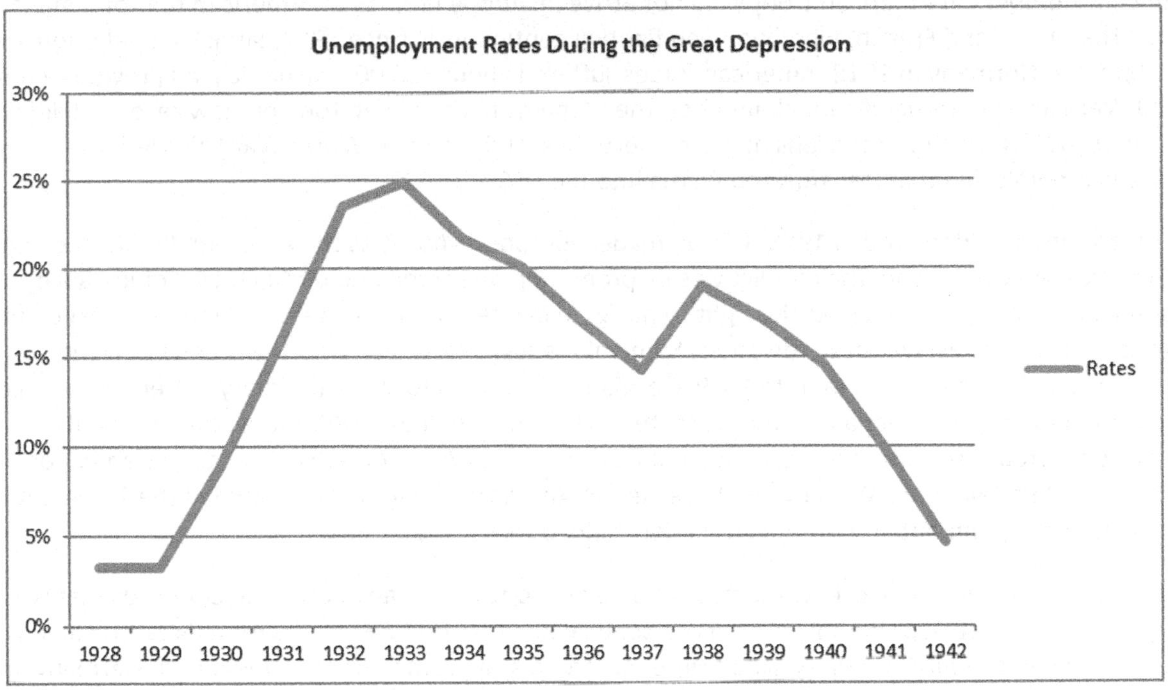

Democratic candidate Franklin D. Roosevelt was elected president in 1932 on his promise to help the economy recover by increasing government spending. After taking office in 1933, Roosevelt introduced a barrage of proposals, called the New Deal, that he hoped would boost employment, stimulate demand, and increase government regulation. Some elements of the New Deal were temporary, such as the Civilian Conservation Corps, which put young men to work improving parks between 1933 and 1942. Other New Deal programs endure to this day, such as the Social Security Administration, which has provided pensions to retirees, temporary payments to unemployed workers, and benefits to handicapped individuals since 1935. In addition, the Securities and Exchange Commission was created in 1934 and continues to regulate stock markets and investment companies. The Wagner Act of 1935 was also an important part of the New Deal because it guaranteed the right of workers to unionize and go on strike. The 21st Amendment was ratified in 1933 and repealed Prohibition, which had been hard to enforce and was unpopular. Roosevelt also hoped it would create jobs and stimulate spending. The New Deal helped reduce unemployment, but the economy did not completely recover until America entered World War II and production increased in order to support the war efforts.

Causes and Consequences of American Participation in World War I & II

World War I began in 1914 with the assassination of Franz Ferdinand, the apparent heir of the Austro-Hungarian Empire. A network of secret alliances meant that most European nations were quickly drawn into the conflict, although President Woodrow Wilson initially tried to keep the United States neutral. The war involved two major European alliances: the Triple Entente of Britain, France, and Russia, and the Central Powers, which included Germany and Austria-Hungary. The British implemented a naval blockade that was very successful, and the Germans retaliated by launching submarine attacks. German submarines attacked any ship carrying supplies to the Triple Entente, including the passenger ship RMS Lusitania in 1915. About 1,200 people died, including more than 100 Americans. The Germans temporarily halted their unrestricted submarine campaign, but eventually resumed the attacks in 1917.

In addition, in 1917, Germany asked Mexico to attack the United States in a communiqué known as the Zimmerman telegram. These events led the United States to join the Triple Entente in 1917, although significant numbers of American troops did not arrive in Europe until 1918. American reinforcement helped the British and French, who had been fighting continuously since 1914, launch a final offensive that defeated Germany in 1918. American forces suffered about 320,000 casualties. As previously noted, World War I also led to significant changes on the home front as women took on new responsibilities, and thousands of African Americans migrated north in search of work. World War I also led to a communist revolution that transformed Russia into the USSR in 1922.

After Germany was defeated in 1918, Wilson made a proposal known as the Fourteen Points and argued that the best way to resolve the conflict was by promoting free trade and democracy. For instance, Wilson wanted nations to respect the right to navigate in international waters and create a League of Nations that would resolve future disputes. Some of his suggestions, such as the League of Nations, were adopted, but many were not. In 1919, Germany was forced to sign the Treaty of Versailles, which imposed harsh economic penalties and restricted the German military. Ultimately, the Treaty of Versailles created resentment in Germany that lead to World War II. America emerged as an important player in world affairs after World War I because the American economy had supplied the Triple Entente with arms and equipment and American soldiers helped to achieve victory.

In the period between the world wars, fascism became popular in many European countries that were ravaged by the Great Depression. Fascism is a political ideology that advocates for a dictatorship in order to provide stability and unity. Adolf Hitler emerged as a prominent fascist leader in Germany and eventually brought the Nazi party to power in 1933. Germany, Italy, and Japan formed an alliance called the Axis and began to threaten other countries. The League of Nations could not diffuse the conflict. World War II broke out when Germany invaded Poland in 1939. Hitler quickly conquered most of Europe, except for Britain, and attacked the USSR in 1941. The United States sent military equipment and weapons to Britain and the USSR, but did not formally join the war until the Japanese attacked Pearl Harbor on December 7, 1941. Again, women played an important role on the home front by working in factories to build guns, tanks, planes, and ships. African Americans, Native Americans, and Japanese Americans also contributed by fighting on the front lines.

American forces first landed in North Africa where they, along with British and French troops, defeated German and Italian forces in 1942. In 1943, Allied forces invaded Italy, and Soviet troops began to push the German army back out of the USSR. Allied troops landed in France in 1944 and the Soviets began to advance on Germany as well. By May 1945, Hitler had committed suicide and Germany had been defeated.

This also brought about an end to the Holocaust. The Holocaust was a genocide committed by Hitler's Nazi Germany and collaborators that resulted in the deaths of more than 6 million Jews and 5 million Romans, gypsies, Afro-Europeans, disabled citizens, and homosexuals. A network of facilities in Germany and its territories were used to house victims for slave labor and mass murder, among other heinous crimes. The Nuremberg trials were part of the aftermath of the Holocaust, which served to prosecute important members of Nazi Germany leadership.

In the Pacific theater, American naval forces defeated the Japanese fleet in several key engagements, including the battle of Midway in 1942. American troops began recapturing territory in the Pacific as well and eventually pushed the Japanese back to their home islands in 1945. The Japanese refused to surrender until American planes dropped atomic bombs on the cities of Nagasaki and Hiroshima in August 1945.

Because World War II devastated most of Europe, the United States and the USSR emerged as the only superpowers when it ended. However, the erstwhile allies were suspicious of each other, which led to the Cold War.

Origins, Developments, and Consequences of the Cold War

Although the United States and the USSR worked together to defeat the Axis powers during World War II, the alliance quickly fell apart. As previously discussed, Americans had been afraid of communist influence since the Russian revolution in 1917. The USSR viewed the United States as a capitalist and imperialist power that threatened Soviet security. The USSR and United States divided Europe into spheres of influence, and this mutual hostility led to the Cold War. For example, the Soviets built a wall around the portion of Berlin, Germany that they occupied. The United States formed a military alliance, called the North Atlantic Treaty Organization, with its allies in Western Europe. The Soviets responded with their own defensive alliance in Eastern Europe, known as the Warsaw Pact. President Harry Truman announced that the United States would try to contain communist influence and would assist countries threatened by communist aggression. The domino theory predicted that once one country succumbed to communism, neighboring nations would also be at risk (thus following like a stack of dominoes). A resurgence of anti-communist sentiment occurred in the early 1950s when Senator Joseph McCarthy pledged to root out spies within the federal government. Known as the Second Red Scare in American history, McCarthy's communist "witch hunts" produced little evidence of his allegations and was censored in 1954 when he refused to reign in his attacks.

The resistance to communism led to a number of indirect conflicts around the globe between the United States and the USSR and China, which had become a communist regime in 1949. For example, Korea was divided into two portions after World War II (at the 38th parallel). When the communist regime in North Korea invaded South Korea in 1950, the United States sent troops to defend South Korea. The USSR and China sent troops, weapons, and equipment to support North Korea. The war ended in a stalemate in 1953, and Korea remains divided to this day. Today, it is divided at a unique demarcation line close to the original 38th parallel separation.

Vietnam was also partitioned into northern and southern regions after World War II. The United States supported South Vietnam and sent troops in ever-increasing numbers. The conflict intensified when North Vietnamese gunboats allegedly attacked a U.S. navy ship in 1964. However, U.S. forces were unable to defeat the Vietnamese communists, who preferred to use guerrilla troops and ambush tactics. The support for the war evaporated in United States as casualties mounted and the draft was unpopular as well. American troops also killed at least 300 civilians in the Vietnamese village of My Lai in 1968. National Guardsmen shot and killed four students and wounded nine others during an anti-war protest at Kent State University in 1970. These scandals made the war extremely unpopular. American troops withdrew in 1973, and South Vietnam was defeated in 1975.

The U.S. and USSR also vied for influence in South America and Africa as well. Some nations refused to pick sides and instead formed the Non-Aligned Movement.

The nuclear arms race and the space race were also important arenas in the Cold War. The Soviets took an early lead in the space race and successfully launched the first satellite into orbit in 1957. The Soviets also put the first man, cosmonaut Yuri Gagarin, into space in 1961. However, the United States surpassed the Soviet Union by landing the first man, Neil Armstrong, on the Moon in 1969.

The United States was the only nuclear power for a brief period after World War II, but the Soviets quickly caught up and detonated their own nuclear bomb in 1949. Both sides developed nuclear missiles during the 1950s. This became a very dramatic issue during the Cuban Missile Crisis. In 1962, President John F. Kennedy learned that the Soviets were installing nuclear missiles in Cuba, which had become a communist regime. The U.S. navy imposed a blockade, and tensions rose as the Soviets refused to back down. Eventually, negotiations ended the crisis and the Soviets agreed to withdraw the missiles in Cuba if the U.S. agreed to withdraw missiles from Turkey that threatened the USSR. Although tensions remained, the nuclear arms race slowed during the 1970s when the U.S. and USSR entered into negotiations. Both the U.S. and USSR promised to reduce nuclear weapons tests and limit their nuclear arsenals. Throughout the Cold War, a concept known as "Mutually Assured Destruction" (MAD) helped prevent nuclear war. Both the United States and the USSR each had thousands of warheads and MAD predicted that no matter who struck first, the other side would have enough surviving firepower to destroy the aggressor.

During the Cold War, a number of protests and demonstrations occurred in the Soviet satellites in Eastern Europe, including Hungary in 1956 and in Czechoslovakia in 1968. The uprisings were suppressed, but demands for reform continued and, in 1985, Mikhail Gorbachev became the leader of the USSR. He promised to make political and economic reforms, but protestors wanted change to occur more rapidly. Revolutions swept through Eastern Europe in 1989, and the communist regimes in Poland, Romania, and elsewhere crumbled. The Berlin Wall fell in 1989, and the Cold War ended when the USSR collapsed in 1991. This left the United States as the sole superpower, although other countries, such as India and China, have become more powerful. Recent scholars, however, are questioning whether the Cold War is once again beginning to heat up with the most recent tensions between Russia and the United States in the early 2000s.

Social, Economic, and Technological Changes Between 1950 and 2000

The post-World War II era led to a number of social, economic, and technological changes in the United States. The counter-culture phenomenon was one of the most powerful social movements in the latter half of the twentieth century in the U.S. The counter-culture movement challenged social norms and rejected traditional authority figures. The movement began in the 1950s with the beatniks, a group of non-conformist writers and artists who were dissatisfied with society. The beatniks sought inspiration in African and Asian cultures and many eschewed materialism.

The counter-culture movement became more popular during the 1960s as millions of children from the Baby Boomers generation entered into adulthood. Veterans came home after World War II and started families, and, by the 1960s, many of these young adults also felt disaffected and rebellious. Their parents criticized them because they began to wear colorful clothing and the boys let their hair grow out. Many members of the counter-culture movement, now called hippies, inherited the beatnik's interest in African and Asian cultures. Writer Ken Kesey traveled around the country on a bus encouraging people to experiment with psychedelic drugs, such as LSD. The counter-culture movement influenced musicians and avant-garde artists.

The counter-culture movement was also closely connected to other protest movements during the 1960s, including the Civil Rights movement, which will be discussed later. Many members of the counter-culture movement during the 1960s also opposed the war in Vietnam. The Baby Boomers could be conscripted to fight in Vietnam whether they wanted to or not. In 1965, young men began burning their draft cards, which was a criminal offense, in protest. Massive demonstrations against the war occurred around the country, especially on college campuses, but many other people also refused to support the war effort, including clergymen and even some veterans who had fought in Vietnam. The counter-culture movement disappeared during the 1970s but had a lasting impact on the social and cultural history of the United States.

Economic Changes

America emerged as one of the most powerful economies in the world after 1945. The US economy, especially manufacturing, was very prosperous during the 1950s and 1960s. The economy successfully switched from wartime production, and consumer demand was very high. During the Great Depression, few families had disposable income. Although most workers earned good wages during World War II, they had little to spend it on because most goods were rationed. Once production of consumer goods resumed, families used their savings to buy cars, household appliances, and televisions. This was good for the economy, and unemployment remained below 5 percent for most of the 1950s and 1960s. However, during the latter part of the 20th century, the manufacturing base in the North and Midwest began to crumble and the area became known as the Rust Belt. Manufacturing jobs began to move from the North and Midwest to states in the South and West, known as the Sun Belt, where land was cheap and wages were low.

The world economy also became increasingly interconnected during the post-World War II era. This accelerated the process of globalization, which is the integration of ideas and products from different cultures. This benefitted the United States economically because businesses, such as McDonald's and Coca-Cola, found many consumers around the world who were eager to consume American goods. However, the process works both ways, and many aspects of foreign culture, such as Japanese cartoons and animation, have become very popular in the United States. Many critics also point out that globalization has hurt the American economy in recent decades because manufacturing jobs have gone overseas to countries in South America and Asia where wages are low.

Technological Changes

Several technological changes have had a significant impact on the U.S. economy as well. The Cold War led to advances in nuclear power and aerospace engineering. The development of computers, in particular, has helped accelerate the transition to a post-industrial economy where information technology and other services have replaced traditional manufacturing jobs. The first computers were used to break coded messages during World War II and had very limited computing power. The invention of transistor technology in 1947 made computers cheaper, smaller, and more reliable. The invention of integrated circuits in the 1960s and 1970s increased computing power and gave birth to the first personal computers. The Internet was created in 1969, but widespread use in business and academia did not begin until the 1980s. These developments have made it much easier to share information and have increased economic opportunities. But, the increasing use of robots, especially in the manufacturing Industry, have also made the economy more efficient while also causing layoffs.

Political Realignments from the New Deal and Great Society Through the Rise of Conservatism

President Franklin D. Roosevelt created the New Deal in order to stimulate the economy and improve government regulation. The New Deal also marked an important shift in American politics because the Democratic Party began to favor government intervention while Republicans opposed it. This was a reversal of the parties' previous platforms. The Democratic Party relied on a coalition of labor unions, Catholics, African Americans, and other minorities. The Republican Party included conservatives, evangelicals, and business leaders.

The Great Society was another major government program that the Democratic Party supported. President Lyndon B. Johnson sought to end poverty and improve education. For example, he raised the minimum wage and created programs to provide poor Americans with job training. The Great Society also implemented a number of Civil Rights laws that will be discussed in greater detail later.

The presidential election of 1980 was another watershed moment. Republican nominee Ronald Reagan carried forty-three states, and the Republicans won a majority in the U.S. Senate after twenty-eight years of Democratic control. Reagan presented an optimistic message and broadcasted a television advertisement that proclaimed "It's morning again in America." He promised to restore America's military power, cut government regulations, and reduce taxes. Reagan enjoyed the support of resurgent conservative Christian evangelicals, who wanted to restore morality to American society. They were particularly concerned about issues such as abortion. The Moral Majority, founded by Baptist minister Jerry Falwell in 1979, was one key group that helped Reagan win the election. This coalition helped realign party loyalties, as more liberal Republicans and conservative Democrats shifted their allegiance.

Impact of Race, Gender, and Ethnicity Throughout American History

Race, gender, and ethnicity have been important themes in American history from the colonial era to the present. Individuals from different races, ethnicities, and genders have had very different experiences throughout the same historical events or eras. It is important to distinguish between race and ethnicity: race refers to a group of people with common ancestry, while ethnicity refers to cultural background, such as language and tradition.

Race played an important part in colonial America because both Caucasians and Africans occupied positions of servitude. White immigrants who could not purchase passage to the New World sometimes agreed to become indentured servants. Their employers paid for their passage across the Atlantic, and in exchange, the indentured servant agreed to work without wages for at least five years. However, African slaves were rarely able to free themselves. The strong connection between slavery and race meant that all blacks, whether free or enslaved, were viewed as inferior. After the American Revolution, most free blacks, even those living in northern states, were denied the right to vote. Although the Civil Rights Movement in the 1960s made great gains, many activists claim more must be done in order to overcome the legacy of racial inequality in America.

Chinese and Japanese have also been the victims of discrimination throughout American history as well. For example, in 1882 Congress prohibited Chinese immigration in an act known as the Chinese Exclusion Act. This was the first law to ever prevent an entire ethnic group from immigrating to the United States. Japanese Americans also experienced discrimination during and after World War II, specifically with the implementation of Japanese internment camps in America. This forced 110,000 to 120,000 Japanese Americans into camps, 62 percent of which were United States citizens.

Discrimination against certain ethnicities is also prominent throughout American history as well. For example, many Americans resented the arrival of German and Irish immigrants during the 1800s because they spoke a different language or practiced different religions. Hispanics were also subject to discrimination, and in 1943, a number of Hispanic youths were attacked during the Zoot Suit Riots.

Gender differences in the United States have also been impossible to ignore. For example, until the 1840s, most married women in the United States were unable to enter into contracts, own property, or retain their own wages. As previously discussed, women were unable to vote until the 19th Amendment was ratified in 1920. The Women's Rights Movement in the U.S. ranged from 1848 to 1920. This movement called for a woman's right to vote, the right to bodily autonomy, freedom from sexual violence, the right to hold public office, the right to work, the right to fair wages and equal pay, and the right to own property and obtain an education. Women continue to demand change during the 21st

century for reasons such as the gender wage gap, better resources for women's health, female reproductive rights, and for protection of basic human rights, such as bringing greater awareness to rape culture, violence against women, and protection against female sex trafficking.

How Participants in the Political Process Engage in Politics and Shape Policy

The Constitution provides for a series of checks and balances between the legislative, executive, and judicial branches of the federal government. Members of Congress debate and vote on legislation, although the president may request that legislators consider a certain proposal. The president may veto legislation that he or she disagrees with, but Congress can override the veto with a two-thirds majority in both chambers. The Supreme Court may review legislation and declare it unconstitutional. The president selects nominees to the Supreme Court but the Senate must confirm them.

Branch	Role	Checks & Balances on Other Branches	
Executive	Carries out the laws	Legislative Branch • Proposes laws • Vetoes laws • Calls special sessions of Congress • Makes appointments • Negotiates foreign treaties	Judicial Branch • Appoints federal judges • Grants pardons to federal offenders
Legislative	Makes the laws	Executive Branch • Has the ability to override a President's veto • Confirms executive appointments • Ratifies treaties • Has the ability to declare war • Appropriates money • Has the ability to impeach and remove President	Judicial Branch • Creates lower federal courts • Has the ability to impeach and remove judges • Has the ability to propose amendments to overrule judicial decisions • Approves appointments of federal judges
Judicial	Interprets the laws	Executive Branch • Has the ability to declare executive actions unconstitutional	Legislative Branch • Has the ability to declare acts of Congress unconstitutional

Constituents, businesses, professional associations, civic organizations, and other interest groups may lobby members of Congress and ask them to propose legislation or support a certain proposal. Interest groups may also lobby the president and other executive branch officials in order to try and influence policies. The president appoints fifteen men and women to head a variety of executive departments, including defense, transportation, education, and many others. These officials are known as the president's cabinet, and they advise the president on various matters. These discussions are used to help formulate policies, and the cabinet members are responsible for putting the decisions into action. The president may also issue executive orders that instruct federal employees how to enforce certain policies. For example, in 1948, President Harry S. Truman issued an executive order that established racial integration within the armed forces.

Elections are an essential part of our democracy. Although members of Congress are prohibited from accepting gifts, individuals and interest groups can make campaign contributions during elections, which occur every two years in the House, four years for the White House, and six years in the Senate. Individuals can give a maximum of $2,700 per year to individual candidates. Since 2010, individuals, corporations, labor unions, and other contributors can give an unlimited amount to organizations known as super PACs (Political Action Committees). Super PACs may not give money to candidates or parties but can air commercials that support a specific issue.

Although President George Washington warned against creating political parties in his farewell address in 1796, they have been a part of American politics since the founding of our country. The Republicans and Democrats hold conventions to nominate candidates for state and national elections. The parties also create a platform, which is a set of goals and principles, at each convention in order to set priorities and inform members about issues. During elections, parties also organize rallies and urge voters to support their candidates and issues. Some Americans belong to either the Republican or Democratic Party, but voters who belong to neither party are known as independents.

Emergence of the United States as a World Power and the Evolving Role of United States in the World

The United States gained prestige and international status after the Spanish-American War of 1898, because the United States defeated Spain and acquired several colonies. American participation in World War I made the United States an economic and financial leader as well. The United States loaned money to Britain and France and supplied weapons and equipment that helped the Triple Entente achieve victory. The United States and USSR emerged from World War II as the only surviving superpowers because so much of the rest of the world had been devastated. This system was described as bipolar because there were two centers of power.

The United States was the leader of the free world during the Cold War and formed military and economic alliances with other nations. With the collapse of the USSR in 1991, the United States was the only surviving world power. This era was a unipolar system because there were no other major powers that could rival the United States.

Although the U.S. was still considered a world power, September 11, 2001 demonstrated that America was nevertheless vulnerable to attacks. The attacks on 9/11 killed more than 3,000 civilians and first-responders. Although American troops have been stationed in Iraq and Afghanistan for more than a decade, both nations are still unstable, and the lack of progress has damaged American prestige. Furthermore, new economic and military powers have risen to challenge American dominance in world affairs. The Chinese economy has grown significantly, and the Chinese government has expanded and improved its armed forces. India has also boosted its manufacturing industry and has purchased new fighter jets and an aircraft carrier. The European Union, Russia, and Brazil have also emerged as potential rivals that might create a multipolar environment. However, the United States is still the world's largest economy and remains a cultural leader.

The Influence of Religion Throughout American History

Religion has also been an important, albeit divisive, theme in American history since the colonial period. The British colonies in North America attracted settlers from many different religions, including Catholics in Maryland, Quakers in Pennsylvania, Puritans in New England, and Anglicans in Virginia. This led to conflict and tension. For example, Puritans in New England expelled dissenters and even executed four Quakers between 1659 and 1661.

In the 1730s and 1740s, a religious revival known as the First Great Awakening swept through the British colonies in North America. This movement emphasized a more personal connection to Christ, and some Protestant preachers, such as Jonathan Edwards, began to present their sermons in a more passionate and emotional style. This "fire and brimstone" form of religious dissemination became the cornerstone of the First Great Awakening. These passionate sermons—and the emotions that they stirred—caused divisions within Protestant congregations. Those who supported the Great Awakening were known as New Lights while those who opposed it were called Old Lights. The Baptists and Methodists became more popular during the revival because they embraced this new style of preaching.

The Second Great Awakening occurred in the early 1800s and urged Protestants to work not only for their own salvation but for the salvation of others as well. This helped fuel a social reform movement that promoted the abolition of slavery, temperance, and prison reform. The question of slavery caused schisms in the Baptist and Methodist churches during the 1840s. The Second Great Awakening, much like the First Great Awakening, inaugurated the creation of several New Religious Movements (NRMs) in the United States, especially in the southern states.

A third revival occurred in the late 1800s that emphasized temperance. As previously discussed, the religious right emerged after World War II and began to play an important part in American politics, especially during the election of President Ronald Reagan in 1980.

Although Catholics were a minority during the colonial period of American history, Catholicism has become the largest religious denomination in the United States. Many colonial governments actually banned Catholicism, but the American Revolution brought more toleration. However, anti-Catholic sentiment renewed in the 1800s as immigrants from Ireland and Germany, many of whom were Catholic, arrived in ever-increasing numbers. The arrival of Italian immigrants in the late 1800s and early 1900s also increased Protestant-Catholic tension in America. Many Americans feared that Catholic immigrants would be more loyal to Pope than they would be to the Constitution. This led to the creation of the Know-Nothings who sought to limit immigration and physically attacked Catholics. Anti-Catholic sentiment remained an issue even until the presidential election of 1960 when John F. Kennedy, a Catholic, won the Democratic nomination. Kennedy helped allay fears by promising to respect the separation of church and state. Since then, anti-Catholicism has largely disappeared.

Small numbers of Jews immigrated to the U.S. during the colonial period, but large numbers of Jews from Eastern Europe began to arrive in the late 19th and early 20th centuries. Jews contributed to the American economy in many different ways but drew criticism from anti-Semites because of their prominence in the financial industry. The Anti-Defamation League was founded in 1913 to combat anti-Semitic sentiments. In the 1920s, the resurgent Ku Klux Klan revived anti-Semitism. The Anti-Defamation League sponsored events after World War II to commemorate the Holocaust and repudiate Holocaust deniers. Anti-Semitism has declined, but the Anti-Defamation League reported that more than 900 anti-Semitic incidents occurred across the country in 2014.

Muslim immigration in the 1800s remained modest. The first mosque was not constructed in the United States until the 20th century. In the latter part of the 20th century, more Muslims, especially from Pakistan, began arriving in the United States. In the wake of the 9/11 attacks, Islamophobic incidents increased, and Muslims were victims of harassment, intimidation, and assaults. The United States' current battle with ISIS in the Middle East, North Africa, and Europe has also increased Islamophobia, paving the way to an anti-refugee right-wing faction in the current Republican Party. The religious morality of the nation has once again become a hot-button topic in the wake of the recent Clinton-Trump debates for the U.S. Presidency.

Major Economic Transformations in the United States

The American economy has changed dramatically since the 1700s, a century where agriculture was the main economic activity. The First Industrial Revolution began in the early 1800s when steam-powered machines were used to increase productivity, especially in the textile industry. The invention of steamboats and railroads made it much cheaper and faster to ship goods across the country in the mid-1800s as well. After the Civil War, the Second Industrial Revolution led to increased productivity and efficiency in the many industries, including metallurgy, chemicals, telecommunications, and energy. This led to significant social changes as immigration and urbanization increased. Workers began to form labor unions in order to demand better wages and working conditions, which led to strikes and conflict with law enforcement officials.

In the early 20th century, Henry Ford introduced the moving assembly line to the automobile manufacturing industry, which made it easier for middle- and working-class families to buy cars. Other industries adopted Ford's methods, which led to lower prices for many consumer goods. The stock market crash in 1929 helped trigger the Great Depression, which resulted in a vicious downward economic spiral. Franklin D. Roosevelt introduced the New Deal to try and boost the economy, but only the outbreak of World War II led to full employment. The United States emerged from World War II as the world's largest economy and pent-up consumer demand fueled prosperity during the post-war era.

The development of computers in the latter part of the 20th century improved communications and led to greater economic efficiency. However, it also marked the beginning of the post-industrial economy in the United States. Traditional manufacturing jobs began to disappear as robots replaced unskilled workers. On the other hand, careers in the information technology sector grew and became a key component of the new high-tech economy. Many unskilled manufacturing jobs also went overseas to countries in Asia and South America as the global economy became more interconnected.

The Causes and Consequences of Changing Immigration Patterns to the United States and Internal Immigration within the United States

Immigration has always played an important role in American history, although patterns have changed over time. Most immigrants came to the United States in search of better economic opportunities, although some have sought religious and political freedom as well. During the colonial period, most immigrants came from Britain, but during the mid-1800s that began to change. In the 1840s, a fungus destroyed the potato crop in Ireland, which led to widespread famine. Many Irish starved, but millions also emigrated, with many heading to the United States. A wave of revolutions also swept across Europe in 1848 and many participants, especially Germans, fled to the United States when the movements failed. This shift led to tension and conflict between immigrants and those born in America. Native-born

Americans resented the immigrants' cultural differences and the increased competition for jobs. In the late 1800s, immigration patterns changed again and arrivals from Southern and Eastern Europe began to increase. In 1924, Congress passed an act that limited immigration from these areas.

In 1965, immigration patterns changed again when Congress passed the Immigration and Nationality Act of 1965 act that changed the way immigration quotas were calculated. Immigrants from Central and South America, as well as Asia, became very numerous. Like their predecessors, most came in search of jobs. Recently, many refugees are fleeing violence that erupted from the U.S. invasion of Iraq in 2003 and the revolutions that swept through the Middle East between 2010 and 2012. Cultural differences and economic competition between immigrants and native-born American citizens continue, especially against Mexicans. Vigilante groups have formed in order to prevent illegal immigrants from crossing the U.S.-Mexico border.

Internal Migration

Migration within the United States has also been an important theme since the colonial period. During the 18th and 19th centuries, the focus was on westward expansion because settlers sought cheap land. This often led to violence between settlers and Native Americans who refused to relinquish their territory.

The 19th century also saw an increase in migration from rural areas to cities as individuals sought employment in factories. This trend continued until the late 20th century and more than 80 percent of Americans now live in cities. World War I led to the Great Migration of African Americans from the South to the North. This influx also created more competition for jobs and housing and resulted in a wave of race riots in 1919.

The Struggles and Achievements of Individuals and Groups for Greater Political and Civil Rights Throughout American History

Although the Declaration of Independence declared "all men are created equal," blacks, women, and other minorities struggled for more than a century to make this dream a reality. The U.S. Constitution legalized slavery, and it was not abolished until the 13th Amendment was ratified in 1865. The 14th Amendment, ratified in 1868, granted African Americans citizenship, and the 15th Amendment, ratified in 1870, explicitly granted them the right to vote. However, white Southerners passed laws, known as the Jim Crow system, that prevented blacks from exercising their rights and, when that failed, they relied on violence and intimidation to oppress African Americans. For example, many Southern states required voters to pass literacy tests and used them to prevent blacks from casting a ballot. Whites were either exempt from the test or were held to much lower standards. Blacks who protested their oppression could be assaulted and even killed with impunity. In the 1896 decision *Plessy vs. Ferguson*, the U.S. Supreme Court ruled that "separate but equal" schools for white and black students were permissible. In reality, black schools were almost always inferior to white schools.

The emergence of the Civil Rights Movement after World War II finally destroyed the Jim Crow system. In the 1954 decision *Brown vs. Board of Education*, the Supreme Court reversed the "separate but equal" doctrine and declared that separate schools were inherently unequal because they stigmatized African American students. In 1957, President Dwight D. Eisenhower used federal troops to force the high school in Little Rock, Arkansas, to integrate and accept nine black students. This encouraged civil rights activists to demand additional reforms. In 1955, Rosa Parks refused to give up her seat on a bus in Montgomery, Alabama, which led to a boycott. Martin Luther King Jr. led the bus boycott and became a national leader in the Civil Rights Movement. In 1960, four students in Greensboro, North Carolina, launched a peaceful sit-in at a segregated lunch counter, which sparked similar protests around the country. White activists from the North went south to help blacks register to vote, and in 1964 three activists were murdered in Mississippi. That same year, King led 250,000 protesters in a march on Washington D.C. where he delivered his famous "I Have a Dream Speech."

Although King advocated for peaceful protests, many other civil rights activists disagreed with him. For example, Malcolm X believed that blacks should use violence to defend themselves. Furthermore, King worked with white activists while Malcolm X rejected any cooperation. Malcolm X was assassinated in 1965, and, despite his reputation as a non-violent leader, King was also gunned down in 1968.

Under mounting pressure, Congress passed several important pieces of legislation. The 1964 Civil Rights Act banned discrimination based on race, color, religion, sex, or national origin. The Voting Rights Act of 1965 prohibited the use of poll taxes or literacy tests to prohibit voting. The Civil Rights Act of 1968 banned housing discrimination. In 1967, Carl Stokes became the first black mayor of a major American city, Cleveland. That same year, Thurgood Marshall became the first African American to serve on the Supreme Court. President Gerald Ford declared February to be black history month. In 1989, Colin Powell became the first black chairman of the Joint Chiefs of Staff. Despite these reforms, activists claim institutional racism is still a problem in the 21st century. The Civil Rights movement inspired women, Latinos, and other groups to make similar demands for equal rights.

<u>Women</u>

In 1776, Abigail Adams urged her husband, founding father John Adams, to advocate for women's rights, but it would take more than a century before women could vote. In 1848, activists organized a convention in Seneca Falls, New York, to organize the women's suffrage movement, and their efforts slowly gained momentum. The ratification of the 19th Amendment in 1920 finally gave women the right to vote.

Although women had achieved political equality, they continued to demand reform throughout the 20th century. In the early 1900s, Margaret Sanger provided women with information about birth control, which was illegal at the time. Women entered the industrial workforce in large numbers during World War II, but when the war ended, they were fired so that veterans would have jobs when they came home. Many women were frustrated when told they had to return to their domestic lives. Simone de Beauvoir, a French writer, published her book "The Second Sex" after World War II, and an English translation was published in 1953. It highlighted the unequal treatment of women throughout history and sparked a feminist movement in the United States. In 1963, Betty Friedan published a book, called "The Feminine Mystique," that revealed how frustrated many suburban wives were with the social norms that kept them at home. During the 1960s, women participated in the sexual revolution and exerted more control over their own sexuality. In 1972, Congress passed Title IX, which prohibited sexual discrimination in education and expanded women's sports programs. In the 1970s, women's rights activists also pushed for greater access to birth control, and in 1973 the Supreme Court issued the landmark decision *Roe vs. Wade* which removed many barriers to abortion services. Women also demanded greater protection from domestic abuse and greater access to divorce.

During the 20th century, many American women made notable achievements, including Amelia Earhart, who was the first woman to cross the Atlantic in an airplane in 1928. In 1981, Sandra Day O'Connor became the first woman to serve on the Supreme Court. In 1983, Sally Ride became the first female astronaut. In 1984, Geraldine Ferraro became the first woman to run for vice-president, although she was unsuccessful. However, many activists continue to demand reform in the 21st century. For example, women only account for 20 percent of the U.S. Senate and House of Representatives. Furthermore, women only earn 79 percent of what men in similar jobs are paid. In 1980, President Jimmy Carter declared March to be women's history month.

Hispanics

After World War II, many Hispanics also began to demand greater equality. In 1949, veterans protested a refusal by a Texas town to bury a Mexican American soldier, who died during World War II, in the local cemetery, because only whites could be buried there. Activists called themselves Chicanos, a term that previously was used as a pejorative to describe Mexican Americans. Cesar Chavez was a labor union activist who organized transient Hispanic agricultural workers in an effort to obtain better working conditions in the 1960s and 1970s. Activists encouraged a sense of pride in Chicano identity, especially in arts and literature. In 1968, President Lyndon B. Johnson declared National Hispanic Heritage Month would run from mid-September to mid-October.

In 1959, biochemist Severo Ochoa became the first Hispanic to win a Nobel Prize. Franklin Chang-Diaz became the first Hispanic astronaut in 1986, and he flew a total of seven space shuttle missions. In 1990, Oscar Hijuelos became the first Hispanic American to win the Pulitzer Prize. Sonja Sotomayor became the first Hispanic to serve on the Supreme Court in 2009.

Native Americans

Native Americans suffered centuries of oppression at the hands of European colonists, and later American settlers as they pushed further west. Native Americans resisted attempts to encroach on their lands but were pushed onto smaller and smaller reservations. The Massacre at Wounded Knee in 1890 was the last major conflict between Native Americans and U.S. forces. However, American officials continued to try and force Native Americans to assimilate into white culture.

In 1968, a group of Native Americans formed the American Indian Movement in order to combat racism and demand greater independence. Between 1969 and 1971, a group of Native American activists occupied the federal prison on Alcatraz Island near San Francisco, although it had been closed since 1963. The activists offered to buy back the island for $9.40 in order to draw attention to how the federal government had forced tribes to sell their lands at low prices. Other activists disrupted Thanksgiving Day ceremonies aboard a replica of the Mayflower in Boston in 1970. In 1971, Native American activists also occupied Mount Rushmore, which is located on ground the Native Americans consider sacred. Violence broke out between activists and law enforcement officials in 1973 when Native Americans occupied the town of Wounded Knee, sight of the famous massacre.

In 1970, President Richard Nixon granted Native American tribes more autonomy. In 1978, Congress passed the American Indian Religious Freedom Act, which guaranteed Native Americans' rights to practice their religious ceremonies and visit sacred sites. In 1990, President George H.W. Bush declared November Native American History Month. In 1969, Navarre Scott Momaday became the first Native American to win a Pulitzer Prize for his book "House Made of Dawn." In 2014, Diane Humetewa, a member of the Hopi tribe, became the first Native American woman to serve as a federal judge. However, many Native American communities still suffer from high rates of unemployment, alcoholism, and domestic abuse.

Asian Americans

Asian Americans also faced discrimination throughout American history and in 1882, Congress passed a law banning all Chinese immigrants. During World War II, more than 100,000 Japanese Americans were interned in concentration camps. In 1982, two American autoworkers beat Vincent Chin to death with a baseball bat because his assailants blamed him for the loss of jobs in the automotive manufacturing industry.

In the 1960s, activists demanded that the term “Asian American” replace the word “oriental,” because it carried a stigma. Asian Americans also promoted a sense of pride in their cultural identity and successfully pushed for the creation of ethnic studies programs. Ellison Onizuka became the first Asian American astronaut in 1985, although he perished in the space shuttle Challenger disaster. In 1990, President George H.W. Bush declared May Asian Pacific American Heritage Month and Sheryl WuDunn became the first Asian American to win a Pulitzer Prize that same year.

Economics

Economics is the study of human behavior in response to the production, consumption, and distribution of assets or wealth. Economics can help individuals or societies make decisions or plans for themselves or communities, dependent upon their needs, wants, and resources. Economics is divided into two subgroups: microeconomics and macroeconomics.

Microeconomics is the study of individual or small group behaviors and patterns in relationship to such things as earning and spending money. It focuses on particular markets within the economy, and looks at single factors that could potentially affect individuals or small groups. For example, the use of coupons in a grocery store can affect an individual’s product choice, quantity purchased, and overall savings that a person may later roll into a different purchase. Microeconomics is the study of scarcity, choice, opportunity costs, economics systems, factors of production, supply and demand, market efficiency, the role of government, distribution of income, and product markets.

Macroeconomics examines a much larger scale of the economy. It focuses on how a society or nation’s goods, services, spending habits, and other factors affect the people of that entity. It focuses on aggregate factors such as demand and output. For example, if a national company moves its production overseas to save on costs, how will production, labor, and capital be affected? Macroeconomics analyzes all aggregate indicators and the microeconomic factors that influence the economy. Government and corporations use macroeconomic models to help formulate economic policies and strategies.

Microeconomics

Scarcity

People have different needs and wants, and the question arises, are the resources available to supply those needs and wants? Limited resources and high demand create scarcity. When a product is scarce, there is a short supply of it. For example, when the newest version of a cellphone is released, people line up to buy the phone or put their name on a wait list if the phone is not immediately available. The product, the new cellphone, may become a scarce commodity. In turn, because of the scarcity, companies may raise the cost of the commodity, knowing that if it is immediately available, people may pay more for the instant gratification—and vice versa. If a competing company lowers the cost of the phone but has contingencies, such as extended contracts or hidden fees, the buyer will still have the opportunity to purchase the scarce product. Limited resources and extremely high demand create scarcity and, in turn, cause companies to acquire opportunity costs.

Choice and Opportunity Costs

On a large scale, governments and communities have to assess different opportunity costs when it comes to using taxpayers' money. Should the government or community build a new school, repair roads, or allocate funds to local hospitals are all examples of choices taxpayers may have to review at some point in time. How do they decide which choice is the best, since each one has a trade off? By comparing the opportunity cost of each choice, they may decide what they are willing to live without for the sake of gaining something else.

Economic Systems

Economic systems determine what is being produced, who is producing it, who receives the product, and the money generated by the sale of the product. There are two basic types of economic systems: market economies (including free and competitive markets), and planned or command economies.

- Market Economies are characterized by:

  Privately owned businesses, groups, or individuals providing goods or services based on demand.

  The types of goods and services provided (supply) are based on that demand.

  Two types: competitive market and free market.

Competitive Market	**Free Market**
Due to the large number of both buyers and sellers, there is no way any one seller or buyer can control the market or price.	Voluntary private trades between buyers and sellers determine markets and prices without government intervention or monopolies.

- Planned or Command Economies:

  In planned or command economies, the government or central authority determines market prices of goods and services.

  The government or central authority determines what is being produced as well as the quantity of production.

  Some advantages to command economies include a large number of shared goods such as public services (transportation, schools, or hospitals).

  Disadvantages of command economies include wastefulness of resources.

Factors of Production

There are four factors of production:

Land: both renewable and nonrenewable resources
Labor: effort put forth by people to produce goods and services
Capital: the tools used to create goods and services
Entrepreneurship: persons who combine land, labor, and capital to create new goods and services

The four factors of production are used to create goods and services to make economic profit. All four factors strongly impact one another.

Supply and Demand

Supply and demand is the most important concept of economics in a market economy. Supply is the amount of a product that a market can offer. Demand is the quantity of a product needed or desired by buyers. The price of a product is directly related to supply and demand. The correlation between the price of a product and the demand necessary to distribute resources to the market go hand in hand in a market economy. For example, when there are a variety of treats at a bakery, certain treats are in higher demand than others. The bakery can raise the cost of the more demanded items as supplies get limited. Conversely, the bakery can sell the less desirable treats by lowering the cost of those items as an incentive for buyers to purchase them.

Market Efficiency and the Role of Government (Taxes, Subsidies, and Price Controls)

Market efficiency is directly affected by supply and demand. The government can help the market stay efficient by either stepping in when the market is inefficient and/or providing the means necessary for markets to run properly. For example, society needs two types of infrastructure: physical (bridges, roads, etc.) and institutional (courts, laws, etc.). The government may impose taxes, subsidies, and price controls to increase revenue, lower prices of goods and services, ensure product availability for the government, and maintain fair prices for goods and services.

The Purpose of Taxes, Subsidies, and Price Controls

Taxes	**Subsidies**	**Price Controls**
-Generate government revenue -Discourage purchase or use of "bad" products such as alcohol or cigarettes	-Lower the price of goods and services -Reassure the supply of goods and services -Allow opportunities to compete with overseas vendors	-Act as emergency measures when government intervention is necessary -Set a minimum or maximum price for goods and services

Distribution of Income

Distribution of income refers to how wages are distributed across a society or segments of a society. If everyone made the same amount of money, the distribution of income would be equal. That is not the case in most societies. The wealth of people and companies varies. Income inequality gaps are present in America and many other nations. Taxes provide an option to redistribute income or wealth because they provide revenue to build new infrastructure and provide cash benefits to some of the poorest members in society.

Product Markets

Product markets are marketplaces where goods and services are bought and sold. Product markets provide sellers a place to offer goods and services to consumers, and for consumers to purchase those goods and services. The annual value of goods and services exchanged throughout the year is measured by the Gross Domestic Product (GDP), a monetary measure of goods and services made either quarterly or annually. Department stores, gas stations, grocery stores, and other retail stores are all examples of product markets. However, product markets do not include any raw, scarce, or trade materials.

Theory of the Firm

The behavior of firms is composed of several theories varying between short- and long-term goals. There are four basic firm behaviors: perfect competition, profit maximization, short run, and long run. Each firm follows a pattern, depending on its desired outcome. Theory of the Firm posits that firms, after conducting market research, make decisions that will maximize their profits since they are for-profit entities.

- Perfect competition:
    - In perfect competition, several businesses are selling the same product at the same time.
    - There are so many businesses and consumers that none will directly impact the market.
    - Each business and consumer is aware of the competing businesses and markets.
- Profit maximization:
    - Firms decide the quantity of a product that needs to be produced in order to receive maximum profit gains. Profit is the total amount of revenue made after subtracting costs.
- Short run:
    - A short amount of time where fixed prices cannot be adjusted
    - The quantity of the product depends on the varying amount of labor. Less labor means less product.
- Long run:
    - An amount of time where fixed prices can be adjusted
    - Firms try to maximize production while minimizing labor costs.

Overall, microeconomics operates on a small scale, focusing on how individuals or small groups use and assign resources.

Macroeconomics

Macroeconomics analyzes the economy as a whole. It studies unemployment, interest rates, price levels, and national income, which are all factors that can affect the nation as a whole, and not just individual households. Macroeconomics studies all large factors to determine how, or if, they will affect future trend patterns of production, consumption, and economic growth.

Measures of Economic Performance

It is important to measure economic performance to determine if an economy is growing, stagnant, or deteriorating. To measure the growth and sustainability of an economy, several indicators can be used. Economic indicators provide data that economists can use to determine if there are faulty processes or if some form of intervention is needed.

One of the main indicators to measure economic performance is the growth of the country's Gross Domestic Product (GDP). GDP growth provides important information that can be used to determine fiscal or financial policies. The GDP does not measure income distribution, quality of life, or losses due to natural disasters. For example, if a community lost everything to a hurricane, it would take a long time to rebuild the community and stabilize its economy. That is why there is a need to take into account more balanced performance measures when factoring overall economic performance.

Other indicators used to measure economic performance are unemployment or employment rates, inflation, savings, investments, surpluses and deficits, debt, labor, trade terms, the HDI (Human Development Index), and the HPI (Human Poverty Index).

Unemployment

Unemployment occurs when an individual does not have a job, is actively trying to find employment, and is not getting paid. Official unemployment rates do not factor in the number of people who have stopped looking for work, unlike true unemployment rates that do, causing them to be higher.

There are three types of unemployment: cyclical, frictional, and structural.

Cyclical
The product of a business cycle. This usually occurs during a recession.
Frictional
The difficulty of matching qualified workers for specific jobs. An example would be a person changing careers.
Structural
When a person no longer qualifies for a specific job, or failing out of a retraining course for a job.

Given the nature of a market economy and the fluctuations of the labor market, a 100 percent employment rate is impossible to reach.

Inflation

Inflation is when the cost of goods and services rises over time. Supply, demand, and money reserves all affect inflation. Generally, inflation is measured by the Consumer Price Index (CPI), a tool that tracks price changes of goods and services over time. The CPI measures goods and services such as gasoline, cars, clothing, and food. When the cost of goods and services increase, the quantity of the product may decrease due to lower demand. This decreases the purchasing power of the consumer. Basically, as more money is printed, it holds less and less value in purchasing power. For example, when inflation occurs, consumers in the United States are spending and saving less because the U.S. dollar is worth less, and therefore the consumer cannot buy or save as much money. However, if inflation occurs steadily over time, the people can better plan and prepare for future necessities.

Inflation can vary from year to year, usually never fluctuating more than 2 percent. Central banks try to prevent drastic increases or decreases of inflation to prohibit prices from rising or falling far from the minimum. Inflation can also vary based on different monetary currencies. Although rare, any country's economy may experience hyperinflation (when inflation rates increase to over 50 percent), while other economies may experience deflation (when the cost of goods and services decrease over time). Deflation occurs when the inflation rate drops below zero percent.

Business Cycle

A business cycle is when the Gross Domestic Product (GDP) moves downward and upward over a long-term growth trend. These cycles help determine where the economy currently stands, as well as where the economy could be heading. Business cycles usually occur almost every six years, and have four phases: expansion, peak, contraction, and trough. Here are some characteristics of each phase:

- Expansion:
  - Increased employment rates and economic growth
  - Production and sales increase
  - On a graph, expansion is where the lines climb.
- Peak:
  - Employment rates are at or above full employment and the economy is at maximum productivity.
  - On a graph, the peak is the top of the hill, where expansion has reached its maximum.
- Contraction:
  - When growth starts slowing
  - Unemployment is on the rise.
  - On a graph, contraction is where the graph begins to slide back down or contract.
- Trough:
  - The cycle has hit bottom and is waiting for the next cycle to start again.
  - On a graph, the trough is the bottom of the contraction prior to when it starts to climb back up.

When the economy is expanding or "booming," the business cycle is going from a trough to a peak. When the economy is headed down and toward a recession, the business cycle is going from a peak to a trough.

Four phases of a business cycle:

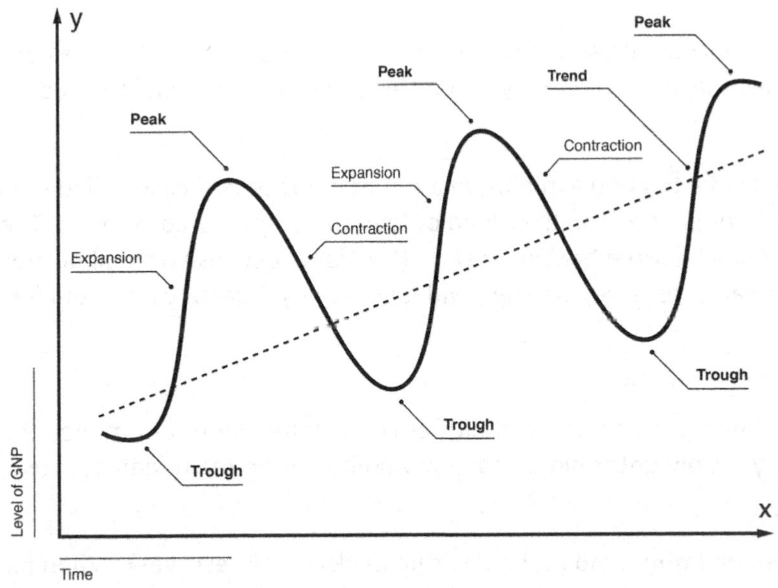

Fiscal Policy

A fiscal policy is when the government is involved in adjusting spending and tax rates to assist the way in which an economy financially functions. Fiscal policies can either increase or decrease tax rates and spending. These policies represent a tricky balancing act, because if the government increases taxes too much, consumer spending and monetary value will decrease. Conversely, if the government lowers taxes, consumers will have more money in their pockets to buy more goods and services, which increases demand and the need for companies to supply those goods and services. Due to the higher demand, suppliers can add jobs to fulfill that demand. While the increase of supply, demand, and jobs are positive for the overall economy, they may result in a devaluation of the dollar and less purchasing power.

<u>Money and Banking</u>
Money is the universal form of currency used throughout goods and services exchanges that holds its value over time. Money provides a convenient way for sellers and consumers to understand the value of their goods and services. As opposed to bartering (when sellers and consumers exchange goods or services as equal trades), money is quick and easy for both buyers and sellers.

There are three main forms of money: commodity, fiat, and bank. Here are characteristics of each form:

- Commodity money: Money as a valuable good, such as precious metals
- Fiat money: The value of the good set by supply and demand rather than the actual value it represents, such as paper money
- Bank money: Money that is credited by a bank to those who deposit it into bank accounts, such as checking and savings accounts or credit

While price levels within the economy set the demand for money, most countries have central banks that supply the actual money. Essentially, banks buy and sell money. Borrowers can take loans and pay back the bank, with interest, providing the bank with extra capital.

A central bank has control over the printing and distribution of money. Central banks serve three main purposes: manage monetary growth to help steer the direction of the economy, be a backup to commercial banks that are suffering, and provide options and alternatives to government taxation.

The Federal Reserve is the central bank of the United States. The Federal Reserve controls banking systems and determines the value of money in the United States. Basically, the Federal Reserve is the bank for banks.

All Western economies have to keep a minimum amount of protected cash called *required reserve*. Once banks meet those minimums, they can then lend or loan the excess to consumers. The required reserves are used within a fractional reserve banking system (fractional because a small portion is kept separate and safe). Not only do banks reserve, manage, and loan money, but they also help form monetary policies.

<u>Monetary Policy</u>
The central bank and other government committees control the amount of money that is made and distributed. The money supply determines monetary policy. Three main features sustain monetary policy:

1. Assuring the minimum amount held within banks (bank reserves). When banks are required to hold more money in reserve funds, banks are less willing to lend money to help control inflation.

2. Adjusting interest rates. For example, if the value of money is low, companies and consumers buy more (products, employees, stocks) because prices are cheap. Just like an investment, it is risky, but can pay off in the long term.

3. The purchase and sales of bonds (otherwise known as open market operations). When buying bonds to increase money and selling bonds to reduce the supply, the central bank helps control the money supply.

In the United States, the Federal Reserve maintains monetary policy. There are two main types of monetary policy: expansionary monetary policy and contractionary monetary policy.

- Expansionary monetary policy:
  - Increases the money supply
  - Lowers unemployment
  - Increases consumer spending
  - Increases private sector borrowing
  - Possibly decreases interest rates to very low levels, even near zero
  - Decreases reserve requirements and federal funds
- Contractionary monetary policy:
  - Decreases the money supply
  - Helps control inflation
  - Possibly increases unemployment due to slowdowns in economic growth
  - Decreases consumer spending
  - Decreases loans and/or borrowing

The Federal Reserve uses monetary policy to try to achieve maximum employment and secure inflation rates. Because the Federal Reserve is the "bank of banks," it truly strives to be the last-resort option for distressed banks. This is because once these kinds of institutions begin to rely on the Federal Reserve for help, all parts of the banking industry—such as those dealing with loans, bonds, interest rates, and mortgages—are affected.

<u>International Trade and Exchange Rates</u>
International trade is when countries import and export goods and services. Countries often want to deal in terms of their own currency. Therefore, when importing or exporting goods or services, consumers and businesses need to enter the market using the same form of currency. For example, if the United States would like to trade with China, the U.S. may have to trade in China's form of currency, the *Yuan*, versus the dollar, depending on the business.

The exchange rate is what one country's currency will exchange for another. The government and the market (supply and demand) determine the exchange rate. There are two forms of exchange rates: fixed and floating. Fixed exchange rates involve government interventions (like central banks) to help keep the exchange rates stable. Floating or "flexible" exchange rates constantly change because they rely on supply and demand needs. While each type of exchange rate has advantages and disadvantages, the rate truly depends on the current state of each country's economy. Therefore, each exchange rate may differ from country to country.

Advantages and Disadvantages of Fixed Versus Floating Exchange Rates			
Fixed Exchange Rate: government intervention to help keep exchange rates stable		Floating or "Flexible" Exchange Rate: Supply and demand determines the exchange rate	
Advantages -Stable prices -Stable foreign exchange rates -Exports are more competitive and in turn more profitable	*Disadvantages* -Requires a large amount of reserve funds -Possibly mispricing currency values Inflation increases	*Advantages* -Central bank involvement is not needed. -Facilitates free trade	*Disadvantages* -Currency speculation -Exchange rate risks -Inflation increases

While each country may have differing economic statuses and exchange rates, countries rely on one another for goods and services. Prices of imports and exports are affected by the strength of another country's currency. For example, if the United States dollar is at a higher value than another country's currency, imports will be less expensive because the dollar will have more value than that of the country selling its good or service. On the other hand, if the dollar is at a low value compared to the currency of another country, importers will tend to defer away from buying international items from that country. However, U.S. exporters to that country could benefit from the low value of the dollar.

<u>Economic Growth</u>

Economic growth is measured by the increase in the Gross National Product (GNP) or Gross Domestic Product (GDP). The increase of goods and services over time indicates positive movement in economic growth. Keep in mind that the quantity of goods and services produced is not necessarily an indicator of economic growth. The value of the goods and services produced matters more than the quantity.

There are many causes of economic growth, which can be short- or long-term. In the short term, if aggregate demand (the total demand for goods and services produced at a given time) increases, then the overall Gross Domestic Product (GDP) increases as well. Not only will the GDP increase, interest rates may decrease. With reduced interest rates, spending and investing will increase. Consumer and government spending will also increase because there will be more disposable income. Real estate prices will rise, and there will be lower income taxes. All of these short-term factors can stimulate economic growth.

In the long term, if aggregate supply (the total supply of goods or services in a given time period) increases, then there is potential for an increase in capital as well. With more working capital, more infrastructure and jobs can be created. With more jobs, there is an increased employment rate, and education and training for jobs will improve. New technologies will be developed, and new raw materials may be discovered. All of these long-term factors can also stimulate economic growth.

Outside of the short- and long-term causes for economic growth, other factors include low inflation and stability. Lower inflation rates encourage more investing versus higher inflation rates that cause instability in the market. Stability encourages businesses to continue investing. If the market is unstable, investors may question the volatility of the market.

Potential Costs of Economic Growth:

- Inflation: When economic growth occurs, inflation tends to be high. If supply cannot keep up with demand, then the inflation rate may be unmanageable.
- Economic booms and recessions: The economy goes through cycles of booms and recessions. This causes inflation to increase and decrease over time, which puts the economy into a continuous cycle of rising and falling.
- Account inefficiencies: When the economy grows, consumers and businesses increase their import spending. The increase of import spending affects the current account and causes a shortage.
- Environmental costs: When the economy is growing, there is an abundance of output, which may result in more pollutants and a reduction in quality of life.
- Inequalities: Growth occurs differently among members of society. While the wealthy may be getting richer, those living in poverty may just be getting on their feet. So while economic growth is happening, it may happen at two very different rates.

While these potential costs could affect economic growth, if the growth is consistent and stable, then growth can occur without severe inflation swings. Also, as technology improves, new ways of production can reduce negative environmental factors as well.

Geography and the World

Map Types and Projections

Geographers utilize a variety of different maps in their study of the spatial world. Projections are maps that represent the entire world (which is spherical) on a flat surface. *Conformal projections* preserve angles locally, maintaining the shape of a small area in infinitesimal circles of varying sizes on a two-dimensional map. Conformal projections tend to possess inherent flaws due to their two-dimensional nature. For example, the most well-known projection, the *Mercator projection*, drastically distorts the size of land areas at the poles. In this particular map, Antarctica, one of the smallest continents, appears massive, almost rivaling the size of North America. In contrast to the poles, the areas closer to the central portion of the globe are more accurate. Other projections attempt to lessen the amount of distortion; the *Equal-area projection*, for example, attempts to equally represent the size of landforms on the globe. Nevertheless, equal-area projections like the *Lambert projection* also inherently alter the size of continents, islands, and other landforms, both close to Earth's center and near the poles. Other projections are a hybrid of the two primary models. For example, the *Robinson projection*, also referred to as the *Goode's homolosine projection*, tries to balance form and area in order to create a more visually accurate representation of the spatial world. Despite the efforts to maintain consistency with shapes, projections cannot provide accurate representations of the Earth's surface, due to their flat, two-dimensional nature. In this sense, projections are useful symbols of space, but they do not always provide the most accurate portrayal of spatial reality.

Unlike projections, *topographic maps* display contour lines, which represent the relative elevation of a particular place and are very useful for surveyors, engineers, and/or travelers. Hikers of the Appalachian Trail or Pacific Crest Trail, for instance, may call upon topographic maps to calculate their daily climbs.

Thematic maps are also quite useful to geographers because they use two-dimensional surfaces to convey complex political, physical, social, cultural, economic, or historical themes.

Thematic maps can be broken down into different subgroups: *dot-density maps* and *flow-line maps*. A *dot-density map* is a type of thematic map that illustrates the volume and density in a particular area. Although most dots on these maps represent the number of people in an area, they don't always have to do that. Instead, these maps may represent the number of events, such as lightning strikes, that have taken place in an area. *Flow-line maps* are another type of thematic map, which utilize both thin and thick lines to illustrate the movement of goods, people, or even animals between two places. The thicker the line, the greater the number of moving elements; a thinner line would, of course, represent a smaller number.

Similar to topographic maps, an *isoline map* is also useful for calculating data and differentiating between the characteristics of two places. In an *isoline map*, symbols represent values, and lines can be drawn between two points in order to determine differences. For example, average temperature is commonly measured on isoline maps. Point A, which is high in the mountains, may have a value of 33 degrees, while point B, which is in the middle of the Mojave Desert, may have a value of 105 degrees. Using the different values, it is easy to determine that temperatures in the mountains are 72 degrees cooler than in the desert. Additionally, isoline maps help geographers study the world by creating questions. For example, is it only elevation that is responsible for the differences in temperature? If not, what other factors could cause such a wide disparity in the two values? Utilizing these, and other sorts of maps, is essential in the study of geography.

Using Mental Maps to Organize Spatial Information

Mental maps are exactly what they sound like—maps that exist within someone's mind. The cognitive image of a particular place may differ from person to person, but the concept of remembering important places does not. For example, the commonalities usually emerge relative to the knowledge of one's workplace, school, home, or favorite restaurants. Furthermore, mental maps also embody the means of travelling from point A to point B. One may know the best route on public transit, the least hilly bike path, or the roadways that have the least amount of traffic. In places where someone has very little interaction, mental maps usually tend to be minimally informative, due to the absence of any personal experience in a particular place.

Maps are also organized through scale. Scale is simply the ratio of a distance on the ground to the corresponding distance on paper. Geographers and cartographers attempt to make the image on paper representative of the actual place. For example, the United States Geological Survey (USGS) utilizes the mathematical ratio of 1/24,000 in all of its topographical maps. This scale means that one inch on the map is equivalent to 24,000 inches—or nearly two-thirds of a mile—on the ground. The two primary types of maps, *large scale* and *small scale*, essentially serve the same purpose, but for two different types of places. Large-scale maps represent a much smaller area with greater detail, while small-scale maps are representative of much larger areas with less detail.

Recognizing and Interpreting Spatial Patterns Presented at Different Scales from Local to Global

Two primary realms exist within the study of geography. The first realm, *physical geography*, essentially correlates with the land, water, and foliage of the Earth. The second realm, *human geography*, is the study of the Earth's people and how they interact with their environment. Like land and water on Earth, humans are also impacted by different forces such as culture, history, sociology, technological advancement and changes, and access to natural resources. For example, human populations tend to be higher around more reliable sources of fresh water. The metropolitan area of New York City, which has abundant freshwater resources, is home to nearly 20 million people, whereas Australia, both a continent and a country, has almost the same population. Although water isn't the only factor in this disparity, it certainly plays a role in a place's *population density*—the total number of people in a particular place divided by the total land area, usually square miles or square kilometers. Australia's population density stands at 8.13 people per square mile, while the most densely populated nation on Earth, Bangladesh, is home to 2,894 people per square mile.

Population density can have a devastating impact on both the physical environment/ecosystem and the humans who live within the environment/ecosystem of a particular place. For example, Delhi, one of India's most populated cities, is home to nearly five million gasoline-powered vehicles. Each day, those vehicles emit an enormous amount of carbon monoxide into the atmosphere, which directly affects the quality of life of Delhi's citizens. In fact, the problem of the smog and pollution has gotten so severe that many drivers are unable to see fifty feet in front of them. Additionally, densely populated areas within third-world nations, or developing nations, struggle significantly in their quest to balance the demands of the modern economy with their nation's lack of infrastructure. For example, nearly as many automobiles operate every day in major American cities like New York and Los Angeles as they do in Delhi, but they create significantly less pollution due to cleaner burning engines, better fuels, and governmental emission regulations.

Although it's a significant factor, population density is not the only source of strain on the resources of a particular place. Historical forces such as civil war, religious conflict, genocide, and government corruption can also alter the lives of a nation's citizens in a profound manner. For example, the war-torn nation on the Horn of Africa, Somalia, has not had a functioning government for nearly three decades. As a result, the nation's citizens have virtually no access to hospital care, vaccinations, or proper facilities for childbirth. Due to these and other factors, the nation's *infant mortality rate*, or the total number of child deaths per 1,000 live births, stands at a whopping 98.39/1000. When compared to Iceland's 1.82/1000, it's quite evident that Somalia struggles to provide basic services in the realm of childbirth and there is a dire need for humanitarian assistance.

Literacy rates, like the infant mortality rate, are also an excellent indicator of the relative level of development in a particular place. Like Somalia, other developing nations have both economic and social factors that hinder their ability to educate their own citizens. Due to radical religious factions within some nations like Afghanistan and Pakistan, girls are often denied the ability to attend school, which further reduces the nation's overall literacy rate. For example, girls in Afghanistan, which spent decades under Taliban control, have a 24.2 percent literacy rate, one of the lowest rates of any nation on Earth that keeps records (Somalia's government is so dysfunctional records don't exist). Although literacy rates are useful in determining a nation's development level, high literacy rates do exist within developing nations. For example, Suriname, which has a significantly lower GDP (Gross Domestic Product) than Afghanistan, enjoys a nearly 96 percent literacy rate among both sexes. Utilizing this and other data, geographers can create questions regarding how such phenomena occur. How is Suriname able to educate its population more effectively with fewer financial resources? Is it something inherent within their culture? Demographic data, such as population density, the infant mortality rate, and the literacy rate all provide insight into the characteristics of a particular place and help geographers better understand the spatial world.

Locating and Using Sources of Geographic Data

Geographic data is essential to fully understanding both the spatial and human realms of geography. In reference to the human population, different factors affect the quality of life one experiences during their lifetime. Geographers attempt to understand why those differences exist through data utilization and comparative analysis. For example, as has been previously mentioned, population density, infant mortality rates, and literacy rates are all useful tools in analyzing human characteristics of a place; however, those are not the only tools geographers utilize. In fact, organizations such as the *Population Reference Bureau* and the *Central Intelligence Agency* both provide an incredible amount of *demographic* data useful to researchers, students, or really anyone curious about the world in which they live.

The *CIA World Factbook* is an indispensable resource for anyone interested in the field of human or physical geography. Providing information such as land area, literacy rates, birth rate, and economic data, this resource is one of the most comprehensive on the Internet. In addition to the CIA World Factbook, the *Population Reference Bureau* (*PRB*) also provides students of geography with an abundant supply of information. In contrast to the CIA source, the *PRB* provides a treasure trove of analyses related to human populations including HIV rates, immigration rates, poverty rates, etc.

In addition to the aforementioned sources, the *United States Census Bureau* provides similar information about the dynamics of the American population. Not only does this source focus on the data geographers need to understand the world, but it also provides information about upcoming classes, online workshops, and even includes an online library of resources for both students and teachers. Websites for each source can be found below:

- Population Reference Bureau: www.prb.orghttp://www.prb.org
- United States Census Bureau: www.census.govhttp://www.census.gov
- CIA World Factbook: https://www.cia.gov/library/publications/the-world-factbook/https://www.cia.gov/library/publications/the-world-factbook/

Spatial Concepts

Location is the central theme in understanding spatial concepts. In geography, there are two primary types of locations that people utilize on a daily basis. The first type, *relative location*, is used frequently and involves locating objects by notating their proximity to another, better known object. For example, directions from person to person may relate directly to massive shopping centers, major highways, or well-known intersections. Although relative location is important, in the modern world, it's common to use digital satellite-based technologies, which rely on *GPS* (*Global Positioning System*). To determine *Absolute Location*, or the exact latitudinal and longitudinal position on the globe, GPS uses sensors that interact with satellites orbiting the Earth. *Coordinates* correspond with the positions on a manmade grid system using imaginary lines known as *latitude* (also known as *parallels*) and *longitude* (also known as *meridians*).

In order to understand latitude and longitude, one should think of a simple X and Y-axis. The *equator* serves as the X-axis at zero degrees, and measures distance from north to south. The Y-axis is at zero degrees and is represented by the *Prime Meridian*.

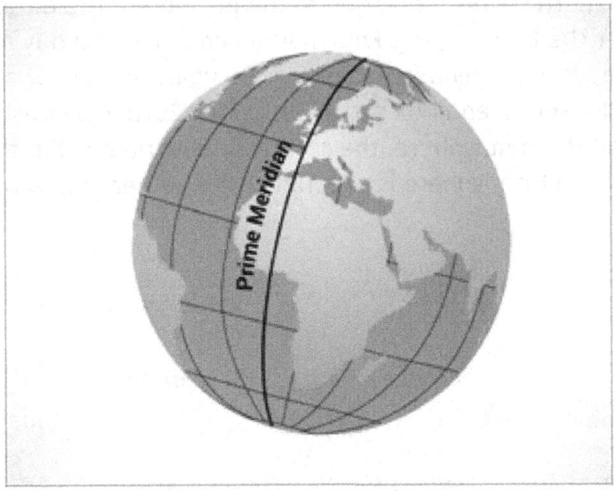

In addition to anchoring the grid system to create the basis for absolute location, these major lines of latitude and longitude also divide the Earth into *hemispheres***.** The Equator divides the Earth into the northern and southern hemispheres, while the Prime Meridian establishes the eastern and western hemispheres. Coordinates are always expressed in the following format:

Degrees north or south, degrees east or west, or 40°N, 50°E. Since lines of latitude and longitude are great distance from one another, absolute locations are often found in between two lines. In those cases, degrees are broken down into *minutes* and *seconds*, which are expressed in this manner: (40° 53' 44" N, 50° 22' 65" E).

In addition to the Equator and the Prime Meridian, other major lines of latitude and longitude exist to divide the world into regions relative to the direct rays of the sun. These lines correspond with the Earth's *tilt*, and are responsible for the seasons. For example, the northern hemisphere is tilted directly toward the sun from June 22 to September 23, which creates the summer season in that part of the world. Conversely, the southern hemisphere is tilted away from the direct rays of the sun and experiences winter during those same months.

The transitions from season to season involve two factors: the 23 ½ degree tilt of the Earth and the movement of the direct rays of the sun relative to the Earth's revolution. To clarify, the area between the *Tropic of Cancer* (23 ½ degrees north) and the *Tropic of Capricorn* (23 ½ degrees south) can be envisioned as the playing field for the direct rays of the sun. These rays never leave the playing field, and, as a result, the area between those two lines of latitude—the *tropics*—tends to be warmer and experience fewer variations in seasonal temperatures. In contrast, the area between the Tropic of Cancer and the *Arctic Circle* (66 ½ degrees north) is in the *middle latitudes*—the region where most of the Earth's population resides. In the Southern Hemisphere, the middle latitudes exist between the Tropic of Capricorn and the *Antarctic Circle* (66 ½ degrees south). In both of these places, indirect rays of the sun strike the Earth, so seasons are more pronounced and milder temperatures generally prevail. The final region, known as the *high latitudes*, is found north of the Arctic Circle and south of the Antarctic Circle. These regions generally tend to be cold all year, and experience nearly twenty-four hours of sunlight during their respective *summer solstice* and twenty-four hours of darkness during the *winter solstice*.

Regarding the seasons, it is important to understand that those in the Southern Hemispheres are opposite of those in the Northern Hemisphere, due to the position of the direct rays of the sun. When the sun's direct rays are over the Equator, it is known as an *equinox*, and day and night are almost of equal length throughout the world. Equinoxes occur twice a year; the fall, or autumnal equinox, occurs on September 22nd, while the spring equinox occurs on March 20th. Obviously, if seasons are opposite of one another depending on the hemisphere, the corresponding names flip-flop depending on one's location (i.e. when the Northern Hemisphere is experiencing summer, it is winter in the Southern Hemisphere).

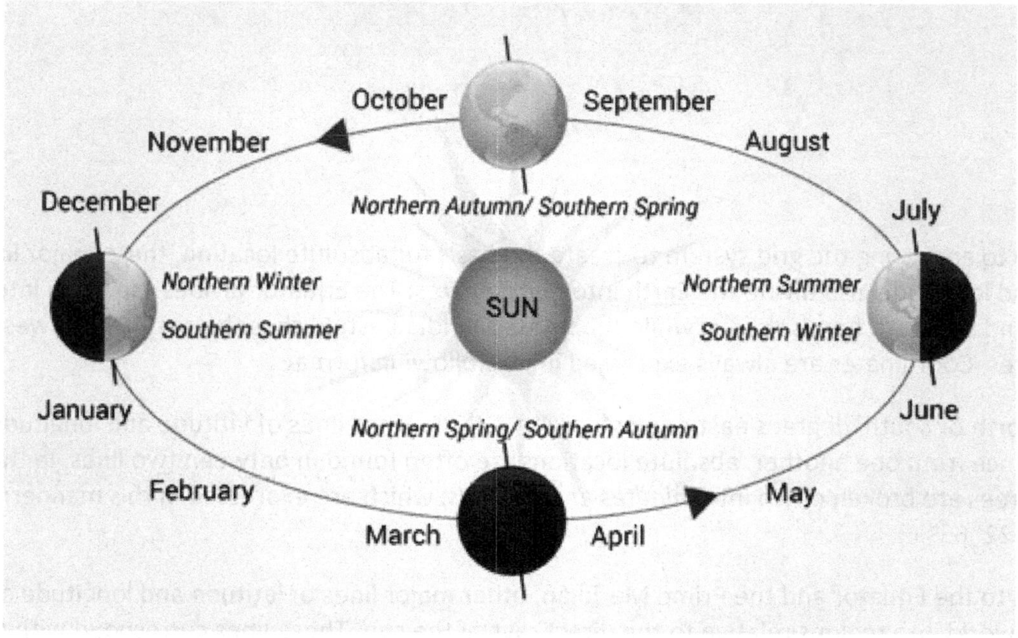

Place

Both absolute and relative location help humans understand their sense of place. Place is a simple concept that helps to define the characteristics of the world around us. For example, people may create *toponyms* to further define and orient themselves with their sense of place. Toponyms are simply names given to locations to help develop familiarity within a certain location. Although not always the case, toponyms generally utilize geographical features, important people in an area, or even wildlife commonly found in a general location. For example, many cities in the state of Texas are named in honor of military leaders who fought in the Texas Revolution of 1836 (such as Houston and Austin), while other places, such as Mississippi and Alabama, utilize Native American toponyms to define their sense of place.

Regions

In addition to location and place, geographers also divide the world into regions in order to more fully understand differences inherent with the world, its people, and its environment. As mentioned previously, lines of latitude such as the Equator, the Tropics, and the Arctic and Antarctic Circles already divide the Earth into solar regions relative to the amount of either direct or indirect sunlight that they receive. Although not the same throughout, the middle latitudes generally have a milder climate than areas found within the tropics. Furthermore, tropical locations are usually warmer than places in the middle latitudes, but that is not always the case. For example, the lowest place in the United States—Death Valley, California—is also home to the nation's highest-ever recorded temperature. Likewise, the Andes Mountains in Peru and Ecuador, although found near the Equator, are also home to heavy snow, low temperatures, and dry conditions, due to their elevation.

Formal regions are spatially defined areas that have overarching similarities or some level of *homogeneity* or *uniformity*. Although not exactly alike, a formal region generally has at least one characteristic that is consistent throughout the entire area. For example, the United States could be broken down into one massive formal region due to the fact that in all fifty states, English is the primary language. Of course, English isn't the only language spoken in the United States, but throughout that nation, English is heavily used. As a result, geographers are able to classify the United States as a formal region; but, more specifically, the United States is a *linguistic region*—a place where everyone generally speaks the same language.

Functional regions are similar to formal regions in that they have similar characteristics, but they do not have clear boundaries. The best way to understand these sorts of regions is to consider large cities. Each large city encompasses a large *market area*, whereby people in its vicinity generally travel there to conduct business, go out to eat, or watch a professional sporting event. However, once anyone travels farther away from that *primate city*, they transition to a different, more accessible city for their needs. The functional region, or *area of influence*, for that city, town, or sports team transitions, depending upon the availability of other primate cities. For example, New York City has two primary professional baseball, basketball, and football teams. As a result, its citizens may have affinities for different teams even though they live in the same city. Conversely, a citizen in rural Idaho may cheer for the Seattle Seahawks, even though they live over 500 miles from Seattle, due to the lack of a closer primate city.

Effects of Physical Processes, Climate Patterns, and Natural Hazards on Human Societies

The Earth's surface, like many other things in the broader universe, does not remain the same for long; in fact, it changes from day to day. The Earth's surface is subject to a variety of physical processes that continue to shape its appearance. In each process, water, wind, temperature, or sunlight play a role in continually altering the Earth's surface.

Erosion can be caused by a variety of different stimuli including ice, snow, water, wind, and ocean waves. *Wind erosion* is a specific phenomenon that occurs in generally flat, dry areas with loose topsoil. Over time, the persistent winds can dislodge significant amounts of soil into the air, reshaping the land and wreaking havoc on those who depend on agriculture for their livelihoods. Erosion can also be caused by water and is responsible for changing landscapes as well. For example, the Grand Canyon was carved over thousands of years by the constant movement of the Colorado River. Over time, the river moved millions of tons of soil, cutting a huge gorge in the Earth along the way. In all cases, erosion involves the movement of soil from one place to another. In water erosion, material carried by the water is referred to as *sediment*. With time, some sediment can collect at the mouths of rivers, forming *deltas*, which become small islands of fertile soil. This process of detaching loose soils and transporting them to a different location where they remain for an extended period of time is referred to as *deposition*, and is the end result of the erosion process.

In contrast to erosion, *weathering* does not involve the movement of any outside stimuli. In this physical process, the surface of the Earth is either broken down physically or chemically. *Physical weathering* involves the effects of atmospheric conditions such as water, ice, heat, or pressure. Through the process of weathering over the course of centuries, large rocks can be broken down with the effects of icy conditions. *Chemical weathering* generally occurs in warmer climates and involves organic material that breaks down rocks, minerals, or soil. This process is what scientists believe led to the creation of fossil fuels such as oil, coal, and natural gas.

Climate Patterns

Weather is defined as the condition of the Earth's atmosphere at a particular time. *Climate* is different; instead of focusing on one particular day, climate is the relative pattern of weather in a place for an extended period of time. For example, the city of Atlanta is in the American South and generally has a humid subtropical climate; however, Atlanta also occasionally experiences snowstorms in the winter months. Despite the occasional snow and sleet storm, over time, geographers, meteorologists, and other Earth scientists have determined the patterns that are indicative to north Georgia, where Atlanta is located. Almost all parts of the world have predictable climate patterns, which are influenced by the surrounding geography.

The Central Coast of California is an example of a place with a predictable climate pattern. Santa Barbara, California, one of the region's larger cities, has almost the same temperature for most of the summer, spring, and fall, with only minimal fluctuation during the winter months. The temperatures there, which average between 75 and 65 degrees Fahrenheit daily regardless as to the time of year, are influenced by a variety of different climatological factors including elevation, location relative to the mountains and ocean, and ocean currents. In the case of Santa Barbara, the city's location on the Pacific Coast and its position near mountains heavily influences its climate. The cold California current, which sweeps down the west coast of the United States, causes the air near the city to be temperate, while the mountains trap cool air over the city and the surrounding area. This pattern, known as the *orographic effect*, or *rain shadow*, also affects temperatures on the leeward side of the mountains by blocking most of the cool air and causing dry conditions to dominate. Temperatures can fluctuate by more than 20 degrees Fahrenheit on opposite sides of the mountain.

Other factors affecting climate include elevation, prevailing winds, vegetation, and latitudinal position on the globe.

Like climate, *natural hazards* also affect human societies. In tropical and subtropical climates, hurricanes and typhoons form over warm water and can have devastating effects. Additionally, tornadoes, which are powerful cyclonic windstorms, also are responsible for widespread destruction in many parts of the United States and in other parts of the world. Like storms, earthquakes, usually caused by shifting plates along faults deep below the Earth's surface, also cause widespread devastation, particularly in nations with a poor or crumbling infrastructure. For example, San Francisco, which experiences earthquakes regularly due to its position near the San Andreas Fault, saw relatively little destruction and deaths (67 total) as a result of the last major earthquake to strike there. However, in 2010, an earthquake of similar magnitude reportedly killed over 200,000 people in the western hemisphere's poorest nation, Haiti. Although a variety of factors may be responsible for the disparity, modern engineering methods and better building materials most likely helped to minimize destruction in San Francisco. Other natural hazards, such as tsunamis, mudslides, avalanches, forest fires, dust storms, flooding, volcanic eruptions, and blizzards, also affect human societies throughout the world.

Characteristics and Spatial Distribution of Earth's Ecosystems

Earth is an incredibly large place filled with a variety of different land and water *ecosystems*. *Marine ecosystems* cover over 75 percent of the Earth's surface and contain over 95 percent of the Earth's water. Marine ecosystems can be broken down into two primary subgroups: *freshwater ecosystems*, which only encompass around 2 percent of the earth's surface; and *ocean ecosystems*, which make up over 70 percent. On land, *terrestrial ecosystems* vary depending on a variety of factors, including latitudinal distance from the equator, elevation, and proximity to mountains or bodies of water. For example, in the high latitudinal regions north of the Arctic Circle and south of the Antarctic Circle, frozen *tundra* dominates. Tundra, which is characterized by low temperatures, short growing seasons, and minimal vegetation, is only found in regions that are far away from the direct rays of the sun.

In contrast, *deserts* can be found throughout the globe and are created by different ecological factors. For example, the world's largest desert, the Sahara, is almost entirely within the tropics; however, other deserts like the Gobi in China, the Mojave in the United States, and the Atacama in Chile, are the result of the orographic effect and their close proximity to high mountain ranges such as the Himalayas, the Sierra Nevada, and the Andes, respectively. In the Middle Latitudes, greater varieties of climatological zones are more common due to fluctuations in temperatures relative to the sun's rays, coupled with the particular local topography. In the Continental United States, *temperate deciduous forest* dominates the southeastern portion of the country. However, the Midwestern states such as Nebraska, Kansas, and the Dakotas, are primarily *grasslands*. Additionally, the states of the Rocky Mountains can have decidedly different climates relative to elevation. In Colorado, Denver, also known as the "Mile High City," will often see snowfalls well into late April or early May due to colder temperatures, whereas towns and cities in the eastern part of the state, with much lower elevations, may see their last significant snowfall in March.

In the tropics, which are situated between the Tropics of Cancer and Capricorn, temperatures are generally warmer, due to the direct rays of the sun's persistence. However, like most of the world, the tropics also experience a variety of climatological regions. In Brazil, Southeast Asia, Central America, and even Northern Australia, tropical rainforests are common. These forests, which are known for abundant vegetation, daily rainfall, and a wide variety of animal life, are absolutely essential to the health of the world's ecosystems. For example, the *Amazon Rain Forest* is also referred to as "the lungs of the world," as its billions of trees produce substantial amounts of oxygen and absorb an equivalent amount of carbon dioxide—the substance that many climatologists assert is causing climate change or *global warming*. Unlike temperate deciduous forests whose trees lose their leaves during the fall and winter months, *tropical rain forests* are always lush, green, and warm. In fact, some rainforests are so dense with vegetation that a few indigenous tribes have managed to exist within them without being influenced by any sort of modern technology, virtually maintaining their ancient way of life in the modern era.

The world's largest ecosystem, the *taiga*, is found primarily in high latitudinal areas, which receive very little of the sun's indirect rays. These forests are generally made up of *coniferous* trees, which do not lose their leaves at any point during the year as *deciduous* trees do. Taigas are cold-climate regions that make up almost 30 percent of the world's land area. These forests dominate the northern regions of Canada, Scandinavia, and Russia, and provide the vast majority of the world's lumber.

Overall, it is important to remember that climates are influenced by five major factors: elevation, latitude, proximity to mountains, ocean currents, and wind patterns. For example, the cold currents off the coast of California provide the West Coast of the United States with pleasant year-round temperatures. Conversely, Western Europe, which is at the nearly the same latitude as most of Canada, is influenced by the warm waters of the *Gulf Stream*, an ocean current that acts as a conveyor belt, moving warm tropical waters to the icy north. In fact, the Gulf Stream's influence is so profound that it even keeps Iceland—an island nation in the far North Atlantic—relatively warm.

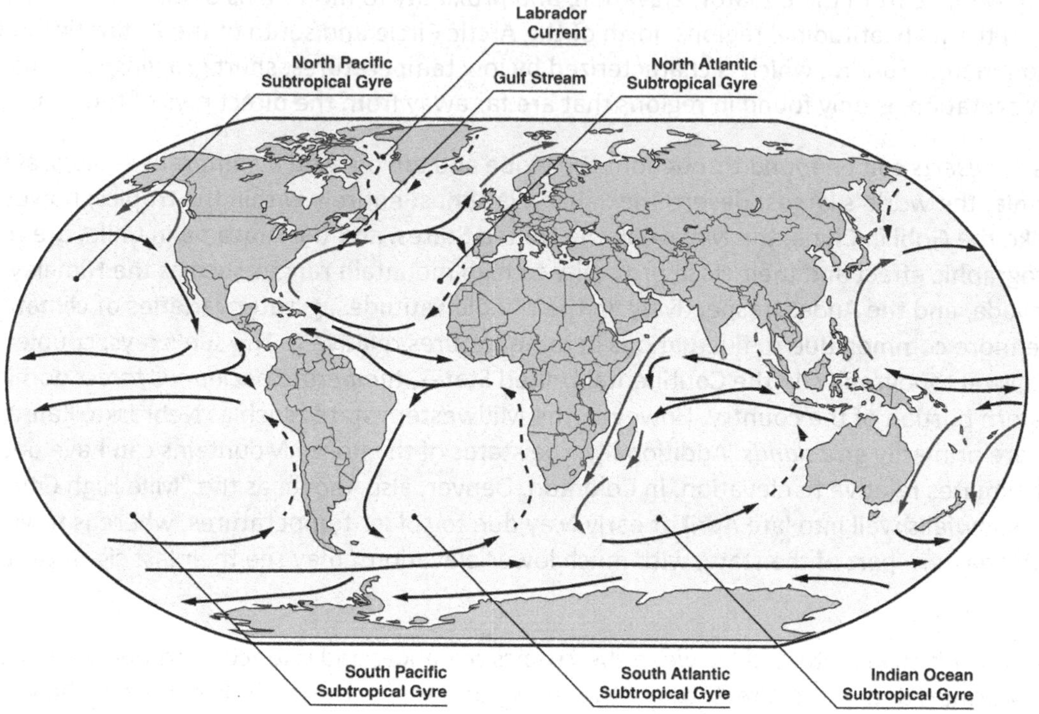

Interrelationships Between Humans and Their Environment

Like any other animal, humans adapt to their environment; but, unlike other animals, humans also adapt their environment to suit their needs. For example, human social systems are created around the goal of providing people with access to what they need to live more productive, fulfilling, and meaningful lives. Sometimes, humans create systems that are destructive, but generally speaking, humans tend to use their environment to make their lives easier. For example, in warmer climates, people tend to wear more comfortable clothing such as shorts, linen shirts, and hats. Additionally, in the excessively sun-drenched nations of the Middle East, both men and women wear flowing white clothing complete with both a head and neck covering, in order to prevent the blistering effects of sun exposure to the skin. Likewise, the native Inuit peoples of northern Canada and Alaska use the thick furs from the animals they kill to insulate their bodies against the bitter cold.

Humans also adapt to their environment to ensure that they have access to enough food and water for survival. Irrigation, or the process of moving water from its natural location to where it's needed, is an example of how humans change their environment in order to survive. For example, the city of Los Angeles, America's second most populous city, did not have adequate freshwater resources to sustain its population. However, city and state officials realized that abundant water resources existed approximately three hundred miles to the east. Rather than relocating some of its population to areas with more abundant water resources, the State of California undertook one of the largest construction projects in the history of the world, the Los Angeles Aqueduct, which is a massive concrete irrigation ditch connecting water-rich areas with the thirsty citizens of Los Angeles.

The Los Angeles Aqueduct is just one example of a human-environment interaction. In other cases, humans utilize what nature provides in close proximity. For example, the very first permanent British Colony in North America, Jamestown, VA, was heavily influenced by its environment. In contrast to the Pilgrims who settled in Plymouth, Massachusetts, Jamestown settlers found themselves in a hot, humid climate with fertile soil. Consequently, its inhabitants engaged in agriculture for both food and profit. Twelve years after Jamestown's foundation in 1607, it was producing millions of dollars of tobacco each year. In order to sustain this booming industry, over time, millions of African slaves and indentured servants from Europe were imported to provide labor. Conversely, the poor soils around Plymouth did not allow for widespread cash crop production, and the settlers in New England generally only grew enough food for themselves on small subsistence farms. Furthermore, slavery failed to take a strong foothold in the New England states, thus creating significantly different cultures within the same country, all due in part to human interaction with the environment.

Renewable and Nonrenewable Resources

When gas prices are high, prices on virtually everything increase. After all, there are very few products that humans can buy that are not transported by either a gasoline- or diesel-powered engine. As a result, an increase in fuel prices leads to an increase in the price of food, goods, or other cargo. Recently, there has been considerable debate regarding the reliance on *nonrenewable resources* like oil, natural gas, and coal. These resources, which are also known as *fossil fuels,* are quite common throughout the world and are generally abundant, and cheaper to use than *renewable resources* like solar, wind, and geothermal energy. While solar energy is everywhere, the actual means to convert the sun's rays into energy is not. Conversely, coal-fired power plants and gasoline-powered engines, which are older technologies in use during the industrial revolution, remain quite common throughout the world. In fact, reliance on non-renewable resources continues to grow, due to the availability coupled with the existing infrastructure. However, use of renewable energy is increasing, as it becomes more economically competitive with nonrenewable resources.

In addition to sources of energy, nonrenewable resources also include anything that can be exhausted. These can include precious metals like gold, silver, and platinum, freshwater underground aquifers, and precious stones such as diamonds, emeralds, and opals. Although abundant, most nonrenewable sources of energy are not sustainable because their creation takes millions of years and can therefore not be reproduced. Renewable resources are sustainable, but must be properly overseen so that they remain renewable. For example, the beautiful African island of Madagascar is home to some of the most amazing rainforest trees in the world. As a result, logging companies cut, milled, and sold thousands of them in order to make quick profits without planning how to ensure the continued health of the forests. As a result of severe deforestation on the island, mudslides became more and more common as the forests gradually shrank from widespread logging. In this case, renewable resources were mismanaged, and thus essentially became nonrenewable, due to the length of time for growth for the replacement of rainforest trees. In the United States, paper companies harvest pine trees to create paper; and because it can take almost twenty years for a pine tree to reach maturity, most of the companies utilize planning techniques to ensure that mature pine trees will always be available. In this manner, these resources remain renewable for human use in a sustainable fashion.

Renewable sources of energy are relatively new in the modern economy. Even though electric cars, wind turbines, and solar panels are becoming more common, they still do not provide enough energy to power the world's economy. As a result, reliance on older, reliable forms of energy continues, which has a devastating effect on the environment. Beijing, China, which has seen a massive boom in industrial jobs, is also one of the most polluted places on Earth. Furthermore, developing nations with very little modern infrastructure also rely heavily on fossil fuels, due to the ease in which they are converted into usable energy. Even the United States, which has one of the most developed infrastructures in the world, still relies almost exclusively on fossil fuels, with only ten percent of the required energy coming from renewable sources.

Spatial Patterns of Cultural and Economic Activities

Spatial patterns refer to where things are in the world. Biomes, regions, and landforms all have spatial patterns regarding where they exist. Additionally, elements of *human geography*—the study of human culture and its effect on the world—also have certain patterns regarding where they appear on Earth.

Ethnicity

An ethnic group, or ethnicity, is essentially a group of people with a common language, society, culture, or ancestral heritage. Different ethnicities developed over centuries through historical forces, the impact of religious traditions, and other factors. Thousands of years ago, it was more common for ethnic groups to remain in one area with only the occasional interaction with outside groups. In the modern world, different ethnicities interact on a daily, if not hourly, basis, due to better transportation resources and the processes of globalization. For example, in the United States, it is not uncommon for a high school classroom to encompass people of Asian, African, Indian, European, or Native descent. That's not to suggest that all American classrooms have ethnic diversity, but, in general, due to a variety of pull-factors, the United States continues to attract people from all over the world. In less developed parts of the world, travel is limited due to the lack of infrastructure. Consequently, ethnic groups develop in small areas that can differ greatly from other people just a few miles away. For example, on the Balkan Peninsula in southeastern Europe, a variety of different ethnic groups live in close proximity to one another. Croats, Albanians, Serbs, Bosnians, and others all share the same land, but have very different worldviews, traditions, and religious influences. In the case of the Balkan Peninsula, such diversity has not always been a positive characteristic. For example, the First World War began there in 1914 related to a dispute regarding Serbia's national independence. Additionally, Bosnia was the scene of a horrible genocide against Albanians in an "ethnic cleansing" effort that continued throughout the late 20th century.

Linguistics

Linguistics, or the study of language, groups certain languages together according to their commonalities. For example, the Romance Languages—French, Spanish, Italian, Romansh, and Portuguese—all share language traits from Latin, the language of the former Roman Empire. These languages, also known as *vernaculars*, or more commonly spoken *dialects*, evolved over centuries of physical isolation on the European continent. The Spanish form of Latin emerged into today's Spanish language. In other parts of the world, the same pattern is true. The Bantu people of Africa travelled extensively and spread their language, now called *Swahili*, which is the first Pan-African language. When thinking of the world as a whole, it is important to understand that thousands of languages exist; however, to interconnect the world, it is important to have a means of communication with which everyone is at least somewhat familiar. A *lingua franca* is essentially the language of business. In other words, when executives from multinational corporations need to communicate regarding business, they often communicate in English, which is considered to be the world's lingua franca, due to the economic dominance of the United States.

Religion

Religion has played a tremendous role in creating the world's cultures. Devout Christians crossed the Atlantic in hopes of finding religious freedom in New England, Muslim missionaries and traders travelled to the Spice Islands of the East Indies to teach about the Koran, and Buddhist monks traversed the Himalayan Mountains into Tibet to spread their faith. In some countries, religion helps to shape legal systems. These nations, termed *theocracies*, have no separation of church and state and are more common in Islamic nations such as Saudi Arabia, Iran, and Qatar. In contrast, even though religion has played a tremendous role in the history of the United States, its government remains *secular*, or nonreligious, due to the influence of European Enlightenment philosophy at the time of its inception. Like ethnicity and language, religion is also a primary way that people self-identify. As a result, religious influences can shape a region's laws, architecture, literature, and music. For example, when the Ottoman Turks, who are Muslim, conquered Constantinople, which was once the home of the Eastern Orthodox Christian Church, they replaced Christian places of worship with mosques. Additionally, different forms of Roman architecture were replaced with those influenced by Arabic traditions.

<u>Economics</u>

Economic activity also has a spatial component. For example, nations with few natural resources generally tend to import what they need from nations willing to export raw materials to them. Furthermore, areas that are home to certain raw materials generally tend to alter their environment in order to maintain production of those materials. In the San Joaquin Valley of California, an area known for extreme heat and desert-like conditions, local residents have engineered elaborate drip irrigation systems to adequately water lemon, lime, olive, and orange trees, utilizing the warm temperatures to constantly produce citrus fruits. Additionally, other nations with abundant petroleum reserves build elaborate infrastructures in order to pump, house, refine, and transport their materials to nations who require gasoline, diesel, or natural gas. Essentially, different spatial regions on Earth create jobs, infrastructure, and transportation systems that seek to ensure the continued flow of goods, raw materials, and resources out of their location, so long as financial resources keep flowing into the area.

Patterns of Migration and Settlement

Migration is governed by two primary causes: *push factors*, which are reasons causing someone to leave an area, and *pull factors*, which are factors luring someone to a particular place. These two factors often work in concert with one another. For example, the United States of America has experienced significant *internal migration* from the industrial states in the Northeast (such as New York, New Jersey, Connecticut) to the Southern and Western states. This massive migration, which continues into the present-day, is due to high rents in the northeast, dreadfully cold winters, and lack of adequate retirement housing, all of which are push factors. These push factors lead to migration to the *Sunbelt*, a term geographers use to describe states with warm climates and less intense winters.

In addition to internal migrations within nations or regions, international migration also takes place between countries, continents, and other regions. The United States has long been the world's leading nation in regard to *immigration*, the process of having people come into a nation's boundaries. Conversely, developing nations that suffer from high levels of poverty, pollution, warfare, and other violence all have significant push factors, which cause people to leave and move elsewhere. This process, known as *emigration*, is when people in a particular area leave in order to seek a better life in a different—usually better—location.

The Development and Changing Nature of Agriculture

Agriculture is essential to human existence. The *Neolithic Revolution*, or the use of farming to produce food, had a profound effect on human societies. Rather than foraging and hunting for food, human societies became more stable and were able to grow due to more consistent food supplies. In modern times, farming has changed drastically in order to keep up with the increasing world population.

Until the twentieth century, the vast majority of people on Earth engaged in *subsistence farming*, or the practice of growing only enough food to feed one's self, or one's family. Over time, due to inventions such as the steel plow, the mechanical reaper, and the seed drill, farmers were able to produce more crops on the same amount of land. As food became cheaper and easier to obtain, populations grew, but rather than leading to an increase in farmers, fewer people actually farmed. After the advent of mechanized farming in developed nations, small farms became less common, and many were either abandoned or absorbed by massive commercial farms producing both foodstuffs, staple crops, and cash crops.

In recent years, agricultural practices have undergone further changes in order to keep up with the rapidly growing population. Due in part to the *Green Revolution*, which introduced the widespread use of fertilizers to produce massive amounts of crops, farming techniques and practices continue to evolve. For example, *genetically modified organisms*, or *GMOs*, are plants or animals whose genetic makeup has been modified using different strands of DNA in hopes of producing more resilient strains of staple crops, livestock, and other foodstuffs. This process, which is a form of *biotechnology*, attempts to solve the world's food production problems through the use of genetic engineering. Although these crops are abundant and resistant to pests, drought, or frost, they are also the subject of intense scrutiny. For example, the international food company, Monsanto, has faced an incredible amount of criticism regarding its use of GMOs in its products. Many activists assert that "rewiring" mother nature is inherently problematic and that foods produced through such methods are dangerous to human health. Despite the controversy, GMOs and biotechnologies continue to change the agricultural landscape by changing the world's food supply.

Like Monsanto, other agribusinesses exist throughout the world. Not only do these companies produce food for human consumption, but they also provide farming equipment, fertilizers, agrichemicals, and breeding and slaughtering services for livestock. While these companies are found all over the world, they are generally headquartered near the product they produce. For example, General Mills, a cereal manufacturer, is headquartered in the Midwestern United States, near its supply of wheat and corn—the primary ingredients in its cereals.

Contemporary Patterns and Impacts of Development, Industrialization, and Globalization

As mentioned previously, *developing nations* are nations that are struggling to modernize their economy, infrastructure, and government systems. Many of these nations may struggle to provide basic services to their citizens like clean water, adequate roads, or even police protection. Furthermore, government corruption makes life even more difficult for these countries' citizens. In contrast, *developed nations* are those who have relatively high *Gross Domestic Products (GDP)*, or the total value of all goods and services produced in the nation in a given year. To elucidate, the United States, which is one of the wealthiest nations on Earth when ranked by overall GDP, has nearly a 19 trillion dollar GDP; while Haiti, one of the poorest nations in the Western Hemisphere, has nearly a nine billion dollar GDP. This is a difference of almost seventeen trillion dollars. This is not to disparage Haiti or other developing nations; the comparison is simply used to show that extreme inequities exist in very close proximity to one another, and it may be difficult for developing nations to meet the needs of their citizens and move their economic infrastructure forward toward modernization.

In the modern world, industrialization is the initial key to modernization and development. For developed nations, the process of industrialization took place centuries ago. England, where the *Industrial Revolution* began, actually began to produce products in factories in the early 1700s. Later, the United States and some nations of Western Europe followed suit, using raw materials brought in from their colonies abroad to make finished products. For example, cotton was spun into fabric on elaborate weaving machines that mass-produced textiles. As a result, nations that perfected the textile process were able to sell their products around the world, which produced enormous profits. Over time, those nations were able to accumulate wealth, improve their nation's infrastructure, and provide more services for their citizens. Similar to the events of the eighteenth and nineteenth centuries, nations throughout the world are undergoing the same process in today's world. China exemplifies this concept. In China, agriculture was once the predominant occupation, and although it is true that agriculture is still a dominant sector of the Chinese economy, millions of Chinese citizens are flocking to major cities like Beijing, Shanghai, and Hangzhou, due to the availability of factory jobs that allow its workers a certain element of *social mobility*, or the ability to rise up out of one's socioeconomic situation.

Due to improvements in transportation and communication, the world has become figuratively smaller. For example, university students on the Indian Subcontinent now compete directly with students all over the world to obtain the skills employers desire to move their companies forward. Additionally, many corporations in developed nations have begun to *outsource* labor to nations with high levels of educational achievement but lower wage expectations. The process of opening the marketplace to all nations throughout the world, or *globalization*, has only just started to take hold in the modern economy. As industrial sites shift to the developing world, so does the relative level of opportunity for those nation's citizens. However, due to the massive amounts of pollution produced by factories, the process of globalization also has had significant ecological impacts. The most widely known impact, *climate change*, which most climatologists assert is caused by an increase of carbon dioxide in the atmosphere, remains a serious problem that has posed challenges for developing nations, who need industries in order to raise their standard of living, and developed nations, whose citizens use a tremendous amount of fossil fuels to run their cars, heat their homes, and maintain their ways of life.

Demographic Patterns and Demographic Change

Demography, or the study of human populations, involves a variety of closely related stimuli. First, as has been previously addressed, economic factors play a significant role in the movement of people, as do climate, natural disasters, or internal unrest. For example, in recent years, millions of immigrants from the war-torn country of Syria have moved as far as possible from danger. Although people are constantly moving, some consistencies remain throughout the world. First, people tend to live near reliable sources of food and water, which is why the first human civilizations sprung up in river valleys like the Indus River Valley in India, the Nile River Valley in Egypt, and the Yellow River Valley in Asia. Second, extreme temperatures tend to push people away, which is why the high latitudinal regions near the North and South Poles have such few inhabitants. Third, the vast majority of people tend to live in the Northern Hemisphere, due to the simple fact that more land lies in that part of the Earth. In keeping with these factors, human populations tend to be greater where human necessities are easily accessible, or at least more readily available. In other words, such areas have a greater chance of having a higher population density than places without such characteristics.

Demographic patterns on earth are not always stagnate. In contrast, people move and will continue to move as both push and pull factors fluctuate along with the flow of time. For example, in the 1940s, thousands of Europeans fled their homelands due to the impact of the Second World War. Today, thousands of migrants arrive on European shores each month due to conflicts in the Levant and difficult economic conditions in Northern Africa. Furthermore, as previously discussed, people tend to migrate to places with a greater economic benefit for themselves and their families. As a result, developed nations such as the United States, Germany, Canada, and Australia have a net gain of migrants, while developing nations such as Somalia, Zambia, and Cambodia generally tend to see thousands of their citizens seek better lives elsewhere.

It is important to understand the key variables in changes regarding human population and its composition worldwide. Religion and religious conflict play a role in where people choose to live. For example, the Nation of Israel won its independence in 1948 and has since attracted thousands of people of Jewish descent from all over the world. Additionally, the United States has long attracted people from all over the world, due to its promise of religious freedom inherent within its own Constitution. In contrast, nations like Saudi Arabia and Iran do not typically tolerate different religions, resulting in a decidedly uniform religious—and oftentimes ethnic—composition. Other factors such as economic opportunity, social unrest, and cost of living also play a vital role in demographic composition.

Basic Concepts of Political Geography

Nations, states, and nation-states are all terms with very similar meanings, but knowing the differences aids in a better understanding of geography. A nation is an area with similar cultural, linguistic, and historical experiences. A state is a political unit with sovereignty, or the ability to make its own decision in a particular area; and a nation-state is an entity that combines states into one, singular government system. For example, in the United States, the state of Texas is not an independent nation-state. Instead, it is part of the United States and thus, is subject to its laws. In a similar fashion, the United Kingdom encompasses four member states: England, Wales, Northern Ireland, and Scotland. Although people in those states may consider themselves to be *sovereign*, or self-governing, the reality is that those states cannot make decisions regarding international trade, declarations of war, or other important decisions regarding the rest of the world. Instead, they are *semi-autonomous*, meaning that they can make some decisions regarding how their own state is run, but must yield more major powers to a centralized authority. In the United States, this sort of system is called *Federalism*, or the sharing of power among Local, State, and Federal entities, each of whom is assigned different roles in the overall system of government.

Nation-states, and the boundaries that define where they are, are not always permanent. For example, after the fall of the Soviet Union in 1991, new nations emerged that had once been a part of the larger entity called the Union of Soviet Socialists Republics. These formerly sovereign nations were no longer forced to be a part of a unifying communist government, and as a result, they regained their autonomy and became newly independent nations that were no longer *satellite nations* of the Soviet Union. In a historical sense, the United States can be seen as a prime example of how national boundaries change. After the conclusion of the American Revolution in 1781, the Treaty of Paris defined the United States' western boundary as the Mississippi River; today, after a series of conflicts with Native American groups, the Mexican government, Hawaiian leadership, the Spanish, and the purchase of Alaska from the Russians, the boundaries of the United States have changed drastically. In a similar fashion, nations in Europe, Africa, and Asia have all shifted their boundaries due to warfare, cultural movements, and language barriers.

In the modern world, boundaries continue to change. For example, the Kurds, an ethnic minority in the Middle East, are still fighting for the right to control their people's' right to *self-determination*, but have not yet been successful in establishing a nation for themselves. In contrast, the oil-rich region of South Sudan, which has significant cultural, ethnic, and religious differences from Northern Sudan, successfully won its independence in a bloody civil war, which established the nation's newest independent nation. In recent years, Russia has made the world nervous by aggressively annexing the Crimean Peninsula, an area that has been part of the Ukraine since the end of the Cold War. Even the United Kingdom and Canada have seen their own people nearly vote for their own rights to self-determination. In 1995, the French-speaking Canadian province of Quebec narrowly avoided becoming a sovereign nation through a tightly contested referendum. In a similar fashion, Scotland, which is part of the UK, also voted to remain a part of the Crown, even though many people in that state see themselves as inherently different from those in other regions within the nation.

Political geography is constantly changing. Boundaries on maps from ten years ago are not consistent with those of 2016 and beyond. Simply looking at a map of Africa from 1950 can give one a sense of the level of change that takes place in a lifetime. For example, a map of Africa before 1950 looks completely different than a map of Africa from 2016. There are fewer European nations in the names on the 2016 map. *Decolonization*, or the removal of dependency on colonizers, has altered the political landscape of Africa, allowed more autonomy for the African people, and has forever redefined the boundaries of the entire continent.

Practice Questions

1. What's the term for the ability of a ruling body to influence the actions, behavior, and attitude of a person or group of people?
   a. Politics
   b. Power
   c. Authority
   d. Legitimacy

2. Which of the following is NOT a shared characteristic sufficient to form a nation?
   a. Culture and traditions
   b. History
   c. Sovereignty
   d. Beliefs and religion

Question 3 is based on the following passage:

> Upon this, one has to remark that men ought either to be well treated or crushed, because they can avenge themselves of lighter injuries, of more serious ones they cannot; therefore the injury that is to be done to a man ought to be of such a kind that one does not stand in fear of revenge.
>
> From Niccolo Machiavelli's *The Prince*, 1513

3. What advice is Machiavelli giving to the prince?
   a. Lightly injured enemies will overthrow the prince.
   b. Seek to injure everyone you meet.
   c. Hurting people is always the correct course of action.
   d. If you are going to cause an enemy some injury, ensure the injury is fatal.

Question 4 is based on the following passage:

> The creed which accepts as the foundation of morals, Utility, or the Greatest-Happiness Principle, holds that actions are right in proportion as they tend to promote happiness, wrong as they tend to produce the reverse of happiness. By happiness is intended pleasure, and the absence of pain; by unhappiness, pain, and the privation of pleasure.
>
> The utilitarian morality does recognise in human beings the power of sacrificing their own greatest good for the good of others. It only refuses to admit that the sacrifice is itself a good. A sacrifice which does not increase, or tend to increase, the sum total of happiness, it considers as wasted.
>
> From John Stuart Mill's *Utilitarianism*, 1861

4. What is the meaning of the "Utility"?
   a. Actions should be judged based on the net total of pleasure.
   b. Actions requiring sacrifice can never be valuable.
   c. Actions promoting sacrifice that increase happiness are more valuable than actions that only increase happiness.
   d. Actions can be valuable even if the pain outweighs the pleasure.

Question 5 is based on the following passage:

> The history of all hitherto existing society is the history of class struggles.
>
> Freeman and slave, patrician and plebeian, lord and serf, guildmaster and journeyman, in a word, oppressor and oppressed, stood in constant opposition to one another, carried on an uninterrupted, now hidden, now open fight, that each time ended, either in the revolutionary reconstitution of society at large, or in the common ruin of the contending classes.
>
> Let the ruling classes tremble at a Communistic revolution. The proletarians have nothing to lose but their chains. They have a world to win.
>
> Workingmen of all countries unite!
>
> Karl Marx and Friedrich Engels, *The Communist Manifesto,* 1848

5. What's the main idea presented in the excerpt?
    a. Working men are morally superior to the ruling class.
    b. Every society will come to an end at some point.
    c. History is defined by class struggle, and working men must now unite and fight the ruling class to gain freedom.
    d. Working men are in the same position as the slave, plebeian, serf, and journeyman.

Question 6 is based on the following image:

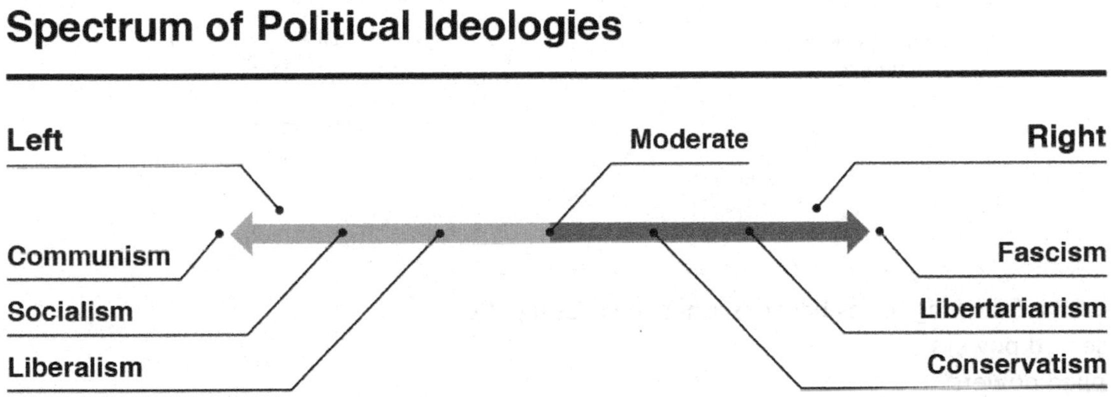

6. Which of the following represents the ideology that advocates for the most radical government intervention to achieve social and economic equality?
    a. Socialism
    b. Liberalism
    c. Libertarianism
    d. Fascism

7. Which of the following represents the ideology that prioritizes stability and traditional institutions within a culture?
    a. Socialism

b. Liberalism
c. Conservatism
d. Libertarianism

8. The central government established under the Articles of Confederation held which of the following powers?
a. The power to impose taxes
b. The power to declare war
c. The power to regulate trade
d. The power to enforce laws enacted by Congress

Question 9 is based on the following diagram:

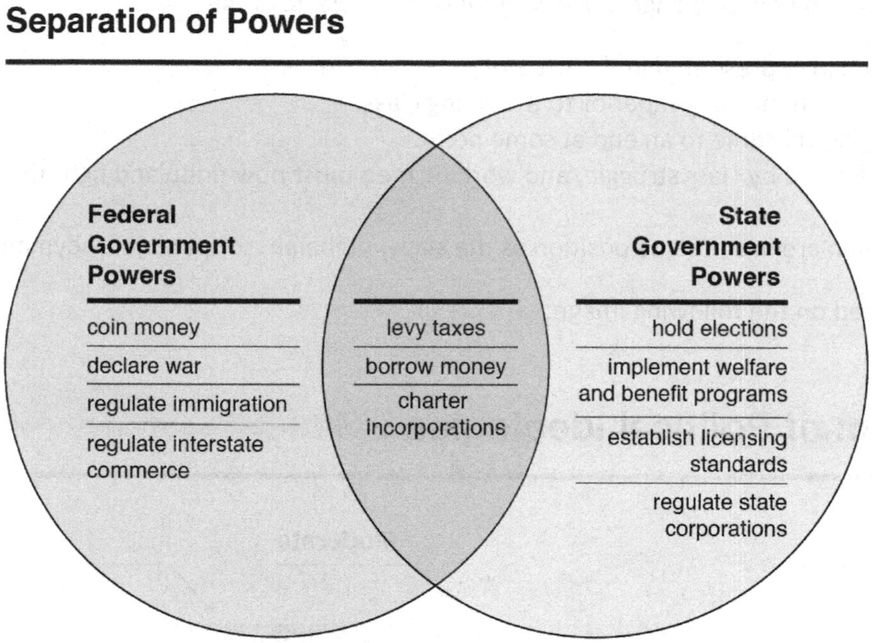

9. Which of the following terms best describes the missing title?
a. Reserved powers
b. Implied powers
c. Delegated powers
d. Concurrent powers

Question 10 is based on the following passage:

> Ambition must be made to counteract ambition. The interest of the man must be connected with the constitutional rights of the place. It may be a reflection on human nature, that such devices should be necessary to control the abuses of government. But what is government itself, but the greatest of all reflections on human nature?
>
> If men were angels, no government would be necessary. If angels were to govern men, neither external nor internal controls on government would be necessary. In framing a government

which is to be administered by men over men, the great difficulty lies in this: you must first enable the government to control the governed; and in the next place oblige it to control itself.

Alexander Hamilton or James Madison, aka *Publius*, "Federalist No. 50," 1788

10. What is the main idea presented in the excerpt?
    a. Men are inherently immoral and abusive.
    b. The best form of government is the type that angels would construct.
    c. Government reflects human nature.
    d. An effective government requires a separation of powers to regulate itself.

Question 11 is based on the following diagram:

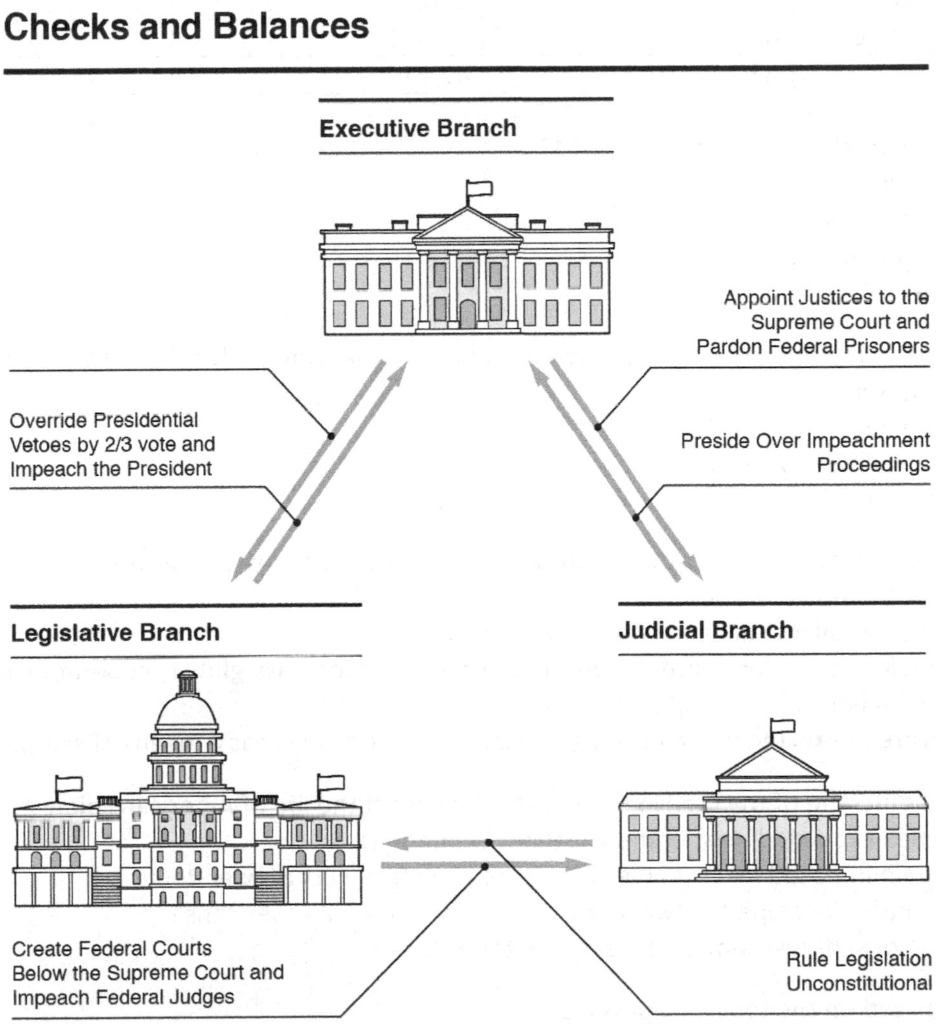

11. Which of the following answer choices best completes the diagram?
    a. Impeach congressmen and veto legislation
    b. Call special sessions of Congress and refuse to enforce laws
    c. Call special sessions of Congress and veto legislation
    d. Impeach congressmen and refuse to enforce laws

12. What amendment guarantees American citizens the right to keep and bear arms?
 a. First Amendment
 b. Second Amendment
 c. Third Amendment
 d. Fourth Amendment

Question 13 is based on the following table:

Presidential Election of 1824			
Candidate	Electoral Votes	Popular Votes	State Votes in the House of Representatives
Andrew Jackson	99	153,544	7
John Quincy Adams	84	108,740	13
William H. Crawford	41	46,618	4
Henry Clay	37	47,136	0

13. Who won the presidential election of 1824?
 a. Andrew Jackson
 b. John Quincy Adams
 c. William H. Crawford
 d. Henry Clay

14. What electoral system can result in a second round of voting commonly referred to as a runoff?
 a. Majority systems
 b. Plurality systems
 c. Single transferable systems
 d. Party list systems

15. In international relations, which of the following is NOT a basic tenet of realism?
 a. States are the central actors.
 b. States act rationally to advance their self-interest.
 c. States should seek to form international organizations to increase global cooperation and respond to international issues.
 d. All states are interested in maintaining or expanding their power as a means of self-preservation.

16. How did the outcome of the French and Indian War impact the life of American colonists?
 a. The colonies expanded west of the Allegheny Mountains.
 b. Great Britain imposed taxes on the colonies to pay off the British war debt.
 c. A lasting peace developed between the colonists and Native Americans.
 d. The power of self-government increased in the colonies.

Question 17 is based on the following passage:

> We hold these Truths to be self-evident: that all Men are created equal; that they are endowed by their creator with certain inalienable rights; that among these are life, liberty, and the pursuit of happiness: that to secure these rights, governments are instituted among men, deriving their just powers from the consent of the governed; that whenever any form of government becomes destructive of these ends, it is the right of the people to alter or abolish it, and to institute new

government, laying its foundation on such principles, and organizing its powers in such form, as to them shall seem most likely to affect their safety and happiness.

Prudence indeed will dictate that governments long established should not be changed for light and transient causes; and accordingly all experience hath shown that mankind are more disposed to suffer while evils are sufferable, than to right themselves by abolishing the forms to which they are accustomed. But when a long train of abuses and usurpations begun at a distinguished period and pursuing invariably the same object, evinces a design to reduce them under absolute despotism, it is their right, it is their duty to throw off such government, and to provide new guards for their future security

Declaration of Independence, adopted July 4, 1776

17. What is the main purpose of the excerpt?
    a. Provide a justification for revolution when the government infringes on "certain inalienable rights"
    b. Provide specific evidence of the "train of abuses"
    c. Provide an argument why "all Men are created equal"
    d. Provide an analysis of the importance of "life, liberty, and the pursuit of happiness"

Question 18 is based on the following map:

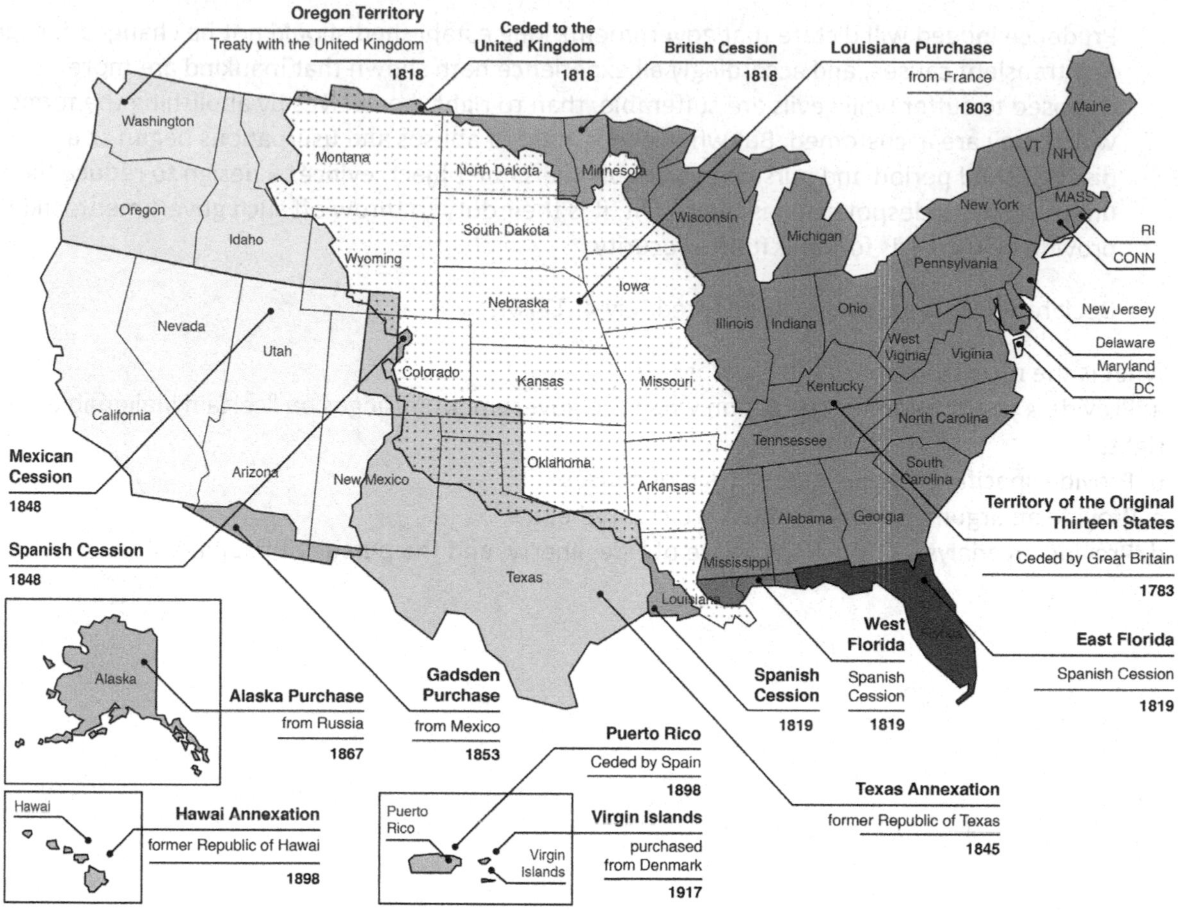

18. What current state did the United States gain through military force with a non-native nation-state?
   a. Nebraska
   b. Missouri
   c. Alaska
   d. Nevada

Question 19 is based on the following passage:

> Now, therefore I, Abraham Lincoln, President of the United States, by virtue of the power in me vested as Commander-in-Chief, of the Army and Navy of the United States in time of actual armed rebellion against the authority and government of the United States, and as a fit and necessary war measure for suppressing said rebellion...
>
> And by virtue of the power, and for the purpose aforesaid, I do order and declare that all persons held as slaves within said designated States, and parts of States, are, and henceforward

shall be free; and that the Executive government of the United States, including the military and naval authorities thereof, will recognize and maintain the freedom of said persons.

President Abraham Lincoln, Emancipation Proclamation, January 1, 1863

19. How does President Lincoln justify freeing the slaves in designated areas of the South?
    a. Emancipation is necessary since slavery is evil.
    b. Emancipation is necessary to boost the morale of the North.
    c. Emancipation is necessary to punish for the South seceding from the Union.
    d. Emancipation is necessary to strengthen the war effort of the North.

20. What was a consequence of the industrialization that followed the Civil War?
    a. Decreased immigration
    b. Increased urbanization
    c. Decreased socioeconomic inequality
    d. Increased rights for workers

21. Which of the following best describes how the Treaty of Versailles contributed to the outbreak of World War II?
    a. Forced Germany to assume responsibility for all damage incurred during the war and pay billions of dollars in reparations.
    b. Failed to adequately end the violence of World War I.
    c. Left large tracts of territory unclaimed by any nation-state.
    d. Created the League of Nations.

Question 22 is based on the following passage:

Hand in hand with this we must frankly recognize the overbalance of population in our industrial centers and, by engaging on a national scale in a redistribution, endeavor to provide a better use of the land for those best fitted for the land. The task can be helped by definite efforts to raise the values of agricultural products and with this the power to purchase the output of our cities. It can be helped by preventing realistically the tragedy of the growing loss through foreclosure of our small homes and our farms. It can be helped by insistence that the Federal, State, and local governments act forthwith on the demand that their cost be drastically reduced. It can be helped by the unifying of relief activities which today are often scattered, uneconomical, and unequal. It can be helped by national planning for and supervision of all forms of transportation and of communications and other utilities which have a definitely public character. There are many ways in which it can be helped, but it can never be helped merely by talking about it. We must act and act quickly.

Finally, in our progress toward a resumption of work we require two safeguards against a return of the evils of the old order: there must be a strict supervision of all banking and credits and investments, so that there will be an end to speculation with other people's money; and there must be provision for an adequate but sound currency.

President Franklin D. Roosevelt, Inaugural Address, March 4, 1933

22. Which of the following best describes President Roosevelt's underlying approach to government?
    a. Government must be focused on redistribution of land.
    b. Government must "act and act quickly" to intervene and regulate the economy.

c. Government must exercise "strict supervision of all banking."
d. Government must prevent the "growing loss through foreclosure."

Question 23 is based on the following passage:

> What, to the American slave, is your 4th of July? I answer: a day that reveals to him, more than all other days in the year, the gross injustice and cruelty to which he is the constant victim. To him, your celebration is a sham; your boasted liberty, an unholy license; your national greatness, swelling vanity; your sounds of rejoicing are empty and heartless; your denunciations of tyrants, brass fronted impudence; your shouts of liberty and equality, hollow mockery; your prayers and hymns, your sermons and thanksgivings, with all your religious parade, and solemnity, are, to him, mere bombast, fraud, deception, impiety, and hypocrisy—a thin veil to cover up crimes which would disgrace a nation of savages. There is not a nation on the earth guilty of practices, more shocking and bloody, than are the people of these United States, at this very hour.
>
> Frederick Douglass, "What to the Slave is the 4th of July?" July 5, 1852

23. What is the specific hypocrisy that Douglass repudiates?
   a. The Declaration of Independence declared that all men are created equal, but Thomas Jefferson owned slaves.
   b. Americans are free, but they do not value their freedom.
   c. The Fourth of July is a celebration about freedom, and slavery remained legal in the United States.
   d. The United States is a Christian nation, but American traditions contradict their faith.

Question 24 is based on the following passage:

> May it please your honor, I shall never pay a dollar of your unjust penalty. All the stock in trade I possess is a $10,000 debt, incurred by publishing my paper—The Revolution—four years ago, the sole object of which was to educate all women to do precisely as I have done, rebel against your man-made, unjust, unconstitutional forms of law, that tax, fine, imprison and hang women, while they deny them the right of representation in the government; and I shall work on with might and main to pay every dollar of that honest debt, but not a penny shall go to this unjust claim. And I shall earnestly and persistently continue to urge all women to the practical recognition of the old revolutionary maxim, that "Resistance to tyranny is obedience to God."
>
> *An Account of the Proceedings on the Trial of Susan B. Anthony on the Charge of Illegal Voting*, 1874.

24. What is the main idea presented in the excerpt?
   a. Taxation without representation is tyranny.
   b. Domestic abuse and violence against women is the cause of tyranny.
   c. Anthony cannot pay her fine due to debt accumulated from fighting for women's rights.
   d. Denying women the right to vote is tyranny and must be resisted.

25. Which of the following most accurately describes the platform of Ronald Reagan?
   a. Christianity, optimism, and preserving social safety nets
   b. Increased defense spending, deregulation, and tax cuts
   c. Moral majority, international cooperation, and compromise
   d. Conservatism, opposition to abortion, and organized labor

26. How do market economies differ from planned economies?
  a. Unlike market economies, planned economies have a larger number of both buyers and sellers.
  b. Unlike market economies, planned economies distribute resources more efficiently.
  c. Unlike planned economies, market economies allow demand to set prices.
  d. Unlike planned economies, market economies prioritize public services.

Question 27 is based on the following passage:

> Those who are opposed to this proposition tell us that the issue of paper money is a function of the bank and that the government ought to go out of the banking business. I stand with Jefferson rather than with them, and tell them, as he did, that the issue of money is a function of the government and that the banks should go out of the governing business.
>
> If they dare to come out in the open field and defend the gold standard as a good thing, we shall fight them to the uttermost, having behind us the producing masses of the nation and the world. Having behind us the commercial interests and the laboring interests and all the toiling masses, we shall answer their demands for a gold standard by saying to them, you shall not press down upon the brow of labor this crown of thorns. You shall not crucify mankind upon a cross of gold.
>
> William Jennings Bryan, "Cross of Gold" speech, 1896

27. What is the main idea presented in the excerpt?
  a. Banks prefer the gold standard.
  b. Most Americans dislike the gold standard.
  c. Violence is justified when the government oppresses the masses.
  d. The government should set the monetary policy based on the will of the people.

Question 28 is based on the following graph:

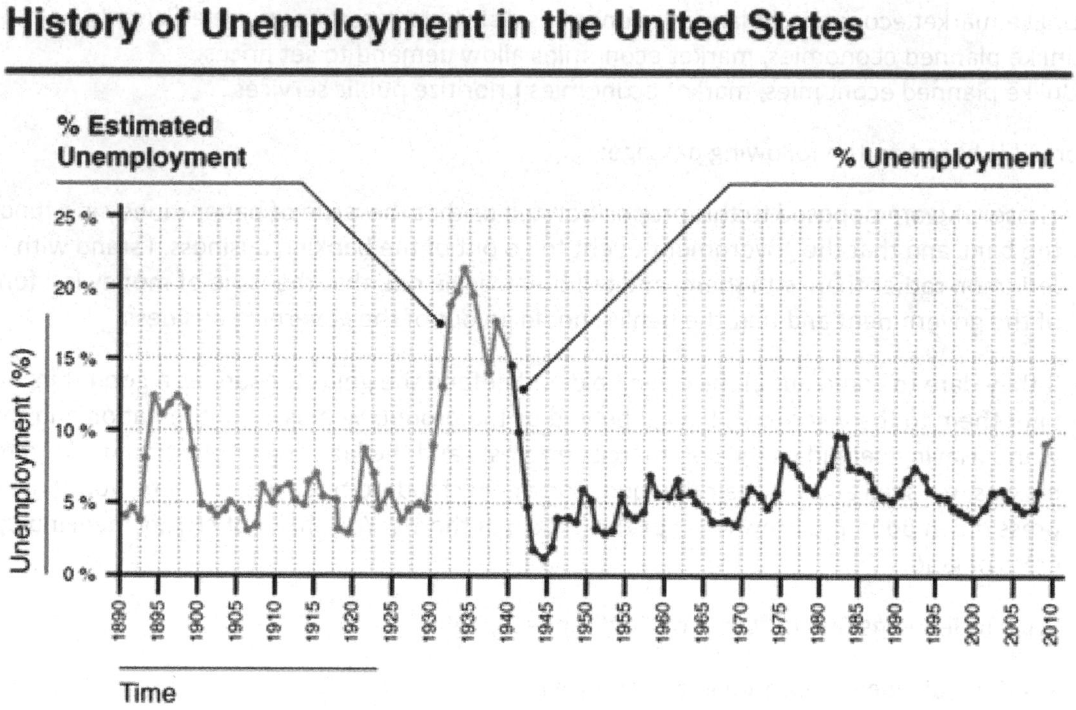

28. Which event caused the second largest increase in unemployment in American history?
    a. Panic of 1893
    b. Depression of 1920
    c. Depression of 1929
    d. Great Recession of 2007

Question 29 is based on the following diagram:

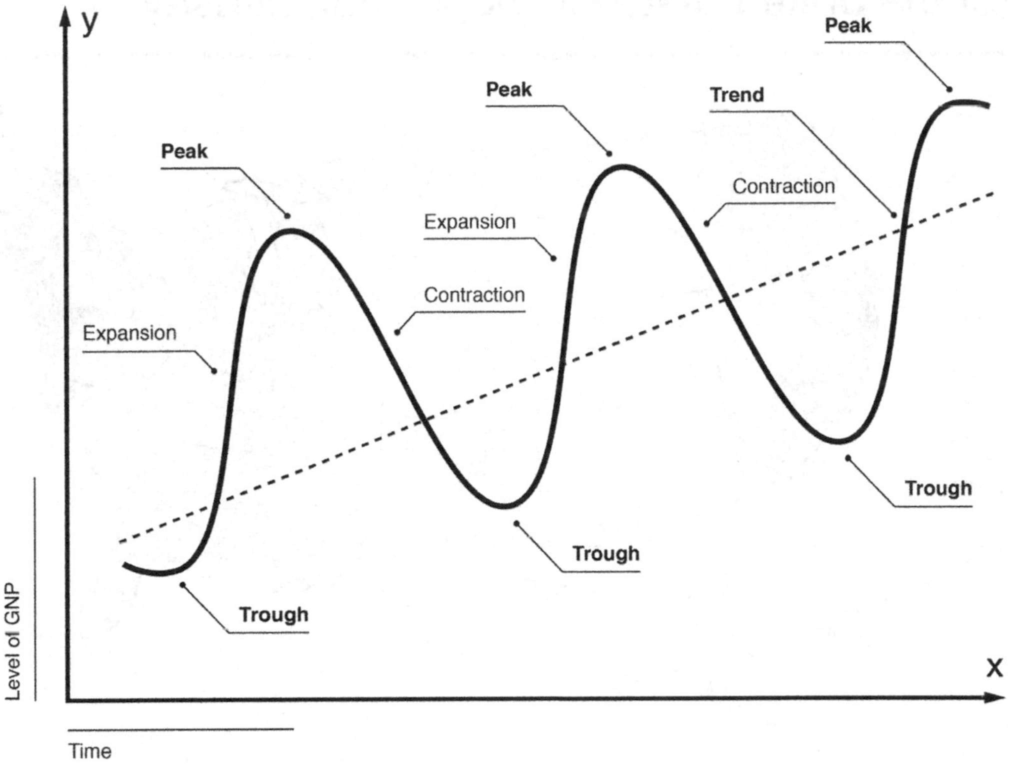

29. Which of the following phases of a business cycle occurs when there is continual growth?
    a. Expansion
    b. Peak
    c. Contraction
    d. Trough

30. Which of the following types of government intervention lowers prices, reassures the supply, and creates opportunity to compete with foreign vendors?
    a. Income redistribution
    b. Price controls
    c. Taxes
    d. Subsidies

31. What type of map would be the most useful for calculating data and differentiating between the characteristics of two places?
    a. Topographic maps
    b. Dot-density maps
    c. Isoline maps
    d. Flow-line maps

Question 32 is based on the following map:

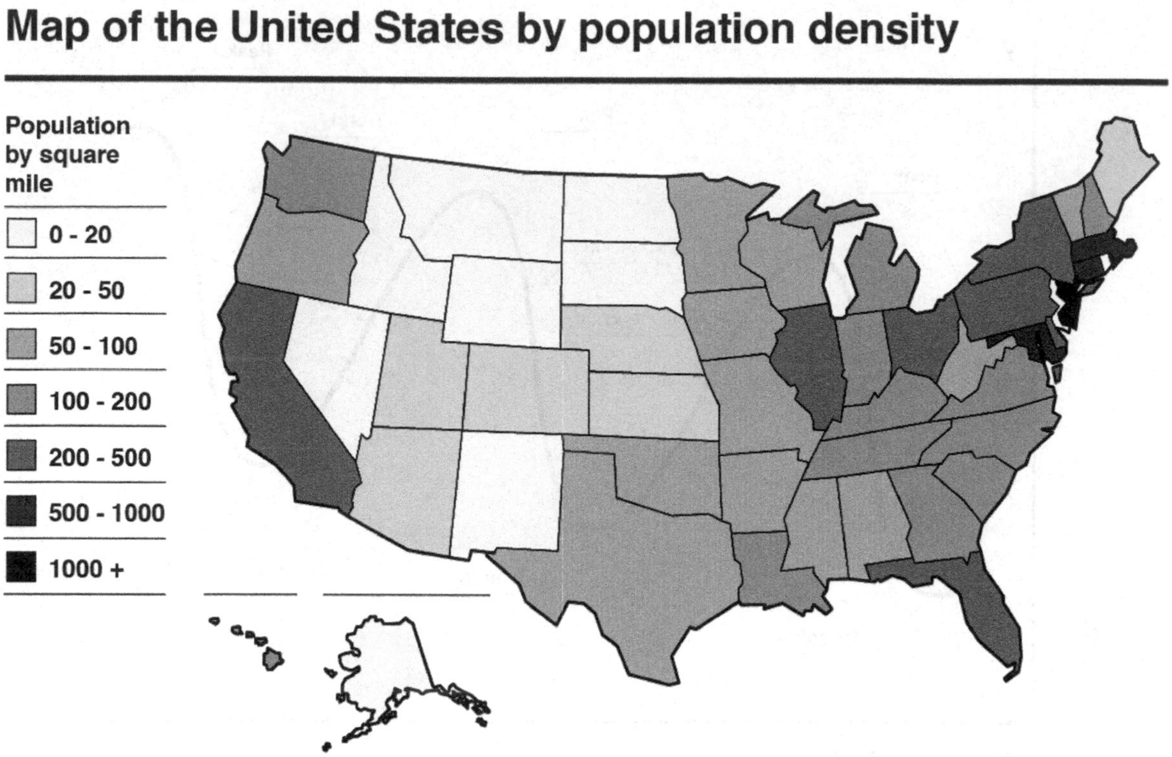

32. According to the map, what area of the United States has the highest population density?
    a. Northwest
    b. Northeast
    c. Southwest
    d. Southeast

33. What accounts for different parts of the Earth experiencing different seasons at the same time?
    a. Differences in the rate of Earth's rotation
    b. Ocean currents
    c. Tilt of the Earth's rotational axis
    d. Elevation

34. Which of the following is NOT a reason why nonrenewable energy sources are used more often than renewables?
    a. Nonrenewable energy is currently cheaper.
    b. Infrastructure was built specifically for nonrenewable sources.
    c. Renewable energy is more difficult and expensive to store for long periods.
    d. Renewable energy cannot be converted into a power source.

Question 35 is based on the following map:

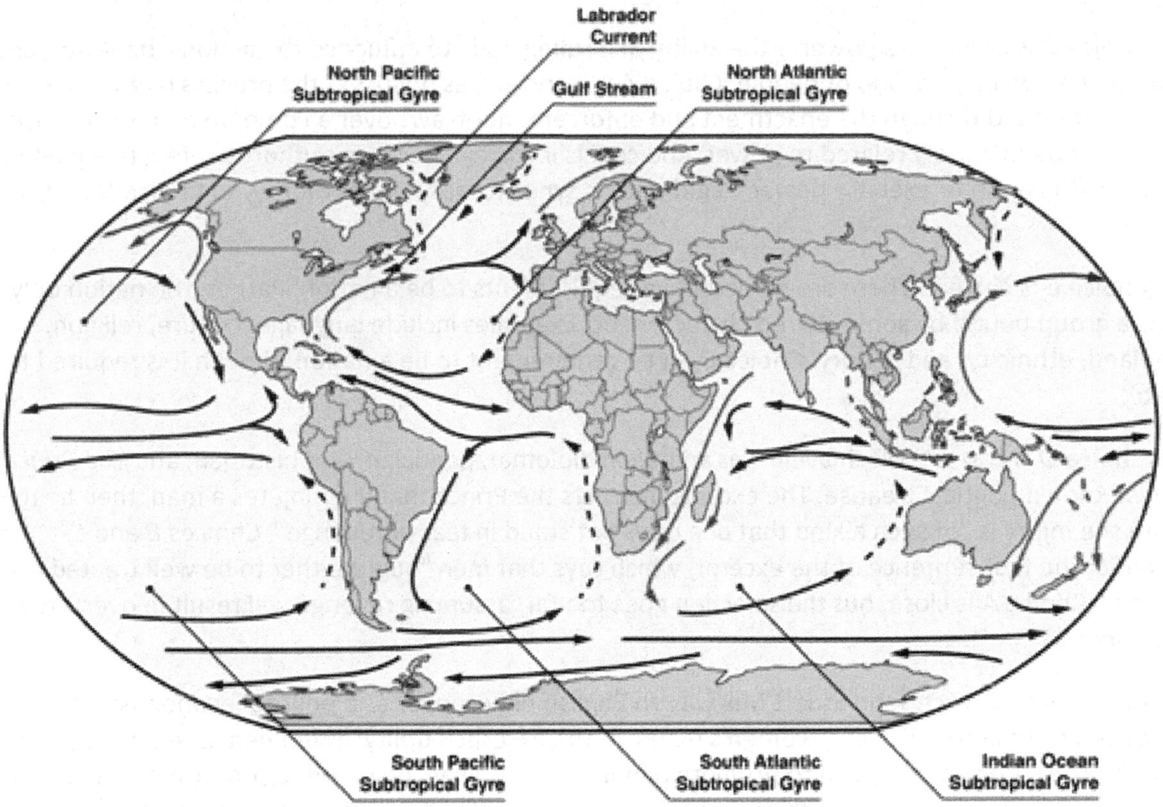

35. Which pair of ocean currents or gyres has the most impact on the weather of the United States?
    a. North Atlantic Subtropical Gyre and South Atlantic Subtropical Gyre
    b. Gulf Stream and North Pacific Subtropical Gyre
    c. North Pacific Subtropical Gyre and South Pacific Subtropical Gyre
    d. Alaskan Current and Indian Ocean Subtropical Gyre

Answer Explanations

1. B: Choice *B* is correct, as power is the ability of a ruling body to influence the actions, behavior, and attitude of a person or group of people. Choice *A* is incorrect, as politics is the process of governance typically exercised through the enactment and enforcement of laws over a community, most commonly a state. Although closely related to power, Choice *C* is incorrect, because authority refers to a political entity's justification to exercise power. Legitimacy is synonymous with authority, so Choice *D* is also incorrect.

2. C: Choice *C* is correct. There are no definitive requirements to be a nation. Rather, the nation only needs a group bound by some shared characteristic. Examples include language, culture, religion, homeland, ethnicity, and history. Choice *C* isn't a requirement to be a nation, though it is required to be a state.

3. D: Choice *D* is correct. Machiavelli was an Italian diplomat, politician, and historian, and *The Prince* is his best-known political treatise. The excerpt instructs the Prince that if he injures a man, then he must ensure the injury is "of such a kind that one does not stand in fear of revenge." Choices *B* and *C* contradict the first sentence of the excerpt, which says that men "ought either to be well treated or crushed." Choice *A* is close, but the selection goes too far, assuming revenge will result in overthrowing the Prince.

4. A: Choice *A* is correct. John Stuart Mill was an English philosopher and political economist who advocated for utilitarianism and women's rights. In the excerpt, "utility" is defined as actions that are "right in proportion as they tend to promote happiness, wrong as they tend to produce the reverse of happiness." The excerpt then explains that happiness is measured by pleasure, and the reverse is pain. Therefore, Mill calls for actions to be evaluated based on the net total of pleasure. Choice *D* contradicts the definition provided in the excerpt. The excerpt doesn't support Choice *C*, as there's no evidence that pleasure-generating sacrifices merit special status. Choice *B* is incorrect because sacrifice can still be valuable if it leads to more pleasure than pain.

5. C: Choice *C* is correct. Karl Marx, a philosopher, social scientist, historian, and revolutionary, is considered the father of communism. All the answer choices contain true statements or reasonable assumptions from the passage; however, Choice *C* best articulates the main idea—society is the history of class struggle, and working men must unite and fight a revolutionary battle like their historical ancestors.

6. A: Choice *A* is correct. On the political spectrum, ideologies on the left side of the axis emphasize socioeconomic equality and advocate for government intervention, while ideologies on the right axis seek to preserve society's existing institutions and oppose government intervention. Therefore, the answer will be the farthest left on the axis, making Choice *A* correct.

7. C: Choice *C* is correct, as it most closely corresponds to the provided definition. Conservatism prioritizes traditional institutions. In general, conservatives oppose modern developments and value stability. Socialism and liberalism both feature the desire to change the government to increase equality. Libertarianism is more concerned with establishing a limited government to maximize personal autonomy.

8. B: Choice *B* is correct. The Articles of Confederation were the first form of government adopted in the American colonies. Under the Articles of Confederation, the central government (the Continental

Congress) was granted very limited powers, rendering it largely ineffective. Although the choices describe what would appear to be basic functions of government, the central government could only declare war.

9. D: Choice *D* is correct. The missing title is in the overlap between federal and state government powers. Concurrent powers are shared between federal and state governments. Reserved powers are the unspecified powers of the states not expressly granted to the federal government or denied to the state by the Constitution, and left to the states by the Tenth Amendment. Implied powers are the unstated powers that can be reasonably inferred from the Constitution. Delegated powers are the specific powers granted to the federal government by the Constitution.

10. D: Choice *D* is correct. The Federalists supported the expansion of the federal government, and the anti-Federalists feared that a stronger central government would weaken the states. *The Federalist Papers* argued for the ratification of the Constitution to establish a more powerful central government. The main idea of this excerpt is to argue that the Constitution establishes a central government powerful enough to rule, while also providing checks and balances to ensure the government doesn't abuse its power. Separation of powers is the concept behind checks and balances, so Choice *D* is the correct answer. Choices *A* and *C* are true statements, but they don't identify the main idea. Choice *B* references a theoretical assertion from the excerpt, but it's not the main idea.

11. C: Choice *C* is the correct answer. Checks and balances refer to the powers granted to ensure other branches don't overstep their authority. The other arrows in the diagram identify checks and balances, so the correct answer is the executive branch's checks and balances on the legislative branch. The executive branch can call special sessions of Congress and veto legislation, so Choice *C* is correct. Unlike the judicial and executive branches, members of the legislative branch cannot be impeached by another branch, though the legislative branch can expel its own members. The executive branch cannot refuse to enforce laws.

12. B: Choice *B* is correct. The Second Amendment states, "A well regulated Militia, being necessary to the security of a free State, the right of the people to keep and bear Arms, shall not be infringed." The First Amendment provides freedom of religion, speech, and the press, the right to assemble, and the right to petition the government. The Third Amendment establishes the right to refuse to house soldiers in times of war. The Fourth Amendment establishes a series of protections for citizens accused and charged with crimes.

13. B: Choice *B* is correct. The Electoral College determines the winner of presidential races, but if a candidate doesn't win a majority of electoral votes, the Twelfth Amendment requires the House of Representatives to decide the presidency, with each state delegation voting as a single bloc. The candidate with the most votes in the House wins the election. The table shows that Andrew Jackson won a plurality of electoral and popular votes, but he didn't receive a majority. John Quincy Adams received the most votes in the House of Representatives, so he won the presidency.

14. A: Choice *A* is correct. Electoral systems dictate how the members of the ruling body are selected, how votes translate into positions, and how seats are filled in the political offices at each level of government. In a majority system, a candidate must receive a majority of votes in order to be awarded a seat, but if none of the candidates reach a majority, a second round of voting occurs, commonly referred to as a runoff.

15. C: Choice *C* is correct. The two major theories of international relations are Realism and Liberalism. Realism analyzes international relations through the interactions of states under the assumption that states act rationally to maintain or expand power a means of self-preservation, which inevitably leads to conflict in an anarchical system. The question asks for the choice that doesn't adhere to Realism, and the other choices state three of the four basic tenets of Realism. In contrast, Choice *C* states a principle of Liberalism. Realists don't value international organizations or prioritize global cooperation.

16. B: Choice *B* is correct. Following the French and Indian War, the British government amassed an enormous war debt, and Great Britain imposed taxes on the colonists to generate more revenue. King George III argued that British resources defended the colonists from French and Native American forces, so the colonists should share in the expenses. The other choices are factually incorrect. The Royal Proclamation of 1763 prevented the colonies from expanding west of the Allegheny Mountains. No lasting peace ever occurred between the colonists and Native Americans. Self-government decreased in the colonies after the French and Indian War.

17. A: Choice *A* is correct. Heavily influenced by the Enlightenment, the Declaration of Independence repudiated the colonies' allegiance to Great Britain. The main purpose of the excerpt is to justify the colonists' revolutionary ambitions due to Great Britain's tyranny and the role of consent in government to protect the natural rights of citizens. Although the excerpt alludes to abuses, the purpose isn't to list specific evidence. This occurs later in the Declaration of Independence. Choices *C* and *D* are supporting evidence for the main purpose.

18. D: Choice *D* is correct. The question asks for a territory that the United States didn't gain from war. Any territory gained via purchase is incorrect. Missouri and Nebraska became American territories through the Louisiana Purchase, and the United States purchased Alaska from Russia. In contrast, Mexico ceded Nevada as part of the peace agreement ending the Mexican-American War.

19. D: Choice *D* is correct. President Lincoln issued the Emancipation Proclamation to free the slaves in the Confederacy, allowing the institution to continue in states and territories that didn't secede. The excerpt justifies the decision as a "fit and necessary war measure for suppressing said rebellion." Therefore, per the excerpt, emancipation was necessary to strengthen the war effort for the North. Choice *C* is the second-best answer, but the excerpt supports the contention that emancipation was part of an active war effort, rather than merely a punishment. Nothing in the excerpt describes the evil of slavery or the effect of emancipation on morale in the North.

20. B: Choice *B* is correct. Industrialization directly caused an increase in urbanization. Factories were located near cities to draw upon a large pool of potential employees. Between 1860 and 1890, the urbanization rate increased from about 20 percent to 35 percent. The other three choices are factually incorrect. Immigration increased during industrialization, as immigrants flooded into America to search for work. Socioeconomic problems plagued the period due to the unequal distribution of wealth and the social ills caused by rapid urbanization. Labor unrest was common as unions advocated for workers' rights and organized national strikes.

21. A: Choice *A* is correct. The Treaty of Versailles contained a clause that required Germany to assume responsibility for damages incurred during the conflict. Thus, the Treaty ordered Germany to pay $31.4 billion, the equivalent of $442 billion in 2017. World War I ravaged the German economy, and the country couldn't afford the war debt. The resulting poverty contributed to the rise of the Nazi Party, leading to World War II.

22. B: Choice *B* is correct. President Franklin D. Roosevelt introduced the New Deal, a series of executive orders and laws passed by Congress in response to the Great Depression. The excerpt describes how President Roosevelt intended to fight poverty by using the government's power to intervene and regulate the economy. Although the other answer choices correctly identify specific activities referenced in the excerpt, they are examples of the underlying philosophy in action. The underlying philosophy is an active role for government in the nation's economic affairs.

23. C: Choice *C* is correct. Frederick Douglass escaped from slavery and worked as an abolitionist for the rest of his life. The excerpt references the hypocrisy of the Fourth of July, as the holiday celebrates freedom in a country with millions of slaves. The other answer choices identify hypocritical aspects surrounding the slavery debate, but Choice *C* directly states the specific hypocrisy attacked in the excerpt.

24. D: Choice *D* is correct. Along with Lucy Stone and Elizabeth Cady Stanton, Susan B. Anthony was one of the most outspoken advocates for women's suffrage. Women couldn't vote in the United States until Congress passed the Nineteenth Amendment in 1920. Choice *D* accurately expresses the main idea of the excerpt. Denying women the right to vote is tyranny, so Anthony will not pay a fine for voting illegally. Choice *A* is the second-best answer, but it's too general to be the main idea of an excerpt specifically about women's suffrage.

25. B: Choice *B* is correct. Ronald Reagan won the presidential election of 1980 and promised to restore America's military power through defense spending, cutting government regulations, and reducing taxes. Evangelical Christians and the Moral Majority fiercely supported President Reagan's agenda, particularly his opposition to abortion and his conservative approach to social issues. The other answer choices include at least one mischaracterization. Choice *A* is incorrect because President Reagan generally opposed social programs. Choice *C* is incorrect because President Reagan valued American leadership more than international cooperation. In addition, his platform was far more radically conservative than compromising. Choice *D* is incorrect because President Reagan fought labor unions on several fronts, most notably when he broke a strike organized by an air traffic controllers' union.

26. C: Choice *C* is correct. In a market economy, privately owned businesses, groups, or individuals price goods or services and set prices based on demand. In contrast, the government or central authority determines prices and quantity of production in a command economy. Of the two economic systems, the market economy more efficiently uses resources. Choice *C* is the only accurate statement.

27. D: Choice *D* is correct. William Jennings Bryan's "Cross of Gold" is one of the most famous speeches in American history, launching his candidacy in the 1896 presidential election. The speech advocates for abolishing the gold standard and adopting a bimetallic system to provide more government control over monetary policy. The excerpt condemns the influence of banks in monetary policy, and without some reform, the masses should act to remove the gold standard. Although the other answer choices accurately state assertions from the excerpt, they aren't the main idea.

28. A: Choice *A* is correct. The Depression of 1929, commonly referred to as the Great Depression, is the largest increase to unemployment, but the question stem asks for the second-largest increase. According to the graph, the Panic of 1893 increased unemployment by approximately ten percent; the Depression of 1920 increased unemployment by approximately six percent; the Depression of 1929 increased unemployment by approximately fifteen percent; and the Great Recession of 2007 increased unemployment by approximately four percent. Thus, the Panic of 1893 marks the second-largest increase to unemployment.

29. A: Choice *A* is correct. A business cycle is when the gross domestic product (GDP) moves downward and upward over a long-term growth trend, and the four phases are expansion, peak, contraction, and trough. An expansion is the only phase where employment rates and economic growth continually grow. Contraction is the opposite of expansion. The peak and trough are the extreme points on the graph.

30. D: Choice *D* is correct. The government can intervene in the economy by imposing taxes, subsidies, and price controls to increase revenue, lower prices of goods and services, ensure product availability for the government, and maintain fair prices for goods and services. Subsidies lower prices, reassure the supply, and create opportunity to compete with foreign vendors, so Choice *D* is correct.

31. C: Choice *C* is correct. Isoline maps are used to calculate data and differentiate between the characteristics of two places. In an isoline map, symbols represent values, and lines can be drawn between two points to determine differences. The other answer choices are maps with different purposes. Topographic maps display contour lines, which represent the relative elevation of a particular place. Dot-density maps and flow-line maps are types of thematic maps. Dot-density maps illustrate the volume and density of a characteristic of an area. Flow-line maps use lines to illustrate the movement of goods, people, or even animals between two places.

32. B: Choice *B* is correct. The map is a density map illustrating population density by state in the United States. Accordingly, the darker areas have higher population density. The darkest area of the map is the Northeast, so Choice *B* is correct.

33. C: Choice *C* is correct. The tilt of the Earth's rotation causes the seasons due to the difference in direct exposure to the Sun. For example, the northern hemisphere is tilted directly toward the Sun from June 22 to September 23, which creates the summer in that part of the world. Conversely, the southern hemisphere is tilted away from the Sun and experiences winter during those months. Choice *A* is factually incorrect—the rate of Earth's rotation is constant. Choice *B* and *D* are factors in determining climate, but differences in climate don't cause the seasons.

34. D: Choice *D* is correct. Nonrenewable energy resources are oil, natural gas, and coal, collectively referred to as fossil fuels. Nonrenewable energy is more widely used due to its abundance and relatively cheap price. In addition, countries have tailored their existing infrastructure to nonrenewable energy. Currently, the technology to store renewable energies for long periods is either nonexistent or expensive. Choice *D* is correct because it's inaccurate. Renewable energy can be converted into a power source, but the issue is scale of use. For example, the United States converts renewable resources to derive ten percent of the country's energy.

35. B: Choice *B* is correct. Ocean currents dramatically impact the climate by storing heat from the Sun and transporting the warmth around the globe. The evaporation of ocean water increases the temperature and humidity in the nearby landmasses. A gyre is a system of circulating currents. Countries are most impacted by the currents and gyres closest to their shores. The question stem asks what currents have the most impact on the United States. According to the map, the North Atlantic Gyre, North Pacific Gyre, California Current, Alaskan Current and Gulf Stream impact the United States. Choice *B* is the only answer with a pair of those currents or gyres.

Photo Credits

FREE Test Taking Tips DVD Offer

To help us better serve you, we have developed a Test Taking Tips DVD that we would like to give you for FREE. **This DVD covers world-class test taking tips that you can use to be even more successful when you are taking your test.**

All that we ask is that you email us your feedback about your study guide. Please let us know what you thought about it – whether that is good, bad or indifferent.

To get your **FREE Test Taking Tips DVD**, email freedvd@studyguideteam.com with "FREE DVD" in the subject line and the following information in the body of the email:

a. The title of your study guide.

b. Your product rating on a scale of 1-5, with 5 being the highest rating.

c. Your feedback about the study guide. What did you think of it?

d. Your full name and shipping address to send your free DVD.

If you have any questions or concerns, please don't hesitate to contact us at freedvd@studyguideteam.com.

Thanks again!